Classic
Papers
in
Child
Abuse

Anne Cohn Donnelly & Kim Oates
Editors

Classic Papers *in* Child Abuse

Sage Publications, Inc.
International Educational and Professional Publisher
Thousand Oaks ■ London ■ New Delhi

For information:

 Sage Publications, Inc.
2455 Teller Road
Thousand Oaks, California 91320
E-mail: order@sagepub.com

Sage Publications Ltd.
6 Bonhill Street
London EC2A 4PU
United Kingdom

Sage Publications India Pvt. Ltd.
M-32 Market
Greater Kailash I
New Delhi 110 048 India

Printed in the United States of America

Library of Congress Cataloging-in-Publication Data

Main entry under title:

Classic papers in child abuse / edited by Anne Cohn Donnelly and Kim Oates.
    p.   cm.
Includes bibliographical references and index.
ISBN 0-7619-1836-1 (cloth: alk. paper) — ISBN 0-7619-1837-X (paper: alk. paper)
1. Child abuse. I. Donnelly, Anne Cohn. II. Oates, Kim.
HV6626.5 .C59 2000
362.76—dc21   99-006922

This book is printed on acid-free paper.

00 01 02 03 04 05 06 7 6 5 4 3 2 1

Acquiring Editor:	Nancy Hale
Editorial Assistant:	Anna Howland
Production Editor:	Sanford Robinson
Editorial Assistant:	Victoria Cheng
Typesetter:	Danielle Dillahunt
Indexer:	Molly Hall

Contents

*This volume is dedicated to C. Henry Kempe and Donna J. Stone,
two pioneers in our collective efforts to understand
and prevent child abuse, and two important mentors.*

Introduction

What makes a classic paper in child abuse? Is it the number of times scholars refer to it in their own writings? Is it one that has influenced the way practitioners work? Perhaps, it is one that has led to a change in policy and practice at a national or even an international level.

Most of us would be able to think of at least one or two published book chapters or articles that have had a major influence on our thinking or understanding and that may have changed the way we work. If a large group of professionals shared their opinions about papers that had influenced them, a number of papers would be regularly mentioned. If we also looked at how often the papers the professionals mentioned were referenced, or cited, in the child abuse literature, then we would end up with some degree of consensus about influential or "classic" papers in child abuse.

This is how we arrived at the 25 classic papers in this volume. First, we surveyed a group of people in leadership positions in child abuse research or clinical work to tell us about the journal papers or book chapters they felt had been most influential to them and to the child protection field as a whole. Once this list was generated, we conducted a larger, international survey of professionals, asking them to rank the papers in what they believed was their order of importance and influence. Finally, we compared the views of this group with the actual number of times these papers had been cited in the literature by searching the Science Citation Index and the Social Science Citation Index for the previous 10 years (Oates & Cohn Donnelly, 1997).

Obviously, the list of papers presented here is not exhaustive. Readers may think of other papers that may have had a major influence on their thinking or on that of others. Some examples include Fontana's (1963) early descriptions of the medical aspects of child abuse, de Francis's (1969) work on child protection, Elmer and Gregg's (1967) study of development following abuse, and Besharov's (1974) early work, which influenced child protection legislation and Fraiberg's work on infancy.

The 25 papers in this volume cover work from 1946 to 1989. They represent the consensus of a large number of professionals about what are the classic papers in child abuse, chosen from among the highest-ranking papers in the professional and citation surveys to give a balanced view of the entire spectrum of abuse: emotional abuse, neglect, deprivation, sexual abuse, and physical abuse. Some papers, such as Klaus's (1972) paper on the importance of maternal attachment, are not specifically about abuse at all but were highly ranked by professionals because of the impact they had in helping us to understand the larger picture of factors that may contribute to or reduce abusive behavior.

Because these papers in general represent the early thinking and early methodologies used to explore child abuse, we wanted to assess their relevance today. To that end, we asked several dozen of our colleagues—none of whom have works represented here, to restudy several papers each and to report on why they believe these papers were so influential in their day, why the papers continue to be influential today, and what cautions they have in using the contents of these papers in today's work. The remarks we gathered from our colleagues are woven into commentaries by the editors before each paper (see List of Commentators).

Although the papers in this volume are arranged in chronological order to show how the evolution of understanding and thinking about child abuse has occurred, it is worth mentioning those papers that appear to have been the most influential of all. Eight papers appeared in the top fifteen in the international survey of professionals and were among the 15 most frequently cited papers. These are: "Multiple Fractures of the Long Bones in Infants Suffering From Chronic Subdural Hematoma" (Caffey, 1946); "The Battered Child Syndrome" (Kempe et al., 1962); "Munchausen Syndrome by Proxy" (Meadow, 1997); "Child Abuse and Neglect: The Myth of Classlessness" (Pelton, 1978); "The Child Sexual Abuse Accommodation Syndrome" (Summit, 1983); "The Prevalence and Incidence of Intrafamilial and Extrafamilial Sexual Abuse Among Women" (Russell, 1983); "Four Conditions: A Model" (Finkelhor, 1984), and "Impact of Child Sexual Abuse: A Review of the Research" (Browne & Finkelhor, 1986).

Why bother to make a collection of classic papers? Few people would have the time to locate these papers individually, making their collection in one volume a useful resource. Just keeping up with the current literature is a major problem recognized by child protective service workers who, although they realize that keeping up would be relevant to their work, often feel that they do not have the time to be familiar with all the literature (Fryer, Poland, Bross, & Krugman, 1988). Although the literature is extensive, not all of it is that relevant to many who work in the area, so that a collection of the classic papers, recognized by a group of peers as being highly relevant, can be a valuable resource.

A collection of the most influential child abuse papers published to date has much to teach. We can be encouraged by seeing how far we have come and how much we have learned since those early descriptions of abused children started to shatter society's complacency that all children have happy, carefree lives. The papers will also challenge us to see that the same problems persist and that although we understand them better, there is still a long way to go before we have a society where all children are truly valued and adequately protected.

But most of all, these papers are highly relevant today. When we re-read these papers, we were impressed that their core insights are just as relevant to today's practice as when they were written.

For those starting to work in the area, these papers provide a wise and thoughtful introduction to the entire scope of child abuse and neglect. To those who are experienced, the papers are a salutary reminder of the importance of learning from past experience as we move into the future.

Many people helped in the production of this volume. Our special thanks go to our friends and colleagues around the world who took part in the survey that resulted in the choice of these classic papers; our colleagues who provided the material for the commentaries on each of the papers; the publishers of the original papers for permission to reprint them; and most important, all of the original authors of these classic papers, who played such a vital role in our understanding of the very complex and compelling issue of child abuse. We also gratefully acknowledge the indispensable assistance of Wendy Nelson as well as that of our Sage colleagues Terry Hendrix, Kassie Gavrilis, Nancy Hale, and Sanford Robinson.

Anne Cohn Donnelly and Kim Oates

REFERENCES

Besharov, D. (1974). Report of the New York State Assembly's Select Committee on Child Abuse. In R. E. Helfer & C. H. Kempe (Eds.), *The battered child* (2nd ed.). Chicago: University of Chicago Press.

de Francis, V. (1969). *Protecting the child victim of sex crimes committed by adults.* Denver, CO: American Humane Association.

Elmer, E., & Gregg, G. (1967). Development characteristics of abused children. *Pediatrics, 40,* 596-602.

Fontana, V. (1963). The maltreatment syndrome in children. *New England Journal of Medicine, 269,* 1389-1394.

Fraiberg, S. (1980). Ghosts in the nursery. In *Clinical studies in infant mental health: The first year of life* (pp. 164-196). New York: Basic Books.

Fryer, G. E., Poland, J. E., Bross, D. C., & Krugman, R. D. (1988). The child protective service worker: A profile of needs, attitudes, and utilization of professional resources. *Child Abuse and Neglect, 12,* 481-490.

Klaus, M. H., Jerauld, G., Kreger, N. C., McAlpine, W., Steffa, M., & Kennell, J. H. (1972). Maternal attachment: Importance of the first post-partum days. *New England Journal of Medicine, 286,* 460-463.

Oates, R. K., & Cohn Donnelly, A. (1997) Influential papers in child abuse. *Child Abuse and Neglect, 21,* 319-326.

Multiple Fractures in the Long Bones of Infants Suffering From Chronic Subdural Hematoma

JOHN I. CAFFEY   1946

Re-reading Caffey's 1946 paper, "Multiple Fractures in the Long Bones of Infants Suffering From Chronic Subdural Hematoma," the diagnosis today seems so obvious. In the six cases documented, Caffey describes children who have subdural hematomas, retinal hemorrhages, multiple fractures of different ages (including spiral fractures), periosteal elevation, and metaphysical chip fractures. In some of these cases, fresh bruising and new fractures appeared after the child's subdural hematoma had been treated and the child discharged from hospital.

Give a description like this to any pediatric intern or medical student today, and you would expect the diagnosis of child abuse as the most likely cause. But, over 50 years ago, the medical profession did not diagnose child abuse. The importance of Caffey's paper is that for the first time he asked "why" and documented a series of puzzling cases. "For many years we have been puzzled by the roentgen disclosure of fresh, healing, and healed multiple frac-

tures in the long bones of infants whose principal disease was chronic subdural hematoma," he wrote, but "in not a single case was there a history of injury to which the skeletal lesions could be attributed."

In two cases, it was reported that injury to the infant had been denied, and, in one case, after being shown the roentgen findings, the mother altered her story. In one case, Caffey raised the question of ill treatment because "the infant was clearly unwanted by both parents."

This paper is an important example of careful observation and documentation of what was then an obscure and unexplained combination of injuries. Caffey had the insight to suggest that the fractures in the long bones may have been caused by the same traumatic forces that were responsible for the subdural hematomas, and although he implied that injury—possibly caused by parents—may have been a possibility, the world of 1946 was not yet ready to accept that parents could deliberately damage their infants in this way.

Now, well over a half century later, the cause of the trauma is no longer a mystery. Caffey's paper was the beginning of the identification of the phenomenon no one wanted, or was able, to admit existed—the severe physical abuse of children by those responsible for their care and nurture.

Fractures of the cranium are not infrequently associated with infantile subdural hematoma, but fractures in the long bones have rarely been reported as complications of this intracranial lesion. An old fracture of the radius is mentioned by Sherwood[1] in his fifth case. Ingraham and Heyl[2] demonstrated greenstick fractures roentgenographically in the radiuses and ulnas of both forearms of one infant (Case 4) in whom there were neither clinical signs of fracture nor history of injury. Dr. Ingraham has written me that in his extensive experience with more than 100 cases of infantile subdural hematoma, fractures were also found in the humerus of one patient, in the femur of another, and in six ribs of a third.[3]

For many years, we have been puzzled by the roentgen disclosure of fresh, healing, and healed multiple fractures in the long bones of infants whose principal disease was chronic subdural hematoma. The subject of this paper is the description of six such patients, who exhibited 23 fractures and four contusions of the long bones. In not a single case was there a history of injury to which the skeletal lesions could reasonably be attributed, and in no case was there clinical or roentgen evidence of generalized or localized skeletal disease which would predispose to pathological fractures.

CASE REPORTS

Case 1. H. D., male, was born March 13, 1925, after a normal gestation and labor; the birth weight was 8 pounds. He gained and developed normally on whole milk formula.

A purulent discharge from the right ear began at 5 months and continued for 2 months. At 7 months, there was a single convulsion which lasted for one-half hour, after which the infant was weak and listless for 3 days and strabismus with stare developed. During this period, fever was present and vomiting was frequent. The mother, who had been with the infant continuously, had not observed injury to the head or extremities. Physical examination disclosed a tense bulging anterior fontanel, internal strabismus, and exaggerated deep reflexes. There were no signs of meningeal irritation. The bones of the left forearms were thickened to palpation, and this finding raised the question of an old fracture with callus. Roentgenograms of the extremities were not made at this time. Forty-five cubic centimeters of cerebrospinal fluid were withdrawn from the lumbar subarachnoid space; the pressure was increased, but the fluid was normal chemically and microscopically. Following lumbar puncture, the signs and symptoms disappeared; the patient was sent home after 3 days, with the diagnosis of hydrocephalus of unknown origin.

Two weeks later, the patient began to vomit, and the bulge over the fontanel reappeared; 35 cc. of lumbar cerebrospinal fluid were found to be crystal clear and normal microscopically and chemically. During the next 5 weeks, 30 to 40 cc. of normal cerebrospinal fluid were withdrawn during each of 12 lumbar punctures. At 9 months of age, subdural punctures yielded 25 cc. of bloody fluid from the right angle and 15 cc. from the left angle of the anterior fontanel.

Originally published in the *American Journal of Roentgenology*. Reprinted by permission of the American Roentgen Ray Society.

Roentgenograms of the skull after the injection of air into the subdural space demonstrated a large cavity which extended over both cerebral hemispheres but which did not appear to communicate with the subarachnoid or ventricular spaces. The patient was discharged December 24 to spend the Christmas holiday at home.

On December 28, the infant was re-admitted for further study and treatment. The 4-day sojourn at home had been uneventful, and re-examination showed that the fontanel was depressed and widely open. A weakness of the right side of the face was noticeable when the patient was crying. The therapeutic lumbar punctures and subdural punctures were discontinued. On January 6, after 9 days of continuous hospital residence, swelling of the right wrist was detected—slight dorsal swelling with ecchymosis and tenderness. No unusual trauma had been observed by any of the hospital attendants. Roentgenograms showed a fresh fracture of the right radius and old fractures of the left ulna and the right femur. The fractured bones were well developed and well mineralized; there were no roentgen signs of scurvy. The fractured radius healed promptly, and at 3 years, the patient appeared to be normal, showing no sequels of the subdural hematoma or the multiple fractures.

Case 2. J. M., a white male born after normal gestation and labor on September 11, 1931, weighed 6 pounds. Two blood transfusions were given during the neonatal period for the treatment of hemorrhagic disease of the newly born. He was breast-fed for 1 month and then fed from a bottle until the 11th month. Cod liver oil was given after the 5th month, and 1 ounces of orange juice were taken daily after the 6th month. Gain in weight was slow; at 1 year, he weighed only 16 pounds.

During the 7th month, the gums became swollen and hemorrhagic. In the 10th month, blood was found in vomitus and feces. At the same time, bluish and black spots appeared on the skin of the face and arms. The patient is said to have taken $1\frac{1}{2}$ ounces of orange juice daily during the 3 months prior to the onset of these hemorrhagic manifestations.

A few weeks later, during the 10th month, the infant suddenly became cyanotic and rigid and remained so for one-half hour. Examination at this time in another hospital disclosed scattered petechiae in the oral mucous membrane and ecchymoses on the skin of the face, arms, and trunk. The left side of the face and the left arm were weak. Numerous hemorrhages were found in the ocular fundi. The subdural space was aspirated through the left side of the anterior fontanel and yielded bloody fluid. At this time, the clotting and bleeding times of the blood were normal, and the blood platelets were normal in number. Hematuria was not demonstrated in several examinations of the urine. Roentgen examination of the extremities was said to have shown some osteoporosis but no changes diagnostic of scurvy and no fractures.

After discharge from the first hospital, convulsions recurred frequently at home, often three and four times daily, until the 15th month, when he was admitted to a second hospital. In examinations there, the patient appeared to be undernourished and pale, and there were numerous old ecchymoses on the head and thighs. The anterior fontanel was still widely open, and mental development was retarded. The ocular fundi were normal. The bleeding and clotting times were not increased, and there were 135,000 platelets per cu. mm. of blood. Fluid, withdrawn from the lumbar subarachnoid space, was yellow and contained 136 erythrocytes per cu. mm. In pneumograms of the skull, the lateral ventricles were dilated and asymmetrical and the cranial sutures were widened. The blood Wassermann test gave a nonsyphilitic reaction. After a hospital residence of 1 month, the patient was discharged improved.

After only 4 days at home and at 16 months of age, the infant was returned to the hospital because of tenderness of the left leg, which was said to have appeared suddenly without injury 4 days previously, on the same day that he had been discharged from the hospital. After re-admission, the left leg was found to be hot, swollen, and tender from the thigh to the ankle. There were purpuric patches on the skin over the left knee and ankle. Roentgen examination disclosed swelling of the soft parts of the left leg but no signs of scurvy or fracture in the bones. Two weeks later, a shell of ectopic subperiosteal bone had formed around the lower three quarters of the shaft of the left femur, but there was still no evidence of fracture.

At 19 months of age, he was re-admitted to the same hospital because of difficulty in moving arms and legs. The skull was trephined, and the diagnosis of subdural hematoma was confirmed.

Convulsions recurred at 22 months, and the left arm became partially paralyzed at the shoulder. Roentgen examination of the long bones showed a complete fracture in the lower third of the left femoral shaft, with overriding of the fragments and a large mass of heavily mineralized callus. At the proximal ends of both humeri, subperiosteal shells of bone surrounded the terminal segments of the shafts. There were no roentgenologic signs of healed or fresh scurvy in the metaphyses.

At 27 months, the patient was admitted for the first time to the Babies Hospital. The head was enlarged, and there was limitation of movement of the extremities, more pronounced on the right side. The ocular fundi were pale. Examination of the blood, urine, and cerebrospinal fluid resulted in normal findings. Pneumograms of the brain disclosed marked dilatation of the ventricular system; there was no evidence of cranial fracture. In roentgenograms of the extremities, the left femur was found to be thickened and deformed at the site of the earlier fracture. The distal end of the left humerus was fragmented and surrounded by externally thickened cortex, and the shaft of the left ulna was cloaked in heavy cortical layers. The findings in the right humerus were similar to those at 22 months, but there was a fresh fracture of the distal end of the right ulna with slight angulation.

Case 3. J. B., a female Negro, was born March 10, 1933, after a normal pregnancy and labor. The birth weight was 5 pounds. She was fed from the breast for 2 months, after which a bottle was given with daily cod liver oil and orange juice. She developed normally.

At 8 months, she had a generalized convulsion and remained unconscious for several hours. After admission to another hospital, two convulsions occurred during a residence there of 6 days. Convulsive seizures recurred at home; after 4 days, the patient was brought to the Babies Hospital. She was found to be poorly nourished (6.7 kilograms) and short (70 cm.), with large head (43 cm. in circumference). The fontanel was not bulging, and there were no signs of meningeal irritation. Multiple fresh hemorrhages were seen in each ocular fundus. Bloody fluid under increased pressure spurted from the needle inserted into the lumbar spine; this fluid was yellow after centrifugation. Subdural punctures on both sides of the anterior fontanel yielded blood-tinged fluid, which remained yellow after centrifugation. Kahn's test on the blood and cerebrospinal fluid resulted in nonsyphilitic reactions. The urine was free of blood in several examinations. Subdural fluid was withdrawn at weekly intervals in the hospital, and although the fluid remained blood tinged, the patient became brighter and more active. After 1 month, the infant was discharged.

Four days later, the mother brought the baby back to the hospital because the right leg had suddenly become tender and swollen and bruises had appeared under the left eye and in other parts of the body. The mother denied that any injury had occurred during the 4 days since discharge from the hospital. Movement in both lower extremities was found to be limited, and the right leg was swollen and tender. There was a large ecchymosis on the left side of the face just beneath the orbit, and numerous petechiae were scattered on the abdominal wall. Several fresh hemorrhagic foci were found in the ocular fundi. Lumbar subarachnoid fluid and subdural fluid, withdrawn from the lateral angles of the anterior fontanel, were discolored with blood. Roentgenograms of the extremities disclosed that the bones in the arms were normal, but five fractures were visible in the shafts of the bones adjacent to the knee joints—one in the distal end of each femur, one in the proximal end of each tibia, and one in the right fibula. These bones were well mineralized, and there were no signs of scurvy in the shafts, the metaphyses or in the epiphyseal ossification centers. In roentgenograms made 18 days later, heavy cortical thickenings surrounded the fractured shafts. The skull was not examined roentgenographically.

The patient remained in the hospital 25 days. The swelling and tenderness gradually subsided and disappeared. There were no later observations.

Case 4. R. M. S., female, was born December 3, 1942, after a normal gestation and labor; she weighed 6 pounds.

Convulsions began at 1 month of age and recurred frequently thereafter. A "blood clot," presumably a subdural hematoma, was removed from the cranial cavity during the 6th month at another hospital. Following the operation, the convulsions ceased, and the vision seemed to improve.

At 12 months, pain and tenderness were first noted in the left arm; these manifestations disappeared after 2 weeks, and they did not recur. The mother stated that injury had not occurred at any time. Examination at another clinic disclosed that the movements of the left arm were limited and painful. The left arm was swollen above the elbow, and extension of the elbow was limited to 165 degrees; flexion was normal. Pronation and supination were limited to 20 degrees.

The patient had resided in hospitals during most of the first year and presumably had received a normal diet with adequate vitamin C. Development was retarded. She failed to sit up or stand alone during the first 15 months of life.

At 15 months of age, she was admitted to the Babies Hospital for the first time; she ap-

peared well nourished. There was a long, healed surgical scar in the scalp; the left arm was flexed at the elbow and hung motionless except when touched. Both active and passive movements of the left arm were painful. Microscopic and chemical examinations of the blood and urine were normal. Kline's test on the blood gave a nonsyphilitic reaction. Clear cerebrospinal fluid withdrawn from the lumbar spine was normal microscopically and chemically. The ocular fundi were pale.

In pneumograms of the skull, the cerebral ventricular system was found to be dilated, and there was considerable irregularity in the density of the parietal bones in the sites of earlier craniotomies, which were done during the 6th month of life. Roentgenograms of the long bones disclosed cortical thickenings in both humeri. At the proximal end of the right humerus, there was a deformity with displacement of a terminal diaphyseal fracture fragment and its attached epiphyseal centers. In contrast, only the distal end of the left humerus was thickened. In the distal end of the right tibia, there was an old transverse metaphyseal fracture with thickenings of the cortex and displacement of the distal fracture fragment and its attached epiphysis. There were no changes suggestive of old or recent scurvy or rickets.

Following discharge from the hospital, the patient did not return for follow-up observations.

Case 5. M. C., male, was born September 4, 1936, after a normal pregnancy and labor; the birth weight was 7 pounds. He thrived on breast milk until the 5th week, when he suddenly became weak and dyspneic and remained so for 3 days when a single convulsion occurred. No injury was observed prior to the onset of these complaints. A few hours after the convulsion, he was admitted to the Babies Hospital and was found to be somnolent but hyper-irritable when disturbed. Respirations were irregular. The anterior fontanel protruded, but the neck was not stiff, and there were no signs of meningeal irritation.

Subdural fluid withdrawn from the left side of the anterior fontanel was blood-tinged, as was subarachnoid fluid obtained from the lumbar spine. The patient became more alert after these punctures, although the fontanel remained full and the sutures became widened. He vomited irregularly.

At 2 months, the cranial circumference measured 42 cm. Bloody subdural fluid was obtained in aspirations from both sides of the anterior fontanel. There were no hemorrhages in the ocular fundi. Roentgenograms of the cranium revealed widening of the great sutures and thinning and osteoporosis of the calvarium, but no fractures were visible. The extremities appeared to be normal clinically; roentgenograms of them were not made.

At 5 months, the patient was re-admitted for 2 weeks, with bilateral purulent otitis media. No abnormalities of the extremities were noted in the physical examination.

The patient re-entered the hospital at 7 months of age. Six days earlier, black and blue spots had appeared on the forehead and face. Similar spots were observed on the hands, feet, and back on the day of admission. Six hours before admission, the left thigh began to swell, and the infant cried out with pain when the thigh was touched or attempts were made to move him. The mother denied that the patient had been injured. Orange juice had been started at 3 months of age and had been taken in daily dosage of approximately 1 ounce.

Scattered ecchymoses were found in the skin of the face and extremities. The left thigh was diffusely swollen and tender; it was held in abduction and flexion. There were no hemorrhages in the ocular fundi. Subdural taps on the right and left side of the anterior fontanel yielded blood-tinged fluid. The blood and urine were normal microscopically and chemically; there was no hematuria. The bleeding time was 2 minutes; the clotting time was 6 minutes; there were 490,000 blood platelets per cu. mm. Kahn's test on the blood gave a nonsyphilitic reaction.

Roentgenograms of the extremities disclosed a fresh, long, spiral fracture of the left femur and an impacted fracture in the proximal metaphysis of the right humerus. Old healed fractures with angular deformities also were evident in the middle thirds of the right radius and ulna. There were no roentgen signs of old or recent scurvy. In the cranium, there were no visible fractures.

The left lower extremity was fixed in traction for 5 weeks, and the femoral fracture healed satisfactorily. The patient was discharged to an institution for chronic care and has not been observed since.

Case 6. A. L., female, was born on December 6, 1942, after cesarean section. She weighed 6 pounds. During the first 2 weeks, she appeared to be normal and suffered no recognized injuries.

Convulsions and projectile vomiting began at the end of the 2nd week. Thereafter convulsions recurred frequently, often as many as four times daily.

During the 6th week the mother noted that the infant's left leg was limp and tender. Injury to the baby was specifically denied; only the mother had cared for the infant. The head was large and measured 17 cm. in circumference. The anterior fontanel was large, full, and tense. Both eyes showed proptosis, and the vision appeared to be poor. Forty-five cc. of bloody subdural fluid were withdrawn from the right side of the anterior fontanel and 15 cc. from the left side. This fluid was yellow after centrifugation. Roentgenograms of the extremities showed a partially healed, complete transverse fracture of the left tibia and fine fragmentation of the distal end of the right femur and the proximal end of the right tibia. Delicate layers of subperiosteal bone overlay the external surfaces of the humeri. There were no roentgen signs of scurvy and no hematuria. In roentgenograms of the skull, the sutures were widened, but there were no fractures. The bones of the thorax and pelvis were normal.

TABLE 1.1 Summary of Important Data in Six Cases

Case	Bones Affected	Total Lesions	Fractures	Contusions	Location Fracture Metaphyseal	Diaphyseal	Following Subdural Hematoma	History Trauma	Remarks
1	Radius Ulna Femur	3	3	0	0	3	1	0	Fracture of radius during hospital residence without recognized injury
2	Femur Humerus (2) Ulna (2)	5	4	1	2	2	5	0	Skeleton normal roentgenographically at onset of subdural hematoma
3	Femurs (2) Tibias (2) Fibulas	5	5	0	5	0	5	0	All fractures located in opposing bones at knee joint
4	Humerus (2) Tibia (2)	4	3	1	3	0	4	0	Clinical signs of fracture aooeared 11 months after first convulsion
5	Femur Tibia Radius Ulna	4	4	0	1	3	2	0	Fractures of radius and ulna probably neonatal; fractures of humerus and femur occurred at 7 months of age
6	Humerus (2) Tibia (2) Femur	6	5	2	3	1	0	0	Cesarean section; first convulsion in second week of life
TOTAL	26	27	23	4	14	9	17	0	

Subdural fluid was withdrawn in large amounts in repeated aspirations, and at 10 weeks, a subdural hematoma was removed after craniotomy. The postoperative course was satisfactory. The patient returned to the care of her private physician.

COMMENT

The skeletal changes are summarized in Table 1.1, and their distribution is depicted schematically in Figure 1.1. In the aggregate, all of the large bones in the upper and lower extremities were fractured, but the small bones of the hands, feet, wrists, and ankles were not affected. The epiphyseal ossification centers were all intact, and fractures were not found in the cranium or in the flat bones of the pelvis and shoulder girdle.

Save for the fractures, the entire skeletons of all patients appeared to be healthy; this was true of the fractured as well as the unfractured bones. There was neither clinical nor roentgen evidence to support the idea that pre-existing systemic or localized skeletal disease weakened the bones and made them unusually vulnerable to trauma.

The large cortical thickenings associated with several of the fractures are similar to the cortical thickenings which develop in many cases of scurvy following subperiosteal hemorrhage. The other roentgen signs which characterize active scurvy are, however, conspicuously absent in these cases—changes in the metaphyses, spongiosa, corticalis, and epiphyseal ossification centers. Moreover, five patients (except Case 1) appeared to have taken adequate vitamin C at the time fractures were found, and none of them exhibited the clinical manifestations of active scurvy. During the first years of life, when the periosteum is normally loosely attached to the underlying corticalis and is normally richly supplied with blood vessels, large subperiosteal hemorrhages commonly develop at the sites of traumatic fractures in nonscorbutic infants. Two

other features make the scorbutic origin of the fractures highly improbable. Nine of the fractures were located deep in the shafts (see ulna, Case 1; femur, Case 2; femur, Case 5; tibia Case 6); scorbutic fractures, in contrast, develop characteristically in the metaphyses near the cartilage-shaft junctions. Furthermore, angular deformities of the fractured bones persisted after healing in several bones (see femur, Case 1; femur, Case 2; humerus, Case 4; radius and ulna, Case 5). Scorbutic fractures in our experience heal without residual angular deformities. Although scurvy has been described in a few cases of infantile subdural hematoma,[4,5] there is no convincing clinical or roentgen evidence that the patients in this group suffered from vitamin C deficiency.

When cortical thickenings were demonstrated in the absence of visible fractures, the lesions have been classified as periosteal contusions (see left humerus, Case 4 and both humeri, Case 5). Trauma to the periosteal blood vessels may cause subperiosteal hemorrhage, elevation of the periosteum, and local cortical thickening in nonscorbutic infants. The causal mechanism is similar to that of traumatic ossifying periostitis of the newly born.[6] It is also possible that fractures were actually present in the sites of the cortical thickenings but were invisible roentgenographically. Such was undoubtedly the case in the femur of our second patient. In an early roentgenogram, a large subperiosteal swelling was visible, but there was no evidence of a fracture line; 6 months later, however, at the same site, a healed complete fracture, overriding of the fragments, and massive callus were all evident.

The traumatic theory of the causation of subdural hematoma has been accepted almost to the exclusion of all other causes[7] despite the fact that a history of injury is lacking in almost one half of the cases.[8] The negative history of trauma in so many cases can probably be best explained by assuming that sometimes lay observers do not properly evaluate ordinary but causally significant accidents especially falls on the head and that other important traumatic episodes pass unnoticed or are forgotten by the time delayed cranial symptoms appear. Putman and Cushing[9] have pointed out that weeks or months may elapse between the original cephalic injury and the onset of the clinical signs of subdural hematoma. Also, recognized injuries may be denied by mothers and nurses because injury to an infant implies negligence on the part of its caretaker.

The absence of history of trauma to the fractured bones cannot be explained in the same way. The injuries which caused the fractures in the long bones of these patients were either not observed or were denied when observed. The motive for denial has not been established. The clinical signs of fractures in the long bones usually appear immediately after injury, and the causal relationship between the traumatic force and damage to the bone is clear. It is unlikely that trivial unrecognizable trauma caused the complete fractures in the femurs in Cases 1, 2, and 5; in the humerus in Case 4; and in the radius in Case 1. Moreover, in several cases, ecchymoses were found near the sites of the fractures. There was a striking similarity in the course of events in Case 2 and Case 3. In each case, unexplained fresh fractures appeared shortly after the patient had arrived home after discharge from the hospital. In one of these cases, the infant was clearly unwanted by both parents, and this raised the question of intentional ill treatment of the infant; the evidence was inadequate to prove or disprove this point. In Case 1, a fresh complete fracture of the radius with ecchymoses in the neighboring soft tissues developed after a continuous residence of 9 days in the hospital, and, notwithstanding, injury was not observed or at least not admitted by the hospital attendants.

It is possible that some of the fractures in the long bones were caused by the same traumatic forces which were presumably responsible for the subdural hematomas. However, this was not the case in the majority of the fractures because 17 fresh fractures appeared many weeks and months after the first clinical manifestations of subdural hematoma and after the withdrawal of bloody fluid from the subdural space. In one patient (Case 4), fractures in the long bones developed 6 months after the subdural tumor had been removed surgically.

We have also considered the possibility that the long bones were injured and fractured during convulsive seizures. There is little evidence to support such a postulate. In not a single case did fresh fractures appear immediately following the convulsive seizure, and complete fractures occurred in patients who had only mild convulsions. It has been demonstrated that the vertebral bodies of children may be fractured during the convulsive seizures of tetanus,[10] but in these circumstances, there were no associated fractures in the extremities. To our knowledge, fractures of convulsive origin in the long bones have never been demonstrated in the common severe convulsive diseases of infancy and childhood such as lead poisoning, meningitis, cerebral neoplasm, and hypocalcemic tetany.

SUMMARY

(1) Six infants with chronic subdural hematoma and associated multiple fractures in the long bones are described.

(2) History of injury to the long bones as well as to the head was lacking in all cases.

(3) There was no roentgen or clinical evidence of general or localized skeletal disease which would have predisposed the bones to pathological fractures.

(4) The majority of the fractures developed after the onset of the subdural hematomas.

CONCLUSIONS

Fractures of the long bones are a common complication of infantile subdural hematoma.

The fractures appear to be of traumatic origin, but the traumatic episodes and the causal mechanism remain obscure.

The presence of unexplained fractures in the long bones warrants investigation for subdural hematoma.

Routine roentgen examination of the long bones in subdural hematoma is necessary for the identification of fractures because many of them are silent clinically.

REFERENCES

1. SHERWOOD, D. Chronic subdural hematoma in infants. *Am. J. Dis. Child.,* 1930, 39, 980.

2. INGRAHAM, F. D., and HEYL, H. L. Subdural hematoma in infancy and childhood. *J. Am. M. Ass.,* 1939, 112, 198-204.

3. INGRAHAM, F. D. Personal communication, May 7, 1945.

4. GILMAN, B. B., and TANZER, R. C. Subdural hematoma in infantile scurvy. *J. Am. M. Ass.,* 1932, 99, 989-991.

5. INGALLS, T. H. The role of scurvy in the etiology of chronic subdural hematoma. *New England J. Med.,* 1936, 215, 1279-1281.

6. SNEDECOR, S. T., KNAPP, R. E., and WILSON, H. B. Traumatic ossifying periostitis of the newborn. *Surg., Gynec. & Obst.,* 1935, 61, 385-387.

7. GROFF, R. A., and GRANT, F. C. Chronic subdural hematoma; collective review. *Internat. Abstr. Surg.,* 1942, 74, 9-20.

8. INGRAHAM, F. D., and MATSON, D. D. Subdural hematoma in infancy. *J. Pediat.,* 1945, 24, 1.

9. PUTNAM, T. J., and CUSHING, H. Chronic subdural hematoma. *Arch. Surg.,* 1925, 11, 329-393.

10. DIETRICH, H. F., KARSHNER, R. G., and STEWART, S. F. Tetanus and lesions of the spine in childhood. *J. Bone & Joint Surg.,* 1940, 22, 43-54.

The Battered-Child Syndrome

C. HENRY KEMPE
FREDERIC N. SILVERMAN
BRANDT F. STEELE
WILLIAM DROEGEMUELLER
HENRY K. SILVER   *1962*

"The Battered-Child Syndrome" has come to be regarded as the single most significant document in the history of child abuse research and treatment. First presented by Dr. C. Henry Kempe, and later published by Dr. Kempe and his colleagues in the Journal of the American Medical Association, the material in this paper created the first real wave of public and professional awareness of and active concern about physical abuse of children.

Donna Rosenberg talks of the raw shock value of this paper, whose authors grabbed attention for its beleaguered subjects by cannily naming the article "The Battered-Child Syndrome." She also explains that the authors withstood the ridicule of their colleagues for mucking about in family concerns, for venturing beyond respectable borders of medical practice, for being alarmists.

There are many firsts in this paper. Kevin Browne says that this paper defined and introduced the term *the battered-child syndrome*, expanding on the work of Caffey introduced in 1946, in which he recognized nonaccidental fractures of bone in children, called "the parent-infant stress syndrome." Susan Hiatt explains that although earlier papers such as Caffey's had documented the phenomenon of physical abuse, this paper was the first to trigger widespread media interest, complete with national magazine cover stories showing pictures of battered children. It also was the first to attempt to establish the incidence of the problem and to allude to the wider variety of forms of maltreatment. Browne points out that in this paper Kempe offers psychiatric considerations and psychological explanations in addition to descriptions of the clinical manifestations of physical abuse. The paper offers techniques for evaluation and diagnosis of physical abuse and begins to consider the management of such cases. Hiatt adds that the concept of intergenerational transmission of child abuse was described, and, for the first time, the paper advocated the use of multidisciplinary teams in the diagnosis and treatment of child abuse.

The legacy of this paper is very evident today. Although the estimates of incidence in this paper were very low (in the hundreds versus a million or more today), it has been the catalyst for so much of the clinical work and research that has followed on the identification, causes, consequences, and management of battered children, specifically, and abused children in general. The result is a vast literature on child abuse that includes a more realistic sense of incidence. The paper also was an important stimulus for public policy, including the adoption in all 50 of the states in the United States of laws mandating the reporting of child abuse. And, according to Hiatt, this paper serves as a constant reminder to look at and respond to the root causes of abuse, not just the presenting problem. The paper calls for us to consider behavior patterns and family history in an inquisitive yet compassionate way, looking at the whole family, not just the child. As Rosenberg concludes, the content of this paper—a series of case studies, has been remarkably durable, an irony given that, if it were submitted for peer review today, it would doubtless be rejected because it doesn't meet today's rigorous standards of research methodology.

A. C. D. and K. O.

The battered-child syndrome is a term used by us to characterize a clinical condition in young children who have received serious physical abuse, generally from a parent or foster parent. The condition has also been described as "unrecognized trauma" by radiologists, orthopedists, pediatricians, and social service workers. It is a significant cause of childhood disability and death. Unfortunately, it is frequently not recognized or, if diagnosed, is inadequately handled by the physician because of hesitation to bring the case to the attention of the proper authorities.

INCIDENCE

In an attempt to collect data on the incidence of this problem, we undertook a nationwide survey of hospitals, which were asked to indicate the incidence of this syndrome in a 1-year period. Among 71 hospitals replying, 302 such cases were reported to have occurred; 33 of the children died, and 85 suffered permanent brain injury. In one third of the cases, proper medical diagnosis was followed by some type of legal action. We also surveyed 77 District Attorneys, who reported that they had knowledge of 447 cases in a similar 1-year period. Of these, 45 died, and 29 suffered permanent brain damage; court action was initiated in 46% of this group. This condition has been a particularly common problem in our hospitals; on a single day, in November 1961, the Pediatric Service of the Colorado General Hospital was caring for four infants suffering from the parent-inflicted battered-child syndrome. Two of the four died of their central nervous system trauma; one subsequently died suddenly in an unexplained manner 4 weeks after discharge from the hospital while under the care of its parents, while the fourth is still enjoying good health.

CLINICAL MANIFESTATIONS

The clinical manifestations of the battered-child syndrome vary widely, from those cases in which the trauma is very mild and is often

exhibit the most florid evidence of injury to the soft tissues and skeleton. In the former group, the patients' signs and symptoms may be considered to have resulted from failure to thrive from some other cause or to have been produced by a metabolic disorder, an infectious process, or some other disturbance. In these patients, specific findings of trauma such as bruises or characteristic roentgenographic changes as described below may be misinterpreted and their significance not recognized.

The battered-child syndrome may occur at any age, but, in general, the affected children are younger than 3 years. In some instances, the clinical manifestations are limited to those resulting from a single episode of trauma, but more often the child's general health is below par, and he shows evidence of neglect including poor skin hygiene, multiple soft tissue injuries, and malnutrition. One often obtains a history of previous episodes suggestive of parental neglect or trauma. A marked discrepancy between clinical findings and historical data, as supplied by the parents, is a major diagnostic feature of the battered-child syndrome. The fact that no new lesions, either of the soft tissue or of the bone, occur while the child is in the hospital or in a protected environment lends added weight to the diagnosis and tends to exclude many diseases of the skeletal or hemopoietic systems in which lesions may occur spontaneously or after minor trauma. Subdural hematoma, with or without fracture of the skull, is, in our experience, an extremely frequent finding even in the absence of fractures of the long bones. In an occasional case, the parent or parent-substitute may also have assaulted the child by administering an overdose of a drug or by exposing the child to natural gas or other toxic substances. The characteristic distribution of these multiple fractures and the observation that the lesions are in different stages of healing are of additional value in making the diagnosis.

In most instances, the diagnostic bone lesions are observed incidental to examination for purposes other than evaluation for possible abuse. Occasionally, examination following known injury discloses signs of other, unsuspected, skeletal involvement. When parental assault is under consideration, radiologic examination of the entire skeleton may provide objective confirmation. Following diagnosis, radiologic examination can document the healing of lesions and reveal the appearance of new lesions if additional trauma has been inflicted.

The radiologic manifestations of trauma to growing skeletal structures are the same, whether or not there is a history of injury. Yet, there is reluctance on the part of many physicians to accept the radiologic signs as indications of repetitive trauma and possible abuse. This reluctance stems from the emotional unwillingness of the physician to consider abuse as the cause of the child's difficulty and also because of unfamiliarity with certain aspects of fracture healing so that he is unsure of the significance of the lesions that are present. To the informed physician, the bones tell a story the child is too young or too frightened to tell.

PSYCHIATRIC ASPECTS

Psychiatric knowledge pertaining to the problem of the battered child is meager, and the literature on the subject is almost nonexistent. The type and degree of physical attack varies greatly. At one extreme, there is direct murder of children. This is usually done by a parent or other close relative, and, in these individuals, a frank psychosis is usually readily apparent. At the other extreme are those cases where no overt harm has occurred, and one parent, more often the mother, comes to the psychiatrist for help, filled with anxiety and guilt related to fantasies of hurting the child. Occasionally, the disorder has gone beyond the point of fantasy and has resulted in severe slapping or spanking. In such cases, the adult is usually responsive to treatment; it is not known whether or not the disturbance in these adults would progress to the point where they would inflict significant trauma on the child.

Between these two extremes are a large number of battered children with mild to severe injury which may clear completely or result in permanent damage or even death after repeated attack. Descriptions of such children have been published by numerous investigators including radiologists, orthopedists, and social workers. The latter have reported on their studies of investigations of families in which children have been beaten and of their work in effecting satisfactory placement for the protection of the child. In some of these published reports, the parents, or at least the parent who inflicted the abuse, have been found to be of low intelligence. Often, they are described as psychopathic or sociopathic characters. Alcoholism, sexual promiscuity, unstable marriages, and minor criminal activities are reportedly common among them. They are immature, impulsive, self-centered, hypersensitive, and quick to react with poorly controlled aggression. Data, in some cases, indicate that such attacking parents had themselves been subject to some degree of attack from their parents in their own childhood.

Beating of children, however, is not confined to people with a psychopathic personality or of borderline socioeconomic status. It also occurs among people with good education and stable financial and social background. However, from the scant data that are available, it would appear that in these cases, too, there is a defect in character structure which allows aggressive impulses to be expressed too freely. There is also some suggestion that the attacking parent was subjected to similar abuse in childhood. It would appear that one of the most important factors to be found in families where parental assault occurs is "to do unto others as you have been done by." This is not surprising; it has long been recognized by psychologists and social anthropologists that patterns of child rearing, both good and bad, are passed from one generation to the next in relatively unchanged form. Psychologically, one could describe this phenomenon as an identification with the aggressive parent, this identification occurring despite strong wishes of the person to be different. Not infrequently, the beaten infant is a product of an unwanted pregnancy, a pregnancy which began before marriage, too soon after marriage, or at some other time felt to be extremely inconvenient. Sometimes, several children in one family have been beaten; at other times, one child is singled out for attack while others are treated quite lovingly. We have also seen instances in which the sex of the child who is severely attacked is related to very specific factors in the context of the abusive parent's neurosis.

It is often difficult to obtain the information that a child has been attacked by its parent. To be sure, some of the extremely sociopathic characters will say, "Yeah, Johnny would not stop crying so I hit him. So what? He cried harder so I hit him harder." Sometimes, one spouse will indicate that the other was the attacking person, but more often, there is complete denial of any knowledge of injury to the child and the maintenance of an attitude of complete innocence on the part of both parents. Such attitudes are maintained despite the fact that evidence of physical attack is obvious and that the trauma could not have happened in any other way. Denial by the parents of any involvement in the abusive episode may, at times, be a conscious, protective device, but in other instances, it may be a denial based upon psychological repression. Thus, one mother who seemed to have been the one who injured her baby had complete amnesia for the episodes in which her aggression burst forth so strikingly.

In addition to the reluctance of the parents to give information regarding the attacks on their children, there is another factor which is of great importance and extreme interest as it relates to the difficulty in delving into the problem of parental neglect and abuse. This is the fact that physicians have great difficulty both in believing that parents could have attacked their children and in undertaking the essential questioning of parents on this subject. Many physicians find it hard to believe that such an attack could have occurred, and they attempt to obliterate such suspicions from their minds, even in the face of obvious circumstantial evidence. The reason for this is not clearly understood. One possibility is that the arousal of the physician's antipathy in response to such situations is so great that it is easier for the physician to deny the possibility of such attack than to have to deal with the excessive anger which surges up in him when he realizes the truth of the situation. Furthermore, the physician's training and personality usually makes it quite difficult for him to assume the role of policeman or district attorney and start questioning patients as if he were investigating a crime. The humanitarian-minded physician finds it most difficult to proceed when he is met with protestations of innocence from the aggressive parent, especially when the battered child was brought to him voluntarily.

Although the technique wherein the physician obtains the necessary information in cases of child beating is not adequately solved, certain routes of questioning have been particularly fruitful in some cases. One spouse may be asked about the other spouse in relation to unusual or curious behavior or for direct description of dealings with the baby. Clues to the parents' character and pattern of response may be obtained by asking questions about sources of worry and tension. Revealing answers may be brought out by questions concerning the baby such as, "Does he cry a lot? Is he stubborn? Does he obey well? Does he eat well? Do you have problems in controlling him?" A few general questions concerning the parents' own ideas of how they themselves were brought up may bring forth illuminating answers; interviews with grandparents or other relatives may elicit additional suggestive data. In some cases, psychological tests may disclose strong aggressive tendencies, impulsive behavior, and lack of adequate mechanisms of controlling impulsive behavior. In other cases, only prolonged contact in a psychotherapeutic milieu

will lead to a complete understanding of the background and circumstances surrounding the parental attack. Observation by nurses or other ancillary personnel of the behavior of the parents in relation to the hospitalized infant is often extremely valuable.

The following two condensed case histories depict some of the problems encountered in dealing with the battered-child syndrome.

▌ REPORT OF CASES ▌

Case 1. The patient was brought to the hospital at the age of 3 months because of enlargement of the head, convulsions, and spells of unconsciousness. Examination revealed bilateral subdural hematomas, which were later operated upon with great improvement in physical status. There had been a hospital admission at the age of 1 month because of a fracture of the right femur, sustained "when the baby turned over in the crib and caught its leg in the slats." There was no history of any head trauma except "when the baby was in the other hospital a child threw a little toy at her and hit her in the head." The father had never been alone with the baby, and the symptoms of difficulty appeared to have begun when the mother had been caring for the baby. Both parents showed concern and requested the best possible care for their infant. The father, a graduate engineer, related instances of impulsive behavior, but these did not appear to be particularly abnormal, and he showed appropriate emotional concern over the baby's appearance and impending operation. The mother, aged 21, a high school graduate, was very warm and friendly and gave all the appearance of having endeavored to be a good mother. However, it was noted by both nurses and physicians that she did not react as appropriately or seem as upset about the baby's appearance as did her husband. From interviews with the father and later with the mother, it became apparent that she had occasionally shown very impulsive, angry behavior, sometimes acting rather strangely and doing bizarre things which she could not explain nor remember. This was their first child and had resulted from an unwanted pregnancy which had occurred almost immediately after marriage and before the parents were ready for it. Early in pregnancy, the mother had made statements about giving the baby away, but by the time of delivery, she was apparently delighted with the baby and seemed to be quite fond of it. After many interviews, it became apparent that the mother had identified herself with her own mother, who had also been unhappy with her first pregnancy and had frequently beaten her children. Despite very strong conscious wishes to be a kind, good mother, the mother of our patient was evidently repeating the behavior of her own mother toward herself. Although an admission of guilt was not obtained, it seemed likely that the mother was the one responsible for attacking the child; only after several months of treatment did the amnesia for the aggressive outbursts begin to lift. She responded well to treatment, but for a prolonged period after the infant left the hospital, the mother was not allowed alone with her.

Case 2. This patient was admitted to the hospital at the age of 13 months with signs of central nervous system damage and was found to have a fractured skull. The parents were questioned closely, but no history of trauma could be elicited. After 1 week in the hospital, no further treatment was deemed necessary, so the infant was discharged home in the care of her mother, only to return a few hours later with hemiparesis, a defect in vision, and a new depressed skull fracture on the other side of the head. There was no satisfactory explanation for the new skull fracture, but the mother denied having been involved in causing the injury, even though the history revealed that the child had changed markedly during the hour when the mother had been alone with her. The parents of this child were a young, middle-class couple who, in less than 2 years of marriage, had been separated, divorced, and remarried. Both felt that the infant had been unwanted and had come too soon in the marriage. The mother gave a history of having had a "nervous breakdown" during her teens. She had received psychiatric assistance because she had been markedly upset early in the pregnancy. Following an uneventful delivery, she had been depressed and had received further psychiatric aid and four electroshock treatments. The mother tended to gloss over the unhappiness during the pregnancy and stated that she was quite delighted when the baby was born. It is interesting to note that the baby's first symptoms of difficulty began the first day after its first birthday, suggesting an "anniversary reaction." On psychological and neurological examination, this mother showed definite signs of organic brain damage, probably of lifelong duration and possibly related to her own prematurity. Apparently, her significant intellectual defects had been camouflaged by an attitude of coy, naive, cooperative sweetness which distracted attention from her deficits. It was noteworthy that she had managed to complete a year of college work despite a borderline IQ. It appeared that the impairment in mental functioning was probably the prime factor associated with poor control of aggressive impulses. It is known that some individuals may react with aggressive attack or psychosis when faced with demands beyond their intellectual capacity. This mother was not allowed to have unsupervised care of her child.

Up to the present time, therapeutic experience with the parents of battered children is minimal. Counseling carried on in social agencies has been far from successful or rewarding. We know of no reports of successful psychotherapy in such cases. In general, psychiatrists feel that treatment of the so-called psychopath or sociopath is rarely successful. Further psychological investigation of the character structure of attacking parents is sorely needed. Hopefully, better understanding of the mechanisms involved in the control and release of aggressive impulses will aid in the earlier diagnosis, prevention of attack, and treatment of parents, as well as give us better ability to predict the likelihood of further attack in the future. At present, there is no safe remedy in the situation except the separation of battered children from their insufficiently protective parents.

TECHNIQUES OF EVALUATION

A physician needs to have a high initial level of suspicion of the diagnosis of the battered-child syndrome in instances of subdural hematoma, multiple unexplained fractures at different stages of healing, failure to thrive, when soft tissue swellings or skin bruising are present, or in any other situation where the degree and type of injury is at variance with the history given regarding its occurrence or in any child who dies suddenly. Where the problem of parental abuse comes up for consideration, the physician should tell the parents that it is his opinion that the injury should not occur if the child were adequately protected, and he should indicate that he would welcome the parents giving him the full story so that he might be able to give greater assistance to them to prevent similar occurrences from taking place in the future. The idea that they can now help the child by giving a very complete history of circumstances surrounding the injury sometimes helps the parents feel that they are atoning for the wrong that they have done. But, in many instances, regardless of the approach used in attempting to elicit a full story of the abusive incident(s), the parents will continue to deny that they were guilty of any wrongdoing. In talking with the parents, the physician may sometimes obtain added information by showing that he understands their problem and that he wishes to be of aid to them as well as to the child. He may help them reveal the circumstances of the injuries by pointing out reasons that they may use to explain their ac-

tion. If it is suggested that "new parents sometimes lose their tempers and are a little too forceful in their actions," the parents may grasp such a statement as the excuse for their actions. Interrogation should not be angry or hostile but should be sympathetic and quiet with the physician indicating his assurance that the diagnosis is well established on the basis of objective findings and that all parties, including the parents, have an obligation to avoid a repetition of the circumstances leading to the trauma. The doctor should recognize that bringing the child for medical attention in itself does not necessarily indicate that the parents were innocent of wrongdoing and are showing proper concern; trauma may have been inflicted during times of uncontrollable temporary rage. Regardless of the physician's personal reluctance to become involved, complete investigation is necessary for the child's protection so that a decision can be made as to the necessity of placing the child away from the parents until matters are fully clarified.

Often, the guilty parent is the one who gives the impression of being normal. In two recent instances, young physicians have assumed that the mother was at fault because she was unkempt and depressed while the father, in each case a military man with good grooming and polite manners, turned out to be the psychopathic member of the family. In these instances, it became apparent that the mother had good reason to be depressed.

RADIOLOGIC FEATURES

Radiologic examination plays two main roles in the problem of child abuse. Initially, it is a tool for case finding, and, subsequently, it is useful as a guide in management.

The diagnostic signs result from a combination of circumstances: age of the patient, nature of the injury, the time that has elapsed before the examination is carried out, and whether the traumatic episode was repeated or occurred only once.

Age. As a general rule, the children are under 3 years of age; most, in fact, are infants. In this age group, the relative amount of radiolucent cartilage is great; therefore, anatomical disruptions of cartilage without gross deformity are radiologically invisible or difficult to demonstrate. Since the periosteum of infants is less securely attached to the underlying bone than in older children and adults, it is more easily and extensively stripped from the shaft by hemorrhage than in older patients. In infancy, massive subperiosteal hematomas may follow injury and elevate the active periosteum so that new bone formation can take place around and remote from the parent shaft.

Nature of injury. The ease and frequency with which a child is seized by his arms or legs make injuries to the appendicular skeleton the most common in this syndrome. Even when bony injuries are present elsewhere, for example, skull, spine, or ribs, signs of injuries to the extremities are usually present. The extremities are the "handles" for rough handling, whether the arm is pulled to bring a reluctant child to his feet or to speed his ascent upstairs or whether the legs are held while swinging the tiny body in a punitive way or in an attempt to enforce corrective measures. The forces applied by an adult hand in grasping and seizing usually involve traction and torsion; these are the forces most likely to produce epiphyseal separations and periosteal shearing. Shaft fractures result from direct blows or from bending and compression forces.

Time after injury that the X-ray examination is made. This is important in evaluating known or suspected cases of child abuse. Unless gross fractures, dislocations, or epiphyseal separations were produced, no signs of bone injury are found during the first week after a specific injury. Reparative changes may first become manifest about 12 to 14 days after the injury and can increase over the subsequent weeks, depending on the extent of initial injury and the degree of repetition. Reparative changes are more active in the growing bones of children than in adults and are reflected radiologically in the excessive new bone reaction. Histologically, the reaction has been confused with neoplastic change by those unfamiliar with the vigorous reactions of young growing tissue.

Repetition of injury. This is probably the most important factor in producing diagnostic radiologic signs of the syndrome. The findings may depend on diminished immobilization of an injured bone leading to recurring macro- and micro-trauma in the area of injury and healing, with accompanying excessive local reaction and hemorrhage, and ultimately, exaggerated repair. Second, repetitive injury may produce bone lesions in one area at one time, and in another area at another, producing lesions in several areas and in different stages of healing.

Thus, the classical radiologic features of the battered-child syndrome are usually found in the appendicular skeleton in very young children. There may be irregularities of mineralization in the metaphyses of some of the major tubular bones, with slight malalignment of the adjacent epiphyseal ossification center. An overt fracture may be present in another bone. Elsewhere, there may be abundant and active but well-calcified subperiosteal reaction with widening from the shaft toward one end of the bone. One or more bones may demonstrate distinctly thickened cortices, residuals of previously healed periosteal reactions. In addition, the radiographic features of a subdural hematoma with or without obvious skull fracture may be present.

Differential diagnosis. The radiologic features are so distinct that other diseases generally are considered, only because of the reluctance to accept the implications of the bony lesions. Unless certain aspects of bone healing are considered, the pertinent findings may be missed. In many cases, roentgenographic examination is only undertaken soon after known injury; if a fracture is found, reexamination is done after reduction and immobilization; and, if satisfactory positioning has been obtained, the next examination is usually not carried out for a period of 6 weeks when the cast is removed. Any interval films that may have been taken prior to this time probably would have been unsatisfactory since the fine details of the bony lesions would have been obscured by the cast. If fragmentation and bone production are seen, they are considered to be evidence of repair rather than manifestations of multiple or repetitive trauma. If obvious fracture or the knowledge of injury is absent, the bony changes may be considered to be the result of scurvy, syphilis, infantile cortical hyperostoses, or other conditions. The distribution of lesions in the abused child is unrelated to rates of growth; moreover, an extensive lesion may be present at the slow-growing end of a bone which otherwise is normally mineralized and shows no evidence of metabolic disorder at its rapidly growing end.

Scurvy is commonly suggested as an alternative diagnosis, since it also produces large calcifying subperiosteal hemorrhages due to trauma and local exaggerations most marked in areas of rapid growth. However, scurvy is a systemic disease in which all of the bones show the generalized osteoporosis associated with the disease. The dietary histories of most children with recognized trauma have not been grossly abnormal, and whenever the vitamin C content of the blood has been determined, it has been normal.

In the first months of life, *syphilis* can result in metaphyseal and periosteal lesions similar to those under discussion. However, the bone lesions of syphilis tend to be symmetrical and are usually accompanied by other stigmata of the disease. Serological tests should be obtained in questionable cases.

Osteogenesis imperfecta also has bony changes which may be confused with those due to trauma, but it too is a generalized disease, and evidence of the disorder should be present in the bones which are not involved in the disruptive-productive reaction. Even when skull fractures are present, the mosaic ossification pattern of the cranial vault, characteristic of osteogenesis imperfecta, is not seen in the battered-child syndrome. Fractures in osteogenesis imperfecta are commonly of the shafts; they usually occur in the metaphyseal regions in the battered-child syndrome. Blue sclerae, skeletal deformities, and a family history of similar abnormalities were absent in reported instances of children with unrecognized trauma.

Productive diaphyseal lesions may occur in *infantile cortical hyperostosis,* but the metaphyseal lesions of unrecognized trauma easily serve to differentiate the two conditions. The characteristic mandibular involvement of infantile cortical hyperostosis does not occur following trauma, although obvious mandibular fracture may be produced.

Evidence that repetitive unrecognized trauma is the cause of the bony changes found in the battered-child syndrome is, in part, derived from the finding that similar roentgenographic findings are present in *paraplegic patients with sensory deficit* and in patients with *congenital indifference to pain;* in both of whom similar pathogenic mechanisms operate. In paraplegic children, unappreciated injuries have resulted in radiologic pictures with irregular metaphyseal rarefactions, exaggerated subperiosteal new bone formation, and ultimate healing with residual external cortical thickening comparable to those in the battered-child syndrome. In paraplegic adults, excessive callus may form as a consequence of the lack of immobilization, and the lesion may be erroneously diagnosed as osteogenic sarcoma. In children with congenital indifference (or insensitivity) to pain, identical radiologic manifestations may be found.

To summarize, the radiologic manifestations of trauma are specific, and the metaphyseal lesions in particular occur in no other disease of which we are aware. The findings permit a radiologic diagnosis, even when the clinical history seems to refute the possibility of trauma. Under such circumstances, the history must be reviewed, and the child's environment carefully investigated.

MANAGEMENT

The principal concern of the physician should be to make the correct diagnosis so that he can institute proper therapy and make certain that a similar event will not occur again. He should report possible willful trauma to the police department or any special children's protective service that operates in his community. The report that he makes should be restricted to the objective findings which can be verified and, where possible, should be supported by photographs and roentgenograms. For hospitalized patients, the hospital director and the social service department should be notified. In many states, the hospital is also required to report any case of possible unexplained injury to the proper authorities. The physician should acquaint himself with the facilities available in private and public agencies that provide protective services for children. These include children's humane societies, divisions of welfare departments, and societies for the prevention of cruelty to children. These, as well as the police department, maintain a close association with the juvenile court. Any of these agencies may be of assistance in bringing the case before the court, which alone has the legal power to sustain a dependency petition for temporary or permanent separation of the child from the parents' custody. In addition to the legal investigation, it is usually helpful to have an evaluation of the psychological and social factors in the case; this should be started while the child is still in the hospital. If necessary, a court order should be obtained so that such investigation may be performed.

In many instances, the prompt return of the child to the home is contraindicated because of the threat that additional trauma offers to the child's health and life. Temporary placement with relatives or in a well-supervised foster home is often indicated in order to prevent further tragic injury or death to a child who is returned too soon to the original dangerous environment. All too often, despite the apparent cooperativeness of the parents and their apparent desire to have the child with them, the child returns to this home only to be assaulted again and suffer permanent brain damage or death. Therefore, the bias should be in favor of the child's safety; everything should be done to prevent repeated trauma, and the physician should not be satisfied to return the child to an environment where even a moderate risk of repetition exists.

SUMMARY

The battered-child syndrome, a clinical condition in young children who have received serious physical abuse, is a frequent cause of permanent injury or death. Although the findings are quite variable, the syndrome should be considered in any child exhibiting evidence of possible trauma or neglect (fracture of any bone, subdural hematoma, multiple soft tissue injuries, poor skin hygiene, or malnutrition) or where there is a marked discrepancy between the clinical findings and the historical data as supplied by the parents. In cases where a history of specific injury is not available, or in any child who dies suddenly, roentgenograms of the entire skeleton should still be obtained in order to ascertain the presence of characteristic multiple bony lesions in various stages of healing.

Psychiatric factors are probably of prime importance in the pathogenesis of the disorder, but our knowledge of these factors is limited. Parents who inflict abuse on their children do not necessarily have psychopathic or sociopathic personalities or come from borderline socioeconomic groups, although most published cases have been in these categories. In most cases, some defect in character structure is probably present; often, parents may be repeating the type of child care practiced on them in their childhood.

Physicians, because of their own feelings and their difficulty in playing a role that they find hard to assume, may have great reluctance to believe that parents were guilty of abuse. They may also find it difficult to initiate proper investigation so as to assure adequate management of the case. Above all, the physician's duty and responsibility to the child requires a full evaluation of the problem and a guarantee that the expected repetition of trauma will not be permitted to occur.

BIBLIOGRAPHY

Altman, D. H., and Smith, R. L.: Unrecognized Trauma in Infants and Children, *J Bone Joint Surg (Amer) 42A:* 407-413 (April) 1960.

Bakwin, H.: Multiple Skeletal Lesions in Young Children Due to Trauma, *J Pediat 49:* 7-15 (July) 1956.

Barmeyer, G. H.; Alderson, L. R.; and Cox, W. B.: Traumatic Periostitis in Young Children, *J Pediat 38:* 184-190 (Feb.) 1951.

Boardman, H. E.: Project to Rescue Children from Inflicted Injuries, *Soc Work* (no. 1) *7:* 43 (Jan.) 1962.

Caffey, J: Multiple Fractures in Long Bones of Infants Suffering from Chronic Subdural Hematoma, *Amer J Roentgenol 56:* 163-173 (Aug.) 1946.

Caffey, J.: Some Traumatic Lesions in Growing Bones Other Than Fractures and Dislocations: Clinical and Radiological Features, *Brit J Radiol 30:* 225-238 (May) 1957.

Elmer, E.: Abused Young Children Seen in Hospitals, *Soc Work* (no. 4) *5:* 98-102 (Oct.) 1960.

Fisher, S. H.: Skeletal Manifestations of Parent-Induced Trauma in Infants and Children, *Southern Med J51:* 956-960 (Aug.) 1958.

Frauenberger, G. S., and Lis, E. F.: Multiple Fractures Associated with Subdural Hematoma in Infancy, *Pediatrics 6:* 890-892 (Dec.) 1950.

Gwinn, J. L.; Lewin, K. W.; and Peterson, H. G., Jr.: Roentgenographic Manifestations of Unsuspected Trauma in Infancy, *JAMA 176:* 926-929 (June 17) 1961.

Miller, D. S.: Fractures Among Children, *Minnesota Med 42:* 1209-1213 (Sept.) 1959; *42:* 1414-1425 (Oct.) 1959.

Silver, H. K., and Kempe, C. H.: Problem of Parental Criminal Neglect and Severe Physical Abuse of Children, *J Dis Child 95:* 528, 1959.

Silverman, F.: Roentgen Manifestations of Unrecognized Skeletal Trauma in Infants, *Amer J Roentgenol 69:* 413-426 (March) 1953.

Smith, M. J.: Subdural Hematoma with Multiple Fractures, *Amer J Roentgenol 63:* 342-344 (March) 1950.

Snedecor, S. T.; Knapp, R. E.; and Wilson, H. B.: Traumatic Ossifying Periostitis of Newborn, *Surg Gynec Obstet 61:* 385-387, 1935.

Snedecor, S. T., and Wilson, H. B.: Some Obstetrical Injuries to Long Bones, *J Bone Joint Surg 31A:* 378-384 (April) 1949.

Weston, W. J.: Metaphyseal Fractures in Infancy, *J Bone Joint Surg (Brit)* (no. 4) *39B:* 694-700 (Nov.) 1957.

Woolley, P. V., Jr., and Evans, W. A., Jr.: Significance of Skeletal Lesions in Infants Resembling Those of Traumatic Origin, *JAMA 158:* 539-543 (June) 1955.

Maternal Attachment

Importance of the First Post-Partum Days

MARSHALL H. KLAUS
RICHARD JERAULD
NANCY C. KREGER
WILLIE McALPINE
MEREDITH STEFFA
JOHN H. KENNELL   *1972*

This paper was published at a time when the battered-child syndrome was becoming well recognized. Professionals around the world were horrified to discover that children with multiple injuries or brain damage had in fact been severely abused at the hands of their own parents. Many of those who were investigating the histories of these families at the time, reports Jacquie Roberts, were struck by the number of times the abuse could have been predicted. Serious child abuse was found to be the outcome of multiple factors, one of which was the relationship between the birth mother and the child. At the time the Klaus et al. article was published, many people were looking for ideas about how to intervene as early as possible in high-risk cases to prevent child abuse.

In their paper, Klaus and colleagues provided some carefully researched evidence that the quality of time a mother and child spend together in the first few days of life makes a difference in that dyad's longer-term relationship. The work, a carefully designed and controlled study of healthy full-term babies and their young primiparous mothers, had a major impact on practice as well as future research. (Earlier research in this area had focused on premature babies.)

For example, prior to 1972, according to Diane Depanfilis, hospital practices generally involved separating full-term new mothers from their infants following birth. Enhanced understanding about the effect of separation on maternal attachment, resulting from this paper, helped to establish the importance of keeping infants with their mothers in the period following birth. The results from this study and others that followed it are used to this day, as hospitals around the globe assist in maternal-child attachment by allowing new mothers to keep their babies close after birth. Jacquie Roberts concurs, adding that the findings also encouraged midwives to allow vulnerable or troubled young parents to take time getting to know their babies. *Bonding* and *attachment* became common parlance. Depanfilis says that the Klaus paper, published the year she became a public child welfare caseworker, also influenced the training of foster parents and their need to attach with children in their care.

In the final paragraph of the paper, the authors suggest that health professionals not rush out and make major changes based on the study until some longer-term work can be done to assess potential long-term side effects. These words were not heeded. The study confirmed many people's belief that the quality of time spent between parents and babies at the time of birth actually matters, and they eagerly acted on the findings—apparently to the benefit of mothers and their babies throughout the world.

A. C. D. and K. O.

I n certain animals such as the goat, cow, and sheep, separation of the mother and infant immediately after birth for a period as short as 1 to 4 hours often results in distinctly aberrant mothering behavior, such as failing to care for the young, butting her own offspring away, and feeding her own and other infants indiscriminately.[1,2] In contrast, if they are together for the first 4 days and are then separated on the 5th day for an equal period, the mother resumes the protective and mothering behavior characteristics for her species when the pair is reunited. Thus, there is a special period immediately after delivery in the adult animal. If the animal mother is separated from her young during this period, deviant behavior may result. An early short period of separation does not produce as severe a distortion of mothering behavior in all species.[3]

In recent years, several investigators have studied whether a similar phenomenon occurs in mothers of premature infants.[4,5] Does the prolonged separation experienced by the mother of a premature infant affect the formation of her affectional bonds and change her mothering behavior months and years after the delivery? Early results from these studies suggest that the long period of physical separation common in most nurseries may adversely affect maternal performance of some women.

Studies of human mothers of premature infants necessarily differ in design from the classic studies of separation in the animal mother. The gestation of the mothers is severely shortened, the infant is small and appears fragile, the period of separation after birth is greatly extended, and it has not been possible to provide close physical contact immediately after birth similar to the natural human and animal situation.

In most nurseries in the United States, however, even full-term mothers are separated from their infants for a short but possibly important time. Thus, it seemed essential to determine whether present hospital practices for the mother of a full-term infant influence later maternal behavior. This report tests the hypothesis that there is a period shortly after birth that is uniquely important for mother-to-infant attachment in the human being.

Originally published in *The New England Journal of Medicine*, 1972, *286*, 460-463.

MATERIAL AND METHODS

We placed each of 28 primiparous mothers of normal full-term infants in one of two study groups, depending on the day of delivery. Neither group knew of this study in advance or to our knowledge was aware of the arrangements made for the other. (The mothers, however, were not questioned on this subject.) The 14 mothers in the control group had the traditional contact with their infants: a glimpse of the baby shortly after birth, brief contact and identification at 6 to 12 hours, and then visits for 20 to 30 minutes every 4 hours for bottle feedings. In addition to this routine contact, the 14 mothers in the extended contact group were given their nude babies, with a heat panel overhead, for 1 hour within the first 3 hours after birth and also for 5 extra hours of contact each afternoon of the 3 days after delivery. (A heat panel was also placed over the control mothers' beds for 1 hour during the 3 three hours.)

To eliminate any influence from the enthusiasm or interest of the nurse that might obscure the results, the special nurses who cared for the mothers during the extended contact period (5 hours per day) spent an equal amount of time with the control mothers. After an initial standardized introductory statement, they only answered questions, did not instruct any of the women in caretaking unless this was requested, and, most of the time, were available just outside the room.

The mean age, socioeconomic and marital status, color, premedication, sex of the infant, and days hospitalized in both groups were nearly identical (Table 3.1). Only mothers who intended to keep their infants and to bottle-feed them were admitted to the study. The mean birth weights of the two groups of infants differed by 110 g.

To determine if this short additional time with the infant early in life altered later behavior, we asked the mothers to return to the hospital a month after delivery for three separate observations. These observations were made between the 28th and 32nd postpartum days and consisted of a standardized interview, an observation of maternal performance during a physical examination of the infant, and a filmed study of the mother feeding her infant.

The first seven questions on the interview concerned the general health of the infant, such as the number of stools and the amount of milk taken. Three separate questions were related to caretaking and were scored 0, 1, 2, 3.

> First: "When the baby cries and has been fed, and the diapers are dry, what do you do?" A score of 0 was given for letting the baby cry it out and 3 for picking up the baby every time. An intermediate score was given for gradations of behavior.
>
> Second question: "Have you been out since the baby was born, and who sat?" A score of 0 was given for "yes," and if the mother felt good and did not think about her infant while she was out. A score of 3 was given if she did not go out or leave the baby with anyone, or if she did go out but thought constantly about the baby.
>
> The third question related to spoiling and could not be scored.

A second measure of maternal behavior was the observation of the mother during a standardized examination of her infant. A score of 3 was allotted if, during the examination of the infant, she was standing by the pediatrician and watching continuously; a score of 0 was given if she remained seated and looked elsewhere. We also noted whether or not the mother attempted to soothe the baby when it cried. If she did not interact with the baby, she was given a score of 0; if she was consistently soothing, she was given a score of 3. The scoring of the interview and observation of maternal performance was then de-

TABLE 3.1 Clinical Data for 14 Mothers in the Extended Contact and 14 in the Control Group

Group	Maternal Characteristics							Nurses' Time	Hospital Stay	Mean Birth Weight	Number of Infants	
	Age	Married	Negro	White	Mean Score[a]							
	Year				A	B	C	Minutes/ Day	Days	Grams	Male	Female
		Number of Mothers										
Extended contact	18.2	4	13	1	6.7	6.7	4.9	13	3.8	3184	6	8
Control	18.6	5	13	1	6.5	6.9	4.9	14	3.7	3074	8	6

a. In this (Hollingshead) scoring system, on a scale of 1 to 7, residence (A) of 7.0 = poorest housing, occupation (B) of 7.0 = unskilled workers, and education (C) of 5.0 = reaching 10th to 11th grade in high school.

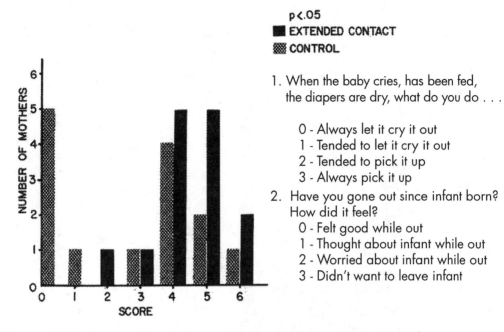

Figure 3.1. Maternal Scores From a Standardized Interview at 1 Month

termined by independent raters who did not know to which group the mothers belonged.

To study maternal behavior in another situation, we made time-lapse films of the mothers feeding their infants. They all knew they were being photographed and were told to spend as much time as they wished. Filming was done through a one-way mirror for 15 minutes at a speed of 60 frames per minute. Mothers' and babies' reactions could then be analyzed in detail at one-second intervals. Each frame of the first 600 was scored by analyzers who did not know which group the mothers were in. We analyzed each frame for 25 specific activities, ranging from caretaking skills (such as the position of the bottle) to measurements of maternal interest and affection such as "en face" (defined as when the mother aligned her face in the same vertical plane or rotation as the infant's[6]), whether the mother's body was touching the infant's trunk, and whether she fondled the infant. (We defined fondling as any active spontaneous interaction initiated by the mother not associated with feeding, such as stroking, kissing, bouncing, or cuddling.) Interobserver reliability coefficients were calculated for the individual behaviors. The average of the reliability coefficients was 0.83 for "en face" and 0.99 for fondling.

RESULTS

$\mathbf{A}$nalysis of the interview data is shown in Figure 3.1. The extended contact group (the solid black bars) had scores of 2 and greater, whereas the control mothers (cross-hatched bars) were at the lower end of the scale. The chance of this occurrence is less than 0.05, with the use of the Mann-Whitney U-test.[7]

The two groups scored differently on the results of the observations during the physical examination (Figure 3.2). The extended contact group did not score below 3, whereas the scores of the control mothers were distributed from 1 to 6 ($p < 0.02$). When the scores on the interview questions and the observations made during the examination are combined (Figure

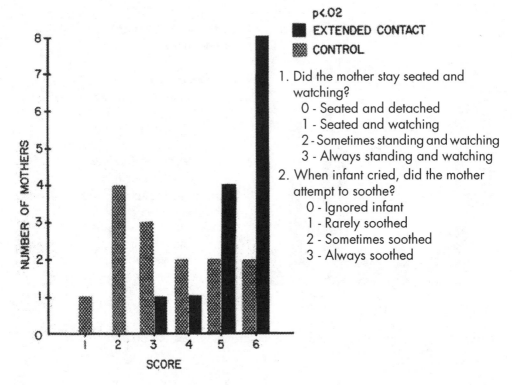

Figure 3.2. Scored Observations of the Mother Made During a Phsyical Examination of Her Infant at One Month

3.3), there is a separation of the scores of the two groups of mothers. The controls have scores of 2 to 10 spread out over the entire range, whereas mothers in the extended contact group have scores ranging from 7 to 12 ($p < 0.002$).

Figure 3.4 indicates the fondling and "en face" scores for both groups of mothers. Although the amount of time the mothers were looking at their babies was not significantly different in the two groups, the extended contact mothers had significantly greater "en face" and fondling (11.6% and 6.1% of the total scored time, as compared to 3.5% and 1.6% in the control group). There were no significant differences in measures of care-taking, although the bottle was held away from the perpendicular more often in the control group. By all three measurements studied, differences between the two groups of mothers are apparent.

DISCUSSION

It is surprising, with the multitude of factors that influence maternal behavior[8] (such as the mother's genetic and cultural background, her relations with her husband and family, the planning and course of her pregnancy, her own mothering as an infant, and her experiences in her family), that just 16 extra hours in the first 3 days had an effect that persisted for 30 days. From our study, we are unable to determine if the initial hour, the 5 hours of additional contact per day, or a combination produced the differences. The previously observed intensive interest of mothers[6,9] in their infants' eyes, matched with the unusual ability of the newborn infant to attend and follow, especially in the first hour of life, suggest that the period immediately after birth may be uniquely important.

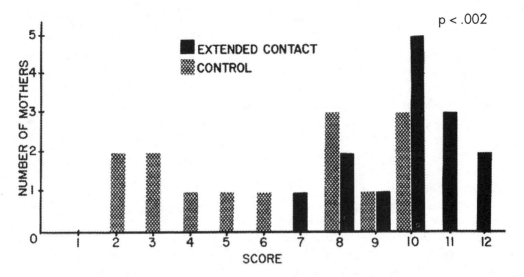

p < .002

Figure 3.3. Summation of Scores of Performance From Both the Interview and the Observation of the Mother During an Office Visit at 1 Month Postpartum

Though these findings suggest a special attachment period in the human mother somewhat similar to that described in animals, it is possible that the early presentation of a baby shortly after birth is taken by a mother as a special privilege or recognition that in itself may have altered her behavior. In either case, it does affect behavior.

Extensive studies have focused on the process by which the infant becomes attached to his mother. Our observations help in describing the process in the opposite direction—the attachment behavior of the mother. It is tempting to consider this a form of imprinting or a critical period for an adult human. However, this process does not fit the precise definition for either imprinting or a critical period.[10] Both processes are defined in terms of the infant animal and refer to events that occur only once in the life of an individual. Our data suggest that this may be a special attachment period for an adult woman—special in the sense that what happens during this time may alter the later behavior of the adult toward a young infant for at least as long as 1 month after delivery. It would

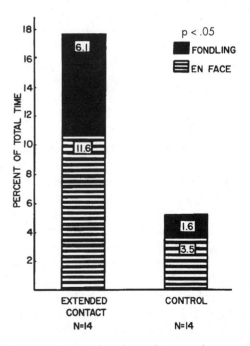

Figure 3.4. Filmed Feeding Analysis at 1 Month, Showing Percentage of "en Face" and Fondling Times in Mothers Given Extended Contact With Their Infants and in the Control Group

be useful to have a special term for this period, such as *maternal sensitive period.*

An understanding of this intricate process may be vital during planning for the mother of the full-term infant as well as for the mother of the high-risk infant or the premature infant, and even the adopting mother. Should the adopting mother receive her baby immediately after delivery to optimize maternal attachment? If there is a "sensitive period," this question and many others require study.

The differences between the two groups in eye-to-eye contact and in tactile stimulation that have probably occurred in the first month in over 200 feedings, and in countless other encounters between mother and infant, may have definite effects on the infant. If these differences in attentiveness and in responsiveness to the babies' cries that we observed are to continue, they could assume additional consequence when taken in the light of the observations of Rubenstein,[11] Bell,[12] and others, who have shown that increased maternal attentiveness facilitates exploratory behavior and the early development of cognitive behavior in infants. Early and extended contact for the human mother may have a powerful effect on her interaction with her infant and consequently its later development.

We do not know whether these differences in maternal behavior will disappear after 2 or 3 months, will be present in other social and economic groups, or will affect the later development of the two groups of infants. Thus, it is premature to make any recommendations regarding which caretaking regimen is preferable. Caution is recommended before any drastic changes are made in hospital policies as a result of this report, particularly in facilities for mother and infant care, where changes have been made in the past without study of the long-term effects on the mother and infant. It has been the custom of health professionals to make major changes affecting behavior and environment to promote what appeared to be a beneficial innovation without a careful study of the side effects.

We are indebted to Harriet Wolfe, Robin White, Susan Davis, and the nursing staff for their helpful ideas and criticism.

REFERENCES

1. Collias NE: The analysis of socialization in sheep and goats. Ecology 37: 228-239, 1956

2. Hersher L, Moore AU, Richmond JB: Effect of post partum separation of mother and kid on maternal care in the domestic goat. Science 128: 1342-1343, 1958

3. Rheingold H: Maternal Behavior in Mammals. New York. John Wiley and Sons, 1963

4. Barnett CR, Leiderman PH, Grobstein R, et al: Neonatal separation: the maternal side of interactional deprivation. Pediatrics 45: 197-205, 1970

5. Klaus MH, Kennell JH: Mothers separated from their newborn infants. Pediatr Clin North Am 17: 1015-1037, 1970

6. Robson K: The role of eye-to-eye contact in maternal-infant attachment. J Child Psychol Psychiatry 8: 13-25, 1967

7. Siegel S: Non-parametric Statistics for the Behavioral Sciences. New York, McGraw-Hill Book Company, 1956

8. Bowlby J: Attachment and Loss. Vol 1, New York, Basic Books Inc. 1969

9. Klaus M, Kennell JH, Plumb N, et al: Human maternal behavior at the first contact with her young. Pediatrics 46: 187-192, 1970

10. Caldwell B: The usefulness of the critical period hypothesis in the study of filiative behavior. Merrill-Palmer Q 8: 229-242, 1962

11. Rubenstein J: Maternal attentiveness and subsequent exploratory behavior in the infant. Child Dev 38: 1089-1100, 1967

12. Bell S: The development of the concept of object as related to infant-mother attachment. Child Dev 41: 291, 1970

On the Theory and Practice of Shaking Infants

Its Potential Residual Effects of Permanent Brain Damage and Mental Retardation

JOHN CAFFEY   1972

"On the Theory and Practice of Shaking Infants" was first read as the Tenth Annual Abraham Jacobi Award Address at the 1972 annual convention of the American Medical Association, and, later that year, it was published in the American Journal of Diseases of Children. The paper was a landmark in defining the shaken baby syndrome and creating awareness of this problem.

Writing for a medical audience, Dr. John Caffey defines the shaken baby problem, cites 27 recorded examples, ponders the causes and prevalence, and explains the possible serious long-term medical consequences. He also raises questions of what to do about the syndrome. Randall Alexander notes that although A. N. Guthkelch reported on infantile subdural hemotoma and its relationship to whiplash injuries in the *British Medical Journal* in 1971, Caffey popularized the notion. He coined the term *whiplash shaken baby syndrome*, says Su-

san Kelley. Both Alexander and Kelley note that Caffey was the first to suggest that shaking alone, in the absence of evidence of skull fractures or extreme head trauma, could lead to serious head and eye injuries. He was the first in the literature to explain that shearing forces from shaking alone result in retinal and intracranial hemorrhaging. Caffey also warned that this type of head injury could be an unrecognized cause of mental retardation.

Alexander points out that the paper helped in describing the specific syndrome of injuries (brain damage, intracranial bleeding, and retinal hemorrhages). The sources and mechanisms of shaking were the keys to understanding how such internal injuries could occur. Caffey's documentation that a child could have no external signs of harm yet have a specific set of internal head injuries was a great help in establishing shaken baby syndrome as a form of child abuse. The biomechanical explanation presented has resulted in considerable subsequent research.

Kelley further notes that Caffey's paper makes a compelling argument for a national campaign to alert parents and other caregivers to the dangers of shaking infants. Because of Caffey's work in this area, and the work of others that followed, various large-scale education efforts have been undertaken, and professionals and parents alike increasingly have become aware of the absolute dangers of shaking infants.

Given the paucity of knowledge at the time, Caffey reasoned from what he did see that minor shaking could cause minor brain injury, resulting in subtle mental or motor problems. That view, according to Dr. Alexander, has created quite a debate today, in the courtroom as well as in public education programs. The questions revolve around what the threshold or degree of force might be to cause an injury to a child and whether, for example, rough play or even playing "horsey" with a very young child could indeed be damaging. Current research addresses this, as well as how best to educate parents about the shaken baby syndrome without unduly worrying them.

A. C. D. and K. O.

In the first modern discussion in 1946 of the parent-infant stress syndrome (PITS), or battered baby syndrome, I described six infants, 13 months or younger, who suffered from the combination of subdural hematomas and characteristic bone lesions.[1] During the last 25 years,[2-5] substantial evidence, both manifest and circumstantial, has gradually accumulated which suggests that the whiplash-shaking and jerking of abused infants are common causes of the skeletal as well as the cerebrovascular lesions; the latter is the most serious acute complication and by far the most common cause of early death.[6]

Today, we invite your attention to the evidence which supports our concept that the whiplash-shaking and jerking of infants are frequently pathogenic and often result in grave permanent damage to infantile brains and eyes. We shall also point out that potentially pathogenic whiplash-shaking is practiced commonly in a wide variety of ways, under a wide variety of circumstances, by a wide variety of persons, for a wide variety of reasons. The most common motive for repeated whip-lash-shaking of infants and young children is to correct minor misbehavior. Such shakings are generally considered innocuous by both parents and physicians. If our concept of the pathogenic significance of whiplash-shaking is valid, it follows that the prevention of such shaking and jerking might substantially reduce the incidence of brain damage and mental retardation. The line of demarcation between pathogenic and nonpathogenic shaking is often vague.

The nature and distribution of the bone lesions in the PITS must be interpreted from the radiographic changes exclusively because they have not been studied systematically at either surgical exploration or necropsy. The metaphyseal avulsions are the most common of these lesions. Some are small fragments of cortical bone torn off the external edge of the cortical wall at the metaphyseal levels where the periosteum is most tightly bound down to the cortex. In most cases, however, they appear to be small chunks of calcified cartilage which have been broken off the edges of the provisional zones of calcification at or near the sites of the attachments of the articular capsules. Often, bones on both the proximal and distal sides of a single joint are affected, especially at the knee. All of these metaphyseal avulsion fragments appear to result from *indirect, traction, stretching, and shearing, acceleration- deceleration stresses on the periosteum and articular capsules,* rather than *direct, impact stresses such as smashing blows on the bone itself.*

Traumatic involucra commonly accompany the metaphyseal avulsions and involve the same terminal segment of the same shaft. They are the largest and most conspicuous of all traumatic lesions in growing bones. Usually, they are not fracture-dependent. They develop due to traction-rupture of the abundant normal perforating blood vessels, which course through the cortical wall between the periosteum and the medullary cavity and which are severed at the junction of the internal edge of the periosteum with the external edge of the cortex. The accumulation of blood internal to the periosteum, but external to the cortical wall, lifts the periosteum off the wall for variable distances and forms subperiosteal hematomas of variable sizes and shapes. Often, these are symmetrical in analogous bones in the two arms or legs, or they affect bones in the arms and forearms only, or sometimes in the thighs and shanks only. Frequently, they involve bones on both the distal and proximal sides of a single joint, especially the knees. At first, they appear radiographically as masses of water density superimposed on the shaft, but after 4 to 10 days, a thin opaque shell of new fibrous bone begins to form around the external edge of the hematoma. The entrapped subperiosteal blood is then gradually resorbed. The nature and distribution of these lesions can be best explained on the basis of *indirect, primary, acceleration-deceleration traction drags* on the periosteum, its vessels, and the joint capsules from manual seizing and gripping the extremities and whiplash-shaking the head. Neither their nature nor their distribution can be satisfactorily explained on the basis of *direct impact stresses (blows) on the bone itself.*

Several observers have noted associated diffuse sclerosis of the shafts of some of the affected bones of some abused infants. This has suggested excessively fragile, brittle, chalk-like bones to some radiologists. In recent biopsies, however, the microscopic examination disclosed the lamellae to be laid down in an irregular woven pattern. This, in my opinion, indicates that the sclerosis is caused by excessive newly formed primitive fibrous or woven bone, which forms regularly under the periosteum following traumatic subperiosteal edema or bleeding or both. Traumatic thickenings of the external subperiosteal edge of the cortical wall are the cause of the sclerosis. The epiphyseal ossification centers and round bones are not sclerotic. These sclerotic shafts are probably stronger than normal shafts.

Traumatic metaphyseal cupping is due to traumatic obstructive injury to the epiphyseal arterioles in the neighboring cartilage plate;[4] and the metaphyseal "loop" deformities[2] are due to stretching and extension of the traumatic involucra terminally. Both of these lesions are best explained on the causal basis of the grabbing, squeezing of the extremities by the assailant's hands, and whiplash-shaking of the infant's head.

Despite the failure of parents and physicians to appreciate the grave significance of whiplash-shaking younger infants, and to record shaking in medical histories, there are several convincing recorded examples of pathogenic and even fatal shaking.

Example 1 (15 Cases). The most gruesome and, at the same time, the most significant examples of proved pathogenic whiplash-shakings and of burpings are recounted in the story of an infant-nurse (*Newsweek* 48(pt 1):90, 1956). She is reported to have killed three infants and maimed 12 others during a period of 8 years, largely by shaking and jolting infantile brains and their blood vessels. These assaults all occurred in the homes of upper-middle-class, well-educated, well-to-do parents, who provided expert medical care by highly trained pediatricians. Her services were said to have been much in demand because she had built up a reputation for being "extravagantly kind" to her infant charges. Both parents and doctors apparently had full confidence in her; in one instance, she was invited back by the parents to care for their second infant after she had shaken their first child to death. After one infant was found dead without satisfactory explanation, the nurse explained that she had only tried to get the bubble up. "I picked him up and tried to get the bubble up. I didn't do anything wrong." After another of her patients had succumbed unexpectedly, she admitted that she "had given him a good shaking." Necropsy disclosed traumatic brain injury. Eventually, she admitted killing three infants and maiming two others. When these admissions became known to the community, parents disclosed that 10 additional infants had been significantly injured by this nurse.

The primary assaulting force in all of the nurse's attacks on infants appears to have been violent whiplash-shaking and excessive whiplash-pounding on the back during burping. One is amazed that she was able to continue her murderous assaults in this much better-than- average social and medical milieu for 8 years. It is likely that she did not realize the full power and violence generated in her shaking of small infants. She weighed 105.32 kg (233 lb) and was said to have had very large hands. The last infant she shook to death weighed 4.97 kg (11 lb). Had the nurse been shaken by a caretaker of corresponding weight and strength, the monster would have weighed 21 times her weight or about 2,226 kg (5,000 lb) and would have had the strength of 21 strong women.

Example 2 (Four Cases). Weston[6] and Steele and Pollock[7] report four cases of pathogenic shaking in battered babies. (1) A girl, 2 years old, was shaken violently because she whined. (2) A girl 4 years of age was shaken violently because of incessant crying. (3) A

girl 4 months of age was shaken fatally, during which her head was banged against the crib. (4) A girl, 2 years old, was shaken and beaten to death with a stick.

Example 3 (Three Cases[8]). (1) A boy of 6 months had unexplained convulsions and fever. His mother was too shocked to speak. A subdural hematoma was excised, and he died 3 days later. Eventually the mother admitted that she had shaken him several times to save him from "choking to death" during a violent paroxysm of coughing. She had attempted to "clear his throat," and he went into convulsions following the shaking. (2) A boy, 6 months old, began to vomit and convulse. There were no external signs of head injury, but retinal hemorrhages were seen in both ocular fundi. Subdural hematomas were treated surgically. (3) A few days later, this patient's twin brother came to the hospital with an unexplained broken femur. Shortly thereafter, the first twin returned with persistent subdural hematoma. By this time, bruises had appeared on both his forearms, which fitted the pads in the fingers and thumbs of the examiner's hands, where the boy's forearms had been gripped by his assailant during the shaking. Eventually, the mother admitted that she and her husband "might have shaken him when he cried at night." Guthkelch[8] opines that a "good shaking" is felt by British parents to be more socially acceptable, and physically less dangerous, than blows or punches to the head.

Example 4 (One Case). Kempe et al.[9] described radiographic bone lesions caused by the repeated parental shaking of a prematurely born twin girl of 7 months, who had been abused by the mother since the second month of life. She was shaken while gripped by the legs and held inverted. Multiple massive involucra and several metaphyseal avulsions developed in her femurs and tibias.

Example 5 (One Case). Swischuk[10] described compression fractures of vertebral bodies in one infant, which were believed to be due to whiplash-shaking.

Example 6 (Three Cases). We have found two examples of protective jerking and one of repeated sibling whiplash-shaking. We have encountered two patients in whom a single, sudden, violent jerk of one extremity apparently produced metaphyseal avulsions and traumatic involucra. (1) A boy, 4 months old, had always been well until his mother grabbed him by one forearm and yanked him upward to prevent his falling to the floor, off a bassinet. Six weeks later, massive involucra of the radius and ulna in the seized forearm were demonstrated radiographically. (2) A girl of 3 weeks was said to have suddenly developed unexplained swelling of the knee and fever. Twelve hours later, a pediatrician diagnosed osteomyelitis of the tibia because of point tenderness at the knee and slight fever and leukocytosis. There were no bruises. Treatment with penicillin was begun. Radiographs showed avulsion fracture fragments at the level of one proximal tibial metaphysis, which indicated trauma. Later films showed the evolution of a long traumatic involucrum on this tibia, when the fever was subsiding. On the 19th day, the mother admitted that, just prior to the appearance of the swelling of the knee, she had grabbed the baby by the leg and jerked her upward to protect her from falling onto a hard wood floor. At the same time, she had fallen forward with her and onto her. The pediatrician was still reluctant to accept the primary diagnosis of a trauma because he was unfamiliar with the frequency of fever and leukocytosis after traumatic internal hemorrhage.[11] (3) This boy of 8 months had unexplained swellings and tenderness and limitation of motion in both legs for several weeks when radiographs of the skeleton disclosed traumatic involucra at the proximal ends of both femurs. The parents rejected the diagnosis of trauma because, other than themselves, no one had been alone with the infant except his 8-year-old brother. He, however, had frequently acted as a lone baby-sitter when the parents went out socially. They found, at the first trial, by secretly watching their son as lone baby-sitter, that soon after their departure he seized the infant by the legs and shook him violently, and swung him, and flung him onto a bed.

Example 7 (Two Cases). These cases involve oculovascular lesions. Gilkes[12] mentions the case of Wallis in which subdural hematoma and retinal hemorrhages resulted from seizing an infant by the legs and swinging him in a circle about the parent's head. He also refers to Breinin's infant patient who developed retinal lesions after a parent had gripped him by the thorax and shaken him violently.

These 27 examples of recorded pathogenic shaking represent only an infinitesimal portion of the uncounted thousands of moderate unadmitted, undetected, and unrecorded whiplash-shakings which probably occur every day in the United States. The actual daily incidence of pathogenic shakings in the United States is unknown, but it is undoubtedly substantial. The admitted pathogenic whiplash-shakings by the infant-nurse, cited above, have a special relevance because they demonstrate conclusively that even repeated murderous whiplash-shaking can be concealed for years without arousing the suspicions of educated parents and well-trained pediatricians, in an optimal medical and socioeconomic environment. This long concealment was due in large part to the fact that shakings, which caused fatal brain damage and intracranial bleedings in the nurse's patients, did not cause suggestive signs of head injury such as bruising of the scalp and face, or cephalhematoma, or bulging of the anterior fontanel, or fractures of the calvarium.

The whiplash-shakings of infants and younger children are precarious, pervasive, prevalent, and pernicious practices which can be observed whenever parents, parent-substitutes, infants, and small children congregate: in the home, on the street, in buses, nurseries, kindergartens, day care centers, orphanages, "preschool" schools, in parks, playgrounds, shopping centers, and even in the waiting rooms of pediatric clinics. Many well-intentioned, responsible parents, who think nothing of giving a small child a "good shaking" or a series of such shakings, would not dream of giving their child a series of "good" blows or punches on the head. Yet, the cumulative pathogenic effects of repeated mild or moderate whiplash-shakings of the head, though unapparent clinically, may be far more grave than single, even if heavy, blows or punches to the head. The history of trauma and the nature of the traumatic force used cannot usually be elicited, sometimes owing to traumatic amnesia of the perpetrators who may not remember the traumatic episode or the kind and amount of violence inflicted on the infant. Steele and Pollock call this kind of amnesia "more or less unconscious defensive forgetting."[7]

The grabbing and gripping of an infant or younger child by the extremities or by one leg or arm and then shaking him seem to be instinctive, almost reflex, violent actions by angry adults in the commission of willful assault or for ordinary discipline of minor misbehavior. Many infants are whipped, beaten, and spanked, as well as shaken. The frequency of whiplash-shaking varies inversely with the age of the infant; apparently, many infants are shaken and jerked, but few are spanked prior to the 7th month of life. Overvigorous pathogenic shaking may be resorted to unwittingly, by a frightened parent or nurse, to dislodge a suspected foreign body from the mouth or pharynx, or to stop violent coughing or protracted crying and whining. Even overvigorous "burping" may be fatal, as demonstrated in the story of the shake-prone infant-nurse. All curative and prophylactic medical procedures which require repeated whiplash-shaking and jerking of the head are potentially pathogenic to the brain and should be banned or used with proper caution. Artificial respiration may include excessively high intracranial and intraocular venous pressures which lead to hemorrhagic

brain and eye damage and pneumomediastinum.

There are several apparently innocent, accepted, habitual practices, other than intentional shaking and jerking, which whiplash the head and brain, and which could lead to permanent brain damage. The infantile head is subjected to some of these stresses during such playful practices as repeated vigorous "tossing the baby into the air"; "riding the horse," in which the infant faces the parent while sitting on his pendulant shin, which is swung ventrodorsally; "cracking the whip," or gripping the infant by his ankles and swinging him in a circle around the parent's head; or spinning him on his own longitudinal axis; and "skinning the cat," in which the younger child is suddenly somersaulted forward, after being gripped by the wrists which have been inserted backward between his thighs. Infants and younger children are often handled too roughly in play by older siblings as well as parents, in such procedures as "shaking or spinning him dizzy." It is obvious that younger, more supple, calvaria of smaller children, of 4 to 8 years, although less pliable than the calvaria of the first weeks and months, were not designed for the habitual jolting of repeatedly diving headfirst into water, water skiing, protracted gymnastic tumbling, and the inevitable brain jolting of such adversary sports as boxing, wrestling, football, and basketball when indulged in repeatedly for several years. In some of these, the training sessions of several hours each week are more hazardous than the games and performances themselves.

Many of the toys and recreational contraptions which generate whiplash-shakes and jolts to the head should be more carefully assayed for their pathogenicity and banned from infantile and early juvenile use if it can be shown that their cumulative effects over protracted periods are pathogenic. These items should include baby bouncers and infant jumpers and, for younger children, the swings, seesaws, and play slides in amusement parks, the powered vibratory training and practice equipment in gymnasia; powered cradles and powered rocking horses; trampolines; skateboards, and sled jumping. The same studious consideration should be given to jolting transport vehicles which carry infants and small children—bicycles and such powered vehicles as motorcycles and motor cars driven rapidly and habitually over rough roads. The recurrent exposure to the snowmobile probably offers the greatest hazard to infantile brains and hearing. The pathogenic, brain-jolting, whiplash potentials for infants and younger children who are carried habitually in speedboats over rough water and in small airplanes in rough weather are manifest. Noise and other vibratory stimuli may be peculiarly pathogenic to infants when they are subjected to them continuously 24 hours a day at home. Mental and emotional disorders are said to be more prevalent around airports with high noise and air vibration levels. It is possible that the noises and air vibrations induced by radio, television, amplified hi-fi sets, air conditioners, telephones, vacuum cleaners, blenders, and garbage disposal and dishwashing units may interfere with the basic rest needs of the infant in his own home when he is overexposed to them continuously for long periods. In small thin-walled apartments, excessive exposure of an infant to pathogenically high-level noises is practically guaranteed.

Some of the more violent forms of endogenous trauma, such as the repeated convulsions in tetanus and epilepsy, or of meningoencephalitis caused by viral infections or by lead poisoning, may induce traumatic whiplash-brain damage and mental retardation. The grave, frequently fatal encephatopathy of infantile pertussis results, in part, from increased intracranial venous pressures caused by severe paroxysms of coughing, which in turn leads to focal cerebral hemorrhages and residual cerebral damage. Rhythmic whiplash habits of the infant himself during the first months of life, such as *head rolling, body rocking,* and *head banging,* may be traumatically pathogenic to

his brain and its veins. Protracted, repeated severe *breath-holding spells* may be similarly damaging to the brain.

Theoretically, the needs of infants who suffer disorders characterized by immaturity of their calvaria such as osteogenesis imperfecta, familial hyperphosphatasemia, hypophosphatasia, lacunar skull, and cleidocranial dysostosis should all be specially vulnerable to whiplash-shaking. This is also true for the infantile disorders associated with weakness of the cervical muscles.

Subdural hematomas are practically always traumatic in origin. They are found commonly in infants younger than 24 months with a peak incidence during the 6th month.[13] This high vulnerability of the neonate and the younger infant to traumatic intracranial bleeding is due to the combination of heavy head and weak neck muscles, which renders his brain especially susceptible to whiplash stresses. Also, his thin, partly membranous calvarium is supple and permits easy stretching of the brain and its veins by the postnatal indirect whiplash-traction stresses of shaking and jerking. The softness of his immature unmyelinated brain adds to its vulnerability. The actual time of onset of the subdural hematoma is usually uncertain during the first weeks and months of life. Much postnatal trauma has long been depreciated because it has been undetected and ascribed to birth injury. Premature infants are very vulnerable, and the vulnerability of full-term infants varies inversely with age. Male infants are twice as vulnerable as females; this is probably due to the relative immaturity of male heads and brains. The hydrocephalic premature infant is maximally vulnerable.

Infantile subdural hematoma frequently remains undiagnosed owing to the customary lack of distinctive diagnostic signs and symptoms. Ingraham and Matson[13] obtained a history of birth injury in only 26% of their 319 patients, and postnatal injury in only 20%. In 54%, the source and nature of the trauma were never determined. Fractures of the skull were identified in only 9%. Regional bruises of the scalp and face were not sufficiently frequent to be included in their tables on clinical findings. The clinical picture was not characteristic; it was made up mainly of fever, convulsions, vomiting, and hyperirritability. These signs are all common to many ordinary infantile disorders. It is probable that practically all of the small cumulative subdural hematomas which result from habitual shaking remain undiagnosed permanently and go on to become chronic subdural hematomas.

Ingraham and Matson[13] state that their mentally retarded and deficient patients, for the most part, were those who suffered from large chronic hematomas associated with marked atrophy of the cerebral hemispheres. The incidence of mental retardation in their pretreated and nontreated patients is not reported. They did find, however, that incomplete removal of the marginal membranes of the hematoma restricted the normal growth of the underlying cerebral cortex and impaired mental growth. This statement implies that the persistence of the membranes in all undetected, untreated patients would impair mental growth in a far greater number in cases of undiagnosed, untreated, chronic subdural hematoma. Ford[14] found cerebral damage and mental deficiency and motor deficits in a large majority of the children who survive after aspiration treatment alone. One can reasonably conclude that whiplash-shaking and jerkings, which are the prime causes of subdural hematoma in diagnosed cases, are also substantial causes of later mental retardation in the countless cases of unrecognized chronic subdural hematoma, in far greater numbers. The frequent bilaterality of subdural hematomas also supports whiplash-shaking as the probable cause.

The retinal lesions caused by shaking will undoubtedly become valuable signs in the diagnosis of subclinical unapparent chronic subdural hematoma, and also become a productive screening test for the prevalence of whiplash-dependent mental retardation and other types of so-called idiopathic brain damage. Kiffney[15] found bilateral retinal detachments in a battered girl of 7 months. Maroteaux and associates[16] found permanent, stable retinal lesions in the peripheries of the ocular fundi of previously battered children. In five battered children, Friendly[17] found retinal hemorrhages associated with intracranial bleedings.

It should be borne in mind that the "needling" of the brain to get diagnostic, subdural, subarachnoid, or intraventricular fluid may in itself be a dangerous procedure[18] and may lead to extensive porencephaly and brain destruction. Smith and Crothers[19] have shown that the injection of air into the lumbar subarachnoid space may cause intracranial bleeding and intracranial subdural hematomas. Overvigorous passive movements of the infantile head—to displace the intracranial gas and place it in optimal positions for diagnosis—expose the bridging veins to additional pathogenic stresses.

Chronic infantile hydrocephalus has not been reported as a residual in the follow-up studies of abused infants but has been found in many cases of chronic subdural hematoma.[14] Since subdural hematoma is a common complication of infant abuse, it is possible that residual hydrocephalus has been present but missed because it was not adequately searched for in the currently available inadequate studies of the late sequels in shaken infants. Cephalic enlargement of idiopathic hydrocephalus may not be noted until several weeks or months after birth, which raises the high probability that some, or even much, of the hydrocephalus which has been attributed to birth injury actually resulted from early postnatal whiplash-shaking. The studies of Laurie and Berne[20] and several others have demonstrated that subarachnoid hemorrhage is an important cause of the hydrocephalus engendered by birth injury; this may be equally true for the postnatal injuries caused by whiplash-shaking.

Russel[21] states that the hydrocephalus-producing gliosis of the brain which follows hemorrhages is so similar microscopically to the hydrocephalus-producing gliosis which follows infections that the two cannot be satisfactorily differentiated. The obstructing subependymal gliosis which surrounds the aqueductus cerebri and causes the most common type of ventricular hydrocephalus in infants may be either infection-dependent or hemorrhage-dependent. The same is true for the neuroglial membranes in the fourth ventricle, which block the foramens of Luschka and Magendie and may cause the cystic hydrocephalus of the fourth ventricle (Dandy-Walker syndrome).

According to Russel,[21] the meninges react similarly to several kinds of particulate matter in the spinal fluid and produce an inflammatory exudate, followed later by a localized gliosis (fibrosis). Blood extravasated into the ventricular and meningeal spaces can, thus, cause obstructions to the flow of cerebrospinal fluid and back pressure dilatations at any and all levels. Russel also cites examples of hydrocephalus due to hemorrhages incidental to brain surgery. There is, therefore, good evidence that hydrocephalus is frequently caused by intracranial hemorrhage and also good evidence that intracranial hemorrhage is a common feature of the whiplash-shaken infant. Hydrocephalus, however, has not been reported as a significant sequel of abused infants (shaken infants). More adequate late studies of large populations of previously traumatized infants are needed for a satisfactory solution of this contradiction.

Mental retardation occurred in high incidence in two small follow-up studies of abused infants. In Elmer's[22] group of 22 infants, 12 had intelligence quotients of less than 80. This incidence of 12 in 22 becomes increased to 17 in 22 (77%), if one adds five more retarded children, who were not available for interviews because they had already been admitted to state institutions for the mentally retarded. None of 67 nonabused children in the control group had similarly low IQs. Morse et al.[23] found the inci-

dence of mental retardation to be 60% in 15 children who had been followed for 3 years after the original injury. Kempe et al. reported brain damage in 25 of 45 fatal cases in 1962.[9] These high incidences in three reports suggest that permanent brain damage and mental retardation develop in a surprisingly high number of infants in whom traumatic abuse has been detected. More detailed studies of large populations with valid controls are needed for determination of the true incidence.

Characteristic, consistent structural changes in the brain have not been demonstrated in so-called idiopathic juvenile mental retardation, which includes 80% to 90% of all cases. In the case of whiplash-shaking cerebral injuries, it is possible that the original, early traumatic cerebral edema, the small cumulative chronic subdural hematomas, the petechial hemorrhages, and even the larger cerebral contusions have all disappeared completely by the time, years later, the brains are available for autopsy. Owing to the frequent lack of comparable degrees of structural changes in the brains of children who are severely retarded mentally, it has been suggested that the original injuries caused irreversible change in the neurons themselves—changes which are not detectable microscopically or chemically.

The cerebral lesions of whiplash-shaken children have not been studied systematically. In some studies of blunt traumatic injuries to the head, the changes in the brain have differed significantly in younger infants from those in older infants, children, and adults. Diffuse gliosis was common in the youngest brains and may have been the residual of earlier traumatic cerebral edema and hemorrhage. The authors point out that mental deficiency and motor defects may be due to the destruction of the matrix cells around the lateral ventricle.

The most striking documented clinical and pathologic example of mental deficiency, induced by repeated whiplash jolts to the head and which are associated with profuse petechial hemorrhages in the brain, is the so-called punch-drunk or slap-happy veteran fist-fighter. He develops severe losses of memory and impairments of judgment, with speech and gait disturbances, from being repeatedly jabbed and beaten over the head during years of exposure in the boxing ring. He may never suffer detectable acute brain injury from a single heavy blow; he does suffer, however, from the cumulative effects of numerous, milder repeated jabs which jolt his brain. If one cared to paraphrase the cruel but realistic lingo of the fight game, one could accurately describe some mentally retarded children as "jolt-dolts" or whiplash-silly.

The exact prevalence of idiopathic juvenile mental retardation in the general child population is not known, but all responsible estimates indicate that it is woefully high—as high as 2 million cases in persons younger than 18 years.[24] The rate during infancy is set at 0.5% to 1%. Ten percent to 15% of children in large metropolitan centers have been classified as mentally subnormal. It is obvious that, if the whiplash-shaking of infants is even a minor cause of such a pervasive and devastating disorder, its prevention would eliminate substantial amounts of massive human suffering and misery, as well as monumental socioeconomic wastage. If one assumes that the average family unit for each retarded child includes two parents and two siblings, we can then appreciate that the lives of 8 to 10 million additional humans are dwarfed and darkened by this most baneful of all chronic human scourges—juvenile mental retardation.

Cerebral palsies and idiopathic epilepsy appear to be due to postnatal trauma in many cases, especially in those cases in which the clinical signs first appear weeks, months, and years after birth. It is probable that postnatal whiplash-shaking plays an important causal role in some or many of these patients. Neither of these disorders has yet been reported as residual effects in the PITS. More, and more comprehensive, studies are needed to determine the causal significance of whiplash injuries to the infantile brain, in residual cerebral palsies and idiopathic epilepsy.

Summary and Conclusions

Shaking is generally disregarded as a type of causal violence in the PITS by both parents and physicians, and it is rarely mentioned in medical histories. Thus, both its frequency and potential pathogenicity are consistently depreciated and ignored.

The radiographic bone changes in the PITS, both their nature and distribution, indicate that they are usually caused largely by rough manhandling of the infantile arms and legs, such as grabbing and then grasping, squeezing, wringing, and jerking, and then whiplash-shaking of the head; all usually occur in the absence of bruises in the skin of the arms and legs.

Several examples of pathogenic jerking of the extremities and whiplash-shaking of the head have now been recorded in the PITS; six of these were fatal.

Whiplash-shaking is widely practiced in all levels of society, by a wide variety of persons, in a wide variety of ways, for a wide variety of motives.

The pathogenicity of ordinary, casual, habitual, customary, repeated shaking of infants is generally unrecognized by physicians and parents.

The infantile head is especially vulnerable to whiplash injuries owing to a combination of the normal relatively heavy head and weak neck muscles, to the plasticity of an immature, partially membranous calvarium, and to the softness of an immature, unmyelinated brain.

Some, perhaps many, of the cerebrovascular injuries which are currently attributed, both clinically and microscopically, to prenatal infections, congenital malformations, birth injuries, and genetic metabolic diseases are undoubtedly caused by undetected, depreciated, and unapparent whiplash-shakings during the first weeks and months of life.

In the follow-up studies of two small groups of previously traumatized children, mental retardation was found to have a surprisingly high incidence. The mental status of these patients was not determined prior to their traumatic abuse.

The evidence on which our concepts of the pathogenicity of infant-shaking is based does not lend itself to satisfactory statistical analysis; "universal" samples of a total population of shaken infants have not been obtained, nor have adequate matching controls of unshaken infants from the same socioeconomic milieu.

1. Whiplash-shaking of the infantile head is always potentially pathogenic to some degree. Its actual incidence is unknown and cannot be even estimated satisfactorily.

2. Whiplash-shaking appears to be practiced widely in all levels of society for many different reasons. It is generally ignored by physicians.

3. The habitual, repeated, relatively mild whiplash-shakings which are inflicted in the ordinary training and disciplining of infants, and which may induce undetected cumulative chronic subdural hematomas and other undetected chronic types of brain damage, are probably more pathogenic than the less frequent but more violent and conspicuous shakings during willful assault, because they are consistently unrecognized and may persist to generate mental retardation and permanent brain damage.

4. There are several features of infantile subdural hematomas which indicate that they are not usually caused by *direct impact injuries* to the head but are caused by *indirect acceleration-deceleration traction stresses* such as whiplash-shaking of the head. These features include bilaterality of subdural hematomas in 85% of infants[13] and frequent bilateral retinal hemorrhages. There is a striking lack of such signs of impact injuries such as blows to the head. Usually, there are no bruises to the face or scalp, no subperiosteal cephalhematomas, and no fractures of the calvarium.

5. There is considerable manifest and much circumstantial evidence which indicates that whiplash-shaking and jolting of infantile heads may be major, unrecognized causes of mental retardation and permanent brain damage. The wide practice of habitual whiplash-shaking for trivial reasons warrants a massive nationwide educational campaign to alert everyone responsible for the welfare of infants on its potential and actual pathogenicity.

6. Trauma is the most important killer and crippler of infants and children, and it warrants aggressive study to insure effective preventive and optimal diagnoses and management. It seems certain that a new pediatric subspecialist will soon emerge, a pediatric traumatologist, who will head trauma teams in the larger medical clinics and attack the problem of traumatic diseases with the same success as other pediatric subspecialists have already achieved in the infectious, neoplasms, metabolics, deficiency, and genetically determined diseases.

The problem and the prevention of whiplash injuries are summarized in the following quatrain:

Hark ye, good parents, to my words true and plain,
When you are shaking your baby, you could be bruising his brain.
So, save the limbs, the brain, even the life of your tot;
By shaking him never; never and not.

Comment. Dr. C. Henry Kempe, University of Colorado, made available data from his new book *Helping the Battered Child and Its Family* (J. B. Lippincott Co). In Chapter 7, by Harold Martin, 42 abused children were followed for 3 years. He found 33% functionally retarded; 93% of these had a history of trauma to the head. Subdural hematomas or skull fractures were found in 31%, and 43% had neurologic residuals. Dr. Martin points out the complexities and interfering factors in attempting to establish exactly the amount of permanent brain damage and mental retardation which results directly from traumatic abuse.

A comprehensive and authoritative biography of Abraham Jacobi by J. S. Leopold can be found in Borden Veeder's *Pediatric Profiles* (C. V. Mosby Co, 1957).

Drs. Bertram Girdany and Albert B. Ferguson generously provided much excellent radiographic and clinical material from the departments of radiology (Dr. Girdany) and orthopedic surgery (Dr. Ferguson), Children's Hospital of Pittsburgh.

REFERENCES

1. Caffey J: Multiple fractures in the long bones of infants suffering from subdural hematoma. *Amer J Roentgen* 56: 163-173, 1946.

2. Caffey J: Some traumatic lesions in the growing skeleton other than fractures and dislocations. *Brit J Radiol* 30: 225-238, 1957.

3. Caffey J: Significance of the history in the diagnosis of traumatic injury to children. *J Pediat* 67: 1000-1014, 1965.

4. Caffey J: Traumatic cupping of the metaphyses of growing bones. *Amer J Roentgen* 108: 451-460, 1970.

5. Caffey J: The parent-infant traumatic stress syndrome; (Caffey-Kempe syndrome), (battered babe syndrome). *Amer J Roentgen* 114: 217-228, 1972.

6. Weston JT: The pathology of child abuse, in Helfer RE, Kempe CH (eds.): *The Battered Child.* Chicago, University of Chicago Press, 1965, pp 77-100.

7. Steele BF, Pollock CB: A psychiatric study of parents who abuse infants and small children, in Helfer RE, Kempe CH (eds.): *The Battered Child.* Chicago, University of Chicago Press, 1965, pp 103-147.

8. Guthkelch AN: Infantile subdural hematoma and its relationship to whiplash injuries. *Brit Med J* 2: 430-431, 1971.

9. Kempe CH, Silverman FN, Steele BF, et al: The battered child syndrome. *JAMA* 181: 17-24, 1962.

10. Swischuk LE: Spine and spinal cord trauma in the battered child syndrome. *Radiology* 92: 733-737, 1969.

11. Staheli LT: Fever following trauma in childhood. *JAMA* 199: 163-165, 1967.

12. Gilkes MJ: Fundi of battered babies. *Lancet* 2: 468, 1967.

13. Ingraham FD, Matson DD: *Neurosurgery of Infancy and Childhood.* Springfield, Ill, Charles C Thomas Publisher, 1954.

14. Ford FR: *Diseases of the Nervous System in Infancy and Childhood and Adolescence,* ed 4. Springfield, Ill, Charles C Thomas Publisher, 1960.

15. Kiffney GT: The eye of the "battered child." *Arch Ophthal* 72: 231-233, 1964.

16. Maroteaux P, et al. The fundi of battered babies, *Presse Med* 75: 711, 1967.

17. Friendly DS: Ocular manifestations of child abuse. *Trans Amer Acad Opthal Otolaryng* 75: 318-332, 1971.

18. Lorber J, Granger RG: Cerebral cavities following ventricular puncture in infants. *Clin Radiol* 14: 98-109, 1963.

19. Smith HV, Crothers B: Subdural fluid as a consequence of pneumoencephalography. *Pediatrics* 5: 375-389, 1950.

20. Laurie H, Berne AS: A contribution on the etiology and pathogenesis of congenital communicating hydrocephalus: The syndrome of delayed hemorrhage into the cisterns of the transverse cerebral fissure of infants. *Neurology* 15: 815-822, 1965.

21. Russel DS: *Observation on the Pathology of Hydrocephalus,* special report series 265, Medical Research Council. London, Her Majesty's Stationery Office, 1949.

22. Elmer E: *Children in Jeopardy: A Study of Abused Minors and Their Families.* Pittsburgh, University of Pittsburgh Press, 1967.

23. Morse CW, Sahler OJZ, Friedman SB: A three-year study of abused and neglected children. *Amer J Dis Child* 120: 439-446, 1970.

24. Christy RA: *Lengthening Shadows.* Report of the American Academy of Pediatrics on the Delivery of Medical Care to Children, 1970, p 60.

On Continuity,
a Child's Sense of Time,
and the Limits of Both
Law and Prediction

J. GOLDSTEIN
ANNA FREUD
A. J. SOLNIT   *1973*

"On Continuity, a Child's Sense of Time, and the Limits of Both Law and Prediction," originally published as Chapter 3 of *Beyond the Best Interests of the Child*, has profoundly influenced the way jurists and others think through legal decisions that influence a child. In this work, Goldstein and his colleagues present a few core principles about child development that the court had historically ignored. Most notable of these are how important continuity of relationships and environment are to children, particularly very young children, and how differently children, compared to adults, experience time. Goldstein and his colleagues then apply these principles to decision making in the courtroom. Subsequent to its publication in 1973, this paper became one of the most widely referenced in the literature, and it continues to be exten-

sively cited—a testament to the importance of the ideas it presents, both for jurists and for professionals who work with children.

Jaap Doek explains the impact this work had on him—it was published just as he was commencing his work as a juvenile court judge in the Netherlands. His comments relate to two notions from this publication, the continuity of relationships and the sense of time.

> For my decisions as a judge, [these notions] meant, first, that I tried as much as possible to assure continuity of relationship and environment for the child—as a result I may not always have returned the child to the biological parents. Second, I made decisions as soon as possible (having learned that a long time of uncertainty could become very negative for the child's

development) and, for example, gave parents of very young children only a limited amount of time to really improve.

Others have been equally influenced by this paper. According to Donald Bross, "Goldstein and his colleagues changed my understanding of how children experience early life . . . they make it difficult for anyone understanding their message to ignore the apparently greater power of the courts to do harm than to do good." Bross notes that, for too long, a child's incapacity has been used to deny a child both choice and protection. He explains that Goldstein emphasized how normal child development must not be impaired by legal procedures responding, often bluntly, to adult conflicts. In so doing, Goldstein and his colleagues make the compelling case for focusing on what is in a child's best interests.

The longer term impact of this piece is evident in so many ways: It has provoked heated debates among law and policy makers and has resulted in changes in laws and procedures in courtrooms and protective service agencies around the world. And, although our knowledge base about early child development distilled from scientific work has flourished in recent years, what we have learned since in no way contradicts the earlier and clearly astute insights of Goldstein and his colleagues.

A. C. D. and K. O.

We propose three component guidelines for decision makers concerned with determining the placement and the process of placement of a child in a family or alternative setting. These guidelines rest on the belief that children whose placement becomes the subject of controversy should be provided with an opportunity to be placed with adults who are or are likely to become their psychological parents.

PLACEMENT DECISIONS SHOULD SAFEGUARD THE CHILD'S NEED FOR CONTINUITY OF RELATIONSHIPS

Continuity of relationships, surroundings, and environmental influence are essential for a child's normal development. Since they do not play the same role in later life, their importance is often underrated by the adult world.

Physical, emotional, intellectual, social, and moral growth does not happen without causing the child inevitable internal difficulties. The instability of all mental processes during the period of development needs to be offset by stability and uninterrupted support from external sources. Smooth growth is arrested or disrupted when upheavals and changes in the external world are added to the internal ones.

Disruptions of continuity have different consequences for different ages:

In *infancy,* from birth to approximately 18 months, any change in routine leads to food refusals, digestive upsets, sleeping difficulties, and crying. Such reactions occur even if the infant's care is divided merely between mother and baby-sitter. They are all the more massive where the infant's day is divided between home and day care center; or where infants are displaced from the mother to an institution, from institutional to foster care, or from fostering to adoption. Every step of this kind inevitably brings with it changes in the ways the infant is handled, fed, put to bed, and comforted. Such moves from the familiar to the unfamiliar cause discomfort, distress, and delays in the infant's orientation and adaptation within his surroundings.

Change of the caretaking person for *infants and toddlers* further affects the course of their emotional development. Their attachments, at these ages, are as thoroughly upset by separations as they are effectively promoted by the constant, uninterrupted presence and attention of a familiar adult. When infants and young children find themselves abandoned by the parent, they suffer not only separation distress and anxiety but also setbacks in the quality of their next attachments, which will be less trustful. Where continuity of such relationships is interrupted more than once, as happens due to multiple placements in the early years, the children's emotional attachments become increasingly shallow and indiscriminate. They tend to grow up as persons who lack warmth in their contacts with fellow beings.

For *young children* under the age of 5 years, every disruption of continuity also affects those achievements which are rooted and develop in the intimate interchange with a stable parent figure, who is in the process of becoming the psychological parent. The more recently the achievement has been acquired, the easier it is for the child to lose it. Examples of this are cleanliness and speech. After separation from the familiar mother, young children are known to have breakdowns in toilet training and to lose or lessen their ability to communicate verbally.[1]

For *school-age children,* the breaks in their relationships with their psychological parents affect above all those achievements which are based on identification with the parent's demands, prohibitions, and social ideals. Such identifications develop only where attachments are stable and tend to be abandoned by the child if he feels abandoned by the adults in question. Thus, where children are made to

wander from one environment to another, they may cease to identify with any set of substitute parents. Resentment toward the adults who have disappointed them in the past makes them adopt the attitude of not caring for anybody; or of making the new parent the scapegoat for the shortcomings of the former one. In any case, multiple placement at these ages puts many children beyond the reach of educational influence and becomes the direct cause of behavior which the schools experience as disrupting and the courts label as dissocial, delinquent, or even criminal.[2]

With *adolescents,* the superficial observation of their behavior may convey the idea that what they desire is discontinuation of parental relationships rather than their preservation and stability. Nevertheless, this impression is misleading in this simple form. It is true that their revolt against any parental authority is normal developmentally since it is the adolescent's way toward establishing his own independent adult identity. But for a successful outcome, it is important that the breaks and disruptions of attachment should come exclusively from his side and not be imposed on him by any form of abandonment or rejection on the psychological parents' part.

Adults who as children suffered from disruptions of continuity may themselves, in "identifying" with their many "parents," treat their children as they themselves were treated—continuing a cycle costly both for a new generation of children and for society itself.[3]

Thus, continuity is a guideline because emotional attachments are tenuous and vulnerable in early life and need stability of external arrangements for their development.

Implications

Some of the implications of this guideline for the laws on adoption, custody, and foster care are that each child placement be final and unconditional and that, pending final placement, a child must not be shifted to accord with each tentative decision. This means that all child placements, except where specifically designed for brief temporary care, shall be as permanent as the placement of a newborn with its biological parents.

Adoption

Once final, adoption is unconditional and thus accords with our continuity guideline. However, the usual waiting period of a year between a child's placement with the adopting family and the final order of adoption conflicts with this guideline. The "waiting period" is, as the name suggests, a period of uncertainty for adult and child. It is a period of probation encumbered by investigative visits and the fear of interruption. It is not, as it ought to be, a full opportunity for developing secure and stable attachments.

For the state, the waiting period may provide an opportunity to interrupt developing relationships for reasons that would not justify intrusion into any permanent parent-child relationship.[4] For some adopting parents, the period may be one in which they place the child on "probation," an intolerable handicap for initiating such a delicate relationship. It may even provide a temptation for some adopting parents (and for some adopted children) not to allow the new relationship to develop. Furthermore, for those families which at the time of adoption already include other children, the knowledge that the state can take the new child away is experienced as a threat. And in those cases where the fear or wish that the new brother or sister be taken away is actually realized, the detrimental impact on the health and well-being of the child who is already a member of the family is incalculable.

We propose, therefore, that the adoption decree be made final the moment a child is actually placed with the adopting family. To accord with the continuity guideline, this would mean that the adoption order would be as final as a birth certificate, not subject to special supervision or open to special challenge by state or agency.[5]

The certainty of final placement should make all of the participants more aware than they often seem to be under current practice of the implications of the decisions to place a child for adoption and for a family to adopt a child. Moreover, as for all "final" placements, whether by birth certificate or adoption, "abuse," "neglect," and "abandonment," for example, could trigger state intervention. But even such placement proceedings must consider the continuity guideline in deciding whether an existing relationship should be altered. The advantages of continuing, ongoing "imperfect" relationships must be weighed even in neglect proceedings against those of the alternative placements that can be made available.

Finally, it should be noted that all of the continuity problems attributable to the waiting period are exacerbated by the lengthy opportunity for appeal following a final decree. A disappointed party or a relinquishing adult who withdraws consent may, by seeking review, extend the uncertainty for years. We do not propose, as we do for the waiting period, that there be no period during which the right to appeal is protected. But the continuity guideline dictates that the period for appeal should be drastically shortened, a proposal we discuss later in relation to a guideline concerning the special meaning of time for a child.[6]

Custody in Divorce and Separation

Child placement in divorce and separation proceedings are never final and often are conditional. The lack of finality, which stems from the court's retention of jurisdiction over its custody decision, invites challenges by a disappointed party claiming changed circumstances. This absence of finality, coupled with the concomitant increase in opportunities for appeal, is in conflict with the child's need for continuity. As in adoption, a custody decree should be final, that is, not subject to modification.[7]

One reason for the retention of continuing jurisdiction by the court is that custody orders may be made on conditions such as a requirement to send a child to religious school, or to provide regular medical examinations. The obligation to enforce such conditions prompts interruption by disappointed parties who claim violation. In addition, certain conditions such as visitations may themselves be a source of discontinuity.[8] Children have difficulty in relating positively to, profiting from, and maintaining the contact with two psychological parents who are not in positive contact with each other. Loyalty conflicts are common and normal under such conditions and may have devastating consequences by destroying the child's positive relationships to both parents. A "visiting" or "visited" parent has little chance to serve as a true object for love, trust, and identification, since this role is based on his being available on an uninterrupted day-to-day basis.

Once it is determined who will be the custodial parent,[9] it is that parent, not the court, who must decide under what conditions he or she wishes to raise the child. Thus, the noncustodial parent should have no legally enforceable right to visit the child, and the custodial parent should have the right to decide whether it is desirable for the child to have such visits.[10] What we have said is designed to protect the security of an ongoing relationship—that between the child and the custodial parent. At the same time, the state neither makes nor breaks the psychological relationship between the child and the noncustodial parent, which the adults involved may have jeopardized. It leaves to them what only they can ultimately resolve.[11]

Even if all custody decisions were unconditional, the guideline of continuity would dictate another alteration of procedure. On appeal pending review of the final decision a child ought not to be shifted back and forth between competing claimants merely to accord with what may prove to be tentative decisions.[12]

Foster and Other Temporary Placements

In foster or other less formal but temporary placements, the continuity guideline should prompt the development of procedures and opportunities in temporary placement for maintaining relationships between child and absent parent. Thus, unlike permanent placements, foster placements should be conditional.[13] This does not mean that foster parents are to remain aloof and uninvolved.[14] Nor does this mean that foster care is to be used as a means of keeping the child from establishing a positive tie with his "temporary" adult custodians by constantly shifting him from one foster setting to another in order to protect an adult's right of reclaim.[15] But once the prior tie has been broken, the foster or other temporary placements can no longer be considered temporary. They may develop into or substantially begin to become psychological parent-child relationships, which in accord with the continuity guideline deserve recognition as a common-law adoption.

The choice between adoption and long-term foster care is complex and involves many factors. One of them is the provision of financial help to foster parents,[16] whereas adoptive parents receive no subsidy. Thus, the recognition of common-law adoptions could be strengthened by providing for subsidized adoption[17] as an alternative to long-term foster care or institutionalization.

PLACEMENT DECISIONS SHOULD REFLECT THE CHILD'S, NOT THE ADULT'S, SENSE OF TIME

A child's sense of time, as an integral part of the continuity concept, requires independent consideration. That interval of separation between parent and child which would constitute a break in continuity for an infant, for example, would be of no or little significance to a school-age youngster. The time it takes to break an old or to form a new attachment will depend upon the different meanings time has for children at each stage of their development.

Unlike adults, who have learned to anticipate the future and thus to manage delay, children have a built-in time sense based on the urgency of their instinctual and emotional needs. As an infant's memory begins to incorporate the way in which parents satisfy wishes and needs, as well as the experience of the reappearance of parents after their disappearance, a child gradually develops the capacity to delay gratification and to anticipate and plan for the future.

Emotionally and intellectually, an infant or toddler cannot stretch his waiting more than a few days without feeling overwhelmed by the absence of parents. He cannot take care of himself physically, and his emotional and intellectual memory is not sufficiently matured to enable him to use thinking to hold on to the parent he has lost. During such an absence, for the child under 2 years of age, the new adult who cares for the child's physical needs is latched onto "quickly"[18] as the potential psychological parent. The replacement, however ideal, may not be able to heal completely, without emotional scarring, the injury sustained by the loss.[19]

For most children under the age of 5 years, an absence of parents for more than 2 months is equally beyond comprehension. For the younger school-age child, an absence of 6 months or more may be similarly experienced. More than 1 year of being without parents and without evidence that there are parental concerns and expectations is not likely to be understood by the older school-aged child and will carry with it the detrimental implications of the breaches in continuity we have already described. After adolescence is fully launched, an individual's sense of time closely approaches that of most adults.

Thus, the child's sense of the passage of time depends on what part of the mind does the measuring. It may be either the sensible, reasoning part, which accepts the laws of the external world, or the impulsive, egocentric part, which ignores the surroundings and is exclusively bent on seeking pleasurable satisfaction. The young child starts in the latter way, with his impulses being incapable of tolerating delay and waiting. Postponement of action and the foreseeing of consequences are introduced very gradually in step with the maturing of the personality. A child will experience a given time period not according to its actual duration, measured objectively by calendar and clock, but according to his purely subjective feelings of impatience and frustration. These will decide whether the intervals set for feeding, or for the absence of the mother, or the duration of hospitalization, and so on, will seem to the child short or long, tolerable or intolerable, and, as a result, will prove harmless or harmful in their consequences.

The significance of parental absences depends, then, upon their duration, frequency, and the developmental period during which they occur. The younger the child, the shorter is the interval before a leave-taking will be experienced as a permanent loss accompanied by feelings of helplessness and profound deprivation. Since a child's sense of time is directly related to his capacity to cope with breaches in continuity, it becomes a factor in determining if, when, and with what urgency the law should act.

Implications

The child's-sense-of-time guideline would require decision makers to act with "all deliberate speed" to maximize each child's opportunity either to restore stability to an existing relationship or to facilitate the establishment of new relationships to "replace" old ones. Procedural and substantive decisions should never exceed the time that the child-to-be-placed can endure loss and uncertainty.

The courts, social agencies, and all the adults concerned with child placement must greatly reduce the time they take for decision.

While the taking of time is often correctly equated with care, reasoned judgment, and the assurance of fairness, it often also reflects too large and burdensome caseloads or inefficiently deployed resources. Whatever the cause of the time-taking, the costs as well as the benefits of the delay to the child must be weighed. Our guideline would allow for no more delay than that required for reasoned judgment. By reasoned judgment, we do not mean certainty of judgment. We mean no more than the most reasonable judgment that can be made within the time available—measured to accord with the child's sense of time. Therefore, to avoid irreparable psychological injury, placement, whenever in dispute, must be treated as the emergency that it is for the child.[20]

The procedures of child placement are not designed to assure a prompt final decision. The process is characterized by extended periods of uncertainty caused by overcautious and overworked administrative agencies; by courts with overcrowded dockets, extended and oft- postponed hearings; and by judges who are inclined to procrastinate before rendering their decisions at trial or on appeal.[21] Yet, when the *physical* well-being of a child or adult may be endangered by delay or when delay may cause irreparable injury to the national security or to a person's right to an education, property, or the free exercise of speech, both administrative and judicial bodies have demonstrated their capacity, if not their obligation, to make prompt and final determinations.[22] When, for example, parents refuse to authorize a blood transfusion for their deathly ill child, hospitals and courts can and do move with great dispatch and flexibility by giving such cases priority. Judges may act in a matter of hours after an application for decision is made—they may even conduct their hearings at bedside in the hospital.[23] The blood transfusion cases may be perceived as emergency child placement cases for a temporary period and a limited purpose. But the model of a procedural scheme for treating all child placements as emergencies may more

readily be taken from another setting. In order to avoid irreparably jeopardizing a motion picture exhibitor's constitutional right to freedom of expression, the U.S. Supreme Court wrote as follows:

> To this end, the exhibitor must be assured . . . that the censor will within a specified brief period either issue a license or go to court to restrain showing the film. Any restraint imposed in advance of a final determination on the merits must similarly be limited to preservation of the status quo for the shortest fixed period compatible with sound judicial resolution.[24]

Were the court to adopt this position to safeguard a child's psychological health, it would have to say:

> To this end, the child must be assured that the placement agency will in a specified brief period either decide not to challenge the current placement, or go to court to arrange a new placement. Any temporary placement imposed in advance of a final determination on the merits must similarly be limited to preservation of the status quo for the shortest fixed period compatible with sound judicial resolution.

We propose, then, that as a matter of normal procedure, a child's placement be treated by agency and court as a matter of urgency which gives consideration to a child's sense of time by granting such cases a high priority, by dealing with them rapidly, and by accelerating the course of review and final decision.

Adoption

For adoption agencies, such a procedural scheme would mean pursuing a policy of early placements. Infants should, if possible, be placed even before birth. Expectant parents who contemplate putting their child up for adoption should receive agency assistance in reaching a firm decision before birth, either to keep or not to keep the child. Adopting families should be investigated and selected in advance of a child's availability for adoption. If anyone is to be kept waiting, it should not be the child but the adults for whom the anticipation may be a positive factor. Before placement, there should not be prolonged periods of observation for gathering information about the newborn in order to certify its physical and intellectual fitness. Adopting families should be prepared to accept the "adopted" child the moment it becomes available. We share the view of Littner, who observed:

> There is no question that the longer we wait, the more we will know. Yet . . . to be able to give complete assurance of normal development we would have to place adults, and not children. [F]or the majority of adopted children, extra information that would come from waiting would *not* have resulted in a different placement. [A]ny program that does not place children early is running the risk of exposing the majority of their children to certain perils of late placement in order to protect the minority from the possible dangers of misplacement.[25]

Of course, the older a child is at the time of adoption, the longer the delay may be to find a placement which will maximize continuity of environment, including life style, relationships with siblings, and educational opportunities.

As for court procedures in adoption, initial hearings should be promptly scheduled and decisions rendered quickly. The period for appeal should be extremely short, not more than a week or two, with a final decision rendered within days after the close of that hearing. Prompt appeal and decision safeguard not only the interest of the child but also those of aggrieved adult parties. If the continuity guideline is to be observed by the court, the longer a child remains with the adult who retains custody pending appeal, the less likely are the chances for an aggrieved party, even if right in principle, to obtain custody.

Separation and Divorce

All that has been said with regard to judicial proceedings in adoption applies as well to child custody in divorce or separation. The child's-sense-of-time guideline would require that all disputes between the parents about the placement of their children be resolved by separate and accelerated proceedings prior to and without waiting for a determination on the merits of the divorce or separation action itself. An aggrieved party's right to appeal the custody decision must be exercised shortly after the initial award, with a hearing and final decision by the appellate court to be rendered not more than a few weeks later. Such placement decisions become final, then, as a result of the appellate review or at the expiration of the time for appeal. To accord with our continuity guideline, it must in no way be contingent upon the ultimate outcome of the divorce or separation action.[26]

We have not attempted to lay down rigid time limits for administrative or judicial decisions in adoption, divorce, or separation placements. Rather, we have sought only to suggest for legislative consideration a possible procedural design which would be sensitive and responsive to a child's differing sense of time.

Abandonment and Neglect

The concept of abandonment or permanent neglect, to turn from procedure to substance, provides another illustration for the application of our guidelines. The law of abandonment, in determining, for example, the eligibility of a child for adoption, rests primarily on the intent of the neglecting parent, not on the duration of his or her absence.[27] It may even rest on how diligent a child care agency has been in its efforts "to encourage and strengthen" the relationship between a child in foster care and the absent biological parent.[28] The failure of an agency to make such an effort can preclude a court from finding that a child has been abandoned in law even though he has been abandoned psychologically for many years.[29]

To the extent that time is a factor, whatever the age of the child, not less than 1 year of neglect is generally required to establish the requisite personal intent to abandon.[30] Moreover, abandonment has been perceived as a continuing process which may be reversed by the absent parent's express declaration of a change of mind.[31]

Application of the child's-sense-of-time guideline would require a shift of focus to the individual child's tolerance of absence and sense of abandonment and away from the adult's intent to abandon or an agency's failure to encourage a relationship. Furthermore, rather than a statutory 1-year period, the time factor would be flexible and vary with a child's maturity at the time of separation and the extent to which the ties with the absent adults have effectively been kept alive.

The process through which a new child-parent status emerges is too complex and subject to too many individual variations for the law to provide a rigid statutory timetable. For the purposes of declaring a child eligible for adoption, or of acknowledging the existence of a common-law adoptive relationship, abandonment in law would have taken place by the time the parents' absence has caused the child to feel no longer wanted by them. It would be that time when the child, having felt helpless and abandoned, has reached out to establish a new relationship with an adult who is to become or has become his psychological parent.[32]

A statute may provide that a finding of abandonment may rest upon evidence that so much time has elapsed from the child's vantage point that the biological or adoptive tie never matured into a psychological tie with the absent adult, or that the developing psychological tie has been broken or damaged and that the child needs to or has already begun to develop a new relationship with another adult. Such a statute would include a presumption that (barring extraordinary efforts to maintain the continuity of a "temporarily interrupted" relationship), the younger the child, the shorter the period of relinquishment before a developing psychological tie is broken and a new relationship has begun. Abandonment or permanent neglect would then be defined to comport with a child's sense of time.

CHILD PLACEMENT DECISIONS MUST TAKE INTO ACCOUNT THE LAW'S INCAPACITY TO SUPERVISE INTERPERSONAL RELATIONSHIPS AND THE LIMITS OF KNOWLEDGE TO MAKE LONG-RANGE PREDICTIONS

Though obvious once said, when left unsaid, the limitations of law often go unacknowledged in discussions about child placement. Too frequently, there is attributed to law and its agents a magical power—a power to do what is far beyond its means. While the law may claim to establish relationships, it can in fact do little more than give them recognition and provide an opportunity for them to develop. The law, so far as specific individual relationships are concerned, is a relatively crude instrument.[33] It may be able to destroy human relationships; but it does not have the power to compel them to develop. It neither has the sensitivity nor the resources to maintain or supervise the ongoing day-to-day happenings between parent and child—and these are essential to meeting ever-changing demands and needs.[34] Nor does it have the capacity to predict future events and needs, which would justify or make workable over the long run any specific conditions it might impose concerning, for example, education, visitation, health care, or religious upbringing. We share the view—one which is too easily ignored in the law and administration of child placement—of Justice Wachenfeld:

The uncertainties of life . . . will always remain to be encountered as long as one lives. . . . Their devious forms and variations are too complicated and numerous to be susceptible of tabulation. Our inability to predict or solve them anchors us closely to nature's intendment. . .

A judicial approach does not make the future more readily foreseeable and the assurance of our decisions, whatever it be, is unfortunately circumscribed by the frailties of human judgment.[35]

The law, then, ought to and generally does prefer the private ordering of interpersonal relationships over state intrusions on them.[36]

Yet, the law does intrude. When it does, it becomes important for decision makers to be guided by an understanding of the limitations not only of the legal process but also of the predictive value of the knowledge on which judgments can be based. Each child placement, even that by birth certificate, is based upon assumptions and predictions about children and the adults who are designated parents. As the continuity and the child's-sense-of-time guidelines suggest, placement decisions can be based on certain generally applicable and useful predictions. We can, for example, identify who, among *presently available* adults, is or has the capacity to become a psychological parent and thus will enable a child to feel wanted. We can predict that the adult most likely suited for this role is the one, if there be one, with whom the child has already had and continues to have an affectionate bond rather than one of otherwise equal potential who is not yet in a primary relationship with the child. Further, we can predict that the younger the child and the more extended the period of uncertainty or separation, the more detrimental it will be to the child's well-being and the more urgent it becomes, even without perfect knowledge, to place the child permanently.

Beyond these, our capacity to predict is limited.[37] No one—and psychoanalysis creates no exception—can forecast just what experi-ences, what events, what changes a child, or for that matter his adult custodian, will actually encounter.[38] Nor can anyone predict in detail how the unfolding development of a child and his family will be reflected in the long run in the child's personality and character formation. Thus, the law will not act in the child's interests but merely add to the uncertainties if it tries to do the impossible—guess the future and impose on the custodian special conditions for the child's care. This merely leads to harmful and threatening discontinuity by leaving the decision for placement open and subject to special challenges by someone who claims that conditions have so changed that the custodian should be replaced. In the long run, the child's chances will be better if the law is less pretentious and ambitious in its aim, that is, if it confines itself to the avoidance of harm and acts in accord with a few, even if modest, generally applicable short-term predictions.

NOTES

1. A large number of the children billeted without their families in wartime England developed enuresis. Many specific examples of regression following separation are recorded by Anna Freud and Dorothy Burlingham in *Infants Without Families: Reports on the Hampstead Nurseries (The Writings of Anna Freud,* Volume III. New York: International Universities Press, 1973).

2. A not uncommon case history of this sort is found in *Carter v. United States,* 252 F. 2d 608 (D.C. Cir. 1957), reprinted in R. C. Donnelly, J. Goldstein, and R. D. Schwartz, *Criminal Law* (New York: Free Press, 1962, pp. 784-788):

Carter was indicted, tried, convicted, and sentenced to death for first-degree murder. . .

At the time of the offense Carter was eighteen years of age. . .

. . .Carter spent the first seven or eight years of his life with his father's sister, a blind woman. . .

. . .Carter's aunt released him to the Child Welfare, Division of the Department of Public Welfare. He was forced to leave his first foster home. After six months at a second foster home he was placed with a Mr. and Mrs. Reed, with whom he stayed about four years. The Reeds found him extremely difficult. He relieved himself in his clothing and bedclothing "just as regularly as if it were the right thing." He often struck smaller children without provocation. . .

Carter left the Reeds in August, 1949, and went to the Industrial Home School at Blue Plains. While there, he forced a child into an act of sodomy, threw a knife at another child, and was in the habit of fighting with smaller children who would not give him their possessions. . . . Upon reaching the age of sixteen (in December, 1952) Carter was placed in another foster home. He stayed there only a short time and then went to live with a Mrs. Gordon, who requested the authorities to remove him from her home after he masturbated in her presence.

Thereafter Carter moved to still another foster home for about one month, after which he was again placed in yet another foster home where he remained for three days and then ran away. He was found seventeen days later . . . and was removed to a Receiving Home for Children. He subsequently left the Receiving Home to live with his father, remaining there about one month. . . . He was apprehended on a complaint charging "disorderly conduct or peeping tom" and was sent back to the Receiving Home. . .

3. See Carl Pollock and Brandt F. Steele, "A Therapeutic Approach to the Parents." In: *Helping the Battered Child and His Family,* ed. By C. Henry Kempe and Ray E. Helfer (Philadelphia: J. B. Lippincott, 1972, pp. 3-22); and Brandt F. Steele, "Parental Abuse of Infants and Small Children." In: *Parenthood: Its Psychology and Psychopathology,* ed. By E. James Anthony and Therese Benedek (Boston: Little Brown & Co., 1970, pp. 449-479); and S. Wasserman, "The Abused Parent of the Abused Child" (*Children,* 14: 5, 1967).

4. Adoption, even when "final," may be conditional and thus in effect subject to the continuing jurisdiction of the courts with power to abrogate. See, e.g., *New York Domestic Relations Law,* §118-a (1970) which provides in pertinent part:

[Any adoptive child]. . .or any person or authorized agency on behalf of such child may make an application to a judge or surrogate of the court in which the original adoption took place for the abrogation of such adoption on the ground of (a) cruelty, (b) misusage, (c) inability or refusal to support, maintain, or educate such child, (d) *an attempt to change or the actual making of a change of or the failure to safeguard the religion of such child* or (e) any other violation of duty on the part of the adoptive parents or parent toward such a child [our italics].

5. If adopting parents change their minds, they could, as can biological parents, activate state processes designed to provide the child with another opportunity to be placed.

The Uniform Adoption Act of 1953 provided in Optional §17 that adoptive parents could petition to annul "If within two years after the adoption a child develops any serious and permanent physical or mental malady or incapacity as a result of conditions existing prior to the adoption and of which the adopting parents had no knowledge or notice. . ."

The Revised Uniform Adoption Act (1969) has no such provision. But see Kentucky Rev. Stat. §199.540(1) (1969), which provides that an adoption can be set aside by a decree of annulment if within 5 years the adopted child "reveals definite traits of ethnological ancestry different from those adoptive parents, and of which the adoptive parents had no knowledge or information prior to adoption."

6. We thus reject the approach taken in the Revised Uniform Adoption Act (1969), which requires a period of at least 6 months after an agency placement before an adoption decree can become final—a longer period is required for other adoptions (Section 12)—and an appeal procedure based on that used in ordinary civil actions (Section 15(a)), which provides:

[Appeal and Validation of Adoption Decree.]

(a) An appeal from any final order or decree rendered under this Act may be taken in the manner and time provided for appeal from a [judgment in a civil action].

(b) Subject to the disposition of an appeal, upon the expiration of [one] year after an adoption decree is issued the decree cannot be questioned by any person including the petitioner, in any manner upon any ground, including fraud, misrepresentation, failure to give any required notice, or lack of jurisdiction of the parties or of the subject matter, unless, in the case of the adoption of a minor, or, in the case of the adoption of an adult, the adult had no knowledge of the decree within the [one] year period.

7. §409(a) of the Uniform Marriage and Divorce Act compromises the continuity concept while trying to respond to it by providing fixed intervals during which decrees may not be modified:

No motion to modify a custody decree may be made earlier than one year after the date of the initial decree. If a motion for modification has been filed, whether or not it was granted, no subsequent motion may be filed within 2 years after disposition of the prior motion, unless the court decides . . . that there is reason to believe that the child's present environment may endanger his physical health or significantly impair his emotional development.

This problem may be greatly exacerbated by conflicting laws between states and between countries. See, e.g., Uniform Adoption Act, §14.

8. If the interrupting visits are not allowed by the custodian, the court may, on that ground alone, create further discontinuity by changing the child's custodian. See, e.g., *Berlin v. Berlin* 21 N.Y. 2d 371, 235 N.E. 2d 109 (1967), where the child is awarded to the father for the sole reason that the mother had not lived up to the visitation requirements of the initial decree that granted her custody.

9. This determination may be made either by agreement between the divorcing parents or by the court in the event each claims custody.

10. We would thus oppose such provisions as the following from the Uniform Marriage and Divorce Act:

§407. [Visitation.]

(a) A parent not granted custody of the child is entitled to reasonable visitation rights unless the court finds, after a hearing, that visitation would endanger the child's physical health or significantly impair his emotional development.

(b) The court may modify an order granting or denying visitation rights whenever modification would serve the best interests of the child; but the court shall not restrict a parent's visitation rights unless it finds that the visitation would endanger the child's physical health or significantly impair his emotional development.

§408 [Judicial Supervision.]

(a) Except as otherwise agreed by the parties in writing at the time of the custody decree, the custodian may determine the child's upbringing, including his education, health care, and religious training, unless the court, after hearing, finds upon motion by the non-custodial parent, that in the absence of a specific limitation of the custodian's authority, the child's physical health would be endangered or his emotional development significantly impaired.

11. It is of interest that much of what we have said in the preceding paragraphs is also contained in The Civil Code of Japan (Supreme Court of Japan, Tokyo, Official English Translation, pp. 152-153), which, e.g., provides,

Article 818. A child who has not yet attained majority is subject to the parental power of its father and mother. . . .

While the father and mother are in matrimonial relations, they jointly exercise the parental power. But, if either the father or the mother is un-able to exercise the parental power, the other parent exercises it.

Article 819. If father and mother have effected divorce by agreement, they shall determine one of them to have the parental power by agreement.

In case of judicial divorces the Court determines a father or mother to have the parental power.

If the father and mother have effected divorce before the birth of child, the parental power is exercised by the mother. But the father and mother may determine the father to have the parental power by agreement after the birth of child. . . .

If no agreement mentioned in any of pars. 1 to 3 and preceding paragraph is reached or possible, the Family Court may render judgment in place of agreement on application of the father or mother. . .

Section II. Effect of Parental Power

Article 820. A person who exercises parental power has the rights and incurs the duty of providing for the custody and education of his or her child.

Article 821. A Child establishes its place of residence in the place designated by the person who exercises parental power.

12. The lack of finality and the "continuity" of discontinuity pending appeal are dramatically illustrated by the following case reported in the *London Times* (February 16, 1973, p. 6, col. 6).

New Divorce Proceeding Prolongs Desramault Case

The case for the custody of Caroline Desramault, who has been a bone of contention for three years between her divorced English mother and French father, has taken yet another legal turn.

It seemed to have been settled finally by the Cour de Cassation's rejection on Tuesday of M. Desramault's appeal against the court decision giving custody of Caroline to her mother. However, the whole ponderous legal machine has been set in motion again by way of new divorce proceedings before the Versailles court.

The Versailles court in May, 1971, had ruled in a provisional order that Caroline should be entrusted for three-monthly periods to her father and mother alternately. M. Desramault did not accept this judgment and refused to hand over the child. Two months later the court of Appeal in Paris annulled the provisional order by the Versailles court and, pending a final decision, entrusted the custody of Caroline to Mme Desramault, her parental grandmother.

M. Desramault wanted to keep the child and hid her. The grandmother then started a new action, and a new judgment entrusted custody of the child provisionally to the father.

In July last year the Versailles tribunal, which had to give a new judgment on the divorce proceedings because the first one was annulled by the Paris Court of Appeals, ordered a new investigation and temporarily entrusted the custody of the child to the mother.

The father, however, fled with the child to Switzerland, and on an action by the mother a Swiss court placed the child in a home, the address of which is kept secret.

13. But see decision of Judgement Polier in *In re Sylvia Clear* 58 Misc. 2d 699, 296 N.Y.S. 2d 184 (Fam. Ct. Juv. Term N.Y. Co. 1969) in which she describes the dangers inherent in the N.Y. Family Ct. Act [1]611, which requires child care agencies to make "diligent efforts to encourage and strengthen the parental relationships." In that case, the court describes the negative reaction of a child in foster placement to her biological parent's visits, which were sponsored in accord with the statute by the child care agency. The right of visitation can, at least as time goes by, become a problem in what initially is perceived as temporary foster placement.

14. In "Young Children in Brief Separation: A Fresh Look" (*The Psychoanalytic Study of the Child,* 26:264-315, New York: Quadrangle Books, 1971), James and Joyce Robertson compare two forms of substitute care for young children whose mothers were confined to the hospital. One group of children received foster care in the home of the Robertsons; another child was placed in a residential nursery. See also the films made by James and Joyce Robertson, *Young Children in Brief Separation* (films Nos. 1, 2, and 4; London: Tavistock Child Development Research Unit: New York: New York University Film Library, 1967-1971) and *John: 17 Months* (film No. 3, ibid., 1969).

15. See, e.g., the dissent of Judge Froessel in *In re Jewish Child Care Association,* 5 N.Y. 2d 222, 156 N.Y. 2d 700 (1959):

Laura was born on June 3, 1953. Her mother delivered her to the Department of Welfare of New York City, who thereupon turned her over to the Agency. On July 30, 1954, the Agency gave the child to the Sanders for boarding care, at which time she was not quite 14 months old. . . . Laura's mother visited her but once a year for the first two years. Small wonder then that the

Sanders thought she had little interest in Laura, and therefore inquired about adopting her, despite the fact that they had been told by the Agency that Laura could not be adopted. Its order having been disobeyed, the Agency sought to place the child in another home. The Sanders were told they "were too attached to the child," they "loved her too much." For that entirely normal human reaction of the average person to the love of a child, Laura is to be transferred to strangers in the sixth year of her life . . . If Laura is to be bandied about meanwhile from family to family until she is transferred to her mother, each such change will be extremely difficult for the child, as testified to without contradiction by the psychiatrist at the hearing. Why multiply the shocks? And if the mother never chooses to take Laura, and that does not appear to the unlikely from the record before us, the child could not find a better home than she now enjoys.

16. See, e.g., the Connecticut agreement, which clearly specifies the financial terms.

17. For an explanation of such a program established in Maryland, see "Guidelines for Subsidized Adoption" issued on July 16, 1969 by the State Department of social Services:

1. Subsidized Adoption: General Intent

Subsidizing adoption is a method which makes it possible for potential parents to adopt a child for whom they can supply all the requisites of good parental care except the financial ability to support an additional dependent.

Subsidization opens up additional resources for many children for whom there are insufficient adoption homes. A home with subsidy payment will be considered for any child for whom this is the best placement resource.

The adoptive family may either be the foster parents of the child or they may be adoptive applicants.

Subsidization, which makes possible permanency and continuity of care and affection, provides important benefits to the child. The agency will usually have guardianship of the child in preadoptive care, with the right to consent to adoption or to adoption and/or long-term care. Some children will have been in regular foster care with no family ties or contacts with parents over a prolonged period of time and for these children guardianship will be obtained, so that adoption may be consummated by the foster families in which the children are settled, or adoptive placement may be made with a new family, depending on the individual situation. It is to be expected that many of the children will be those who were hard to place because they were part of a sibling group, or because of age, minority race, or handicap.

Reprinted in Monrad G. Paulsen, Walter Wadlington, Julius Goebel, Jr., *Domestic Relations* (Mineola, N.Y.: Foundation Press, 1970, pp. 737f.).

18. We should be alert to the fact that time words such as *quickly* express an adult's sense of time. Were the infant to write the sentence in the text, it would read "latched onto after a *prolonged period* of time."

19. See, e.g., Anna Freud and Dorothy Burlingham, *Infants Without Families: People on the Hampstead Nurseries (The Writings of Anna Freud,* Vol. III. New York: International Universities Press, 1973, pp. 182-183), where they describe the violent reactions of a small child to the parting of his mother:

The child feels suddenly deserted by all the known persons in his world to whom he has learned to attach importance. His new ability to love finds itself deprived of the accustomed objects, and his greed for affection remains unsatisfied. His longing for his mother becomes intolerable and throws him into states of despair which are very similar to the despair and distress shown by babies who are hungry and whose food does not appear at the accustomed time. For several hours or even for a day or two this psychological craving of the child, the "hunger" for his mother, may override all bodily sensations. There are some children of this age who will refuse to eat or to sleep. Very many of them will refuse to be handled or comforted by strangers.

The children cling to some object or to some form of expression which means to them at that moment memory of the material presence of the mother. Some will cling to a toy which the mother has put into their hands at the moment of parting; others to some item of bedding or clothing which they have brought from home. Some will monotonously repeat the word by which they are used to call their mothers.

Observers seldom appreciate the depth and seriousness of this grief of a small child. Their judgment of it is misled for one main reason. This childish grief is short-lived. Mourning of equal intensity in an adult person would have to run its course throughout a year; the same process in the child between 1 and 2 years will normally be over in 36 to 48 hours. It is a psychological error to conclude from this short duration that the reaction is only a superficial one and can be treated lightly.

See also Anna Freud, "The Concept of the Rejecting Mother" (*The Writings of Anna Freud,* Vol. IV. New York: International Universities Press, 1968, pp. 596-597).

The first attempt at object love has been destroyed; the next one will not be of quite the same quality, will be more demanding, more intent on immediate wish fulfillments, i.e., further removed from the more mature forms of "love."

20. Three months may not be a long time for an adult decision maker. For a young child, it may be forever.

21. See, e.g., *In re Lem* 164 A. 2d 345 (D.C. Mun. Ct. App. 1960):

[Raver, C. J.] The mother of Cecelia Lem, . . . appeals from an order committing her daughter to the legal custody and guardianship of the Department of Public Welfare until her 21st birthday, and permanently depriving her of custody in order that the Welfare Department may consent to the adoption of the child. . .

The child was born January 11, 1956. Paternity has not been established. . . . For about four months after the birth of the child a private social welfare agency sought to advise the mother as to the best course for her to follow, but she resisted any definite planning other than foster care for the child. At the expiration of four months, and apprehending that long-term planning would be required, the agency referred the case to the Department of Public Welfare. On May 4, 1956, the child came into "emergency care" of the child Welfare Division of the Welfare Department and was placed in a home for infants.

During the next 14 months the Division sought either to work out a plan whereby the mother would actively assume custody and responsibility for her child, or to persuade her to surrender it for adoption. She cooperated with the Division so long as she was not forced to make a definite decision. When pressed for some definitive action, however, she would state that her psychiatrist had cautioned her about being "rushed" into making a decision, and would become uncommunicative, withdrawn, and unavailable.

On July 3, 1957, the Child Welfare Division, pursuant to the provisions of Code 1951, §11-908, filed a petition in the Juvenile Court charging that the child was without adequate parental care. Code 1951 §11-906(a)(6). In an accompanying report it related the mother's history of vacillation and indecisiveness concerning the rearing of the child and recommended that the later be committed to the Department of Public Welfare for three months "In order to give the mother this additional time either to make her decision to release Cecelia for permanent planning or to offer a satisfactory plan of care for her independent of Child Welfare Division." On July 10, 1957, a hearing was held with the mother's court-appointed counsel present; the court found the child was without adequate parental care and committed her to the department of Public Welfare until October 9, 1957. This period appears to have been inadequate to accomplish its purpose, and the court on November 11, 1957, after a hearing with the mother and counsel present, committed the child to the Welfare Department for two years until November 4, 1959. The mother consented to this action.

At the end of the latter commitment period a hearing was again held on November 25, 1959. At that time counsel for the mother indicated it was his intention to ask for more time for his client to formulate her plans. The court replied that it would hear no arguments for further temporary commitment but would confine the hearing to resolving the issue of permanent custody in the mother or the Welfare Department. Counsel for the mother acquiesced in this ruling and the hearing proceeded on that basis.

. . .The mother visited her about once every two months throughout the period. . .

The mother herself testified that she loved her daughter very much and had developed a close attachment for her during her visits; she also expressed concern about the child's welfare. She said she never thought about the possibility that the child would be taken from her, but since that was the course this hearing was taking, she was now willing to assume custody and responsibility for the child rather than lose her permanently.

This was the first time she evidenced any decisiveness in the matter, and thus we have pointed up the fundamental issue in the case—whether her decision has come too late. The child was by then almost four years old and so far as the record indicates, never had been under the care of the mother for any length of time. . .

. . . At the conclusion of the hearing the court ruled against the mother. . .

No reasonable mind could question the proposition that a child deprived of the care and attention of its natural mother and committed to the care of welfare agencies for the first four years of its life is a neglected child within the meaning of the statute. We think the evidence was completely adequate to sustain the court's finding.

22. See, e.g.. *O'Brien v. Brown,* 409 U.S. 1 (1973) (presidential primary-political process); *New York Times v. United States,* 403 U.S. 713 (1971) (national security and freedom of speech); *Freedom v. Maryland,* 380 U.S. 51 (1964) (freedom of speech); *Cooper v. Aaron,* 358 U.S. 1 (1958) (right to education); *Youngstown Co. v. Sawyer,* 343 U.S. 579 (1951) (national security): *United States v. United Mine Workers,* 330 U.S. 258 (1947) (national security).

23. See, e.g., *In re Clark* 210.0.2d 86, 90 O.L.A. 21 (1962):

> [Kenneth Clark, aged 3 years, was suffering second and third degree burns over 40 percent of his body.] [T]he child's parents refused to authorize [blood transfusions] because the religious sect to which they belong (Jehovah's Witnesses) forbids it. . . . Ohio's Juvenile Code empowers the Juvenile Court to protect the rights of a child in this condition:
>
> §2152.33, Revised Code ***Upon the certificate of one or more reputable practicing physicians, the court may summarily provide for emergency medical and surgical treatment which appears to be immediately necessary for any child concerning whom a complaint or an application for care has been filed, pending the service of a citation upon its parents, guardian, or custodian.***
>
> Even without this specific authorization we believe the court would have had ample power to act summarily under its broad equitable jurisdiction.

And see *Georgetown College Inc.* 221 F.2d 1000.n. 15, p. 1007 (D.C. Cir.1964) Cert. Den. 377 U.S. 978 (1964).

24. *Freedman v. Maryland* 380 U.s. $1, 58-59 (1964). The court refers to a New York procedure that, if applied to child placement, not film censorship, would preclude interruption of an ongoing relationship until a hearing before a court, which must be provided 1 day after notice of the dispute about placement is given; the judge must hand down his decision within 2 days after termination of the hearing. No mention is made of similarly expeditious determinations on appeal. Such provisions would, of course, have to be made in child placement.

25. Ner Littner, "Discussion of a Program of Adoptive Placement for Infants under Three Months" (*American Journal of Orthopsychiatry,* 26:577, 1956).

26. Such a proposal comports with the concept of divisible divorce, which recognizes that the official severance of personal relationships between the adult parties is divisible from (and need not be conditioned on or await a final determination of) property and support rights. *Estin v. Estin,* 334 U.S. 541 (1948). Where an adult party to a divorce has sought to preclude a final decree of divorce until a final property settlement has been reached, courts have observed, e.g., "society will be little concerned if the parties engage in property litigation of however long duration; it will be much concerned if two people are forced to remain legally bound to one another when this status can do nothing but engender additional bitterness and unhappiness." *Hall v. Superior Court of Los Angeles County,* 54 Cal. 2d 139 352 P2d 161 (1960). Ending disputes about the child-adult relationships seems an equally if not a more compelling reason for in-

voicing the divisible divorce concept. *May v. Anderson,* 345 U.S. 528 (1953). That concept is implicit in the continuing jurisdiction courts retain over custody decisions, which, of course, we oppose.

27. See 35 ALR 2d 662, 668 (189) and *Winnans v. Luppie* 4/ N.J. Eg. 302, 305 (1890); Hazuke's case 345 Pa. 432 (1942) ; and *Lett v. Family and Children's Society,* Sup. Ct. of N.J. (1953) reprinted in J. Goldstein and J. Kats, *The Family and the Law (supra,* p. 1115).

28. See, e.g., the N.Y. Family Ct. Act. Art. VI, 611, which provides in pertinent part: "permanent neglect [is established when] the parent . . . has failed for a period of more than one year following the placement . . . substantially and continuously or repeatedly to maintain contact with and plan for the future of the child, although physically and financially able to do so, not withstanding the [child care] agency's diligent efforts to encourage and strengthen the parental relationship."

29. Judge Polier, construing the provision in *In re Sylvia Clear,* 58 Misc. 2d 699, 296 N.Y.S. 184 (Fam. Ct. Juv. Term N.Y. Co. 1969) with regard to a caseworker's decision not to encourage visits by a biological mother (see note 12), said,

> Visits with the mother were soon seen as disturbing to the child. . . . There is no basis for criticizing the action of the agency whose first responsibility was the well-being of the child. The agency could not have sought to strengthen the parental relationship without violating its responsibility for the welfare of the child in its custody. Yet that is what the present statute requires as a condition to terminating parental rights.

> Although this court is satisfied it would be in the best interest of the child to terminate parental rights, it cannot find that the statute empowers it to do so. The mother has continued to visit the child, has persistently rejected the idea of surrender, and the mother continues to speak of making a home for both of her children in the future when she feels stronger. While this court finds no evidence to sustain this expressed hope and is satisfied that the mother is not competent to care for this child, the evidence does not warrant a finding that the present statutory requirement has been met.

30. See, e.g., California Civil Code 232a (1961) which provides in pertinent part:

> Sec. 232. Persons entitled to be declared free from parental custody and control. An action may be brought for the purpose of having any person under the age of 21 years declared free from the custody and control of either or both of his parents when such person . . . has been left by either or both of his parents in the care and custody of another without any provision for his support, or without communication from either or both of his

parents, for the period of one year with the intent on the part of such parent or parents to abandon such person. Such failure to provide, or such failure to communicate for the period of one year, shall be presumptive evidence of the intent to abandon.

31. See, e.g., *Davis Adoption Case* 353 Pa. (1946). *In re Graham* 239 Mo. App. 1036 (1947).

32. While the process through which a new child-parent status emerges is too complex and subject to too many individual variations for the law to know just when "abandonment" may have occurred, the law can generally verify that the biological tie never matured into an affirmative psychological tie for the child or that a developing psychological tie has been broken or damaged and whether a promising new relationship has developed and is being formed.

33. See Jeremy Bentham, *Theory of Legislation* (supra, 1840, Vol. I, p. 254).

> The natural arrangement, which leaves the choice, the mode, and the burden of education to the parents, may be compared to a series of experiments for perfecting the general system. Every thing is advanced and developed by the emulation of individuals, and by differences of ideas and of genius; in a word, by the variety of particular impulses. But let the whole be cast into a single mould; let instruction everywhere take the form of legal authority; errors will be perpetuated, and there will be no further progress.

34. It has taken the law a long time, for example, to realize that its power to deny divorce cannot establish a healthy marriage, or preclude the parties from separating, or even prevent new "relationships" from maturing. See J. Goldstein and M. Gitter, "On the Abolition of Grounds for Divorce: A Model Statute and Commentary" (*Family Law Quart.,* 3:75-99, 1969).

35. See *Lott v. Family and Children's Society* (cited in note 25, *supra*).

36. The law, seeking to safeguard the privacy of family relationships and the private ordering of one's life, has adopted a policy of minimum state intervention consistent, of course, with the state's goal of safeguarding the well-being of children, protecting them from exploitation by adults. See J. Goldstein and M. Gitter (*supra,* note 32).

37. See, e.g., J. D. Watson, professor of molecular biology at Harvard (*New York Times,* March 22, 1973, col. 3, p. 43):

> We must never forget that for the most part we have little insight about the truly unknown—the world we live in is immensely complicated and on the whole its natural phenomena are remarkably unpredictable. Only after a chemical reaction within a cell has been observed, do we usu-

ally find a reason for its existence. Thus it is almost impossible to plan far ahead what the future will bring.

38. See Anna Freud, "Child Observation and Prediction of Development: A Memorial Lecture in Honor of Ernst Kris" (*The Psychoanalytic Study of the Child,* Vol. 13, pp. 97-98; New York: International Universities Press, 1958):

> I name three [factors which] make prediction difficult and hazardous. (1) There is no guarantee that the rate of maturational progress on the side of ego development and drive development will be an even one; and whenever one side of the structure outdistances the other in growth, a variety of unexpected and unpredictable deviations from the norm will follow. (2) There is still no way to approach the quantitative factor in drive development, nor to foresee it; but most of the conflict solutions within the personality will, in the last resort, be determined by quantitative rather than by qualitative factors (3) The environmental happenings in a child's life will always remain unpredictable since they are not governed by any known laws.

Unraveling Child Abuse

‖ DAVID G. GIL   *1975* ‖

"Unraveling Child Abuse," published in 1975, is without question a seminal article in the field of child abuse. David Gil provides a comprehensive examination of child abuse from a sociological perspective. In doing so, Gil is the first to argue for the need to interpret child abuse and neglect holistically rather than along single causal lines. His paper makes the case for eradicating child abuse rather than just ameliorating some individual cases. Sadly, his very cogent arguments have gone largely unheeded and unused by policy makers.

The paper describes the manifestation of abuse and the levels of causation and calls for a primary prevention approach. In explaining its manifestation, Gil was one of the first to expand the definition of child maltreatment beyond that committed by family members. He adds many forms of institutional abuse, including corporal punishment in the schools, inadequate welfare support, practices that allowed children to languish in the foster care system, and treatment in institutions for the mentally ill.

In articulating the various causes of maltreatment, Gil describes a multidimensional reality of the human condition, stating that child abuse can best be understood as emanating from a combination of biological, psychological, social, and economic factors. This perspective was a pioneering one.

And, with regard to prevention, Gil suggests that the eradication of child abuse—what he describes as the only relevant goal of prevention—requires fundamental changes in all of the factors leading to maltreatment, including changes in social philosophy and values, in human relationships and conceptions of children's rights. Gil states that only if society is willing to provide social equity for all children, which would include the elimination of poverty, will we be able to stop child abuse. These were powerful statements at the time and were not met with favor by those working to respond to the child abuse problem one case at a time.

Policy makers and many in the field have stayed far away from Gil's proposed paradigm. Yet, as suggested by Susan Kelley, Gil's comprehensive discussion of the confluence of factors associated with child maltreatment has had substantial influence, notably by providing an early and solid foundation for subsequent knowledge development in the field.

Charles Wilson also comments on the influence of Gil's work. He states that, at the time this article was published, professional attention was largely focused on the individual characteristics of those who abuse children. Gil raised the argument that abuse exists on the institutional and societal levels, as well. In doing so, he became and has remained a strong voice suggesting that society's failure to address the underlying issues of poverty and injustice contributes to the abuse of children. This attribution of responsibility for abuse to society, according to Wilson, has been used by some to successfully shift the professional focus in certain interventions from individual short-comings to more positive family-focused approaches. From this movement to reduce the blame for abuse on the individual has come a whole body of programmatic efforts including family preservation and family-based services. These interventions do not address the underlying causes of abuse so eloquently articulated by Gil, nor do they address his call for a purely primary prevention focus. However, they are nonetheless important outgrowths of his writings.

A. C. D. and K. O.

This paper is an attempt to clarify the sources and dynamics of child abuse and to suggest approaches to its primary prevention. To gain understanding of any social problem one needs to view it in the total societal context within which it evolves, rather than, as is so often done, as an isolated, fragmented phenomenon. Furthermore, one needs to avoid the fallacious tendency of interpreting its dynamics along single causal dimensions such as biological, psychological, social, economic, and so on, a tendency which in our society is usually weighted in favor of individual interpretations and which thus leads to ameliorative programs designed to change individuals rather than pathogenic aspects of the social order.

A VALUE-BASED DEFINITION OF CHILD ABUSE

Understanding and overcoming the dynamics of social problems also requires specification of, and a societal commitment to, certain value premises, and a definition logically linked to such premises. I have suggested such a value-based definition of child abuse at hearings on the *Child Abuse Prevention Act* (S. 1191 of 1973) before the Subcommittee on Children and Youth of the U.S. Senate. This definition views child abuse as inflicted gaps or deficits between circumstances of living which would facilitate the optimal development of children, to which they should be entitled, and their actual circumstances, irrespective of the sources or agents of the deficit:

> Every child, despite his individual differences and uniqueness is to be considered of equal intrinsic worth, and hence should be entitled to equal social, economic, civil, and political rights, so that he may fully realize his inherent potential and share equally in life, liberty, and happiness. Obviously, these value premises are rooted in the humanistic philosophy of our Declaration of Independence.
>
> In accordance with these value premises, then, any act of commission or omission by individuals, institutions, or society as a whole, and any conditions resulting from such acts or inaction which deprive children of equal rights and liberties and/or interfere with their optimal development, constitute, by definition, abusive or neglectful acts or conditions.

Originally published in the *American Journal of Orthopsychiatry*, 1975, *45*, 346-356. Reprinted with permission of the American Orthopsychiatric Association, Inc.

ANALYTIC CONCEPTS

The definition of child abuse presented above suggests the use of two related analytic concepts for studying the nature of child abuse and for developing effective policies and programs for its prevention. These concepts will be referred to here as "levels of manifestation" and "levels of causation" or "causal dimensions." The levels of manifestation identify the agents and the settings in which children may experience abuse. The levels of causation unravel the several causal dimensions, the interactions of which result in abusive acts and abusive conditions at the levels of manifestation. The distinction implicit in these analytic concepts, between the levels at which abuse occurs and the forces that underlie the occurrences, is important, for these levels and forces are not the same. They do, however, complement each other and interact with each other in multiple ways. Moreover, interaction also takes place among the levels themselves and among the forces. Clarifying the nature of child abuse means, essentially, tracing these multiple interactions among the levels of manifestation and the causal dimensions.

LEVELS OF MANIFESTATION

Three levels of manifestation of child abuse may be distinguished. The most familiar one is abusive conditions in the home and abusive interaction between children and their caretakers. Abuse on this level consists of acts of commission or omission by individuals, which inhibit a child's development. The perpetrators are parents, permanent or temporary parent substitutes, or others living in a child's home regularly or temporarily. Abuse in the home may be intentional and conscious or unintentional and also unconscious. Abuse may result from supposedly constructive, disciplinary, educational attitudes and measures or

from negative and hostile feelings toward children. Abusive acts in the home may be one-time events, occasional incidents, or regular patterns. So far, child abuse at this level of manifestation has been the dominant focus of scholarly, professional, and public concern with this destructive phenomenon.

A second level at which child abuse occurs is the institutional level. This includes such settings as day care centers, schools, courts, child care agencies, welfare departments, and correctional and other residential child care settings. In such settings, acts and policies of commission or omission that inhibit, or insufficiently promote, the development of children, or that deprive children of, or fail to provide them with, material, emotional, and symbolic means needed for their optimal development, constitute abusive acts or conditions. Such acts or policies may originate with an individual employee of an institution, such as a teacher, child care worker, judge, probation officer, or social worker, or they may be implicit in the standard practices and policies of given agencies and institutions. In the same way as in the home, abusive acts and conditions in institutional settings may also result from supposedly constructive or from negative and hostile attitudes toward children, and they may be one-time or occasional events or regular patterns.

Institutional child care settings such as schools are often perceived by parents as bearers of cultural norms concerning child-rearing practices and discipline. Hence, when schools and other child care settings employ practices that are not conductive to optimal child development, for example, corporal punishment and other demeaning and threatening negative disciplinary measures, they convey a subtle message to parents—namely, that such measures are appropriate, as they are sanctioned by educational authorities and "experts." Influence also flows in the other direction, from the home to the institutional level. Teachers and child care personnel will frequently adopt child-rearing practices and disciplinary measures similar to those practiced in the homes of children in their care, on the assumption that this is what the children are used to, what they expect, and to what they respond. In this way, methods conducive or not conducive to optimal child development tend to be transmitted back and forth, and reinforced, through interaction between the home and the institution.

When child abuse is viewed as inflicted deficits between a child's actual circumstances and circumstances that would assure his optimal development, it seems to be endemic in most existing institutional settings for the care and education of children, since these settings usually do not facilitate the full actualization of the human potential of all children in their care. Analysis of institutional child abuse reveals that this form of abuse is not distributed randomly throughout the population. Schools and institutions serving children of minority groups, children from deprived socioeconomic backgrounds, handicapped children, and socially deviant children are less likely to facilitate optimal development of children's inherent potential than are schools and institutions serving children of majority groups, "normal" children, and children from affluent families and neighborhoods. However, even settings serving children from privileged backgrounds rarely encourage the optimal development of all children in their care. They, too, tend to inhibit the children's spontaneity and creativity and to promote conformity rather than critical, independent thought. Only rarely will children in these settings develop all their inherent faculties and their unique individuality.

Worse, though, than the educational system, with its mind-stifling practices and its widespread use of corporal punishment and other demeaning and threatening forms of discipline, is the legally sanctioned, massive abuse of children under the policies and practices of the public welfare system, especially the Aid to Families With Dependent Children (AFDC) program. This system of grossly inadequate income maintenance—inadequate even by measures of minimal needs as published by the U.S. Bureau of Labor Statistics—virtually

condemns millions of children to conditions of existence under which physical, social, emotional, and intellectual development are likely to be severely handicapped.

Similarly destructive versions of legally sanctioned abuse on the institutional level are experienced by several hundred thousands of children living in foster care, in training and correctional institutions, and in institutions for children defined as mentally retarded. That these settings of substitute child care usually fail to assure optimum development for the children entrusted to them has been amply demonstrated[1, 5] and does not require further documentation here.

The massive manifestations of institutional child abuse tend to arouse much less public concern and indignation than child abuse in the home, although the abusive conditions and practices of public education, public welfare, and child placement are endemic to these systems and are visible to all who care to see. Perhaps, the enormity of institutional abuse dulls our sensibilities in the same way in which the fate of inmates of concentration camps tends to arouse a lesser response than does the killing of a single individual with whom we are able to identify.

Institutional child abuse is linked, intimately, to the third level at which child abuse is manifested, namely, the societal level. On this level originate social policies which sanction, or cause, severe deficits between the actual circumstances of children and conditions needed for their optimal development. As direct or indirect consequences of such social policies, millions of children in our society live in poverty and are inadequately nourished, clothed, housed, and educated; their health is not assured because of substandard medical care; their neighborhoods decay; meaningful occupational opportunities are not available to them; and alienation is widespread among them. No doubt, these destructive conditions, which result, inevitably, from the normal workings of the prevailing social, economic, and political order and from the value premises which shape that order and its human dynamics, cannot fail to inhibit severely the development of children exposed to them.

Of the three levels of child abuse sketched here, the societal level is certainly the most severe. For what happens at this level determines not only how children fare on the institutional level, but also, by way of complex interactions, how they fare in their own homes.

LEVELS OF CAUSATION

Before discussing the causal dimensions of child abuse, it should be reiterated that the conventional dichotomy between individual and societal causation of social problems distorts the multidimensional reality of human phenomena. We know that psychological forces which shape individual behavior evolve out of the totality of life experiences in specific historical, cultural, social, economic, and political contexts. Individual motivation and behavior are thus always rooted in a societal force field. Yet, societal forces are always expressed, or mediated, through the behavior of individuals, for societies cannot act except through their individual members. Clearly, then, any human phenomenon, at any moment, involves both social and individual elements. In real life, these elements are inseparable. Their separation in theory is merely a product of scholarly, or rather pseudo-scholarly, abstraction.

Based on this reasoning, child abuse, at any level of manifestation, may be understood as acts or inactions of individuals, on their own or as institutional agents, whose behavior reflects societal forces mediated through their unique personalities.

The most fundamental causal level of child abuse consists of a cluster of interacting elements, to wit, a society's basic social philosophy, its dominant value premises, its concept of humans; the nature of its social, economic, and political institutions, which are shaped by its philosophy and value premises and which in turn reinforce that philosophy and these values; and, finally, the particular quality of human relations prevailing in the society, which derives from its philosophy, values, and institutions. For, in the final analysis, it is the philosophy and value premises of a society, the nature of its major institutions, and the quality of its human relations that determine whether or not individual members of that society will develop freely and fully in accordance with their inherent potentialities.

To discern a society's basic social philosophy and values and its concept of humans, one needs to ascertain whether it considers everyone to be intrinsically of equal worth in spite of his or her uniqueness and, hence, entitled to the same social, economic, and political rights; or whether everyone in the society considers himself, and those close to himself, of greater worth than anyone else, and hence entitled to more desirable or privileged circumstances. The former, egalitarian philosophy would be reflected in institutional arrangements involving cooperative actions in pursuit of common existential interests. Every individual, and that includes every child, would be considered an equally entitled subject who could not be exploited and dominated by any other individual or group and whose right to fully and freely develop his individuality would be assured and respected, subject to the same right of all others. The latter, non-egalitarian philosophy, on the other hand, as we know so well from our own existence, is reflected in institutional structures which encourage competitive behavior in pursuit of narrowly perceived, egotistical interests. Everyone strives to get ahead of others, considers himself entitled to privileged conditions and positions, and views and treats others as potential means to be used, exploited, and dominated in pursuit of his egotistical goals.

Analysis of these contrasting social philosophies, societal institutions, and modes of human relations suggests that full and free development of every child's inherent potential may be possible only in a society organized

consistently around egalitarian and cooperative value premises, since the equal right to self-
actualization is implicit in an egalitarian philosophy, while such a right is incompatible with a
non-egalitarian philosophy. In a society organized on non-egalitarian and competitive principles, full and free development for all children is simply impossible, as, by definition,
there must always be losers in such societies,
whose chances to realize their inherent potential will be severely limited. Hence, significant
developmental deficits for large segments of the
population, or high levels of socially structured
and sanctioned abuse of children, are endemic
in such societies.

A second, more specific, level of causation
of child abuse may be intrinsic to the social
construction, or definition, of childhood prevalent in a society. Obviously, this level is closely
related to the first level. How does a society
view its children, all its children, and how does
it define their rights? How much obedience,
submission, and conformity does it expect of
children? Does it process children through
caste-like channels of socialization into relatively closed and inflexible social and occupational structures, or does it encourage them,
within limits of reason, to discover and develop
their individuality and uniqueness and to shape
their lives accordingly? Obviously, optimal development of the inherent potential of all children is a function of the extent to which a society's processes of socialization are permeated
with a commitment to such self-actualization
for all. When this commitment is lacking alto-
gether, or when it varies with such factors as
sex, race, and social and economic position of a
family, then different children will experience
varying deficits in realizing their potential.
Presently, in our society, social policies that
sustain different levels of rights for children
from different social and economic backgrounds are a major, direct cause of many forms
of child abuse on the societal and institutional
levels and an indirect cause of abuse on the
family level.

A further causal dimension of child abuse is
a society's attitude toward the use of force as a
legitimate means for attaining ends, especially
in imbalanced, interpersonal relations such as
master-slave, male-female, guard-prisoner,
and adult-child. The tendency to resort to the
use of force for dealing with conflicts in our society seems to require no documentation here,
nor does it seem necessary to document the
specific readiness to use force, or the threat of
it, as a means to maintain authority and discipline in adult-child relations in the public domain, such as schools and other child care settings, and in the private domain of the family.
The readiness to use physical force for disciplinary objectives is certainly endemic in our
society.

It should be noted that the readiness to use
force in general, and in adult-child relations in
particular, is intimately linked to a society's
basic philosophy and value premises and to its
concept of humans and their rights. A non-
egalitarian philosophy is much more likely to
sanction the use of force than is an egalitarian
one, since the use of force against other humans constitutes the strongest possible nega-
tion of equality. The use of force toward children is also related to the manner in which
childhood and the rights of children are defined by a society and in turn tends to reinforce
that definition.

As mentioned earlier, the use of force toward children is widespread in our society on
the institutional and family levels. Attempts to
limit and outlaw it in public institutions have
had only limited success so far. It may be
noted, in this context, that because of the com-
patibility between the use of physical force, on
the one hand, and a non-egalitarian philosophy
and competitive social, economic, and political institutions, on the other, corporal punishment and the threat of it may actually be highly
functional in preparing children for adult roles
in a non-egalitarian and competitive social order. For, were our children reared in a harmoni-
ous fashion without threats, insults, and physi-

cal force, they might not be adequately prepared and conditioned for adult roles in our non-egalitarian, competitive reality.

Whenever corporal punishment in child rearing is sanctioned, and even subtly encouraged by a society, incidents of serious physical abuse and injury are bound to happen, either as a result of deliberate, systematic, and conscious action on the part of perpetrators or under conditions of loss of self-control. In either case, but especially in the latter, physical attacks on children tend to relieve tensions and frustrations experienced by the perpetrators. Clearly, then, these attacks are carried out to meet emotional needs of the perpetrators rather than educational needs of the victims, as is often claimed by advocates of corporal punishment.

The next causal dimension may be referred to as "triggering contexts." These contexts operate jointly with the societal sanction of the use of physical force in adult-child relations. Adults who use force toward children do not do so all the time but only under specific circumstances which serve as triggers for their abusive behavior. In general, abusive attacks tend to be triggered by stress and frustration, which may cause reduction or loss of self-control. Stress and frustration may facilitate abusive attacks even without causing a reduction or loss of self-control, as long as the appropriateness of the use of force in child rearing is accepted.

One major source of stress and frustration for adults in our society is the multifaceted deprivations of poverty and its correlates: high density in overcrowded, dilapidated, inadequately served neighborhoods; large numbers of children, especially in one-parent, mainly female-headed households; and the absence of child care alternatives. Having identified poverty and its correlates as an important triggering context of child abuse in the home, we may now note that social policies which sanction and perpetuate the existence of poverty among large segments of the population, including millions of children, are thus indirect sources of child abuse in the home. It should be emphasized, though, that poverty, per se, is not a direct cause of child abuse in the home but operates through an intervening variable, namely, concrete and psychological stress and frustration experienced by individuals in the context of culturally sanctioned use of physical force in child rearing.

Poverty is not the only source of stress and frustration triggering child abuse in the home. Such abuse is known to occur frequently in many homes in adequate and even affluent economic circumstances. One other important source of stress and frustration in our society is the alienating circumstances in most workplaces, be the work manual labor, skilled and unskilled occupations, or administrative, managerial, and professional work through all levels and sectors of business, academic, and government bureaucracies. A recent report by a task force of the U.S. Department of Health, Education, and Welfare[6] documented the seriousness of work alienation experienced by constantly growing segments of the working population. This government report reached conclusions similar to those voiced by many severe critics of our economic system in recent years—that the prevailing competitive and exploitative human relations in the workplace, and its hierarchical and authoritarian structures, tend to cause psychological stress and alienation for nearly every working person. These pressures may lead to various forms of deviant behavior, such as alcoholism, drug addiction, mental illness, white-collar crime, and so on. Perhaps the most frequent locus for discharging feelings of stress and frustration originating in the formal world of work is the informal world of primary relations, the home and the family. Conflicts between spouses are one form this discharge may take. Child abuse in the form of violent physical outbursts is another.

Here, then, we identify once again a triggering context for child abuse on the interpersonal level, which is rooted deeply in societal forces, namely, the alienating quality of our society's economic and productive system, complemented by the culturally sanctioned use of physical force in child rearing.

The final causal dimension of child abuse on the interpersonal level in the home and in child care settings is made up of intrapsychic conflicts and various forms of psychopathology on the part of perpetrators. Child abuse literature is largely focused on this dimension, and thus little needs to be said here to document it. What needs to be stressed, however, is that psychological disturbances and their manner of expression are not independent factors but are deeply rooted in, and constantly interact with, forces in the social environment of the disturbed individual. To the extent that psychopathology is not rooted in genetic and biochemical processes, it derives from the totality of the life experiences of the individual, which are shaped by continuous interactions between the person and his social setting, his informal and formal relations in primary and secondary contexts. However, it is not only the etiology of intrapsychic conflicts and disturbances that is conditioned, in part, by social forces, but also the manner in which these conflicts and disturbances are expressed in social relations. The symptoms of emotional disturbance and mental illness are not randomly generated phenomena but derive from normal behavioral traits in a culture. These normal traits appear in exaggerated or negated forms in behavior which is considered deviant, neurotic, and psychotic. Hence, one may assume that in a society in which the use of physical force in general, and toward children in particular, is not sanctioned, intrapsychic conflicts and psychopathology would less often be expressed through violence against children. It follows from these considerations that the "battered baby" syndrome,[3,4] and other forms of child abuse associated with psychological disturbance of one kind or another, are not independent of societal forces, although the perpetrators of these acts may be emotionally ill individuals. We are thus again led to the con-

clusion that abusive acts and conditions, irrespective of the level of manifestation, can be understood not in terms of one specific causal dimension but only in terms of complex interactions among the several causal dimensions sketched here.

PRIMARY PREVENTION

According to a general conceptual model, primary prevention proceeds from identification toward elimination of the causal context from which specified undesired phenomena derive. It needs to be realized that the prevention of undesired phenomena may also result in the elimination of other phenomena whenever such other phenomena derive from, or are part of, the same causal context. The likelihood of simultaneous prevention of several phenomena could lead to serious dilemmas if some of the phenomena are desired, while others are considered undesirable, or when groups in a society differ in their respective evaluation of the desirability of the several phenomena. Decisions concerning primary prevention of social phenomena and of "social problems" are thus essentially political choices.[2]

Turning now to the primary prevention of child abuse, we may begin by summarizing our conclusions so far. Child abuse, conceived of as inflicted deficits on a child's right to develop freely and fully, irrespective of the source and agents of the deficit, was found to occur on several related levels: on the interpersonal level in the home and in child care settings; on the institutional level through the policies and practices of a broad array of child care, educational, welfare, and correctional institutions and agencies; and on the societal level, where the interplay of values and social, economic, and political institutions and processes shapes the social policies by which the rights and lives of all children, and of specific groups of children, are determined. The causal dimensions of child abuse are, first of all, the dominant social philosophy and value premises of a society, its social, economic, and political institutions, and the quality of human relations to which these institutions, philosophy, and values give rise; other causal dimensions are the social construction of childhood and the social definition of children's rights; the extent to which a society sanctions the use of force in general and, more specifically, in the child-rearing context; stress and frustration resulting from poverty and from alienation in the workplace, which may trigger abusive acts; and expressions of intrapsychic conflicts and psychopathology which, in turn, are rooted in the social fabric. While child abuse, at any particular level, may be more closely related to one rather than another causal dimension, none of these dimensions are independent, and they exert their influence through multiple interactions with each other.

This analysis suggests that primary prevention of child abuse, on all levels, would require fundamental changes in social philosophy and value premises, in societal institutions, and in human relations. It would also require a reconceptualization of childhood, of children's rights, and of child rearing. It would necessitate rejecting the use of force as a means for achieving societal ends, especially in dealing with children. It would require the elimination of poverty and of alienating conditions of production, major sources of stress and frustration which tend to trigger abusive acts toward children in adult-child interaction. And, finally, it would necessitate the elimination of psychological illness. Because of the multiple interactions among the several causal dimensions, progress in overcoming the more fundamental dimensions would also reduce the force of other dimensions. Thus, transforming the prevailing non-egalitarian social philosophy, value premises, and institutions, and the kind of human relations they generate, into egalitarian ones would also result in corresponding modifications of children's rights, elimination of poverty and alienation of work, and rejection of the use of force. It would indirectly influence psychological well-being and would

thus eliminate the processes that now trigger child abuse in interpersonal relations.

Effective primary prevention requires working simultaneously toward the transformation of all the causal dimensions. Fragmented approaches focused on one or the other causal dimension may bring some amelioration, but one should entertain no illusions as to the effectiveness of such piecemeal efforts. Even such important and necessary steps as outlawing corporal punishment in schools and other child care settings would have only limited, though highly desirable, results. There simply is no way of escaping the conclusion that the complete elimination of child abuse on all levels of manifestation requires a radical transformation of the prevailing unjust, non-egalitarian, irrational, competitive, alienating, and hierarchical social order into a just, egalitarian, rational, cooperative, humane, and truly democratic, decentralized one. Obviously, this realization implies that primary prevention of child abuse is a political issue which cannot be resolved through professional and administrative measures.

Primary prevention of child abuse would bring with it the prevention of other equally undesirable and inevitable consequences or symptoms of the same causal context, including many manifestations of social deviance. However, it would also result in the complete transformation of the prevailing social, economic, and political order with which large segments of our society are either identified or drifting along, because this order conforms to their accustomed mental sets and because they seem reluctant, due to inertia, to search actively for alternative social, economic, and political institutions that might be more conductive to human fulfillment for all. Some or many members of our society may even be consciously committed to the perpetuation of the existing order, not realizing how destructive that order may be to their own real interests.

Whatever one's attitude may be toward these fundamental political issues, one needs to recognize and face the dilemmas implicit in them and, hence, in primary prevention of child abuse. If one's priority is to prevent all child abuse, one must be ready to part with its many causes, even when one is attached to some of them, such as the apparent blessings, advantages, and privileges of inequality. If, on the other hand, one is reluctant to give up all aspects of the causal context of child abuse, one must be content to continue living with this social problem. In that latter case, one ought to stop talking about primary prevention and face the fact that all one may be ready for is some measure of amelioration.

▌ REFERENCES ▌

1. GIL, D. 1970. *Violence Against Children.* Harvard University Press, Cambridge, Mass.

2. GIL, D. 1973. *Unraveling Social Policy.* Schenkman Publishing Co., Cambridge, Mass.

3. HELFER, R. AND KEMPE, C., eds. 1968. *The Battered Child,* University of Chicago Press, Chicago.

4. KEMPE, C. AND HELFER, R., eds. 1972. *Helping the Battered Child and His Family.* Lippincott, Philadelphia.

5. SCHORR, A., ed. 1974. *Children and Decent People.* Basic Books, New York.

6. TASK FORCE TO THE SECRETARY OF HEW. 1973. *Work in America.* MIT Press, Cambridge, Mass.

Nonorganic Failure to Thrive

A Long-Term Follow-Up

IAN W. HUFTON
R. KIM OATES   *1977*

"Nonorganic Failure to Thrive: A Long-Term Follow-Up," when published in 1977, brought into focus an important dimension of the longer-term consequences of a child's failure to thrive, a dimension that had previously been inadequately appreciated by the medical community. By conducting a long-term follow-up study on children who had been diagnosed with failure to thrive, Ian Hufton and Kim Oates were able to offer important new insights into a perplexing and not very well understood phenomenon. As a result of their work, they recognized that the social and developmental consequences of failure to thrive were ultimately more significant than the failure to gain weight or to sustain linear growth. Kevin Browne explains that their work followed on that of Elmer and Chase and Martin and others who had earlier identified developmental delays in children who had suffered nonorganic failure to thrive.

As reported by Martin Finkel, what makes this paper significant is the authors' recognition and eloquent articulation that the adverse long-term impact of deprivation ultimately involves changes in personality, verbal intelligence including reading ability, and behavior more than changes in traditional growth parameters (e.g., height and weight). The authors also found evidence of what is widely understood today but was not at the time: that these children were most likely being raised in environments characterized by family instability and economic difficulty. Thus, this was as much an individual as a community problem.

Stephen Ludwig describes the importance of this paper: It identified for the medical community the notion that poor weight gain and low growth parameters were not medical conditions in isolation but rather markers of more pervasive family dysfunction. The finding that many children, years later, still had intellectual and developmental deficiencies despite adequate weight gain was a startling and important one. Browne believes that this paper has prompted further studies in this important area, with findings that emphasize the need for follow-up and longer-term intervention for children who in the past have suffered from nonorganic failure to thrive.

Finkel comments that this paper represents one of the fundamental building blocks of our understanding of the full spectrum of consequences that result from failure to provide adequate care. Recent research on early brain development is beginning to demonstrate the serious long-term consequences of deprivation and maltreatment. The interdependence of the human brain and the external environment for optimal growth is becoming more fully understood. Deprivation adversely influences the neurobiology of the brain and shapes its clinical expression in terms of development and behavior. These authors, concludes Finkel, made a contribution that is evident in their early charge to medical colleagues to complement the traditional medical approach to failure to thrive with intensive social support. Their observations are as poignant today as when they were first described.

A. C. D.

Nonorganic failure to thrive has been defined as the presence of growth retardation with, or without, associated development deficit and the absence of organic disorders sufficient to account for these deviations.[1] The syndrome has been thoroughly investigated in the past and the status of the child in the family at the time of admission or shortly after, the presence of environmental deprivation, low socioeconomic class, and marital instability have been documented.[2-6]

In 1971, Fischoff and coworkers[7] reported that a high proportion of the mothers of these children have character disorders. They suggested that these disorders in the mothers are in part responsible for the difficulties encountered in trying to treat these families.

In 1970, a review was made of 24 of the 30 children with nonorganic failure to thrive admitted to a unit of the Royal Alexandra Hospital for Children, Sydney, between January 1967 and December 1969.[6] On review, 50% of these children were below the 10th percentile for weight and 30% were below the 10th percentile for both height and weight. It was noted that the index child was usually the youngest in the family and, in 60% of cases, had been born within 18 months of a sibling. The parents of the children usually came from large families, which were often disrupted. Ten families in the group were no longer intact. Three children had been surrendered for adoption.

Preventive medical care had been poor, with one third of the families having no family doctor but preferring to use hospital emergency rooms. Only one half of the children were fully immunized. Sixty percent of the children's fathers were semiskilled or unskilled workers.

The present study was designed to review these 24 children. A protocol was designed to review: (1) Physical progress and health of the children; (2) educational progress of the children, using the Wechsler Intelligence Scale for Children[8] (WISC), a graded reading vocabulary test,[9] and reports from school teachers; (3) emotional status of the children using a questionnaire[10] completed by teachers; (4) the mother's attitudes towards the child, using a personality questionnaire,[10] and the mother's subjective comments on the child; (5) the personalities of the mothers, using the Minnesota Multiphasic Personality Inventory[11] (MMPI) and personal interview; and (6) the present socioeconomic circumstances of the child and family.

Twenty-one of the original 24 children were located, including two of the three adopted children. Fourteen lived in the metropolitan area and seven lived in the country. All the chil-

Originally published in *Pediatrics* 1977, *57*, 73-77. Copyright 1977. Reprinted by permission of *Pediatrics*.

TABLE 7.1 Wechsler Intelligence Scale for Children (WISC) Scores

WISC Score	>110	90 to 110	< 90
Verbal and performance subtests within 19 points	1	7	3
Performance exceeds verbal score by 20 to 29 points			
Performance exceeds verbal score by more than 30 points		2	

dren living in the city and two of the country families were seen and interviewed by one of the authors (I.W.H.). The other five families were interviewed by local community health nurses, using a standard questionnaire. One child of the original 24 had died in suspicious circumstances, and two families could not be found despite extensive searching. There was considerable difficulty in locating most of the families in the survey, as 15 of the 21 families had changed address at least once since the last review. Three families had moved five times in that period. It was our impression that those families who were better adjusted were the easiest to trace and the most cooperative.

The average interval from discharge to review was 6 years 4 months (range, 5 years 5 months to 8 years 1 month). The average age of the children on review was 7 years 10 months (range, 5 years 10 months to 11 years 9 months).

RESULTS

Physical and Health Status

Only five children remained below the 10th percentile for weight, while their heights were in the normal range. Only one child was below the 10th percentile for height, when corrected for mid-parent height,[12] compared to eight such children in 1970.

Since the last review, four of the children had been admitted to a hospital with gastrointestinal upsets. The other children had been well. Three children were incompletely immu-

nized, and one other child had received no immunization at all. No serious accidents had been recorded, apart from one child with a fractured skull and another with a fractured arm. Review of the hospital records of these accidents did not indicate any suspicion of child abuse. One child had died in January 1975 after convulsions at home. This occurred 2 weeks after the mother's common-law husband had been charged with assaulting the mother and the child. An autopsy showed facial and head bruising and cerebral edema but no evidence of further intracranial or other pathology. One child in the original series died prior to review in 1970 as a result of head injuries inflicted by a relative.[6]

Educational Status

The WISC[8] was given to the 14 children living in the city (Table 7.1). One child had a full-scale score of more than 110 points, and three had full-scale scores of less than 90 points, with comparable scores on the verbal and performance subtests. The remaining 10 children had full-scale scores between 90 and 110 points. Of these, 3 children had performance scores that were 20 points or more higher than their verbal scores. In two cases, this differences was more than 30 points. Ten of the children were described by their teacher as functioning below average.

A graded vocabulary test[9] was given to 18 of the children. This showed that two thirds had a reading age 1 or 2 years behind their

TABLE 7.2 Graded Reading Vocabulary Test Scores

Reading Age	WISC[a] ≥ 90	WISC < 90
1 year or more above chronological age	1	
Within 1 year of chronological age	5	
Between 1 and 2 years below chronological age	6	2
More than 2 years below chronological age	6	1

a. Wechsler Intelligence Scale for Children.

chronological age (Table 7.2). It is interesting to note that one of the adopted children had a reading age 18 months ahead of his chronological age and that his verbal scale score on the WISC was 19 points higher than his performance score.

Emotional Status

The children's personalities were assessed by a questionnaire[10] completed by the child's teacher. This questionnaire, designed to be completed by school teachers, detects deviant personalities and separates them into neurotic, antisocial, or undifferentiated types. Ten children were classified as having abnormal personalities. Five of these had antisocial and five had neurotic characteristics.

To see if the mothers perceived these children as different from their other children, they were asked to complete this questionnaire for the index child and for the next oldest and youngest sibling. Sixteen of the 18 mothers who completed the questionnaire scored their index children as abnormal. In one half of these cases, the siblings received a normal score. The mother's subjective comments on the children's personalities were also noted (Table 7.3). There was a high incidence of complaints about speech problems, lying, temper tantrums, enuresis, and overactivity. Of the eight children with speech difficulties, three had a stammer. The other speech difficulties included delayed speech and lisp.

Family Profile

These families had a high degree of marital instability. At the time of review, 12 of the 19 natural families were still intact. Seven mothers were divorced, separated, or had never been married. Of these, five were living in a common-law relationship.

In 13 cases, the mother's personality was assessed, using the MMPI in conjunction with a personal interview. The MMPI showed three abnormal profiles. One mother showed extreme defensiveness, another showed moderate depression, and one showed a hysteroid, passive, somatizing profile.[13] Three mothers had attempted suicide unsuccessfully, and two of these attempts had occurred since the last review in 1970. Overdose of prescribed tablets was the method used in each case. Nine moth-

TABLE 7.3 Mothers' Subjective Comments

Behavior[a]	Number
Speech problems	8
Frequent lying	8
Bad temper tantrums	7
Emotional, insecure, or nervous	7
Enuresis	7
Overactive	5
Attention-seeking	4
Stealing	3
Encopresis	1

a. Several characteristics may apply to one child.

ers described themselves as suffering from "nerves" or depression. Two women were being treated for depression.

Of the 12 natural fathers who were still married, one was a recognized paranoid schizophrenic receiving treatment and one was an aggressive man who is known to have physically abused at least one of his children.

At the last review, it was noted that most of the children were the youngest in a large family, and it was suggested that this extra child was more than the mother's already overburdened resources could manage.[6] Ten of the families now have further children. The majority of these children have normal physical growth. At least three of these siblings have psychological disturbances. One has been admitted to a psychiatric hospital in the past 12 months. This child has been physically abused by his father.

Socioeconomic Aspects

Nine families were dependent on welfare benefits for all or part of their incomes. Ten families described themselves as having financial difficulties. Twelve families lived in rented accommodations, and the remainder owned or were buying their own homes. Six families described their homes as inadequate. In eight of the homes, at least one bedroom had three or more people in it.

Five families relied on hospital emergency rooms for medical care and had no family physician. Two families were not covered by hospital or medical insurance. The remaining families were either insured or covered by welfare benefits.

DISCUSSION

This review suggests that children with nonorganic failure to thrive remain at risk in the areas of physical growth, personality development, and education. In most cases,

physical growth was satisfactory, but three children of the original group of 30 are known to have suffered physical abuse from either a relative or a father surrogate, and two of these have died. Failure to thrive and child abuse often represent different parts of the same spectrum,[14] and many of the features of the families in this series have been found in battering families.[15]

Emotionally, 10 of the children were considered abnormal, using a standardized questionnaire[10] completed by their teachers. Ninety percent of mothers using the same questionnaire gave the child an abnormal personality score. The mothers also complained of a high incidence of behavior disturbances. This suggests that these mothers may perceive these children as being difficult and unpleasant. This may partly account for their caloric and emotional understimulation in early childhood. The disparity between the performance and verbal scores on the WISC further suggests that some of these children may be subjected to a lack of appropriate emotional and intellectual stimulation in their homes. This is also suggested by the delayed reading age in the nine children with normal intelligence. It might help if these children could be placed on a special education register when they are admitted to a hospital with nonorganic failure to thrive. This would provide early recognition of their potential educational problems so that remedial teaching and reading could be instituted at the appropriate times.

Family analysis reveals the instability of marriages in this group and the high incidence of depression in the mothers. It was felt that the MMPI is of little value applied so long after the initial crisis situation. We agree with Fischoff et al.[7] that an unstructured interview at the time of admission may be of considerable benefit in determining personality deficits in the mother. The results of this survey confirm the findings of Elmer et al.,[4] who followed 15 children with nonorganic failure to thrive. In that series, there were similar family problems, and 13 of the 15 children were regarded as functioning below normal in at least one of the areas of physical development, intellectual development, or behavior.

On their original hospital admission, the children in this series were thoroughly investigated medically. When no organic cause was found, they were nutritionally improved and sent home. Very little in-depth social work investigation was done during admission, and little continuing support was provided after discharge. Fifty percent of the families failed to keep follow-up appointments at the hospital, and contact was then lost.

These parents would be unlikely to benefit from a problem-solving psychotherapeutic approach.[7] Character modification could only be achieved with prolonged psychiatric treatment, during which time the child remains at risk. An alternative is to provide a more active program of direct support for the mother so that she can be encouraged to cope with her infant herself rather than have the child fed in the hospital and then returned to her. Taking the child from the mother to be cared for adequately by other women in the hospital only serves to reinforce her feelings of inadequacy. Close rapport must be established with the mother and a warm, supporting relationship built up in hospital and continued at home.

Since March 1974, a coordinated management program for these families has been instituted at this hospital. All children with failure to thrive under 1 year of age are seen early by the social worker for a detailed social history. From the outset, the mother and, if possible, the father are involved in the treatment of the child. The emphasis from all members of the ward team is on management of the mother and child together. The mother is encouraged to feed and care for her child as part of the therapeutic team. The mother is praised for her efforts, and the remainder of the team sees that she gets the credit for the progress the child

makes in the hospital. Multidisciplinary case conferences are held weekly.

After organic causes of failure to thrive have been excluded and the child is gaining weight, arrangements are made to continue care at home. Close liaison has been established with community nurses, baby health clinic sisters, and community social workers. When the child is discharged from the hospital, home visits to provide the mother with support in a benign, nonthreatening manner are made by one of these community workers. Initially, home visits are made daily and continued at least twice weekly. Communication is maintained between the community workers and the hospital personnel.

It is hoped that this plan of intensive support and follow-up for these families will partially prevent the long-term sequelae of deranged physical, educational, and emotional development that occur in this condition.

REFERENCES

1. Togut M, Allen JE, Lelchuck L: A psychological exploration of the non-organic failure to thrive syndrome. Dev Med Child Neurol 11: 601, 1969.

2. Leonard FS, Rhymes JP, Solnit AJ: Failure to thrive in infants: A family problem. Am J Dis Child 111: 600, 1966.

3. Shaheen E, Alexander D, Truskowsky M, Barbero GJ: Failure to thrive—A retrospective profile. Clin Pediatr 7: 255, 1968.

4. Elmer E, Gregg G, Ellison P: Late results of the failure to thrive syndrome. Clin Pediatr 8: 584, 1969.

5. Glaser HH, Heagarty MC, Bullard DM, Pivchik EC: Physical and psychological development of children with early failure to thrive. J Pediatr 73: 690, 1969.

6. Oates RK, Yu JS: Children with non-organic failure to thrive: A community problem. Med J Aust 2: 199, 1971.

7. Fischoff J, Whitten CF, Pettit MG: A psychiatric study of mothers of infants with growth failure secondary to maternal deprivation. J Pediatr 79: 209, 1971.

8. Wechsler D: Wechsler Intelligence Scale for Children. New York, Psychological Corporation, 1949.

9. Schonell AJ, Schonell FE: Diagnostic and Attainment Testing, ed 2. Edinburgh, Oliver & Boyd, 1952, p 38.

10. Rutter M: A children's behaviour questionnaire for completion by teachers. J Child Psychol Psychiatry 8: 1, 1967.

11. Hathaway SR, McKinley JC: Minnesota Multiphasic Personality Inventory. New York, Psychological Corporation, 1967.

12. Tanner JM, Goldstein N, Whitehouse RH: Standards for children's height at ages 2-9 years allowing for height of parents. Arch Dis Child 45: 755, 1970.

13. Gilberstadt H, Duker J: A Handbook for Clinical and Actuarial MMPI Interpretation. Philadelphia, WB Saunders, 1965.

14. Koel BS: Failure to thrive and fatal injury as a continuum. Am J Dis Child 118: 565, 1969.

15. Steele BF, Pollock CB: A psychiatric study of parents who abuse infants and small children. In, Helfer RE, Kempe KH (eds): The Battered Child. Chicago, University of Chicago Press, 1974.

Munchausen Syndrome by Proxy

The Hinterland of Child Abuse

| **ROY MEADOW   1977** |

Sir Roy Meadow, the recently knighted author of "Munchausen Syndrome by Proxy: The Hinterland of Child Abuse," offered the medical community a way to see something that was right in front of them and, thereby, opened an important door on one of the most hidden aspects of child maltreatment. Through the dissection of two cases in which children repeatedly appeared for medical care with confusing, unexplained diagnoses, Dr. Meadow concluded that the children's parents were falsifying the children's symptoms and even tampering with the children's specimens and interfering with hospital observations (a phenomenon reminiscent of the Munchausen Syndrome, in which patients falsified their own conditions). He labeled the phenomenon Munchausen syndrome by proxy. In doing so, Meadow helped deliver many children from perpetual torture and even a premature and harrowing death.

The power of the paper is clear. Donna Rosenberg reports that, on reading this paper shortly after it was published in 1977, it occurred to her that a certain "mystery disease" of one of her own patients had prob-

ably been illness falsification. She says, "Not only had I missed the diagnosis during my month-long tenure as the child's doctor, I doubt the diagnosis would ever have occurred to me, however long I had remained his pediatrician." In addition to that one case, many hundreds have now been described in the medical literature, and probably thousands more have been diagnosed. Susan Hiatt adds that the paper helped remind professionals that even parents can be perpetrators—despite the fact that the battered-child syndrome had been recognized more than a decade earlier.

The paper clearly has led to significant changes in clinical diagnosis and to additional research on this facet of child maltreatment. Despite all the work prompted by this significant paper, according to Rosenberg, the field is still far from a satisfactory explanation as to what truly motivates the parents who engage in this behavior. Thus, our practice today includes a well-developed pediatric diagnosis of the child but not a psychiatric diagnosis of the perpetrator. In discussing the impact of this paper on subsequent research, Hiatt says that this paper confirms the value of case studies in furthering our knowledge, a helpful alternative to large-scale clinical trials in times of funding limitations.

Rosenberg graciously quarrels with one of Meadow's points. He suggests that parents who perpetrate Munchausen syndrome by proxy are indeed otherwise loving parents; based on the cases she has seen, Rosenberg acknowledges that love can take many forms, but Munchausen syndrome by proxy is not one of them.

A. C. D. and K. O.

Doctors dealing with young children rely on the parents' recollection of the history. The doctor accepts that history, albeit sometimes with a pinch of salt, and it forms the cornerstone of subsequent investigation and management of the child.

A case is reported in which over a period of 6 years, the parents systematically provided fictitious information about their child's symptoms, tampered with the urine specimens to produce false results, and interfered with hospital observations. This caused the girl innumerable investigations and anesthetic, surgical, and radiological procedures in three different centers.

The case is compared with another child who was intermittently given toxic doses of salt, which again led to massive investigation in three different centers and ended in death. The behavior of the parents in these two cases was similar in many ways. Although in each case, the end result for the child was "non- accidental injury", the long-running saga of hospital care was reminiscent of the Munchausen syndrome, in these cases by proxy.

CASE REPORTS

First Case

Kay was referred to the pediatric nephrology clinic in Leeds at the age of 6 be-cause of recurrent illnesses in which she passed foul-smelling, bloody urine. She had been investigated in two other centers without the cause being found.

In the child's infancy, her mother had noticed yellow pus on the nappies, and their doctor had first prescribed antibiotics for suspected urine infection when Kay was 8 months old. Since then, she had had periodic courses of antibiotics for presumed urine infection. Since the age of 3, she had been on continuous antibiotics, which included co-trimoxazole, amoxycillin, nalidixic acid, nitrofurantoin, ampicillin, gentamicin, and uticillin. These treatments had themselves caused drug rashes, fever, and candidiasis, and she had continued to have intermittent bouts of lower abdominal pain associated with fever and foul-smelling, infected urine, often containing frank blood. There was intermittent vulval soreness and discharge.

The parents were in their late 30s. Father, who worked mainly in the evenings and at night, was healthy. The mother had had urinary-tract infections. The 3-year-old brother was healthy.

At the time of referral, Kay had already been investigated at a district general hospital and at a regional teaching hospital. Investigations had included two urograms, micturating cystourethrograms, two gynecological examinations under anesthetic, and two cystoscopies. The symptoms were unexplained and continued unabated. She was being given steadily more toxic chemotherapy. Bouts were recurring more often, and everyone was mystified by the intermittent nature of her complaint and the way in which purulent, bloody urine specimens were followed by completely clear ones a few hours later. Similarly, foul discharges were apparent on her vulva at one moment, but later on the same day, her vulva was normal.

On examination, she was a healthy girl who was growing normally. The urine was blood-stained and foul. It was strongly positive for blood and albumin and contained a great many leucocytes and epithelial cells. It was heavily infected with *Escherichia coli.*

The findings strongly suggested an ectopic ureter or an infected cyst draining into the urethra or vagina. Yet, previous investigations had not disclosed this. Ectopic ureters are notoriously difficult to detect, and, after consultation with colleagues at the combined pediatric/urology clinic, it was decided to investigate her immediately she began to pass foul urine. No sooner was she admitted than the foul discharge stopped before cystoscopy could be done. More efficient arrangements were made for the urological surgeon concerned to be contacted immediately she should arrive in Leeds, passing foul urine. This was done three times (including a bank holiday and a Sunday). No source of the discharge was found. On every occasion, it cleared up fast. Efforts to localize the source included further radiology, vaginogram, urethrogram, barium enema, suprapubic aspiration, bladder catheterization, urine cultures, and exfoliative cytology. During these investigations, the parents were most cooperative, and Kay's mother always stayed in hospital with her (mainly because they lived a long way away). She was concerned and loving in her relationship with Kay and yet sometimes not quite as worried about the possible cause of the illness as were the doctors. Many of the crises involved immediate admission and urgent anesthetics for examinations or cystoscopy, and these tended to occur most at weekend holiday periods. On one bank holiday, five consultants came into the hospital specifically to see her.

The problem seemed insoluble, and many of the facts did not make sense. The urinary pathogens came and went at a few minutes' notice; there would be one variety of *E. coli* early in the morning and then, after a few normal specimens, an entirely different organism such as *Proteus or Streptococcus fæcalis* in the evening. Moreover, there was something about the mother's temperament and behavior that was reminiscent of the mother described in Case 2, so we decided to work on the assumption that everything about the history and investigations were false. Close questioning revealed that most of the abnormal specimens were ones that, at some stage or other, had been left unsupervised in the mother's presence.

This theory was tested when Kay was admitted with her mother, and all urine specimens were collected under strict supervision by a trained nurse, who was told not to let the urine out of her sight the moment it passed from Kay's urethra to it being tested on the ward by a doctor and then delivered to the laboratory. On the fourth day, supervision was deliberately relaxed slightly so that one or two specimens were either left for the mother to collect or collected by the nurse and then left in the mother's presence for a minute before being taken away. On the first 3 days, no urine specimen was abnormal. On the first occasion that the mother was left to collect the specimen (having been instructed exactly how to do so), she brought a heavily blood-stained specimen containing much debris and bacteria. A subsequent specimen collected by the nurse was completely normal. This happened on many occasions during the next few days. During a 7-day period, Kay emptied her bladder 57 times; 45 specimens were normal, all of these being collected and supervised by a nurse; 12 were grossly abnormal, containing blood and different organisms, all these having been collected by the mother or left in her presence. All the specimens were meant to be collected in exactly the same way as complete specimens, and the mother was using the same sort of uten-sils as were the nurses. On one evening, the pattern was as shown here:

Time	Appearance	Collection
5.00 p.m.	Normal	By nurse
6.45 p.m.	Bloody	By mother
7.15 p.m.	Normal	By nurse
8.15 p.m.	Bloody	By mother
8.30 p.m.	Normal	By nurse

On that day, the mother was persuaded to provide a specimen of urine from herself. She produced a very bloody specimen, full of de-bris and bacteria which resembled the speci-mens she had been handing in as Kay's urine. The mother was menstruating. Kay was given xylose tablets so that we could identify which urine came from her. All the specimens handed in by the mother contained xylose, which meant that each specimen contained some of Kay's urine. The help of the Yorkshire Police forensic laboratory was obtained. Kay and her mother had similar blood groups, but erythro-cyte acid phosphatase in the blood in the urine specimens was of group Ba, which was simi-lar to the mother's but not to Kay's.

At this stage, there was enough evidence to support the theory that the mother's story about her daughter was false and that she had been adding either her own urine or menstrual dis-charge to specimens of her daughter's urine. Other abnormal findings could similarly be ex-plained by the deliberate actions of the mother.

The consequences of these actions for the daughter had included 12 hospital admissions, seven major X-ray procedures (including in-travenous urograms, cystograms, barium en-ema, vaginogram, and urethrogram), six exam-inations under anesthetic, five cystoscopies, unpleasant treatment with toxic drugs, and eight antibiotics, catheterizations, vaginal pes-saries, and bactericidal, fungicidal, and oestro-gen creams; the laboratories had cultured her urine more than 150 times and had done many other tests; 16 consultants had been involved in her care.

The various fabrications occupied a major part in the mother's life, and arrangements were made for her to see a psychiatrist at a hospital near her home. At first, she denied interfering with the management of her daughter. How-ever, during the period of psychiatric outpa-tient consultation, Kay's health remained good. The urinary problems did not recur, and her parents said that they felt that "since going to Leeds, Kay had been much better and their prayers had been answered".

Later, it emerged that the mother had a more extensive personal medical history than she had admitted and that during investigation of her own urinary tract, she had been suspected of altering urine specimens, altering tempera-ture charts, and heating a thermometer in a cup of tea. She was a caring and loving mother for her two children. Kay was a long-awaited baby (in the hope of which the mother had taken a fertility drug), but after the birth, the mother sometimes felt that her husband was more in-terested in the child than in her.

Second Case

Charles had had recurrent illnesses associ-ated with hypernatremia since the age of 6 weeks. He was the third child of healthy par-ents. The attacks of vomiting and drowsiness came on suddenly, and on arrival in hospital, he had plasma-sodium concentrations in the range 160 to 175 mmol/l. At these times, his urine also contained a great excess of sodium. The attacks occurred as often as every month; between attacks, he was healthy and develop-ing normally. Extensive investigations took place in three different centers. He was sub-jected to radiological, biochemical, and other pathological procedures during several hospi-tal admissions. These showed no abnormality between attacks, and his endocrine and renal systems were normal. When given a salt load, he excreted it efficiently. The attacks became more frequent and severe, and by the age of 14 months, it became clear that they only happened at home. During a prolonged hospital stay in which the mother was deliberately excluded, they did not happen until the weekend when she was allowed to visit. Investigation proved that the illness must be caused by sodium administration, and the time relationship clearly incriminated the mother. We did not know how she persuaded her toddler to ingest such large quantities of salt (20 g of sodium chloride given with difficulty by us raised the serum-sodium to 147 mmol/l only). The mother had been a nurse and was presumably experienced in the use of gastric feeding tubes and suppositories.

During the period in which the local pediatrician, psychiatrist, and social services department were planning arrangements for the child, he arrived at hospital one night, collapsed with extreme hypernatremia, and died.

Necropsy disclosed mild gastric erosions "as if a chemical had been ingested." The mother wrote thanking the doctors for their care and then attempted suicide.

She too was a caring home-minded mother. She had an undemonstrative husband, a shift worker who did not seem as intelligent as she. As a student, she had been labeled hysterical and, during one hospital admission, had been thought to be interfering with the healing of a wound.

DISCUSSION

These two cases share common features. The mothers' stories were false, deliberately and consistently false. The main pathological findings were the result of the mothers' actions and, in both cases, caused unpleasant and serious consequences for the children. Both had unpleasant investigations and treatments, both developed illnesses as a result of the malpractice and the treatments, and the second child died.

Both mothers skillfully altered specimens and evaded close and experienced supervision. In Case 1, a specimen of the child's urine col-

lected under "close supervision" was abnormal, but it emerged that the mother had momentarily persuaded the nurse to leave the cubicle and leave the specimen unguarded for about a minute. Expressed breast milk collected from the mother of Case 2 early in the course of the illness had a very high sodium content. It had been collected under supervision for chemical analysis, but when the supervisory nurse was instructed not to leave the specimen between its emergence from the mother's breast and its delivery to the laboratory, the next specimen was normal.

During the investigation of both these children, we came to know the mothers well. They were very pleasant people to deal with, cooperative and appreciative of good medical care, which encouraged us to try all the harder. Some mothers who choose to stay in hospital with their child remain on the ward slightly uneasy, overtly bored, or aggressive. These two flourished there, as if they belonged, and thrived on the attention that staff gave to them. It is ironic to conjecture that the cause of both these children's problems would have been discovered much sooner in the old days of restricted visiting hours and the absence of facilities for mothers to live in hospital with a sick child. It is also possible that, without the excellent facilities and the attentive and friendly staff, the repetitive admissions might not have happened. Both mothers had a history of falsifying their own medical records and treatment. Both had at times been labeled as hysterical personalities who also tended to be depressed. We recognize that parents sometimes exaggerate their child's symptoms, perhaps to obtain faster or more thorough medical care of their child. In these cases, it was as if the parents were using the children to get themselves into the sheltered environment of a children's ward surrounded by friendly staff. The mother of Case 1 may have been projecting her worries about her own urinary tract problems onto the child in order to escape from worries about herself. She seemed to project her own worries onto the child in many different ways, once informing another hospital that a specialist from Switzerland was coming to see her daughter in Leeds because she had an incurable kidney tumor which emptied into the vagina, causing the discharge.

This sort of fabricated story is reminiscent of the Munchausen syndrome. The parents described share some of the common features of that syndrome, in which the persons have traveled widely for treatment and the stories attributed to them are both dramatic and untruthful. But those with Munchausen syndrome have more fanciful stories, which are different at different hospitals. They tend to discharge themselves when the game is up. They cause physical suffering to themselves but not usually to their relatives. Munchausen syndrome has been described in children, the confabulations being made by the child.[1] Case 1 seems to be the first example of "Munchausen syndrome by proxy."

The repetitive poisoning of a child by a parent (Case 2) has been described before. Rogers and colleagues[2] described six cases in 1976, and they suggested that such poisoning was "an extended form of child abuse." Larsky and Erikson[3] suggested marital conflict as a possible cause for such poisoning, one spouse harming a child who was considered to be unfairly favored by the other. The resulting illness of the child tended to restore marital relations at the child's expense.

None can doubt that these two children were abused, but the acts of abuse were so different in quality, periodicity, and planning from the more usual non-accidental injury of childhood that I am uneasy about classifying these sad cases as variants of non-accidental injury.

Whatever label one chooses to describe them, these cases are a reminder that, at times, doctors must accept the parents' history and indeed the laboratory findings with more than usual skepticism. We may teach, and I believe should teach, that mothers are always right; but at the same time, we must recognize that when mothers are wrong, they can be terribly wrong.

Asher began his paper on Munchausen's syndrome[4] with the words, "Here is described a common syndrome which most doctors have seen, but about which little has been written". The behavior of Kay's mother has not been described in the medical literature. Is it because that degree of falsification is very rare or because it is unrecognized?

This paper is dedicated to the many caring and conscientious doctors who tried to help these families, and who, although deceived, will rightly continue to believe what most parents say about their children, most of the time.

REFERENCES

1. Sneed, R. C., Bell, R. F. *Pediatrics,* 1976, **58,** 127.

2. Rogers, D., Tripp, J., Bentovin, A., Robinson, A., Berry, D., Goulding, R. *Br. med. J.* 1976, i, 793.

3. Larsky, S. B., Erikson, H. M. *J. Am. Acad. Child Psychiat.* 1974, **13,** 691.

4. Asher, R. *Lancet,* 1951, i, 339.

Child Abuse and Neglect

The Myth of Classlessness

LEROY H. PELTON   *1978*

"Child Abuse and Neglect: The Myth of Classlessness" rocked the commonly held beliefs of many when it was published in 1978. At the time, widespread media reports and professional discussions about child abuse and neglect emphasized that it occurs among families from all socioeconomic levels, religious groups, races, and nationalities. In this paper, Pelton argues that such a viewpoint served professional interests by allowing for an understanding of child maltreatment in the context of the medical model—it is a disease that needs to be treated. It also served political interests by removing the label of child maltreatment as just another manifestation of poverty—at a time when the poverty issue had lost its appeal. Pelton referred to this view as "the myth of classlessness," a conclusion he reached both through analysis of existing data on the child maltreatment phenomenon (which showed a very high proportion of all cases coming from low-income families) and through reason (e.g., it made sense that low-income families would have a harder time providing for their children's needs). Furthermore, Pelton argued that by denying the strong connections between child abuse and class, attention was diverted away from the real nature of the problem and the full range of the underlying causes, and thus from useful solutions. In so doing, Pelton built on and broadened the earlier work of Gil.

Patricia Schene notes a number of reasons why this has been such an influential paper. First, the paper cogently argued that the then-prevalent view of child maltreatment as a classless phenomenon resulted in a field that focused on personal pathology, and thus therapeutic or punitive interventions, rather than changes required in the societal structure, such as the pattern of income distribution or the availability of social supports. Thus, the paper served as a warning bell for the field and helped to set the direction in which it would move. Second, even as this article helped build the knowledge base in the field by reporting on a variety of early studies related to the demographics of child maltreatment, it also opened up new lines of research by asking more complex questions than databases addressed at the time.

Schene further states that Pelton's work made her more oriented toward interventions that are supportive to parents in concrete material ways. It also increased her awareness of and interest in understanding the ways stress and environments affect child maltreatment as mediating factors connecting poverty to child abuse and neglect.

Pelton's wake-up call did not fall on entirely deaf ears. Increasingly, the field has studied and taken account of economic and environmental factors as it develops an understanding of and response to child maltreatment, particularly neglect. And, if anything, the concern today may be more that child maltreatment is seen entirely as an issue associated with poverty, producing "the myth of class."

A. C. D. and K. O.

Child abuse is not a black problem, a brown problem, or a white problem. Child abusers are found in the ranks of the unemployed, the blue-collar worker, the white-collar worker, and the professional. They are Protestant, Catholic, Jewish, Baptist and atheist.[7]

Child abuse and neglect occur among families from all socioeconomic levels, religious groups, races, and nationalities.[16]

The problem of child abuse is not limited to any particular economic, social, or intellectual level, race or religion.[6]

Child abuse and child neglect afflict all communities, regardless of race, religion, or economic status.[4]

While such oft-repeated statements are true, they are often half-true. Child abuse and neglect have indeed been found among all socioeconomic classes and within all of the other groupings mentioned. But these statements seem to imply that child abuse and neglect occur without regard to socioeconomic class, or are distributed proportionately among the total population. The impression that these problems are democratically distributed throughout society is increasingly being conveyed by professionals writing in academic journals, and to the public through the news media, despite clear evidence to the contrary.

This paper will be concerned primarily with three issues: (1) the extent and nature of the evidence associating child abuse and neglect with social class, (2) the reasons why the myth of classlessness continues to be promulgated, and (3) the damaging effects of the myth on our ability to understand and deal with the problems.

WHAT THE STUDIES SHOW

Substantial evidence of a strong relationship between poverty and child abuse and neglect currently exists. Every national survey of officially reported child neglect and abuse incidents has indicated that the preponderance of the reports involves families from the lowest socioeconomic levels.

In the first of these studies, a nationwide survey of child abuse reports made to central registries, Gil[8] found that nearly 60% of the

Originally published in *American Journal of Orthopsychiatry*, 1978, *48*, 608-617. Reprinted by permission of the American Orthopsychiatric Association, Inc.

families involved in the abuse incidents had been on welfare during or prior to the study year of 1967, and 37.2% of the abusive families had been receiving public assistance at the time of the incident. Furthermore, 48.4% of the reported families had incomes below $5,000 in 1967, as compared with 25.3% of all American families who had such low incomes. Only 52.5% of the fathers had been employed throughout the year, and at least 65% of the mothers and 55.5% of the fathers did not graduate from high school. On the other side of the coin, only 3% of the families had incomes of $10,000 or over (as compared with 34.4% of all American families for the same year), and only 0.4% of the mothers and 2.2% of the fathers had college degrees.

More recent data have been collected by the American Humane Association (AHA) through its national study of official child abuse and neglect reporting. For the year 1975,[2] family income information was provided by 20 states and territories on a total of 12,766 validated reports. For 53.2% of these reports, the yearly income was under $5,000, and 69.2% of the families had incomes of less than $7,000. In fact, less than 11% of the families had incomes of $11,000 or over.

The AHA 1976 data[1] on 19,923 validated reports, from a greater number of states and territories, show that 49.6% of the families had incomes under $5,000, and 65.4% under $7,000. Forty-two percent of the families were receiving public assistance, mostly Aid to Families with Dependent Children (AFDC). Only 14.9% of the reports indicated family incomes of $11,000 or over, and only 9% of the families had incomes of $13,000 or above. The median family income was $5,051 (which is at the 1976 poverty level for a family of four), as compared with about $13,900 for all American families in 1976. For reports of neglect only, the median income dipped slightly to $4,250, and it rose slightly to $6,882 for abuse only.

More geographically limited but in-depth studies substantiate this poverty picture. In her classic study of child abuse and neglect in the early 1960s, Young[20] examined the case records of 300 families, taken from the active files of child protection agencies in several different urban, suburban, and rural areas of the country. She found that "most of the families studied were poor, many of them very poor." Her data indicate that 42.7% of the families had been on public assistance at some time and that only 10.7% of all of the families "were financially comfortable and able to meet their physical needs." In 58% of the families, the wage earner had not held one job continuously for as long as 2 years; in 71% of the families, the wage earner was an unskilled laborer. Furthermore, few of the families lived in adequate housing: "Poorly heated, vermin-ridden, in various states of disrepair, much of the housing was a hazard to health."

A recent study[14] in which a random sample of active cases from the state child protection agency caseload in Mercer County, New Jersey, was carefully screened for abuse and neglect, and the case records thoroughly analyzed, revealed that 81% of the families had received public welfare benefits at some time. Seventy-nine percent of the families had an income of $7,000 or less at the time of case acceptance. Two thirds of the mothers had left school by the end of the 10th grade.

Many more statistics are available that lead to the same unmistakable conclusion: The lower socioeconomic classes are disproportionately represented among all child abuse and neglect cases known to public agencies, to the extent that an overwhelming percentage— indeed, the vast majority—of the families in these cases live in poverty or near-poverty circumstances.

Those who uphold the myth of classlessness do not generally dispute such findings. Rather, they offer several disclaimers. Poor people, it is suggested, are more available to public scrutiny, more likely to be known to social agencies and law enforcement agencies, whose workers have had the opportunity to enter their households. The family lives of middle-class and upper-class people, on the other hand, are less open to inspection by public officials; they are less likely than people in poor neighborhoods to turn to public agencies when help is needed. Thus, injuries to children of the middle and upper classes are less likely to arouse outside suspicion of abuse and neglect; even when they do, the private physicians whom the parents consult, and with whom they may have a rather personal relationship, will be reluctant to report their suspicions to public authorities.

Therefore, it is claimed, the socioeconomic distribution of *reported* child abuse and neglect cases does not reflect that of *all* cases. It is further implied that there are proportionately more *unreported* cases among the middle and upper classes than among lower-class families, to such an extent that child abuse and neglect are more or less proportionately distributed among all socioeconomic classes.

While the premises are valid—poor people *are* more subject to public scrutiny—the conclusions do not follow logically from them. We have no grounds for proclaiming that if middle-class and upper-class households were more open to public scrutiny, we would find proportionately as many abuse and neglect cases among them. Undiscovered evidence is no evidence at all.

Although poor people are more susceptible to public scrutiny, there is substantial evidence that the relationship between poverty and child abuse and neglect is not just an anomaly of reporting systems. The public scrutiny argument cannot explain away the real relationship that exists.

First, while it is generally acknowledged that greater public awareness and new reporting laws have led to a significant increase in reporting over the past few years, the socioeconomic pattern of these reports has not changed appreciably. The findings already reviewed here indicate that an expanded and more vigilant public watch has failed, over the years, to produce an increased proportion of reports from above the lower class.

Second, the public scrutiny argument cannot explain why child abuse and neglect are related to *degrees* of poverty, even *within* that same lower class that is acknowledged to be more open to public scrutiny. In studying only poor families, Giovannoni and Billingsley[9] found the highest incidence of child neglect to have occurred in families living in the most extreme poverty. A large, more recent study[19] in northern New Jersey compared AFDC recipient families known to the state child protection agency, and identified as having abused or neglected their children, with AFDC families not known to that agency. The maltreating families were found to be living in more crowded and dilapidated households, to have been more likely to have gone hungry, and, in general, to be existing at a lower material level than the other AFDC families. The mothers in the maltreating families had fewer years of education than the mothers in the other families. The investigators concluded that the abusing and neglecting families are the poorest of the poor.

Third, the public scrutiny argument cannot explain why, among the reported cases, the most severe injuries have occurred within the poorest families. In his study of child abuse reports, cited earlier, Gil[8] found that injuries were more likely to be fatal or serious among families whose annual income was below $3,500.

Severity certainly seems an important factor in this regard. If definitions of child abuse and neglect are viewed on a long continuum and stretched to their most innocuous limits, it may indeed be concluded that, by "definition," child abuse and neglect are rampant throughout society. Moreover, the myth itself conveys the impression that severity, as well as frequency, of abuse is distributed proportionately among the classes. But, as Gil[8] pointed out, officially reported incidents are more likely than unreported incidents to involve severe injury, since severity is an important criterion of reporting; as we have seen, the relationship between poverty and severity of injury obtains even among the reported incidents.

A British study[15] of 134 battered infants and children under 5 years of age, most of whom had been admitted to hospitals, found that the parents were predominantly from the lower social classes. The investigators concluded that "battering is mainly a lower class phenomenon." They further stated that

> As the criteria for referral of cases were medical we are reasonably confident that if more children from high social class families had been admitted with unexpected injuries then consultant pediatricians would have referred them.

The most severe and least easily hidden maltreatment of children is that which results in death. As a forensic pathologist associated with the Office of the Medical Examiner in Philadelphia, Weston[17] reviewed the mortality of all children under 16 years of age in that city from 1961 through 1965. During this 5-year period, 60 deaths due to child abuse and neglect were found. Among the 24 deaths due to neglect, Weston noted that more than 80% of the families had received some form of public assistance. The investigator divided the abuse victims into two categories, according to prior trauma. Of the 13 children with no previous injury (36% of the abuse victims), he reported that "more than half" came from middle-class homes. As for the 23 children with a history of repetitive trauma (64% of the abuse victims), he noted that, with few exceptions, most came from "homes of extremely low socioeconomic level," and none came from upper-middle or upper-class families.

Kaplun and Reich[11] studied 112 of the 140 apparent homicides of children under 25 years of age recorded by New York City's Chief Medical Examiner, which occurred in that city during 1968 and 1969. Over two thirds of the assailants in these homicides were parents or paramours. The authors found,

> Most of the families of the murdered children (70%) lived in areas of severe poverty,

and almost all were known to the city's public welfare agency.

Thus, we can conclude from these studies that the vast majority of the fatal victims of child abuse and neglect are from poor families.

Unlike certain other injuries to children, in only rare instances can death be hidden. Because of its greater severity and openness to public scrutiny than other injuries, its true causes, too, are less likely to go undetected. Death will prompt an investigation. However, it is probable that some child homicides have been successfully passed off as accidents by the parents, and some people will argue that investigative authorities have been more readily deceived by middle-class and upper-class parents than by lower-class parents.

Yet, there is simply a massive amount of evidence, from our country and many others, that

> the overwhelming majority of homicides and other assaultive crimes are committed by persons from the lowest stratum of a social organization.[18]

As Magura[12] noted, the source of such evidence is not limited to official statistics and, moreover, any presumed bias in the detection of offenses cannot explain the fact that official crime rate differences between social classes are substantially greater for physically aggressive crimes than for property offenses. If anything, as Magura pointed out, since the seriousness of an offense is known to be related to the probability of police intervention, the role of a bias in police recognition of offenses would be expected to be least influential in the detection of the most serious offenses. The rate differentials can only mean that, in actuality, crimes of violence are far more prevalent among the lowest socioeconomic classes. There is little reason to believe that child abuse (leaving aside, for the moment, child neglect, which is an act of a different nature than most violent crimes) conforms to any different socioeconomic pattern than that of violent crimes in general. In fact, the available evidence, including that pertaining to fatal child abuse, indicates that it does not.

WHY THE MYTH PERSISTS

That belief in the classlessness of child abuse and neglect has taken hold with such tenacity among professionals and the public, despite evidence and logic to the contrary, suggests that it serves important functions for those who accept it. Maintenance of the myth permits many professionals to view child abuse and neglect as psychodynamic problems, in the context of a medical model of "disease," "treatment," and "cure," rather than as predominantly sociological and poverty-related problems. Moreover, like the popular conception of an epidemic disease, afflicting families without regard to social or economic standing, the myth allows the problems of abuse and neglect to be portrayed as broader than they actually are; indeed, as occurring in "epidemic" proportions.

Boehm[5] has pointed out that the strong psychodynamic orientation in the field of social work has led to the assumption that neglect is a classless phenomenon. Conversely, it can be said that the assumption of classlessness plays a key role in upholding the psychodynamic orientation, as well as the medical model of treatment.

The mystique of psychodynamic theories has captivated many helping professionals, who seem to view the espousal and practice of such theories as conferring status and prestige upon themselves. Unfortunately, the mundane problems of poverty and poverty-related hazards hold less fascination for them; direct, concrete approaches to these problems appear to be less glamorous professionally than psychologizing about the poor and prescribing the latest fashions in psychotherapy. Although concrete services are the ones most attractive to prospective lower-class consumers, they are the services that are least appealing to the middle-class helping professionals immersed in the "psychological society."[10]

Thus the myth serves several functions. It supports the prestigious and fascinating psychodynamic medical-model approach and, by disassociating the problems from poverty, accords distinct and separate status to child abuse and neglect specialists. The myth holds that child abuse and neglect are not, for the most part, mere aspects of the poverty problem. Ultimately, by encouraging the view that abuse and neglect are widespread throughout society, the myth presumably aids in prying loose additional federal funds for dealing with these problems.

Politicians, for their part, have been amenable to the myth of classlessness because it serves certain functions for them. The questioning of David Gil by then-Senator Walter Mondale at the 1973 Senate hearings on the Child Abuse Prevention and Treatment Act was most revealing of this preference. Invoking the public scrutiny argument, Mondale pressed hard to establish that child abuse "is not a poverty problem." As Patti[13] noted,

> It seems that the Senator wished to avoid treating child abuse as another manifestation of poverty out of a concern that the poverty issue had lost its political appeal.

Berleman[3] commented on the same hearings:

> Some legislators wished to be reassured that abuse was not disproportionately distributed according to socioeconomic class; they were particularly anxious not to have the problem become identified with the lower class. Many witnesses also gave the impression that the problem was not class-related.

Thus, both professional and politician, each for his own reasons, is disinclined to see the problems as poverty-related: the former to increase his chances of gaining funding for a medical model approach, the latter to increase his own chances of getting a bill passed and thus being seen as aggressively dealing with the phenomenon of child "battering," which the public already perceives as a "sickness."

But the ends (obtaining increased funding) cannot justify the means (presenting a picture of child abuse and neglect not supported by the evidence) even on tactical grounds. When certain claims are made in order to secure funding, these claims will determine the disposition of the funds. If it is asserted that there are millions of undiscovered abuse and neglect cases among the middle classes, then legislators must reasonably conclude that money should be earmarked for finding them. And if it is claimed that the problems are unrelated to poverty, then money and attention will be diverted from poverty-oriented services.

Well-meaning mental health professionals may be drawn to the myth of classlessness, believing that the association of child abuse and neglect with poverty constitutes one more insulting and discriminatory act toward poor people, one more way to "stigmatize" them unjustly. In fact, the myth does a disservice to poor people and to the victims of child abuse and neglect; it undermines development of effective approaches to deal with their real and difficult problems and directs us toward remedies more oriented to the middle classes.

To say that child abuse and neglect are strongly related to poverty is not to say that poor people in general abuse and neglect their children. On the contrary, only a tiny minority of lower-class parents do so.[14] But the myth of classlessness diverts our attention from the "subculture of violence,"[18] the stresses of poverty that can provoke abuse and neglect, and the hazardous poverty environment that heightens the dangerousness of child neglect.

HOW THE MYTH SERVES AS A SMOKESCREEN

In the face of the evidence that child abuse and neglect, especially in their most severe forms, occur disproportionately among the lower socioeconomic classes, proponents of the myth of classlessness have provided little substance for their beliefs. Nonetheless, as suggested above, the myth is persistent and powerful enough to blind many of us to the real poverty-related problems of most abuse and neglect cases. For poverty is not merely "associated" with child abuse and neglect; there is good reason to believe that the problems of poverty are causative agents in parents' abusive and negligent behaviors and in the resultant harm to children.

As Gil[8] has pointed out, the living conditions of poverty generate stressful experiences that may become precipitating factors of child abuse, and the poor have little means by which to escape from such stress. Under these circumstances, even minor misbehaviors and annoyances presented by powerless children may trigger abuse. Such poverty-related factors as unemployment, dilapidated and overcrowded housing, and insufficient money, food, recreation, or hope can provide the stressful context for abuse. This is not to say that middle-class parents never experience stresses that might lead to child abuse, or that abuse is always contributed to by environmental stress. Nor does it mean that the additional stresses of poverty cause most impoverished families to maltreat their children. But, given the established fact that poverty is strongly related to child maltreatment, we find that there are sensible explanations as to why poverty might be a partial determinant of it.

Child neglect is a far more pervasive social problem than is abuse, occurring in more than twice as many cases.[1,14] Moreover, when harm to the child severe enough to have required hospitalization or medical attention has occurred, it is from one-and-a-half to two times as likely to have been due to neglect than to abuse. In addition, neglect is somewhat more strongly related to poverty than is abuse.[1, 14]

Like abuse, neglect may partially result from poverty-related stresses. In leading to neglect, these stresses may produce the mediating factor of despair rather than anger when, for example, a single parent attempts to raise a large family in cramped and unsafe living quarters with no help and little money. The relationship can be seen most clearly in those cases in which a terrible incident, such as a fire devastating the home, also destroys the mother's capacity to cope with poverty any longer.

However, no matter what the origins of neglectful behavior, there is a more immediate way in which poverty causes harm to neglected children. Poverty itself directly presents dangers for children, and very often neglect merely increases the likelihood that those dangers will result in harm.

Neglectful irresponsibility more readily leads to dire consequences when it occurs in the context of poverty than when that same behavior is engaged in by middle-class parents.[14] In middle-class families, there is some *leeway* for irresponsibility, a luxury that poverty does not afford. A middle-class mother can be careless with her money and squander some of it but still have enough so that her children will not be deprived of basic necessities. Identical lapses in responsibility on the part of an impoverished mother might cause her children to go hungry during the last few days of the month. The less money one has, the better manager of money one has to be.

Leaving a child alone or unattended is the most prevalent form of child neglect, occurring in 50% of all neglect cases.[14] A middle-class parent's inadequate supervision will not put the children in as great danger as will that of the impoverished parent, because the middle-class home is not as drastically beset with health and safety hazards. The context of poverty multiplies the hazards of a mother's neglect. Thus,

poor people have very little margin for irresponsibility or mismanagement of either time or money.

In some cases, the mother does not have much choice but to leave her children alone. A welfare mother with many children cannot easily obtain or pay for a baby-sitter every time she must leave the house to do her chores; in addition, she may find it more difficult to do her shopping than would a middle-class mother. If she leaves her children alone, she is taking a gamble with their safety; if she stays with them, it may mean being unable to provide proper food or other immediate necessities. Thus, some mothers are caught up in difficult and dangerous situations that have less to do with their adequacy and responsibility as parents than with the hard circumstances of their lives.

The myth of classlessness diverts attention from the environmental problems of poor households that make neglect so much more dangerous to children than it would be in middle-class homes. Recognition of the impoverished context of child neglect points us to the need for concrete services directed at the dangers of poverty, services such as house finding, rat control, in-home baby-sitter services, installation of window guard-rails, and emergency cash for the repair of boilers or plumbing, the payment of gas and electric bills, a security deposit on a new apartment, or the purchase of food, crib, playpen, and so on. Such measures will often directly prevent harm to children in protective services cases and obviate the need for immediate child placement. In addition, reducing the immediate stresses of poverty may have a rapid and positive impact upon the parents' behavior.

Although the stresses of poverty certainly have psychological effects, the strong relationship between poverty and child abuse and neglect suggests that remediation of situational defects should take precedence over psychological treatments. These parents' behavior problems are less likely to be symptoms of unconscious or intrapsychic conflicts than of concrete antecedent environmental conditions, crises, and catastrophes. It is these root causes that must be addressed.

Child welfare agencies can neither enter the housing industry nor raise clients' welfare benefits. But they can seek to remedy many of the health and safety hazards that attend poverty and inadequate housing and that, in combination with parental factors produced in part by those very hazards, place children in danger of harm and abuse.

CONCLUSION

Both evidence and reason lead to the unmistakable conclusion that, contrary to the myth of classlessness, child abuse and neglect are strongly related to poverty, in terms of prevalence and severity of consequences. This is not to say that abuse and neglect do not occur among other socioeconomic classes, or that, when they do occur, they never have severe consequences. However, widespread reports suggesting that abuse and neglect are classless phenomena are unfounded and misleading. The myth of classlessness persists not on the basis of evidence or logic, but because it serves certain professional and political interests. These interests do not further the task of dealing with the real problems underlying abuse and neglect; adherence to the myth diverts attention from the nature of the problems and diverts resources from their solution.

REFERENCES

1. AMERICAN HUMANE ASSOCIATION. 1978. *National Analysis of Official Child Neglect and Abuse Reporting.* American Humane Association, Denver.

2. AMERICAN HUMANE ASSOCIATION. *Statistics for 1975.* American Humane Association, Denver.

3. BERLEMAN, W. 1976. *An analysis of issues related to child abuse and neglect as reflected in Congressional hearings prior to the enactment of the Child Abuse Prevention and Treatment Act of 1974.* Center for Social Welfare Research, School of Social Work, University of Washington.

4. BESHAROV, D. AND BESHAROV, S. 1977. "Why do parents harm their children?" *National Council of Jewish Women* (Winter): 6-8.

5. BOEHM, B. 1964. "The community and the social agency define neglect." *Child Welfare* 43: 453-464.

6. FONTANA, V. 1977. In statement printed in Senate hearings on extension of the Child Abuse Prevention and Treatment Act, April 6-7: 505.

7. FRASER, B. 1976-77. "Independent representation for the abused and neglected child: the guardian ad litem." *Calif. Western Law Rev.* 13.

8. GIL, D. 1970. *Violence Against Children.* Harvard University Press, Cambridge, Mass.

9. GIOVANNONI, J. AND BILLINGSLEY, A. 1970. "Child neglect among the poor: a study of parental inadequacy in families of three ethnic groups." *Child Welfare* 49: 196-204.

10. GROSS, M. 1978. *The Psychological Society.* Random House, New York.

11. KAPLUN, D. AND REICH, R. 1976. "The murdered child and his killers." *Amer. J. Psychiat.* 133: 809-813.

12. MAGURA, S. 1975. "Is there a subculture of violence?" *Amer. Sociol. Rev.* 40: 831-836.

13. PATTI, R. 1976. *An analysis of issues related to child abuse and neglect as reflected in Congressional hearings prior to the enactment of the Child Abuse Prevention and Treatment Act of 1974.* Center for Social Welfare Research, School of Social Work, University of Washington.

14. PELTON, L. 1977. *Child abuse and neglect and protective intervention in Mercer County, New Jersey: a parent interview and case record study.* Bureau of Research, New Jersey Division of Youth and Family Services.

15. SMITH, S., HANSON, R. AND NOBLE, S. 1975. "Parents of battered children: a controlled study." In *Concerning Child Abuse,* A. Franklin, ed. Churchill Livingstone, Edinburgh.

16. STEELE, B. 1975. "Working with abusive parents: a psychiatrist's view." *Children Today* 4: 3.

17. WESTON, J. 1974. "The pathology of child abuse." In *The Battered Child* (2nd ed.), R. Helfer and C. Kempe, eds. University of Chicago Press, Chicago.

18. WOLFGANG, M. 1967. "Criminal homicide and the subculture of violence." In *Studies in Homicide,* M. Wolfgang, ed. Harper and Row, New York.

19. WOLOCK, I. AND HOROWITZ, B. 1977. "Factors relating to levels of child care among families receiving public assistance in New Jersey." *Final Report,* Vol. 1, June 30, 1977 (grant No. 90-c-418). Submitted to the National Center on Child Abuse and Neglect, DHEW.

20. YOUNG, L. 1971. *Wednesday's Children.* McGraw-Hill, New York.

10

The Elusive "Crime"
of Emotional Abuse

| JAMES GARBARINO   1978 |

"The Elusive 'Crime' of Emotional Abuse" was pivotal in establishing a foundation for defining emotional maltreatment as well as stimulating and guiding further work in this area. Stuart Hart explains that, in the paper, Garbarino expresses, early in the field's evolution, the realization among child development and child maltreatment specialists that emotional abuse exists and has pathogenic influences and significant negative developmental consequences. Theresa Reid comments that this paper makes a major contribution by organizing disparate and poorly conceived ideas about emotional abuse into the beginnings of a coherent framework. Furthermore, the paper includes operational definitions of "actionable" emotional abuse, building on the earlier work of McClelland and his model of competence.

It is important that Garbarino recognizes how central the socialization process is in understanding emotional abuse and its effects, and thus the value of looking at emotional abuse as a developmental and social problem. The paper also captures the frustration of the few who were cognizant of the

problem at the time over what very little progress was being made in understanding and handling it. In identifying the need for progress, the paper calls for a fuller conceptualization of the issue, the development of operational definitions, and the use of a developmental approach, all of which were subsequently achieved. The paper prompted much research and other activities, such as the 1983 International Conference on the Psychological Abuse of Children. These efforts, in turn, produced a critical mass of interest in the topic and subsequent advances in our understanding of and ability to deal with emotional abuse. Also, the paper predicted the now more common use of the term *psychological abuse* in place of emotional abuse.

Garbarino's work, as presented in 1978, came to be seen as too narrow (by himself and others); his actionable criteria for emotional abuse did not include acts of omission (emotional neglect), which are regularly included today. Although our definition of emotional abuse, and our knowledge about it, has expanded significantly since 1978, the paper challenges the

reader in ways which are still of value today. Reid cites the example of Garbarino's
anticipation of cultural difference issues.
The paper discusses how parental behavior
has different effects depending on the family context and the child's temperament and
experience; Garbarino insists that standards of parental behavior be applied contextually, by people who are "inside" the
family system. This is a model today for intervention in families of different cultural
backgrounds.

A. C. D. and K. O.

Emotional abuse has been discussed and
debated, but it has not been operationally defined. Nor have appropriate intervention strategies been designed. It well deserves to be called "the elusive crime."
Professionals in the fields of social work, psychology, psychiatry, and even law enforcement
seem to believe that emotional abuse does exist, even if they are unable to reach consensus
in defining it. Emotional abuse (or "psychological abuse" as it is often called) has been addressed in child abuse legislation (cf. Katz et
al., 1976), in formal discussions by students of
child maltreatment (National Conference on
Child Abuse and Neglect, 1977), and by child
protective services practitioners in the
"trenches" (e.g., Nebraska Association of Social Workers, 1977). The goal of this paper is to
improve upon past efforts and define emotional abuse. This will provide a basis for further research and interventive action.

A recent "state of the art" panel on the topic
of emotional abuse brought together a
multi-disciplinary group of experts for a serious attempt to make some progress in this frustrating and difficult area (Lourie and Kent,
1977). The results were disappointing. Very
little that was substantive and virtually nothing
conclusive emerged. To quote from the summary of this panel's report:

> Although a precise definition of emotional
> abuse and a process by which the definition
> would be implemented were not formu-
> lated, it was generally agreed that emotional

abuse and neglect have not been adequately
defined in current law and regulations, but
that they are definable.

These results are similar to what has been
produced in informal brain-storming sessions
by child protective service practitioners in
workshop programs sponsored by the National
Center on Child Abuse and Neglect and by
other such groups around the country.

One such session (Nebraska Association of
Social Workers, 1977), presumably typical of
most others, was a particularly poignant
illustration of the problem. The following
descriptions were supplied by participants in
response to the leader's call for associations with
the term *psychological or emotional abuse*:

> put downs
> labeling
> unrealistic expectations
> humiliation
> scapegoating
> name calling
> excessive responsibility
> seductive behaviors
> fear-inducing techniques
> extreme inconsistency
> ignoring
> rejection
> lying

All these terms ring true intuitively. Each
one evokes an image of psychological dam-

Originally published in *Child Abuse and Neglect*, 1978, Vol. 2, pp. 89-99. Reprinted with permission from Elsevier Science.

age to the target child. The participating child protective service workers were responding to the leader's request as best they could, from their day-to-day experiences with psychologically unhealthy parent-child relations. Each of the behaviors noted above has clear clinical relevance as a pathogenic influence (cf. Millon, 1969). Moreover, these behaviors are among those discouraged in a variety of preventive and remedial parent education programs.

While this list of behaviors does have a measure of validity as a composite indicator of psychological abuse, it lacks conceptual organization and a clear developmental perspective. The issue of emotional abuse is manifest in these behaviors, but it cannot be understood through them alone. The conclusion that practitioners and researchers alike are stumbling around in the dark on this issue is all but inescapable. Emotional abuse is truly an elusive crime. It's definitely there in the lives of children, but it's very difficult to establish adequate conceptual and operational definitions that are linked to existing and potential child development research.

What's the problem here? Whenever a problem doesn't yield to sustained interdisciplinary frontal assault, one is compelled to stand back from the issue and seek a reconceptualization to break through the impasse. This, it seems, is what is needed to advance our understanding of what psychological or emotional abuse is and how we can best deal with it in theory and practice. As a society, we need such an advance, and if this necessity is mother to our invention, growing encouragement by professional colleagues is the father.

A PERSPECTIVE FROM WHICH TO VIEW PSYCHOLOGICAL ABUSE

Archimedes maintained that if given an appropriate place to set his fulcrum, he could move the world. In the intellectual realm, we often lose sight of the power of a theoretical fulcrum

to permit progress in solving social problems. Our characteristic orientation is, of course, the pragmatic, positivistic stance reflected in that most American of maxims, "Don't just stand there, do something!" This approach has served us well in many ways in many areas, but it does have its limitations, as is illustrated by our present quandary over the meaning of emotional abuse. Perhaps, at this point, having been stymied in the positivist mode, we can profitably turn to another tradition.

In his efforts to redirect the thinking and behavior of developmental psychologists, Bronfenbrenner (1977a, 1977b) has argued for a return to the tradition exemplified by Kurt Lewin's maxim, "There is nothing so practical as a good theory." In the present case, this statement is particularly appropriate. What is lacking in our attempts to understand emotional abuse, and thus define it in policy and practice, is a suitable theoretical perspective (in the Lewinian sense).

A previous general analysis of child maltreatment (Garbarino, 1977) identified some basic necessary and sufficient conditions for abuse as a pyschosocial phenomenon. That review reconceptualized maltreatment as a problem of inadequate timing and sequencing of important events in family development. Early students of child abuse adopted a model dominant in clinical work that focused primarily on "defective person" theories. Adoption of this model may have impaired our understanding of maltreatment as a *developmental* and *social* problem (cf. Friedmann, 1976). This state of affairs has only recently begun to be rectified in theoretical and empirical work (cf. Friedmann, 1976; Garbarino, Crouter, and Sherman, 1978; Parke and Collmer, 1975). To understand the phenomenon of emotional abuse, it is likewise necessary to move away from the limitations of a narrow clinical orientation. It is necessary to adopt a perspective emphasizing both developmental and social aspects of the issue. What does this mean in specific terms?

When placed in a broad developmental and social perspective, *emotional abuse is the willful destruction or significant impairment of a child's competence.* The theoretical underpinnings for competence as a unifying theme in studying human development have emerged sporadically in recent decades but have increasingly come together into an integrated approach (e.g., Goldberg, 1977; White, 1959). It is to this tradition that we can turn for a developmental perspective on emotional abuse.

The general elements of human competence go beyond "adaptivity," as intelligence is conceptualized by Caldwell (1967), Piaget (1952), Binet and Simon (1916), and others. McClelland (1973) has set forth a suggestive analysis suitable for the present purpose. In his view, competence (i.e., successful performance in specific social contexts) typically consists of the following abilities.

1. Communication Skills: "a person be able to communicate accurately by word, look, or gesture just what he intends or what he wants done"
2. Patience: "response delay"
3. Moderate Goal Setting: "in most life situations it is distinctly preferable to setting goals either too high or too low, which leads more often to failure"
4. Ego Development: "a general kind of competence" (McClelland, 1973, p. 10)

McClelland's definition of competence suggests a fulcrum with which to move the problem of emotional abuse. It permits us to evaluate parental behavior (or parent-child relations, or teacher-student relations) in light of a developmental criterion, namely, its contribution to the development of competence. It sets goals for the socialization process, as Inkeles (1966) and others have argued is necessary. To evaluate socialization practices, we must know what will be demanded through the life course. The general goal of socialization is, of course, competence (as McClelland defines it). This is the key to understanding emotional abuse. If we start with this conception of competence as the "currency" of development, we can proceed toward an under-

standing of emotional abuse as both a scientific issue and a problem for practice.

EMOTIONAL ABUSE IN THE LIVES OF CHILDREN

The overall issue of child abuse pushes our scientific credibility to its extreme limits. By any common language usage, child abuse is not simply "less than optimal" child rearing. It is a pattern of behavior that drastically violates both moral and scientific norms concerning child care. In the United States, a parent is free to engage in any and all forms of child care up to the point at which a "clear and present danger" to the child's welfare arises. In the opinion of many observers (e.g., Gil, 1970; Zigler, 1976), these lower limits are generally very low indeed.

It should be noted at the outset that adults must be held accountable for behaviors that are developmentally damaging if these behaviors are engaged in willfully. Just as it is no excuse for a parent to maintain that he or she was "simply disciplining" a child by burning him with cigarettes, it is no adequate defense to argue that one is only "toughening the child up" when engaging in emotionally destructive behavior. What this does, however, is to highlight the responsibility of educational, health care, and other service institutions to make sure that lower-limit norms of child care are clearly communicated to everyone who cares for children. When this responsibility is not met, these institutions become accomplices in the abusive pattern. In law and custom, it is the task of society's institutions to guard against violations of the norms concerning minimal child care.

Whatever we may think of this "lower limit" approach to parental autonomy, it does obtain in fact, in law, and in cultural practice. How can we set some lower limits as criteria for "actionable" psychological abuse? How can we operationally define a "clear and present danger" to a child's developing competence? This is a pressing task for progress in producing a policy science of child development (Wald, 1976).

If we return directly to McClelland's (1973) suggested components of competence, the task becomes one of specifying dangers to communication skills, patience, moderate goal setting, and ego development. Whether "scientists" like it or not, the operational decisions in these matters will be made in the trenches of family life—that is, by a variety of medical, child care, police, social work, and legal personnel. Can we offer them something that will "stand up in court"—the overarching criterion for people in the field (Wald, 1976)?[1]

We can certainly direct their attention to specific outcomes—a child with a nonorganic communication disorder, an impatient youngster who cannot cope with everyday frustrations, a student who is wildly inappropriate in his goal setting, a child with drastically inadequate self-esteem. There are two problems with such an approach, of course. First, we must be able to specify when a parent is culpable for the psychologically damaged child, that is, when there is evidence that the parent is directly and willfully contributing to the maladaptive condition of the child. There are many non-parental and non-culpable causes for the conditions mentioned earlier. In fact, it is common for a child's aversive idiosyncratic behavior to act as a stimulus for abnormal parental behavior, as in the case of a colicky infant, or a preschooler's oppositional tantrums (Patterson and Reid, 1970). Second, we need to be able to intervene *before* the damage is done, or at least before it is permanently debilitating. These issues exactly parallel those faced in working with physical abuse, where both *unequivocal* diagnosis of risk and preventive intervention are often impossibly difficult tasks (cf. Friedman, 1976).

As others have recognized (e.g., Lourie and Kent, 1977, with respect to the issue of emotional abuse), there are always two interests to be served by the process of diagnosis in cases of child maltreatment. First and foremost, ideally and in practice, diagnosis serves the function of identifying a need for service. Second, diagnosis provides a basis for invoking the coercive resources of the State when the provision of service cannot meet the protective needs of the child or the parent refuses to accept services offered.

Both aspects of diagnosis are designed to produce "actionable" evidence of maltreatment. Because of the adversary nature of the legal proceedings involved in bringing to bear the coercive resources of the State (e.g., court-ordered participation in parent education programs, removal of the child-victim to foster care, etc.), the criteria for diagnostic proof in this latter case are much more procedurally stringent and require more extensive documentation than when providing service is the goal. While prevention is always preferable to treatment in dealing with child maltreatment (cf. Gray et al., 1977), we must make progress in defining actionable criteria for psychological abuse to ensure that families are restored to healthy functioning and children are protected.

One last caveat is necessary before plunging into the task of specifying actionable criteria for emotional abuse. This is the necessity to recognize the importance of individual differences—for example, the impact of the child's "temperament" in shaping the outcome of parent-child relations. While in the case of physical abuse, there are at least some universals—a broken bone is a broken bone is a broken bone—in the matter of emotional abuse, there are few, if any. As developmental psychology has grudgingly recognized, the impact of any specific parental behavior is to some degree dependent upon the child toward whom it is directed. Temperament and experience produce a context in which parental behavior acts upon development (Bronfenbrenner, 1977b; Bronson, 1972; Kagan, 1971; Thomas, Chess, and Birch, 1970).

How then can we hope to define actionable emotional abuse? We must specify some transcontextual standards for parental behavior. While this is difficult, we can suggest some principles to be applied contextually by people "inside" the family system, people with detailed personal knowledge of the context and its meanings. This suggestion presupposes a view of "information" and its relation to parent-child relations (Garbarino, 1977).

First, information consists of both regular feedback on parent-child relations and general knowledge of appropriate norms, expectations, and techniques concerning child rearing. Second, adequate information depends upon the presence of the following three factors: (1) day-to-day, regularized observation and discussion of parent-child relations; (b) informal folk wisdom based on extensive historically validated firsthand experience; and, (3) formal, "professional" expertise, particularly in the areas of solving behavior problems. Third, the need for information is a direct function of situational demands that are both internal and external to the parent-child relationship. As these demands increase, so does the need for information. Fourth, formal institutions can become effective sources of information, insofar as they are actively linked to the family's social network—either directly (through the parent) or indirectly (through the parent's relationship with some other person who, in turn, links him with formal institutions).

This conception leads directly to the conclusion that actionable evidence of emotional abuse is *necessarily* the result of applying general principles concerning the development of competence to specific family systems. This requires a source of information *from* as well as *to* the family. To advance our understanding of emotional abuse, we need to study these mechanisms. Applying a set of general principles concerning child care to specific children requires observation and evaluation by *both* lay (e.g., family, neighbors, friends) and professional family support systems. Furthermore, investigators must be able to study these processes. In light of the model of competence noted earlier, four principles can be suggested. Each of them refers to a significant aspect of emotional abuse because it can be presumed to present a clear and present danger to the child's

developing competence. It thus represents actionable behavior—first, as a basis for initiating service, and second, as a basis for legal coercion.

Four Aspects of Psychological Abuse

Infancy:

Principle 1: Punishment of positive, operant behaviors such as smiling, mobility, exploration, vocalization, and manipulation of objects is emotional abuse.

Research from a variety of contexts has demonstrated that caregiver behavior can have a direct impact on the performance of these "building blocks" of human development (cf. Brackbill, 1958; Foss, 1965). There is an operant drive to mastery or motive for effectance (Goldberg, 1977; White, 1959). To punish this drive and its accompanying behaviors is a clear and present danger to the child's development of competence.

Principle 2: Discouraging caregiver-infant bonding is emotional abuse.

Caregiver-infant bonding has emerged as one of the central issues in child development (Klaus and Kennell, 1976). Disruptions of bonding have been linked to physical abuse (Kennell, Voos, and Klaus, 1976), failure to thrive (Spitz, 1945), and a variety of competence deficits (Bronfenbrenner, 1977a). Systematic efforts to discourage bonding, therefore, pose a direct threat to adequate development. They can be treated as actionable grounds for diagnosing emotional abuse.

Childhood and Adolescence:

Principle 3: Punishment of self-esteem is emotional abuse.

Self-esteem is the positive valuing of one's characteristics, a positive identity. Self-esteem rises and falls in response to the behavior of others, and it is linked to a variety of pro-social characteristics (Coopersmith, 1967). To discourage self-esteem is to attack a fundamental component of competent development. It is thus emotionally abusive.

> *Principle 4*: Punishing interpersonal skills necessary for adequate performance in nonfamilial contexts such as schools, peer groups, and so on is emotional abuse.

Burgess and Conger (1977) observe that families involved in child maltreatment do not provide positive reinforcement for key interpersonal behaviors. Others have noted that abusive parents typically discourage normal social relations among their children—for example, the formation of friendships outside the home (cf. Friedmann, 1976; Garbarino, 1977; Parke and Collmer, 1975). In developing a set of actionable components, therefore, we must include systematically discouraging behaviors needed for competence in non-familial settings. This pattern corresponds to what has been called the "World of Abnormal Rearing." To create such a world and force the child to live in it is emotionally abusive.

As a matter of primary prevention, parents should be steered away from each of these behavior patterns. When *informed* observation identifies grounds for suspecting that one or more of these conditions obtains, there is prima facie evidence that the child's competence is being undermined. These become actionable grounds for offering services, and ultimately for initiating coercive action, if the offer of services is not successful. The key, of course, is having access to the family and thus being able to provide the necessary data. The pressing need, then, is to develop appropriate procedures for gaining valid lay and professional "testimony" concerning the character of parent-child interaction. The task for research, then, is to better understand the flow of information to and from the family. We need to learn how it operates and how it can be modified to perform more effectively on behalf of children.

The elusive crime of emotional abuse can only be grasped—both conceptually and practically—if this can be done.

❙ NOTE ❙

1. The author expresses his appreciation to members of the Child Protection Team at the University of Nebraska Medical Center and his students at the University of Nebraska School of Social Work, who have brought this point home to him in the course of consultation and teaching.

❙ REFERENCES ❙

Binet, A. and Simon, T. *The development of intelligence in children* (Kite, E.S., Trans.) (Baltimore: Williams and Wilkins, 1916.)

Brackbill, Y. Extinction of the smiling response in infants as a function of reinforcement schedule. *Child Development*, 1958, *29*, 114-124.

Bronfenbrenner, U. Lewinian space and ecological substance. Paper presented at the 85th Annual Convention of the American Psychological Association, San Francisco, California, August 26-31, 1977a.

Bronfenbrenner, U. Towards an experimental ecology of human development. *American Psychologist*, 1977b, *32*, 513-531.

Bronson, W. C. The role of enduring orientations to the environment in personality development. *Genetic Psychology Monographs*, 1972, *86*, 3-80.

Burgess, R. and Conger, R. Family interaction patterns related to child abuse and neglect. *Child Abuse and Neglect*, 1977, *1*, 269-278.

Caldwell, B. What is the optimal learning environment for the young child? *American Journal of Orthopsychiatry*, 1967 *37*, 8-21.

Coopersmith, S. *The antecedents of self-esteem* (San Francisco: Freeman, 1967).

Foss, B. M. (Ed.) *Determinants of infant behavior* (London: Methuen, 1965).

Friedmann, R. Child abuse: a review of the psychosocial research. In Herner and Company (Eds), *Four Perspectives on the Status of Child Abuse and Neglect Research*. (Washington, D.C.: National Center on Child Abuse and Neglect, 1976.)

Garbarino, J. The human ecology of child maltreatment: a conceptual model for research. *Journal of Marriage and the Family*, 1977, *39*, 721-736.

Garbarino, J., Crouter, A., and Sherman, D. Screening neighborhoods for intervention: a research based model for child protective services. *Journal of Social Service Research*, 1978.

Gil, D. *Violence against children: physical child abuse in the United States.* Cambridge, Mass.: Harvard University Press, 1970.

Goldberg, S. Social competence in infancy: a model of parent-infant interaction. *Merrill-Palmer Quarterly,* 1977, *23,* 164-177.

Gray, J., Cutler, C., Dean, J., and Kempe, C. H. Prediction and prevention of child abuse and neglect. *Child Abuse and Neglect,* 1977, *1,* 45-58.

Inkeles, A. "Social structure and the socialization of competence." *Harvard Education Review,* 1966, *36,* 279-285.

Kagan, J. *Change and continuity in infancy* (New York: Wiley, 1971).

Katz, S., Ambrosino, L., McGrath, M. and Sawitslsy, K. The laws on child abuse and neglect: a review of the research. In Herner and Co., (Eds), *Four Perspectives on the Status of Child Abuse and Neglect Research.* (Washington, D.C.: U.S. Department of Commerce, National Technical Information Service, 1976.)

Kennell, J., Voos, D. and Klaus, M. Parent-infant bonding. In R. Helfer and C.H. Kempe (Eds.) *Child Abuse and Neglect: the Family and the Community* (Cambridge, Mass.: Ballinger, 1976, pp. 25-54).

Klaus, M. and Kennell, J. *Maternal-infant bonding* (St. Louis, Missouri: C. V. Mosby Company, 1976.)

Lourie, I. and Kent, J. Defining emotional abuse. Symposium presented at the Second Annual National Conference on Child Abuse and Neglect, Houston, Texas, April 17-20, 1977.

McClelland, D. "Testing for competence rather than intelligence," *American Psychologist,* 1973, *28,* 1-14.

Millon, T. *Modern psychopathology,* (Philadelphia: Saunders, 1969).

National Conference on Child Abuse and Neglect, *Program.* (Houston, Texas: Resource Center on Child Abuse and Neglect, 1977.)

Nebraska Association of Social Workers, Child abuse and neglect training project. Lincoln, Nebraska, May 18-20, 1977.

Parke, R. and Collmer, C.W. Chilc abuse an interdisciplinary analysis. In E. M. Hetherington (Ed.), *Review of Child Development Research, Volume 5.* (Chicago: University of Chicago Press, 1975.)

Patterson, G. R. and Reid, J. B. Reciprocity and coercion: two facets of social systems. In C. Neuringer and J. Michael (Eds.). *Behavior Modification in Clinical Psychology.* (New York: Appleton-Century-Crofts, 1970, pp. 133-177.)

Piaget, J. *The origins of intelligence in children* (Cook, M. trans.). (New York: International Universities Press, 1952.)

Spitz, R. Hospitalism: the genesis of psychiatric conditions in early childhood. *Psychoanalytic Studies of the Child, Volume 1* (New York: International Universities Press, 1945, pp. 53-24).

Thomas, A., Chess, S., and Birch, H.G. The origin of personality. *Scientific American,* 1970, *223,* 102-109.

Wald, M. Legal policies affecting children: A lawyer's request for aid. *Child Development,* 1976, *47,* 1-5.

White, R. The concept of competence. *Psychological Review* 1959, *66,* 297-333.

Zigler, E. Controlling child abuse in America: an effort doomed to failure. Mary Elaine Meyer O'Neal Award Lectureship, Meyer Children's Rehabilitation Institute, University of Nebraska Medical Center, Omaha, Nebraska, May 25, 1976.

Sexual Abuse

Another Hidden Pediatric Problem

C. HENRY KEMPE   1978

Although it was not the first paper in the literature on child sexual abuse, "Sexual Abuse: Another Hidden Pediatric Problem" may well be the most important early paper, both because of the message and the messenger. Presented to an audience of pediatricians in 1977 as the C. Anderson Aldrich Lecture and published the next year, this paper or address by C. Henry Kempe identifies child sexual abuse as a significant hidden pediatric problem and describes its nature, types, clinical manifestations, and treatment possibilities. It does so boldly and humanely. As suggested by Howard Dubowitz, this paper was presented at a time when there was relatively little attention to or belief in the existence of the sexual abuse of children. Kempe, because of his stature in the world of pediatrics, created quite a stir in addressing, in front of his peers, this most distress-ing form of maltreatment. Sexual abuse of children, at least for professionals, came out of the closet as a result.

Dubowitz goes on to praise this important piece for other reasons, as well. He explains that Kempe was an astute clinician who learned a great deal from his experiences. At the time, there had been little research on the topic, yet, Kempe described this phenomenon in astounding detail and depth. The lesson here may be that much can be gleaned from careful, thoughtful observation.

Another lesson cited by Dubowitz is Kempe's openness to consider a distasteful subject, at a time when it was not widely recognized. His courage to speak out was impressive. As he described various cases in his address to an audience of pediatricians, he even cited an example of a pediatrician molesting his patients. His insights on why addressing this issue is so difficult are as pertinent today as they were then.

His humanity and his concern for all, including the perpetrators of sexual abuse, are quite evident in this paper. The caring tone is exemplary. At the same time, Dubowitz reminds us, Kempe offers practical advice and never loses sight of the child victim's needs. These same messages apply today.

This paper clearly helped to build the foundation for recognizing and examining the all too common phenomenon of child sexual abuse while offering explanations for perpetrators' motives and parental roles. The paper discusses the need to include the non-offending parent in treatment and raises questions about the value of a punitive approach.

The paper's value is every bit as strong today as it was when first presented. At the same time, it is good to recognize that this paper is a speech, not a carefully crafted academic analysis. As such, it is missing the usual academic cautions and caveats that would otherwise accompany the kinds of sweeping generalizations it contains. These omissions are more than adequately made up for in subsequent writing on this topic by Kempe and his colleagues. And this paper remains exemplary of the work of a man whose keen observations, openness, courage, humanity, and concern with optimal practice made him such an important role model and made his writing so very influential.

A. C. D. and K. O.

Pediatrics started, about a hundred years ago, around the single critical issue of deaths due to diarrhea, caused by unsafe milk. Pediatrics has progressed to a comprehensive approach to child health, with intermittent episodes of acute illness and the skilled management of chronic illnesses. The modern pediatrician, modeling himself after Dr. Aldrich, will attempt to return the child to his normal and optimal state of health as soon as possible and to try to minimize the deleterious effects of illness on the normal growth and development of the child, from both the emotional and the physical point of view.

I have chosen to speak on the subject of sexual abuse of children and adolescents as another hidden pediatric problem and a neglected area. More and more clinical problems related to sexual abuse come to our attention every year. In our training and in our practice, we pe-

diatricians are insufficiently aware of the frequency of sexual abuse; it is, I believe, just as common as physical abuse and the failure-to-thrive syndrome.

Just as the "battered-child syndrome" rang a responsive chord among pediatricians 20 years ago, it is my hope that with this brief discussion, I might stimulate a broader awareness among pediatricians of the problems of sexual abuse. I shall try to do so from a developmental point of view, since the child's stage of development profoundly influences the evaluation and treatment we give.

During last year's influenza vaccination campaign, a 10-year-old girl was seen in consultation with the possible diagnosis of Guillain-Barré syndrome. She was, in fact, suffering from hysterical paralysis. Everyone was relieved by what she did not have, but not so impressed with the discovery that her hysteri-

Originally published in *Pediatrics,* 1978, *62,* 382-389. Copyright 1978. Reprinted by permission of *Pediatrics.*

cal paralysis stemmed from the fact that she had been the subject of an incestuous relationship with her father. This had become increasingly intolerable to her, with the resulting symptoms. Physicians and, surprisingly, nurses generally shunned her and were not very sympathetic. She was somehow in the wrong. There was some discussion that she was "seductive" and that she "might have been asking for it." Another group didn't believe the diagnosis in the first place. I found her to be a lonely and almost suicidal youngster in need of immediate rescue through active intervention. Her masked depression was characterized by inability to eat or sleep.

Sexual abuse is defined as the involvement of dependent, developmentally immature children and adolescents in sexual activities that they do not fully comprehend, to which they are unable to give informed consent, or that violate the social taboos of family roles.

Sexual abuse includes pedophilia (an adult's preference for or addiction to sexual relations with children), rape, and all forms of incest. *Sexual exploitation* is another term frequently used, and it is true that these children are "exploited," because sexual abuse robs the child and adolescent of their developmentally determined control over their own bodies, and they are further robbed of their own preference, with increasing maturity, for sexual partners on an equal basis. This is so regardless of whether the child has to deal with a single overt, and perhaps violent, act, often committed by a stranger, or with incestuous acts, often continued for many years, which may be carried out under actual or threatened violence or may be nonviolent or even tender, insidious, collusive, and secretive.

Scientific studies of incidence are even rarer in the field of sexual abuse than in the field of physical abuse. Data collection has been impaired by what has been euphemistically referred to as a "family affair." In discovered acts of pedophilia, such as occurs in fon-

dling or exhibitionism, the child complains to his parents, the police are involved, and an incidence report is made. The same holds true of child rape. In these situations, incidence data are at least minimally correct. As far as the child is concerned, family and professional support for the victim is strong, and criminal conviction rates are relatively high. Pediatricians here are often informed early on, and they do participate in the diagnosis and even the early treatment of victims. In instances of nonviolent pedophilia, particularly a single act involving a stranger, simple reassurance of the child and more massive reassurance of the parents are all that is required. Forcible sexual abuse and child rape involving strangers, aside from the management of the sexual injuries, often call for long-term supportive therapy to each member of the family.

The discovery of incest, on the other hand, finds the family and the community reacting in a different way. If reports are made by the victim, they rarely result in family support, nor do they often result in successful criminal prosecution. Moreover, it is common for children, who are regularly cared for by their pediatrician, to be involved in incest for many years without their physician knowing. Incest makes pediatricians and everyone else very uncomfortable.

Some physicians routinely ascribe specific complaints of incest, and even incestous pregnancy, to adolescent fantasy. Often, pediatricians will simply not even consider the diagnosis of incest in making an assessment of an emotionally disturbed child or adolescent of either sex. Still, a history of incest is so commonly found among adults coming to the attention of psychiatrists, marriage counselors, mental health clinics, the police, and the courts—10 or 15 years after the events—that the failure to consider the diagnosis early on is somewhat surprising. Most of the youngsters we now see are under the care of a pediatrician in private practice or a clinic setting. With remarkable regularity, they represent the children of professionals, white- and blue-collar workers, as well as of the poor, in a way that reflects a cross-section of our community. And so it is with the racial distribution, which, contrary to published reports from welfare departments and the police, reflects that no race in Denver is overrepresented in sexual abuse, provided one considers all levels of society who come to our attention.

Underreporting is massive. In incest, there is often long-standing active or passive family collusion and support. Disruption of the ongoing set relationships is generally resisted, and understandably so; disclosure will result in public retribution, with the firm expectation of total family disruption, unemployment and economic disaster, loss of family and friends for the victim, and likely incarceration for the perpetrator, at least until bail is posted. There is also the public shame of failure for each person involved in his or her own role as father, mother, and child, with resulting further loss of self esteem by all. The Children's Division of the American Humane Society reported 5,000 cases of sexual abuse for the United States in 1972. Since only a small fraction of instances of sexual abuse are reported at the time of occurrence, as opposed to those that come to light 10 or more years later, it is our view that the true incidence must be at least 10 times higher. In the first 6 months of this year, the Denver General Hospital alone saw 89 cases. We are increasingly seeing younger and younger children who require urgent care. The group of children from birth to age 5 years has increased in recent years from 5% to 25% of the total, while the incidence during the latency age period from 5 to 10 has remained stable at 25%. Between 1967 and 1972, the number of sexually abused children increased 10-fold in our hospital.

Incest is usually hidden for years and comes to public attention only as a result of a dramatic change in the family situation, such as adolescent rebellion or delinquent acts, pregnancy, venereal disease, a great variety of psychiatric

illnesses, or something as trivial as a sudden family quarrel. One half of our adolescent runaway girls were involved in sexual abuse, and many of them experienced physical abuse as well.

NATURE OF SEXUAL ABUSE

Pedophilia

Pedophilia often involves nonviolent sexual contact by an adult with a child, and it may consist of genital fondling, orogenital contact, or genital viewing.

Case 1. A brilliant young lawyer, father of two children, on several occasions engaged in genital fondling of 6- to 8-year-old girls who were friends of his children. The neighbors contacted us with a view toward stopping this behavior, while at the same time wanting to prevent the ruin of this attractive family and to get psychiatric help for the patient. Much of this compassionate and nonpunitive view was the result of their affection for the patient's young wife, whom they greatly liked. They insisted, however, that the family promptly leave the neighborhood. The patient moved to a distant city, where he entered psychotherapy and has had a long-term cure of his addictive pedophilia. His professional and family life has remained stable.

Case 2. A 53-year-old physician was accused of fondling the genitalia of his preadolescent male patients. A hearing before the medical board confirmed that he regularly measured the penis of all his male patients, much as he would examine their weight. His defense was that measurements such as these are part of comprehensive care, but the board held that the procedure was not routine anywhere, except when the specific medical problem concerned the size of the penis, as is the case in some hormonal disorders. He voluntarily resigned his license to practice but refused offers of help.

Violent Molestation and Rape

While all sexual exploitation of minors is illegal, society is particularly concerned with retribution to prevent repetition when rape or other forcible molestation occurs. It is not necessary for hymenal rupture or vaginal entry to occur to have the rape statute apply; frequently, vaginal tears and/or evidence of sperm or a type-specific gonococcal infection can be the ultimate proof. However, perineal masturbatory action often leads to emission of sperm outside the vagina, on the skin or the anus. Many molesters experience premature ejaculation, and others are impotent. We find sperm less than 50% of the time. Orogenital molestation may leave no evidence, except the child's story. This must be believed! Children do not fabricate stories of detailed sexual activities unless they have witnessed them, and they have, indeed, been eyewitnesses to their abuse.

Case 3. The 23-year-old unemployed boyfriend of a divorced middle-class woman was baby-sitting for the woman's two daughters, aged 6 and 14. He first began to sexually assault the 14-year-old girl and raped her, despite her efforts to resist by screaming, hitting, and biting. While she ran for help to distant neighbors, he raped the 6-year-old and fled. When captured, he told the police that he had two beers and remembered nothing of the events. The children both required hospital care for emotional as well as medical reasons. The 6-year-old had a 2.5-cm vaginal tear that was repaired. The older child had a hymenal tear and many bruises. Both had semen in the vagina, and both required antibiotics to prevent gonorrhea with which the attacker was afflicted. Loving and supportive nursing and, later, psychiatric care were given to both victims, who seemed to view the event as "a bad accident." The mother had much reason to feel guilt, since she had known of her friend's inability to handle alcohol without becoming violent. The psychiatric diagnosis of the perpetrator was "violent and sociopathic personality,

not likely to change at any time." He remains in prison for an indeterminate sentence, but he is a model prisoner to date and will eventually be paroled.

Incest

Father-daughter incest accounts for approximately three fourths of cases of incest, while mother-son, father-son, mother-daughter, and brother-sister incidents account for the remaining one fourth. It is our belief that incest has been increasing in the United States in recent years, perhaps because of the great changes in family life: increasing divorce rates, birth control, abortion, and an increasingly more tolerant view of sexual acts between blood-related household members who come from divorced or previously separated homes. This is particularly true as it affects brother-sister incest between stepchildren, who are living as a family but are not related. We believe that cultural attitudes in regard to this latter group of adolescents are rapidly changing to a less concerned stance.

Father-daughter incest tends to be nonviolent, but in the preadolescent and early adolescent, the coexisting relationship between physical abuse and sexual exploitation is often striking but rarely discussed. It is not uncommon for acting-out adolescent girls to be suffering from both physical and sexual abuse. We find men with psychopathic personalities and indiscriminate sexuality who view children as objects, and these men are often violent. Some nonviolent abuse is seen in pedophiles who seduce both their own and other children. Most fathers involved incestuously with their daughters have introverted personalities, tend to be socially isolated, and have an intrafamily orientation. Many are gradually sliding toward incestuous behavior, with the extra push given, often, by a wife who either abets or arranges situations likely to make privacy between father and daughter easier. She may, for example, arrange her work schedule to take her away from home in the evenings and tell her daughter to "take care of Dad" or to "settle him down." It is not hard to see how a very loving and dependent relationship between father and daughter might result, first, in acceptable degrees of caressing, and later, in increasingly intimate forms of physical contact. The silent agreement between husband, wife, and daughter is a triad in which each plays a role and which is generally free of marked guilt or anger unless a crisis occurs. One of these crises is public discovery. A daughter is, of course, robbed of her developmentally appropriate sexuality and is often caught in the dilemma of forcing an end to a now-embarrassing affair in order to live a more usual life with her peers and of losing her family security which, she believes, her compliance has assured her, her mother, and her siblings. It is a terrible burden to carry for these immature women, and relief may not come until they leave home and try to build a new life.

Writers have, for the most part, stressed unduly the seductive nature of young girls involved sexually with fathers or brothers, as opposed to the more important participatory role played by mothers. Our experience suggests that the seduction that some young girls tend to experiment with to a certain degree and usually safely, within the family, is usually normal and does not explain incest, which is not initiated by the child but by the adult male, with the mother's complicity. Stories by mothers that they "could not be more surprised" can generally be discounted; we have simply not seen an innocent mother in cases of long-standing incest. Still, the mother escapes the punishment her husband will likely suffer.

Why do mothers play such an important role in incest between father and daughter? Often, a very dependent mother is frantic to hold her man to the family for her needs and the financial support he provides. The sexual role of the daughter is seen as one way of providing him a younger, more attractive bond within the family than she can provide. This is especially true if she is frigid, rejected sexually, or is herself promiscuous. Rationalizations for incest

abound and must be dealt with in a direct manner. The "I only wanted to show her how to do it" school is often talked about but rarely encountered. The same is true for the "he just needs a lot of sex" attitude. The vast majority of incest situations find people literally caught up in a lifestyle from which they find no easy way out and in which discovery must at all cost be avoided. In order to preserve the family, even after discovery has occurred, admission is often followed by denial, and the immediate family tends to condemn the victim if she is the cause of discovery. She is then bereft of all support and has few choices. Far more often, of course, there is no immediate discovery and only after some time does the victim's emotional need bring about an understanding of her difficult past.

Case 4. An 18-year-old college student with many minor physical complaints and episodes of insomnia told freely of her anger at her father who, on her leaving for college, was having an incestuous affair with her younger sister. She maintained that she was not jealous but rather wanted him stopped: as she said, "I have given my best years to him to keep us together."

Her father, a judge, had begun to sexually stimulate her at bedtime when she was 12 and commenced regular intercourse when she was 14, often six times each week. Her mother knew of these acts from the start, encouraged them subtly at first, and then simply would not discuss the matter. Whenever the patient threatened to leave home, she was told by her mother that she kept the family together and that her two younger siblings would be forever grateful to her for preventing a divorce. The patient had had no boyfriends and few girlfriends and was anxious until she left home to "have things stay the same." On discussion with the mother, it appeared that she was frightened and angry, denied that her husband, "an important man in this community," could be so ungratefully accused, asked that he not be contacted, and disowned her daughter as a chronic liar.

Her father admitted, in medical confidence, that his daughter was totally correct and that he was, indeed, involved with his second daughter. He entered therapy with an experienced psychiatrist and has, over the past years, been able to desist from all incestuous relationships. His eldest daughter will not see him, and he accepts this. He blames himself fully, is puzzled by his craving for love from his daughters, and finally blames himself for his wife's frigidity. He is chronically depressed and takes medication, and he has been a borderline alcoholic in recent years.

Case 5. A 14-year-old girl was seen on request by the police because her 16-year-old brother, when arrested as a runaway, had told them that his father had an incestuous relationship with his sister. The parents denied the allegation and, initially, so did the patient. But on the second interview, she began to discuss her fears about pregnancy and venereal diseases and, with reassurance, described her 4-year involvement with her father, a 35-year-old computer programmer with a college education. The patient was placed in foster care but repeatedly ran away. The father lost his job when he was first arrested and, while awaiting trial, attempted suicide. Subsequently, criminal prosecution was deferred, and both parents received joint treatment around their failing marriage and their relationship with both children. Both children elected to remain in different foster homes until graduation from high school. Criminal charges were eventually dropped, and employment was resumed. The marriage was stabilized. Both children, who are in college now, seem to be on friendly terms with both parents, although they never visit overnight.

Case 6. A 14-year-old girl was seen with a history of marked weight loss and a diagnosis of anorexia nervosa. Her 16-year-old brother was extremely worried about her deteriorating condition and confessed to his father that he had carried on a brief incestuous relationship with her for 4 months and that he wondered if he had caused her illness. The patient recovered promptly, and both youngsters received individual therapy. Each requested a therapist of his/her own sex. Both remained in the household, and both have done well personally and professionally.

Case 7. A 16-year-old girl was seen because an unrelated household member, a boy of 16, had been treated for gonorrhea and listed her as one of his sexual contacts. She was asymptomatic, but her vaginal and rectal cultures were also positive, although for a distinctly different strain of the gonococcus organism. The remaining members of the large family were then cultured. Her stepfather was positive for gonorrhea with the same strain, as were her 14-year-old and 18-year-old stepsisters. Throat cultures for the gonococcus were positive in her 9-year-old stepbrother, as was his anal culture. Her mother was culture-negative, as were two cousins and another, younger stepbrother. It is likely, but was not admitted, that the stepfather, who had a criminal record, and not the 16-year-old boy had infected by sodomy and vaginal intercourse the index patient, who was not clinically ill. The stepfather had further, through fellatio by his stepson on himself and by sodomy, infected the 9-year-old boy and caused vaginal infections in the 14- and 18-year-old girls. The health department administered curative doses of penicillin to all members found to be infected. They noted, wryly, that the initial report of the 16-year-old boy was not related to the family infection and ignored all other implications of this family's chaotic incestuous life.

AGE OF PARTNERS

In pedophilia or child rape, the age of the child tends to be between 2 years and early adolescence, while incestuous relationships may begin at the toddler age and continue into adult life. The median age for incestuous behavior in recent years has been between 9 and 10 years, well within the age group routinely seen by pediatricians, including those pediatricians who shun the care of the adolescent patient.

Society tends to be more concerned with fathers sleeping with or genitally manipulating daughters or sons than mothers doing the same to sons or, rarely, daughters. This double standard is most likely based on the belief that the sheltering mother is simply prolonging, perhaps unusually but not criminally, her previous nurturing role. That mothers who regularly sleep with their school-age sons, referring to them as "lovers" and sexually stimulating them, are very seriously mentally ill, as are their children, is quite clear to us, but intervention is difficult because mothers are given an enormous leeway in their actions, while fathers and brothers are not.

Violent acts of sexual exploitation or rape are usually perpetrated by males under the age of 30, while father-daughter incest tends to involve middle-aged men between 30 and 50. Other incestuous relationships, such as those between siblings, can vary from mutual genital play in early childhood and during the school-age years to attempted and sometimes successful intercourse in adolescence. A grandson-grandmother relationship involved a boy, age 18, and an exceedingly wealthy woman, age 70. At least three physicians dealt with the emotional problems of the delinquent grandson, but none of them was prepared to accept the diagnosis readily admitted to by both patients.

Girls involved with fathers or stepfathers are often the first daughters in preadolescence or early adolescence.

SUBTLE CLINICAL FINDINGS

In cases in which the parents report a single episode caused by either a stranger, a baby-sitter, a relative, or a household member other than the parents, the diagnosis is made before the physician is ever involved. More troubling are those subtle manifestations that are not ordinarily thought to relate to the diagnosis and that call forth the pediatrician's best diagnostic acumen.

In the child under 5 years of age, aggressive sexual abuse, that is, any forced sexual act, often results in fear states and night terrors, clinging behavior, and some form of developmental regression. The pediatrician's role is to provide reassurance. In a stable family setting, it is the parents rather than the child who need repeated help. It may be that, from time to time, the event will have to be worked through with the child once again, but this can often be done in a nursery school setting with active support from loving teachers and parents, and again in adolescence, if needed.

In the school-age child, subtle clinical manifestations may include sudden onset of anxiety, fear, depression, insomnia, conversion hysteria, sudden massive weight loss or weight gain, sudden school failure, truancy, or running away.

In adolescence, serious rebellion, particularly against the mother, is often the presenting finding. The physician who is aware of a specific estrangement between the mother and daughter should consider this diagnosis. Girls involved in incest often will eventually forgive their fathers, but rarely will they forgive their mothers, who failed to protect them. Further, if the pediatrician notices that the daughter has suddenly been assigned virtually all the functions ordinarily taken by a mother within the family group, by looking after the house and siblings, the diagnosis is often made. Parents have reassigned to the daughter the mother's function, both in the kitchen and in bed. These youngsters must be given an opportunity to share their secret with a sympathetic person.

As children get older, we often find more serious delinquency, including massive loss of self-esteem ("I am a whore," "I am a slut"). We see prostitution, along with chronic depression, social isolation, and increasing rebellion and runaways. There are, on the other hand, some very compliant and patient youngsters who carry the load of the family on their frail shoulders, at great sacrifice to their personal development and happiness. These adolescents are in a terrible dilemma. They are in no way assured of ready help from anyone, but they risk losing their family and feel guilty and responsible for bringing it harm if they share their secret. Youngsters may come to the attention of the health care system or the law only through pregnancy, prostitution, venereal disease, drug abuse, or antisocial behavior.

TREATMENT OF SEXUAL ABUSE

There is a chance, particularly when dealing with nonviolent sexual exploitation, to use the criminal justice system to initiate treatment, when the condition is treatable. Filing of criminal charges and a deferred prosecution to await evaluation and treatment are possible, provided certain requirements are met:

1. Exploitation must assuredly be stopped and for good.
2. Law enforcement officials must be involved in planning and must agree to the proposed treatment plan.
3. The prosecuting attorney and the court must feel that the criminal system is not being thwarted but that rehabilitation is an acceptable course, if it is under the supervision, even if remote, of the probation department or law enforcement.
4. Treatment failure, including nonparticipation in an agreed-to program, should bring the criminal process back at once, because, while the bypass process is recognized as an option for the legal system, it is strictly limited to effecting a better outcome than can be foreseen by incarceration following conviction.

Pedophilia may never be cured, but it is often possible to bring all illegal acts under control (Case 1). There is no certain cure for the aggressive sociopath who engages in violent sexual molestation and rape. Until we know what to do for such people, we must be certain that they never have control of a child, who is always defenseless in their presence. Moreover, they are often a menace to all, and, in many cases, nothing but prison is left for their management if they are convicted, or psychiatric commitment to a secure setting if they are judged to be legally insane and unable to stand trial.

The treatment of incest, on the other hand, is far more likely to be successful and to result in the three desired goals: (1) stopping the incest; (2) providing individual and, later, group treatment to victim and each parent; and (3) healing the victim's wounds so that he/she grows up as a whole person, with the ability to enjoy normal sexuality.

In our experience, it has not been possible to reunite families after incest has been stopped through either placing the child or removing the offender unless two conditions have been met: (1) the mother must be shown to be willing and able to protect her children and (2) both parents must admit to the problem and have a shared desire to remedy it, while at the same time either improving their failing marriage or divorcing. Ultimately, treatment can be judged to be successful only many years later, when the child has grown up and made a success of life.

Projective psychological tests reveal that incest victims see themselves as defenseless, worthless, guilty, at risk, and threatened from all sides, particularly from their father and mother, who would be expected to be their protectors. Improvement in these projective tests is a useful aid to progress of therapy. Projective tests also clearly differentiate the angry wrongful accuser from the rather depressed incestuous victim and are therefore most useful in early family evaluation when the facts of incest are denied. Questions to be answered early on are these: Can the child forgive the perpetrators? Can the child regain self-confidence and self-esteem and have a better self-image?

In a report from Santa Clara County, California, 90% of the marriages were saved, 95% of the incestuous daughters returned home, and there was no recidivism in families receiving a minimum of 10 hours of treatment. Regrettably, we have been far less successful! In my experience, between 20% and 30% of the families have not been reunited, no matter what we have attempted, and I have come to feel that they should not be reunited. Reuniting families should not be the overriding goal. Rather, the best interests of the child should be served. Many adolescent girls do far better as emancipated minors, in group homes, or in carefully selected foster home settings. Once they have broken the bond of incest, society must not condemn these victims to an additional sentence, but it must provide loving protection and supportive adults who are better models than their fathers and mothers can ever hope to be. They will, of course, still have ties of affection to their family, but they will see them in a more mature, compassionate way. In any case, the dependency on the family is over somewhat sooner than it would normally be.

Much less is known about the treatment of mother-son or homosexual incest between a parent and child, but these general observations can be made. The gray area of incest in preadolescent cuddly behavior is not without danger. Even quite early, children receive cues about their role vis-à-vis each parent, and sexual models can be normal or highly distorted. After adolescence has begun, guilt, fear of discovery, low self-esteem, isolation, all extract a frightful toll. These problems must always be faced, either sooner or later, and later is generally much worse.

PROGNOSIS OF SEXUAL EXPLOITATION

A one-time sexual molestation by a stranger, particularly of a nonviolent kind, such as a pedophilic encounter, appears to be harmless to normal children living with secure and reassuring parents. The event still needs to be talked out and explained at an age-appropriate level, and all questions need to be answered. Fierce admonishment such as "Don't let anyone touch you there!" or "All men are beasts" is, at most, not helpful.

All victims of violent molestation and rape need a great deal of care. For many reasons, a brief, joint hospital stay with the mother may help to take care of injuries, such as a vaginal tear, and to satisfy the legal requirements for criminal evidence in a setting that is sympathetic and supportive. During examination, the presence of the mother, sister, or grandmother is essential. A female physician-gynecologist who is gentle and who explains the examination is equally important. With her help, a vaginal specimen can be obtained for possible identification of semen (which can be typed and compared to the accused offender's) and for cultures for venereal diseases. The culture findings can be of use in understanding the chain of transmission within the family and in influencing treatment. At times, children are so afraid and in such pain that an almost equally violent form of rape occurs in the emergency room on the part of inexperienced and rough physicians and nurses. It is far better to take time and try to do all that is needed under gentle guidance and among faces that are familiar to and beloved by the frightened child than to attempt force. It is best, at times, to give the child a brief anesthetic to allow for examination and obtaining samples while she is asleep. In any event, a terrifying experience must not be made even worse by those providing treatment. We have tended to resist the request for physical examination in nonviolent abuse cases. In children under 12, the story given or the acts demonstrated by children are to be believed because of the very nature of their detail and clarity of description. This is not fantasy!

Incest occurring before adolescence and then stopped appears to cause less havoc than incest continuing into or throughout adolescence. The principal and major exception to this is the not uncommon situation in which a very young girl is trained to be a sexual object and to give and receive sexual pleasure as the one way to receive approval. These girls make each contact with any adult male an overt sexual event, with genital stimulation sought, supplied, and rewarded. They have, in short, been trained for the profession of prostitution. Nothing is more pathetic and more difficult to manage, because these girls are far too knowing and provocative to be acceptable in most foster or adoptive homes. They are socially disabled until cared for, at length, by a mature and understanding couple. We have found that fathers involved in this form of early "training incest" are not curable. The outlook for the children also is not good, even with treatment, because of the timing and prolonged imprinting nature of their exploitation.

Incest during adolescence is especially traumatic because of the heightened awareness of the adolescent and the active involvement in identity formation and peer group standards. Frigidity, conversion hysteria, promiscuity, phobias, suicide attempts, and psychotic behavior are some of the chronic disabilities one sees in some women who experienced adolescent incest without receiving help. It is only in retrospect that these histories are obtained many years later, and, generally the affair never came to the notice of anyone outside the family.

Boys do much worse than girls! Either mother-son (or grandmother-grandson) or father-son incest leaves a boy with such severe emotional insult that it blocks normal emotional growth. These boys tend to be severely restricted and may be unable to handle any stress without becoming frankly psychotic. Incest is ruinous for the male but can be overcome with or without help by many girls. In general, workers agree that early and humane working through of the complex emotions and distorted relationships is curative and that late discovery after serious symptoms have appeared is far less satisfactory. The focus of treatment is the family, but sometimes there really is no functional family, and the youngster must try to build an independent life with sympathetic help from others.

In contemporary society, many explain the incest taboos as having no function other than the prevention of close inbreeding, with its deleterious genetic effects. Where this explanation has been accepted as sufficient, it has meant a weakening of the sanctions that, in the past, protected the relation between adults and children, including stepchildren. Mead feels that where the more broadly based sanctioning system has broken down, the household may become the setting for cross-generational reciprocal seduction and exploitation, rather than fulfilling its historic role of protecting the immature and permitting the safe development of the strong affectional ties in a context where sex relationships within the family are limited to spouses. Home must be a safe place!

We believe that *all* sexual exploitation is harmful and that it must be stopped!

This does not imply that criminal sanctions must always follow, though they are often an expression of public fury and demand for retribution. What is clear is that the child may need weeks and months of individual or group psychotherapy to come to terms with the event and to integrate the sometimes puzzling, sometimes frightening, and sometimes guilt-laden occurrence back into a normally progressing and safe environment. The growing child and adolescent increasingly assumes charge of his or her control over body and mind. Failure to treat the victim is a far more serious societal act than failure to punish the perpetrator.

CONCLUSION

Each week, we find among our pediatric-adolescent patients, among youngsters at the Kennedy Child Development Center, and among the children seen at our child psychiatric service, increasing numbers of sexually abused children whose presenting chief complaint is nonspecific.

The nonspecific symptoms I have described may be the only clues we physicians have that we may be dealing with sexual abuse. One requires sensitive attention to the patient, good listening, taking time, and always going beyond the presenting "chief complaint."

The runaway who is simply asked "Why did you run away?" will say, "I had a fight with my folks." The next question is "What was your fight about?" The answer, "I was out late." Most professionals stop right there, but that's where we should all start. We simply have to know more. One needs to lead up to the relationships with the child's mother and father, and then, one finally has to ask some direct questions, in as kind a way as possible, in order to give the child permission to relate his/her loneliness, shame, and fears.

Sexual abuse should always be viewed from a developmental point of view, and it is the point of each child's development which determines the ultimate impact that sexual abuse has. Early and decisive intervention, rescue, and supportive therapy work well, even if the family is not reunited. The child deserves a chance at therapy just as much as if there were any other insult to development.

Pediatricians routinely try to find children who have hearing and speech problems. Should we not be equally open and ready, intellectually and emotionally, for the condition of incest, which is the last taboo?

Thank you for allowing me to share with you this hour honoring the late Dr. Aldrich. I hope that I have done him honor.

12

Prediction and Prevention of Child Abuse and Neglect

JANE D. GRAY
CHRISTY A. CUTLER
JANET G. DEAN
C. HENRY KEMPE   *1979*

In 1979, when Jane Gray and her colleagues published the results of their research on predicting and preventing child abuse, the idea that it might be possible to predict who would abuse their children was little more than an unsupported hypothesis. So was the notion that certain interventions might keep those parents from ever crossing the line. As such, "Prediction and Prevention of Child Abuse and Neglect" presented the first credible evidence that both prediction, through observation of interactions between new parents and their babies, and prevention, through the use of home visitors, were possible. The paper set the stage for a later explosion of activity in this area.

Working with just 200 new parents and two alternative methods for assessing risk and the services of lay home visitors (the use of videotaping real-life interaction and interviewing about social supports and childhood experiences and parenting views), the study was both elegantly simple in design and inexpensive. The findings were important. Among other things, the study specifically suggested that it is possible to prevent very serious forms of physical child abuse in the first year of life.

The findings, as powerful as they were, have not always been used as one might have expected. As David Chadwick points out, the importance of the paper is not the use of videotaping; rather, it is the intervention strategy—offering support to new parents in their own homes.

Martha Erickson reports that this work has helped her make the case for researching prospective parents well before the birth of their babies, as well as actually engaging such families in service. For Helen Agathonos, this paper laid the foundation for further work in the field of prevention through its unique combination of sound methodology with observation, as well as its emphasis on early assessment and parent/child interaction.

Erickson points out that there have been dramatic changes in the management and delivery of health care services over the past decade or so—resulting in less continuity of care, greater concerns about privacy, greater time demands on providers, and less communication among providers.

Given these changes, there would seem to be great value in revisiting the basis of this work. And yet, as Chadwick points out, today's researchers can learn a great deal from the elegance, economy, and simplicity of this work. And, says Agathonos, the importance of this paper withstands the test of time because it grounds us in the great importance and possibilities of prevention.

A. C. D. and K. O.

Child abuse is a major problem affecting many thousands of children from all social strata. Increasing knowledge of the general factors that operate in causing children to be abused has resulted in earlier and more accurate diagnosis. Effective therapy is now being instituted at the first indication of injuries in an attempt to break the cycle of parent-induced child abuse and neglect. Although the overall dynamics operating to produce child abuse and neglect are becoming better understood, the specific factors that allow us to predict abnormal child-rearing patterns in certain families have not been generally established. The ability to make accurate predictions of abnormal parenting practices will greatly facilitate the initiation of effective intervention before significant damage has been allowed to occur.

This study examines the feasibility of predicting the potential for some abnormal child-rearing practices, of which child abuse and neglect is one extreme. It concentrates on the perinatal and early neonatal periods, since these offer an excellent opportunity to make assessments of a newborn infant's behavior, to observe the mother's and father's responses to

their child, and to study the interaction between them. The perinatal period also provides easy accessibility to individuals as they become a family, permits observations of the mother and child during a critically sensitive time [1], and allows pediatric intervention to begin early whenever there is indication that potentially harmful child-rearing patterns may occur. Intervention at this time can be aimed at increasing strengths within the family so that a child may have the opportunity to reach his physical, emotional, and intellectual potential.

METHODS

From November 1971 to March 1973, a population sample was drawn from 350 mothers who were having either their first or second child at Colorado General Hospital. Infants with neonatal conditions severe enough to require transfer to the neonatal intensive care unit were excluded from the study.

Some or all of the following screening procedures were carried out to determine which of them were most likely to be predictive of "abnormal parenting practices."

Acknowledgments: The authors wish to thank Gary O. Zerba, Ph. D., Department of Biometrics, University of Colorado Medical Center, for his valuable assistance in the statistical determinations. This study was supported by the Grant Foundation, Inc.

Originally published in *Child Abuse and Neglect,* 1977, Vol. 1, pp. 45-58. Reprinted with permission from Elsevier Science.

1. *Collection of prenatal information.* Data were gathered regarding the parents' upbringing, feelings about this pregnancy, expectations for the unborn child, attitudes toward discipline, availability of support systems, and the present living situations. (Table 12.1a)

2. *Administration of a questionnaire* [2]. A 74-item questionnaire was administered to the mother during the prenatal or early postnatal period. The questions covered information similar to that obtained in the prenatal interview (see No. 1 above).

3. *Assessment of labor and delivery room information.* These data were collected by one or more of the following methods:

   a. Mother-infant interaction forms were completed by the labor and delivery room nurses. The nurses recorded the parents' verbal and nonverbal interactions with their child during their first encounter with him/her (Table 12.1b). The nurse also added any additional pertinent observations about the parents' behavior.

   b. In a number of instances, with the parents' permission, videotapes were made of mothers' and infants' interaction so as to be able to carry out a more thorough assessment of the quality of this interaction and to check the accuracy of observations made by labor and delivery room nurses and physicians.

   c. The delivery room staff was encouraged to provide anecdotal information regarding their observations of the parents and children. This information was also used to assess parenting potential (Table 12.1b).

4. *Observations and/or interview during the postpartum period.* During the postpartum period, the parents were again interviewed to obtain or expand on information gained during the prenatal interview (see No. 1 above and Table 12.1c). Information obtained from direct observation of the mother-infant interaction during the postpartum stay in the hospital was also recorded.

From the data gathered in two or more of these areas, parents were assessed as to their parenting potential. One hundred mothers identified as having psychological, interactional, and lifestyle dynamics [3-5] which might result in "abnormal parenting practices" were randomly assigned to a High-Risk Intervene group ($N = 50$) or a High-Risk Nonintervene group ($N = 50$). Fifty mothers who also delivered their first or second child at the hospital in the same time period and who were assessed as low-risk in terms of abnormal parenting potential were selected as controls.

Intervention in this study meant the provision of pediatric care by one pediatrician at the Medical Center where the child was born. This pediatrician examined the infant during his stay in the newborn nursery, talked with the parents on the postpartum ward, and scheduled the first pediatric clinic visit to take place before the infant was 2 weeks old. Thereafter, the pediatrician saw the child at scheduled bimonthly visits. Additional pediatric visits took place whenever the doctor or the mother felt that the child should be seen. In addition to seeing the child during visits to the clinic, the pediatrician also contacted the family by telephone 2 or 3 days after discharge from the hospital, as well as during the subsequent weeks when a clinic visit was not scheduled. Additional telephone calls were initiated by the pediatrician to ascertain the status of any problems that may have become apparent in previous clinic visits and/or telephone conversations. The physician also contacted the family to provide support to them whenever a medical or other crisis was known to be present. It was not pointed out to the study families that this service was exceptional; it was simply provided as part of the child's well-baby care.

In addition to the contact between the pediatrician and the family, "intervention" also included weekly visits to the home by public health nurses. The public health nurses had been notified of the pertinent findings obtained by the interview, assessment of the delivery room interaction, and the questionnaires. Whenever necessary, referrals were made to other medical facilities or mental health clin-

TABLE 12.1 Warning Signs

These are *indications* of possible problems. A high-risk situation is created by varying combinations of these signs, the family's degree of emphasis upon them, and the family's willingness to change. The interviewer must take into consideration the mother's age, culture, and education, as well as observations of her affect and the significance of her feelings. Many of these signs can be observed throughout the perinatal period; they are listed in this order because they are found most commonly at these times.

A. *Observations During the Prenatal Period*
    The mother seems overly concerned with the baby's sex or performance.
    The mother exhibits denial of the pregnancy (not willing to gain weight, no plans for the baby, refusal to talk about the situation).
    This child could be "one too many."
    The mother is extremely depressed over the pregnancy.
    The mother is very frightened and alone, especially in anticipation of delivery. Careful explanations do not seem to dissipate the fears.
    There is lack of support from husband and/or family.
    The mother and/or father formerly wanted an abortion or seriously considered relinquishment and have changed their minds.
    The parents come from an abusive/neglectful background.
    The parents' living situation is overcrowded, isolated, unstable, or is intolerable to them.
    They do not have a telephone.
    There are no supportive relatives and/or friends.

B. *Observations During Delivery*
    Written form with baby's chart of parent's reaction at birth.
    How does the mother LOOK?
    What does the mother SAY?
    What does the mother DO?
    When the father attends delivery, record his reactions as well.
    Passive reaction, either verbal or non-verbal: mother doesn't touch, hold, or examine baby, nor talk in affectionate terms or tones about the baby.
    Hostile reaction, either verbal or non-verbal: mother makes inappropriate verbalizations, glances, or disparaging remarks about the physical characteristics of the child.
    Disappointment over sex of the baby.
    No eye contact.
    Non-supportive interaction between the parents.
    If interaction seems dubious, talk to the nurse and doctor involved with delivery for further information.

C. *Observations During the Postpartum Period*
    The mother doesn't have fun with the baby.
    The mother avoids eye contact with the baby and avoids the direct *en face* position.
    The verbalizations to the infant are negative, demanding, harsh, and so on.
    Most of the mother's verbalizations to others about the child are negative.
    The parents remain disappointed over the sex of the child.
    Negative identification of the child: significance of name, who he/she looks like and/or acts like.
    The parents have expectations developmentally far beyond the child's capabilities.
    The mother is very bothered by crying; it makes her feel hopeless, helpless, or like crying herself.
    Feedings: the mother sees the baby as too demanding; she is repulsed by his messiness, or ignores his demands.
    Changing diapers is seen as a very negative, repulsive task.
    The mother does not comfort the baby when he cries.
    The husband's and/or family's reactions to the baby have been negative or non-supportive.
    The mother is receiving little or no meaningful support from anyone.
    There are sibling rivalry problems or a complete lack of understanding of this possibility.
    The husband is very jealous of the baby's drain on mother's time, energy, and affection.
    The mother lacks control over the situation. She is not involved, nor does she respond to the baby's needs, but relinquishes control to the doctors or nurses.
    When attention is focused on the child in her presence, the mother does not see this as something positive for herself.
    The mother makes complaints about the baby that cannot be verified.

ics. Lay health visitors (6) (lay persons who visited in the homes to assess the general health status of the child, to offer emotional support to the entire family, and to provide liaison with the professional health system) were utilized whenever indicated.

Nonintervention meant that the investigators did nothing directly for the family after discharge. However, all of the available information was routinely shared with attending hospital staff, community agencies such as visiting nurse service, and the family physician or clinic.

When a child was between the ages of 17 and 35 months (mean age 26.8 months), a home visit was made to 25 randomly selected families in each of the three categories: High-Risk Intervene (HRI), High-Risk Nonintervene (HRN), and Low-Risk (LR). During this home visit, the mother was interviewed, and medical and social information involving the entire family was collected. Also, observations of mother-child interaction were made, and the Denver Developmental Screening Test (DDST) was administered to the child.

The incidence of various findings was determined for each child during the first 17 months of life (at the time of detailed evaluation, the youngest child was 17 months old). In order to determine whether a group at risk for deficient parenting had actually been predicted, children were assessed for the presence of incidents of abnormal parenting practices, which included all verified reports of abuse and neglect to the Central Child Abuse Registry, injury secondary to lack of adequate care and supervision, injuries suspicious for inflicted trauma, failure to thrive which was thought to be secondary to deprivation [7], relinquishments, foster care placements, and parental kidnaping. Children were also assessed as to the number of incidents of trauma thought to be true accidents, reasons why children were no longer in their biologic homes, their immunization status, and their performance on the DDST.

Central Child Abuse Registry reports and indications of abnormal parenting practices in-

volving medical concerns were categorized for all three study groups as a comparison of the effect of intervention.

Data were also compiled to help indicate which of the four screening procedures (prenatal interview, questionnaires, labor and delivery room observations, or postpartum interviews and observations) resulted in the greatest percentage of correct predictions of "parenting potential."

The three groups were compared by ordinary chi square tests appropriate for 3 by 2 contingency tables. These total chi squares were partitioned into single degrees of freedom chi squares appropriate for comparing the two high-risk groups with the low-risk group (HR vs. LR) and the High-Risk Intervene group with the High-Risk Nonintervene group (HRI vs. HRN), as discussed by Kastenbaum [8]. (See Table 12.4.)

RESULTS

The Ability to Predict

1. Indications of abnormal parenting. By the time of detailed evaluation, there were 22 indications of abnormal parenting practices in the high-risk groups (25 HRI and 25 HRN) and 2 indications in the control group of 25. The high-risk groups differed significantly from the low-risk group ($p < .01$). In the total population sample (150 children), eight high-risk children and no low-risk children were reported to the Central Child Abuse Registry ($p < .04$).

There were three cases of failure to thrive (weight below the third percentile, height and head circumference above the third percentile) thought to be secondary to deprivation [7] in the HRI group. Although children in the HRN group were not followed as closely, information was obtained by chart review and contact with the child's physician that two of these children exhibited failure to thrive thought to

TABLE 12.2 Positive Family Circumstances

1. Parents see likeable attributes in baby, see baby as separate individual.
2. Baby is healthy and not too disruptive to parents' lifestyle.
3. Either parent can rescue the child or relieve the other in a crisis.
4. Marriage is stable.
5. Parents have a good friend or relative to turn to, a sound "need-meeting" system.
6. Parents exhibit coping abilities; that is, capacity to plan and understand need for adjustments because of new baby.
7. Mother's intelligence and health are good.
8. Parents had helpful role models when growing up.
9. Parents can have fun together and enjoy personal interests or hobbies.
10. This baby was planned or wanted.
11. Future birth control is planned.
12. Father has stable job.
13. Parents have their own home and stable living conditions.
14. Father is supportive to mother and involved in care of baby.

be secondary to deprivation. There were no such cases in the low-risk group.

2. *Accidents.* There were 31 children in the high-risk groups and 11 children in the low-risk group who had sustained at least one accident which required medical attention during the time period of the study. During the first 17 months of life, 22 children in the high-risk groups and 4 children in the low-risk group had at least one accident requiring medical attention ($p < .02$).

3. *Immunization status.* At 1 year of age, 47 out of the 50 high-risk children (25 HRI and 22 HRN) were up-to-date with their immunizations. In the low-risk group, 24 of 25 had similar immunization status. The difference in the groups is not statistically significant.

4. *Denver Developmental Screening Test.* DDST assessment of high-risk children revealed that there were 3 whose results were recorded as questionable, 3 children who were untestable, and 44 who were normal [9]. In the low-risk group, all 25 were normal. There is no statistically significant difference between these groups. If the results of the DDST are examined by counting the number of clear failures (test items to the left of the child's chronological age), 10 high-risk chil-

dren versus no low-risk children had clear failures ($p < .02$).

5. *Reasons for no evaluation.* There was a significantly increased incidence ($p < .04$) of infants assessed as being at risk for abnormal parenting practices not being in their biologic home at the time of the follow-up evaluation. All low-risk children were in their biologic homes; but eight high-risk children either were in foster care, were permanently living with relatives, or had been legally relinquished.

Results of Intervention on the Incidence and Outcome of Abnormal Parenting Practices

1. Incidence. Between the HRI group and the HRN group, there were no significant statistical differences on the basis of Central Child Abuse Registry reports, indications of abnormal parenting practices, accidents, immunizations, or Denver Developmental Screening Test scores.

2. *Outcome.* Another way to measure the effect of intervention within the high-risk groups is to describe the quality of differences in the types of abnormal parenting practices

TABLE 12.3 Special Well-Child Care for High-Risk Families

1. Promote maternal attachment to the newborn.
2. Contact the mother by telephone on the second day after discharge.
3. Provide more frequent office visits.
4. Give more attention to the mother.
5. Emphasize nutrition.
6. Counsel discipline only around accident prevention.
7. Emphasize accident prevention.
8. Use compliments rather than criticism.
9. Accept phone calls at home.
10. Provide regular home visits by Public Health Nurse or Lay Health Visitor.

that occurred. No child in the low-risk group and no child in the HRI group suffered an injury thought to be secondary to abnormal parenting practices that was serious enough to require hospitalization for treatment. However, five children in the HRN group required inpatient treatment for serious injuries ($p < .01$). These injuries included a fractured femur, a fractured skull, barbiturate ingestion, a subdural hematoma, and third-degree burns. Although these five injuries were treated in local hospitals, only two of them had been reported to the Central Child Abuse Registry.

Screening Procedures

Information from observations of labor and delivery room interactions was analyzed individually and resulted in 76.5% correct predictions of parenting potential. The questionnaire alone resulted in 57.5% correct predictions. The prenatal interview alone resulted in 54.4% correct predictions, and the postpartum interview/observations resulted in 54% correct predictions. If all four parameters are included together, they resulted in 79% correct predictions.

During the initial interviews and observations, four factors were considered as possible indicators of high risk: the mother's race, the

family's socioeconomic status (as determined by the hospital's financial ratings), the mother's marital status, and the mother's age. In the study population, the mother's race did not prove to be a significant variable. There was a trend toward financial difficulty in mothers in the high-risk groups. The mother's marital status and age differed significantly between the high-risk groups and the low-risk group; single and young mothers were considered to be at higher risk for abnormal parenting practices.

DISCUSSION

Child abuse is now being reported approximately 300,000 times each year in our country. The figure rises to 1 million if neglect is included. About 60,000 children have significant injuries; about 2,000 die, and 6,000 have permanent brain damage [6]. Multidisciplinary research (sociologic, pediatric, nursing, psychiatric, and legal) has made possible earlier diagnosis and more successful treatment programs; however, as in many other aspects of medicine, prevention is the ultimate goal.

Medical and nursing staff who work in the prenatal, labor and delivery area, and the neonatal nursery are ideally situated to make sensitive observations of a family's interactional behavior. The assessment of attitudes and feelings has been a part of pediatrics for many years. It is now time to formally utilize these assessments in the implementation of supportive intervention for families in need. Systematic use of a prenatal interview, questionnaire, labor and delivery observations, and postpartum interviews/observations can identify a population at risk for abnormal parenting practices. These data show that accurate prediction of families in need of extra services is possible, as evidenced by the statistical differences between the high-risk groups and the low-risk group in the areas of abnormal parenting practices, Central Child Abuse Registry reports, the number of accidents (by 17 months of age),

TABLE 12.4 Summary of Statistical Analysis

Item	High-Risk, Intervention	High-Risk, Non-intervention	Low Risk	High-Risk/ Low-Risk	High-Risk, Intervention/ High-Risk Non-intervention	Total
					Partitioned χ^2 Results	
Total study population (150):						
Central Registry reports	6	2	0	$p < .04$	$p < .08$	$p < .03$
Detailed evaluation of population (25 in each category)						
Central Registry reports						
at time of home evaluation (mean 26.8 months)	2	1	0	$p < .22$	$p < .48$	$p < .36$
by 17 months of age	1	1	0	$p < .60$	$p < .99$	$p < .30$
Indications of abnormal parenting practices						
by time of home evaluation	11	11	2	$p < .01$	$p < .99$	$p < .01$
by 17 months of age	10	10	0	$p < .01$	$p < .99$	$p < .01$
Failure to thrive	3	2	0	$p < .20$	$p < .60$	$p < .30$
Denver Developmental Screening Test not normal						
by test manual (see reference 9)	3	3	0	$p < .08$	$p < .99$	$p < .20$
by failed items	7	3	0	$p < .02$	$p < .10$	$p < .02$
Accidents						
by time of home evaluation	16	15	11	$p < .14$	$p < .78$	$p < .33$
by 17 months of age	12	10	4	$p < .02$	$p < .56$	$p < .05$
Not in biologic home	5	3	0	$p < .04$	$p < .36$	$p < .07$
Appropriate immunization status						
at one year	25	22	24	$p < .72$	$p < .16$	$p < .16$
Inpatient treatment for injury	0	5	0	$p < .11$	$p < .01$	$p < .01$

children no longer in their biologic homes, and children exhibiting clear failures on the DDST.

It is a belabored point that battering parents tend to lack motivation toward initiating helping services. However, when the health care providers (pediatricians, public health nurses, and lay health visitors) initiate an outreach approach with high-risk families, a comprehensive medical program can be successful.

Recently, there has been an increased awareness of the abnormal behavior characteristics and the developmental lags seen in abused children [10,11]. This has been observed in the children after documentation of abuse, but

with the assumption that the children have been living in an abusive environment prior to the physical abuse. In this study, 20% of children thought prospectively to be at risk for abnormal parenting had at least one clear failure on the DDST. These are children thought to be living in an environment deficient in parenting.

Now that it is largely possible to identify a population at risk for abnormal parenting practices, the next step is to determine the success and practicality of initiating early intervention with these families. Although there was no statistically significant difference in the incidence of abnormal parenting practices between the HRI and the HRN groups, there was a qualitative difference in the injuries in the study groups. In the HRI and the low-risk groups, no child required hospitalization for treatment of a serious injury thought to be secondary to abnormal parenting practices. However, in the HRN group, five children required treatment for trauma or poisoning. One of the five serious injuries (the burns) was preceded by relatively minor inflicted trauma, including cigarette burns, scratch marks, and strap marks. These all received medical attention but were never reported, nor was an attempt made to involve other helping agencies in an effort to prevent further injuries. There is a possibility that the third-degree burns and the resulting contractures could have been prevented if intervention had been initiated promptly. In another case, a subdural hematoma and its resulting intellectual deficit and neurologic handicap might have been prevented if intervention had been instituted during a "social admission" to a hospital just prior to the injury. If appropriate interventions to alleviate social pressure had been undertaken at this point, there is a possibility that the injury would not have occurred. In the low-risk group, injuries (a minor burn and a metacarpal fracture) thought to have occurred because of negligence both involved children over 2 years of age. These children were well into the accident-prone toddler years, whereas injuries in the high-risk groups occurred at younger ages.

There was also an increased incidence of failure to thrive in the high-risk groups. Early identification and effective intervention in one case of failure to thrive in the HRI group was therapeutic for that child. This baby was promptly hospitalized at 5 weeks of age when failure to thrive was discovered. The weight gain was re-established in the hospital, and failure to thrive was completely resolved by 4 months of age. On the 2-year follow-up, the child had normal growth parameters.

Therefore, in the HRI group, it appears that modest intervention precluded any injuries severe enough to require hospitalization for treatment and any injury that resulted in prolonged disability. The less serious injuries and the failure-to-thrive baby in the HRI group were promptly reported and effective community intervention established, which may have prevented subsequent, more serious problems.

The concept of early preventive pediatric and community intervention will, it is hoped, lead to progress in prevention of the harmful effects of child abuse and neglect. Families identified as being in need of extra services must have access to intensive, continuous intervention which is both positive and supportive. It makes little sense to provide excellent prenatal, obstetrical, and neonatal pediatric care in our hospitals, only to abandon the most needy young families at the hospital door and leave to chance, or to parent motivation, the needed access to helping professionals.

SUMMARY

In this study, information gained from observers in the delivery room was most accurate in predicting potential for abnormal parenting practices. The questionnaire did not add significantly to the accuracy of prediction. If delivery room observation is not feasible and only one opportunity for evaluation exists, the early postpartum period affords the best opportunity for collection and analysis of prenatal, labor and delivery, and postpartum observations. Such observations are non-invasive and should be part of obstetrical and postpartum routine.

Immediate, effective intervention by physicians, public health nurses, and/or lay health visitors can significantly decrease many abnormal parenting practices. In this study, such intervention prevented serious injury in a high-risk population.

REFERENCES

1. Klaus, M. et al., Maternal attachment: importance of the first postpartum days, *N. Engl. J. Med.* 286, 460 (1972).

2. Schneider, C. et al., The predictive questionnaire: a preliminary report in *Helping the Battered Child and His Family,* ed. Kempe, C. H., and Helfer, R., Lippincott, Philadelphia, p. 271 (1972).

3. Steele, B., and Pollock, C., A psychiatric study of parents who abuse infants and small children, in *The Battered Child,* ed. Helfer, R., and Kempe, C. H., University of Chicago Press, p. 89 (1968).

4. Pollock, C., Early case finding as a means of prevention of child abuse, in *The Battered Child,* ed. Helfer, R., and Kempe, C. H., University of Chicago Press, p. 149 (1968).

5. Riser, S., The fourth stage of labor: family integration, *Amer. J. Nurs.* 74, 870 (1974).

6. Kempe, C. H., Approaches to preventing child abuse: the health visitor concept, *Amer. J. Dis. Child.* 130, 941 (1976).

7. Schmitt, B. D., and Kempe, C. H., The pediatrician's role in child abuse and neglect, in *Current Problems in Pediatrics* Monograph, Year Book Medical Publishers, Chicago (1975).

8. Kastenbaum, M. A., A note on the additive partitioning of chi square in contingency tables, *Biometrics* 16, 416 (1960).

9. Frankenburg, W. et al., *The Denver Developmental Screening Test* (revised), University of Colorado Medical Center, Denver (1970).

10. Martin, H. et al., The development of abused children, in *Advances in Pediatrics,* vol. 21, ed. Schulman, I., Year Book Medical Publishers, Chicago, p. 25 (1974).

11. Martin, H. et al., *The Abused Child: A Multidisciplinary Approach to Developmental Issues and Treatment,* Ballinger Press, Cambridge, Mass. (1976).

13

Isolation of the Neglectful Family

NORMAN A. POLANSKY
MARY ANN CHALMERS
ELIZABETH BUTTENWIESER
DAVID P. WILLIAMS   *1979*

"Isolation of the Neglectful Family" represents some of the earliest work to systematically investigate the problem of child neglect. Presenting the results of a study comparing the extent of social isolation in neglectful and non-neglectful families, this 1979 paper demonstrates dramatically the extreme isolation of neglectful families, including their lack of support from family and friends and their lack of connection in their communities. According to John Leventhal, although these findings of social isolation and uninvolvement and detachment seem like old news today when describing neglectful families, they were not in 1979. However, they confirmed early clinical observations.

The paper is an important building block in our understanding of the most widespread form of maltreatment. As explained by Donald Bross, Polansky and his colleagues peer deeply into the haze of child neglect, providing early and crucial insights into this type of human misery. They combined clinical insight with rigorous empirical study. Their work examines genera-

tion-to-generation communication and both social and psychological isolation, echoing important insights from the study of the physically battered child without oversimplifying the problem of neglect or its solution.

While the authors indicate where intervention may succeed, according to Leventhal, they also provide a warning about the difficulties of intervening with neglectful families because of their "lifelong patterns of nonparticipation." Jaap Doek adds that in all of Polansky's early work on neglect, the reader is made constantly aware of the difficulties of trying to help neglectful families and the need to reach out to them.

The early insights of Polansky and his colleagues certainly served as a catalyst for subsequent study of neglect and for new interventions with neglectful families, such as intensive family preservation services and reunification programs. Yet, as noted by Leventhal, neglect continues to be understudied. Despite the prevalence of neglect in cases reported to public protective service agencies, for example, methodologically sound evaluations of programs aimed at helping neglectful families remain unavailable. Ongoing problems include the difficulty of providing clear definitions and effective interventions that can substantially influence such isolated parents, as well as the fact that neglect is usually chronic and occurs in families with multiple problems. However, as Polansky and his colleagues made clear so many years ago, we must intensify our efforts to understand clearly the basis for their isolation and to develop more accessible services.

A. C. D. and K. O.

For clients requesting emergency assistance, traditional social work practice has been to help them "review their own resources." Among the latter has commonly been included assistance that might be provided by relatives and friends. Implicit in this procedure is the assumption that most people are members of "helping networks," which are informal but reliable. Is such an assumption valid for families implicated in child neglect? A number of investigators have noted the social isolation typical of abusive families;[3,4,5,7] however, we have thus far had little research relevant to the issue of child neglect.

We have recently completed in Philadelphia a study that was first done in rural southern Appalachia.[6] Evidence will be presented that neglectful families are not, typically, in helping networks to the same extent as are others of similar social position. Their isolation, moreover, extends to other forms of formal and informal social participation. A possible explanation of these deficits, and their implications for practice, will also be presented.

STUDY DESIGN

The study compared a sample of families identified by local social agencies as neglectful with a sample of families in similar circumstances, not identified as neglectful. In keeping with the earlier Appalachian study, all families were low-income and white, and each included at least one child between the ages of 4 and 7, living in the home. Neglectful families were referred to the study through a two-stage process calculated to respect their privacy and other rights. Control families were recruited by advertising in neighborhood newspapers and other means. All families were paid $50 for participating. For a variety of reasons, ours was a numerically unbalanced design. The neglect sample included 22 families with the legal father or a regular male partner present and 24 headed by a woman. Fifty of the control families were two-parent; in the other 29, there was no male figure in the house. It is important to the present interest to note that the neglectful and non-neglectful samples were matched on a number of socioeconomic variables, including household income. Data to be reported here represent interviews with all mothers in the study and all but four of the fathers.

RESULTS

The Family Support Index

Each mother and father was interviewed in detail about the geographic accessibility of potential intimates, paying particular attention to family members since, at least in the community studied, relatives are usually the core of

Originally published in *American Journal of Orthpsychiatry,* 1979, *49,* 146-152. Reprinted by permission of the American Orthopsychiatric Association, Inc.

TABLE 13.1 Comparison of Neglect and Control Groups on the Family Support Index

Index	Mothers Only		Fathers Only		Family	
	Neglect	Control	Neglect	Control	Neglect	Control
1. Completely isolated	13	3	6	7	10	3
2. Family dyad	2	2	5	4	3	2
3. Friend dependent	6	2	2	4	6	1
4. Family bound	11	6	4	5	12	5
5. Family and friend related	7	8	1	3	7	6
6. Supported	6	58	3	24	7	62
Insufficient data	1	0	1	3	1	0

one's helping network. Questions dealt with frequency of contact; several concerned help given or received during the past year. By combining responses to several questions, each parent, and then each family, could be assigned a position on an ordinal scale, which we term the Family Support Index:

1. *Completely isolated.* No one helps, or client stated that the only person to be counted on was a social worker or similar professional helper.
2. *Family dyad.* One parent or one sibling can be counted on to help.
3. *Friend dependent.* No family member can be counted on; only one friend can be called on.
4. *Family bound.* Two or more immediate family members (parents or siblings) only can be called upon for help.
5. *Family and friend related.* At least one member of the immediate family and one friend or more distant relative can be called upon for help.
6. *Supported.* At least one immediate family member and at least two friends or more distant relatives can be called upon for help.

Placements on the Family Support Index (FSI) for mothers and for fathers, individually, are given in Table 13.1. The score for

Family was arrived at by putting together the contacts of both parents in intact households; scores for female-headed families were, of course, identical with those for *Mother Only*.

Data in Table 13.1 demonstrate that the assumption that a client will prove to be embedded in a helping network is not unjustified. Of these low-income, white families, 62 of 79 (86%) in the control group were rated as *supported*. But the neglect sample was distributed throughout the scale, with over a fifth classified as *completely isolated*. The proportion of those low on the FSI (rated 1, 2, or 3) was compared with those ranked high (4, 5, and 6). Difference between neglect and control mothers was significant at beyond .001 by chi-square test; between fathers at .01; and between families at .001. In terms of having intimates readily available to help, neglectful parents are *not* in an average-expectable working-class position.

Formal and Informal Social Participation

Does their isolation from helping networks reflect a more general pattern? How about involvements with formal organizations? Here, it was especially important to have a reasonably well-matched control group, since it has been found repeatedly that membership in formal social organizations is positively related to socioeconomic status. Respondents were grouped into three categories. Low meant either no memberships or only pro forma belonging, as in a parish or a compulsory union. Activity in one organization plus membership in another was rated Medium. High included respondents active in two or more groups. Of the neglectful mothers, 74% were rated Low; of the controls, only 16% were so rated. Of the neglectful fathers, 85% were rated Low, compared with 32% of the controls. Nonparticipation in formal organizations proved to be the norm for the parents implicated in neglect to a degree that cannot be explained as typical of their social class or income groups.

How about informal social participation—visiting, partying, and the like? A Going-Out scale was developed, on which parents were again classified as *Low, Medium,* or *High.* Of the neglectful mothers, 44% rated *Low,* compared to only 10% of the controls. Differences between the fathers were not so marked but were in the same direction (24% vs. 13% *Low*). Indeed, although the scoring of each index was, of course, independent of scores on the others, all three scales—the FSI, participation in formal organizations, and the Going-Out index—were significantly intercorrelated.

In the Appalachian study,[6] we came to suspect that neglectful families were socially isolated; the urban study confirmed our impression. Moreover, the lack of informal sources of help among our neglectful parents appears to be but one aspect of a general tendency to be uninvolved and detached.

DISCUSSION

How might we explain the relative isolation of those parents identified as neglectful? In examining mobility, we find the majority of these parents were third-generation Philadelphians. Over 60% came from families with four or more siblings. The only relevant situational difference between our families is that those in the neglect group averaged 3.4 moves during the present marriage, compared to 1.2 moves among controls. But, even this willingness to rupture neighborly attachments might reflect psychological detachment quite as much as it explains it. Our most promising explanatory leads point to the enduring personalities of the parents. Case judges read narratives describing our research social workers' contacts and then rated the mothers and fathers on the presence of what we term *Apathy-Futility*[6] elements in their personalities. We found that, for all mothers, the presence of schizoid futility and withdrawal in the personality was negatively related to score on the Family Support Index ($r = -.60$); the same was true for fathers ($r = -.62$). Indeed, we infer from other evidence that the roots of the relative detachment probably go back to childhood, to high incidences of placements and feelings of being unwanted. But these are only leads; the dynamics remain to be uncovered by clinical work and other means.

As for implications for practice, it is obvious that neglectful parents are individuals; it would be unwise to infer a universal treatment from factor loadings or average differences discovered in statistics. But we can prepare each worker, and our overall treatment programs, to meet problems shown to be highly prevalent in this client group. The pattern we label isolation is experienced by the majority of these parents as loneliness and vulnerability. For, whatever their brittle defenses, most meet difficult day-to-day problems without help.

Given their lifelong patterns of nonparticipation, they appear poor prospects for general programs of family support or family life education. Their deficits in ordinary social skills require us to meet them well over half way; their unresponsiveness contributes to worker burnout. Still, one often encounters some readiness to trust, so the proffering of personal concern that is so much part of all good social work may be gratefully received. A number of thoughtful workers[1] have designed group experiences to be offered the mothers. Work thus far indicates such socialization groups can attract and hold a fair proportion, leading to surprising gains in mothers' self-esteem. Since so little warmth appears to radiate toward them from their own families of orientation, the burgeoning movement to join neglectful families with volunteers, working one-on-one, is also promising.

But, just as they have often proved to be too much for initially sympathetic neighbors, so there is a residuum of neglectful parents beyond the reach of volunteers and, ultimately, of mental health professionals. In short, their isolation reminds us that there are too many neglectful parents who remain beyond the grasp of our current methods of offering help. We must intensify the effort to understand clearly the bases of their isolation and to develop new services that will render them more accessible.

REFERENCES

1. AMBROSE, B. 1976. Patient rehabilitation and enrichment project. Unpublished paper, School of Social Welfare, State University of New York at Albany.

2. CANTOR, M. 1975. The formal and informal social support system of older New Yorkers. Presented to the Tenth International Congress of Gerontology, Jerusalem.

3. ELMER, E. 1967. Children in Jeopardy. University of Pittsburgh Press, Pittsburgh, Pa.

4. HELPER, R. 1973. The etiology of child abuse. Pediatrics 51: 777-779.

5. MARTIN, H. 1976. The Abused Child. Ballinger, Cambridge, Mass.

6. POLANSKY, N., BORGMAN, R. AND DE SAIX, C. 1972. Roots of Futility. Jossey-Bass, San Francisco.

7. SMITH, S., HANSON, R. AND NOBLE, S. 1974. Social aspects of the battered baby syndrome. Brit. Psychiat. 125: 568-582.

Failure of "Bond Formation" as a Cause of Abuse, Neglect, and Maltreatment

BYRON EGELAND
BRIAN VAUGHAN   *1981*

The enthusiasm for the concepts in another classic paper in this volume, "Maternal Attachment: Importance of the First Postpartum days," published in 1972 by Klaus et al., led Egeland and Vaughn 9 years later to question the importance of early postpartum separation. One of the problems of a new concept such as the importance of early postpartum contact is that it is likely to become quickly adopted and overstated by others. Egeland and Vaughan's contribution was rated a classic paper because it challenged what had rapidly become the prevailing dogma, that prematurity and early separation at birth were significant risk factors for later child abuse.

Earlier studies had been based largely on finding a relatively high proportion of premature births in a sample of abused children and then concluding that prematurity (or bonding failure) was the cause of the abuse. Egeland and Vaughan point out that looking backward in time always provides what appears to be a cause but that there is not necessarily a linear relationship. They designed a prospective study of 267 primiparous women and showed that prematurity and other indices of "bonding failure" did not occur with greater frequency among a subsample of mothers who mistreated their children than among a similar subgroup providing adequate care.

However, although they found no evidence of a relationship between child abuse and complications of delivery, infant illness, or prematurity, their study did suggest that early and extended contact of the mother and infant may enhance the relationship. It is quite clear that the majority of premature children are not later abused. While the work of Klaus and colleagues was a major milestone in changing obstetric hospital behavior and in supporting the early attachment between mother and child, Egeland and Vaughan prevented the pendulum from swinging too far by urging researchers to look for multiple causes of child abuse and neglect rather than just pinpointing one single, early event.

A. C. D. and K. O.

There is probably no more graphic example of the failure of adequate mother-infant bonding than physical abuse or neglect of an infant or young child. It is bewildering and upsetting to most adults to find that a mother could be responsible for the physical abuse, or condone the abuse by another, of her own infant. Yet, the incidence of cases of abuse and neglect seems to be on the rise. Interest in the etiology of abuse and neglect, especially in the etiology of "bonding," which may be directly implicated in the increases in the incidence of abuse and neglect, has to a large extent been an outgrowth of the work of Klaus, Kennell, and their colleagues,[4,9,10] who have been particularly interested in the initial development of the mother-infant bond. Their observations of mothers and newborn infants has led them to hypothesize that early separations during the immediate postpartum period (such as occasioned by typical hospital routines in the United States) may result in difficulties in establishing the normal mother-infant bond. Further, they have suggested that this initial failure to establish an appropriate bond may lead to disorders of mothering, the extreme form of which is abuse and neglect.

Drawing on the theoretical work of Bowlby,[2] Klaus and Kennell[9] defined attachment as "a unique relationship between two people that is specific and endures through time." While the term *bonding* was never specifically defined, it carries the implication that there is a sensitive or "critical" period in the first few minutes or hours after the birth of the infant during which close physical contact between the neonate and the parents is necessary if the appropriate "bond" is to be formed. Though bonding was discussed as if it were a form of imprinting, Klaus et al.[11] pointed out that their conceptualization of the bonding process does not fit a precise definition of imprinting.[7] They suggested that the period of early contact between the mother and her infant during the immediate postpartum period is special in that what the mother does during this time may alter her later behavior with the infant during the first few years of life.

As noted above, Klaus and associates argued that the prevailing hospital practice of separating infants (even healthy, full-term babies) from their mothers may have long-term effects on the mother's attitudes and behavior toward the infant.[1,9,12] They suggested that there is an increased likelihood of abuse and neglect following separation. In part, they based their argument on the fact that there is a disproportionately high number of premature and unhealthy infants in samples of neglected children.[4,8,10] They have further buttressed their arguments concerning the deleterious effects of early separations of infants and mothers with studies of many animals.[16]

Unfortunately, studies that have attempted to implicate bonding failure in the etiology of child abuse and neglect have been plagued with methodological problems and by inadequate measures of bond formation. Consequently, there is no direct evidence to support the notion that failure to form a bond was the cause of later child abuse. For example, Fanaroff et al.[4] followed up a group of 146 infants who had been in a nursery longer than 14

Originally published in *American Journal of Orthopsychiatry*, 1981, *51*, 78-84. Reprinted by permission of the American Orthopsychiatric Association, Inc.

days. Within the group of infants, 38 had received visits from their mothers less than three times, and from that group of 38, there were 11 identified cases of "disorders of mothering." The authors concluded that visiting is an indicator of the strength of mother-infant bonding. While the number of visits to the intensive care nursery may well be an appropriate indicator of the mother's attitudes and ambivalence toward her sick infant, there is good reason to question its validity as an index of the strength of the mother's present and future bond with the infant.

In another study, Lynch and Roberts[14] examined the birth records of 50 children who were later abused and found that 21 of these children had been admitted to intensive care. As a comparison, only 5 children from a control sample of nonabused children had been admitted to intensive care as neonates. Their conclusion was that mothers whose infants were placed in intensive care were not able to form the normal bonding, which they defined as the failure to develop normal parent-child love. A problem in interpreting this study is that there was no systematic attempt to assess the bonding process during infancy. Physical abuse was taken as prima facie evidence that there had been either a breakdown of the parent-infant bond or a failure to form such a bond at the outset. The observation that many of the abused infants had a history of intensive care as neonates makes an attractive post hoc explanation of the later abuse; however, it is likely that quite different results would have been found had the entire sample of children admitted to intensive care been followed up. Certainly, the vast majority of neonates admitted to intensive care nurseries are not subsequently abused or neglected by their parents.

The problem with an easy acceptance of the conclusion that separations during the newborn period—whether resulting from routine hospital practices or from delivery complications or from health problems of the neonate such as prematurity—lead to poor mother-infant bonding and subsequently to disorders of mothering is the lack of indication that an actual bonding problem exists. Neither is there evidence that such potential bonding problems are the *causes* of later abuse and neglect. One might readily argue that it is not an attachment problem per se that is implicated in the etiology of the mothering disorder, but that certain personality characteristics of the mother, present prior to the birth of her infant, affect her ability to become bonded to her baby and her subsequent mothering. It is possible that such mothers were more irresponsible concerning prenatal care than other mothers and, as a result, were more likely to have premature or otherwise vulnerable infants. The infrequent visits noted by Fanaroff et al.[4] may have been simply a further manifestation of an immature mother's irresponsible behavior toward her offspring. If this were indeed the case, then the failure to form a bond would simply be another symptom of a more pervasive problem and not necessarily the cause of later mothering disorders.

Another plausible explanation for the finding that premature and unhealthy infants are overrepresented in populations of abused and neglected infants is that such infants are particularly difficult to care for, regardless of the level of skill of the caretaker. Such infants may well frustrate attempts to provide adequate care, with the result that their parents come to dislike them.

It is clearly the case that the available data do not provide definite answers to the question of the role of bonding failures or early separations during the neonatal period in the etiology of child abuse and neglect. There is a great need for prospective research in these areas. The present investigation was designed to examine prospectively certain conditions related to early separations (and presumed failure to establish appropriate bonds) in two groups of mothers who were identified from a larger group of mothers and infants participating in a longitudinal study of the antecedents of child abuse and neglect. One of the groups is comprised of all the mothers from the larger sample who have met the criteria for a disorder of mothering during the infant's first year; the second group consists of those mothers who have been identified as providing optimal care for their infants during the first year of life. Specifically, our intent is to examine whether there are differences between the two groups in the proportions of infants born prematurely or having perinatal complications resulting in unusual separations, or in the length of stay in the hospital following delivery.

METHOD

Sample

A sample of 267 primiparous women receiving prenatal care at the Maternal and Infant Care Clinics, Minneapolis Health Department, was enrolled during the last trimester of pregnancy. The families are from lower socioeconomic backgrounds (the majority were on welfare), and the mean number of years of education at the time of delivery was 11.9 (range 7 to 22 years). The base rate for abuse and neglect in the Public Health Clinic population is approximately 1% to 2%, which is considerably higher than reported for the state in general. The mothers were quite young (mean age 20.4 years), and 62% were unwed at the time of delivery.

Within the sample of 267, 32 infants have been identified as not receiving adequate care, in that the mother (or other caretaker) is to some extent irresponsible in managing the day-to-day child care activities. While the problems may not be as severe as those found in children referred to child protection, there is reason to expect some adverse psychological impact due to their early experiences. Ratings and observations made by home observers are similar to ratings made on families who have been referred to the child protection agency. At each visit to the homes (at 3, 6, and 9 months after delivery) observers completed the Child Care Rating Scale,[3] which involves ratings of

any evidence of violence in the household, particularly toward the child; poor physical care; bad living conditions; neglect; and failure to thrive. Actual physical abuse was noted in four cases, neglect and abuse in three cases, and severe neglect in 25 cases, which also included three cases of failure to thrive. The Child Care Rating Scale[a] was filled out by the tester after each scheduled visit to the home.

A group of 33 mothers offering high-quality care to their children was identified, based on tester observations and results from the Child Care Rating Scales. These mothers all provided adequate care in terms of feeding, meeting the child's health care needs, protecting the child from possible dangerous situations in the home, and not leaving the baby alone or with unknown baby-sitters. The group of 32 mothers who abused, neglected, or in some way mistreated their child is referred to as the inadequate care group; the group of 33 mothers offering high-quality care is referred to as the adequate care group. Comparisons on certain indices of bonding were made between these two groups.

Data Gathering

From the detailed medical records regarding birth, delivery, and the neonatal period, the following information was obtained: length of labor, gestational age, birth weight, days in hospital, delivery complications, number of newborns with delivery complications, number of newborns with medical problems, physical anomalies, and number born prematurely, defined as having a birth weight of less than 2,500 grams.

RESULTS

Prematurity, difficulties at birth resulting in the newborn being separated from the mother over and above routine hospital procedures (e.g., placement under fluorescent lights due to hyperbilirubin anemia), and length of stay

TABLE 14.1 Pregnancy, Delivery, and Infant Data for Optimal and Nonoptimal Care Groups and Total Sample

Measure	Optimal Care (N = 33)	Nonoptimal Care (N = 32)	Total Sample (N = 267)
Premature (frequency)	2	2	30
Length of labor (hours)	12.05 (8.77)	12.25 (5.53)	12.79 (7.80)
Gestational age (weeks)	40.10 (.91)	39.87 (1.41)	39.66 (1.59)
Birth weight (grams)	3454 (552)	3324 (592)	3261 (540)
Unplanned pregnancy	71%	92%	86%
Days in hospital	3.32 (range 1—8)	3.89 (range 1—12)	
Mothers enrolled in midwife program (N)	14	1	52
Delivery complications	45%	52%	52%
Newborns with medical problems (N = 24)	9%	12%	10%
Newborns with physical anomalies (N = 51)	24%	22%	21%

in the hospital (after the mother was discharged) were used as the criteria for potential bonding failure. These data are displayed in Table 14.1 for both of the study groups and for the sample as a whole. As can be seen from Table 14.1, there are no differences between the adequate and the inadequate·care groups in the proportions of infants born prematurely, extent of delivery complications, prorportion born with medical problems requiring separations from the mother, or number of newborns with physical anomalies (e.g., six digits on a hand). Not only were there nonsignificant differences between the two groups, they were indistinguishable from the sample as a whole on these criteria. Further, data presented in Table 14.1 indicate that the two study groups were not different in terms of the infants' mean gestational ages or birth weight or mothers' length of labor. There was a trend toward longer hospital stays in the inadequate care group of *both* mothers and infants but not simply for infants after the mother had been discharged. This trend was due to the fact that six of the mothers in the adequate care group were discharged from the hospital within 2 days after delivery. There were three mothers in the adequate care group and four mothers in the inadequate care group who were in the hospital for 5 or more days, and in each case, contact was limited or did not occur during the first 2 days of the infant's life.

These data, though somewhat tentative, provide no evidence to support the notion that premature status, perinatal problems, or other indices of limited contact immediately after birth are implicated in the etiology of abuse, neglect, or other forms of mistreatment by mothers. Nor do they support the conclusions from previous research that there is a sensitive period immediately following birth during which contact is necessary if appropriate bonds are to be formed between a mother and her infant.

DISCUSSION

From the present data, it is not possible to conclude that limited contact between mother and infant immediately after birth results in bonding failure, which in turn causes disorders of mothering. The findings did not support a relationship between child abuse and neglect and the typical indices of bonding failure: prematurity, delivery complications, infant illness, and anomalies. These data suffer from the same problem that exists in other studies of bonding, namely the questionable nature of the measures used to infer bonding and bonding failure. Before any definite conclusions can be drawn, bonding needs to be defined objectively and measured systematically, and its relationship to later patterns of parenting looked at prospectively.

The strength of this investigation is its prospective design. Finding a relatively high proportion of premature births in a sample of abused children and concluding that prematurity (or bonding failure) causes child abuse is misleading. The conclusions drawn from such retrospective studies suffer from what Garmezy[5] referred to as "etiological error." Looking backward in time always provides a cause, but the inferred linearity is misleading. It may be the case, as some investigators have shown, that a number of abused children are premature. But, as the current results have demonstrated, the vast majority of premature children are not subsequently abused. This is an excellent example of etiological error, in which it is clear that a simple linear model of maltreatment will not suffice.

Even though we found no evidence to support the notion that bonding failure is implicated in the etiology of abuse and neglect, a closer examination of the adequate care group suggests the possibility that early and extended contact of the mother with her infant may enhance their relationship. Over one third (14) of the mothers in the adequate care group had volunteered to participate in the midwife program available through the county general hospital where all of the infants were delivered. This program provided extensive prenatal education; in addition, the mother was offered physical contact with her infant immediately after delivery, and the infant roomed with the mother. During the rooming-in period, mothers were

encouraged to touch, fondle, and engage the infant in eye-to-eye contact. Because these mothers had volunteered for the program and because, as a group, they were older, better educated, and in better health and had expressed more interest in the birth of their infants, we do not feel that the extended contact with their infants was the sole cause for the optimal care that these mothers provided. Further, it should be pointed out that participation in the midwife program did not insure optimal care since one of the midwife-delivered mothers was in the inadequate care group. Most likely, participation in the midwife program just reflects mother's interest in her child. Similarly, it is likely that the indices used to infer bonding, such as parents' visiting patterns,[4] amount of time with child and length of visit,[12] mother's behavior during physical exam of her child,[8] and interview data,[11] just reflect mother's interest in her child.

The development of an optimal bond or attachment between the mother and her infant has a complex etiology. This attachment develops slowly over the first year of the infant's life, and a number of mother and infant factors may facilitate or interfere with its development. One of these factors is early and extended contact between mother and infant. We are aware that many researchers and pediatricians have demonstrated some benefits of early contact between the mother and her infant.[9,15] O'Connor et al.[15] randomly assigned high-risk mothers to rooming-in or routine postpartum contact. When the infants were approximately 17 months of age, significantly more routine hospital care mothers were experiencing problems of parenting, which included referral to child protection and giving the child up for adoption. Although the results were significant, the small number of mothers experiencing parenting problems ($N = 10$) suggested the need for caution in interpreting the results. The rooming-in procedure used in the O'Connor et al. study is probably not a test of the effects of bonding, since the mothers did not experience early contact with their infants. The earliest the infants were given to their mothers was 7 hours after birth.

There can be no doubt that any hospital procedure that makes the mother feel more comfortable or more competent to care for her new baby will be a positive influence on the development of the maternal bond. However, to imply that lack of contact between mothers and their newborns is indicative of a current failure to bond with the infant, or is predictive of later breakdowns in the mother-infant bond, is a disservice to the millions of mothers and infants who have developed perfectly healthy bonds and attachments under the current hospital regimen. Finally, when parent-child bonds do break down, as in cases of abuse and neglect, researchers should look for multiple causes rather than pinpointing some very early event as the predisposing single trauma. Past experience with single causes (e.g., anoxia in the 1950s[6]) should keep us wary of assigning "blame" for the failure of bonds to early separations.

NOTE

a. Information regarding the development and use of the Child Care Rating Scale can be obtained from the first author.

REFERENCES

1. BARNETT, C. ET AL. 1970. Neonatal separation: the maternal side of interactional deprivation. Pediatrics 45: 197-205.

2. BOWLBY, J. 1969. Attachment and Loss, Vol. 1: Attachment. Basic Books, New York.

3. EGELAND, B. AND DEINARD, A. 1975. Child Care Rating Scale. University of Minnesota, Minneapolis.

4. FANAROFF, A., KENNELL, H. AND KLAUS, M. 1972. Follow-up of low birthweight infants: the predictive value of maternal visiting patterns. Pediatrics 49: 287-290.

5. GARMEZY, N. 1977. Parents, patience, and schizophrenia. Frieda Fromm-Reichman Lecture, Washington, D.C.

6. GRAHAM, F. ET AL. 1957. Anoxia as a significant perinatal experience: a critique. J. Pediat. 50: 556-569.

7. HESS, E. 1970. Ethology and developmental psychology. *In* Carmichael's Manual of Child Psychology, P. Mussen, ed. John Wiley, New York.

8. KENNELL, J. ET AL. 1974. Maternal behavior one year after early and extended post-partum contact. Devlpm. Med. Child Neurol. 16: 172-179.

9. KLAUS, M. AND KENNELL, J. 1976. Maternal-Infant Bonding. C.V. Mosby, St. Louis.

10. KLAUS, M. AND KENNELL, J. 1970. Mothers separated from their newborn infants. Pediat. Clin. N. A. 17: 1015-1037.

11. KLAUS, M. ET AL. 1972. Maternal attachments: importance of the first post-partum days. New Eng. J. Med. 286: 460-463.

12. LAMPE, J., TRAUSE, M. AND KENNELL, J. 1977. Parental visiting of sick infants: the effect of living at home prior to hospitalization. Pediatrics 59: 294-296.

13. LEIFER, A. ET AL. 1972. Effects of mother-infant separation on maternal attachment behavior. Child Devlpm. 43: 1203-1218.

14. LYNCH, M. AND ROBERTS, J. 1977. Predicting child abuse: signs of bonding failure in the maternity hospital. Brit. Med. J. 1: 624-626.

15. O'CONNOR, S. ET AL. 1970. Reduced incidence of parenting disorders following rooming-in. Unpublished manuscript, Vanderbilt University.

16. TRAUSE, M., KLAUS, M. AND KENNELL, J. 1976. Maternal behavior in mammals. *In* Maternal-Infant Bonding, M. Klaus and J. Kennell, eds. C.V. Mosby, St. Louis.

15

The Incidence and Prevalence of Intrafamilial and Extrafamilial Sexual Abuse of Female Children

DIANE E. H. RUSSELL   1983

By the early 1980s, the magnitude of the child sexual abuse problem was widely recognized. Several dozen studies independently suggested that the problem was widespread in the population. Yet, the first findings based on a representative sample were not available until 1983, when Diane Russell published the results of a survey of 930 female residents of San Francisco, randomly selected and interviewed about any experiences of sexual abuse they may have had at any time in their lives. The resulting paper, "The Incidence and Prevalence of Intrafamilial and Extrafamilial Sexual Abuse of Female Children," had a profound impact on our understanding of just how widespread the problem could be, as well as on subsequent methods used to study the problem. The study also provoked the kind of debate that has helped in refining our definitions of sexual abuse of children.

The alarmingly high rates of sexual abuse reported in this study led to as much skepticism and debate as to belief. The author herself is quite confident the study's findings are not overstated. In her conclusions, she states, "Although we can be virtually certain that some of our random sample of 930 women were unwilling to disclose experiences of child sexual abuse, and although it seems reasonable to assume that there may be a significant number of women who have repressed such experiences from their conscious memories, and despite the fact that the definitions used in our study were narrower than those used in other major surveys, astonishingly high rates of child sexual abuse were nonetheless disclosed." The use of carefully selected and trained female interviewers undoubtedly contributed to the rates documented.

The work presented in this paper, coupled with findings from comparable studies published soon after this one, was like a match in the tinderbox. The concern about child sexual abuse exploded almost overnight, fueled by individual reports in the media that high-profile individuals shared this experience. A near-hysteria seemed to erupt, resulting in the proliferation of hundreds and hundreds of educational efforts targeting on young children to teach them how to avoid becoming the victims of sexual abuse. On a more measured front, the methodology used in this study became the subject of much study and replication. It can be credited with contributing toward the increased sophistication of prevalence and incidence studies in the more narrow field of sexual abuse and the broader one of child maltreatment.

A. C. D. and K. O.

There is no consensus among researchers and practitioners about what sex acts constitute sexual abuse, what age defines a child, nor even whether the concept of child sexual abuse is preferable to others such as sexual victimization, sexual exploitation, sexual assault, sexual misuse, child molestation, sexual maltreatment, or child rape. Furthermore, these terms have frequently been limited to sexual behavior that occurs between adults and children [1,2,3]. Consequently, cases in which children are raped or otherwise sexually abused by their peers, younger children, or children less than 5 years older than themselves are often discounted as instances of child sexual abuse. The terms *sexual abuse* and *sexual victimization* will be used interchangeably in this article; these terms should be understood to include sexual abuse by peers or other children.

LITERATURE REVIEW OF INCIDENCE AND PREVALENCE

Both the incidence and prevalence of child sexual abuse, in the family and outside of it, are unknown [4]. Weinberg, in his classic study originally published in 1955, estimated that there was one case of incest per million persons per year in English-speaking countries [5]. Ferracuti estimated in 1972 that between one and five cases of incest per million persons occur every year throughout the world [6]. Many other estimates have been made, but none of them are based on representative samples. Meiselman attempted to list all studies of incest with samples larger than five published in this country [7]. The highly select and nonrepresentative nature of the samples used in all 36 studies listed is very apparent. Studies of extrafamilial abuse are equally unrepresentative.

The National Incidence Study, which includes cases known to other investigatory bodies besides child protective service agencies, as well as other professionals in schools, hospitals, and major agencies, estimated a rate of 0.7 cases of child sexual exploitation per 1,000 children per year, as compared with 3.4 cases of other physical assault, 2.2 cases of emotional abuse, 1.7 cases of physical neglect, 2.9 cases of educational neglect, and 1.0 case of emotional neglect per 1,000 children per year. The number of substantiated cases of sexual exploitation was 44,700 [8]. Surprisingly, there were proportionately more serious injuries associated with sexual exploitation than

Acknowledgment: The author would like to thank Patricia Mrazek and David Finkelhor for their useful suggestions in response to an earlier draft of this manuscript, Karen Trocki and Bill Wells for their assistance with the data analysis, and Jan Dennie for her help in the preparation of this article.
Originally published in *Child Abuse and Neglect,* 1983, Vol. 7, pp. 133-146. Reprinted with permission from Elsevier Science.

with physical assault [9]. This finding suggests that only the most serious cases of sexual abuse were seen as qualifying for inclusion. Just as so many cases of reported rapes are "unfounded" every year by the police, it appears that many legitimate cases of child sexual abuse were "unsubstantiated."

Most other estimates have focused on the prevalence of incest and/or other child sexual abuse rather than the incidence. Herman presents data from five surveys that have been undertaken on the prevalence of sexual abuse of female children since 1940. She points out that cumulatively, these studies have recorded information from over 5,000 women from many different regions of the United States and primarily from the more privileged strata [10]. According to Herman,

> The results of these five surveys were remarkably consistent. One-fifth to one-third of all women reported that they had had some sort of childhood sexual encounter with an adult male. Between four and twelve percent of all women reported a sexual experience with a relative, and one woman in one hundred reported a sexual experience with her father or stepfather [10].

However, none of these surveys were based on representative samples. A major objective of the research reported here was to obtain a more valid basis on which to arrive at estimates of both intrafamilial and extrafamilial child sexual abuse.

METHODOLOGY [11]

The Sample

A probability sample of 930 women residents of San Francisco 18 years and older were interviewed during the summer of 1978 about any experience of sexual abuse they might have had at any time throughout their lives. San Francisco was selected because, among other

reasons, it was believed that women in that city would be more willing to disclose such experiences than women in many other parts of the country. The probability sample of households was drawn by Field Research Associates, a respected public opinion-polling organization in San Francisco. Carefully trained women interviewers enumerated households to find out whether a woman 18 years or older resided there. If there was more than one eligible woman in a given household, a procedure was applied to randomly select the one to be interviewed. Detailed interviews, the average length of which was 1 hour and 20 minutes, were then arranged with the selected women.

The Interview

Because it appeared that many prior surveys suffered from under-disclosure of sexual assault experiences, every effort was made to discourage this from occurring in this study. The interview schedule was carefully designed to encourage good rapport with the respondent. Interviewers were selected for their sensitivity to the issue of sexual assault as well as for their interviewing skills. They received 65 hours of intensive training that included education about rape and incestuous abuse, as well as desensitization to sexual words and rigorous training in administering the interview schedule. Interviews were held in private, and whenever possible, race and ethnicity of interviewer and respondent were matched. Each respondent was paid $10 for her participation.

Refusal Rate

Nineteen percent of the women who were selected as respondents refused to participate, after being informed that the crimes to be discussed were rape and other sexual assault. An additional 17% of people, men as well as women, declined to give a listing of those in the household prior to being told about the topic to be studied. This amounts to a refusal rate of

36%. However, if one also takes into account all households where no one was ever at home, or where the interviewer could not gain access to the house because of locked gates, fierce watchdogs, and the like, as well as those where the women randomly selected to be interviewed simply were never available because they were out of town, or because their husbands or some other persons would not give the interviewer access to the women, or for some other reason, then the refusal rate was 50%. Although this refusal rate is higher than desired, it must be remembered that Kinsey and his colleagues [12], Masters and Johnson [13], as well as Hite [14], all based their studies on volunteers because they considered a random sample unfeasible. Even an imperfect random household sample such as ours is still unprecedented for research in the area of sex or sexual abuse.

The Definitions

For purposes of our survey, extrafamilial child sexual abuse was defined as one or more unwanted sexual experiences with persons unrelated by blood or marriage, ranging from petting (touching of breasts or genitals or attempts at such touching) to rape, before the victim turned 14 years, and completed or attempted forcible rape experiences from the ages of 14 to 17 years (inclusive).

Since intrafamilial child sexual abuse was expected to be generally more upsetting and traumatic than extrafamilial child sexual abuse, and since the issue of whether or not the sexual contact was wanted or not is so much more complex in intimate relationships, a broader definition of what constitutes intrafamilial sexual abuse was used. More specifically, *intrafamilial child sexual abuse* was defined as any kind of exploitive sexual contact that occurred between relatives, no matter how distant the relationship, before the victim turned 18 years old. Experiences involving sexual contact with a relative that were wanted *and* with a peer were

regarded as nonexploitive, for example, sex play between cousins or siblings of approximately the same ages. An age difference of less than 5 years was the criterion for a peer relationship [15].

It should be noted that our definitions of these two forms of child sexual abuse are narrower than those used by some other researchers, who include exhibitionism and/or other experiences that may involve no actual contact, for example, a sexual advance or proposition that is not acted upon or which is successfully avoided [1, 16, 17].

Initially, the age of 13 and younger was chosen as the criterion for child sexual abuse, because law in California, the state in which this research was undertaken, defined child molestation in 1978 as "all sex acts upon children under age of fourteen, when the intent of sexually stimulating either party is involved" [18]. Other researchers have used other ages; for example, Finkelhor defined a child as a person under 17 years of age [1], and the National Child Abuse and Neglect publications use 18 years as their criterion [3]. Eighteen is, of course, the age of consent in many states, and it is also the age specified in the child abuse and neglect reporting statute. However, since it seems inappropriate to regard many 16- and 17-year-olds as children, both because of their physical and emotional maturity, prevalence rates will be reported for both the ages of 13 and under, and 17 and under.

The Interview Schedule

Extensive pre-testing revealed that when a number of different questions are asked in a wide variety of ways, the chances of tapping memories stored under many different categories are greatly facilitated. The questions used to elicit memories of child sexual abuse experiences were as follows:

1. Before you turned 14, were you ever upset by anyone exposing their genitals?

2. Did anyone ever try or succeed in having any kind of sexual intercourse with you against your wishes before you turned 14?

3. In those years, did anyone ever try or succeed in getting you to touch their genitals against your wishes (besides anyone you've already mentioned)? [19]

4. Did anyone ever try or succeed in touching your breasts or genitals against your wishes before you turned 14 (besides anyone you've already mentioned)?

5. Before you turned 14, did anyone ever feel you, grab you, or kiss you in a way you felt was sexually threatening (besides anyone you've already mentioned)?

6. Before you turned 14, did you have any (other) upsetting sexual experiences that you haven't mentioned yet?

The following few questions, including the two questions on intrafamilial sexual abuse, did not stipulate age limit but nevertheless yielded many experiences of child sexual abuse.

7. At *any* time in your life, have you ever had an unwanted sexual experience with a girl or a woman?

8. At any time in your life, have you ever been the victim of a rape or attempted rape?

9. Some people have experienced unwanted sexual advances by someone who had authority over them, such as a doctor, teacher, employer, minister, therapist, policeman, or much older person. Did *you ever* have *any* kind of unwanted sexual experience with someone who had authority over you, at *any* time in your life?

10. People often don't think about their relatives when thinking about sexual experiences, so the next two questions are about relatives. At *any* time in your life, has an uncle, brother, father, grandfather, or female relative ever had *any kind* of sexual contact with you?

11. At any time in your life, has anyone less closely related to you, such as a stepparent, stepbrother, or stepsister, in-law, or first cousin, had *any* kind of sexual contact with you?

12. In general, have you *narrowly missed* being sexually assaulted by someone at any time in your life (*other* than what you have already mentioned)?

13. And have you *ever* been in any situation where there was violence or threat of violence, where you were also afraid of being *sexually* assaulted—again, *other* than what you (might) have already mentioned?

14. Can you think of any (other) unwanted sexual experiences (that you haven't mentioned yet)?

Separate questionnaires were administered for all the more serious cases of sexual abuse. Interviewers were instructed to obtain descriptions of the sexual contact(s) sufficiently detailed to insure that the level of intimacy violated could be precisely coded.

FINDINGS

Prevalence Figures

As may be seen in Table 15.1, 16% of the sample of 930 women reported at least one experience of intrafamilial sexual abuse before the age of 18 years. These 152 women reported a total of 186 experiences with different perpetrators. Twelve percent (108) of these women had been sexually abused by a relative before 14 years of age. These prevalence figures exclude eight cases of intrafamilial sexual abuse where information on the age of the respondent at the time it occurred was missing, as well as two cases where it was not known whether actual sexual contact occurred between the respondent and her relative. Hence, these figures err on the side of underestimation, even presuming that all respondents were willing to disclose their experiences of intrafamilial sexual abuse; this is undoubtedly a poor presumption.

Using the more stringent definition of extrafamilial sexual abuse, *31% of the sample of 930 women reported at least one experience of sexual abuse by a non-relative before the age*

TABLE 15.1 Different Measures of the Prevalence and Incidence of Intrafamilial and Extrafamilial Child Sexual Abuse (Separated)

	Women who Had at Least One Experience (Prevalence)(N = 930)		Number of Experiences of Sexual Abuse With Different Perpetrators (Incidence)[a]
	Sample Percentage	Number	Number
Intrafamilial abuse of females involving sexual contact (17 years and under)[b]	16	152	186
Intrafamilial abuse of females involving sexual contact (13 years and under)[b]	12	108	134
Extrafamilial sexual abuse of females involving petting or genital sex (17 years and under)	31	290	461
Extrafamilial sexual abuse of females involving petting or genital sex (13 years and under)	20	189	255

a. Multiple attacks by the same perpetrators are only counted once; abuse involving multiple perpetrators are also counted as only one experience.
b. Eight cases of intrafamilial abuse are excluded because of missing data on the age of the respondent.

of 18 years. These 290 women reported a total of 461 experiences with different perpetrators. *Twenty percent (189) of these women had been sexually abused by a non-relative before 14 years of age* (see Table 15.1).

As might be expected, there is some overlap between the respondents who have experienced intrafamilial and extrafamilial child sexual abuse. When both these categories of child sexual abuse are combined, *38% (357) of the 930 women reported at least one experience of intrafamilial and/or extrafamilial sexual abuse before the age of 18 years, and 28% (258) reported at least one such experience before 14 years of age* (see Table 15.2).

While these prevalence figures for child sexual abuse are already shockingly high, it would be interesting to know how much higher they would be, had broader definitions of both intrafamilial and extrafamilial child sexual abuse more comparable to some other studies been adopted. Although the two questions asked about intrafamilial sexual abuse specifi-

cally stipulated sexual contact as the criterion, some respondents replied by describing experiences that did not involve actual physical contact. While we can be sure that many other respondents would have told us about their non-contact experiences had they been asked about them, these inadvertently obtained data are valuable despite their incompleteness. Additional quantitative data were also obtained on other non-contact experiences in childhood, such as being upset by someone exposing their genitals. In the case of extrafamilial child sexual abuse, there were additional quantitative data on unwanted kisses, hugs, and other non-genital touching that did not meet our definition of sexual abuse by non-relatives.

When applying these broader definitions of intrafamilial and extrafamilial child sexual abuse, which include experiences with exhibitionists as well as other unwanted non-contact sexual experiences, *54% (504) of the 930 women reported at least one experience of intrafamilial and/or extrafamilial sexual abuse before they*

TABLE 15.2 Different Measures of the Prevalence of Intrafamilial and Extrafamilial Child Sexual Abuse of Females (Combined)

	Women Who Had at Least One Experience (N = 930)	
	Sample Percentage	Number
Intrafamilial and/or extrafamilial sexual abuse of females under 18 years	38	357
Intrafamilial and/or extrafamilial sexual abuse of females under 14 years	28	258
Intrafamilial and/or extrafamilial sexual abuse of females under 18 years—broad definition (includes non- contact experiences, e.g., exhibitionism, sexual advances not acted upon, etc.)	54	504
Intrafamilial and/or extrafamilial sexual abuse of females under 14 years—broad definition (as above)	48	450

reached 18 years of age, and *48% (450) reported at least one such experience before 14 years of age* (see Table 15.2).

The narrower definitions of intrafamilial and extrafamilial child sexual abuse will be used throughout the remainder of this article.

The Perpetrators of Intrafamilial Child Sexual Abuse

Forty percent (74 cases) of intrafamilial child sexual abuse occurred within the nuclear family in our survey (i.e., the perpetrators were parents or siblings). Forty-two women reported an incestuous relationship with their fathers before the age of 18 [including 27 biological fathers, 15 step, 1 foster, and 1 father by adoption. Since two women were sexually abused by both their biological and stepfathers, the count includes two more perpetrators (44) than victims (42).] This constitutes 4.5% of our random sample of 930 women (see Table 15.3).

Sexual abuse by uncles is only very slightly more prevalent than father-daughter incestuous abuse, with 4.9% of the women in the sample reporting at least one such experience before the age of 18. Three percent of the women surveyed reported a sexually abusive experience with a first cousin before they turned 18, all but two of whom were male. Just over 2% of the women reported at least one incestuous experience with a brother, 0.9% with a male in-law, 0.9% with a grandfather, 0.3% with a sister, 0.1% with a mother, and 1.8% with some other male or female relative, not including grandmothers or aunts, with whom not a single case of sexual abuse was reported.

Had males as well as females been interviewed, the percentage of female perpetrators would likely have been higher. Nevertheless, it is of interest that in this random sample survey, only eight female perpetrators of intrafamilial child sexual abuse were reported, that is, only 4% of all incestuous perpetrators.

The Perpetrators of Extrafamilial Child Sexual Abuse

As may be seen in Table 15.4, only 15% of the perpetrators of extrafamilial child sexual abuse were strangers, while 42% were acquaintances, and 41% were more intimately

TABLE 15.3 Women Under 18 Years Reporting Intrafamilial Sexual Abuse by Type of Perpetrator

	Number of Women[a]	Percentage of Women in Sample (N = 930)	Number of Incidents With Different Perpetrators
Father (biological, step, foster, or adoptive)	42	4.5	44
Mother (biological, step, foster, or adoptive)	1	0.1	1
Grandfather	8	0.9	8
Grandmother	0	0	0
Brother	20	2.2	26
Sister	3	0.3	3
Uncle	46	4.9	48
Aunt	0	0	0
In-law (male only)	8	0.9	9
First cousin (male or female)	28	3.0	28
Other relative (male or female)	18	1.8	19

a. If a woman was sexually abused by more than one category of relative, she is included in each.

related to their victims (friends of the respondent, friends of the family, dates, boyfriends, and lovers). Forty percent of these perpetrators were also classified as authority figures. Two thirds of them were so classified because they were much older adults, including strangers, acquaintances, friends of the family, parent's lovers, household employees, and neighbors [20].

Those who abused female children not related to them in our survey were overwhelmingly male: As may be seen in Table 15.4, only 4% were females. This is exactly the same percentage of female perpetrators as was found for intrafamilial child sexual abuse.

The Perpetrators of All Child Sexual Abuse Combined

While it is becoming more widely recognized that most child sexual abuse is perpetrated by those known to the victims, our survey reveals that when all cases of intrafamilial and extrafamilial child sexual abuse are combined, the majority of the perpetrators were not relatives. More specifically, 11% were total

strangers, 29% were relatives, and 60% were known to the victims but unrelated to them.

Seriousness of Intrafamilial Child Sexual Abuse

The experiences of intrafamilial sexual abuse included in our survey range from unwanted but non-forceful kissing by a cousin to forcible rape by a biological father. Eighteen different categories of sexual abuse were differentiated according to whether or not force was used as well as the degree of sexual violation involved. For purposes of simplification, this 18-category typology was collapsed into the following three categories: (1) Very Serious Sexual Abuse, including experiences ranging from forced penile-vaginal penetration to attempted fellatio, cunnilingus, analingus, anal intercourse—not by force; (2) Serious Sexual Abuse, including experiences ranging from forced digital penetration of the vagina to nonforceful attempted breast contact (unclothed) or simulated intercourse; and (3) Least Serious Sexual Abuse, including experiences ranging from forced kissing, intentional

TABLE 15.4 Perpetrators of Extrafamilial Sexual Abuse of Females Under 18 Years

	Male Perpetrators		Female Perpetrators	
	Percentage	Number	Percentage	Number
Stranger	15	(71)	0	(0)
Acquaintance	40	(185)	2	(8)
Friend of family	14	(64)	0	(2)
Friend of respondent	9	(43)	2	(7)
Date	9	(40)	0	(0)
Boyfriend, lover, husband[a]	7	(33)	0	(0)
Authority figure (not classifiable)	2	(8)	0	(0)
Total	96	(444)	4	(17)

a. Five women who were raped by their husbands before they turned 18 are included here, since, although they are relatives, clearly sexual abuse by husbands cannot be regarded as incestuous.

sexual touching of the respondent's buttocks, thigh, leg or other body part, including contact with clothed breasts or genitals, to attempts at any of the same acts without the use of force. The frequency with which these different degrees of intrafamilial child sexual abuse occurred in our survey is presented in Table 15.5, along with the relationship between the victim and the perpetrator and the sex of the latter.

This table reveals that 23% of all incidents of intrafamilial sexual abuse were classified as *Very Serious,* 41% as *Serious,* and 36% as *Least Serious.* When differentiating between forceful and non-forceful forms of intrafamilial child sexual abuse, 41% (77) of the cases involved force and 59% (109) involved no force. Note that force includes threat of force as well as the inability to consent due to being unconscious, drugged, asleep, or in some other way, totally helpless. Only one of the eight female perpetrators, a distant female relative, used force, and none were reported to be involved in the most serious category of sexual violation.

It is apparent from the data reported in Table 15.5 that when stepfathers abuse their daughters, they are much more likely than any other relative to abuse them at the most serious level.Ml(1) *Very Serious Sexual Abuse,* including experiences ranging from forced penile-vaginal penetration to attempted fellatio, cunnilingus, analingus, anal intercourse—*not* by force [21]. In almost half the cases of sexual abuse by stepfathers (47%), *Very Serious* abuse was reported, as compared with 26% of biological fathers and a range of from 17% to 29% for other male relatives. In addition, since many more females are accessible to biological fathers than stepfathers, the fact that as many as 15 stepfathers (8% of all incestuous perpetrators) were reported by these women, as compared with 27 biological fathers (15% of all incestuous perpetrators), confirms the widespread belief that stepfathers are more likely to abuse their daughters than biological fathers.

Table 15.5 also reveals that when intrafamilial sexual abuse occurs within the same generation, the *Least Serious* incidents are much less likely to be reported. Only 12% of the incidents with brothers and 19% with first cousins involved abuse at this level, as compared with 75% of the incidents with grandfathers and 54% with uncles. It may be that even relatively mild experiences will be remembered because they are more disturbing when they are cross-generational than when they are not. Or it could be that the incest taboo is weaker for brothers and cousins, so that, like stepfathers, they are more likely to engage in

TABLE 15.5 Seriousness of Intrafamilial Child Sexual Abuse by Relationship With the Perpetrator (Under 18 Years)

	Male Perpetrator								Female Perpetrator				Total
	Biological Father	Step, Adoptive Father	Grandfather	Brother	Uncle	In-Law	First Cousin	Other Male Relative	Biological Mother	Sister	First Cousin	Other Female Relative	
1. Very Serious Sexual Abuse													
Completed and attempted vaginal, oral, anal intercourse, cunnilingus, analingus, forced and unforced[a]	7 26%	8 47%	0	7 27%	8 17%	2 22%	6 23%	5 29%	0	0	0	0	43 23%
2. Serious Sexual Abuse													
Completed and attempted genital fondling, simulated intercourse, digital penetration, forced and unforced	9 33%	5 29%	2 25%	16 62%	14 29%	1 11%	15 58%	7 41%	1	3	1	2	76 41%
3. Least Serious Sexual Abuse													
Completed and attempted acts of intentional sexual touching of buttocks, thigh, leg or other body part, clothed breasts or genitals, kissing, forced and unforced	11 41%	4 24%	6 75%	3 12%	26 54%	6 67%	5 19%	5 29%	0	0	1	0	67 36%
Total	27°	17	8	26	48*	9	26	17	1	3	2	2	186

NOTE: Eight cases of intrafamilial sexual abuse are excluded because of missing information on the age of the respondent at the time of the abuse, and two cases (1 biological father and 1 uncle) because of missing information on the seriousness of the sexual abuse. Categories of relatives where there were no incidents of sexual abuse are omitted.
a. The term *force* includes physical force, threat of physical force, or inability to consent because of being unconscious, drugged, asleep, or in some other way totally helpless.

148

more seriously abusive behavior if they so desire.

Seriousness of Extrafamilial Child Sexual Abuse

When the same differentiation is made between the Very Serious, Serious, and Least Serious incidents of extrafamilial child sexual abuse, 53% (243) were classified as Very Serious, 27% (125) as Serious, and 20% (93) as Least Serious (see Table 15.6). When these percentages are compared with those reported for intrafamilial child sexual abuse, it is apparent that children who are sexually abused outside the family are abused in a significantly more serious manner. It may be that the incest taboo, though frequently violated, serves to restrain those who abuse their relatives. Or it may be a consequence of our methodology, since from the ages of 14 to 17, only incidents of rape and attempted rape are included for extrafamilial child sexual abuse. Also, more minor episodes of sexual contact were included for relatives.

Table 15.6 reveals that authority figures are by far the most likely perpetrators to engage in the less serious kinds of sexual abuse. Only 25% of them were involved in *Very Serious* sexual abuse, as compared with 90% of dates, 88% of boyfriends/lovers, 73% of strangers, 72% of acquaintances, 70% of friends of the respondent, and 50% of friends of the family.

Reporting to the Police

Only 4 cases (2%) of intrafamilial child sexual abuse and only 26 cases (6%) of extrafamilial child sexual abuse were ever reported to the police. These extremely low figures provide powerful evidence that reported cases are only the very tip of the iceberg. This finding is all the more alarming when we see, in addition, that in 32% of the cases of intrafamilial child sexual abuse, the respondent reported that the perpetrator had also sexually abused one or more other relatives (16% of the respondents said they did not know if this had occurred, and 53% said that another relative had not been sexually abused by the person who abused them) [22].

Comparisons With Other Studies

Since Finkelhor's research on the sexual abuse of children was also based on survey data—albeit a population of students who were not randomly selected—his findings regarding those who abuse their young female relatives are the most comparable with ours [1]. In terms of prevalence, Finkelhor stated that 26% of the students surveyed reported a sexual experience with a relative, as compared with only 16% who reported a childhood sexual experience with an older person [23]. The latter experiences included both intrafamilial and extrafamilial child sexual abuse. It will be remembered that our notion of child sexual abuse was not limited to child-adult contacts. With regard to incestuous abuse, our prevalence rate of 16% for females 17 years and under is substantially lower than Finkelhor's. This difference is partially due to his not applying any age limit in cases of incest.

In general, it is apparent that far more cross-generational intrafamilial child sexual abuse was reported in our survey than in Finkelhor's. If we exclude the categories of "other" male and female relatives, since generation is not self-evident for them, then 60% of the intrafamilial child sexual abuse in our survey is cross-generational, as compared with only 14% in Finkelhor's study. More specifically, 24% of the perpetrators of intrafamilial sexual abuse in our San Francisco survey were fathers (including stepfathers, 1 adoptive and 1 foster father) and 26% were uncles, as compared with only 4% fathers and 9% uncles in Finkelhor's sample [24].

One striking similarity is that no aunts were reported as sexually abusive in either study,

TABLE 15.6 Seriousness of Extrafamilial Child Sexual Abuse by Relationship With the Perpetrator (Under 18 Years)

	Male Perpetrator							Female Perpetrator			
	Stranger	Acquaintance	Friend of Family	Friend of Respondent	Date	Boyfriend, Lover	Authority Figure	Acquaintance	Friend of Respondent	Authority Figure	Total
1. Very Serious Sexual Abuse											
Completed and attempted vaginal, oral, anal intercourse, cunnilingus, analingus, forced and unforced[a]	37 73%	54 72%	10 50%	30 70%	36 90%	29 88%	45 25%	0	2	0	243 53%
2. Serious Sexual Abuse											
Completed and attempted genital fondling, simulated intercourse, digital penetration, forced and unforced	7 14%	7 9%	7 35%	7 16%	3 7%	3 9%	80 44%	1	4	6	125 27%
3. Least Serious Sexual Abuse											
Completed and attempted acts of intentional sexual touching of clothed breasts or genitals, forced and unforced	7 14%	14 19%	3 15%	6 14%	1 3%	1 3%	57 31%	3	1	0	93 20%
Total	51	75	20	43	40	33	182	4	7	6	461

NOTE: Categories of perpetrators where there were no incidents of sexual abuse are omitted.
a. The term force includes physical force, threat of physical force, or inability to consent because of being unconscious, drugged, asleep, or in some other way totally helpless.

and only one mother in both studies. In general, there was a minority of female abusers in both studies. However, in our survey, there were only 8 cases of female abusers (4% of all abusers), compared with 35 cases (19%) reported by Finkelhor [24].

One reason for the very large disparities in the findings of our survey and Finkelhor's is that his definition of what constitutes incest is much broader than ours. For example, he included "an invitation to do something sexual"; "other people showing his/her sexual organs to you"; and "you showing your sex organs to other person" [25]. Only experiences that involved some direct physical contact qualified as incestuous abuse in our study. Second, Finkelhor did not differentiate between abusive and non-abusive experiences [26]. Experiences that do not involve actual sexual contact are much more likely to be nonabusive, particularly when they occur between peers. Finally, some of the differences in the findings of these two surveys may also have occurred because women may be less likely to disclose the more taboo experiences of father-daughter and other cross-generational incestuous abuse on a self-administered questionnaire completed in a classroom situation, as was required by Finkelhor's methodology, than in a face-to-face interview with well-trained interviewers who have had an opportunity to build good rapport with the respondent.

Another dramatic difference between the findings of our representative survey and other non-representative surveys is that while only 11% of the perpetrators of child sexual abuse in our sample were total strangers, this figure is much lower than the 24% reported by Finkelhor [1], the 58% reported by Gagnon [13], and the 65% reported by Landis [14]. Similarly, 60% of these perpetrators in our sample were neither total strangers nor related, compared with 26% in Gagnon's study, and 33% in Finkelhor's.

One explanation for these differences may be that our survey tapped into more of the types of experiences that are usually never detected

or divulged, including those not volunteered to agencies or researchers.

SUMMARY, CONCLUSION, AND IMPLICATIONS

Although we can be virtually certain that some of our random sample of 930 women were unwilling to disclose experiences of child sexual abuse, and although it seems reasonable to assume that there may be a significant number of women who have repressed such experiences from their conscious memories, and despite the fact that the definitions used in our study were narrower than those used in other major surveys, astonishingly high rates of child sexual abuse were nevertheless disclosed. One of the reasons for this uncommonly high disclosure is undoubtedly due to the methodology employed, for example, the use of female interviewers only, the careful selection of the interviewers, the inclusion of training sessions to sensitize them to the issue of child sexual abuse, the creation of an interview schedule that facilitated the development of effective rapport before broaching the topic, and the multiplicity of questions asked.

Finkelhor commented on his estimate of a 1% prevalence rate of father-daughter incest as follows:

> One percent may seem to be a small figure, but if it is an accurate estimate, it means that approximately three-quarters of a million women eighteen and over in the general population have had such an experience, and that another 16,000 cases are added each year from among the group of girls aged five to seventeen [27].

In fact, the rate of father-daughter incestuous abuse reported in our survey is close to five times higher than Finkelhor's 1% estimate. The rate of other intrafamilial and extrafamilial child sexual abuse is similarly very much higher than any prior study had led us to believe. More specifically: (1) 16% of the sample of 930 women reported at least one experience of intrafamilial sexual abuse before the age of 18 years, and 12% reported at least one such experience before the age of 14 years; (2) 31% reported at least one experience of extrafamilial sexual abuse before the age of 18 years, and 20% reported at least one such experience before the age of 14 years; (3) when both categories of sexual abuse are combined, 38% reported at least one experience before the age of 18 years, and 28% reported at least one such experience before the age of 14 years.

These alarming prevalence rates are based on the first random sample survey ever conducted on this subject. Although the study was undertaken in the city of San Francisco, there is no reason to believe that the sexual abuse of female children would be any more prevalent there than in other cities of comparable size. Assuming that the findings are indicative of the prevalence of child sexual abuse in other areas, this means that over one quarter of the population of female children have experienced sexual abuse before the age of 14, and well over one third have had such an experience by the age of 18 years. Furthermore, this study confirms the fact that only a minute percentage of cases ever get reported to the police (2% of intrafamilial and 6% of extrafamilial child sexual abuse cases). It is imperative that the magnitude of this problem in the United States be addressed, and it is urgent that more effective preventive strategies be developed and implemented.

▌ NOTES AND REFERENCES ▌

1. FINKELHOR, D. *Sexually Victimized Children.* The Free Press, New York (1979).

2. MRAZEK, P. B. and KEMPE, C. H. (Eds.), *Sexually Abused Children and their Families,* Pergamon Press, New York (1981) p. 12.

3. NATIONAL CENTER ON CHILD ABUSE AND NEGLECT, *Study Findings: National Study of the Incidence and Severity of Child Abuse and Neglect.* DHHS Pub. #(OHDS) 81-30325, Washington, D.C. (1981) pp. 4-5.

4. For purposes of this analysis, *incidence* will refer to cases of child sexual abuse that occurred within a specified period of time, and *prevalence* will refer to the percentage of children victimized by such an experience, whether once or many times.

5. WEINBERG, S. K. *Incest Behavior.* Citadel Press, Secaucus, NJ (1955, rev. 1976).

6. FERRACUTI, F. Incest between father and daughter. In: *Sexual Behaviors,* H. L. P. Resnick and M. E. Wolfgang (Eds.), Little, Brown and Co., Boston (1972) pp. 169-183.

7. MEISELMAN, K. C. *Incest.* Jossey-Bass Publishers, San Francisco, CA (1978) pp. 45-49.

8. NATIONAL CENTER ON CHILD ABUSE AND NEGLECT, DHHS Pub. #(OHDS) 81-30325, p. 18.

9. NATIONAL CENTER ON CHILD ABUSE AND NEGLECT, DHHS Pub. #(OHDS) 81-30325, p. 22.

10. HERMAN, J. *Father-Daughter Incest.* Harvard University Press, Cambridge, MA (1981) p. 12.

11. A more detailed account of the methodology of this study is described in Russel, D. E. H. *Rape in Marriage.* Macmillan, New York (1982) pp. 27-41.

12. KINSEY, A. C., POMEROY, W. B., MARTIN, C. E. and GEBHARD, P. H. *Sexual Behavior in the Human Female.* W. B. Saunders Co., Philadelphia (1948).

13. MASTERS, W. H. and JOHNSON, V. *Human Sexual Response.* Little, Brown and Co., Boston (1966).

14. HITE, S. *The Hite Report: A Nationwide Study of Female Sexuality.* Dell Publishing, New York (1976).

15. The 40 cases of exploitive sexual contact between relatives where the respondent was 18 years or older when it started are excluded from this analysis of child sexual abuse.

16. GAGNON, J. Female child victims of sex offenses. *Social Problems 13:* 176-192 (1965).

17. LANDIS, J. T. Experience of 500 children with adult's sexual deviance. *Psychiatric Quarterly Supplement30:* 91-109 (1956).

18. PUBLIC EDUCATION AND RESEARCH COMMITTEE OF CALIFORNIA, *Sex Code of California: A Compendium.* Graphic Arts of Marin, Sausalito, CA (1973) p. 160.

19. The sections in parentheses were read by the interviewer only if the respondent had already mentioned a childhood sexual experience.

20. Obviously, authority figures such as medical physicians, employers, and professors are almost always much older adults in the case of children, as well as having authority by virtue of their profession. The criterion for determining whether someone qualified as a "much older adult" was not strictly based on the age of the perpetrator nor the age difference between this person and the victim. Instead, an attempt was made to ascertain, from

what respondents said, what had determined the perpetrators' status as an authority figure in their eyes. While this method is somewhat subjective, both on the part of the coders and the respondents, this seemed less disadvantageous than applying age criteria that, while "objective," are arbitrary and whose meaning may be dubious.

21. Although step-, adoptive and foster fathers are included in the same category, experiences with only one foster father and one adoptive father were reported.

22. These figures add to 101% because of rounding to the nearest whole number.

23. FINKELHOR, D., *Sexually Victimized Children,* p. 86.

24. FINKELHOR, D., *Sexually Victimized Children,* Table 6-1, p. 87.

25. FINKELHOR, D., *Sexually Victimized Children,* p. 178.

26. FINKELHOR, D., *Sexually Victimized Children,* p. 84.

27. FINKELHOR, D., *Sexually Victimized Children,* p. 88.

The Child Sexual Abuse Accommodation Syndrome

ROLAND C. SUMMIT   1983

When Roland Summit's paper appeared in 1983, it helped us to understand and accept the complex position in which the child victim is placed and, in particular, to understand why a child who has revealed sexual abuse may later deny that it occurred. Summit described five stages: first, the secrecy in which the abuse occurs; second, the helplessness of the child, who is required to be obedient to an adult entrusted with that child's care, and the threats the abuser uses to maintain secrecy; third, the entrapment and accommodation, where the child has no option but to learn to accept the situation and accommodate to the reality of continuing and escalating sexual abuse, and where the child has both the power to destroy the family and the responsibility to hold it together; fourth, the disclosure, which is delayed, complicated, and unconvincing; and a fifth phase of retraction, where the enormous family pressures on the child may lead the child to decide that the only course left is to say that the abuse did not happen after all.

David Chadwick says that if any single publication can be selected as the most important and defining one for the issue of child sexual abuse in the 20th century, this is the one. He points out that, for the first time, Summit explores in detail the variety of predicaments faced by children who are sexually exploited by people who also hold power over them and who give them other forms of sustenance and support. This paper allows us to see the dilemma through the child's eyes and to learn that all of the options available to the child are unattractive.

A. C. D. and K. O.

Child sexual abuse has exploded into public awareness during a span of less than 5 years. More than 30 books [1-34] on the subject have appeared, as well as a flood of newspapers, magazines, and television features. According to a survey conducted by Finkelhor [35], almost all American respondents recalled some media discussion of child sexual abuse during the previous year.

The summary message in this explosion of information is that sexual abuse of children is much more common and more damaging to individuals and to society than has even been acknowledged by clinical or social scientists. Support for these assertions comes from first-person accounts and from the preliminary findings of specialized sexual abuse treatment programs. There is an understandable skepticism among scientists and a reluctance to accept such unprecedented claims from such biased samples. There is also a predictable counterassertion that while child sexual contacts with adults may be relatively common, the invisibility of such contacts proves that the experience for the child is not uniformly harmful but rather neutral or even beneficial [20, 36-40]. Whatever the merits of the various arguments, it should be clear that any child trying to cope with a sexualized relationship with an adult faces an uncertain and highly variable response from whatever personal or professional resources are enlisted for help.

The explosion of interest creates new hazards for the child victim of sexual abuse since it increases the likelihood of discovery but fails to protect the victim against the secondary assaults of an inconsistent intervention system. The identified child victim encounters an adult world which gives grudging acknowledgment to an abstract concept of child sexual abuse but which challenges and represses the child who presents a specific complaint of victimization. Adult beliefs are dominated by an entrenched and self-protective mythology that passes for common sense. "Everybody knows" that

adults must protect themselves from groundless accusations of seductive or vindictive young people. An image persists of nubile adolescents playing dangerous games out of their burgeoning sexual fascination. What everybody does not know, and would not want to know, is that the vast majority of investigated accusations prove valid and that most of the young people were less than 8 years old at the time of initiation.

Rather than being calculating or practiced, the child is most often fearful, tentative, and confused about the nature of the continuing sexual experience and the outcome of disclosure. If a respectable, reasonable adult is accused of perverse, assaultive behavior by an uncertain, emotionally distraught child, most adults who hear the accusation will fault the child. Disbelief and rejection by potential adult caretakers increase the helplessness, hopelessness, isolation, and self-blame that make up the most damaging aspects of child sexual victimization. Victims looking back are usually more embittered toward those who rejected their pleas than toward the one who initiated the sexual experiences. When no adult intervenes to acknowledge the reality of the abusive experience or to fix responsibility on the offending adult, there is a reinforcement of the child's tendency to deal with the trauma as an intrapsychic event and to incorporate a monstrous apparition of guilt, self-blame, pain, and rage.

Acceptance and validation are crucial to the psychological survival of the victim. A child molested by a father or other male in the role of parent and rejected by the mother is psychologically orphaned and almost defenseless against multiple harmful consequences. On the other hand, a mother who can advocate for the child and protect against reabuse seems to confer on the child the power to be self-endorsing and to recover with minimum sequellae [22,41].

Without professional or self-help group intervention, most parents are not prepared to be-

Originally published in *Child Abuse and Neglect,* 1983, Vol. 7, pp. 177-193. Reprinted by permission of Elsevier Science.

lieve their child in the face of convincing denials from a responsible adult. Since the majority of adults who molest children occupy a kinship or a trusted relationship [8,22,49,50], the child is put on the defensive for attacking the credibility of the trusted adult and for creating a crisis of loyalty which defies comfortable resolution. At a time when the child most needs love, endorsement, and exculpation, the unprepared parent typically responds with horror, rejection, and blame [22,42].

The mental health professional occupies a pivotal role in the crisis of disclosure. Since the events depicted by the child are so often perceived as incredible, skeptical caretakers turn to experts for clarification. In present practice, it is not unusual for clinical evaluation to stigmatize legitimate victims as either confused or malicious. Often, one evaluation will endorse the child's claims and convince prosecutors that criminal action is appropriate, while an adversary evaluation will certify the normalcy of the defendant and convince a judge or jury that the child lied. In a crime where there is usually no third-party eyewitness and no physical evidence, the verdict, the validation of the child's perception of reality, acceptance by adult caretakers, and even the emotional survival of the child may all depend on the knowledge and skill of the clinical advocate. Every clinician must be capable of understanding and articulating the position of the child in the prevailing adult imbalance of credibility. Without awareness of the child's reality, the professional will tend to reflect traditional mythology and to give the stamp of scientific authority to continuing stigmatization of the child.

Clinical study of large numbers of children and their parents in proven cases of sexual abuse provides emphatic contradictions to traditional views. What emerges is a typical behavior pattern or syndrome of mutually dependent variables which allows for immediate survival of the child within the family but which tends to isolate the child from eventual acceptance, credibility, or empathy within the larger society. The mythology and protective

denial surrounding sexual abuse can be seen as a natural consequence, both of the stereotypic coping mechanisms of the child victim and the need of almost all adults to insulate themselves from the painful realities of childhood victimization.

The accommodation process intrinsic to the world of child sexual abuse inspires prejudice and rejection in any adult who chooses to remain aloof from the helplessness and pain of the child's dilemma or who expects that a child should behave in accordance with adult concepts of self-determinism and autonomous, rational choices. Without a clear understanding of the accommodation syndrome, clinical specialists tend to reinforce the comforting belief that children are only rarely legitimate victims of unilateral sexual abuse and that among the few complaints that surface, most can be dismissed as fantasy, confusion, or a displacement of the child's own wish for power and seductive conquest.

Clinical awareness of the sexual abuse accommodation syndrome is essential to provide a counterprejudicial explanation to the otherwise self-camouflaging and self-stigmatizing behavior of the victim.

The purpose of this paper then, is to provide a vehicle for a more sensitive, more therapeutic response to legitimate victims of child sexual abuse and to invite more active, more effective clinical advocacy for the child within the family and within the systems of child protection and criminal justice.

SOURCES AND VALIDITY

This study draws in part from statistically validated assumptions regarding prevalence, age relationships, and role characteristics of child sexual abuse and in part from correlations and observations that have emerged as self-evident within an extended network of child abuse treatment programs and self-help organizations. The validity of the accommodation syndrome as defined here has been tested over a period of 4 years in the author's practice, which specializes in community consultation to diverse clinical and para-clinical sexual abuse programs. The syndrome has elicited strong endorsements from experienced professionals and from victims, offenders, and other family members.

Hundreds of training symposia shared with specialists throughout the United States and Canada have reached thousands of individuals who have had personal and/or professional involvement in sexual abuse. Discussion of the syndrome typically opens a floodgate of recognition of previously uncorrelated or disregarded observations. Adults who have guarded a shameful secret for a lifetime find permission to remember and to discuss their childhood victimization. Family members who have disowned identified victims find a basis for compassion and reunion. Children still caught up in secrecy and self-blame find hope for advocacy. And professionals who had overlooked indications of sexual abuse find a new capacity for recognition and involvement.

A syndrome should not be viewed as a procrustean bed which defines and dictates a narrow perception of something as complex as child sexual abuse. Just as the choice to sexualize the relationship with a child includes a broad spectrum of adults acting under widely diverse motivations and rationalizations [43], the options for the child are also variable. A child who seeks help immediately or who gains effective intervention should not be discarded as contradictory, any more than the syndrome should be disregarded if it fails to include every possible variant. The syndrome represents a common denominator of the most frequently observed victim behaviors.

In the current state of the art, most of the victims available for study are young females molested by adult males entrusted with their care. Young male victims are at least as frequent, just as helpless, and even more secretive than young females [9,44,45].

Because of the extreme reluctance of males to admit to sexual victimization experiences and because of the greater probability that a boy will be molested by someone outside the nuclear family, less is known about possible variations in accommodation mechanisms of sexually abused males. Various aspects of secrecy, helplessness, and self-alienation seem to apply, as does an even greater isolation from validation and endorsement by incredulous parents and other adults. There is an almost universal assumption that a man who molests a boy must be homosexual. Since the habitual molester of boys is rarely attracted to adult males [46], he finds ready exoneration in clinical examination and character endorsements. While there is some public capacity to believe that girls may be helpless victims of sexual abuse, there is almost universal repudiation of the boy victim.

For the sake of brevity and clarity, the child sexual abuse accommodation syndrome is presented in this paper as it applies to the most typical female victim. There is no intent to minimize nor to exclude the substantial hardships of male victims or to ignore the conspicuously small minority of offenders who are female. A more comprehensive discussion of role variants within an extended syndrome is presented elsewhere [47]. In the following discussion the feminine pronoun is used generically for the child rather than the more cumbersome he/she. This convention is not meant to discourage application of the accommodation syndrome to male victims or to the shared experience of males and female co-victims wherever clinical experience indicates appropriate correlations.

THE CHILD SEXUAL ABUSE ACCOMMODATION SYNDROME

The syndrome includes five categories, two of which are preconditions to the occurrence of sexual abuse. The remaining three categories are sequential contingencies which take on increasing variability and complexity. While it can be shown that each category reflects a compelling reality for the victim, each category represents also a contradiction to the most common assumptions of adults. The five categories of the syndrome are:

1. Secrecy
2. Helplessness
3. Entrapment and accommodation
4. Delayed, conflicted, and unconvincing disclosure
5. Retraction

Secrecy

Initiation, intimidation, stigmatization, isolation, helplessness, and self-blame depend on a terrifying reality of child sexual abuse: It happens only when the child is alone with the offending adult, and it must never be shared with anyone else.

Virtually no child is prepared for the possibility of molestation by a trusted adult; that possibility is a well-kept secret, even among adults. The child is, therefore, entirely dependent on the intruder for whatever reality is assigned to the experience. Of all the inadequate, illogical, self-serving, or self-protective explanations provided by the adult, the only consistent and meaningful impression gained by the child is one of danger and fearful outcome based on secrecy [22,48]. "This is our secret; nobody else will understand." "Don't tell anybody." "Nobody will believe you." "Don't tell your mother; (a) she will hate you, (b) she will hate me, (c) she will kill you, (d) she will kill me, (e) it will kill her, (f) she will send you away (g) she will send me away, or (h) it will break up the family and you'll all end up in an orphanage." "If you tell anyone (a) I won't love you anymore, (b) I'll spank you, (c) I'll kill your dog, or (d) I'll kill you."

However gentle or menacing the intimidation may be, the secrecy makes it clear to the child that this is something bad and dangerous. The secrecy is both the source of fear and the promise of safety: "Everything will be all right if you just don't tell." The secret takes on magical, monstrous proportions for the child. A child with no knowledge or awareness of sex and even with no pain or embarrassment from the sexual experience itself will still be stigmatized with a sense of badness and danger from the pervasive secrecy.

Any attempts by the child to illuminate the secret will be countered by an adult conspiracy of silence and disbelief. "Don't worry about things like that; that could never happen in our family." "Nice children don't talk about things like that." "Uncle Johnnie doesn't mean you any harm; that's just his way of showing how he loves you." "How could you ever think of such a terrible thing?" "Don't let me ever hear you say anything like that again!"

The average child never asks and never tells. Contrary to the general expectation that the victim would normally seek help, the majority of the victims in retrospective surveys had never told anyone during their childhood [22,42,49,50]. Respondents expressed fear that they would be blamed for what had happened or that a parent would not be able to protect them from retaliation. Many of those who sought help reported that parents became hysterical or punishing or pretended that nothing had happened [42].

Yet, adult expectation dominates the judgment applied to disclosures of sexual abuse. When the child does not immediately complain, it is painfully apparent to any child that there is no second chance. "Why didn't you tell me?" "How could you keep such a thing secret?" "What are you trying to hide?" "Why did you wait until now if it really happened so long ago?" "How can you expect me to believe such a fantastic story?"

Unless the victim can find some permission and power to share the secret, and unless there is the possibility of an engaging, non-punitive response to disclosure, the child is likely to spend a lifetime in what comes to be a self-imposed exile from intimacy, trust, and self-validation.

Helplessness

The adult expectation of child self-protection and immediate disclosure ignores the basic subordination and helplessness of children within authoritarian relationships. Children may be given permission to avoid the attentions of strangers, but they are required to be obedient and affectionate with any adult entrusted with their care. Strangers, "weirdos," kidnappers, and other monsters provide a convenient foil for both child and parent against a much more dreadful and immediate risk: the betrayal of vital relationships, abandonment by trusted caretakers, and annihilation of basic family security. All available research is remarkably consistent in a discomforting statistic: A child is three times more likely to be molested by a recognized, trusted adult than by a stranger [9,42,44,50]. The risk is not at all remote. Even the most conservative survey implies that about 10% of all females have been sexually victimized as children by an adult relative, including almost 2% involving the man in the role of father [42]. The latest and most representative survey reports a 16% prevalence of molestation by relatives. Fully 4.6% of the 930 women interviewed reported an incestuous relationship with their father or father-figure [50].

A corollary to the expectation of self-protection is the general assumption that uncomplaining children are acting in a consenting relationship. This expectation is dubious even for the mythic seductive adolescent. Given the assumption that an adolescent can be sexually attractive, seductive, and even deliberately provocative, it should be clear that no child has equal power to say no to a parental figure or to anticipate the consequences of sexual involvement with an adult caretaker. Ordinary ethics demand that the adult in such a mismatch bear sole responsibility for any clandestine sexual activity with a minor [51].

In reality, though, the child partner is most often neither sexually attractive nor seductive in any conventional sense. The stereotype of the seductive adolescent is an artifact both of delayed disclosure and a prevailing adult wish to define child sexual abuse within a a model that approximates logical adult behavior.

We can believe that a man might normally be attracted to a nubile child-woman. Only perversion could explain attraction to an undeveloped girl or boy, and the men implicated in most ongoing sexual molestations are quite obviously not perverted. They tend to be hardworking, devoted family men. They may be better educated, more law-abiding, and more religious than average.

As clinical experience in child sexual intervention has increased, the reported age of initiation has decreased. In 1979, a typical average was a surprisingly prepubescent 9 years. By 1981, the federally funded national training models reported the average age of initiation as 7 years [52]. At the Harborview Sexual Assault Center in Seattle, 25% of the children presenting for treatment are 5 years of age or younger [53].

The prevailing reality for the most frequent victim of child sexual abuse is not a street or school-ground experience and not some mutual vulnerability to oedipal temptations, but an unprecedented, relentlessly progressive intrusion of sexual acts by an overpowering adult in a one-sided victim-perpetrator relationship. The fact that the perpetrator is often in a trusted and apparently loving position only increases the imbalance of power and underscores the helplessness of the child.

Children often describe their first experiences as waking up to find their father (or stepfather, or mother's live-in companion) exploring their bodies with hands or mouth. Less frequently, they may find a penis filling their mouth or probing between their legs. Society allows the child one acceptable set of reactions to such an experience. Like the adult victim of rape, the child victim is expected to forcibly resist, to cry for help, and to attempt to escape the intrusion. By that standard, almost every child fails.

The normal reaction is to "play possum," that is to feign sleep, to shift position, and to pull up the covers. Small creatures simply do not call on force to deal with overwhelming threat. When there is no place to run, they have no choice but to try to hide. Children generally learn to cope silently with terrors in the night. Bed covers take on magical powers against monsters, but they are no match for human intruders.

It is sad to hear children attacked by attorneys and discredited by juries because they claimed to be molested yet admitted they had made no protest nor outcry. The point to emphasize here is not so much the miscarriage of justice as the continuing assault on the child. If the child's testimony is rejected in court, there is more likely to be a rejection by the mother and other relatives, who may be eager to restore trust in the accused adult and to brand the child as malicious. Clinical experience and expert testimony can provide advocacy for the child. Children are easily ashamed and intimidated both by their helplessness and by their inability to communicate their feelings to uncomprehending adults. They need an adult clinical advocate to translate the child's world into an adult-acceptable language.

The intrinsic helplessness of a child clashes with the cherished adult sense of free will. Adults need careful guidance to risk empathizing with the absolute powerlessness of the child; they have spent years repressing and distancing themselves from that horror. Adults tend to despise helplessness and to condemn anyone who submits too easily to intimidation. A victim will be judged as a willing accomplice unless compliance was achieved through overwhelming force or threat of violence. Adults must be reminded that the wordless action or gesture of a parent is an absolutely compelling force for a dependent child, and the threat of loss of love or loss of family security is more frightening to the child than any threat of violence.

Questions of free will and compliance are not just legal rhetoric. It is necessary for the emotional survival of the child that adult custodians give permission and endorsement to the helplessness and noncomplicity of the initiate's role. Adult prejudice is contagious. Without a consistent therapeutic affirmation of innocence, the victim tends to become filled with self-condemnation and self-hate for somehow inviting and allowing the sexual assaults.

As an advocate for the child, both in therapy and in court, it is necessary to recognize that no matter what the circumstances, the child had no choice but to submit quietly and to keep the secret. No matter if mother was in the next room or if siblings were asleep in the same bed. The more illogical and incredible the initiation might seem to adults, the more likely it is that the child's plaintive description is valid. A caring father would not logically act as the child describes; if nothing else, it seems incredible that he would take such flamboyant risks. That logical analysis contains at least two naive assumptions: (1) the molestation is thoughtful and (2) it is risky. Molestation of a child is not a thoughtful gesture of caring but a desperate, compulsive search for acceptance and submission [54]. There is very little risk of discovery if the child is young enough and if there is an established relationship of authority and affection. Men who seek children as sexual partners discover quickly something that remains incredible to less impulsive adults: Dependent children are helpless to resist or to complain.

A letter to Ann Landers illustrates very well the continuing helplessness and pervasive secrecy associated with incestuous abuse:

Dear Ann:

Last week my 32-year-old sister told me she had been sexually molested by our father from age 6 to 16. I was stunned because for 20 years I had kept the same secret from anyone. I am now 30. We decided to talk to our three other sisters, all in their 20's. It turned out that our father had sexually molested each and every one of us. We all thought we were being singled out for that humiliating, ugly experience, and were too ashamed and frightened to tell anyone, so we all kept our mouths shut.

Father is now 53. To look at him, you would think he was the all-American dad. Mom is 51. She would die if she had any idea of what he had been doing to his daughters all these years. [55]

Entrapment and Accommodation

For the child within a dependent relationship, sexual molestation is not typically a one-time occurrence. The adult may be racked with regrets, guilt, fear, and resolutions to stop, but the forbidden quality of the experience and the unexpected ease of accomplishment seem to invite repetition. A compulsive, addictive pattern tends to develop which continues either until the child achieves autonomy or until discovery and forcible prohibition overpower the secret [22].

If the child did not seek or did not receive immediate protective intervention, there is no further option to stop the abuse. The only healthy option left for the child is to learn to accept the situation and to survive. There is no way out, no place to run. The healthy, normal, emotionally resilient child will learn to accommodate to the reality of continuing sexual abuse. There is the challenge of accommodating not only to escalating sexual demands but to an increasing consciousness of betrayal and objectification by someone who is ordinarily idealized as a protective, altruistic, loving parental figure. Much of what is eventually labeled as adolescent or adult psychopathology can be traced to the natural reactions of a healthy child to a profoundly unnatural and unhealthy parental environment. Pathological dependency, self-punishment, self-mutilation, selective restructuring of reality, and multiple personalities, to name a few, represent habitual vestiges of painfully learned childhood survival skills. In dealing with the accommodation mechanisms of the child or the vestigial scars of the adult survivor, the therapist must take care to avoid reinforcing a sense of badness, inadequacy, or craziness by condemning or stigmatizing the symptoms.

The child faced with continuing helpless victimization must learn to somehow achieve a sense of power and control. The child cannot safely conceptualize that a parent might be ruthless and self-serving; such a conclusion is tantamount to abandonment and annihilation. The only acceptable alternative for the child is to believe that she has provoked the painful encounters and to hope that by learning to be good she can earn love and acceptance. The desperate assumption of responsibility and the inevitable failure to earn relief set the foundation for self-hate and what Shengold [56] describes as a vertical split in reality testing.

> If the very parent who abuses and is experienced as *bad* must be turned to for relief of the distress that the parent has caused, then the child must, out of desperate need, register the parent—*delusionally*—as good. Only the mental image of a good parent can help the child deal with the terrifying intensity of fear and rage which is the effect of the tormenting experiences. The alternative—the maintenance of the overwhelming stimulation and the bad parental imago—means annihilation of identity, of the feeling of the self. So the bad has to be registered as good. This is a mind-splitting or a mind fragmenting operation. [56]

Shengold's use of the word *delusionally* does not assume a psychotic process or a defect in perception but rather the practiced ability to reconcile contradictory realities. As he continues later on the same page,

> I am not describing schizophrenia . . . but the establishment of isolated divisions of the mind that provides the mechanism for a pattern in which contradictory images of the self and of the parents are never permitted to coalesce. (This compartmentalized 'vertical splitting' transcends diagnostic categories; I am deliberately avoiding bringing in the correlatable pathological formations of Winnicott, Kohut, and Kernberg.) [56]

The sexually abusing parent provides graphic example and instruction in how to be good, that is, the child must be available without complaint to the parent's sexual demands.

There is an explicit or implicit promise of reward. If she is good and if she keeps the secret, she can protect her siblings from sexual involvement ("It's a good thing I can count on you to love me; otherwise I'd have to turn to your little sister"), protect her mother from disintegration ("If your mother ever found out, it would kill her"), protect her father from temptation ("If I couldn't count on you, I'd have to hang out in bars and look for other women"), and, most vitally, preserve the security of the home ("If you ever tell, they could send me to jail and put all you kids in an orphanage").

In the classic role reversal of child abuse, the child is given the power to destroy the family and the responsibility to keep it together. The child, *not the parent,* must mobilize the altruism and self-control to insure the survival of the others. The child, in short, must secretly assume many of the role functions ordinarily assigned to the mother.

There is an inevitable splitting of conventional moral values. Maintaining a lie to keep the secret is the ultimate virtue, while telling the truth would be the greatest sin. A child thus victimized will appear to accept or to seek sexual contact without complaint.

Since the child must structure her reality to protect the parent, she also finds the means to build pockets of survival where some hope of goodness can find sanctuary. She may turn to imaginary companions for reassurance. She may develop multiple personalities, assigning helplessness and suffering to one, badness and rage to another, sexual power to another love and compassion to another, and so on. She may discover altered states of consciousness to shut off pain or to dissociate from her body, as if looking on from a distance at the child suffering the abuse. The same mechanisms which allow psychic survival for the child become handicaps to effective psychological integration as an adult.

If the child cannot create a psychic economy to reconcile the continuing outrage, the intolerance of helplessness and the increasing feeling of rage will seek active expression. For the girl, this often leads to self-destruction and reinforcement of self-hate; self-mutilation, suicidal behavior, promiscuous sexual activity, and repeated runaways are typical. She may learn to exploit the father for privileges, favors, and material rewards, reinforcing her self-punishing image as "whore" in the process. She may fight with both parents, but her greatest rage is likely to focus on her mother, whom she blames for abandoning her to her father. She assumes that her mother must know of the sexual abuse and is either too uncaring or too ineffectual to intervene. Ultimately, the child tends to believe that she is intrinsically so rotten that she was never worth caring for. The failure of the mother-daughter bond reinforces the young woman's distrust of herself as a female and makes her all the more dependent on the pathetic hope of gaining acceptance and protection with an abusive male.

For many victims of sexual abuse, the rage incubates over years of facade, coping, and frustrating, counterfeit attempts at intimacy, only to erupt as a pattern of abuse against offspring in the next generation. The ungratifying, imperfect behavior of the young child and the diffusion of ego boundaries between parent and child invite projection of the bad introject and provide a righteous, impulsive outlet for the explosive rage.

The male victim of sexual abuse is more likely to turn his rage outward in aggressive and antisocial behavior. He is even more intolerant of his helplessness than the female victim and more likely to rationalize that he is exploiting the relationship for his own benefit. He may cling so tenaciously to an idealized relationship with the adult that he remains fixed at a preadolescent level of sexual object choice, as if trying to keep love alive with an unending succession of young boys. Various admixtures of depression, counterphobic violence, misogyny (again, the mother is seen as non-caring and unprotective), child molestation, and rape seem to be part of the legacy of rage endowed in the sexually abused boy [45].

Substance abuse is an inviting avenue of escape for the victim of either gender. As Myers recalls: "On drugs, I could be anything I wanted to be. I could make up my own reality: I could be pretty, have a good family, a nice father, a strong mother, and be happy . . . drinking had the opposite effect of drugs. . . . Drinking got me back into my pain; it allowed me to experience my hurt and my anger" [57].

It is worth restating that all these accommodation mechanisms—domestic martyrdom, splitting of reality, altered consciousness, hysterical phenomena, delinquency, sociopathy, projection of rage, even self-mutilation—are part of the survival skills of the child. They can be overcome only if the child can be led to trust in a secure environment which can provide consistent, *noncontigent* acceptance and caring. In the meantime, anyone working therapeutically with the child (or the grown-up, still-shattered victim) may be tested and provoked to prove that trust is impossible [22] and that the only secure reality is negative expectations and self-hate. It is all too easy for the would-be therapist to join the parents and all of adult society in rejecting such a child, looking at the results of abuse to assume that such an "impossible wretch" must have asked for and deserved whatever punishment had occurred, if indeed the whole problem is not a hysterical or vengeful fantasy.

Delayed, Conflicted, and Unconvincing Disclosure

Most ongoing sexual abuse is never disclosed, at least not outside the immediate family [8,22,49,50]. Treated, reported, or investigated cases are the exception, not the norm. Disclosure is an outgrowth either of overwhelming family conflict, incidental discovery by a third party, or sensitive outreach and community education by child protective agencies.

If family conflict triggers disclosure, it is usually only after some years of continuing sexual abuse and an eventual breakdown of accommodation mechanisms. The victim of incestuous abuse tends to remain silent until she enters adolescence, when she becomes capable of demanding a more separate life for herself and challenging the authority of her parents. Adolescence also makes the father more jealous and controlling, trying to sequester his daughter against the "dangers" of outside peer involvement. The corrosive effects of accommodation seem to justify any extreme of punishment. What parent would not impose severe restrictions to control running away, drug abuse, promiscuity, rebellion, and delinquency?

After an especially punishing family fight and a belittling showdown of authority by the father, the girl is finally driven by anger to let go of the secret. *She seeks understanding and intervention at the very time she is least likely to find them.* Authorities are alienated by the pattern of delinquency and rebellious anger expressed by the girl. Most adults confronted with such a history tend to identify with the problems of the parents in trying to cope with a rebellious teenager. They observe that the girl seems more angry about the immediate punishment than about the sexual atrocities she is alleging. They assume there is no truth to such a fantastic complaint, especially since the girl did not complain years ago when she claims she was forcibly molested. They assume she has invented the story in retaliation against the father's attempts to achieve reasonable control and discipline. The more unreasonable and abusive the triggering punishment, the more they assume the girl would do anything to get away, even to the point of falsely incriminating her father.

Unless specifically trained and sensitized, average adults, including mothers, relatives, teachers, counselors, doctors, psychotherapists, investigators, prosecutors, defense attorneys, judges, and jurors, cannot believe that a normal, truthful child would tolerate incest without immediately reporting or that an apparently normal father could be capable of repeated, unchallenged sexual molestation of his own daughter. The child of any age faces an unbelieving audience when she complains of ongoing sexual abuse. The troubled, angry adolescent risks not only disbelief but scapegoating, humiliation, and punishment as well.

Not all complaining adolescents appear angry and unreliable. An alternative accommodation pattern exists in which the child succeeds in hiding any indications of conflict. Such a child may be unusually achieving and popular, eager to please both teachers and peers. When the honor student or the captain of the football team tries to describe a history of ongoing sexual involvement with an adult, the adult reaction is all the more incredulous. "How could such a thing have happened to such a fine young person?" "No one so talented and well-adjusted could have been involved in something so sordid." Obviously, it did not happen or, if it did, it certainly did not harm the child.

So there is no real cause for complaint. Whether the child is delinquent, hypersexual, countersexual, suicidal, hysterical, psychotic, or perfectly well-adjusted, and whether the child is angry, evasive, or serene, the immediate affect and the adjustment pattern of the child will be interpreted by adults to invalidate the child's compliant.

Contrary to popular myth, most mothers are not aware of ongoing sexual abuse. Marriage demands considerable blind trust and denial for survival. A woman does not commit her life and security to a man she believes capable of molesting his own children. The "obvious" clues to sexual abuse are usually obvious only in retrospect. Our assumption that the mother "must have known" merely parallels the demand of the child that the mother must be in touch intuitively with invisible and even deliberately concealed family discomfort.

The mother typically reacts to allegations of sexual abuse with disbelief and protective denial. How could she not have known? How could the child wait so long to tell her? What kind of mother could allow such a thing to happen? What would the neighbors think? As someone substantially dependent on the approval and generosity of the father, the mother in the incestuous triangle is confronted with a mind-splitting dilemma analogous to that of the abused child. Either the child is bad and deserving of punishment, or the father is bad and unfairly punitive. One of them is lying and unworthy of trust. The mother's whole security and life adjustment and much of her sense of adult self-worth demand a trust in the reliability of her partner. To accept the alternative means annihilation of the family and a large piece of her own identity. Her fear and ambivalence are reassured by the father's logical challenge, "Are you going to believe that lying little slut? Can you believe I would do such a thing? How could something like that go on right under your nose for years? You know we can't trust her out of our sight anymore. Just when we try to clamp down and I get a little rough with her, she comes back with a ridiculous story like this. That's what I get for trying to keep her out of trouble."

Of the minority of incest secrets that are disclosed to the mother or discovered by the mother, very few are subsequently reported to outside agencies [50]. The mother will either disbelieve the complaint or try to negotiate a resolution within the family. Now that professionals are required to report any suspicion of child abuse, increasing numbers of complaints are investigated by protective agencies. Police investigators and protective service workers are likely to give credence to the complaint, in which case all the children may be removed immediately into protective custody pending hearing of a dependency petition. In the continuing paradox of a divided judicial system, the juvenile court judge is likely to sustain out-of-home placement in the "preponderance of the evidence" that the child is in danger, while no charges are even filed in the adult court which would consider the father's criminal responsibility. Attorneys know that the uncorroborated testimony of a child will not convict a respectable adult. The test in criminal court requires specific proof "beyond a reasonable doubt," and every reasonable adult juror will have reason to doubt the child's fantastic claims. Prosecutors are reluctant to subject the child to humiliating cross-examination just as they are loath to prosecute cases they cannot win. Therefore, they typically reject the complaint on the basis of insufficient evidence.

Out-of-family molesters are also effectively immune from incrimination if they have any amount of prestige. Even if several children have complained, their testimony will be impeached by trivial discrepancies in their accounts or by the countercharge that the children were willing and seductive conspirators.

The absence of criminal charges is tantamount to a conviction of perjury against the victim. "A man is innocent until proven guilty," say adult-protective relatives. "The kid claimed to be molested but there was nothing to it. The police investigated and they didn't even file charges." Unless there is expert advocacy for the child in the criminal court, the child is likely to be abandoned as the helpless custodian of a self-incriminating secret which no responsible adult can believe.

The psychiatrist or other counseling specialist has a crucial role in early detection, treatment intervention, and expert courtroom advocacy. The specialist must help mobilize skeptical caretakers into a position of belief, acceptance, support, and protection of the child. The specialist must first be capable of assuming that same position. The counselor who learns to accept the secrecy, the helplessness, the accommodation, and the delayed disclosure may still be alienated by the fifth level of the accommodation syndrome.

Retraction

Whatever a child says about sexual abuse, she is likely to reverse it. Beneath the anger of impulsive disclosure remains the ambivalence of guilt and the martyred obligation to preserve the family. In the chaotic aftermath of disclosure, the child discovers that the bedrock fears and threats underlying the secrecy are true. Her father abandons her and calls her a liar. Her mother does not believe her or decompensates into hysteria and rage. The family is fragmented, and all the children are placed in custody. The father is threatened with disgrace and imprisonment. The girl is blamed for causing the whole mess, and everyone seems to treat her like a freak. She is interrogated about all the tawdry details and encouraged to incriminate her father, yet the father remains unchallenged, remaining at home in the security of the family. She is held in custody with no apparent hope of returning home if the dependency petition is sustained.

The message from the mother is very clear, often explicit. "Why do you insist on telling those awful stories about your father? If you send him to prison, we won't be a family anymore. We'll end up on welfare with no place to stay. Is that what *you* want to do to us?"

Once again, the child bears the responsibility of either preserving or destroying the family. The role reversal continues, with the "bad" choice being to tell the truth and the "good" choice being to capitulate and restore a lie for the sake of the family.

Unless there is special support for the child and immediate intervention to force responsibility on the father, the girl will follow the "normal" course and retract her complaint. The girl "admits" she made up the story. "I was awful mad at my dad for punishing me. He hit me and said I could never see my boyfriend again. I've been really bad for years and nothing seems to keep me from getting into trouble. Dad had plenty of reason to be mad at me. But I got real mad and just had to find some way of getting out of that place. So I made up this story about him fooling around with me and everything. I didn't mean to get everyone in so much trouble."

This simple lie carries more credibility than the most explicit claims of incestuous entrapment. It confirms adult expectations that children cannot be trusted. It restores the precarious equilibrium of the family. The children learn not to complain. The adults learn not to listen. And the authorities learn not to believe rebellious children who try to use their sexual power to destroy well-meaning parents.

DISCUSSION

It should be obvious that, left unchallenged, the sexual abuse accommodation syndrome tends to reinforce both the victimization of children and societal complacency and indifference to the dimensions of that victimization. It should be obvious to clinicians that the power to challenge and to interrupt the accommodation process carries an unprecedented potential for primary prevention of emotional pain and disability, including an interruption in the intergenerational chain of child abuse.

What is not so obvious is that mental health specialists may be more skeptical of reports of sexual abuse and more hesitant to involve themselves as advocates for children than many professionals with less specific training. The apparent cause-and-effect relationships and the emphasis on unilateral intrusions by powerful adults may seem naive and regressive to anyone trained in more sophisticated family dynamics, where events are viewed as an equilibrium of needs and provocations within the system as a whole [58]. Freud led a trend from the victim-perpetrator concept to a more universal and intellectually stimulating view in 1897 when he renounced his own child seduction theory of hysteria for the seductive child thesis of the Oedipus complex [16, 59-61]. Even if a substantial number of descriptions of sexual victimization prove to be valid, how can they be distinguished from those that should be treated as fantasy or deception? Rosenfeld [62] has addressed these questions in a general sense, but a nagging uncertainty persists.

The victim of child sexual abuse is in a position somewhat analogous to that of the adult rape victim prior to 1974. Without a consistent clinical understanding of the psychological climate and adjustment patterns of rape, women were assumed to be provocative and substantially responsible for inviting or exposing themselves to the risk of attack. The fact that most women chose not to report their own victimization only confirmed the unchallenged suspicion that they had something to hide. Those who reported often regretted their decision, as they found themselves subjected to repeated attacks on their character and credibility.

The turnaround for adult victims came with publication of a landmark paper in the clinical literature during a time of aroused protest led by the women's movement. *Rape Trauma Syndrome* by Burgess and Holmstrom appeared in 1974 [63]. It provided guidelines for recognition and management of the traumatic psychological sequellae and established a logical sequence of the victim's shame, self-blame, and secrecy, which so typically camouflaged the attack. Its publication initiated what proved to be a trend toward more sympathetic reception of rape victims both in clinics and in courts.

A similar reception is long overdue for juvenile victims [24]. Ironically, the same clinical study that defined the rape trauma syndrome led the authors to describe a related set of circumstances observed in children treated within the Boston Hospital Victim Counseling Program. *Sexual Trauma of Children and Adolescents: Pressure, Sex, and Secrecy* was published in 1975 [64]. The first paragraph concludes, "The emotional reactions of victims result from their being pressured into sexual activity and from the added tension of keeping the act secret."

The narrative describes the elements of helplessness and the pressure to maintain secrecy. The fear of rejection and disbelief is documented by poignant clinical vignettes, as are several mechanisms of accommodation and the traumatic effects of unsupported disclosure. The discussion challenges earlier studies indicating willing or seductive participation.

In reviewing our data on child and adolescent victims, we have tried to avoid traditional ways of viewing the problem and instead to describe, from the victim's point of view, the dynamics involved between offender and victim regarding the issues of inability to consent, adaptive behavior, secrecy, and the disclosure of the secret. . . . Our data clearly indicates that a syndrome of symptom reaction is the result of pressure to keep the activity secret as well as the result of the disclosure. . . . It may be speculated that there are many children with silent reaction to sexual trauma. The child who responds to the pressure to go along with the sexual activity with adults may be viewed as showing an adaptive response for survival in the environment. [65]

If there had been an aroused protest for protection of children in 1975, the vanguard observations of Burgess and Holmstrom might have marked a turnaround for more sympathetic reception of child victimization. Since child advocacy suffers in competition with adult interests, there has been at best an evolutionary rather than a revolutionary response within the clinical and judicial fields. It is, therefore, appropriate to recall the rape trauma syndrome as a model for increasing the sensitivity of counselors and of legal counselors and to restate the sexual trauma of children and adolescents as seen with an additional 8 years of multiagency experience and nationwide correlation.

CONCLUSION

Sexual abuse of children is not a new phenomenon, although its true dimensions are emerging only through recent awareness and study. Children have been subject to molestation, exploitation, and intimidation by supposed caretakers throughout history [66]. What is changing most in our present generation is the sensitivity to recognize exploitation, to identify blatant inequities in parenting among otherwise apparently adequate families, and to discover that such inequities have a substantial impact on the character development, personality integration and emotional well-being of the more deprived and mistreated children.

Freud could find no precedent in 1897 for any number of respectable parents victimizing their children. "Then there was the astonishing thing that in every case. . .blame was laid on perverse acts by the father, and the realization of the unexpected frequency of hysteria, in every case of which the same applied, though it was hardly credible that perverted acts against children were so general" [67].

In the 1980s, we can no longer afford to be incredulous of basic realities of child abuse. The growing body of literature emanating from the now classic paper, *The Battered Child Syndrome* [68], published in 1962, gives ample precedent and a 20-year perspective for the certain recognition that perverted acts against children are, in fact, so general.

Sexual molestation was called the last frontier in child abuse in 1975 by Sgroi, an internist, who was already in a position to identify the reluctance of many clinicians to accept the problem [69].

Recognition of sexual molestation in a child is entirely dependent on the individual's inherent willingness to entertain the possibility that the condition may exist. Unfortunately, willingness to consider the diagnosis of suspected child sexual molestation frequently seems to vary in inverse proportion to the individual's level of training. That is, the more advanced the training of some, the less willing they are to suspect molestation.

It is urgent, in the interests both of treatment and of legal advocacy and for the sake of primary, secondary, and tertiary prevention of diverse emotional disabilities, that clinicians in every field of the behavioral sciences be more aware of child sexual abuse. It is countertherapeutic and unjust to expose legitimate victims to evaluations or treatment by therapists who cannot suspect or "believe in" the possibility of unilateral sexual victimization of children by apparently normal adults.

The sexual abuse accommodation syndrome is derived from the collective experience of dozens of sexual abuse treatment centers in dealing with thousands of reports or complaints of adult victimization of young children. In the vast majority of these cases, the identified adult claimed total innocence or admitted only to trivial, well-meaning attempts at "sex education," wrestling, or affectionate closeness. After a time in treatment, the men almost invariably conceded that the child had told the truth. Of the children who were found to have misrepresented their complaints, most had sought to *understate* the frequency or duration of sexual experiences, even when reports were made in anger and in apparent retaliation against violence or humiliation. Very few children, no more than two or three per *thousand,* have ever been found to exaggerate or to invent claims of sexual molestation [70]. It has become a maxim among child sexual abuse intervention counselors and investigators that children never fabricate the kinds of explicit sexual manipulations they divulge in complaints or interrogations [8].

The clinician with an understanding of the child sexual abuse accommodation syndrome offers the child a right to parity with adults in the struggle for credibility and advocacy. Neither the victim, the offender, the family, the next generation of children in that family, nor the well-being of society as a whole can benefit from continuing secrecy and denial of ongoing sexual abuse. The offender who protects an uneasy position of power over the silent victims will not release his control unless he is confronted by an outside power sufficient to demand and to supervise a total cessation of sexual harassment [13, 22, 25, 32, 71].

The counselor alone cannot expect cooperation and recovery in an otherwise reluctant and unacknowledged offender. The justice system alone can rarely prove guilt or impose sanctions without preparation and continuing support of all parties within an effective treatment system. All agencies working as a team give maximum promise of effective recovery for the victim, rehabilitation of the offender, and survival of the family [24,71].

The child sexual abuse accommodation syndrome provides a common language for the several viewpoints of the intervention team and a more recognizable map to the last frontier in child abuse.

NOTES AND REFERENCES

1. ARMSTRONG, L. *Kiss Daddy Goodnight.* Hawthorn Books, New York (1978).
2. BURGESS, A., GROTH, A. N., HOLMSTROM, L. and SGROI, S. *Sexual Assault of Children and Adolescents.* Lexington Books, Lexington, MA (1978).
3. BUTLER, S. *Conspiracy of Silence.* New Glide Publications, San Francisco, CA (1978).
4. FORWARD, S. *Betrayal of Innocence.* Tarcher, New York (1978).
5. GEISER, R. *Hidden Victims.* Beacon, Boston (1978).
6. MEISELMAN, K. *Incest.* Jossey-Bass, San Francisco (1978).
7. BRADY, K. *Father's Days.* Seaview Books, New York (1979).
8. MULDOON, L. (Ed.). *Incest: Confronting the Silent Crime.* Minnesota Program for Victims of Sexual Assault, Saint Paul, MN (1979).
9. FINKELHOR, D. *Sexually Victimized Children.* Free Press, New York (1979).
10. JUSTICE, B. and JUSTICE, R. *The Broken Taboo.* Human Sciences Press, New York (1979).
11. SCHULTZ, L. *The Sexual Victimology of Youth.* Charles C Thomas, Springfield, IL (1979).
12. ALLEN, C. *Daddy's Girl.* Wyndham Books, New York (1980).
13. BULKLEY, J. and DAVIDSON, H. *Child Sexual Abuse-Legal Issues and Approaches.* American Bar Association, Washington, D.C. (1980).
14. MacFARLANE, K., JONES, B. and JENSTROM, L. (Eds.), *Sexual Abuse of Children: Selected Readings.* National Center on Child Abuse and Neglect, Office of Human Development Services, U.S. Department of Health and Human Services, Washington, D.C. (1980).
15. MRAZEK, P. B., and KEMPE, C. H. (Eds.), *Sexually Abused Children and their Families.* Pergamon, Oxford (1981).
16. RUSH, F. *The Best Kept Secret.* Prentice Hall, New York (1980).

17. SANFORD, L. *The Silent Children, A Parent's Guide to the Prevention of Child Sexual Abuse.* Anchor Press/Doubleday, New York (1980).

18. ADAMS, C. and FAY, J. *No More Secrets.* Impact Publishers, San Luis Obispo, CA (1981).

19. BULKLEY, J. (Ed.). *Child Sexual Abuse and the Law.* National Legal Resource Center for Child Advocacy and Protection, American Bar Association, Washington, D.C. (1981).

20. CONSTANTINE, L. L. and MARTINSON, F. M. (Eds.). *Children and Sex: New Findings, New Perspectives.* Little, Brown and Co., Boston (1981).

21. HALLIDAY, L. *The Silent Scream: The Reality of Sexual Abuse.* Sexual Abuse Victims Anonymous, R.R. No. 1, Campbell River, B.C., Canada V9W 3S4 (1981).

22. HERMAN, J. L. *Father-Daughter Incest.* Harvard University Press, Cambridge, MA (1981).

23. BULKLEY, J., (Ed). *Innovations in the Prosecution of Child Sexual Abuse Cases.* National Legal Resource Center for Child Advocacy and Protection, American Bar Association, Washington, D.C. (1982, 2nd Edition).

24. BULKLEY, J. *Recommendations for Improving Legal Intervention in Intrafamily Child Sexual Abuse Cases.* National Legal Resource Center for Child Advocacy and Protection, American Bar Association, Washington, D.C. (1982).

25. GIARRETTO, H. *Integrated Treatment of Child Sexual Abuse: A treatment and Training Manual.* Science and Behavior Books, Inc., Palo Alto, CA (1982).

26. GOODWIN, J. *Sexual Abuse: Incest Victims and their Families.* John Wright PSG Inc., Littleton, MA (1982).

27. LIST, S. *Forgiving.* E. P. Dutton, Inc., New York (1982).

28. MARTIN, L. and HADDAD, J. *We Have a Secret.* Crown Summit Books, Newport Beach, CA (1982).

29. MORRIS, M. *If I Should Die Before I Wake.* J. P. Tarcher, Inc., Los Angeles (1982).

30. O'BRIEN, S. *We Can! Combat Child Sexual Abuse.* College of Agriculture. The University of Arizona, Tucson (1982).

31. RICKS, C. *Carol's Story: The Sin Nobody Talks About.* Tyndale House Publishers, Inc., Wheaton, IL (1982).

32. SGROI, S. M. *Handbook of Clinical Intervention in Child Sexual Abuse.* Lexington Books, Lexington, MA (1982).

33. *Social Work and Child Sexual Abuse,* Vol. *I.* No. 1/2, *Journal of Human Sexuality and Social Work* (1982).

34. ARMSTRONG, L. *The Home Front: Notes from the Family War Zone.* McGraw-Hill Book Co., New York (1983).

35. FINKELHOR, D., *Sexual abuse: A sociological perspective.* Paper presented at the Third International Congress on Child Abuse and Neglect, Amsterdam (1981).

36. NOBILE, P., Incest, the last taboo. *Penthouse* December, pp. 117-118, 126, 157-158 (1977).

37. RAMEY, J., Dealing with the last taboo. *Siecus Report VII* (5): 1-2, 6-7 (1979).

38. Attacking the last taboo: Researchers are lobbying against the ban on incest. *Time,* April 14: 72 (1980).

39. DE MOTT, B., The pro-incest lobby. *Psychology Today 13* (10): 11-16 (1980).

40. LEO, J. Cradle-to-grave intimacy: Some researchers openly argue that "anything goes" for children. *Time* Sept 7, pp. 69 (1981).

41. McMANMON, M. T. Personal communication (1979).

42. FINKELHOR, D., Risk factors in the sexual victimization of children. *Child Abuse & Neglect 4*: 265-273 (1980).

43. SUMMIT, R. and KRYSO, J., Sexual abuse of children: A clinical spectrum. *American Journal of Orthopsychiatry.* 48: 237-251 (1978).

44. GROTH, A.N., Patterns of sexual assault against children and adolescents. In: *Sexual Assault of Children and Adolescents,* A. Burgess, A. N. Groth, L. Holmstrom, and S. Sgroi (Eds.), Lexington Books, Lexington, MA (1978).

45. GROTH, A. N. *Men who Rape: The Psychology of the Offender.* Plenum Press, New York (1979).

46. GROTH, A. N. and BIRNBAUM, B., Adult sexual orientation and attraction to underage persons. *Archives of Sexual Behavior 7*: 175-181 (1978).

47. SUMMIT, R., Recognition and treatment of child sexual abuse. In: *Providing for the Emotional Health of the Pediatric Patient,* C. Hollingsworth (Ed.), Spectrum Publishers, New York (1983).

48. SUMMIT, R. C., Review of Herman, J. L., Father-Daughter Incest. *American Journal of Orthopsychiatry.* 52: 725-729 (1982).

49. GAGNON, J., Female child victims of sex offenses. *Social Problems 13*: 176-192 (1965).

50. RUSSELL, D. E. H., The incidence and prevalence of intrafamilial and extrafamilial sexual abuse of female children. *Child Abuse & Neglect 7* (1983).

51. FINKELHOR, D., What's wrong with sex between adults and children? Ethics and the problem of sexual abuse. *American Journal of Orthopsychiatry 49*: 692-697 (1979).

52. MacFARLANE, K. Personal communication (1981).

53. BERLINER, L. Personal communication (1981).

54. Note: Classification of offenders and differential diagnosis of pedophilic behavior are beyond the scope of this article. In the present discussion of intra-family sexual abuse, it is assumed that the intruder is acting within a regressive crisis and that he is not a practiced, habitual molester of children. See Groth [45] for further discussion.

55. LANDERS, A., Sisters discover dad molested all five of them. Field Newspaper Syndicate, Chicago, IL, May 21 (1980).

56. SHENGOLD, L., Child abuse and deprivation: Soul murder. *Journal of American Psychoanalytic Association 27*: 533-599 (1979).

57. MYERS, B., Incest: If you think the word is ugly, take a look at its effects. In: *Sexual Abuse of Children: Selected Readings,* K. MacFarlane, B. Jones and L. Jenstrom (Eds.), National Center on Child Abuse and Neglect, Office of Human Development Services, U.S. Department of Health and Human Services, Washington, D.C. (1980).

58. LUSTIG, N., DRESSER, J.W., SPELLMAN, S.W. and MURRAY, T. B., Incest: A family group survival pattern. *Archives of General Psychiatry 14*: 31-40 (1966).

59. PETERS, J., Children who are victims of sexual assault and the psychology of offenders. *American Journal of Psychotherapy 30*: 398-412 (1976).

60. ROSENFELD, A., Sexual misuse and the family. *Victimology II (2):* 226-235 (1977).

61. RUSH, F., The Freudian cover-up. *Chrysalis 1*: 31-45 (1977).

62. ROSENFELD, A., NADELSON, C., and KRIEGER, M., Fantasy and reality in patient reports of incest. *Journal of Clinical Psychiatry 40*: 159-164 (1979).

63. BURGESS, A. and HOLMSTROM, L., Rape trauma syndrome. *American Journal of Psychiatry 131*: 981-986 (1974).

64. BURGESS, A. and HOLMSTROM, L., Sexual trauma of children and adolescents: Pressure, sex and secrecy. *Nursing Clinics of North America 10*: 551-563 (1975).

65. BURGESS and HOLMSTROM, *Nursing Clinics of North America 10:* 562 (1975).

66. DE MAUSE, L. (Ed.) *The History of Childhood.* Psychohistory Press, New York (1974).

67. FREUD, S. In: *The Origins of Psychoanalysis: Letters to Wilhelm Fliess, Drafts and Notes: 1887-1902.* M. BONPARTE, A. FREUD, and E. KRIS, (Eds.) (Translated by E. Mosbacher and J. Strachey). Basic Books, New York. p. 217 (1954).

68. KEMPE, C. H., SILVERMAN, F. N., STEELE, B. F., DROEGEMUELLER, W. and SILVER, H., The battered child syndrome. *Journal of the American Medical Association 181*: 17-24 (1962).

69. SGROI, S., Sexual molestation of children: The last frontier in child abuse. *Children Today 4*: 18-21, 44, (1975).

70. GIARRETTO, H., Personal communication (1979).

71. SUMMIT, R., Sexual child abuse, the psychotherapist and the team concept. In: *Dealing with sexual child abuse, Vol. 2,* H. Donovan and R. J. Beran (Eds.), National Committee for the Prevention of Child Abuse (1978).

Four Preconditions

A Model

| **DAVID FINKELHOR**   *1984* |

In 1984, with the publication of his book, *Child Sexual Abuse,* and its seminal chapter, "Four Preconditions: A Model," David Finkelhor wrote "there is a pressing need for new theory in the field of sexual abuse." He then proceeded to explain the shortcomings of existing theor and articulated a new one in response.

His four preconditions constituted the first comprehensive, multidisciplinary paradigm for thinking about, understanding, studying, assessing, and eventually treating and preventing sexual abuse. The four include: a potential offender's motivation to abuse, a potential offender overcoming internal inhibitions to abuse, a potential offender overcoming external impediments, and, a child's resistance to abuse being undermined or overcome. It has become the underpinning of much of the subsequent work done in this area.

Finkelhor's paper reminds us all of the maxim, "nothing is as useful as a good theory." As Howard Dubowitz explains, long after the problem of child sexual abuse was well recognized, most professionals remained uncertain how or why this behavior occurred. In his paper, Finkelhor synthesizes the knowledge available at the time about sexual abuse into a highly cogent explanation of the contributing factors. He took account of both psychological and sociological factors. The implications of his theory have been far reaching, and the theory remains as useful today as it was when first published.

Finkelhor's theory has been pivotal in guiding research efforts to better understand the underlying causes of child sexual abuse. It has fostered recognition of the multiple factors that need to be considered and the complex ways in which they may interact. It draws attention to the need to carefully consider an array of factors and to resist simplistic explanations.

In recognition of the power and influence of this particular paper, Dubowitz explains that this work helped him appreciate the complexity of the phenomenon of sexual abuse of children—a complexity he has, as a result, taken account of in both his research and clinical life. He says, "I have long admired David's ability to weave to-gether different strands of knowledge in such a rich and textured way!"

A. C. D. and K. O.

There is a pressing need for new theory in the field of sexual abuse. What theory we have currently is not sufficient to account for what we know. Nor is it far-reaching enough to guide the development of new empirical research.

Two types of theory currently prevail in the field. On the one hand, there is a collection of partially developed ideas, catalogued in the previous chapter, about what creates a child molester. On the other hand, there is a highly specific family-systems model of father-daughter incest.

Taken as a whole, the current level of theoretical development displays a number of important shortcomings. For one, the theories we have are not very useful for collating what is known about offenders with what is known about victims and their families. Research and theory about offenders have been developed by psychologists working with offenders in prison settings, in isolation from other workers who were protecting and treating children.

For another, currently available theories are not comprehensive. The theories about offenders have been developed from work mostly with men who molested multiple children outside their own families. In contrast, the family-systems theories have been developed almost exclusively from work with father-daughter incest families. Unfortunately, there is much sexual abuse, such as that committed by older brothers, uncles, and neighbors, which falls outside either domain. Theory to account for such abuse is missing.

Finally, currently available theories tend to neglect sociological factors. They have mostly developed from clinical work and are aimed at helping to direct therapeutic interventions. However, sexual abuse as a widespread social problem has sociological dimensions that need to be included in theory.

In this chapter, we build on the foundation of the last chapter and propose a model of sexual abuse that tries to address these shortcomings. It brings together knowledge about offenders, victims, and families. It is at a level of generality capable of accommodating many different types of sexual abuse, from father-daughter incest to compulsive and fixated molesting. Finally, it incorporates explanations at both the psychological and sociological level. The model is called the Four Preconditions Model of Sexual Abuse.

The model was developed by reviewing all the factors that have been proposed as contributing to sexual abuse (Lukianowicz, 1972; Lystad, 1982; Tierney & Corwin, 1983), including factors related to victims and families, as detailed in Chapter 3, and factors related to offenders, as detailed in Chapter 4. This review suggested that all factors relating to sexual abuse could be grouped as contributing to one of four preconditions that needed to be met before sexual abuse could occur:

1. A potential offender needed to have some motivation to abuse a child sexually.
2. The potential offender had to overcome internal inhibitions against acting on that motivation.
3. The potential offender had to overcome external impediments to committing sexual abuse.
4. The potential offender or some other factor had to undermine or overcome a child's possible resistance to the sexual abuse.

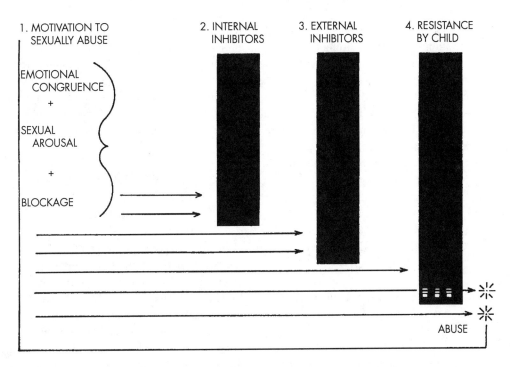

Figure 17.1. Four Preconditions of Sex Abuse

These factors suggested a model of sexual abuse portrayed in Figure 17.1. What follows is a more detailed description of the components of the model and how it operates to account for a wide variety of sexual abuse.

PRECONDITION 1: MOTIVATION TO SEXUALLY ABUSE

A model of sexual abuse needs to account for how a person (an adult or adolescent) becomes motivated for or interested in having sexual contact with a child. This question is essentially the one we took up in the previous chapter. Following along the lines of the previous chapter, we suggest that there are three components to the source of this motivation: (1) emotional congruence—relating sexually to the child satisfies some important emotional need; (2) sexual arousal—the child co-

mes to be the potential source of sexual gratification for that person; and (3) blockage— alternative sources of sexual gratification are not available or are less satisfying. (The fourth factor from the previous chapter— disinhibition—is isolated as a separate precondition for reasons detailed below.)

These three components are not themselves preconditions. That is, some contribution from each is not required in order for the sexual abuse to occur. For example, an offender may sexually abuse a child without necessarily being sexually aroused by the child; he may do so simply because such abuse satisfies an emotional need to degrade. Or an offender may sexually abuse a child for the sake of variety without necessarily being blocked from alternative sources of gratification.

However, in many cases, elements are present from each of the three components in accounting for the motivation. As we illustrated in the previous chapter, the mixture of elements may help explain a variety of aspects of the motivation: whether it is strong and persistent or weak and episodic, whether it focuses primarily on boys or girls or both.

The first section of Table 17.1 lists some factors that may help account for the presence of Precondition 1. These are some of the more common theories catalogued here, apportioned according to whether they occur at the individual or social-cultural level.

PRECONDITION 2: OVERCOMING INTERNAL INHIBITION

In order for sexual abuse to occur, a potential offender not only needs to be motivated to commit abuse, but the offender must overcome internal inhibitions against acting on those motives. We presume that most members of society have such inhibitions. If there are those who do not, then the absence of inhibitions needs to be explained.

This precondition is essentially the same as the disinhibition factor identified in Chapter 4. It is established as a precondition separate from the other three factors relating to offenders for two reasons. First, emotional congruence, sexual arousal, and blockage are sources of the motivation to sexually abuse. Disinhibition is not in itself a source of motivation but the reason the motivation is unleashed. It is not sufficient in itself to create abuse. A person who has no inhibitions against sexual abuse, but also no inclination to do so, will not abuse.

Second, unlike the other three, disinhibition itself *is* a requirement for sexual abuse. No matter what the motivation to abuse sexually, if a potential offender is inhibited by social taboos from acting, then abuse will not occur. Many people probably have a strong sexual interest in children but do not commit abuse precisely because they are inhibited. To account for the abuse, we need to account for why the inhibitions were overcome. The disinhibition

may have been temporary, and the person may ordinarily have very strong controls, but an explanation for the disinhibition is an important element in a full explanation of sexual abuse.

Table 17.1 also lists the major reasons for disinhibition of sexually abusive behavior as found in the literature reviewed in Chapter 4.

PRECONDITION 3: OVERCOMING EXTERNAL INHIBITORS

The first two preconditions try to account for the behavior of perpetrators. But it is quite clear that such accounts do not fully explain to whom or why abuse occurs. A man fully motivated to abuse sexually who is also disinhibited may not do so, and he certainly may not do so with a particular child. There are factors outside himself that control whether he abuses and whom he abuses. Preconditions 3 and 4 are about these.

Precondition 3 concerns external inhibitors in the environment outside the offender and outside the child. The most important of these external forces is the supervision a child receives from other persons. Family members, neighbors, and children's own peers all exert a restraining influence on the actions of a potential abuser.

It might appear that, given an offender motivated to commit abuse, the supervision of other persons is a rather fragile form of deterrent. A child cannot always be in the presence of others. Yet, it is interesting how frequently, in both the clinical and empirical literature, the influence of third parties appears as an important factor in creating a vulnerability to abuse. Some of the most important external inhibitors of sexual abuse noted in the literature are included in the table of preconditions.

Mothers appear to be especially crucial in protecting children from abuse. Of course, there has been criticism that mothers have been blamed too frequently for abuse. This criticism has some validity, which was discussed in

TABLE 17.1 Preconditions for Sexual Abuse

	Level of Explanation	
	Individual	*Social/Cultural*
Precondition 1: *Factors related to* *motivation to sexually abuse*		
Emotional congruence	Arrested emotional development Need to feel powerful and controlling Re-enactment of childhood trauma to undo the hurt Narcissistic identification with self as a young child	Masculine requirement to be dominant and powerful in sexual relationships
Sexual arousal	Childhood sexual experience that was traumatic or strongly conditioning Modeling of sexual interest in children by someone else Misattribution of arousal cues Biologic abnormality	Child pornography Erotic portrayal of children in advertising Male tendency to sexualize all emotional needs Repressive norms about masturbation and extramarital sex
Blockage	Oedipal conflict Castration anxiety Fear of adult females Traumatic sexual experience with adult Inadequate social skills Marital problems	
Precondition 2: Factors *predisposing to overcoming* *internal inhibitors*	Alcohol Psychosis Impulse disorder Senility Failure of incest inhibition mechanism in family dynamics	Social toleration of sexual interest in children Ideology of patriarchal privileges for fathers Social toleration for deviance committed while intoxicated Child pornography Male inability to identify with needs of children
Precondition 3: Factors *predisposing to overcoming* *external inhibitors*	Mother who is absent or ill Mother who is not close to or protective of child Mother who is dominated or abused by father Social isolation of family Unusual opportunities to be alone with child Lack of supervision of child Unusual sleeping or rooming conditions	Lack of social supports for mother Barriers to women's equality Erosion of social networks Ideology of family sanctity
Precondition 4: Factors *predisposing to overcoming* *child's resistance*	Child who is emotionally insecure or deprived Child who lacks knowledge about sexual abuse Situation of unusual trust between child and offender Coercion	Unavailability of sex education for children Social powerlessness of children

Chapter 3 and will be discussed further later in context of the full four-preconditions model. But findings related to the importance of mothers in protecting children appear too regularly to be dismissed simply as sexism. There is growing evidence that when mothers are incapacitated in some way, children are more vulnerable to abuse.

That incapacitation may take various forms. When a mother is absent from a family because of divorce, death, or sickness, as seen in Chapter 3, children appear to suffer more abuse. (See also Kaufman, Peck & Tagiuri, 1954; Machotka, Pittman & Flomenhaft, 1966; Maisch, 1972; Raphling, Carpenter & Davis, 1967). Mothers may also be psychologically absent because they are alienated from children or husband or suffering from other emotional disturbances, with similar consequences.

One form of maternal incapacitation, it is also interesting to note, may come from the relationship between mother and father. Mothers may be unable to protect children because they themselves are abused and intimidated by tyrannical and domineering men. Even large power imbalances that may stem from differences in education may undercut a woman's ability to be an ally for her children.

Just what are all the forms of protection that a mother provides is not entirely clear. Supervision does not mean simply being present with the child at all times. It also includes knowing what is going on for a child, knowing when a child is troubled, and being someone to whom the child can readily turn for help. It can be seen how a potential offender might well be inhibited from abusing a child if he realized that the mother would quickly suspect or know what was going on. Judith Herman (1981) has found that the main difference between families where father and daughter have a "seductive" relationship and families where that relationship becomes actual incest is that in the incestuous families, the mother is incapacitated in some way. In the seductive relationship situation, mothers seem to exert some inhibiting force.

Other people besides mothers act as deterrents to sexual abuse. To the degree that neighbors, siblings, friends, and teachers interact closely with a child and are familiar with his or her activities, they also inhibit abuse. This idea would appear to be supported by findings that children who live in isolated settings or who have few friends and few social contacts are at greater risk to abuse (Henderson, 1972). The absence of general public scrutiny of family and children may be one of the factors that accounts for the reportedly high level of abuse in the stereotypical "backwoods" family environments (Summit & Kryso, 1978).

One other form that external inhibition may take is simply the absence of physical opportunity for abuser and child to be alone together. In situations where such opportunities are more available, abuse is more likely to occur. The literature on sexual abuse has, for example, mentioned household conditions as factors which may facilitate abuse. When family members are required to sleep together in the same bed or in the same room, abuse may be facilitated. Similarly, one of the reasons why a father's unemployment may precipitate abuse is that, in addition to lowering his internal inhibitions because of emotional stress, it leaves him at home alone with a child for extended periods. When a potential abuser and a child are left alone in the absence of supervising persons, it may help to overcome the *external inhibitions* that often exist against sexual abuse.

PRECONDITION 4: OVERCOMING THE RESISTANCE OF THE CHILD

Children themselves play an important role in whether or not they are abused, and any full explanation of why abuse occurs needs to take into account factors related to the child. Children have a capacity to avoid or resist abuse. Unfortunately, since professionals are mostly in contact with children who were abused, the importance of this capacity is not often realized. If professionals dealt with more children who had had close calls but escaped, this capacity might be more apparent. Some of the factors noted in the literature as compromising children's capacity to resist are listed in Table 17.1.

The notion of a capacity to resist or avoid must not be seen in a narrow way. It means much more than a child who says no to a potential abuser when asked to play a sexual game, or who runs away or fights back when accosted. It involves many subtle aspects related to children's behavior and personality.

Much abuse is undoubtedly short-circuited without the child's knowing anything about it because a potential abuser chooses not to approach that particular child but goes on to another. This even occurs within a family, where some children will be molested by a father while others are left alone. Abusers undoubtedly sense that some children do not make good targets. They sense that a child will not play along, will not keep a secret, will say no, cannot be intimidated. One might call this a "front of invulnerability." Some molesters who pick victims out in public situations, such as in school yards, have been quoted as saying they know almost instinctively who is a promising target and who is not. Many children may resist abuse without even being aware they are resisting.

A great many things may overcome the ability of children to avoid or resist becoming victims of abuse, and usually one or more of these things are present in every abuse situation. One large class of risk factors is anything that makes a child feel emotionally insecure, needy, or unsupported (Burton, 1968; DeFrancis, 1969; Weiss et al., 1955). A child who feels needy will be more vulnerable to the ploys of a potential abuser: the offers of attention, affection, or bribes. A child who feels unsupported will not have someone to turn to about the abuse or will be more afraid to tell. Children who are emotionally abused, who are disabled or disadvantaged, or who have poor relationships to their parents are all at-risk for these reasons. Several of the factors we found associated with abuse in Chapter 3—having few friends, not receiving physical affection from a father, not being close to a mother, or having her be punitive—fall into this category. They all erode a child's ability to resist.

Children's ability to resist or avoid abuse may be undercut because they are young, are naive, or lack information. It may also be undercut because they have a special relationship to the potential offender. A child who might object to a sexual game when proposed by a stranger may comply because the proposal comes from a family member, a person the child trusts. Because the adult knows the child, the adult may frame the proposal in such a way that the child will agree. That same familiarity may allow the adult to formulate a threat which will thwart any resistance by the child.

Of course, it is important to recognize that however the child behaved or whatever the child did may not make a difference in some situations. All that may have been simply irrelevant because the adult used force and coercion to involve the child in sexual activity. In such cases, the factor overcoming a child's resistance had nothing to do with the child or the child's relationship with the adult. The key factor was force.

Whether or not force was present, it is important in understanding why abuse occurs to account for factors related to the victims. Such factors will continue to appear among those which are found empirically to predict a child's risk of becoming a victim of sexual abuse. These factors seem to be best conceptualized as explaining something about the ability of children to resist or avoid abuse. The absence of such resistance or its being overcome in some fashion are a fourth precondition to the occurrence of sexual abuse.

OPERATION OF THE MODEL

The operation of the four-preconditions model is illustrated in Figure 17.1. It suggests that the various preconditions come into play in a logical sequence.

Only some individuals have strong motivation to become sexually involved with children. Of those that do, only some overcome their internal inhibitions to act on these motives. Of those who overcome their internal inhibitions, only some overcome external inhibitions—the surveillance of other family members or the lack of opportunity—and act on the motives.

At this point, three things can happen. (1) Any particular child may resist either directly or indirectly, for example by running away or by having a confident, assertive, or invulnerable demeanor, and in such a way avoid abuse. This is shown by the arrow that stops before Precondition 4. (2) Any particular child may fail to resist and be abused. This is shown by the lowest line in the figure. (3) Any particular child may resist but may have his or her resistance overcome through coercion. This is shown by the line drawn through Precondition 4.

All four preconditions have to be fulfilled for the abuse to occur. The presence of only one condition, such as lack of protection by a mother or social isolation or emotional deprivation, *is not enough in itself to explain abuse. To explain abuse requires the presence of all four prior conditions.*

This model of sexual abuse, with its four preconditions, is useful for categorizing and integrating many of the suggestions in the literature about individual, family, and cultural factors which predispose to sexual abuse. But the model also has other uses.

NO DISTINCTION BETWEEN INTRA- AND EXTRAFAMILIAL ABUSE

As we indicated earlier, much prior theorizing about sexual abuse has revolved around either (1) the psychodynamics of sex abusers or (2) the family-systems model of father-daughter incest. However, a great deal of sexual abuse falls in neither category. Many children are abused by members of their extended family who are not pedophiles and not fathers: for example, brother, uncles, and grandfathers. No current theory even attempts to explain why this abuse occurs. Many other children are abused by baby-sitters and neighbors who are also not pedophiles. Moreover, the family-systems theory, which is entirely about father-daughter incest, is virtually useless in trying to account for the sexual abuse of boys in their own family (Conte, 1982).

By contrast, the four-preconditions model is at a sufficiently general level that all kinds of abuse can be integrated within it. It suggests that abuse by fathers and abuse by pedophiles both require an explanation of how the sexual interest in the child arose, why there were no effective inhibitors, and why a child's resistance was either absent or insufficient. It is an approach which applies to both "fixated" and "regressed" offenders (Groth, 1979), both intrafamilial and extrafamilial sexual abuse.

FAMILY SYSTEMS MODEL

The four-preconditions model should not be seen necessarily as an alternative to the family-systems model. Rather the family-systems model is just one particular instance of the four-preconditions model, an instance that applies to the dynamics of father-daughter incest. All the dynamics of the family-systems model are encompassed within the four-preconditions model. The four-preconditions model is simply at a higher level of generality.

If the family-systems model is reformulated in terms of the four-preconditions model, it sounds something like the following:

Precondition 1. Father is motivated to take a sexual interest in his daughter because his relationship with his wife has deteriorated (blockage). Perhaps, he sees in his daughter someone who has qualities similar to what he liked in his wife, but someone who can give him uncritical admiration and whom he can manipulate easily to fulfill his sexual and emotional needs (emotional congruence). Father may have himself been sexually abused but certainly has fantasized about daughter and perhaps masturbated to these fantasies (sexual arousal).

Precondition 2. Father's internal inhibitions against committing abuse are overcome, either by alcohol or by a setback in his job or career aspirations. He rationalizes to himself that he really loves his daughter, or that no great harm will be caused, or that committing incest is preferable to having an affair.

Precondition 3. External inhibitions against committing abuse are low because mother is not readily protective of daughter. Father may have cultivated a rivalry between mother and daughter. Or mother may be alienated from daughter for her own reasons. Daughter does not feel close to or readily confide in mother.

Precondition 4. Daughter's resistance to father's advances is undermined because she trusts him, because she enjoys the attention, affection, and favored status. She may even feel she is holding the whole family together.

This is just one example of how family dynamics can be encompassed within the four-preconditions model. In other families, somewhat different dynamics prevail. But the basic mechanisms are the same.

PUTTING RESPONSIBILITY IN PERSPECTIVE

One of the most persistent criticisms of explanations of sexual abuse is that they tend to take responsibility for the abuse off the offenders and displace it onto either victims, third parties, or society as a whole (Armstrong, 1978, 1983; Conte, 1982). For example, the family-systems model, which finds that mothers are unsupportive and unprotective of daughters in many incestuous families, is frequently criticized for blaming the mother (McIntyre, 1981; Nelson, 1982). Similarly, research that has found that emotionally deprived children are more vulnerable to abuse has been criticized for putting unnecessary blame on the victims.

The four-preconditions model of sexual abuse puts the issue of responsibility into a somewhat better perspective. In this model, the problem of a mother's failing to protect her child or a child's failing to resist victimization is taken seriously as a contributing element. However, it is clear that these factors are not germane to the situation until after the potential offender has already taken some giant strides on the road toward committing the offense. The matter of victim's and mother's behavior are relevant only because the offender is already embarked on an antisocial train of events, better showing where responsibility lies.

COMBINING PSYCHOLOGICAL AND SOCIOLOGICAL EXPLANATIONS

Another advantage to the four-preconditions model is that it is able to accommodate explanatory factors at both a psychological and a sociological level. This seems to be an important prerequisite for a model that can adapt to new developments in our knowledge about sexual abuse. A great deal of the theorizing about sexual abuse occurred at a time when it was believed to be a rather unusual problem. These theories reflected the ideas of abnormal psychology mentioned earlier. However, since that time we have come to realize how many adults molest children and how many children suffer abuse. A problem that is so widespread certainly needs to be accounted for in sociological as well as psychological terms.

Social factors can be incorporated into the four-preconditions model just as easily as psychological ones. Some of these factors have already been illustrated in the discussion of offenders.

Precondition 1. Identifiable characteristics of our society tend to motivate adult men to interact sexually with children. These include the erotic premium that males place on youth, smallness, and submissiveness in sexual partners and the tendency of males to eroticize all their affectionate relationships. Such social factors make sexual relations with children more emotionally congruent for potential offenders.

In Chapter 3, we also mentioned social factors related to other components of the motivation to abuse. For example, pornography plays a possible role in the conditioning of sexual arousal to children. Repressive social norms about masturbation and alternative sexual outlets may also contribute to the blockage that directs offenders toward children.

Precondition 2. Social factors may influence large groups of men to ignore or discount conventional social inhibitions against becoming sexually involved with children. These include child pornography, again, which promotes the idea that sex with adults is enjoyable and educational for children. The social norm that a father has the prerogative to demand what he wants from his children may act as a disinhibitor of sexual abuse within the family. Another such social factor may be the widespread belief that people are not socially accountable for behavior they engage in while drunk (McCaghy, 1968). Such a belief may facilitate the disinhibition of sexually abusive behavior among adults while they are drinking.

Precondition 3. Several social factors in particular may help account for the failure of ex-

ternal inhibitors to protect large numbers of children. First, to the extent that mothers are dependent on husbands and deprived of social resources by virtue of their sex, they are less effective protectors of children. Second, as traditional, stable communities and neighborhoods have disappeared, many children have fewer adults who supervise and monitor their activities and thus serve as protectors. Finally, a traditional ideology of family sanctity deters outsiders from interfering in family affairs on behalf of children whom they might suspect of being abused.

Precondition 4. Social factors play a role in undermining the ability of many children to resist or avoid the enticements of sexual abusers. For example, a pervasive society-wide anxiety about sex makes it common for children not to receive important information about human sexual behavior that would alert them to abuse situations before they occurred.

By drawing attention to sociological factors that contribute to sexual abuse, the model also highlights proposals for changing social systems in ways that would reduce the prevalence of abuse.

USE OF THE MODEL IN TREATMENT

The four-preconditions model also has implications for working with abusive families and abusive individuals. It suggests that evaluation and intervention can operate at four separate sites to prevent sexual abuse from re-occurring. Therapists can evaluate the strengths of each of the four mechanisms in the individual or family situation and develop strategies that can be useful in reinforcing areas that are weak.

For example, in the case of a father who has been abusing his daughter, a clinician might use the model as follows:

Precondition 1. What motivates the offender to take a sexual interest in his daughter? In many cases of incest, therapists conclude that the emotional congruence and sexual arousal elements of the situation are not strong and that the blockage of relationship to the wife is the key to understanding why the husband turns to the daughter. However, the model urges clinicians to look carefully at these other sources of sexual interest. The relationship with the daughter may be fulfilling very strong emotional needs for the father (emotional congruence) that arise from much earlier life experiences. They may be the reason why the relationship with the wife is poor. Without the daughter, the father may simply turn to other inappropriate partners, including other children. The clinician needs to look also at the component of sexual arousal, since some research indicates that incestuous fathers have or develop deviant sexual arousal patterns that make them similar to non-incest pedophiles (Abel et al., 1981). To avoid repetition of the abuse, it may be appropriate for the therapist to consider specific behavioral manipulation of the father's sexual proclivities.

Precondition 2. An evaluation of the strength and quality of the offender's internal inhibitions may be the key to assessing how likely he is to re-abuse. He may be a generally well-controlled individual who acted under intense stress and who feels great guilt about his actions. On the other hand, he may be full of denial or be someone whose inhibitions are readily overwhelmed by frustrations or alcohol. Of course, the strength of the inhibitions must be examined in the context of the strength of the motives. Even some strongly inhibited offenders are overwhelmed by powerful compulsions. The strength of the internal inhibitors will probably be a good index of how motivated an offender is to participate in treatment voluntarily.

Precondition 3. Many of the immediate issues for child welfare workers concern evaluation of factors related to external inhibitors. Workers want to know whether, now that the abuse has been uncovered, other adults are capable of protecting the child from re-abuse. The child's welfare seems better assured when the mother reacts by believing the child, kicking the father out of the household, and allowing the father access to the daughter only under supervised conditions. If the mother sides with the father, refuses to acknowledge the abuse, or appears ineffectual and emotionally devastated, then workers will worry that external inhibitors to re-abuse are weak. They will look for other adults, such as grandparents, who can help to protect the child. Or they can remove the child from the family. Removal from access to the perpetrator is the ultimate external inhibitor. But in general, external inhibitors are the ones easiest to manipulate and thus most readily assessed in crisis intervention.

Precondition 4. Clinicians sometimes neglect to analyze the degree to which children are capable of protecting themselves. Sometimes the revelation of the abuse gives the child knowledge and support that reinforce the ability to resist the offender. Knowing she or he can tell the caseworker that it has happened again may be just enough to help the child stand up to the father. Some treatment programs find it very valuable to train victims in abuse prevention skills. If the child now knows that adults clearly should not do such things and has practiced saying no in various situations, the child may be much less vulnerable to re-abuse. If, on the other hand, the child is filled with guilt and remorse for creating problems for the family, this may be a sign that ability to resist is not yet great.

By using the four-preconditions model as a framework for assessment, clinicians may be able to plan the most effective strategy in working with a family. The model directs attention to a variety of vulnerable points. A comprehensive strategy will try to address them all. Some preconditions are easier to manipulate than others. A worker may be able to create external inhibitors to re-abuse much more quickly than reduce an offender's motivation to abuse. On the other hand, some interventions promise more comprehensive results. To simply introduce more external inhibitors may protect some children, but the offender, still motivated to abuse and still disinhibited, may simply turn to other children.

Decisions about the advisability of criminal prosecution can also be made in the context of the model. The threat of criminal action may be exactly the kind of external constraint that will deter an offender from abusing again. On the other hand, if other constraints are as effective and prosecution risks traumatizing the child, then it may not be called for.

The model has a great many other uses as a guide for assessment and intervention, and we have given only some brief illustrations here as an encouragement to others to adopt it and utilize it.

CONCLUSION

This chapter has integrated much of what we currently know about child sexual abuse into a four-preconditions model. Models of this sort have a variety of uses beyond simply being a way of organizing knowledge to make it useful and accessible, uses which we have tried to illustrate here.

One thing this model should do is remind us that sexual abuse is a complex phenomenon. Factors at a number of levels, regarding a number of individuals, come into play in determining its occurrence. Keeping such a model in mind should keep us from being seduced by simple explanations.

At the same time, this model should help us to keep from getting discouraged by that complexity. Sexual abuse is a problem with causes and explanations. Many of these we do not yet fully understand. The four-preconditions model is open-ended; new findings and new ideas can be added to it. By having given some structure to what is already known, this model enables us to use that knowledge.

REFERENCES

ABEL, G., BECKER, J., MURPHY, W. D. & FLANAGAN, B. Identifying dangerous child molesters. In R. B. Stuart (Ed.), *Violent behavior.* New York: Brunner/Mazel, 1981.

ARMSTRONG, I. *Kiss daddy goodnight.* New York: Hawthorn, 1978.

———— *The home front.* New York: McGraw Hill, 1983.

BURTON, L. *Vulnerable children.* London: Routledge and Kegan Paul, 1968.

CONTE, J. R. Sexual abuse of children: Enduring issues for social work. In J. R. Conte & D. Shore (Eds.), *Social work and child sexual abuse.* New York: Haworth, 1982.

DE FRANCIS, V. *Protecting the child victim of sex crimes committed by adults.* Denver: American Human Association, 1969.

GROTH, N. *Men who rape.* New York: Plenum, 1979.

HENDERSON, J. Incest: A synthesis of data. *Canadian Psychiatric Association Journal,* 1972, *17:* 299-313.

HERMAN, J. *Father-daughter incest.* Cambridge: Harvard, 1981.

KAUFMAN, I., PECK, A., & TAGIURI, C. K. The family constellation and overt incestuous relations between father and daughter. *American Journal of Orthopsychiatry,* 1954, *24:* 266-279.

LUKIANOWICZ, N. Incest. *British Journal of Psychiatry,* 1972, *120:* 301-313.

LYSTAD, M. H. Sexual abuse in the home: A review of the literature. *International Journal of Family Psychiatry,* 1982.

MACHOTKA, P., PITTMAN, F. S. & FLOMENHAFT, K. Incest as a fmily affair. *Family Process,* 1966, *6:* 98-116.

MAISCH, H. *Incest.* New York: Stein & Day, 1972.

McCAGHY, C. H. Drinking and deviance disavowal: The case of child molesters. *Social Problems,* 1968, *16:* 43-49.

McINTYRE, K. Role of mothers in father-daughter incest: A feminist analysis. *Social Work,* 1981, *26:* 462-466.

NELSON, S. *Incest: Fact and myth.* Edinburgh: Stramullion, 1982.

RAPHLING, D., CARPENTER, B. & DAVIS, A. Incest: A geneological study. *Archives of General Psychiatry,* 1967, *16:* 505-511.

SUMMIT, R. & KAYSO, J. Sexual abuse of children: A clinical spectrum. *American Journal of Orthopsychiatry,* 1978, *48:* 237-251.

TIERNEY, K. & CORWIN, D. Exploring intra-familial child sexual abuse: A systems approach. In D. Finkelhor, R. Gelles, G. Hotaling, & M. Straus (Eds.), *The dark side of families: Current family violence research.* Beverly Hills: Sage, 1983.

WEISS, J., ROGERS, E., DARWIN, M. & DUTTON, C. A study of girl sex victims. *Psychiatric Quarterly,* 1955, *29:* 1-2.

18

Violence Toward Children in the United States and Sweden

RICHARD J. GELLES
AKE W. EDFELDT   1986

M̲ost of the published research attempting to establish the incidence of child abuse prior to 1986 dealt with the problem in the United States; prior to 1986 little to no survey research had been done attempting to compare maltreatment rates in different countries. The Gelles and Edfeldt paper represents an important milestone in efforts to understand child maltreatment across countries. This cross-cultural study reinforces the earlier writings of anthropologist Jill Korbin and others on the importance of culture in understanding child abuse.

This paper reports the results of a comparison of two nationally representative samples—from the United States and Sweden. Using the Conflict Resolution Scales, the study gathered data on abuse and violence and documented lower rates of violence in general in Sweden but equal rates of severe abuse in both countries. As Patricia Schene observes, this work addresses the differences across cultures in the meaning and value of children, in the acceptance of violence in human interactions, and in patterns of impulse control and the relative influence of the presence of child abuse and neglect. This work, she says, has helped us focus on our own society and its mores and their relationship to the presence of violence toward children.

A unique feature of the study is its use of a nationally representative sample, rather than studying cases or reports. As such, it offers a far more complete and thus useful understanding of the distribution of the maltreatment problem. The findings underscore the role of social factors, not just parental pathology. For example, in Sweden, Gelles and Edfeldt found fewer unwanted babies, more supportive services such as day care and universal health care, less sanction for corporal punishment, fewer guns, less violence on TV, and more homogeneity in the population. As Schene notes, by showing a lower likelihood in Sweden of "minor" forms of violence toward children, yet an equal likelihood of more severe forms of violence, the study provides useful insights into the complexity of the relationship between social and cultural variables and the use of physical violence.

This paper has continued value today. The comparative, cross-national findings still have relevance. But more important, the paper instructs us in the usefulness of looking at other countries to better understand our own. The paper also teaches us about the necessity and possibility of methodological rigor even in cross-national studies.

A. C. D. and K. O.

Much of the research carried out on child abuse and violence toward children has focused on the problem in the United States. Yet, students of child maltreatment have long been aware that American children are not the only, or even the most likely, victims [1-3].

While there has been a tremendous growth of an international perspective on abuse and neglect, there have been few actual cross-cultural studies conducted or published [4]. Problems with definitions, costs, and access have limited the ability of researchers to field cross-cultural investigations. This paper reports the results of a cross-cultural study of violence toward children in the United States and Sweden. A comparison of the incidence and patterns of violence toward children in the United States and Sweden is presented.

BACKGROUND

Sweden and the United States offer important contrasts when it comes to cultural and social factors which may be related to violence and abuse. Child abuse has not generally appeared to be an overwhelming problem in Scandinavian countries, including Sweden. Vesterdal lists four reasons [5]. First, social conditions are generally good. Second, there is widespread use of contraceptives and free abortions, reducing the number of unwanted babies. Third, many mothers work and leave their children in day care institutions. Last, premature babies are kept in a neonatal ward until they are a certain weight. The babies are released only when their parents are taught to handle a newborn.

There are stark contrasts between the United States and Sweden in terms of social attitudes toward violence. While in the United States the majority of states permit the corporal punishment of school children, corporal punishment has been outlawed in Sweden since 1952. Legislation prohibiting the spanking of children was passed in 1979 and has since been adopted in all other Scandinavian countries. Firearm ownership is rigorously controlled in Sweden. While nearly half of all American households contain guns, mostly handguns, gun ownership in Sweden is mostly limited to weapons used for hunting. Television violence offers another important contrast. American children witness as many as 15,000 killings each year on television; violent programming in Sweden is severely restricted. (Actually, Swedish television is barely on the air as many hours as the average American child watches television in a week.) The level of concern for children's programming in Sweden can be seen in the decision to limit the popular American movie, *ET*, to audiences over 11 years of age. A final contrast is in public violence. Capital punishment is banned in Sweden, but it is allowed and growing in use and popular support in the United States.

There is considerable difference in one area of social complexity. While the United States is a heterogenous nation which is made up of

Originally published in *Child Abuse and Neglect*, 1986, Vol. 10, pp. 501-510. Reprinted by permission of Elsevier Science.

numerous ethnic, religious, and cultural groups and communities, Sweden is more homogenous in terms of such cultural and social attributes. There are, of course, innumerable similarities in the lives of children and families in the United States and in Sweden. However, the contrasts, especially in the area of attitudes toward violence, make a compelling case for comparing the level of violence toward children in the two countries.

Measures of Extent of Abuse and Violence

Research in the United States. Various techniques have been used to measure the extent of child abuse and violence toward children in the United States [6,7]. Two of the most widely cited studies are the National Center on Child Abuse and Neglect report titled Recognition and Reporting of Child Maltreatment [8] and the National Analysis of Official Child Neglect and Abuse Reporting, published yearly by the American Humane Association. Both studies provide interesting data on officially recognized cases of abuse and neglect that come to public attention. However, the studies do not provide a direct measure of the true incidence of the occurrence of abusive events. As Burgdorf admits, a study of reported cases of maltreatment only identifies the "tip of the iceberg of child maltreatment" [8]. Measures of reported child abuse tend to focus on the more injurious forms of violence toward children. Such research cannot be used to examine the total range of violent acts experienced by children.

Not only do official report data fail to inform us about the true extent of violence toward children, such data also do not offer an accurate representation of the factors related to violence and abuse of children. Official reports of child abuse include a number of biases. Certain individuals and families are more likely to be reported due to the nature of the injury, social status of the alleged abuser, and social

characteristics of the victim. Minority, poor, and single parents are more likely to be correctly and incorrectly reported as abusers than are wealthy, white, and intact families [9-11]. Infants are more likely to be identified as victims than are teenagers [9].

Research in Sweden. The State Board of Social Welfare in Sweden undertook two national investigations in which they tried to establish the extent and character of child abuse in Sweden. The first study, which was reported in 1969, examined the period from 1957 to 1966. Data were collected from all general hospitals and all surgical, children's surgical, neurological, pediatric, and children's and youth psychiatric clinics. In addition, data were collected from all medico-legal centers in Sweden. In all, 178 places were contacted as part of the survey. Two cases were reported in 1957; by 1966, there were 66, with an average of 11.9 cases annually for the 10-year period.

A second report was published in 1975 and described the conditions during the period 1969 to 1970. For this period, there was an average of 147 cases of bodily abuse each year and 7 cases titled "sexual outrage."

Sweden, like all countries with the exception of the United States and Canada, does not have laws mandating the reporting of child abuse and neglect [12]. Thus, most of the iceberg of child maltreatment remains below the surface of official recognition in Sweden.

METHODS

The U.S. Survey

One source of data which is not biased by official reports or awareness and which examines a range of violent acts experienced by children is the National Family Violence Survey carried out in 1976 by Murray Straus, Richard J. Gelles, and Suzanne Steinmetz [13]. This survey served as the comparison data for a national survey of violence toward Swedish children conducted by Ake Edfeldt.

A full description of the National Violence Survey in the United States, and specifically the portion of the survey which focused on violence toward children, has been published elsewhere [13]. This section briefly reviews the definitions, measurement, and sample used in the survey.

Defining violence and abuse. Violence was nominally defined as "an act carried out with the intention, or perceived intention, of physically injuring another person." The injury could range from slight pain, as in a slap, to murder. The motivation might range from concern for a child's safety (as when a child is spanked for going into the street) to hostility so intense that the death of the child is desired [14]. Abusive acts were those acts which had a high probability of causing an injury to the child (an injury did not have to actually occur).

Operationalizing violence and abuse. Violence was operationalized through the use of the Conflict Tactics Scales (CTS). First developed at the University of New Hampshire in 1971, this technique has been modified extensively and used in numerous studies of family violence [15-20]. The Conflict Tactics Scales contain items to measure three variables: (1) use of rational discussion and argument (discussed the issue calmly; got information to back up one's side; brought in/tried to bring in someone to help settle things); (2) use of verbal and nonverbal expressions of hostility (insulted or swore at the other; sulked or refused to talk about it; stomped out of the room or house; did or said something to spite the other; threatened to hit or throw something at the other; or threw, smashed, hit or kicked something); and (3) use of physical force or violence as a means of managing the conflict (threw something at the other; pushed, grabbed, shoved the other; slapped or spanked; kicked,

bit, or hit with a fist; hit or tried to hit with something; beat up the other; threatened with a knife or gun; or used knife or gun). The abuse items were those acts that had a high probability of causing an injury: kicked, bit, or hit with a fist; beat up; threatened with a knife or gun; or used a knife or gun.

The Conflict Tactics Scales were presented to subjects in the order enumerated, and the subjects were asked to say how often they used each technique when they had a disagreement or were angry with a child, both in the previous year and in the course of the relationship with the child.

The Conflict Tactics Scales' definition of violence and abuse is different from traditional definitions of child abuse. First, in one sense, the definition is broader than most definitions since it is not limited to acts of violence that only result in injury (operational definitions of child abuse that rely on official reports almost invariably are limited to instances of violence that result in a diagnosable injury). In another sense, the Conflict Tactics Scales are narrower than many definitions of abuse because the scales are limited to a specific list of violent acts. Omitted, for example, are burnings or scaldings of children. Another limitation of the scales is that they rely on the parents' recollection and willingness to report specific acts of violence.

Reliability and validity. The reliability and validity of the Conflict Tactics Scales has been assessed over the 15-year period of its development and modification. A full discussion of reliability and validity can be found elsewhere [13,21]. There is evidence of adequate internal consistency reliability, concurrent validity, and construct validity.

Sample. A national probability sample of 2,143 households comprised the National Family Violence Survey [13]. In each family where there were two caretakers present and there was at least one child at home between the ages of 3 and 17, a referent child was selected using a random procedure. An important limitation of the sample was the omission of referent children under the age of 3 years and single parents. Many experts believe that children under 3 years of age and children of single parents are at the greatest risk of physical abuse [22-24]. Because the examination of violence toward children was imbedded in a larger survey designed to measure all forms of family violence, including violence between couples and violence between siblings, single parents and children less than 3 years of age were excluded from the sample (acts perpetrated by children younger than 3 years of age could not be considered violence in the same way as acts committed by older children).

Of the 2,143 families interviewed, 1,146 had two caretakers and children between the ages of 3 and 17 living at home. The data on parent-to-child violence in the United States are based on the analysis of these 1,146 parent-child relationships.

The Survey in Sweden

Sample. A basic sample of 1,618 individuals representative of Swedish children aged 3 to 17 was purchased by the research team in Sweden. The list contained the name, address, and national registration number of the children, as well as an identifier which indicated who was officially responsible for the household. The head of the household's name, address, and national registration number were obtained also. (In Sweden, the male partner in a two-parent household is automatically identified as the head of the household; thus, a female name automatically indicated a single-parent household.) As the Swedish survey was not concerned with violence between partners, the Swedish sample included two-parent and single-parent households.

There was an initial loss of 3.3% of the sample due to incorrect or insufficient identification data. Forty-one households (2.5%) refused to participate in the survey, although

telephone interviews were completed with 11 of these individuals. Additional cases were lost due to language barriers. Interviews were completed with 78.9% of the sample—a higher completion rate than the U.S. survey. However, a random subsample of 171 completed interviews were lost in transit between two offices of the Swedish State Data Processing Unit. Due to the complete anonymity of the survey, researchers were unable to identify and recontact these individuals.

A final completion rate of 68% was obtained for 1,105 usable interviews. There were 255 single-parent households (only 3 of which were headed by men) and 850 two-parent households. The age and regional distribution of the sample approximated the distribution in Sweden.

Differences Between the Two Surveys

Although the Swedish survey was designed as a replication of the study in the United States, there were some important differences. First, the U.S. survey was conducted in 1976, while the Swedish survey was completed 4 years later in 1980. Second, while both studies collected data by using in-person interviews in the homes of the respondents, the U.S. investigators employed a professional survey research company and professional interviewers. The Swedish interviews were conducted by trained psychologists.

The Conflict Tactics Scales were translated into Swedish. In the process, there were two changes from the original scales. Whereas the American research group asked how often did you threaten/use a gun or knife, the Swedish project asked how often did you threaten/use a weapon. The American version of the scales asked about slapping or spanking, while the Swedish version asked about hitting. In America, respondents were asked how often they hit or tried to hit their children with objects. These items could include attempted and/or com-

TABLE 18.1 Violence Toward Children in the United States and Sweden

Type of Violence	United States		Sweden	
	1975	Ever	1980	Ever
1. Threw things at	5.4%	9.0%	3.6%	13.2%
2. Pushed, grabbed, or shoved	40.5	46.0	49.4	63.3
3. Hit (spanked or slapped)	58.2	71.0	27.5	51.2
4. Kicked, bit, or hit with a fist	3.2	8.0	2.2	8.4
5. Hit with an object[a]	13.4	20.0	2.4	7.7
6. Beat up	1.3	4.0	3.0	8.0
7. Threatened with a weapon	0.1	2.8	0.4	1.5
8. Used a weapon	0.1	2.9	0.4	1.3
All forms of violence (3-8)	63.0	73.0	29.8	66.0
Severe Violence (Index A: 4 thru 8)	14.2		4.6	
Severe Violence (Index B: 4, 6 thru 8)	3.6		4.1	

a. In the United States, this item referred to attempted or completed hits. In Sweden, the item referred only to completed hits.

pleted hits. In Sweden, the interviewers qualified this item by measuring only completed hits.

RESULTS

Because of the contrasts between the United States and Sweden, especially with regard to social and cultural attitudes about violence, and because the Swedish survey was conducted a year after the passage of the anti-spanking law, we expected that the reported rates of violence toward children would be lower in Sweden than in the United States. The results, however, do not generally support this hypothesis.

Physical Punishment

In addition to the administration of the Conflict Tactics Scales, respondents in the United States and Sweden were asked whether they had used any form of physical punishment toward their children in the previous year. Slightly more than half (51.3%) of the Swedish parents reported using physical punishment, compared to more than three quarters (79.2%) of the Americans.

Violence Toward Children

The responses to the Conflict Tactics items offer a more precise comparison as shown in Table 18.1. In general, Swedish parents reported less use of violence toward their children during 1980 than the American respondents reported in 1975 (29.8% vs. 63%). Swedish parents reported less violent conflict tactics during the course of raising their children than the Americans, but the difference here is smaller than for the 1-year recall period.

There is no significant difference between Swedish and American parents in the reported use of severe or abusive violence (kicking, biting, hitting with a fist, beating up, threatening or using a weapon—gun or knife). If one includes hitting (or trying to hit) with an object, there are differences; but these differences are not reliable since the Swedish item only examined completed hits while the item in the United States asked about trying to hit as well.

A rate of abusive violence of 4% in Sweden means that each year 62,000 of the more than 1.5 million Swedish children 3 to 17 years of age are at risk of physical abuse (considering sampling error, the range is from 39,000 to 84,000). In the United States, between 1.4 and 1.9 million children 3 to 17 years of age living with two caretakers were at risk for physical abuse during the survey year.

An item-by-item examination of the two surveys reveals that Swedish parents report more pushing, grabbing, or shoving than American parents (which accounts for the difference between the Swedish previous year figures) and double the rate of beating children, both in the last year and over the course of raising their children. American parents report more spanking (about double the rate of Swedish parents in the previous year, a bit less than 50% more over the course of the child's life). In general, there were far more similarities in the two countries than there were differences.

Factors Associated With Violence Toward Children

A complete profile of the factors associated with violence toward children in the United States has been previously published [13,25]. This section briefly compares the factors found related to violence and abusive violence which are comparable in the two countries.

Age. In both the United States and Sweden, younger parents are more likely to use violence toward their children than older parents.

Marital status. Only intact families were surveyed in the United States. However, much of the child abuse literature claims that single parents are at a greater risk for abusing and striking their children due to higher stress and low income [25-27]. There were no significant differences in the rates of violence toward children between Swedish parents who were married and those who were single parents at the time of the interview.

Education. A curvilinear relation was found between violence toward children and education in the United States—those parents with the highest (at least some college) and lowest (no high school) levels of education were the least likely to use violence. In Sweden, education was unrelated to the rate of abusive violence toward children. Those who had the highest levels of education actually were more likely to report using some form of violence toward their children.

Parents' backgrounds. Violence begets violence, we are told. And, to a certain degree this is borne out in both surveys. Being spanked as a teenager and observing one's parents hit one another raises the chances that a person will be a violent parent, both in the United States and in Sweden.

▎ DISCUSSION ▎

The results of the comparison of violence toward children in the United States and Sweden are complex and do not generally support the hypothesis that Swedish parents are less likely to use violence than American parents. However, Swedish parents tend to be less likely to use the least harmful forms of violence. There is less spanking and slapping in Sweden than there is in the United States. There were no appreciable differences in the rates of abusive violent acts between the two countries.

What accounts for the differences and similarities? First, there are methodological artifacts that may have entered into the comparison study.

Methodological Factors

There were important differences in the qualifications of the interviewers employed in the United States and Sweden. The Swedish interviewers were trained psychologists. We know that they were able to obtain a higher response rate than the American survey research firm. They may have been more successful in eliciting more truthful answers from the respondents. Thus, the rate of violence toward children may be larger in Sweden because the Swedes were more inclined to provide accurate reports of their use of violence, while American respondents systematically under-reported violence.

If one continues to assume that Swedish parents are indeed less violent, then this too could have produced more accurate reporting. If violence is indeed unusual in Sweden, then Swedish parents may have been more likely to remember these unusual behaviors. If violence is "as American as apple pie," then American parents may have been more likely to underreport the routine use of all forms of violence. Thus, Swedish parents may be less violent toward their children than American parents, even though a combination of methodological biases produced similar rates for the abusive forms of violent behavior.

Cultural Factors

In the absence of certain known biases, researchers are trained to believe their data. Thus, even though methodological explanations are a plausible explanation for the findings, we still must accept another plausible explanation: that the similarities and differences are real. If this is the case, why are Swedish parents more moderate in their use of spanking, slapping, general hitting, and throwing things than American parents, but as likely to beat, kick, bite, punch, and even use weapons?

A close examination of the yearly rates of violence compared to the "ever" reports, pro-vides some evidence that the anti-spanking law has had some impact on the lives and behavior of Swedish parents. While the differences between the yearly rates of spanking, slapping, pushing, grabbing, and throwing things are small in the United States, the differences are much greater in Sweden. Since 1980 was the first year that the anti-spanking law was in force (the year of the Swedish survey), parental use of the less harmful forms of violence may have begun to decline.

Spanking, slapping, pushing, and grabbing tend to be the more instrumental forms of violence used by parents. Thus, when hitting children became illegitimate in Sweden, parents may have found it easier to moderate their use of violence as an instrumental technique. Kicking, biting, punching, beating, and using weapons could be considered either more expressive forms of violence (i.e., expressed out of anger or rage) or forms of violence consciously designed to inflict serious injury on a child. These behaviors may be less amenable to control by imposing a cultural standard that spanking is wrong (note the anti-spanking law carries with it no punishment for violation).

At the risk of over-generalizing from a cross-sectional survey, Swedish parents may be responding to the anti-spanking law and lowering their use of the less harmful forms of physical punishment. The more abusive forms of violence appear to be less sensitive to change, at least in the short run.

The fact that there are essentially no differences in the use of abusive violence is still surprising given the differences in cultural attitudes, cultural complexity, and social support in the two countries. One simple explanation is that the attitude changes and levels of social support (e.g., day care, health care) have not gone far enough in Sweden to curtail the use of abusive violence. A more complex formulation is that the differences between the two countries are not nearly as major as one would think. The similarities are those factors which are related to the use of abusive violence toward children. Both societies are Western industrial nations—Sweden tending more toward a socialist economy than the United States. Family life in both countries conforms to the norm of Western industrial nations. Nuclear residence and a premium on family privacy and family rights are the cultural norm for both nations. An exchange/social control explanation of family violence [28] explains that privacy and primacy of the family limits the amount of external social control (formal and informal) that is exerted on family members. With limited social control, the costs of using abusive violence are frequently quite minimal—even if there is a public anti-spanking law. In the extensive report from the Swedish study, another more sophisticated explanation is given to the obvious similarities in the two national samples [29].

Injurious Physical Violence

One of the important limitations of the Conflict Tactics Scales used to measure violence toward children in the United States and Sweden is that it does not measure whether a child was actually ever injured or harmed by the physical violence. While we can measure violent behavior in the two countries, we have little insight into the actual harm inflicted on children. Official reporting records on child maltreatment in the United States are useful means of measuring the harm inflicted on children (at least the harm that comes to public attention). Unfortunately, there is no official reporting of child maltreatment in Sweden, and therefore, there is no opportunity to compare levels of harm experienced by children.

We do have at least some anecdotal data that would seem to imply that, although Swedish and American children are about equally likely to experience violence that could cause harm, there is less of what one would call classic child abuse in Sweden.

At the U.S. and Swedish Symposium on Physical and Sexual Abuse of Children, held in Satra Bruk, Sweden, in June 1985, the Ameri-

can pediatrician, Eli Newberger, presented a report on hospital management of physical abuse. He described a number of cases, including slides of various physically abused children. All Swedish participants agreed that, while they had occasionally seen similar abuse cases in the past, they were no longer seeing these types of cases in 1985.

Thus, although we cannot empirically verify this claim, the changes in social attitudes and social support in Sweden may have been successful in reducing the outrageous, grievous injuries experienced by children. Although Swedish parents are still violent, the violence is not allowed to escalate to the point of injury. However, it is just as possible that, since data on physical abuse are not routinely reported and tabulated in Sweden, the rates of injurious violence are the same in both countries (as our data suggest), but abusive violence in Sweden is simply not recognized or reported as such.

CONCLUSION

Research often tends to raise as many questions as are answered. Such was the case with this first cross-cultural comparison of the rate of violence toward children. We thought that the rates of violence would be lower in Sweden than in the United States, but we found a more complex pattern. Clearly, the relationship between social and cultural attitudes, social support, and societal complexity and the use of physical violence toward children is not simple or unitary. Only with continued and expanded cross-cultural research will we be able to refine our understanding of the sociocultural factors that relate to the physical abuse of children.

REFERENCES

1. GELLES, R. J. and CORNELL, C. *International Perspectives on Family Violence.* Lexington Books, Lexington, MA (1983).

2. KEMPE, C. H. Recent developments in the field of child abuse. *Child Abuse & Neglect 2:* 261-267 (1978).

3. KORBIN, J. (Ed.). *Child Abuse and Neglect: Cross Cultural Perspectives.* University of California Press, Berkeley (1981).

4. STRAUS, M. A. Methodology of collaborative cross-national research on child abuse. Unpublished paper presented at the Swedish/American Symposium on Physical and Sexual Abuse of Children, Satra Bruk, Sweden (1985).

5. VESTERDAL, J. Handling of child abuse in Denmark. *Child Abuse & Neglect:* 193-198 (1977).

6. GELLES, R. J. Violence towards children in the United States. *American Journal of Orthopsychiatry 48:* 580-592 (1978).

7. GELLES, R. J. and CORNELL, C. *Intimate Violence in Families.* Sage, Beverly Hills, CA (1985).

8. BURGDORF, K. *Recognition and Reporting of Child Maltreatment.* Westat, Rockville, MD (1980).

9. GELLES, R. J. The social construction of child abuse. *American Journal of Orthopsychiatry 45:* 363-371 (1975).

10. NEWBERGER, E., REED, R. B., DANIEL, J. H., HYDE, J. N. and KOTELCHUCK, M. Pediatric social illness: Toward an etiologic classification. *Pediatrics 60:* 178-185 (1977).

11. TURBETT, J. P. and O'TOOLE, R. Physician's recognition of child abuse. Unpublished paper presented at the annual meetings of the American Sociological Association, New York (1980).

12. KAMERMAN, S. Eight countries: Cross national perspectives on child abuse and neglect. *Children Today 4:* 34-37 (1975).

13. STRAUS, M. A., GELLES, R. J. and STEINMETZ, S. K. *Behind Closed Doors: Violence in the American Family.* Anchor/Doubleday, Garden City, NY (1980).

14. GELLES, R. J. and STRAUS, M. Determinants of violence in the family: Toward a theoretical integration. In: *Contemporary Theories about the Family,* (Vol. 1), W. R. Burr, R. Hill, F. I. Nye, and I. Reiss (Eds.), pp. 549-581. The Free Press, New York (1979).

15. ALLEN, C. and STRAUS, M. Resources, power and husband-wife violence. Unpublished paper presented to the National Council on Family Relations in Salt Lake City (1975).

16. CATE, R. M., HENTON, J. M. CHRISTOPHER, F. S. and LLOYD, S. Premarital abuse: A social psychological perspective. *Journal of Family Issues 3:* 79-90 (1982).

17. HENTON, J., CATE, R., KOVAL, J., LLOYD, S. and CHRISTOPHER, S. Romance and violence in dating relationships. *Journal of Family Issues 4:* 467-482 (1983).

18. HORNUNG, C., McCULLOUGH, B. and SUGIMOTO, T. Status relationships in marriage: Risk factors in spouse abuse. *Journal of Marriage and the Family 43:* 679-692 (1981).

19. JORGENSEN, S. Societal class heterogamy, status striving, and perception of marital conflict: A partial replication and revision of Perlin's contingency hypothesis. *Journal of Marriage and the Family 43:* 679-692 (1977).

20. STRAUS, M. A. Leveling, civility, and violence in the family. *Journal of Marriage and the Family 36:* 13-30 (1974).

21. STRAUS, M. A. Measuring intrafamily conflict and violence: The Conflict Tactics (CT) scales. *Journal of Marriage and the Family 41:* 75-88 (1979).

22. FERGUSSON, D.M., FLEMING, J. and O'NEIL, D. *Child Abuse in New Zealand* Research Division, Department of Social Work, Wellington NZ (1972).

23. GIL, D. *Violence Against Children: Physical Child Abuse in the United States.* Harvard University Press, Cambridge, MA (1970).

24. JOHNSON, C. *Child Abuse in the Southeast: An Analysis of 1172 Reported Cases.* Welfare Research, Athens, GA (1974).

25. GELLES, R. J. Violence in the family: A review of research in the seventies. *Journal of Marriage and the Family 42:* 873-885 (1980).

26. PARKE, R. D. and COLLMER, C. Child abuse: An interdisciplinary analysis. In: *Review of Child Development Research,* (Vol. 5), M. Hetherington (Ed.), pp. 1-102. University of Chicago Press, Chicago (1975).

27. MADEN, M. F. and WRENCH, D. F. Significant findings in child abuse research. *Victimology 2:* 196-224 (1977).

28. GELLES, R. J. An exchange/social control theory, In: *The Dark Side of Families: Current Family Violence Research,* D. Finkelhor, R. Gelles, M. Straus, and G. Hotaling (Eds.), pp. 151-165. Sage, Beverly Hills, CA (1983).

29. EDFELDT, A. Research and theory on violence towards children in Sweden. Unpublished paper presented at the Sweden/American Symposium on Physical and Sexual Abuse of Children, Satra Bruk, Sweden (1985).

Preventing Child Abuse and Neglect

A Randomized Trial of Nurse Home Visitation

DAVID L. OLDS
CHARLES R. HENDERSON, JR.
ROBERT CHAMBERLIN
ROBERT TATELBAUM   *1986*

"Preventing Child Abuse and Neglect: A Randomized Trial of Nurse Home Visitation" had a significant impact on both the knowledge base of the field and thoughts about best practice methodology. As David Olds and his colleagues report, despite the growing interest in prevention in the early 1980s, only a handful of controlled studies had been completed on specific, promising prevention strategies, and none had been randomized. Through their work, published in 1986, the authors implemented a carefully designed randomized trial of nurses' home visitations for high-risk, first-time, young new mothers, thereby expanding the knowledge base about how to prevent child abuse.

Martha Erickson states that the Olds study constitutes a breakthrough in rigorous evaluation of a specific approach to the prevention of child abuse. The strategies to be evaluated were carefully explained, elegant in their simplicity, and "do-able" in the real world of service. Both the service and research were grounded in an ecological approach that recognizes the importance of variables at different levels. The rigorous methodology is still a benchmark for other studies: randomized, solid measures, analysis of outcomes by level of risk, assessment of the additive effects of different components of treatment. Diane DePanfilis adds that this paper is one of the most frequently cited today both because of the findings (e.g., the positive effects of home visitation in preventing abuse) and because the methodology and study design used were so good—this work has served as a model for many subsequent studies. Erickson adds that the study is a significant reminder of the importance of quality, integrity, and careful documentation of service. The findings remind us about the complexity of such studies and the need to be cautious about interpretation.

Caution has not always been used in applying the findings from this study. Both Depanfilis and Erickson note that the results of this study have too often been used to suggest that any and all home visitation could potentially yield similar results. Professionals and policy makers alike too often take away the simple notion that home visiting works, without regard to who offers the service and to whom, what goes on during a visit, what kind of community the visits are offered in, and how often the visits occur. Yet, at the same time, the study has helped to prompt a veritable plethora of thoughtfully designed programs around the world aimed at helping new parents get off to a good start. This Olds study has also spawned other studies by Olds and many other colleagues. As a result, there has been significant growth in the number of practitioners and researchers working to develop more effective prevention interventions and to promote strong parent-child relationships.

A. C. D. and K. O.

During the last 20 years, public concern about child abuse and neglect has grown dramatically.[1-3] Within the past decade, a National Center on Child Abuse and Neglect has been established by the federal government, a National Committee for the Prevention of Child Abuse has been created in the private sector, and the media routinely convey the message that abuse and neglect are preventable. Two recent surveys have suggested a sharp increase in child abuse and neglect reports in the last 6 years.[4,5] These reports indicate that hundreds of thousands of children and families are in crisis and emphasize the importance of preventive research efforts.[6] In view of these developments, it is disturbing that little is known about the prevention of maltreatment.[7]

Four previous controlled trials of abuse and neglect prevention have produced mixed results. One investigation in this series studied the impact of extended postpartum contact (rooming-in) between mothers and newborns and found a reduction in subsequent caregiving dysfunction.[8] In a second investigation, the effect of early and extended contact was compared to home visitation and a no treatment control[9]; although modest benefits in the area of mother-child interaction were detected for the early contact group, no other benefits were observed for either early contact or home visiting. Treatment effects that may have been intensified for higher risk groups within their samples were not studied. This is unfortunate, because an intensification of treatment effect for higher risk families has been reported in one study of early contact that did not examine child abuse and neglect as an outcome.[10]

In a third controlled trial, from Bradford, England, a group of families at risk for childrearing dysfunction was judged to be unaffected by the provision of preventive services.[11]

Acknowledgment: This research was supported by grants from the Bureau of Community Health Services (HHS-MCR-360403-06), the Robert Wood Johnson Foundation (grant 5263), and the W. T. Grant Foundation (grant 0723-80). We thank Karen Hughes, Jean Thom, Janice Sheppard, and Elizabeth Bement for their help with preparing the manuscript and processing the data; Urie Bronfenbrenner, Robert Cole, Jim Garbarino, Zorika Petic Henderson, Robert Hoekelman, Howard Foye, Gregory Liptak, Elizabeth McAnarney, and Cassie Stevens for offering helpful comments on the manuscript; John Shannon for his administrative support of the project; and Elizabeth Chilson, Diane Farr, Georgianna McGrady, Jacqueline Roberts, and Lyn Scazafabo for their work with the families enrolled in the program.
Originally published in *Pediatrics*, 1986, *78*, 65-78. Reprinted by permission of *Pediatrics*. Copyright 1986.

TABLE 19.1 Services Provided (+) in Each of the Four Treatment Groups

	Treatment Group			
Service Provided	1 (n = 90)	2 (n = 94)	3 (n = 100)	4 (n = 116)
Sensory and developmental screening when children 12 and 24 months of age	+	+	+	+
Free transportation to regular prenatal and well-child visits		+	+	+
Nurse home visitation during pregnancy			+	+
Nurse home visitation during the child's first 2 years of life				+

The services (contact by the project social worker after mothers' and newborns' discharge from the hospital, creation of a drop-in center open 1 day a week, and provision of the project secretary's phone number) did not affect the complex, interrelated factors that undermine parents' capacities to care for their children.

The fourth study examined the effects of providing intensive pediatric consultation plus home visitation to a sample of women at risk for child abuse and neglect and found a reduction in hospitalization for serious injury. The findings are weakened, however, because evaluation follow-up was carried out on only half of the families, and there were no other treatment differences in abnormal parenting practices.[12] It is evident that a variety of problems with research and program design make it difficult to interpret the earlier work in abuse and neglect prevention.

Home visitation has been postulated to be a potent means of preventing maltreatment.[13-16] A comprehensive program of prenatal and postpartum nurse home visitation was evaluated in the present study; it was designed to prevent a wide range of childhood health and developmental problems, including abuse and neglect.

▌ DESIGN AND METHOD ▌

The study design consisted of a randomized clinical trial. Families were assigned at random to one of the four treatment conditions (Table 19.1).

Treatment Conditions

Treatment 1. Families in the first condition served as a control. During pregnancy, no services were provided through the research project. When the babies were 1 and 2 years of age, an infant specialist hired by the research project screened them for sensory and developmental problems. Suspected problems were referred to other specialists for further evaluation and treatment.

Treatment 2. Families in the second condition were provided free transportation for regular prenatal and well-child care at local clinics and physicians' offices through a contract with a local taxicab company. Sensory and developmental screening, as in Treatment 1, was provided when the babies were 1 and 2 years of age.

Treatment 3. In the third condition, families were provided a nurse home-visitor during pregnancy in addition to screening and transportation services. The nurses visited families approximately once every 2 weeks and made an average of nine visits during pregnancy, each of which lasted approximately one hour 15 minutes.

Treatment 4. Families assigned to the fourth condition received the same services as those in Treatment 3, but, in addition, the nurse continued to visit until the child was 2 years of age. For 6 weeks following delivery, the nurses visited families every week; from 6 weeks to 4 months, every 2 weeks; from 4 to 14 months, every 3 weeks; from 14 to 20 months, every 4 weeks; and from 20 to 24 months, every 6 weeks. When predetermined crisis conditions existed, they visited weekly. The visits lasted approximately one hour 15 minutes.

Postnatal Home Visitation Program

During their postnatal home visits, the nurses carried out three major activities that they had begun during pregnancy: parent education regarding fetal and infant development, the involvement of family members and friends in child care and support of the mother, and the linkage of family members with other health and human services. A central aspect of the nurses' approach was to emphasize the strengths of the women and their families.

In their home-based education program, the nurses provided parents with information on infant development, with the ultimate objective of improving parental behavior that theoretically affects the child's well-being. Specific objectives included improving parents' understanding of the following topics: the infant's temperament, especially crying behavior and its meanings; the infant's socioemotional and cognitive needs, including his or her need for responsive caregiving and for progressively more complex motor, social, and intellectual experiences; the infant's physical health care needs, such as dietary requirements and bathing, how to take the baby's temperature and manage common health problems, and the need for routine health care and immunizations. The nurses used a detailed curriculum to guide their educational activities but tailored the content of their visits to the individual needs of each family.

The second major activity of the nurses was to enhance the informal support available to the women during early child rearing. As during pregnancy, the nurses encouraged the women's close friends and relatives to participate in the home visits, to help with household responsibilities, to aid in the care of the child, and to reinforce the advice of the nurses in their absence.

The nurses also connected families with community health and human service agencies. Parents were urged to keep well-child care appointments and to call the physician's office when a health problem occurred, so that the office staff might help them make decisions about whether office or emergency room visits were necessary. The nurses sent two regular reports of their observations regarding medical, social, and emotional conditions to the private physicians who provided the babies' pediatric care. When visiting families' homes, the nurses also clarified and reinforced the physicians' recommendations. When necessary, parents were referred to other services, such as vocational training programs, Planned Parenthood, mental health counseling, legal aid, and the nutritional supplementation program for women, infants, and children (WIC).

Each of the program components—parent education, enhancement of informal support, and linkage of families with health and human services—was designed to work in an integrated, complementary way to improve conditions for bearing and rearing children in socially disadvantaged families.

Detailed record-keeping systems and regular case reviews were used to ensure that the home visit protocol was followed by each nurse. Detailed descriptions of the program are provided elsewhere.[15-17]

Setting

The study was carried out in a small, semirural county of approximately 100,000 residents in the Appalachian region of New York State. At the time the study was initiated, the community was well served from the standpoint of both health and human services. Prenatal care was available through nine private obstetricians and a free antepartum clinic sponsored by the health department. Pediatric care was provided by two sophisticated pediatric practices (with a total of 11 pediatricians) and eight physicians in family practice. A variety of social services was available for children and families. In spite of an abundance of health and human services, the community has consistently exhibited the highest rates of reported and confirmed cases of child abuse and neglect in the state.[18] Moreover, in 1980, the community was rated the worst Standard Metropolitan Statistical Area in the United States in terms of its economic conditions.[19]

Sample

Women were actively recruited if, at intake, they had no previous live births and had any one of the following characteristics that predispose to infant health and developmental problems: (1) young age (< 19 years), (2) single-parent status, (3) low socioeconomic status. The study design, however, allowed any woman who asked to participate and who was bearing a first child to be enrolled. This avoided creating a program that was stigmatized as being exclusively for the poor and, by creating sample heterogeneity, it enabled us to determine whether the effects of the program were greater for families at higher risk. All women were enrolled prior to the 30th week of pregnancy. They were recruited through the health department antepartum clinic, the offices of private obstetricians, Planned Parenthood, the public schools, and a variety of other health and human service agencies. Approximately 10% of the target population was missed due to late registration for prenatal care. An additional 10% was missed because some eligible women from the offices of private obstetricians were not referred. Of 500 women inter-

viewed between April 1978 and September 1980, 400 were enrolled. There were no differences in age, marital status, or education between those women who participated and those who declined. Of the nonwhite women (mostly blacks), 94% enrolled as opposed to 80% of the whites ($P = .02$). At registration, 47% of the participating women were younger than 19 years of age, 62% were unmarried, and 61% came from families in Hollingshead's[20] social class IV and V (semiskilled and unskilled laborers; Hollingshead's index was adapted slightly to accommodate the variety of household compositions found in our sample). Eighty-five percent of the women met at least one of the age, marital status, or socioeconomic status criteria, and 23% possessed all three risk characteristics.

Forty-six nonwhite women were removed from the analyses reported here because the sample of nonwhite women was too small to cross-classify race with other variables of importance in the statistical analyses. Results for these nonwhite cases are presented elsewhere.[21]

Treatment Assignment

Families enrolled in the program were stratified by marital status, race, and seven geographic regions within the county (based on census tract boundaries). These families were assigned at random to one of the four treatment conditions. At the end of the intake interview, the women drew their treatment assignments from a deck of cards. The stratification was executed by using separate decks for the groups defined by the women's race, marital status at intake, and, for white women, the geographic region in which they resided. To ensure reasonably balanced subclasses, the decks were reconstituted periodically to overrepresent those treatments with smaller numbers of subjects, a procedure similar to Efron's[22] biased-coin designs. Women in Treatments 3 and 4 subsequently were assigned on a rotating basis, within their stratification blocks, to one of five home visitors.

There were two deviations from the randomization procedure. First, in six cases, women who enrolled were living in the same household as other women already participating in the study. To avoid potential horizontal diffusion of the treatment in the case of different assignment within households, the six new enrollees were assigned to the same treatment as their housemates.

Second, during the last 6 months of the 30-month enrollment period, the number of cards representing Treatment 4 was increased in each of the decks to enlarge the size of that group and to enhance the statistical power of the design to compare the infancy home-visiting program with Treatments 1 and 2 on infant health and developmental outcomes. Analysis of selected dependent variables confirmed that this slight confounding of treatments with time did not alter the pattern of treatment effects reported here.

Data Collection

Interviews and infant assessments were carried out at registration (prior to the 30th week of pregnancy), and at 6, 10, 12, 22, and 24 months of the infant's life. Medical records were abstracted for the infant's first 2 years of life, and the records of child abuse and neglect registries for 15 states in which families had lived were reviewed. Reliability of the medical record review procedure was checked on a systematic and regular basis and was found to be acceptable.[21]

Except in a small number of cases in which participating women inadvertently disclosed their treatment assignments, all interview and medical record data were collected by staff members who were unaware of the families' treatment assignments. The workers who reviewed the child abuse and neglect registries did not know whether families were in a nurse-visited group.

At registration, prior to their assignment to one of the treatment conditions, the women were interviewed to determine their family characteristics, psychological resources, health conditions, health habits, the availability of informal support, and childhood histories.

During infancy, the babies were brought to the project office at 6, 12, and 24 months for weighing and measuring. The infants also were administered developmental tests in the project offices, using the Bayley scales at 12 months and the Cattell scales at 24 months. At each of these assessments, the mothers were interviewed concerning common infant behavioral problems, such as feeding difficulties and crying, and how the mothers responded to these problems. When the babies were 6 months of age, the mothers were administered an infant temperament Q-sort procedure.[23]

When the infants were 10 and 22 months old, the mothers were interviewed in their homes, and the Caldwell Home Observation checklist and interview procedure was completed. The Caldwell and Bradley[24] procedure evaluates qualities of the home environment and parental caregiving according to six dimensions, including the mother's avoidance of restriction and punishment and the provision of appropriate play materials. Rates of interobserver agreement for the Caldwell procedure on individual items ranged from 82% to 100%.[21]

A list containing the names of all participating women and their children, their children's ages, and their addresses was given to state department of social service workers, who thoroughly reviewed the department records for the presence of "indicated" (i.e., verified) cases of abuse or neglect. Verified cases consisted of those that were reported for abuse or neglect and investigated by a department caseworker who determined that an episode of abuse or neglect, as defined by state law, had indeed occurred. Those cases were then reviewed by department workers to abstract standard information such as age of the child at the time of the first confirmed report, the specific type of abuse and neglect, the alleged perpetrator, and source of the maltreatment report. The names of children and parents who moved to 15 other states during the investigation were sent for review. Fourteen states cooperated, leaving only one case (a nurse-visited nonrisk family with no indication of maltreatment from the local records) that had to be omitted from the sample because of incomplete data.

Statistical Model and Methods of Analysis

For all analyses, a core statistical model was derived that consisted of a 3 2 2 2 factorial structure (leading to 24 smallest subclasses): treatments (1 and 2 versus 3 versus 4) maternal age (< 19 versus ≥ 19 years) marital status social class (Hollingshead classes IV and V versus I, II, and III). Two covariates measured at registration (maternal sense of control and reported husband/boyfriend support) also were included in the model for most analyses to adjust for chance differences between treatment groups for certain at-risk subsamples and to reduce error variance.

Treatments 1 and 2 were combined for purposes of analysis after it was determined that there were no differences between these two groups in their use of routine prenatal and well-child care, the primary means by which transportation was hypothesized to affect pregnancy and infancy outcomes. We refer to the combination of Treatments 1 and 2 as the comparison group and to Treatment 4 as the nurse-visited group. In the tables, Treatment 3 is labeled *nurse-visited: pregnancy,* and Treatment 4 is labeled *nurse-visited: infancy.* Planned comparisons focused on the contrast of the nurse-visited versus the comparison group for the whole sample and for those subsamples defined as being at risk: the teenagers (< 19 years of age), the unmarried, the poor, and the group with all three risk characteristics.

Dependent variables for which a normal distribution was assumed were analyzed in the general linear model, the one dichotomous outcome (presence or absence of abuse and ne-

glect) in the logistic-linear model (assuming a binomial distribution), and low-incidence outcomes in the form of counts (number of emergency room visits) in the log-linear model (assuming a Poisson distribution). No formal tests of distributional assumptions were performed. Estimates and tests were adjusted for all covariates, classification factors, and interactions. Analysis was by our own computer programs, except that in the logistic- and log-linear cases, the model-fitting algorithm of GLIM[25] was invoked as a subroutine. These programs have been developed over many years and have been subjected to rigorous accuracy tests.

The means presented correspond directly to the tests: They are equally weighted averages of the 24 smallest-subclass means, adjusted for the covariates. In the logistic- and log-linear cases, means are given in incidence form because this corresponds more closely to the presentation of general linear model results than would, for example, log odds ratios. Hypothesis tests are unaltered by the form of presentation.

A thorough investigation was carried out for each covariate to determine whether its relationship with the dependent variable was the same for contrasting groups defined by levels of the classification factors, that is, whether the slopes were parallel (the regressions were homogeneous). Nonhomogeneous regressions represent an interaction between the covariate and one or more categorical variables, and certain tests of means depend on the covariate in that a different test exists for each value of the covariate.[26]

For tests that depend on the covariate, the situation can be shown pictorially by plotting the separately estimated regression lines for the groups being compared. With the effects of other covariates and relevant subclasses subsumed in the intercept of the equation, the vertical distance between the lines represents the estimated mean difference at a given covariate value. A test of the mean difference can be carried out for any specified value, or, alternatively, a region can be computed within which means differ statistically. Because the region provides information about a continuum of covariate values, the used of simultaneous statistical inference is appropriate. [27-29]

In the current analysis, we have extended these methods to dependent variables with binomial and Poisson error distributions. The relationship between certain outcomes (child abuse or neglect and emergency room visits) and maternal sense of control differed depending on whether the women were visited by a nurse or assigned to the comparison group. For these dependent variables, results are first presented without adjustment for maternal sense of control; then, the regions of significant treatment differences, delimited by values of this covariate, are shown. We used a significance level of .10 in computing these regions. It sometimes is suggested that a significance level higher than the conventional .05 be used in simultaneous inference, where achieving significance is more difficult.[30] As a comparison, we also present the value of "sense of control" at which treatments differ at the .05 level for a single test.

RESULTS

Preintervention Equivalence of Treatment Conditions

The treatment conditions were examined carefully to determine their equivalence at registration. The nurse-visited and comparison group women were equivalent on all standard sociodemographic characteristics (Table 19.2). On psychological and social support variables, however, in contrast to their comparison group counterparts, there was a trend for the nurse-visited women to expect less accompaniment to labor and delivery ($P = .10$); the unmarried women assigned a nurse had a significantly greater sense of control over their lives ($P = .04$); and the poor, unmarried teenagers assigned a nurse reported greater support from their boy-

friends ($P = .03$). Because sense of control and husband/boyfriend support were related more consistently to the outcomes of this study than was expected accompaniment to labor and delivery, the potential bias created by this initial nonequivalence was handled by including the two former variables in the statistical model as covariates.

Attrition

During the first 2 years of the children's lives, the rates of attrition varied from 15% to 21%, and there were no differences across treatments in the proportion of subjects with completed assessments. In the nurse-visited condition, however, the women who discontinued tended to have a greater sense of control than those who discontinued the comparison group ($P = .06$). An examination of the reasons for these women's discontinuation showed that they had either moved or miscarried. Because women with greater sense of control were more likely to discontinue the nurse-visited group than the comparison group, the preintervention treatment difference for unmarried women in sense of control was not significant in the sample available for assessment at the child's second birthday. Even though more women with greater sense of control dropped out of the nurse-visited group than from the comparison group, the women who remained in the comparison and nurse-visited groups at the end of the program remained essentially equivalent.

Child Abuse and Neglect

During the first 2 years of the children's lives, 19% of the comparison group at greatest risk (the poor, unmarried teens) and 4% of their nurse-visited counterparts had abused or neglected their children ($P = .07$; Table 19.3). (There also was a trend [$P = .07$] for the nurse-visited teenagers to have fewer confirmed reports of abuse and neglect than the teenagers in the comparison group. Because there was little corroborating evidence to support the interpretation that the program was effective with all teenagers, irrespective of their marital status and poverty, we have not emphasized this finding in the remainder of the report.) Although the treatment contrasts for the groups at lower risk did not reach statistical significance, virtually all of the contrasts were in the expected direction. Moreover, in the comparison condition the incidence of abuse and neglect increased as the number of risk factors accumulated, but in the nurse-visited condition, the incidence of abuse and neglect remained relatively low, even in those groups at higher risk. Also, the incidence of maltreatment in Treatment 3 (nurse-visited: pregnancy) in general, was between the infancy nurse-visited and comparison conditions. (This pattern, in which the means of the nurse-visited: pregnancy group was between the other two groups, as indicated below, also held for most of the other outcomes.)

A qualitative review of the eight cases of abuse and neglect among the poor, unmarried teenagers in the comparison condition indicated that four of the eight cases consisted of neglect alone, whereas the remaining four involved a combination of abuse and neglect. In five of the eight cases, the mother was the sole perpetrator; in the three remaining cases, the mother and father shared responsibility for the incidents. Five of the eight families were reported by nonmandated sources (e.g., neighbors, family members), and the remaining three were reported by mandated sources (professionals required by law to report suspected maltreatment). The one nurse-visited case consisted of a combination of abuse and neglect in which both the mother and her boyfriend were the perpetrators. This case was reported by a mandated source. Because the child abuse finding was only marginally significant and subject to potential reporting bias, it was important to determine the extent to which the finding was corroborated by other evidence.

Reports of Infant Temperature and Behavioral Problems and Maternal Concern, Conflict, Scolding, and Spanking

In contrast to women assigned to the comparison condition, nurse-visited women reported that their babies had more positive moods (happier, less irritable dispositions) ($P = .04$) but that their babies had more frequent episodes of resisting eating ($P = .01$) (Table 19.4). There was a trend for the nurse-visited poor, unmarried teenagers to report that their babies cried less frequently ($P = .07$). In response to their 6-month-old infants' behavioral problems, nurse-visited women, irrespective of their risk status, reported greater concern ($P = .05$), whereas there were trends for the nurse-visited poor, unmarried teenagers to report less conflict with and scolding of their babies than their comparison group counterparts ($P = .06$ and $P = .09$, respectively).

Provision of Appropriate Play Materials and Avoidance of Restriction and Punishment

Within the group at greatest risk (the poor, unmarried teenagers), the nurse-visited women were observed in their homes, when their babies were 10 and 22 months of age, to punish and restrict their children less frequently than were their counterparts in the comparison group ($P = .007$ and $P = .04$, respectively) (Table 19.5). Similarly, the nurse-visited poor, unmarried teenagers provided their children with a larger number of appropriate play materials than did the poor, unmarried teenagers in the comparison group ($P = .01$ and $P = .002$, respectively).

Developmental Quotient

As illustrated in Table 19.6, at 12 and 24 months of life, there were trends for the babies

TABLE 19.2 Preintervention Treatment Differences and 95 Percent Confidence Intervals for Maternal Background Characteristics

	Sample			
	Whole		Poor, Unmarried Teenagers (<19 yr of age at registration)	
Dependent Variable and Treatment Group	$\bar{x}$	n	$\bar{x}$	n
Proportion in Hollingshead's social classes IV and V				
Comparison	0.61	165	1.00	32
Nurse-visited:pregnancy	0.62	90	1.00	19
Nurse-visited:infancy	0.60	99	1.00	23
Comparison minus nurse-visited (infancy)	0.01 ± 0.12		0.00 ± 0.24	
Proportion unmarried				
Comparison	0.57	165	1.00	32
Nurse-visited:pregnancy	0.59	90	1.00	19
Nurse-visited:infancy	0.60	99	1.00	23
Comparison minus nurse-visited (infancy)	−0.03 ± 0.12		0.00 ± 0.24	
Proportion <19 years of age				
Comparison	0.41	165	1.00	32
Nurse-visited:pregnancy	0.47	90	1.00	19
Nurse-visited:infancy	0.49	99	1.00	23
Comparison minus nurse-visited (infancy)	−0.08 ± 0.12		0.00 ± 0.24	
Proportion with no risk characteristics				
Comparison	0.17	165	0.00	32
Nurse-visited:pregnancy	0.17	90	0.00	19
Nurse-visited:infancy	0.14	99	0.00	23
Comparison minus nurse-visited (infancy)	0.03 ± 0.09		0.00 ± 0.18	
Maternal education (years completed)				
Comparison	11.25	165	9.78	32
Nurse-visited:pregnancy	11.58	90	10.16	19
Nurse-visited:infancy	11.32	99	9.87	23
Comparison minus nurse-visited (infancy)	−0.07 ± 0.32		−0.09 ± 0.62	
Maternal sense of control[a]				
Comparison	12.21	165	11.93	32
Nurse-visited:pregnancy	12.31	90	12.47	19
Nurse-visited:infancy	12.44	99	12.48	23
Comparison minus nurse-visited (infancy)	−0.23 ± 0.41		−0.55 ± 0.78	
Number of people/helping network				
Comparison	5.30	165	4.75	32
Nurse-visited:pregnancy	5.16	90	3.95	19
Nurse-visited:infancy	5.01	99	4.87	23
Comparison minus nurse-visited (infancy)	0.29 ± 0.66		−0.12 ± 1.26	
Number of intimates/helping network				
Comparison	1.75	165	1.56	32
Nurse-visited:pregnancy	2.08	90	1.79	19
Nurse-visited:infancy	1.57	99	1.39	23
Comparison minus nurse-visited (infancy)	0.18 ± 0.40		0.17 ± 0.81	
Number of kin/helping network				
Comparison	3.42	165	2.69	32
Nurse-visited:pregnancy	3.09	90	1.85	19
Nurse-visited:infancy	3.09	99	1.96	23
Comparison minus nurse-visited (infancy)	0.33 ± 0.51		0.73 ± 0.97	

TABLE 19.2 *Continued*

	Sample			
	Whole		Poor, Unmarried Teenagers (<19 yr of age at registration)	
Dependent Variable and Treatment Group	$\bar{x}$	*n*	$\bar{x}$	*n*
Expected accompaniment to labor and delivery				
Comparison	9.66	165	9.30	32
Nurse-visited:pregnancy	9.36	90	9.50	19
Nurse-visited:infancy	9.04	99	8.68	23
Comparison minus nurse-visited (infancy)	0.62 ± 0.74*		0.62 ± 1.46	
Husband/boyfriend support[b]				
Comparison	0.85	165	−5.22	32
Nurse-visited:pregnancy	1.55	90	−2.41	19
Nurse-visited:infancy	0.34	99	−0.94	23
Comparison minus nurse-visited (infancy)	0.51 ± 2.03		−4.28 ± 3.87**	
Grandmother support[c]				
Comparison	0.12	165	4.37	32
Nurse-visited:pregnancy	−1.07	90	−2.22	19
Nurse-visited:infancy	−0.07	99	3.62	23
Comparison minus nurse-visited (infancy)	0.19 ± 1.45		0.75 ± 2.79	
Predicted positive parenting[d]				
Comparison	0.61	165	0.41	32
Nurse-visited:pregnancy	0.57	90	0.37	19
Nurse-visited:infancy	0.54	99	0.48	23
Comparison minus nurse-visited (infancy)	0.07 ± 0.10		−0.07 ± 0.19	

a. Scale measuring extent to which women felt control over their life circumstances, using a short-form variant of Rotter's[31] locus of control instrument.
b. Scale characterizing availability, contact, and anticipated help with pregnancy and child rearing from the women's husbands or boyfriends.
c. Scale characterizing availability, contact, and anticipated help with pregnancy and child rearing from the women's own mothers.
d. Scale derived from discriminant analysis to predict quality of caregiving, based on weighted sum of mother's reports of being yelled at, spanked, and treated restrictively in her own childhood; the level of psychosocial stress in her family of origin; her level of ego development; her prepregnant level of smoking; the economic status of her current household; and a housing-crowdedness index.
$*P < .10.$ $** P < .05.$

of poor, unmarried teenagers assigned to the nurse-visited condition to have higher developmental quotients than the babies of their counterparts assigned to the comparison group ($P = .06$ and $P = .08$, respectively).

Emergency Room Visits

During the first year of life, the babies of nurse-visited women, especially the babies of poor, unmarried teenagers, were seen in the emergency room fewer times than their counterparts in the comparison group ($P = .04$ for both contrasts) (Table 19.7). A detailed review of the medical records revealed that these differences were explained by a reduction in visits for upper respiratory tract infections. During the second year of life, the babies of nurse-visited women were seen in the emergency room fewer times ($P = .01$) and presented with fewer accidents and poisonings than their counterparts in the comparison condition ($P = .03$).

TABLE 19.3 Treatment Differences and 95 Percent Confidence Intervals for Child Abuse and Neglect—Adjusted for Husband/Boyfriend Support

| | Sample | | | | | | | | | | | | | | | | | |
| | Whole | | Nonrisk | | Nonpoor | | Married | | Older (< 19 years) | | Poor | | Unmarried | | Teenager (< 19 years) | | Poor Unmarried Teenagers | |
Treatment Group	x̄	n	x̄	n	x̄	n	x̄	n	x̄	n	x̄	n	x̄	n	x̄	n	x̄	n
Comparison	0.10	161	0.05	27	0.08	62	0.10	69	0.05	94	0.12	99	0.10	92	0.15	67	0.19	32
Nurse-visited:pregnancy	0.08	86	0.00	11	0.00	31	0.09	35	0.10	45	0.17	55	0.08	51	0.07	41	0.18	18
Nurse-visited:infancy	0.05	95	0.00	14	0.04	40	0.04	38	0.06	48	0.07	55	0.06	57	0.05	47	0.04	22
Comparison minus nurse-visited:infancy	0.05 ±0.09		0.05 ±0.10		0.04 ±0.06		0.06 ±0.13		-0.01 ±0.12		0.05 ±0.08		0.04 ±0.07		0.10 ±0.11*		0.15 ±0.16*	

NOTE: For the whole sample, the teenagers, the unmarried, the poor, and the group for which all three risk characteristics were present, the comparisons of treatments were planned. Tests shown in this table are not independent; they are not to be interpreted as individual findings but are presented to illustrate in detail the pattern of results.

*P < .10.

TABLE 19.4 Treatment Differences and 95 Percent Confidence Intervals for Reports of Infant Temperament, Behavioral Problems, and Maternal Reaction to Behavioral Problems at 6 Months of Age—Adjusted for Husband/Boyfriend Support and Maternal Sense of Control

	Sample			
	Whole		Poor, Unmarried Teenagers	
Dependent Variable and Treatment Group	$\bar{x}$	n	$\bar{x}$	n
Positive mood[a]				
Comparison	2.29	135	2.12	28
Nurse-visited:pregnancy	2.34	64	2.20	13
Nurse-visited:infancy	2.40	74	2.32	14
Comparison minus nurse-visited (infancy)	−0.11 ± 0.10**		−0.20 ± 0.20*	
Crying (number of episodes last 2 weeks)				
Comparison	3.93	107	4.51	22
Nurse-visited:pregnancy	4.05	57	4.22	12
Nurse-visited:infancy	3.44	56	3.53	11
Comparison minus nurse-visited (infancy)	0.49 ± 0.59		0.98 ± 1.17*	
Resist eating (number of episodes last 2 weeks)				
Comparison	1.72	107	1.88	22
Nurse-visited:pregnancy	2.01	57	1.83	12
Nurse-visited:infancy	2.29	56	1.89	11
Comparison minus nurse-visited (infancy)	−0.57 ± 0.45***		−0.01 ± 0.90	
Night awake (number of episodes last 2 weeks)				
Comparison	2.83	107	3.43	22
Nurse-visited:pregnancy	3.25	57	3.15	12
Nurse-visited:infancy	2.69	56	3.44	11
Comparison minus nurse-visited (infancy)	0.14 ± 0.66		−0.01 ± 1.30	
Worry or concern (sum of positive responses for behavioral problems)				
Comparison	0.54	107	0.52	22
Nurse-visited:pregnancy	0.61	57	0.34	12
Nurse-visited:infancy	0.83	56	0.84	11
Comparison minus nurse-visited (infancy)	−0.29 ± 0.28**		−0.32 ± 0.55	
Conflict (sum of positive responses for behavioral problems)				
Comparison	0.25	107	0.68	22
Nurse-visited:pregnancy	0.27	57	0.50	12
Nurse-visited:infancy	0.29	56	0.28	11
Comparison minus nurse-visited (infancy)	−0.04 ± 0.20		0.40 ± 0.40*	
Yell or scold (number of times last 2 weeks)				
Comparison	7.90	103	8.45	22
Nurse-visited:pregnancy	7.56	48	10.48	10
Nurse-visited:infancy	3.99	56	0.70	10
Comparison minus nurse-visited (infancy)	3.91 ± 5.00		7.75 ± 8.82*	
Spank or hit (number of times last 2 weeks)				
Comparison	1.09	103	1.89	22
Nurse-visited:pregnancy	1.71	48	2.00	10
Nurse-visited:infancy	0.19	56	−0.02	10

a. One of five dimensions of infant temperament measured. The others include adaptability, approach, activity level, and rhythmicity.
*$P < .10$. **$P < .05$. ***$P < .01$.

TABLE 19.5 Treatment Differences and 95 Percent Confidence Intervals for Avoidance of Restriction and Punishment and Provision of Play Materials When Infants Were 10 and 22 Months of Age—Adjusted for Husband/Boyfriend Support and Maternal Sense of Control

	Sample			
	Whole		Poor, Unmarried Teenagers	
	$\bar{x}$	n	$\bar{x}$	n
Avoidance of restriction and punishment (10 months)[a]				
Comparison	5.60	123	5.06	27
Nurse-visited:pregnancy	5.77	61	5.63	10
Nurse-visited:infancy	5.40	68	6.26	16
Comparison minus nurse-visited (infancy)	0.20 ± 0.46		.20 ± 0.87**	
Provision of appropriate play materials (10 months)[b]				
Comparison	7.26	128	5.94	28
Nurse-visited:pregnancy	7.45	67	6.70	11
Nurse-visited:infancy	7.36	73	7.35	16
Comparison minus nurse-visited (infancy)	−0.10 ± 0.56		−1.41 ± 1.08**	
Avoidance of restriction and punishment (22 months)[a]				
Comparison	6.28	115	5.28	24
Nurse-visited:pregnancy	5.53	56	6.12	8
Nurse-visited:infancy	5.82	65	6.45	15
Comparison minus nurse-visited (infancy)	0.46 ± 0.60		−1.17 ± 1.11*	
Provision of appropriate play materials (22 months)[b]				
Comparison	8.65	126	7.76	26
Nurse-visited:pregnancy	8.66	64	8.35	11
Nurse-visited:infancy	8.68	72	8.59	15
Comparison minus nurse-visited (infancy)	−0.03 ± 0.26		−0.83 ± 0.52**	

a. Scale consisting of sum of eight yes/no items observed in home (e.g., mother does not shout at child during visit; mother neither slaps nor spanks child during visit).
b. Scale consisting of sum of nine yes/no items (e.g., child has one or more muscle toys or pieces of equipment; child has push or pull toys).
*P < .05. **P < .01.

Maternal Sense of Control as a Conditioner of Treatment Effects

Among the poor, unmarried teenagers, the treatment difference in child abuse and neglect was greater at lower levels of maternal sense of control. For the comparison group, the incidence of maltreatment increased as maternal sense of control declined ($P = .005$), but among the nurse-visited women, a decline in maternal sense of control did not lead to an increase in abuse and neglect ($P = .75$). The test of the difference between the two regression lines pro-

duced a probability of .11, a level low enough to have a significant effect on the interpretation of treatment mean differences.[26]

The estimated regressions of number of emergency room visits during the second year of life on the women's reported sense of control, for all nurse-visited and comparison-group women irrespective of their sociodemographic risk status, were calculated. For the comparison group, the incidence of emergency room visits increased as maternal sense of control declined ($P = .004$); but among the nurse-visited women, there was no such rela-

TABLE 19.6 Treatment Differences and 95 Percent Confidence Intervals for Infant Developmental Quotients at 12 and 24 Months of Life—Adjusted for Husband/Boyfriend Support and Maternal Sense of Control

	Sample			
	Whole		Poor, Unmarried Teenagers	
Dependent Variable and Treatment Group	$\bar{x}$	n	$\bar{x}$	n
Bayley Mental Development Index (12 months)				
Comparison	109.94	131	104.13	26
Nurse-visited:pregnancy	105.44	68	105.86	13
Nurse-visited:infancy	111.23	73	115.01	15
Comparison minus nurse-visited (infancy)	−1.29 ± .53		−10.88 ± 11.12*	
Cattell (24 months)				
Comparison	106.49	122	101.94	25
Nurse-visited:pregnancy	105.73	64	96.02	12
Nurse-visited:infancy	109.34	71	110.56	16
Comparison minus nurse-visited (infancy)	−2.85 ± 5.23		−8.62 ± 9.64*	

*$P < .10$.

tion ($P = .53$). The difference between these regression lines was significant ($P = .02$). A nearly identical pattern emerged for the regression of number of second-year emergency room visits for accidents and poisonings on women's sense of control.

DISCUSSION

The pattern of results from this investigation provides evidence that nurse home-visitors are capable of preventing a number of caregiving dysfunctions, including child abuse and neglect. The positive effects of the program were concentrated on those women at greatest risk for caregiving dysfunction, and the finding of abuse and neglect prevention was supported by a variety of sources: department of social service records, maternal reports of child behavior and maternal caregiving, observations of maternal caregiving, the children's developmental tests, and emergency room records.

As coherent as these results appear to be, they must be viewed with caution for two reasons. First, the nurse-visited unmarried women reported greater sense of control over their lives at the start of the study than did their counterparts in the comparison group. The intensification of treatment effects for the child maltreatment and emergency room outcomes among women with decreasing sense of control over their lives may be a product of this initial nonequivalence.

It should be noted, nevertheless, that these preintervention differences were attenuated, because women with greater sense of control were more likely to discontinue the nurse-visited condition than the comparison condition. Moreover, it is theoretically coherent that the positive effects of the program would intensify as the vulnerability of the population increases. It was only in the case of the dichotomous and low-frequency count data (the abuse and neglect and emergency room outcomes) that we encountered nonhomogeneous regressions by treatments—an intensification of the treatment effect on the given outcome as ma-

TABLE 19.7 Treatment Differences and 95 Percent Confidence Intervals for Emergency Room Visits (Total and for Accidents and Poisonings) for the First and Second Years of Life—Adjusted for Husband/Boyfriend Support

	Sample			
	Whole		Poor, Unmarried Teenagers	
	n	$\bar{x}$	n	$\bar{x}$
Number of emergency room visits (first year of life)				
Comparison	1.02	136	1.66	29
Nurse-visited:pregnancy	1.12	69	1.27	13
Nurse-visited:infancy	0.74	87	0.95	21
Comparison minus nurse-visited (infancy)	0.28 ± 0.20*		0.71 ± 0.64*	
Number of emergency room visits for accidents and poisonings (first year of life)				
Comparison	0.06	136	0.12	29
Nurse-visited:pregnancy	0.12	69	0.07	13
Nurse-visited:infancy	0.12	87	0.09	21
Comparison minus nurse-visited (infancy)	−0.06 ± 0.14		0.03 ± 0.18	
Number of emergency visits (second year of life)				
Comparison	1.09	121	1.27	27
Nurse-visited:pregnancy	1.04	64	1.19	12
Nurse-visited:infancy	0.74	75	0.90	16
Comparison minus nurse-visited (infancy)	0.35 ± 0.28**		0.37 ± 0.67	
Number of emergency visits for accidents and poisonings (second year of life)				
Comparison	0.34	121	0.33	27
Nurse-visited:pregnancy	0.32	64	0.23	12
Nurse-visited:infancy	0.15	75	0.26	16
Comparison minus nurse-visited (infancy)	0.19 ± 0.17*		0.07 ± 0.42	

$*P < .05. **P < .01.$

ternal sense of control declined. This intensification occurred, in large part, because the incidence of these adverse outcomes was relatively infrequent in the nurse-visited group, whereas the incidence increased among comparison group women who had little sense of control over their lives. For other caregiving outcomes, the regressions on maternal sense of control were homogeneous for treatments. Thus, tests of treatment differences could be made with conventional adjustments for biasing background characteristics.

The presence of treatment differences for reports of infant crying behavior, positive mood, maternal conflict with and scolding of the child, play materials, and observations of punishment and restriction (variables for which there is no interaction of treatments with sense of control) increases our confidence that the treatment differences for child abuse and emergency room visits are products of the nurse intervention.

Moreover, it should be emphasized that we were unable to detect any other preintervention treatment differences in a careful examination of the sample on a wide range of theoretically important background characteristics that predispose to caregiving dysfunction. A scale was constructed, for example, to predict the extent to which women would provide optimal care to their children. It included data on the women's own child-rearing histories (including information related to their having been abused and neglected), their current level of psychological functioning, their prenatal health habits, and the level of stress in their current household. There were no preintervention treatment differences on this measure (Table 19.2).

The second reason for caution in interpretation is that these findings may be the result of systematic reporting bias. For each of the sources of data, one can construct an alternative explanation for specific findings. For example, the nurse-visited women may have been taught by nurses to give more socially desirable answers and to behave more appropriately in front of the interviewers. Their friends, neighbors, and relatives may have been more reluctant to report them for abuse and neglect than were associates of women in the comparison group. The finding of superior care giving for the highest risk nurse-visited women over their comparison group counterparts comes from a variety of sources, however, and it is unlikely that each of these sources could have its own idiosyncratic bias and still produce the same pattern of results overall. Assuming that the treatment differences observed are truly a reflection of the nurses' work, how do these pieces of evidence fit together?

The nurse-visited women reported less crying and fussiness on the part of their babies. Because reports of temperament and behavioral problems may be just as much a reflection of the mother's characteristics as the child's,[32,33] we interpret reports of excessive crying and irritability as a problem in the parent-child relationship. One previous intervention study, which focused on adolescent parents of high-risk newborns, found more favorable reports of infant temperament as a result of intervention.[34] It is not surprising that we detected treatment differences in parents' reports of their infants' temperaments and crying behavior in the present study because the nurses spent a considerable portion of their prenatal and postpartum visits helping parents appreciate and manage differences in the temperaments of young infants. Beginning during pregnancy and following with a Brazelton[35] examination after delivery, the nurses encouraged parents to anticipate and recognize differences in infant temperament, especially crying behavior, so that they would not misinterpret the babies' cries as either caregiving failure on their own part or as an indication that the infants were intentionally trying to disrupt their lives. We suspect that the nurse-visited poor, unmarried teenagers were able to interpret their infants' cries more correctly and respond more appropriately, thus forming the basis for secure attachments, which may protect children from abuse and neglect.[36-38]

This interpretation is supported by the pattern of results derived from the interviewers' assessments of the highest risk mothers' treatment of their children and the provision of appropriate play materials during the 10th- and 22nd-month interviews. In the extreme, restriction and punishment are abusive, and the absence of appropriate play materials is a form of neglect.

Additional corroboration for the nurses' prevention of child abuse and neglect is provided by the reduction in emergency room visits. Although the treatment difference in emergency room visits during the first year of life was attributable to the comparison group mothers taking their babies more frequently for upper respiratory tract infections, the more appropriate use of the emergency room on the part of nurse-visited women can be viewed as indirect corroboration, because it shows that the program was working as intended. Moreover, the reduction in emergency room visits for accidents and poisonings for nurse-visited women during their infants' second year of life provides more direct corroboration of the child abuse and neglect finding, because accidents and poisonings are tied more closely to the quality of parental care.[39-41]

Although there clearly is some overlap, the underlying factors leading to child maltreatment and excessive use of the emergency room, even for accidents and poisonings, in many cases are quite different. Overuse of the emergency room, in large part, probably reflects heightened parental concern about the child's well-being and little knowledge about where to turn for help, factors that are likely to be present in a broad portion of the socially disadvantaged population. Abuse and neglect, on the other hand, appear to be the products of converging psychological, economic, and social risks, factors that are limited to a much smaller segment of that population. This probably explains why the treatment difference in abuse and neglect was concentrated on the highest risk subsample, whereas the treatment difference in emergency room visits was present for the whole sample. That we observe treatment differences consistent with these general models of risk, as well as with the objectives of the program, lends credibility to the pattern of results overall.

Finally, the improved intellectual functioning of 9 to 11 points on the developmental tests for children from the highest risk families, although only marginally significant statistically, is of clinical importance. Treatment effects in this range are consistent with those obtained for children of this age enrolled in intensive early childhood intervention programs aimed specifically at enhancing cognitive development.[42]

It is important to emphasize that the home-visiting service tested in this investigation was in several ways unlike conventional community health nursing, at least as it is practiced today.[43] The program called for the nurses to visit frequently enough to establish rapport with families and to identify and reinforce family strengths, the content of the curriculum was structured and yet flexible, and it called for the nurses to summon both formal and informal community support for parents. By addressing these factors in this way, the nurses were able to achieve considerable leverage in improving not only the qualities of caregiving but pregnancy outcomes[44] and maternal life-course development (such as rates of employment, education, and fertility) as well.[21]

Because of its service intensity, the present program is more expensive than most other home-visiting programs. Preliminary cost-benefit analyses suggest that a major portion of the cost for home visitation can be offset by avoided foster care placements, hospitalizations, emergency room visits, and child protective service worker time incurred during the same period that the home-visiting program is provided. The long-range financial savings to the community are in all likelihood substantially greater, as is the reduction in human suffering.

REFERENCES

1. Gil D: *Violence Against Children: Physical Child Abuse in the United States.* Cambridge, MA, Harvard University Press, 1973

2. Garbarino J, Stocking S (eds): *Protecting Children From Abuse and Neglect.* San Francisco, Jossey-Bass, 1980

3. Gerbner G, Ross C, Zigler E (eds): *Child Abuse: An Agenda for Action.* New York, Oxford University Press, 1980

4. *Annual Report, 1983: Highlights of Official Child Neglect and Abuse Reporting.* Denver, American Humane Association, 1985

5. National Center on Child Abuse and Neglect: *National Study of the Incidence and Severity of Child Abuse and Neglect.* US Department of Health and Human Services, Department of Health and Human Services publication No. (OHDS) 81-30325, 1981

6. US Senate: *Child Abuse Prevention and Treatment and Adoption Reform Amendments of 1983,* Report from the Committee on Labor and Human Resources (to accompany S. 1003), Report No. 98-246. US Government Printing Office, 1983

7. Helfer R: A review of the literature on the prevention of child abuse and neglect. *Child Abuse Negl* 1982; 6: 251-261

8. O'Connor S, Vietze PM, Sherrod KB, et al: Reduced incidence of parenting inadequacy following rooming-in. *Pediatrics* 1980; 66: 176-182

9. Siegel E, Bauman KE, Schaefer ES, et al: Hospital and home support during infancy: Impact on maternal attachment, child abuse and neglect, and health care utilization. *Pediatrics* 1980; 66: 183-190

10. Anisfeld E, Lipper E: Early contact, social support, and mother-infant bonding. *Pediatrics* 1983; 72: 79-83

11. Lealman G, Haigh D, Phillips J, et al: Prediction and prevention of child abuse-An empty hope? *Lancet* 1983; 1: 1423-1424

12. Gray J, Cutler C, Dean J, et al: Prediction and prevention of child abuse and neglect. *J Soc Issues* 1979; 35: 127-139

13. Kempe C: Approaches to preventing child abuse: The health visitor concept. *Am J Dis Child* 1976; 130: 941-947

14. Belsky J: Child maltreatment: An ecological integration. *Am Psychol* 1980; 35: 320-335

15. Olds D: Improving formal services for mothers and children, in Garbarino J, Stocking S (eds): *Protecting Children From Abuse and Neglect: Developing and Maintaining Effective Support Systems for Families.* San Francisco, Jossey-Bass Publishers, 1981, pp 173-197

16. Olds D: An intervention program for high-risk families, in Hoekelman R (ed): *Minimizing High-Risk Parenting.* Media, PA, Harwal Publishing Company, 1983, pp 249-268

17. Olds D: The prenatal/early infancy project: An ecological approach to prevention of developmental disabilities, in Belsky J (ed): *In the Beginning.* New York, Columbia University Press, 1982, pp 270-285

18. New York State Department of Social Services: *Annual Report of Child Protective Services in New York State.* Albany, New York State Department of Social Services, 1973-1982

19. Boyer R, Savageau D: *Places Rated Almanac.* New York, Rand McNally, 1981

20. Hollingshead AB: Four-factor index of social status. Working paper. New Haven, CT, Yale University, 1976

21. Olds D, Henderson C, Birmingham M, et al: Final report to The Maternal and Child Health and Crippled Children's Services Research Grants Program, Bureau of Community Health Services, Health Services Administration, Public Health Service, Department of Health and Human Services, Grant MCJ-36040307, November 1983

22. Efron B: Forcing a sequential experiment to be balanced. *Biometrika* 1971; 58: 403-417

23. Pedersen FA, Anderson BJ, Cain RL: A methodology for assessing parent perception of infant temperament. Presented at the Fourth Biennial Southeastern Conference on Human Development, Nashville, April 1976

24. Caldwell B, Bradley R: Home observation for measurement of the environment. Little Rock, AR, University of Arkansas, 1979

25. Baker R, Nelder J: *The GLIM System-Release Three: Generalized Linear Interactive Modeling.* Oxford, England, Numerical Algorithms Group, 1978

26. Henderson C: Analysis of covariance in the mixed model: Higher level, nonhomogeneous, and random regressions. *Biometrics* 1982; 38: 623-640

27. Johnson PO, Neyman J: Tests of certain linear hypotheses and their application to some educational problems. *Stat Res Memoirs* 1936; 1: 57-93

28. Potthoff RF: On the Johnson-Neyman technique and some extensions there of. *Psychometrics* 1964; 29: 241-256

29. Miller RG Jr: *Simultaneous Statistical Inference.* New York, McGraw Hill, 1966

30. Scheffé H: *The Analysis of Variance.* New York, John Wiley & Sons, Inc, 1959

31. Rotter JB: Generalized expectancies for internal versus external control of reinforcement. *Psychol Monog Gen Appl* 1966; 80: 1

32. Vaughn B, Taraldson B, Crichton L, et al: The assessment of infant temperament: A critique of the Carey Infant Temperament Questionnaire. *Infant Behav Dev* 1981; 4: 1-17

33. Sameroff A, Seifer R, Elias P: Sociocultural variability in infant temperament ratings. *Child Dev* 1982; 53: 164-173

34. Field T, Widmayer S, Stringe S, et al: Teenage, lower-class, black mothers and their preterm infants: An infant and developmental follow-up. *Child Dev* 1980; 51: 426-436

35. Brazelton TB: *Neonatal Behavioral Assessment Scale (Clinics in Developmental Medicine,* No. 50). Philadelphia, JB Lippincott, 1973

36. Ainsworth M: Attachment and child abuse, in Gerbner G, Ross C, Zigler E (eds): *Child Abuse: An Agenda for Action.* New York, Oxford University Press, 1980, pp 35-47

37. Egeland B, Sroufe A: Attachment and early maltreatment. *Child Dev* 1981; 52: 44-52

38. Schneider-Rosen K, Cicchetti D: The relationship between affect and cognition in maltreated infants: Quality of attachment and the development of visual self-recognition. *Child Dev* 1984; 55: 648-658

39. Newberger EH, Reed RB, Daniel JH, et al: Pediatric social illnesses: Toward an etiologic classification. *Pediatrics* 1977; 60: 178-185

40. Miller F, Court S, Walton W, et al: *Growing Up in New Castle Upon Tyne,* London, Oxford University Press, 1960.

41. Wheatley GM: Childhood accidents 1952-1972: An overview. *Pediatr Ann* 1973; 2: 10-30

42. Ramey C, Campbell F: The prevention of developmental retardation in high-risk children, in Mittler P (ed): *Research to Practice in Mental Retardation.* Baltimore, University Park Press, vol 1: *Care and Intervention,* 1977, pp 157-164

43. Buhler-Wilkerson K: Public health nursing: In sickness or in health? *Am J Public Health* 1985; 75: 1155-1172

44. Olds DL, Henderson CR Jr, Tatelbaum R, et al: Improving the delivery of prenatal care and outcomes of pregnancy: A randomized trial of nurse home visitation. *Pediatrics* 1986; 77: 16-28

Impact of Child Sexual Abuse

A Review of the Research

ANGELA BROWNE
DAVID FINKELHOR   *1986*

At the time "Impact of Child Sexual Abuse: A Review of the Literature" was published, there was only an emerging body of research literature on the short- and long-term impacts of child sexual abuse. The foundation of our understanding of the impact of this form of abuse was just being formed. A great deal of controversy over the mental health impact of child sexual abuse existed. Browne and Finkelhor sought to discern the common ground in this controversy.

As explained by Finkel, through an analysis of 48 clinical studies in the literature and a synthesis of their findings, Browne and Finkelhor identified the significant stepping stones in our understanding of the impact of child sexual abuse. They identified reactions to sexual abuse in at least the majority of victims, which included fear, anxiety, depression, anger and hostility, aggression, and self-destructive behavior. They sought to begin to explain which types of sexual abuse were the most traumatic. For a society still in denial about child sexual abuse, this consolidation of information

about its negative short- and long-term impacts was most important. And, while clarifying our understanding of its impact, the authors also set an early research agenda for the child sexual abuse field and called for improvements in the methodologies used.

Finkel points out that over half of the clinical studies analyzed in this paper reflected observations of child sexual abuse gleaned in the 1970s. This was a time when there was little standardization of terminology, and studies were plagued by small size as well as design and measurement errors. In brief, the studies that had been done to date generally lacked scientific rigor. Little thought had been given to what a research agenda for this area might consist of (e.g., what might be the most important questions, from the perspectives of prevention and treatment, to address).

This paper is seminal in that it is the first to critically analyze a divergent body of literature and, despite that literature's shortcomings, to articulate common threads and thereby bring clarity to what had been regarded as an enormously complex, almost incomprehensible subject matter. In this paper, the authors manage to provide thoughtful and constructive analysis, which has certainly helped to set the direction for our current understanding of child sexual abuse and the research that has been conducted in the interim to establish this understand-

ing. Most notably, the authors call for significant methodological improvements in sample selection and size, in the use of control groups, and in the selection and use of measures. Subsequent to this article's publication, all of these have been accomplished.

A. C. D. and K. O.

Although clinical literature suggests that sexual abuse during childhood plays a role in the development of other problems, ranging from anorexia nervosa to prostitution, empirical evidence about its actual effects is sparse. In this article, we review the expanding empirical literature on the effects of child sexual abuse, discuss its initial and long-term effects, review studies on the impact of different kinds of abuse, and conclude with a critique of the current literature and some suggestions for future research.

Child sexual abuse consists of two overlapping but distinguishable types of interaction: (a) forced or coerced sexual behavior imposed on a child and (b) sexual activity between a child and a much older person, whether or not obvious coercion is involved (a common definition of "much older" is 5 or more years). As might be expected, not all studies relevant to our purposes share these parameters. Some have focused on experiences with older partners only, excluding coerced sexual experiences with peers. Others have looked only at sexual abuse that was perpetrated by family members. Such differences in samples make comparisons among these studies difficult. However, we include all the studies that looked at some portion of the range of experiences that are bounded by these two criteria. (See Table 20.1 for a breakdown of sample composition of the studies reviewed.)

Two areas of the literature are not included in our review. A small number of studies on the effects of incest (e.g., Farrell, 1982; Nelson, 1981), as well as one review of the effects of child sexual experiences (Constantine, 1980), combine data on consensual, peer experiences with data that involve either coercion or age disparity. Because we were unable to isolate sexual abuse in these studies, we had to exclude them. Second, we decided to limit our review to female victims. Few clinical, and even fewer empirical, studies have been done on male victims (for exceptions, see Finkelhor, 1979; Rogers & Terry, 1984; Sandfort, 1981; Woods & Dean, 1984), and it seems premature to draw conclusions at this point.[1] Under "empirical" studies, we include any research that attempted to quantify the extent to which a sequelae to sexual abuse appeared in a specific population. Some of these studies used objective measures, whereas others were based primarily on the judgments of clinicians.

INITIAL EFFECTS

By initial effects, we mean those reactions occurring within 2 years of the termination of abuse. These early reactions are often called *short-term* effects in the literature. We prefer the term *initial* effects, however, because *short-term* implies that the reactions do not

Originally published in *Psychological Bulletin*, 1986, *99*, 66-76. Reprinted by permission of *Psychological Bulletin*.

persist—an assumption that has yet to be substantiated.

Emotional Reactions and Self-Perceptions

Although several empirical studies have given support to clinical observations of generally negative emotional effects resulting from childhood sexual abuse, only two used standardized measures and compared subjects' scores to general population norms. In an early study of the effects of sexual abuse on children, DeFrancis (1969) reported that 66% of the victims were emotionally disturbed by the molestation: 52% mildly to moderately disturbed, and 14% seriously disturbed. Only 24% were judged to be emotionally stable after the abuse. However, because this sample was drawn from court cases known to Prevention of Cruelty to Children services or to the police, and because the subjects came primarily from low income and multiple-problem families who were on public assistance, these findings may have little generalizability.

In investigating a different type of special population, Anderson, Bach, and Griffith (1981) reviewed clinical charts of 155 female adolescent sexual assault victims who had been treated at the Harborview Medical Center in Washington and reported psychosocial complications in 63% of them. Reports of "internalized psychosocial sequalae" (e.g., sleep and eating disturbances, fears and phobias, depression, guilt, shame, and anger) were noted in 67% of female victims when the abuse was intrafamilial and 49% when the offender was not a family member. "Externalized sequelae" (including school problems and running away) were noted in 66% of intrafamilial victims and 21% of extrafamilial victims. However, no standardized outcome measures were used, so the judgments of these effects may be subjective.

In what is probably the best study to date, researchers affiliated with the Division of Child Psychiatry at the Tufts New England Medical Center gathered data on families involved in a treatment program restricted to those children who had been victimized or revealed their victimization in the prior 6 months. Standardized self-report measures—the Louisville Behavior Checklist (LBC), the Piers-Harris Self-Concept Scale, the Purdue Self-Concept Scale, and the Gottschalk Glesser Content Analysis Scales (GGCA)—with published norms and test validation data were used, so that characteristics of sexually abused children could be contrasted with norms for general and psychiatric populations. Subjects ranged in age from infancy to 18 years and were divided into preschool, latency, and adolescence age groups. Data were gathered on four areas: overt behavior, somaticized reactions, internalized emotional states, and self-esteem.

In evaluating the initial psychological effects of child sexual abuse, Tufts (1984) researchers found differences in the amount of pathology reported for different age groups. Seventeen percent of 4- to 6-year-olds in the study met the criteria for "clinically significant pathology," demonstrating more overall disturbance than a normal population but less than the norms for other children their age who were in psychiatric care. The highest incidence of psychopathology was found in the 7- to 13-year-old age group, with 40% scoring in the seriously disturbed range. Interestingly, few of the adolescent victims exhibited severe psychopathology, except on a measure of neuroticism.

Friedrich, Urquiza, and Beilke (in press) also used a standardized measure in their study of 61 sexually abused girls. Subjects were referred by a local sexual assault center for evaluation or by the outpatient department of a local hospital. Children in this sample had been abused within a 24-month period prior to the

TABLE 20.1 Studies of Effects of Sexual Abuse

Study	Source of Sample	N	Gender	Age of Respondents	Focus of Study	Comparison Group
Anderson, Bach, & Griffith, 1981	Sexual assault center	227	F = 155 M = 72	Ad	I, E	No
Bagley & Ramsay, 1985	Random sample	679	F = 401 M = 278	A	I, E	Yes
Benward & Densen-Gerber, 1975	Drug treatment center	118	F = 118	Ad, A	I	No
Briere, 1984	Community health center	153	F = 153	A	I, E	Yes
Briere & Runtz, 1985	College students	278	F = 278	Ad, A	I, E	Yes
Courtois, 1979	Ads and mental health agencies	31	F = 31	A	I	No
DeFrancis, 1969	Court cases	250	F = 217 M = 33	C, Ad	I, E	No
DeYoung, 1982	College students, therapy patients, and others	80	F = 72 M = 8	C, Ad, A	I	No
Fields, 1981	Prostitutes recruited after arrest	85	F = 85	A	I	Yes
Finkelhor, 1979	College students	796	F = 530 M = 266	Ad, A	I, E	Yes
Friedrich, Urquiza, & Beilke, in press	Sexual assault center, group therapy	64	F = 49 M = 15	C	I, E	No
Fromuth, 1983	College students	482	F = 482	Ad, A	I, E	Yes
Harrison, Lumry, & Claypatch, 1984	Dual disorder treatment program	62	F = 62	A	I, E	Yes
Herman, 1981	Clients in therapy	60	F = 60	Ad, A	I	Yes
James & Meyerding, 1977	Prostitutes selected from arrest records					
Study 1		92	F = 92	Ad, A	I, E	No
Study 2		136	F = 136	A	I, E	No
Landis, 1956	College students	950	F = 726 M = 224	A	I, E	Yes
Langmade, 1983	Mental health centers, private clinics	68	F = 68	A	I	Yes
Meiselman, 1978	Clinical records, psychiatric clinic	108	F = 97 M = 11	C, Ad, A	I	Yes
Peters, J., 1976	Rape crisis center	100		C	I	No

TABLE 20.1 *Continued*

Study	Source of Sample	N	Gender	Age of Respondents	Focus of Study	Comparison Group
Peters, S., 1984	Follow-up, community random sample	119	F = 119	A	I, E	Yes
Russell, in press	Random sample	930	F = 930	A	I, E	Yes
Sedney & Brooks, 1984	College students	301	F = 301	Ad, A	I, E	Yes
Seidner & Calhoun, 1984	College students	152	F = 118 M = 34	A	I, E	Yes
Silbert & Pines, 1981	Prostitutes recruited by ads	200	F = 200	Ad, A	I, E	No
Tsai, Feldman- Summers, & Edgar, 1979	Ads	90	F = 90	A	I, E	Yes
Tufts study, 1984	Clinical referrals	156	F = 122 M = 34	C, Ad	I, E	No

NOTE: F = female and M = male. C = child, Ad = adolescent, and A = adult. I = intrafamilial and E = extrafamilial.

study. Using the Child Behavior Check List (CBCL; see Achenbach & Edelbrock, 1983, for a description of this measure), Friedrich et al. reported that 46% of their subjects had significantly elevated scores on its Internalizing scale (including fearful, inhibited, depressed, and overcontrolled behaviors), and 39% had elevated scores on its Externalizing scale (aggressive, antisocial, and undercontrolled behaviors). This was compared with only 2% of the normative sample who would be expected to score in this range. Younger children (up to age 5) demonstrated a tendency to score high on the Internalizing scale, whereas older children (ages 6-12) were more likely to have elevated scores on the Externalizing scale.

Breaking down emotional impact into specific reactions, we find that the most common initial effect noted in empirical studies, similar to reports in the clinical literature, is that of fear. However, exact proportions vary from a high of 83% reported by DeFrancis (1969) to 40% reported by Anderson et al. (1981). Because of its use of standardized measures, we would give the most credence to the Tufts

(1984) study, which found that 45% of the 7- to 13-year-olds manifested severe fears as measured by the LBCs, compared with 13% of the 4- to 6-year-olds. On the adolescent version of the LBC, 39% of the 14- to 18-year-olds had elevated scores on "ambivalent hostility," or the fear of being harmed.

Another initial effect in children is reactions of anger and hostility. Tufts (1984) researchers found that 45% to 50% of the 7- to 13-year-olds showed hostility levels that were substantially elevated on measures of aggression and antisocial behavior (LBC), as did 35% on the measure of hostility directed outward (GGCA). Thirteen percent to 17% of 4- to 6-year-olds scored above the norms on aggression and antisocial behavior (LBC), whereas 25% of 4- to 6-year-olds and 23% of the adolescents had elevated scores on hostility directed outward (GGCA). In his study of court cases, DeFrancis (1969) noted that 55% of the children showed behavioral disturbances such as active defiance, disruptive behavior within the family, and quarreling or fighting with siblings or classmates. DeFrancis's sample might have been thought to overselect for hostile re-actions; however, these findings are not very different from findings of the Tufts study for school-age children.

Guilt and shame are other frequently ob-served reactions to child sexual abuse, but few studies give clear percentages. DeFrancis (1969) observed that 64% of his sample ex-pressed guilt, although this was more about the problems created by disclosure than about the molestation itself. Anderson et al. (1981) re-ported guilt reactions in 25% of the victims. Similarly, depression is frequently reported in the clinical literature, but here, too, specific figures are rarely given. Anderson et al. (1981) found that 25% of female sexual assault vic-tims were depressed after the abuse.

Sexual abuse is also cited as having an ef-fect on self-esteem, but this effect has not yet been established by empirical studies. Fifty-eight percent of the victims in the DeFrancis (1969) study expressed feelings of inferiority or lack of worth as a result of having been victimized. However in a surprising find-ing, Tufts (1984) researchers, using the Purdue Self-Concept Scale, found no evidence that sex-ually abused children in any of the age groups had consistently lower self-esteem than a nor-mal population of children.

Physical Consequences and Somatic Complaints

Physical symptoms indicative of anxiety and distress are noted in the empirical litera-ture as well as in clinical reports. In their chart review of female adolescent victims, Anderson et al. (1981) found that 17% had experienced sleep disturbances and 5% to 7% showed changes in eating habits after the victimiza-tion. J. Peters (1976), in a study of child vic-tims of intrafamilial sexual abuse, reported that 31% had difficulty sleeping and 20% experi-enced eating disturbances. However, without a comparison group, it is hard to know if this is seriously pathological for any group of chil-

dren, or for clinical populations in particular. Adolescent pregnancy is another physical con-sequence sometimes mentioned in empirical literature. DeFrancis (1969) reported that 11% of the child victims in his study became preg-nant as a result of the sexual offense; however, this figure seems far too high for a contempo-rary sample. Meiselman (1978), in analyzing records from a Los Angeles psychiatric clinic, found only 1 out of 47 incest cases in which a victim was impregnated by her father.

Effects of Sexuality

Reactions of inappropriate sexual behavior in child victims have been confirmed by two studies using standardized measures (Friedrich et al., in press; Tufts, 1984). In the Tufts (1984) study, 27% of 4- to 6-year-old children scored significantly above clinical and general popu-lation norms on a sexual behavior scale that in-cluded having had sexual relations (possibly a confounding variable in these findings), open masturbation, excessive sexual curiosity, and frequent exposure of the genitals. Thirty-six percent of the 7- to 13-year-olds also demon-strated high levels of disturbance on the sexual behavior measure when contrasted to norms for either general or clinical school-age popu-lations. Similarly, Friedrich et al. (in press), us-ing the CBCL to evaluate 3- to 12- year-olds, found that 70% of the boys and 44% of the girls scored at least one standard deviation above a normal population of that age group on the scale measuring sexual problems. Interest-ingly, sexual problems were most common among the younger girls and the older boys.

Effects on Social Functioning

Other aftereffects of child sexual abuse mentioned in the literature include difficulties at school, truancy, running away from home, and early marriages by adolescent victims. Herman (1981) interviewed 40 patients in ther-apy who had been victims of father-daughter incest and compared their reports with those from a group of 20 therapy clients with seductive, but not incestuous, fathers. Of the incest victims, 33% attempted to run away as adolescents compared with 5% of the comparison group. Similarly, Meiselman (1978) found that 50% of the incest victims in her sample had left home before the age of 18, compared with 20% of women in a comparison group of nonvictimized female patients. Younger children often went to a relative, whereas older daughters ran away or eloped, sometimes making early marriages in order to escape the abuse. Two studies, neither with comparison groups, mentioned school problems and truancy. Ten percent of the child victims in J. Peters's (1976) study quit school, although all of his subjects were under the age of 12 at the time. Anderson et al. found that 20% of the girls in their sample experienced problems at school, including truancy or dropping out.

A connection between sexual abuse, running away, and delinquency is also suggested by several studies of children in special treatment or delinquency programs. Reich and Gutierres (1979) reported that 55% of the children in Maricopa County, Arizona, who were charged with running away, truancy, or listed as missing persons were incest victims. In addition, in a study of female juvenile offenders in Wisconsin (1982), researchers found that 32% had been sexually abused by a relative or other person close to them.

Summary of Initial Effects of Child Sexual Abuse

The empirical literature on child sexual abuse, then, does suggest the presence—in some portion of the victim population—of many of the initial effects reported in the clinical literature, especially reactions of fear, anxiety, depression, anger and hostility, and inappropriate sexual behavior. However, because many of the studies lacked standardized outcome measures and adequate comparison groups, it is not clear that these findings reflect the experience of all child victims of sexual abuse or are even representative of those children currently being seen in clinical settings. At this point, the empirical literature on the initial effects of child sexual abuse would have to be considered sketchy.

LONG-TERM EFFECTS

Emotional Reactions and Self-Perceptions

In the clinical literature, depression is the symptom most commonly reported among adults molested as children, and empirical findings seem to confirm this. Two excellent community studies are indicative of this. Bagley and Ramsay (1985), in a community mental health study in Calgary utilizing a random sample of 387 women, found that subjects with a history of child sexual abuse scored more depressed on the Centre for Environmental Studies Depression Scale (CES-D) than did nonabused women (17% vs. 9% with clinical symptoms of depression in the last week), as well as on the Middlesex Hospital Questionnaire's measure of depression (15% vs. 7%). S. Peters (1984), in a community study in Los Angeles also based on a random sample, interviewed 119 women and found that sexual abuse in which there was physical contact was associated with a higher incidence of depression and a greater number of depressive episodes over time and that women who had been sexually abused were more likely to have been hospitalized for depression than nonvictims. In a multiple regression that included both sexual abuse and family background factors (e.g., a poor relationship with the mother), the variable of child sexual abuse made an independent contribution to depression.

The link between child sexual abuse and depression has been confirmed in other nonclinical samples as well. Sedney and Brooks

(1984), in a study of 301 college women, found a greater likelihood for subjects with childhood sexual experiences to report symptoms of depression (65% vs. 43% of the control group) and to have been hospitalized for it (18% of those depressed in the childhood experience group vs. 4% of women in the control group). These positive findings are surprising, in that the researchers used an overly inclusive definition of sexual experiences that may not have screened out some consensual experiences with peers. Their results are consistent, however, with those from a carefully controlled survey of 278 undergraduate women by Briere and Runtz (1985), using 72 items of the Hopkins Symptom Checklist, which indicated that sexual abuse victims reported that they experienced more depressive symptoms during the 12 months prior to the study than did nonabused subjects.

Studies based on clinical samples (Herman, 1981; Meiselman, 1978) have not shown such clear differences in depression between victims and nonvictims. For example, although Herman (1981) noted major depressive symptoms in 60% of the incest victims in her study, 55% of the comparison group also reported depression. Meiselman (1978) reported depressive symptoms in 35% of the incest victims whose psychiatric records she reviewed, compared with 23% of the comparison group; again, this difference was not significant.

Both clinical and nonclinical samples have shown victims of child sexual abuse to be more self-destructive, however. In an extensive study of 153 "walk-ins" to a community health counseling center, Briere (1984) reported that 51% of the sexual abuse victims, versus 34% of nonabused clients, had a history of suicide attempts. Thirty-one percent of victims, compared with 19% of nonabused clients, exhibited a desire to hurt themselves. A high incidence of suicide attempts among victims of child sexual abuse has been found by other clinical researchers as well (e.g., Harrison, Lumry, & Claypatch, 1984; Herman, 1981). Bagley and Ramsay (1985), in their commu-

nity study, noted an association between childhood sexual abuse and suicide ideation or deliberate attempts at self-harm. And Sedney and Brooks (1984) found that 39% of their college student sample with child sexual experiences reported having thoughts of hurting themselves, compared with 16% of the control group. Sixteen percent of these respondents had made at least one suicide attempt (vs. 6% of their peers).

Another reaction observed in adults who were sexually victimized as children is symptoms of anxiety or tension. Briere (1984) reported that 54% of the sexual abuse victims in his clinical sample experienced anxiety attacks (compared with 28% of the nonvictims), 54% reported nightmares (vs. 23%), and 72% had difficulty sleeping (compared with 55% of the nonvictims). In their college sample, Sedney and Brooks (1984) found 59% with symptoms indicating nervousness and anxiety (compared with 41% of the controls); 41% indicated extreme tension (vs. 29% of the controls), and 51% had trouble sleeping (compared with 29% of the controls). These findings are supported by results from community samples, with Bagley and Ramsay (1985) noting that 19% of their subjects who had experienced child sexual abuse reported symptoms indicating somatic anxiety on the Middlesex Hospital Questionnaire, compared with 9% of the nonabused subjects.

The idea that sexual abuse victims continue to feel isolated and stigmatized as adults also has some support in the empirical literature, although these findings come only from the clinical populations. Sixty-four percent of the victimized women in Briere's (1984) study reported feelings of isolation, compared with 49% of the controls. With incest victims, the figures are even higher: Herman (1981) reported that all of the women who had experienced father-daughter incest in her clinical sample had a sense of being branded, marked, or stigmatized by the victimization. Even in a community sample of incest victims, Courtois (1979) found that 73% reported they still suffered from moderate to severe feelings of isolation and alienation.

Although a negative self-concept was not confirmed as an initial effect, evidence for it as a long-term effect is much stronger. Bagley and Ramsay (1985) found that 19% of the child sexual abuse victims in their random sample scored in the "very poor" category on the Coopersmith self-esteem inventory (vs. 5% of the control group), whereas only 9% of the victims demonstrated "very good" levels of self-esteem (compared to 20% of the controls). Women with very poor self-esteem were nearly four times as likely to report a history of child sexual abuse as were the other subjects. As might be expected, self-esteem problems among clinical samples of incest victims tended to be much greater: Eighty-seven percent of Courtois's (1979) community sample reported that their sense of self had been moderately to severely affected by the experience of sexual abuse from a family member. Similarly, Herman (1981) found that 60% of the incest victims in her clinical sample were reported to have a "predominantly negative self-image," as compared with 10% of the comparison group with seductive but not incestuous fathers.

Impact on Interpersonal Relating

Women who have been sexually victimized as children report problems in relating both to women and men, continuing problems with their parents, and difficulty in parenting and responding to their own children. In DeYoung's (1982) sample, 79% of the incest victims had predominantly hostile feelings toward their mothers, whereas 52% were hostile toward the abuser. Meiselman (1978) found that 60% of the incest victims in her psychotherapy sample disliked their mothers, and 40% continued to experience strong negative feelings toward their fathers. Herman (1981) also noted that the rage of incest victims in her sample was often directed toward the mother and observed that

they seemed to regard all women, including themselves, with contempt.

In addition, victims reported difficulty trusting others that included reactions of fear, hostility, and a sense of betrayal. Briere (1984) noted fear of men in 48% of his clinical subjects (vs. 15% of the nonvictims), and fear of women in 12% (vs. 4% of those who had not been sexually victimized). Incest victims seem especially likely to experience difficulty in close relationships: Sixty-four percent of the victims in Meiselman's (1978) clinical study, compared with 40% of the control group, complained of conflict with or fear of their husbands or sex partners, and 39% of the sample had never married. These results are supported by findings from Courtois's (1979) sample, in which 79% of the incest victims experienced moderate or severe problems in relating to men, and 40% had never married.

There is at least one empirical study that lends support to the idea that childhood sexual abuse also affects later parenting. Goodwin, McCarthy, and Divasto (1981) found that 24% of mothers in the child abusing families they studied reported incest experiences in their childhoods, compared with 3% of a nonabusive control group. They suggested that difficulty in parenting results when closeness and affection are endowed with a sexual meaning and observed that these mothers maintained an emotional and physical distance from their children, thus potentially setting the stage for abuse.

Another effect on which the empirical literature agrees is the apparent vulnerability of women who have been sexually abused as children to be revictimized later in life. Russell (in press), in her probability sample of 930 women, found that between 33% and 68% of the sexual abuse victims (depending on the seriousness of the abuse they suffered) were raped later on, compared with 17% of women who were not childhood victims. Fromuth (1983), in surveying 482 female college students, found evidence that women who had been sexually abused before the age of 13 were especially likely to later become victims of nonconsensual sexual experiences. Further evidence of a tendency toward revictimization comes from a study conducted at the University of New Mexico School of Medicine on 341 sexual assault admittances (Miller et al., 1978). In comparing women who had been raped on more than one occasion with those who were reporting a first-time rape, researchers found that 18% of the repeat victims had incest histories, compared with only 4% of first-time victims.

In addition to rape, victims of child sexual abuse also seem more likely to be abused later by husbands or other adult partners. Russell (in press) found that between 38% and 48% of the child sexual abuse victims in her community sample had physically violent husbands, compared with 17% of women who were not victims; in addition, between 40% and 62% of the abused women had later been sexually assaulted by their husbands, compared with 21% of nonvictims. Similarly, Briere (1984) noted that 49% of his clinical sexual abuse sample reported being battered in adult relationships, compared with 18% of the nonvictim group.

Effects on Sexuality

One of the areas receiving the most attention in the empirical literature on long-term effects concerns the impact of early sexual abuse on later sexual functioning. Almost all clinically based studies show later sexual problems among child sexual abuse victims, particularly among the victims of incest. However, there have not yet been community-based studies on the sexual functioning of adults molested as children, as there have been of other mental health areas such as depression.

Of the clinical studies, Meiselman (1978) found the highest percentage of incest victims reporting problems with sexual adjustment. Eighty-seven percent of her sample were classified as having had a serious problem with sexual adjustment at some time since the molestation, compared with 20% of the comparison group (women who had been in therapy at the same clinic but had not been sexually victimized as children). Results from Herman's (1981) study are somewhat less extreme: Fifty-five percent of the incest victims reported later sexual problems, although they were not significantly different from women with seductive fathers on this measure. Langmade (1983) compared a group of women in therapy who had been incest victims with a matched control group of nonvictimized women and found that the incest victims were more sexually anxious, experienced more sexual guilt, and reported greater dissatisfaction with their sexual relationships than the controls. In his study of a walk-in sample to a community health clinic, Briere (1984) found that 45% of women who had been sexually abused as children reported difficulties with sexual adjustment as adults, compared with 15% of the control group. Briere also noted a decreased sex drive in 42% of the victims studied, versus 29% of the nonvictims.

Two nonclinical studies show effects on sexual functioning as well. Courtois noted that 80% of the former incest victims in her sample reported an inability to relax and enjoy sexual activity, avoidance of or abstention from sex, or, conversely, a compulsive desire for sex. Finkelhor (1979), studying college students, developed a measure of sexual self-esteem and found that child sexual abuse victims reported significantly lower levels of sexual self-esteem than their nonabused classmates. However, Fromuth (1983), in a similar study also with a college student sample, found no correlation between sexual abuse and sexual self-esteem, desire for intercourse, or students' self-ratings of their sexual adjustment. Virtually all (96%) of Fromuth's respondents were unmarried, and their average age was 19, so it is possible that some of the long-term sexual adjustment problems reported by women in the clinical and community samples were not yet in evidence in this younger population. Still, this does not explain the discrepancy from the Finkelhor findings.

In another study, Tsai, Feldman-Summers, and Edgar (1979) compared three groups of women on sexual adjustment measures: sexual abuse victims seeking therapy, sexual abuse victims who considered themselves well-adjusted and had not sought therapy, and a nonvictimized matched control group. Results indicated that the "well-adjusted" victims were not significantly different from the control group on measures of overall and sexual adjustment, but the victims seeking therapy did show a difference. They experienced orgasm less often, reported themselves to be less sexually responsive, obtained less satisfaction from their sexual relationships, were less satisfied with the quality of their close relationships with men, and reported a greater number of sexual partners. It is hard to know how to interpret findings from a group of victims solicited on the basis of feeling "well-adjusted." This seems far different from a comparison group of victims who were not in therapy, and thus these results are questionable.

A long-term effect of child sexual abuse that has also received a great deal of attention in the literature is an increased level of sexual behavior among victims, usually called promiscuity (e.g., Courtois, 1979; DeYoung, 1982; Herman, 1981; Meiselman, 1978). Herman noted that 35% of the incest victims in her sample reported promiscuity and observed that some victims seemed to have a "repertoire of sexually stylized behavior" that they used as a way of getting affection and attention (p. 40). DeYoung (1982) reported that 28% of the victims in her sample had engaged in activities that could be considered promiscuous; Meiselman (1978) found 25%. However, in her study of 482 female college students, Fromuth (1983) found no differences in this variable and observed that having experienced child sexual abuse only predicted whether subjects would describe themselves as promiscuous,

not their actual number of partners. This potentially very important finding suggests that the "promiscuity" of sexual abuse victims may be more a function of their negative self-attributions, already well documented in the empirical literature, than their actual sexual behavior; thus, researchers should be careful to combine objective behavioral measures with this type of self-report.

Another question that has received comment but little empirical confirmation concerns the possibility that sexual abuse may be associated with later homosexuality in victims. Although one study of lesbians found molestation in their backgrounds (Gundlach, 1977), Bell and Weinberg (1981), in a large-scale, sophisticated study of the origin of sexual preference, found no such association. Studies from the sexual abuse literature have also found little connection (Finkelhor, 1984; Fromuth, 1983; Meiselman, 1978).

Effects on Social Functioning

Several studies of special populations suggest a connection between child sexual abuse and later prostitution. James and Meyerding (1977) interviewed 136 prostitutes and found that 55% had been sexually abused as children by someone 10 or more years older, prior to their first intercourse. Among adolescents in the sample, 65% had been forced into sexual activity before they were 16 years old. Similarly, Silbert and Pines (1981) found that 60% of the prostitutes they interviewed had been sexually abused before the age of 16 by an average of two people for an average of 20 months. (The mean age of these children at the time of their first victimization was 10.) They concluded that "the evidence linking juvenile sexual abuse to prostitution is overwhelming" (p. 410). However, Fields (1981) noted that, although 45% of the prostitutes in her sample had been sexually abused as children, this did not differentiate them from a comparison group of nonprostitutes matched on age, race, and education, of which 37% had been abused. Although there was no difference in prevalence between the two groups, Fields did find that the prostitutes were sexually abused at a younger age—14.5 versus 16.5—and were more apt to have been physically forced.

An association between child sexual abuse and later substance abuse has also received empirical support. S. Peters (1984), in a carefully controlled community study, found that 17% of the victimized women had symptoms of alcohol abuse (vs. 4% of nonvictimized women), and 27% abused at least one type of drug (compared with 12% of nonvictimized women). Herman (1981) noted that 35% of the women in her clinical sample with incestuous fathers abused drugs and alcohol (vs. 5% of the women with seductive fathers). Similarly, Briere (1984), in his walk-in sample from a community health center, found that 27% of the childhood sexual abuse victims had a history of alcoholism (compared with 11% of nonvictims), and 21% had a history of drug addiction (vs. 2% of the nonvictims). College student samples appear more homogeneous: Sedney and Brooks (1984) found a surprisingly low reported incidence of substance abuse and no significant differences between groups.

Summary of Long-Term Effects

Empirical studies with adults confirm many of the long-term effects of sexual abuse mentioned in the clinical literature. Adult women victimized as children are more likely to manifest depression, self-destructive behavior, anxiety, feelings of isolation and stigma, poor self-esteem, a tendency toward revictimization, and substance abuse. Difficulty in trusting others and sexual maladjustment in such areas as sexual dysphoria, sexual dysfunction, impaired sexual self-esteem, and avoidance of or abstention from sexual activity have also been reported by empirical researchers, although

agreement between studies is less consistent for the variables on sexual functioning.

IMPACT OF SEXUAL ABUSE

In light of the studies just reviewed, it is appropriate to evaluate the persistent controversy over the impact of sexual abuse on victims. It has been the continuing view of some that sexual abuse is not traumatic or that its traumatic impact has been greatly overstated (Constantine, 1977; Henderson, 1983; Ramey, 1979). Proponents of this view contend that the evidence for trauma is meager and based on inadequate samples and unwarranted inferences. Because of the general lack of research in this field, clinicians have only recently been able to substantiate their impressions that sexual abuse is traumatic with evidence from strong scientific studies. However, as evidence now accumulates, it conveys a clear suggestion that sexual abuse is a serious mental health problem, consistently associated with very disturbing subsequent problems in some important portion of its victims.

Findings of long-term impact are especially persuasive. Eight nonclinical studies of adults (Bagley & Ramsay, 1985; Briere & Runtz, 1985; Finkelhor, 1979; Fromuth, 1983; S. Peters, 1984; Russell, in press; Sedney & Brooks, 1984; Seidner & Calhoun, 1984), including three random sample community surveys, found that child sexual abuse victims in the "normal" population had identifiable degrees of impairment when compared with non-victims. Although impairments in these non-clinical victims are not necessarily severe, all the studies that have looked for long-term impairment have found it, with the exception of one (Tsai et al., 1979).

These findings are particularly noteworthy in that the studies were identifying differences associated with an event that occurred from 5 to 25 years previously. Moreover, all these studies used fairly broad definitions of sexual abuse that included single episodes, experiences in which no actual physical contact occurred, and experiences with individuals who were not related to or emotionally close to the subjects. In all four studies that used multivariate analyses (Bagley & Ramsay 1985; Finkelhor, 1984; Fromuth, 1983; S. Peters, 1984), differences in the victimized group remained after a variety of background and other factors had been controlled. The implication of these studies is that a history of childhood sexual abuse is associated with greater risk for mental health and adjustment problems in adulthood.

Unfortunately, although the studies indicate higher risk, they are not so informative about the actual extent of impairment. In terms of simple self-assessments, 53% of intrafamilial sexual abuse victims in Russell's (in press) community survey reported that the experience resulted in "some" or "great" long-term effects on their lives. Assessments with standardized clinical measures show a more modest incidence of impairment: In Bagley and Ramsay's (1985) community survey, 17% of sexual abuse victims were clinically depressed as measured by the CES-D, and 18% were seriously psychoneurotic. Thus, most sexual abuse victims in the community, when evaluated in surveys, show up as slightly impaired or normal. It is possible, however, that some of the impairment associated with childhood molestation is not tapped by these survey evaluations.

Summarizing, then, from studies of clinical and nonclinical populations, the findings concerning the trauma of child sexual abuse appear to be as follows: In the immediate aftermath of sexual abuse, from one-fifth to two-fifths of abused children seen by clinicians manifest pathological disturbance (Tufts, 1984). When studied as adults, victims as a group demonstrate impairment when compared with their nonvictimized counterparts, but under one fifth evidence serious psychopathology. These findings give reassurance to victims that extreme long-term effects are not inevitable. Nonetheless, they also suggest that the risk of initial and long-term mental health

impairment for victims of child sexual abuse should be taken very seriously.

EFFECTS BY TYPE OF ABUSE

Although the foregoing sections have been concerned with the various effects of abuse, there are also important research questions concerning the effects of various kinds of abuse. These have usually appeared in the form of speculation about what types of abuse have the most serious impact on victims. Groth (1978), for example, on the basis of his clinical experience, contended that the greatest trauma occurs in sexual abuse that (a) continues for a longer period of time, (b) occurs with a more closely related person, (c) involves penetration, and (d) is accompanied by aggression. To that list, MacFarlane (1978) added experiences in which (e) the child participates to some degree, (f) the parents have an unsupportive reaction to disclosure of the abuse, and (g) the child is older and thus cognizant of the cultural taboos that have been violated. Such speculations offer fruitful directions for research. Unfortunately, however, only a few studies on the effects of sexual abuse have had enough cases and been sophisticated enough methodologically to look at these questions empirically. Furthermore, the studies addressing these issues have reached little consensus in their findings.

Duration and Frequency of Abuse

Although many clinicians take for granted that the longer an experience goes on, the more traumatic it is, this conclusion is not clearly supported by the available studies. Of nine studies, only four found duration associated with greater trauma. (We are treating duration and frequency synonymously here because they tend to be so highly correlated.) Three found no relation, and two even found some evidence that longer duration is associated with less trauma.

Russell's (in press) study reported the clearest association: In her survey of adult women, 73% of sexual abuse that lasted for more than 5 years was self-rated as extremely or considerably traumatic by the victims, compared with 62% of abuse lasting 1 week to 5 years and 46% of abuse occurring only once. Tsai et al. (1979) found duration and frequency associated with greater negative effects, when measured with the Minnesota Multiphasic Personality Inventory and a problems checklist, at least in their group of adult sexual abuse victims who sought counseling. Bagley and Ramsay (1985) found that the general mental health status of adult victims—measured by a composite of indicators concerning depression, psychoneurosis, suicidal ideation, psychiatric consultation, and self-concept—was worse for longer-lasting experiences. Finally, Friedrich et al. (in press), studying children, found that both duration and frequency predicted disturbances measured by the CBCL, even in multivariate analysis.

However, other studies have not found such relations. Finkelhor (1979), in a retrospective survey of college students, used a self-rating of how negative the experience was in retrospect and found no association with duration. Langmade (1983) reported that adult women seeking treatment who had had long- or short-duration experiences did not differ on measures of sexual anxiety, sexual guilt, or sexual dissatisfaction. In addition, the Tufts (1984) study, looking at child victims with more comprehensive measures than Friedrich et al. (in press), could find no association between duration of abuse and measures of distress, using the LBC and the Purdue Self-Concept Scale, as well as other measures.

Finally, some studies indicated a completely reversed relation. Courtois (1979), surprisingly, found that adult victims with the longest-lasting experiences reported the least trauma. In addition, in their college student sample, Seidner and Calhoun (1984) reported

that a high frequency of abuse was associated with higher self-acceptance (but lower social maturity) scores on the California Psychological Inventory.

In summary, then, the available studies reach quite contradictory conclusions about the relation between duration and trauma. However, duration is closely related to other aspects of the abuse experience—for example, age at onset, a family relationship between victim and offender, and the nature of the sexual activity. Some of the contradictions may be cleared up when we have better studies with well-defined multivariate analyses that can accurately assess the independent effect of duration.

Relationship to the Offender

Popular and clinical wisdom holds that sexual abuse by a close relative is more traumatic than abuse by someone outside the family. Empirical findings suggest that this may be the case, at least for some types of family abuse. Three studies have found more trauma resulting from abuse by relatives than by nonrelatives: Landis (1956), in an early study asking students about how they had recovered; Anderson et al. (1981), in a chart review of adolescents in a hospital treatment setting; and Friedrich et al. (in press), in their evaluation of young victims. However, other researchers (Finkelhor, 1979; Russell, in press; Seidner & Calhoun, 1984; Tufts, 1984) found no difference in the impact of abuse by family members versus abuse by others.

It must be kept in mind that how closely related a victim is to the offender does not necessarily reflect how much betrayal is involved in the abuse. Abuse by a trusted neighbor may be more devastating than abuse by a distant uncle or grandfather. Also, whereas abuse by a trusted person involves betrayal, abuse by a stranger or more distant person may involve more fear and thus be rated more negatively. These factors may help explain why the relative-nonrelative distinction is not necessarily a consistent predictor of trauma.

What has been more consistently reported is greater trauma from experiences involving fathers or father figures compared with all other types of perpetrators, when these have been separated out. Russell (in press) and Finkelhor (1979) both found that abuse by a father or stepfather was significantly more traumatic for victims than other abuse occurring either inside or outside the family. The Tufts (1984) study also reported that children abused by stepfathers showed more distress, but, for some reason, it did not find the same elevated level of distress among victims abused by natural fathers. Bagley and Ramsay (1985) found a small but nonsignificantly greater amount of impairment in women molested by fathers and stepfathers.

Type of Sexual Act

Results of empirical studies generally suggest, with a couple of important exceptions, that the type of sexual activity is related to the degree of trauma in victims. Russell's (in press) findings on long-term effects in adult women are the most clear-cut: Fifty-nine percent of those reporting completed or attempted intercourse, fellatio, cunnilingus, analingus, or anal intercourse said they were extremely traumatized, compared with only 36% of those who experienced manual touching of unclothed breasts or genitals and 22% of those who reported unwanted kissing or touching of clothed parts of the body. The community study by Bagley and Ramsay (1985) confirms this, in a multivariate analysis that found penetration to be the single most powerful variable explaining severity of mental health impairment, using a composite of standardized instruments.

Moreover, four other studies confirm the relation between type of sexual contact and subsequent effects by demonstrating that the least serious forms of sexual contact are associated with less trauma (Landis, 1956; S. Peters, 1984; Seidner & Calhoun, 1984; Tufts, 1984). However, some of these studies did not find the clear differentiation that Russell and Bagley and Ramsay did between intercourse and genital touching. The Tufts (1984) study, for example, using measures of children's anxiety, found children who had been fondled without penetration to be more anxious than those who actually suffered penetration. Moreover, there are three additional studies (Anderson et al., 1981; Finkelhor, 1979; Fromuth, 1983) that do not show any consistent relation between type of sexual activity and effect. Thus, a number of studies concur that molestation involving more intimate contact is more traumatic than less intimate contact. However, there is some disagreement about whether intercourse and penetration are demonstrably more serious than simple manual contact.

Force and Aggression

Five studies, three of which had difficulty finding expected associations between trauma and many other variables, did find an association between trauma and the presence of force. With Finkelhor's (1979) student samples, use of force by an abuser explained more of a victim's negative reactions than any other variable, and this finding held up in multivariate analysis. Fromuth (1983), in a replication of the Finkelhor study, found similar results. In Russell's (in press) study, 71% of the victims of force rated themselves as extremely or considerably traumatized, compared with 47% of the other victims.

The Tufts (1984) study found force to be one of the few variables associated with children's initial reactions: Children subjected to coercive experiences showed greater hostility and were more fearful of aggressive behavior in others. Tufts researchers reported that physical injury (i.e., the consequence of force) was the aspect of sexual abuse that was most consistently related to the degree of behavioral disturbances manifested in the child, as indicated by the LBC and other measures. Similarly, Friedrich et al. (in press) found the use of physical force to be strongly correlated with both internalizing and externalizing symptoms on the CBCL.

Three other studies present dissenting findings, however. Anderson et al. (1981), in studying initial effects, concluded that "the degree of force or coercion used did not appear to be related to presence or absence of psychosocial sequelae" in the adolescents they evaluated (p. 7). Seidner and Calhoun (1984), in an ambiguous finding, noted that force was associated with lower social maturity but higher self-acceptance. In addition, Bagley and Ramsay (1985) found that force was associated with greater impairment, but this association diminished to just below the significance level in multivariate analysis. Despite these findings, we are inclined to give credence to the studies showing force to be a major traumagenic influence, especially given the strong relation found by Finkelhor, Friedrich et al., Fromuth, Russell, and the Tufts study. Although some have argued that victims of forced abuse should suffer less long-term trauma because they could more easily attribute blame for abuse to the abuser (MacFarlane, 1978), empirical studies do not seem to provide support for this supposition.

Age at Onset

There has been a continuing controversy in the literature about how a child's age might affect his or her reactions to a sexually abusive experience. Some have contended that younger children are more vulnerable to trauma because of their impressionability. Others have felt that their naiveté may protect them from some negative effects, especially if they are ignorant of the social stigma surrounding the kind of victimization they have suffered. Unfortunately, findings from the available studies do not resolve this dispute.

Two studies of long-term effects do suggest that younger children are somewhat more vulnerable to trauma. Meiselman (1978), in her chart review of adults in treatment, found that 37% of those who experienced incest prior to puberty were seriously disturbed, compared with only 17% of those who were victimized after puberty. Similarly, Courtois (1979), in her community sample, assessed the impact of child sexual abuse on long-term relationships with men and the women's sense of self and also found more effects from prepubertal experiences.

However, four other studies found no significant relation between age at onset and impact. Finkelhor (1979), in a multivariate analysis, found a small but nonsignificant tendency for younger age to be associated with trauma. Russell (in press) also found a small but nonsignificant trend for experiences before age 9 to be associated with more long-term trauma. Langmade (1983) could find no difference in sexual anxiety, sexual guilt, or sexual dissatisfaction in adults related to the age at which they were abused. Bagley and Ramsay (1985) found an association between younger age and trauma, but that association dropped out in multivariate analysis, especially when controlling for acts involving penetration.

The Tufts (1984) study gave particular attention to children's reactions to abuse at different ages. Tufts researchers concluded that age at onset bore no systematic relation to the degree of disturbance. They did note that latency-age children were the most disturbed, but this finding appeared more related to the age at which the children were evaluated than the age at which they were first abused. They concluded that the age at which abuse begins may be less important than the stages of development through which the abuse persists.

In summary, studies tend to show little clear relation between age of onset and trauma, especially when they control for other factors. If there is a trend, it is for abuse at younger ages to be more traumatic. Both of the initial hypotheses about age of onset may have some validity, however: Some younger children may be protected by naiveté, whereas others are more seriously traumatized by impressionability. However, age interacts with other factors like relationship to offender, and until more sophisticated analytical studies are done, we cannot say whether these current findings of a weak relation mean that age has little independent effect or is simply still masked in complexity.

Sex of Offender

Perhaps because there are so few female offenders (Finkelhor & Russell, 1984), very few studies have looked at impact according to the sex of the offender. Two studies that did (Finkelhor, 1984; Russell, in press) both found that adults rated experiences with male perpetrators as being much more traumatic than those with female perpetrators. A third study (Seidner & Calhoun, 1984) found male perpetrators linked with lower self-acceptance, but higher social maturity, in college-age victims.

Adolescent and Adult Perpetrators

There are also very few studies that have looked at the question of whether age of the perpetrator makes any difference in the impact of sexual abuse on victims. However, two studies using college student samples (Finkelhor, 1979; Fromuth, 1983) found that victims felt significantly more traumatized when abused by older perpetrators. In Finkelhor's multivariate analysis (which controlled for other factors such as force, sex of perpetrator, type of sex act, and age of the offender), age of the offender was the second most important factor predicting trauma. Fromuth (1983) replicated these findings. Russell (in press), with a community sample, reported consistent, but qualifying, results: In her survey, lower levels of trauma were reported for abuse with perpetrators who were younger than 26 or older than 50. The conclusion that experiences with ado-

lescent perpetrators are less traumatic seems supported by all three studies.

Telling or Not Telling

There is a general clinical assumption that children who feel compelled to keep the abuse a secret in the aftermath suffer greater psychic distress as a result. However, studies have not confirmed this theory. Bagley and Ramsay (1985) did find a simple zero-order relation between not telling and a composite measure of impairment based on depression, suicidal ideas, psychiatric consultation, and self-esteem. However, the association became nonsignificant when controlled for other factors. Finkelhor (1979), in a multivariate analysis, also found that telling or not telling was essentially unrelated to a self-rated sense of trauma. Further, the Tufts (1984) researchers, evaluating child subjects, reported that the children who had taken a long time to disclose the abuse had the least anxiety and the least hostility. Undoubtedly, the decision to disclose is related to many factors about the experience, which prevents a clear assessment of its effects alone. For example, although silence may cause suffering for a child, social reactions to disclosure may be less intense if the event is long past. Moreover, the conditions for disclosure may be substantially different for the current generation than they were for past generations. Thus, any good empirical evaluation of the effects of disclosure versus secrecy needs to take into account the possibility of many interrelationships.

Parental Reaction

Only two studies have looked at children's trauma as a function of parental reaction, even though this is often hypothesized to be related to trauma. The Tufts (1984) study found that when mothers reacted to disclosure with anger and punishment, children manifested more behavioral disturbances. However, the same study did not find that positive responses by mothers were systematically related to better adjustment. Negative responses seemed to aggravate, but positive responses did not ameliorate, the trauma. Anderson et al. (1981) found similar results: They noted 2 times the number of symptoms in the children who had encountered negative reactions from their parents. Thus, although only based on two studies of initial effects, the available evidence indicates that negative parental reactions aggravate trauma in sexually abused children.

Institutional Response

There is a great deal of interest in how institutional response may affect children's reactions to abuse, but little research has been done. Tufts (1984) researchers found that children removed from their homes following sexual abuse exhibited more overall behavior problems, particularly aggression, than children who remained with their families. However, the children who were removed in the Tufts study were also children who had experienced negative reactions from their mothers, so this result may be confounded with other factors related to the home environment.

Summary of Contributing Factors

From this review of empirical studies, it would appear that there is no contributing factor that all studies agree on as being consistently associated with a worse prognosis. However, there are trends in the findings. The preponderance of studies indicate that abuse by fathers or stepfathers has a more negative impact than abuse by other perpetrators. Experiences involving genital contact seem to be more serious. Presence of force seems to result in more trauma for the victim. In addition, when the perpetrators are men rather than women, and adults rather than teenagers, the effects of sexual abuse appear to be more disturbing. These findings should be considered tentative, however, being based on only two

studies apiece. When families are unsupportive of the victims, and/or victims are removed from their homes, the prognosis has also been shown to be worse; again, these findings are based on only two studies.

Concerning the age of onset, the more sophisticated studies found no significant relation, especially when controlling for other factors; however, the relation between age and trauma is especially complex and has not yet been carefully studied. In regard to the impact of revealing the abuse, as opposed to the child keeping it a secret, current studies also suggest no simple relation. Of all these areas, there is the least consensus on the effect of duration of abuse on impact.

DISCUSSION

Conclusions from the foregoing review must be tempered by the fact that they are based on a body of research that is still in its infancy. Most of the available studies have sample, design, and measurement problems that could invalidate their findings. The study of the sexual abuse of children would greatly benefit from some basic methodological improvements.

Samples. Many of the available studies are based on samples of either adult women seeking treatment or children whose molestation has been reported. These subjects may be very self-selected. Especially if sexual abuse is so stigmatizing that only the most serious cases are discovered and only the most seriously affected victims seek help, such samples could distort our sense of the pathology most victims experience as a result of this abuse. New studies should take pains to expand the size and diversity of their samples and, particularly, to study victims who have not sought treatment or been reported. Advertising in the media for "well-adjusted" victims, as Tsai et al. (1979) did, however, does not seem an adequate solution, as this injects a different selection bias into the study.

We favor sampling for sexual abuse victims within the general population, using whole communities—as in Russell's (in press), S. Peters's (1984), and Bagley and Ramsay's (1985) designs—or other natural collectivities (high school students, college students, persons belonging to a health plan, etc.). Obtaining such samples may be easier with adult than with child victims. If identified child victims must be used, care should be taken to sample from all such identified children, not just the ones who get referred for clinical assessment and treatment and who may therefore represent the most traumatized group.

Control groups. Some of the empirical studies cited here did not have comparison groups of any sort. Such a control is obviously important, even if it is only a group of other persons in treatment who were not sexually victimized (e.g., Briere, 1984; Meiselman, 1978). In some respects, however, this control procedure may actually underestimate the types and severities of pathology associated with sexual abuse, because problems that sexual abuse victims share with other clinical populations will not show up as distinctive effects. An as-yet untried, but we believe fruitful, approach is to match victims from clinical sources with other persons who grew up with them: that is, schoolmates, relatives, or even unvictimized siblings.

Measurement. Most of the studies we reviewed used fairly subjective measures of the outcome variables in question (e.g., guilt feelings, fears, etc.). We are encouraged by the appearance of studies such as the Tufts (1984) study and Bagley and Ramsay's (1985) survey, which used batteries of objective measures. However, empirical investigations need to go even further. To test for the specific and diverse sequelae that have been associated with child sexual abuse, it would appear that special sexual abuse outcome instruments now need to be developed. Instruments designed specifically to measure the aftereffects noted by clinicians might be more successful at showing the true extent of pathology related to the experience of sexual abuse in childhood.

Sexual abuse in deviant subpopulations. Some of the studies purporting to show effects of child sexual abuse are actually reports of prevalence among specialized populations, such as prostitutes (James & Meyerding, 1977; Silbert & Pines, 1981), sex offenders (Groth & Burgess, 1979), or psychiatric patients (Carmen, Rieker, & Mills, 1984). To conclude from high rates of abuse in deviant populations that sexual abuse causes the deviance can be a misleading inference. Care needs to be taken to demonstrate that the discovered rate of sexual abuse in the deviant group is actually greater than in a relevant comparison group. In at least one study of sex offenders, for example, although abuse was frequent in their backgrounds, even higher rates of prior abuse were found for prisoners who had not committed sex crimes (Gebhard, Gagnon, Pomeroy, & Christenson, 1965). It is important to recognize that such data do not indicate that sexual abuse caused the deviance, only that many such offenders have abuse in their backgrounds.

Developmentally specific effects. In studying the initial and long-term effects of sexual abuse, researchers must also keep in mind that some effects of the molestation may be delayed. Although no sexual difficulties may be manifest in a group of college student victims (as in Fromuth, 1983), such effects may be yet to appear and may manifest themselves in studies of older groups. Similarly, developmentally specific effects may be seen among children that do not persist into adulthood, or that may assume a different form as an individual matures. The Tufts (1984) study clearly demonstrated the usefulness of looking at effects by defined age groupings.

Disentangling sources of trauma. One of the most imposing challenges for researchers is to explore the sources of trauma in sexual abuse. Some of the apparent effects of sexual abuse may be due to premorbid conditions, such as family conflict or emotional neglect, that actually contributed to a vulnerability to abuse and exacerbated later trauma. Other effects may be due less to the experience itself than to later social reactions to disclosure. Such questions need to be approached using careful multivariate analyses in large and diverse samples or in small studies that match cases of sexual abuse that are similar except for one or two factors. Unfortunately, these questions are difficult to address in retrospective long-term impact studies, as it may be difficult or impossible to get accurate information about some of the key variables (e.g., how much family pathology predated the abuse).

Preoccupation with long-term effects. Finally, there is an unfortunate tendency in interpreting the effects of sexual abuse (as well as in studies of other childhood trauma) to overemphasize long-term impact as the ultimate criterion. Effects seem to be considered less "serious" if their impact is transient and disappears in the course of development. However, this tendency to assess everything in terms of its long-term effect betrays an "adulto-centric" bias. Adult traumas such as rape are not assessed ultimately in terms of whether they will have an impact on old age: They are acknowledged to be painful and alarming events, whether their impact lasts 1 year or 10. Similarly, childhood traumas should not be dismissed because no "long-term effects" can be demonstrated. Child sexual abuse needs to be recognized as a serious problem of childhood, if only for the immediate pain, confusion, and upset that can ensue.

NOTE

1. The whole literature on sexual abuse poses problems for differentiating according to gender of victims. As Table 20.1 shows, many studies contain a small number of men included in a larger sample of women. Unfortunately, many of these studies do not specifically mention which effects apply to men, so it is possible that some of the sequalae described apply only to the men. However, we believe that most of the sequelae described apply primarily to women.

REFERENCES

Achenbach, T. M., & Edelbrock, C. (1983). *Manual for the child behavior checklist.* Burlington: University of Vermont.

Anderson, S. C., Bach, C. M., & Griffith, S. (1981, April). *Psychosocial sequelae in intrafamilial victims of sexual assault and abuse.* Paper presented at the Third International Conference on Child Abuse and Neglect, Amsterdam, The Netherlands.

Bagley, C., & Ramsay, R. (1985, February). *Disrupted childhood and vulnerability to sexual assault: Long-term sequels with implications for counselling.* Paper presented at the Conference on Counseling the Sexual Abuse Survivor, Winnipeg, Canada.

Bell, A., & Weinberg, M. (1981). *Sexual preference: Its development among men and women.* Bloomington: Indiana University Press.

Benward, J., & Densen-Gerber, J. (1975, February). *Incest as a causative factor in anti-social behavior: An exploratory study.* Paper presented at the meeting of the American Academy of Forensic Science, Chicago, IL.

Briere, J. (1984, April). *The effects of childhood sexual abuse on later psychological functioning: Defining a "post-sexual-abuse syndrome."* Paper presented at the Third National Conference on Sexual Victimization of Children, Washington, DC.

Briere, J., & Runtz, M. (1985, August). *Symptomatology associated with prior sexual abuse in a non-clinical sample.* Paper presented at the annual meeting of the American Psychological Association, Los Angeles, CA.

Carmen, E., Rieker, P. P., & Mills, T. (1984). Victims of violence and psychiatric illness. *American Journal of Psychiatry, 141,* 378-383.

Constantine, L. (1977). *The sexual rights of children: Implications of a radical perspective.* Paper presented at the International Conference on Love and Attraction, Swansea, Wales.

Constantine, L. (1980). Effects of early sexual experience: A review and synthesis of research. In L. Constantine & F. M. Martinson (Eds.), *Children and sex* (pp. 217-244). Boston: Little, Brown.

Courtois, C. (1979). The incest experience and its aftermath. *Victimology: An International Journal, 4,* 337-347.

De Francis, V. (1969). *Protecting the child victim of sex crimes committed by adults.* Denver, CO: American Humane Association.

DeYoung, M. (1982). *The sexual victimization of children.* Jefferson, NC: McFarland.

Farrell, W. (1982). *Myths of incest: Implications for the helping professional.* Paper presented at the International Symposium on Family Sexuality, Minneapolis, MN.

Fields, P. J. (1981, November). Parent-child relationships, childhood sexual abuse, and adult interpersonal behavior in female prostitutes. *Dissertation Abstracts International, 42,* 2053B.

Finkelhor, D. (1979). *Sexually victimized children.* New York: Free Press.

Finkelhor, D. (1984). *Child sexual abuse: New theory and research.* New York: Free Press.

Finkelhor, D., & Russell, D. (1984). Women as perpetrators of sexual abuse: Review of the evidence. In D. Finkelhor (Ed.), *Child sexual abuse: New theory and research* (pp. 171-187). New York: Free Press.

Friedrich, W. N., Urquiza, A. J., & Beilke, R. (in press). Behavioral problems in sexually abused young children. *Journal of Pediatric Psychology.*

Fromuth, M. E. (1983, August). *The long term psychological impact of childhood sexual abuse.* Unpublished doctoral dissertation, Auburn University, Auburn, AL.

Gebhard, P., Gagnon, J., Pomeroy, W., & Christenson, C. (1965). *Sex offenders: An analysis of types.* New York: Harper & Row.

Goodwin, J., McCarthy, T., & Divasto, P. (1981). Prior incest in mothers of abused children. *Child Abuse and Neglect, 5,* 87-96.

Groth, N. A. (1978). Guidelines for assessment and management of the offender. In A. Burgess, N. Groth, S. Holmstrom, & S. Sgroi (Eds.), *Sexual assault of children and adolescents* (pp. 25-42). Lexington, MA: Lexington Books.

Groth, N. A., & Burgess, A. W. (1979). Sexual trauma in the life histories of rapists and child molesters. *Victimology: An International Journal, 4,* 10-16.

Gundlach, R. (1977). Sexual molestation and rape reported by homosexual and heterosexual women. *Journal of Homosexuality, 2,* 367-384.

Harrison, P. A., Lumry, A. E., & Claypatch, C. (1984, August). *Female sexual abuse victims: Perspectives on family dysfunction, substance use and psychiatric disorders.* Paper presented at the Second National Conference for Family Violence Researchers, Durham, NH.

Henderson, J. (1983). Is incest harmful? *Canadian Journal of Psychiatry, 28,* 34-39.

Herman, J. L. (1981). *Father-daughter incest.* Cambridge, MA: Harvard University Press.

James, J., & Meyerding, J. (1977). Early sexual experiences and prostitution. *American Journal of Psychiatry, 134,* 1381-1385.

Landis, J. (1956). Experiences of 500 children with adult sexual deviation. *Psychiatric Quarterly Supplement, 30,* 91-109.

Langmade, C. J. (1983). The impact of pre- and postpubertal onset of incest experiences in adult women as measured by sex anxiety, sex guilt, sexual satisfaction, and sexual behavior. *Dissertation Abstracts International, 44,* 917B. (University Microfilms No. 3592)

MacFarlane, K. (1978). Sexual abuse of children. In J. R. Chapman & M. Gates (Eds.), *The victimization of women* (pp. 81-109). Beverly Hills, CA: Sage.

Meiselman, K. (1978). *Incest.* San Francisco: Jossey-Bass.

Miller, J., Moeller, D., Kaufman, A., Divasto, P., Fitzsimmons, P., Pather, D., & Christy, J. (1978). Recidivism among sexual assault victims. *American Journal of Psychiatry, 135,* 1103-1104.

Nelson, J. (1981). The impact of incest: Factors in self-evaluation. In L. Zakus & F. Mahlon (Eds.), *Children and sex* (pp. 163-174). Boston: Little, Brown.

Peters, J. J. (1976). Children who are victims of sexual assault and the psychology of offenders. *American Journal of Psychotherapy, 30,* 398-421.

Peters, S. D. (1984). *The relationship between childhood sexual victimization and adult depression among Afro-American and white women.* Unpublished doctoral dissertation, University of California, Los Angeles.

Ramey, J. (1979). Dealing with the last taboo. *Sex Information and Education Council of the United States, 7,* 1-2, 6-7.

Reich, J. W., & Gutierres, S. E. (1979). Escape/aggression incidence in sexually abused juvenile delinquents. *Criminal Justice and Behavior, 6,* 239-243.

Rogers, C. M., & Terry, T. (1984). Clinical intervention with boy victims of sexual abuse. In I. Stewart and J. Greer (Eds.), *Victims of Sexual Aggression* (pp. 1-104). New York: Van Nostrand, Reinhold.

Russell, D. E. H. (in press). *The secret trauma: Incest in the lives of girls and women.* New York: Basic Books.

Sandfort, T. (1981). *The sexual aspect of paedophile relations.* Amsterdam: Pan/Spartacus.

Sedney, M. A., & Brooks, B. (1984). Factors associated with a history of childhood sexual experience in a nonclinical female population. *Journal of the American Academy of Child Psychiatry, 23,* 215, 218.

Seidner, A., & Calhoun, K. S. (1984, August). *Childhood sexual abuse: Factors related to differential adult adjustment.* Paper presented at the Second National Conference for Family Violence Researchers, Durham, NH.

Silbert, M. H., & Pines, A. M. (1981). Sexual child abuse as an antecedent to prostitution. *Child Abuse and Neglect, 5,* 407-411.

Tsai, M., Feldman-Summers, S., & Edgar, M. (1979). Childhood molestation: Variables related to differential impact of psychosexual functioning in adult women. *Journal of Abnormal Psychology, 88,* 407-417.

Tufts' New England Medical Center, Division of Child Psychiatry (1984). *Sexually exploited children: Service and research project.* Final report for the Office of Juvenile Justice and Delinquency Prevention. Washington, DC: U.S. Department of Justice.

Wisconsin Female Juvenile Offender Study (1982). *Sex abuse among juvenile offenders and runaways. Summary report.* Madison, WI: Author.

Woods, S. C., & Dean, K. S. (1984). *Final report: Sexual abuse of males research project* (Contract No. 90 CA/812). Washington, DC: National Center on Child Abuse and Neglect.

Psychodynamic Factors in Child Abuse

| BRANDT F. STEELE   1987 |

"Psychodynamic Factors in Child Abuse," a chapter in the third edition of *The Battered Child*, offered the field an important understanding of factors leading to abusive behavior from a psychiatric perspective. The 1987 paper provided a compilation of the research and clinical observations to date on this topic. While recognizing the complexities of child maltreatment, its many types, and the fact that no two abusers are identical, this esteemed colleague in the field offered a way of cataloging or categorizing the psychodynamic characteristics that appeared to be common to most if not all abusers. And, as noted by Jill Korbin, Steele set high standards for compassion rather than condemnation of abusive parents.

Steele cautions the reader not to disregard the importance of a variety of social and other factors—referred to as life stresses (e.g., poor education, alcoholism, poverty)—in understanding child abuse. And he argues that the purpose of this paper is to discern why under similarly stressful circumstances, such as poverty, some parents will abuse and some will not. Thus,

this paper does not emphasize social factors in its explanation of child maltreatment. By focusing on a deeper, more subtle psychodynamic understanding, Steele is able to describe the intrapsychic state necessary to abuse and thus a basic matrix of abusive behavior.

Korbin notes the importance at the time of publication of the recurrent patterns of psychic functioning described by Steele, notably the importance of parent-to-child attachment, including negative attachment and the residuals of one's own childhood experiences, while also acknowledging that the field today has expanded its understanding of child abuse to encompass individual factors in a broader ecological perspective. Acknowledging that Steele's work has long been the leading statement on the psychodynamic nature, etiology, and consequences of child maltreatment, Gary Melton points out that it is not wholly supported by more recent, systematic empirical research—notably in the areas of role reversal and attachment. Furthermore, Melton emphasizes the absence in Steele's paradigm of the abused child's own mental

health needs, the characteristics and circumstances of older abused children (e.g.
adolescents), and the underemphasis on
neglect.

Steele's paper clearly had a major impact at the time of its publication on the way
professionals in the field understood the underpinnings of child maltreatment. The paper maintains its value today, if read with
the understanding that it is, as its title suggests, strictly a psychodynamic analysis.

A. C. D. and K. O.

Since our previous reports (1-3) of abusive parents, we have continued to study
the behaviors, life histories, and psychological functioning of those parents and other
persons who abuse the infants and children for
whom they are providing care. Although our
original work began in relation to the seriously
injured children described under the title "the
battered-child syndrome," we soon began including children who were less severely physically injured, those who were diagnosed as
failing to thrive as a result of maternal deprivation, or those suffering from other forms of neglect. We have also seen those who were primarily suffering from emotional abuse and,
particularly during the last few years, older
children who have been sexually abused. We
have evaluated and treated their caretakers.
Thus, over the past two decades, we have covered a wide range of forms of maltreatment of
children and studied a great variety of those
parents or other caretakers who carry out their
tasks in less than desirable or adequate ways.

The term *child abuse* will be used in this
chapter to cover this whole spectrum of maltreatment of children. It is an extremely complex group of human behaviors characterized
by maladaptive interactions between infants
and children of all ages and their caretakers.
We speak of it as maldaptive in the direct biological sense. After ensuring his or her own
survival, the prime task of any individual is to
take part in the production of the next generation of individuals in a condition most likely to
ensure survival of the species. Child abuse is
therefore maladaptive in the sense that, to a
greater or lesser degree, it damages immature
members of our species in such a way as to interfere with their optimum development and to
impair their adaptive survival abilities. Abuse
involves children of all ages, from infancy
through adolescence, and caretakers of both
sexes, all ages, and with various kinds of relationships to the child. The caretakers who
abuse are most often biological parents, but
they may also be step-parents, adoptive parents, foster parents, grandparents, siblings,
other relatives, baby-sitters, parental paramours, or other nonrelated persons, such as
teachers, either in or out of the household, who
are involved in the child-caring tasks. Exceptions to this usual pattern of the caretakers being the abusers are the cases of infanticide and
of serious injuries inflicted upon children by
psychotic or seriously mentally disturbed
strangers and the sexual abuse of children perpetrated by strangers, often with the use of
force.

COMMON CHARACTERISTICS OF ABUSIVE BEHAVIOR

In the face of such a variety of interactions
and participants, it would seem difficult to
find any common factors in abusive behavior.
Yet, it is possible, through careful study of the
life histories and behaviors of the many kinds

of abusers, to discern common themes and recurrent patterns of psychic function. In our work with abusive caretakers over the past two decades, we have never seen two who were exactly alike. Despite all their differences, however, they share a number of characteristics which they exhibit in varying degrees. These characteristics will be discussed in some detail below.

Child abuse is an extremely complex problem and, in addition to the impact it has on both its victims and perpetrators, it has many ramifications in the fields of medicine, social work, law, psychology, child development, psychiatry, and anthropology. All of these disciplines have something valuable to contribute to the elucidation and comprehension of child abuse phenomena. Our own personal bias is to understand the problem within the framework of human psychology and, more specifically, according to psychoanalytic concepts of human development and mental functioning. While we thus follow what is essentially a psychiatric approach to the problem of child abuse, we do not mean to imply by this that the child abuse syndrome is a mental illness in the usual sense of that term, nor can it be easily subsumed under any of the commonly accepted psychiatric nosological entities. Some caretakers who abuse children may also show characteristic symptoms of schizophrenia or depression or any of the various kinds of neuroses and character disorders. These occur with approximately the same frequency as they do in the general population, and the abuse is not necessarily a part of such psychic states. Many abusers have emotional problems which are also commonly seen in what are called *narcissistic character disorders* or *borderline states*. Yet, child abuse is not necessarily associated with either of these two entities. In general, it seems to be useful to consider child abusive behavior as a group of abnormal patterns of caretaker-child interactions related to psychological characteristics which can exist concurrently, but quite independently, of any psychiatric disorder or even in otherwise relatively healthy personalities. Abusive, neglecting behavior is not considered to be purely haphazard or impulsive, but rather to be understood as a particular constellation of emotional states and specific adaptive responses which have their roots in the earliest months of life.

By describing the intrapsychic state as the most necessary and basic matrix of abusive behavior, we do not mean to disregard the importance of other factors. Depending upon what particular population of abusers is studied or sampled, it can be shown with statistical significance that abusive, neglecting behavior can be precipitated or escalated by such things as poverty, bad housing, unemployment, marital strife, alcoholism, drug abuse, difficult pregnancies and deliveries, lack of education, lack of knowledge of child development, prematurity and illness of infants, deaths in the family, and a host of other things. Any of these can become a critical stress, precipitating a crisis, ending in abuse or neglect. An excellent review of social factors in abuse is that by Straus (4). In every case, such factors warrant our most intense concern and all our efforts toward alleviation. At the same time, we must realize that awareness of the importance of such social factors in situations of abuse does not answer what we consider more basic questions: Why, under circumstances of stress, do some persons respond with abusive behaviors, while others do not? Why do the majority of people in a low socioeconomic group treat their offspring with adequate kindness, consideration, and love without abuse, even in critical times? And, conversely, why do some people with adequate housing and wealth seriously harm their infants? We feel, in our efforts to answer these and similar questions, that it is necessary to turn to a deeper, more subtle psychological understanding of these individuals. As noted above, no two abusers are exactly alike, but we commonly find among them a certain constellation of emotional states and patterns of reaction which we consider to be essential, basic ingredients in the usual syndromes of abuse and neglect.

History of Abuse in Early Life

As reported in previous studies (1-3), it is common for abusive or neglectful caretakers to give a history of having experienced some significant degree of neglect, with or without accompanying physical abuse. In our experience, it is quite rare to see an abuser who does not relate this history if questioned appropriately. This finding has been confirmed by other investigators (5-9), but it has also been questioned by other workers who have not obtained the history of early life neglect or abuse with as much frequency as we did. We have noted some things which may account for at least a certain number of those who do not claim a history of physical abuse in early life. We have seen several persons who, during evaluation for maltreatment of their children, stoutly denied having been mistreated themselves as children. Upon further questioning as to who did the disciplining in the family and what disciplinary measures were used, they freely described being whipped or beaten to the point of lacerations or bruising, but in no way did they consider this abuse, because the discipline was "appropriate punishment for misbehavior." Others will, for some time, maintain a denial of having been abused because of a persistent fear that, even though they are now adults, their parents might again attack them if they complain or criticize parental actions. Others hesitate to give a true history, lest the family be brought into some sort of difficulty or be disgraced in the community. More rarely, there is a genuine amnesia for the unpleasant events of childhood as a result of unusually strong repression. For example:

Jack S., aged 25, freely admitted bruising and breaking the arm of his 2-year-old daughter during a hassle over an error in toilet training. Although he recalled his father whipping him once when he was an early teenager for joyriding on an illegally "borrowed" motorcycle, he firmly denied any possibility of abuse early in life. Later, he reported talking to his sister about his "crazy psychiatrist" who kept wondering if he had been abused as a child and seemed to doubt his denials. His sister responded by saying, "Jack, do you mean to tell me you've forgotten how father used to take you down to the coal bin in the basement and whip you until you were black and blue and mother was afraid he would kill you?" (Note that the mother, although concerned, was not described as intervening.) Following this revelation, Jack's amnesia gradually lifted, and he recalled many other events of his early life.

There are others who, although they actually remember maltreatment, find it too painful to deal with and comfort themselves by maintaining a fantasy that their parents really were good to them. Such fantasies, of course, can gain a good deal of support from the fact that the parents were, in reality, "good enough," at least part of the time, and the uncomfortable side of the ambivalence can be disregarded.

We have often found it more difficult to establish evidence of neglect in early life than to uncover the history of physical abuse, because it is much harder for people to describe how much love and care were *not* there than to recall how often they were hit. The common expressions we hear from abusive parents, both men and women, are variations on such themes as "I never felt my mother ever really loved me or cared about me" or "My parents never listened to me or paid any attention to what I felt or what was important to me" or "I was the black sheep of the family, always left out" or, very commonly, "I never in my life felt close to either mother or father" or "It was never safe to ask for anything; I just did what I was told or what was wanted of me, but nobody ever really appreciated what I did or thought it was good enough." Another common source of feeling uncared for was the failure of one parent to interfere or protect the child while he was being beaten by the other parent. The child felt that neither one really cared about him. Similarly, girls, when trying to complain to their mothers about being sexually abused by males in the family, were often told they were lying or else "making it up" to cause trouble, or that it was all their fault anyway. And their mothers did nothing about the problem. This left the girls feeling hopeless and uncared for. Other, more obvious deprivations are often glossed over as just some of the "misfortunes of life" without recognition of the serious emotional impact which such things have on the growing child. We ascribe such events to a profound depression in the mother, an absence of the mother as a result of sickness or death, placements of the child with unsympathetic relatives or in unloving foster homes, absence of a father, an overburdened mother without enough time for any of her children, or multiple sicknesses with hospitalization in infancy and childhood. These and other similar experiences in early life can leave long-lasting feelings of deprivation and loneliness, even though they may be intellectually understood and accepted.

Lack of Empathy for Child

The history of neglect and abuse in the early years of the life of the abusive caretaker has been stressed because we believe that therein lies the source of the caretaker's later inability to provide empathic care for infants and children. By empathy, we mean a caretaker's sensitive awareness of a child's state and needs and the ability to instigate appropriate responses thereto. Abuse and neglect are the outward behavioral evidences of a caretaker's inadequate empathy for the child. We believe such inadequate empathy is the tragic deficit present in the caretaker in all situations of abuse and neglect. Excessive punitive expression of aggression or neglectful disregard of a child's basic needs could not occur if normal, adequate empathy existed in the caretaker. As a corollary to this lack of empathic awareness of the child and appropriate responses to it, we find that in times of stress or crisis the caretaker gives priority to his or her own needs and ideas, while the child's needs are given only secondary consideration or are completely disregarded. This phenomenon is seen with striking clarity in cases of sexual abuse of small children. The child is exploited by being drawn into sexual activity which is primarily oriented toward the satisfaction of the adult caretaker, while, at the same time, little or no attention is paid to the child's age-appropriate needs and abilities. The child's obedient, submissive cooperation with the adult in the sexual activity and the pleasure which some children seem to derive from it have led many observers to minimize or disregard this nonempathic exploitation of the child.

Excessively High Expectations

It is quite common, in situations of abuse and neglect, to find the caretakers expecting their infants and small children to behave and perform tasks with unusual efficiency much too early in the child's life, while, at the same time, disregarding the child's own feelings and wants. This phenomenon has been well described by Morris and Gould (10) as role reversal. The child is treated as if he were an adult while the caretaker expects satisfactions of his or her own desires to be cared for.

> An example is Mrs. G., a young woman whose 1-year-old baby girl had been severely burned by scalding water in the bathtub. She also had a boy 2 years old, and when asked about him she responded, "Oh, Buddy is very active. He's on the go all the time. He acts older than he is. He cleans the house, cleans my room, sweeps the floor in his room. He wants to help cook, but I think he's too young for that. Sometimes he's too helpful. He's never been with kids his own age, but it is helpful with him like that. It's not boring. Other kids his age just sit in the corner. He does watch kiddy shows, but he's up 'til 2 or 3 in the morning often helping me, and then he's up again at 7:30 or 8. He only takes a nap once every 2 or 3 days. If I tell him to do something, he will do it. He makes his bed if I tell him to do it. If he

doesn't, I bribe him. I'll send him to his room if he has a fit." When asked if Buddy was considerate of her moods, she replied, "Yeah, if I'm on the couch he gets a blanket and pillow, and brings me some water. He thinks that he made me sick and says, 'I sorry.' He even helps others too." When asked if he helped her take care of the baby, she said, "Oh, yeah, he bathes her, puts powder on her. He hunts for a bottle when she cries. Once there was no bottle. He took a whole half-gallon of milk out of the refrigerator and took it to her. He pushes her in her swing. He's very protective of her. He tells other kids that she's sleeping because he's afraid that they might hurt her, and he slaps kids if he thinks they will. He brings me clean diapers and throws the old ones out. He changed her once, but he did a goofy job of it. He wants to drive a car now." This mother also spoke of how she thought her step-parents were rather cruel to Buddy and said that, as a result, she found it hard to "holler at him." However, she added, "I did give him a licking last night. He knows by the tone of my voice if I'm mad. All I have to do is show him a belt lying around and he shapes up immediately." She claimed that while she was gone to a neighbor's, leaving Buddy to bathe himself, he got out of the tub and put his baby sister in water which was too hot.

It is obvious in this brief vignette that this mother gained satisfaction from the precocious pursuit of adult behavior she expected from her 2-year-old boy. It is obvious that she was critical and punitive toward him if he did not meet expectations, that his own needs to live like a normal 2-year-old boy were not considered. It is also significant to note how energetically this small boy devoted all his efforts toward trying to please his mother. Despite the fact that she loved her children and, in general, took very good care of them, this mother demonstrates a pervasive lack of empathy. She showed no real spontaneous, intuitive, sensitive feelings toward her infants. In talking about her boy, she uses no warm, loving words and says essentially nothing about

what kind of human being he really is. She describes only what he does that is related to his usefulness to her and the household. Leaving her 1-year-old daughter in the precarious care of the 2-year-old brother while she goes visiting indicates a very disturbing lack of awareness of her children's needs and behavior and their need for guidance and protection.

It is very common for physical abuse to occur as a "justified" action or "appropriate disciplinary punishment" when children fail to meet excessively high caretaker expectations. It is also possible to see significant neglect occur as a result of a child's failure to perform well enough to satisfy caretaker expectations. An infant who fails to respond to mother's inept or inappropriately timed feedings or other caretaking procedures is perceived as being defective, negativistic, generally unfit, or no good and is then deemed not worth caring for, resulting in "failure to thrive" or other forms of neglect. Thus, although both abusive and neglectful parents have the same pattern of high expectations of the child, their responses to the child's failure to meet expectations are quite different. In the one case, the child is perceived as failing to follow through to his full capabilities and therefore is punished to make him "shape up" and do better. In other case, the child is seen as incapable of proper response, as worthless, and therefore is given only cursory, inadequate care or almost totally disregarded.

Another young mother, Holly, was similar to Mrs. G. but showed even more significant misperceptions of her children. She had a 22-month-old boy, whom she described as a great help around the household, although not so efficient as Buddy. While in the office with me, she frequently slapped little Sammy on his rear and would alternately tell him, "Stop doing that, come here" and "Stop bothering me, go away." In the midst of this, he emptied my ashtray, wiped it with Kleenex, and replaced it on the desk. When I remarked on this behavior, his mother was obviously pleased and proud of his accomplishments. However, she had not allowed him to have any pleasure or freedom during this visit. She also had a 5-month-old boy in the hospital with a fractured skull and fractured pelvis inflicted during punishment for being stubborn and lazy. She told of how he had been a very good baby at first but had gradually become very unsatisfactory. He would "do nothing for himself," would get sick deliberately to frustrate her, and would look at her with great anger in his eyes. This intelligent young woman was not completely unaware of normal child development, but this did not counteract her misperceptions. The punishment had occurred when she was under more than average stress due to marital difficulties and feeling very much alone and uncared for and, therefore, especially needy of compliant, helpful behavior from her two boys. Some understanding of her behavior could be gained from her statement, "My mother never cared about me, never listened to me or what I wanted. I was never anything but a servant in her house." Her inadequate empathy was documented on another occasion when she described how important it was not to spoil children by giving into them too much or by picking them up when they cried. Then she added, "But I know children need to be loved, too, so I've always made it a practice to pick my little babies up and hold them for 10 minutes twice a day." She at other times also alluded to rather severe physical punishment during her early years.

It is obvious that Holly is severely deficient in empathy for her two children and that her behavior as a parent has been profoundly influenced by her own early life experience, especially by her relationship to her mother.

Impaired Parent-Child Attachment

Not all abusive parents show the high expectations, lack of empathy, and punitive attitude toward failure with the unusual clarity demonstrated in the two cases above. But they do expect simple, obedient, correct, appreciative responses from their infants and small children during the ordinary tasks of feeding,

bathing, toilet training, diapering, and taking naps, all according to parental desires of the moment, and they have other misperceptions of the child's abilities and intentions. The child's failure to please or obey is met by physical attack or verbal criticism or subsequent neglect. Indications of this disordered pattern of parental behavior can be observed at the time of the birth of the baby or in the immediate postpartum period. Gray and her colleagues (11) have clearly demonstrated that a most reliable sign of possible future difficulty in parenting is the evidence of poor attachment seen in the perinatal period. It is seen especially clearly in the mother's behavior toward her newborn baby immediately after delivery and during the first few feedings. It is possible to observe poor attachment by the father as well. Poor attachment is soon evidenced by the unempathic manner in which the parent performs the caretaking tasks. Caretaking is done mechanically, largely according to the caretaker's convenience and without any warm, sensitive interaction oriented toward satisfying the infant's needs and without proper responses according to the infant's state. In some ways, the abusive syndrome can be considered a disorder of attachment with all its subsequent repercussions. Recent research (12-18) has amply illustrated the importance of mother-infant attachment in parent-child bonding and its effect on subsequent parent-child interactions and child development. Two processes are involved. One is the attachment of the infant to the caretaker and the other is that of the caretaker to the infant. Disturbances can occur in either part of the process, and the factors which interfere with the infant's ability to attach well to the caretaker will be discussed later in this chapter. It is our strong belief, however, that it is the impairment of parent-to-child attachment that is most important in situations of abuse and neglect.

The propensity and ability of humans to attach to infants is not uniform or simple. In its most uncomplicated form, it has been best understood as the more or less automatic or instinctual response of a mother to her newborn infant during the first hour after delivery, during the infant's quiet-alert state, and in the subsequent interactions between them during feeding and general care. This is true as far as it goes and is undoubtedly the most characteristic, biologically appropriate time for a mother and infant to establish a bond of relationship between them. However, this paradigm of attachment in no way accounts for the equally strong, although subtly different, attachments that occur with those who have not been involved with the actual processes of pregnancy and delivery. We refer here to the strong attachment that can occur between father and infant, between adoptive parents and infant, as well as others. It is our firm conviction that those persons who have had a good early childhood experience themselves have the empathic ability to attach well to their infants in later years and that those who have suffered from abuse and neglect in early years have poor empathy and are unable to attach well. We thus see some of the dynamics which are so basic in the abuse and neglect cycle: caretakers who have been subject to unempathic care in their earliest years cannot attach well or be empathic to their own offspring and, hence, do not attach well and do not provide empathic care, thus providing the basic matrix for the next generation of abuse and neglect (2, 19). Obviously, this cannot be a completely rigid, inescapably determined process of repetition. Other factors can and do enter in to enhance or diminish the likelihood and severity of the cyclic recurrence. It is characteristic of human development that good and bad experiences in later childhood and after can influence, for better or for worse, psychological and behavioral trends established in the earliest years.

It is of interest to understand the mode of transmission and ramifications of the poor attachment and lack of empathy which we consider to be the basic core of the maladaptive, abusive, neglectful behavior of caretakers. Inasmuch as we see abusive caretakers repeating in their parental behavior the ways in which they themselves were treated as children, plus the fact that we see poor attachment immediately after the birth of the infant, it seems that the basic rudiments of the behavior are acquired at the very beginning of life. Benedek (20) has described how the experience of becoming a parent activates two sets of memories which are largely unconscious. One is the memory of how one was parented, and the other is what it was like to be a small child. These two deeply embedded psychic representations provide the templates to guide caretaking behavior. The caretaker is identified with his own parents, and the new baby is endowed, through reverse identification, with the attributes of the caretaker himself as a small child. These very early, primitive identifications are intensified by the day-to-day interactions between caretaker and infant during the ensuing months and early years. We feel that the basic pattern which can appear later in the adult as abusive, neglectful behavior is firmly established by the third year, although it can also be further modified by ensuing experiences of the child with the same or other caretakers. This acquisition of behavioral patterns by the child, which are similar to those of his caretaker, can also be appropriately understood in the frameworks of social learning theory and role modeling. Yet, we believe the more basic determinants of caretaking behavior are established during the affect-laden identification experience of the first few months before the development of more truly cognitive learning can exert an influence. This process is, in itself, not deviant. It is a normal mode of establishing the basic ingredients of caretaking behavior for all persons. Those who have had a very good experience in the first months of being cared for empathically are quite likely to attach well and to have adequate empathy in their own, later, caretaking activities. Those who have not had such a good experience of positive attachment and empathic care in their beginning lives are severely hampered in their later caretaking ability because of the identification resulting from poor attachment and deficient empathy. This early origin of the adult's ability to be empathic with children has also been noted by Olden (21, 22), Josselyn (23), and others. It accounts for the fact that sensitive, empathic mothering is not something confined to biological mothers but can exist in persons of both sexes, of all ages, as a behavioral expression determined by their own early life experience with either biological parents or other caretakers.

Deficits in the empathic care which all infants need for optimal growth and development are followed by specific psychological effects. In the normal, healthy, caretaker-infant dyad, there is a mutually rewarding, symbiotic relationship in which the caretaker sensitively becomes aware of appropriate responses to the infant's state and needs. As a result, the growing infant develops a feeling of what Benedek called "confidence" and Erikson described as "basic trust," a sense that the world and the people in it will be adequately good to one. In situations where there is lack of empathic care and experience of abuse and neglect, the symbiotic phase is highly distorted. Care is oriented much more toward the whims and convenience of the caretakers, with less appropriate response to the child. In this situation, it is impossible for the child to develop any sense that the world or the people in it in any way reliably respond to his own needs. Hence, he cannot develop basic trust but, on the other hand, will view the world with some degree of doubt and suspicion. Later, facing impossible expectations from caretakers with inevitable failure followed by punishment, criticism, and disregard, he will have learned to pay little attention to his own inner feelings, because they are of diminished value in his dealings with surroundings. Constantly under primary control of the caretaker and plagued with the necessity to deny the self and adapt to caretakers, there will be marked difficulty in the separation and individuation phases of development. It is not surprising, therefore, that as a result of these experiences in childhood, we see adults who are somewhat socially isolated and have a great deal of difficulty in reaching out to others for help and assistance. They have no basic trust and have some fear that the very people to whom they will look for help will be the ones most likely to attack. They also feel their own deepest needs have never been and never will be fully satisfied. There is a low sense of self-esteem and some degree of chronic, low-grade, depressive feeling. Under these circumstances, it is not surprising that we find very commonly in descriptions of adult, abusive, neglectful caretakers characterizations of these people as dependent, immature, and having a poor sense of identity, low self-esteem, a pseudoparanoid attitude of fear of being attacked, a reluctance to form lifelines or seek help in family and community, and a very suspicious attitude toward authority and a wish to avoid it. These characteristics of maltreating caretakers are all direct residuals of childhood experiences and are transferences to the present-day milieu of the feelings and attitudes which were appropriate toward the original caretakers of early years. It is important to understand the early origin and development of many of these characteristics, because it will help us understand the abusive, neglectful behavior of the caretakers and what strategies of management or therapy would be the most useful in helping them improve their child-caring abilities. It also points a way toward the use of helpful interventions in the perinatal period as a most effective time to help a family and to prevent the recurrence of abuse and neglect and the transmission of the pattern to still another generation.

CIRCUMSTANCES OF ATTACK

Physical abuse is usually not a constant or daily occurrence. There are often many days, weeks, or even months between attacks. To be sure, there may be almost daily emotional abuse in the form of yelling and verbal castigation, belittlement, and criticism, as well as disregard and lack of attention. But it is the physical attacks occurring intermittently in discrete episodes which give us the clearest picture of the abusive phenomenon. There are four conditions which seem necessary for abuse to occur:

1. A caretaker who has the predisposition for abuse related to the psychological residues of neglect or abuse in his or her own early life.
2. A crisis of some sort placing extra stress on the caretaker.
3. Lack of lifelines or sources of help for the caretaker, because either he or she is unable to reach out or the facilities are not available.
4. A child who is perceived as being in some way unsatisfactory.

These four factors interact in a mutually reinforcing way. Abusive parents live in a state of precarious balance between emotional supply and demand. They are more needy because of their low self-esteem, but less able to reach out for pleasure and support, and so turn with increased need to those who are least able to provide full satisfaction, their infants. Any crisis, even a small one such as a broken washing machine, becomes unmanageable because of the parent's poor coping techniques and inability or reluctance to seek help. Financial and housing crises are very upsetting, but most devastating are emotional crises related to loss or abandonment by important persons or the emotional desertion of a spouse after marital conflict. It is the infant's disturbing behavior during ordinary caretaking, excessive crying, or his errors during toilet training which are the common stimuli to parental turmoil that culminates in the abusive act. The following discussion drawn from our previous study (2) presents our understanding of the circumstances of abusive attacks.

The parent approaches each task of infant care with three incongruous attitudes: first, a healthy desire to do something good for the infant; second, a deep, hidden yearning for the infant to respond in such a way as to fill the emptiness in the parent's life and bolster his or her low self-esteem; and third, a harsh, authoritative demand for the infant's correct response, supported by a sense of parental rightness. If the caring task goes reasonably well and the infant's response is reasonably adequate, no attack occurs, and no harm is done except for the stimulation of aggression and accompanying strict superego development in the infant. But, if anything interferes with the success of the parental care or enhances the parent's feelings of being unloved and inferior, the harsh, authoritative attitude surges up, and an attack is likely to occur. The infant's part in this disturbance is accomplished by persistent, unassuaged crying, by failing to respond physically or emotionally in accordance with parental needs, or by actively interfering through obstructive physical activity. At times, the parent may be feeling especially inferior, unloved, needy, and angry and, therefore, unusually vulnerable because some important figure such as the spouse or a relative has just criticized or deserted him or her or because some other facet of life has become unmanageable.

On a deeper psychological level, the events begin with the parent's identification of the cared-for infant as a need-gratifying object equivalent to a parent who will replace the lacks in the abusive parent's own being-parented experience. Since the parent's past tells him that those to whom he looked for love were also the ones who attacked him, the infant is also perceived as a critical parental figure. Quite often abusing parents tell us, "When the baby cries like that, it sounds just like mother (or father) yelling at me, and I can't stand it." The perception of being criticized stirs up the parent's feeling of being inferior. It also increases the frustration of his need for love, and anger mounts. At this time, there seems to be a strong sense of guilt, a feeling of helplessness and panic becomes overwhelming, and the haziness is most marked. Suddenly, a shift in identifications occurs. The superego identification with the parent's own punitive parent takes over. The infant is perceived as the parent's own bad childhood itself. The built-up aggression is redirected outward, and the infant is hit with full superego approval.

This sudden shift in identifications is admittedly difficult to document. Our patients cannot clearly describe all that happened in the midst of such intense emotional turmoil. We interpret it as regression under severe stress to an early period of superego development when identification with the aggressor established a strict, punitive superego with more effective strength than the gentler ego ideal. In such a regressive state, the stronger, punitive superego inevitably comes to the fore.

Following the attack, some parents may maintain a strict, righteous attitude, express no sense of guilt about the aggression, insist they have done nothing wrong, and may be very resentful toward anyone who tries to interfere with their affairs. On the other hand, some parents are filled with remorse, weep, and quickly seek medical help if the child has been seriously hurt.

It has not been possible to obtain a clear story from all patients of what they actually did to the child at the time a serious injury occurred, even though abuse is admitted. They insist they did nothing differently than usual. In some cases, this may be a defensive forgetting. In others, we think it is probably a true statement. They have been hitting or yanking the child routinely and are not aware of the extra force used at the time of fracture.

The following condensed case histories, when added to the fragments already quoted, will illustrate the mainstreams of the patient's lives related to the ultimate abusive behavior.

Amy, 26, is the wife of a successful junior executive engineer. She requested help for feelings of depression, fear she was ruining her marriage, and worry over being angry and unloving with her baby boy. She was born and raised in a well-to-do family in a large city on the West Coast. Her parents were brilliant, active intellectuals who apparently had minimal involvement in the earliest years of their children's lives. She and her younger sister and brother were cared for by governesses, about whom Amy has vague, fragmentary memories. One was very warm, kind, and loving. She recalls another who was demanding, stern, and mean and who roughly washed Amy's long hair as a punishment and held her nose to make her eat. We suspect, without adequate documentation, that the governesses raised the infants as much to meet the high behavior standards of the parents as to meet the variable needs and whims of their charges.

As a child, Amy had more interaction with her mother, but she could not feel close to or really understood by either parent. Both parents had compulsive traits of wanting everything in perfect order and tasks done "at once." Her father was quite aloof, uninterested in children because they could not talk to him on any worthwhile level. When Amy was about 13, both mother and father had psychotherapy. Since then, her father has been warmer and has some liking for small children, but he still maintains a pattern of wanting to be the center of the stage and have people pay attention primarily to him, not only in the family, but in all social situations. In recent years, Amy has felt closer to her mother and has felt that they could talk more frankly and openly with each other. During her childhood, Amy felt inept, awkward, ugly, unable to be liked by other people, and somewhat dull intellectually. Even though she made good grades in school, they never seemed good enough to gain approval. (Her IQ is in the upper normal range.)

Although not physically punished or overtly severely criticized, Amy felt great lack of approval and developed a deep sense of inferiority, inability to please, and worthlessness; she thought of herself as almost "retarded." In college, she was capable, but not outstanding, and after graduation, she worked for a while, gaining a significant amount of self-respect and self-assurance. She had become a quite attractive, adequately popular girl and had made a good marriage. She and her husband are well-liked, active members of their social set.

Of her first-born child, Lisa, now age 2 and doing well, Amy says, "I did not like her too well at first and didn't feel close to her until she was several months old and more responsive." By the time Lisa was a year old, with much maternal encouragement, she was talking and beginning to talk and Amy began to think much more highly of her, and for the most part, they get along well with each other. However, if Lisa has tantrums or does not behave well, whines or cries too much, Amy occasionally still shakes her and spanks her rather violently. Their second child, Billy, was born not quite a year and a half after Lisa. He was delivered by cesarean section, 1 month premature. He did not suck well at first and feeding was a problem. Also, Amy was sick for a while after delivery. She never felt warm or close or really loved him and had even less patience with him than with Lisa. His "whining" drove her "crazy" and made her hate him. Because of his crying and lack of adequate response, she would grow impatient with him and leave him or punish him roughly. She spent little time cuddling or playing with him, and he became, as a result, somewhat less responsive and did not thrive as well as he might have. When he was 7 months old, during a routine checkup, the pediatrician unfortunately said to Amy, "Maybe you have a retarded child here." Amy immediately felt intense aversion to Billy, hated the sight of him, couldn't pick him up or feed him easily, and began more serious physical abuse that evening. She felt depressed, angry, and irritable. Billy also seemed to stop progressing. However, when checked by another pediatrician, he was said to be quite normal. Amy felt reassured, but not convinced. She became aware that Billy was responsive and alert if she felt all right and loving toward him, but he acted "stupid" if she were depressed or angry at him. This awareness of her influence on him served only to enhance her feelings of worthlessness and guilt. At times when he was unresponsive or seemed to be behaving in a "retarded" way, and especially if he cried too much or whined, she roughed him up, shook him, spanked him very severely, and choked him violently. No bones had been broken, but there were bruises. Amy described alternating between feelings of anger at Billy because he was "retarded" and feeling very guilty because she had "squashed him" by her own attitudes and behavior.

Amy described being inadequately prepared for and overwhelmed by the tasks of motherhood. This was enhanced by her feeling that she was trying to accomplish the mothering tasks without the help that her mother had had in bringing up her children. Further difficulty arose because her husband, although overtly quite sympathetic with her difficulties and expressing wishes of helping her, would also withdraw from her in times of crisis and imply a good deal of criticism of the way she dealt with the children. She also felt that there had been no one to whom she could really turn to air her troubles and get comfort and help without too much admonition and criticism. Further, Amy had a cousin who was retarded, and she felt devastated by fantasies of the burden of bringing up a retarded child.

This case shows the identification of the abusive parent with her own parents' attitudes toward children, the premature, high expectation and need for the infant to perform responsively, and the inability to cope with the lack of good response. Most clearly, it shows the parental misperception of the infant as the embodiment of those bad behavioral traits (being "retarded") for which the parent herself was criticized as a young child. During treatment, Amy's depressive feelings and sense of worthlessness were ameliorated. She began to interact more happily with her children, and they responded well to her change in behavior. Billy, particularly, began to thrive, grew rapidly, and became a happier, more rewarding baby. Amy and her husband began to communicate a little more effectively, and her aggressive behavior toward her children almost completely disappeared. After 6 months, treatment had to be terminated because of her husband's transfer to another city. We had the good fortune to see her and the children 4 years later. Amy was doing very well, and the two children were active, happy, bright youngsters. Wisely, we believe, they have had no more children. The improvement that occurred in this situation is partly due to our therapeutic intervention, but we would guess that it is also due to the passage of time, which enabled the children to grow up and inevitably become more behaviorally and conversationally rewarding to their mother.

Larry, age 27, is a quiet, shy, unassuming, little man who works as a welder's assistant. Since childhood, he has been plagued by a deep sense of inferiority, unworthiness, and unsureness of himself in his work and in all human relations. There is also a deep resentment, usually very restrained, against a world which he feels is unfair.

He was brought up on a dairy farm, the third of five children. The oldest, a sister, is 10 years his senior. He has never been able to find out the truth about her from his parents or other relatives but thinks all the evidence indicates she is a half-sister and an illegitimate child of his mother's before her marriage. Some resentment against his mother is based on this situation. His two younger sisters he felt were bothersome and annoying during their childhood. His brother, 2 years older, took advantage of him, and his parents always took the brother's side, allowing him to do many things for which Larry was criticized or punished. This brother was quite wild, and while on leave from the Navy, he was in a serious auto accident. Larry said, "Too bad he wasn't killed" but then found out his brother had been killed. Overwhelmed by guilt and grief, Larry took leave from the Army to take his brother's body home for burial.

Larry's parents were deeply religious. He imagined his mother became fanatically so following her illegitimate pregnancy. She was against cigarettes, alcohol, coffee, tea, and most of the usual forms of amusement. Even after his marriage, his mother told his wife not to make coffee for him. Larry felt she was always much more strict with him than with his siblings. She forced him to at-

tend Sunday school and frequent church services, much against his will. She berated him for minor misdeeds and constantly nagged and criticized him to the point where he felt everything he did was wrong and that he could never do right in her eyes. He occasionally rebelled by smoking or drinking. Larry's father drank moderately but became a teetotaler after his son's death. He often had outbursts of temper and once beat Larry with a piece of 2-by-4 lumber for a minor misdeed. Larry does not recall either mother or father spanking as a routine, but there were constant verbal attacks and criticism. He felt that neither of his parents, particularly his mother, really listened to him or understood his unhappiness and his need for comfort and consideration.

While he was in the army, Larry and Becky planned to marry. She was to come to where he was stationed, and they were to be married at Christmas time. He waited all day at the bus station, but she never appeared. Sad and hopeless, he got drunk. Months later, a buddy told him she had married somebody else the first of January. He saw her again a year later when home on leave. She had been divorced; so they made up and got married. She had a child, Jimmy, by her first marriage.

Larry has been dependent on Becky and fears losing her. Seeing Jimmy reminds him of her previous desertion. He feels she favors Jimmy; he is critical of Jimmy and occasionally spanks him. Becky has threatened to leave Larry over his aversion to Jimmy. During their 5 years of marriage, they have been in financial straits, and at such times, Becky and Larry have gone to their respective family homes for help until he could find a new job. Becky resented these episodes and criticized Larry for being an inadequately capable and providing husband.

They have had three more children of their own. Mary, age 4, is liked very much by both parents, although Larry is more irritated by her than by their next child, David, age 2 ½. David is "a very fine, active, alert, well-mannered little boy." He is quite responsive, and both parents like him and are good with him. Maggie, 4 ½ months old, was thought by both parents to be "a bit different" from birth. She seemed to look bluer and cried less strongly than their other babies and was also rather fussy. Becky is fond of Maggie and gives her good mothering. Larry is irritated by her, much as he is by Mary, and more than by David, but he does not dislike her as much as he does Jimmy.

Maggie was admitted to the hospital with symptoms and signs of bilateral subdural hematoma. She had been alone with her father when he noticed a sudden limpness, unconsciousness, and lack of breathing. He gave mouth-to-mouth respiration, and she was brought to the hospital by ambulance. There was a history of a similar episode a month before when Maggie was 3 months old; when alone with her father she had become limp, followed by vomiting. Medical care was not sought until a week later. Following this, there was a question of increasing head size. No fractures of skull or long bones were revealed by X-ray. Two craniotomies were done for the relief of Maggie's subdural hematomas. During the month she was in hospital, we had frequent interviews with the parents. We were impressed by Becky's warmth, responsiveness, and concern over Maggie's welfare. Larry, however, maintained a more uneasy, aloof, evasive attitude, although he was superficially cooperative. What had happened to Maggie was not clearly established, but it seemed obvious she was the victim of trauma. We thought Larry was likely to have been the abuser, despite his maintenance of silence and innocence. We felt we had adequate, although meager, rapport with Larry and Becky and allowed them to take Maggie home with the adamant provision that she never be left alone with Larry.

A week later Larry called urgently for an appointment. Filled with shame, guilt, and anxiety, he poured out his story. President Kennedy had been assassinated 2 days before. Larry was shocked, then flooded with feelings of sympathy for Kennedy and his family, anger at the assassin, grief over the unfair, unnecessary loss of an admired figure, and a sense of communal guilt. In this emotional turmoil, he had a few beers at a tavern, went home and confessed to Becky what he had done to Maggie, and then phoned us. The circumstances of the attack were as follows:

Larry's boss told him that his job was over. The construction contract had been suddenly canceled, and there was no more work. Feeling discouraged, hopeless, and ignored, Larry went home, shamefacedly told Becky he had lost his job, and asked her if she wanted to go with the children to her family. Saying nothing, Becky walked out of the house leaving Larry alone with Maggie. The baby began to cry. Larry tried to comfort her, but she kept on crying; so he looked for her bottle. He could not find the bottle anywhere; the persistent crying and his feelings of frustration, helplessness, and ineffectuality became overwhelming. In a semiconfused "blurry" state, he shook Maggie severely and then hit her on the head. Suddenly aware of what he had done, he started mouth-to-mouth resuscitation; then Becky came home and Maggie was brought to the hospital.

Recurrent in Larry's life are the themes of feeling disregarded and deserted and of being helplessly ineffectual in his attempts to meet expectations. These concepts of himself as worthless and incapable express the incorporation into his superego of the attitudes of his parents toward him during childhood; they have been enhanced by his later reality experiences of failure. He has further strong identifications with the aggressive parental attitudes of criticizing and attacking the weak, the helpless, and the maimed.

The attack on Maggie occurred when several of Larry's vulnerabilities were activated at the same time. He had experienced a lack of being considered and a feeling of failure in losing his job, his wife "deserted" him again with implications of criticism, he felt helpless to cope with the crying demands of the baby, and his own deep yearnings for love and care could not be spoken. Frustration and anger mounted, and the baby was struck. Larry said that in the "blurry" state, he had a fleeting, queer feeling that he had hit himself.

Later, we found similar circumstances were present when Maggie had been less severely injured a month before. Becky had started working evenings to supplement Larry's inadequate income. She would depart soon after he came home from his job, leaving him alone to fix supper, wash the dishes, and put the children to bed. He found the tasks difficult and was upset by the children's crying, particularly Maggie's. One evening, feeling overwhelmed, helpless, and unable to seek help, he attacked.

Larry's relationship to Becky was highly influenced by his unconscious tendency to identify her with his mother. This transference was facilitated by the reality that Becky had a child by a previous liaison, urged Larry to be more involved with the church, took Jimmy's side while disregarding Larry, frequently criticized Larry for failure to meet her expectations, and had several times deserted him, both emotionally and physically. Most basic and potent was Larry's urgent, dependent need to find in Becky the motherliness he had never known. Constantly, despite disappointments, he yearningly looked to her to satisfy the unmet needs of all his yesterdays. When she failed him, there were only the children to look to for responses which would make him feel better.

The preceding case material depicts the four cardinal features of abuse—the psychological set of the parent, the presence of a crisis, the misperception of a child, and the unavailability of help. It also illustrates another factor. Even in cases where one parent is the sole abuser, the spouse is invariably, albeit often unconsciously, instigating, approving, condoning, or passively not interfering with the abuse. This connivance is not surprising, as it is a common observation that persons who have the potential for abuse tend to marry those with similar backgrounds and potential, a process of assortative mating. Young parents have told us they grew tired of following pediatric advice which was spoiling the baby and had decided to "bring it up the way we were brought up," following which the baby was punished and injured. Such marriages seem held together more

by desperate, dependent neediness than by shared respect and love. Both partners have low self-esteem, which leads them to believe they could never find anything better and they must cling to whatever they have. We believe that in marriages where only one partner has the abusive potential, there is little likelihood of abuse or, if there is abuse, that it will be promptly discovered and treated.

FAILURE TO THRIVE

Among all the forms of child neglect, including failure to provide cleanliness, medical care, clothing, and emotional stimulation, the most clear-cut clinical syndrome is that of the "failure to thrive due to maternal deprivation." The term *maternal deprivation* should be understood not as applying only to biological mothers, but rather as a descriptive term referring to the lack of empathic, sensitive awareness and response to an infant by its primary caretaker, whether it be mother, father, nurse, or other person (24). In some ways, the condition is quite similar to *hospitalism,* described by Spitz (25, 26), and it also resembles the state of infants in institutions reported by Provence and Lipton (27). The parents of infants who fail to thrive are essentially not much different from parents who abuse their offspring. Although the mother is predominantly involved with the infant, the father tends to be indifferent to the child's condition and is either uninterested or unable to intervene on the child's behalf. The mother shows the characteristics noted before in abusive mothers and, in fact, may often abuse the child physically concurrently with neglectful behavior producing failure to thrive, or she may abuse the child at other times when the other needs of the child are being met. Koel has reported on failure to thrive and fatal injury as a continuum (28), and we, too, have seen many children with evidences of both malnutrition and physical injuries.

We have found no consistent, significant, across-the-board, qualitative difference between mothers whose infants are injured and those who fail to thrive. There is a tendency, however, for failure-to-thrive mothers to show a higher degree of depression, lower self-esteem, and poorer coping ability in general. Not rarely do they take very poor care of themselves physically and neglect their personal appearance. They also seem to have more suppressed anger, which is not so righteously directed against the environment, as it is in many cases of physical abuse, but rather is internalized with much self-depreciation and an enhancement of a sense of worthlessness. This sense of worthlessness and ineptitude is deep and has been embedded in their character structure since early years. It seems to have been instigated by the recurring criticisms for failure to meet excessive parental demands and has been many times reinforced by the real failures of adult life, which are inevitable because of the person's diminished ability to cope, to learn from experience, to ask for help. Each failure has led to more unsureness, depression, and apathy, thereby paving the way for even more failures in the future. These mothers tend to see their children more negatively, as being somehow defective, inefficient, recalcitrant, or somehow subtly deviant. Even in organically handicapped infants, the mothers seem to exaggerate the deficits and cope with them poorly. Curiously, they may at the same time fail to see or respond to the obvious facts that the infant is significantly underweight, pale, wan, and apathetic. Their response to the infant is that the situation is hopeless, that the baby is not really worth caring for and is, therefore, significantly neglected and underfed. This misperception of the infant is related unconsciously to the mother's own perception of herself as a worthless human being. These behavioral patterns and character states, as well as the almost universal history of emotional deprivation or physical abuse in early childhood, have been reported by others (29-33).

It has sometimes been assumed that lack of knowledge of child development and inexperience in child care can account for cases of failure to thrive. While this may be true in some very young mothers and some culturally deprived persons, it is certainly not routine and is belied by the fact that many mothers of failure-to-thrive children have been able to take care of other babies without difficulty and that many such mothers are quite intelligent and well educated and competent in other areas of their lives. The problem lies in the mother's lack of empathic ability rather than in a cognitive deficit. We believe the programs for enhancing parental skills, which can be quite successful, are so largely because of the emotional support and approval provided rather than solely because of the technical knowledge gained. For instance, a young mother who was a physician and has had some experience in pediatrics delivered a normal infant, which she breast-fed and of which she was happily quite proud. However, after 6 weeks, it was evident the baby had gained practically no weight and was beginning to look seriously malnourished and apathetic. She seemed oblivious of her baby's poor condition, and her husband hesitated to intervene lest she would feel criticized. On further investigation, it became evident she was unconsciously extremely unsure of her ability to be a mother, a concept related to her own poor experience of being mothered as a small child, and she was fearful of being discovered as ineffectual. It was surprising and gratifying to her and to the staff that she responded quickly to support from her pediatrician and to loving encouragement from husband and friends. Soon, the baby was plump, happy, and developing normally.

In failure-to-thrive cases, more often than in physical abuse, there is a history of the mother having had difficulties during pregnancy or delivery, or there is some abnormality of the baby or prematurity. These extra stresses in the prenatal and perinatal periods, added to the already existing poor psychological set of the mother and her much diminished ability to cope, make it difficult for the mother to attach and to be adequately motherly, and failure to thrive can easily ensue. The following case report illustrates the complex interaction of residuals of childhood deprivation, depression, current emotional difficulties, problems in pregnancy, and misperceptions of the infant.

A very well-educated, generally capable young woman consulted us because of depression, embarrassment over her failure to take good care of her baby, and anxiety over punitive behavior toward the child. She had never had a close empathic relationship with her own mother and had a lifelong feeling of being uncared for. After marriage, she lived in another city, and her pregnancy went well until the last few weeks when she returned to the city where her mother lived. She then became anxious and depressed; her relations with her husband were cold (he was absent, working on a new job), and her mother was either unconcerned or intrusive and inconsiderate. She developed mild pre-eclampsia and had a cesarean section. The baby was slightly small for gestational age and had mild, temporary, respiratory difficulty. Because of the baby's slight abnormalities, but more because of her own medical problems, the mother had little contact with her new infant and did not establish a good attachment. In the ensuing weeks, she did not regain full physical health, remained depressed, had difficulty feeding her baby, and would often lose patience with him, sometimes shaking and choking him, with the production of minor bruises. She saw her baby as somehow inadequate, vaguely defective, and as stubbornly refusing to cooperate with her efforts to care for him. On a home visit, we observed the interaction during feeding. Mother very nicely picked up her baby boy, cuddled him in her arms, and put a spoonful of cereal in his mouth, which he eagerly accepted. However, before he had a chance to really mouth his food and swallow it, she had another spoonful of cereal, trying to push it between his closed lips. He turned his head away and refused the proffered food. Mother looked at him angrily, got up, and said, "See, he won't eat," and threw him an-

grily down in his crib. It is not surprising that this baby looked wan, apathetic, significantly underweight, and was behind in his development. Fortunately, the mother responded quite well to treatment. The baby quickly improved. She later had another child under better circumstances, attached well, and was a very good mother.

As noted above, failure-to-thrive parents, particularly mothers, have a very poor self-image and are particularly dubious about their abilities to be good parents. This sense of being inadequate or ineffectual can be greatly enhanced by delivering a baby with some abnormality or having a child who is sickly or unresponsive. Glaser and Bentovim (34) have reported that handicapped or chronically ill infants are more likely to be maltreated in the form of omission of care, and that within this group, the neglect was worse with increase of social and emotional disturbance of the caretakers and family. They also found that nonhandicapped children were more likely to be physically abused. These observations seem to be in agreement with our idea that defective or ill children are perceived as more worthless and less deserving of care, while physically normal children are assumed to be able to perform well and deserve punishment if they do not do so.

ROLE OF THE CHILD IN ABUSE AND NEGLECT

High-Risk Children

A great deal of information has been gained in recent years concerning the different kinds of infants and children who are at risk or who are most likely to be abused and neglected (18, 35-38). Included are essentially normal infants who are the product of a difficult pregnancy or delivery, born at an inconvenient time from an unplanned pregnancy, illegitimate, of the wrong sex, too active, too passive, the child of an unloved father, or born during a period of severe family stress and crisis. Other infants at risk are those who for some reason are more or less "abnormal." Included are infants both with significant prematurity; those who are small for gestational age; those who have various congenital deficiencies, abnormalities, and perinatal illnesses, particularly those which require hospitalization; and those who have later chronic or recurrent illness, again, especially if there is hospitalization. There is a third group of children who can be either essentially normal physically or show very mild deficiencies, but who are described as being "difficult" or "different." They are hyperactive, fussy, difficult to feed, hard to cuddle, have abnormal sleep patterns, cry excessively, and are seen as generally being inadequately responsive to caretaking efforts. Adopted children seem to be at some risk, as there is a higher incidence of adoptive children in the population of abused and neglected infants than is warranted by their incidence in the general population. Finally, there are children, usually somewhat older, described as deliberately provoking or "asking for abuse" when in foster care, just as they did in their own homes.

It is true that all the children enumerated above are at high risk for abuse and neglect. Valid statistics indicate that they are overrepresented in the observed populations of abused and neglected children, but it must also be noted that only a minor percentage of all the premature, congenitally defective, sickly, and difficult children are abused or neglected and, also, that only a small proportion of the total population of abused and neglected children comes from this group of excessively high-risk infants. It is our experience that a majority of abused and neglected children had originally been quite normal and that many of the emotional difficulties, evidences of retardation, and behavioral problems are the results of previous abuse and neglect rather than "causes" of it.

It has been distressing to note that some investigators have subtly implied that the observed abuse and neglect of these high-risk infants can not only be understood, but almost forgiven, inasmuch as the infant's fault explains the parental action. We are quite aware that some of these children are extremely difficult and place an enormous burden on their caretakers. Sometimes, the experienced nurses on our wards, who are accustomed to and expert in taking care of extremely difficult cases, find that some of these children try their patience to the breaking point. But abuse and neglect can never be considered a permissible or appropriate response in such situations. To us, it is obvious that punishment or neglect of an infant can never, in any circumstance, be considered correct response to a fussy, premature baby or to the feeding problems resulting from a cleft palate. All of these high-risk circumstances are ones which call for much more attention and careful monitoring of the parent-infant dyad and the provision of extra services to the caretakers, who are faced with coping with enormous extra burdens.

How then can we account for the fact that some caretakers abuse some infants who, through no fault of their own, have "conditions which place them at high risk"? One of the basic tenets of the abusive parent is the conviction or belief that a child's primary role is to behave and respond in such a way as to please and satisfy parents. Thus, we see the very early and excessive expectation of performance which was noted above. It is also the parental belief that children who fail to perform adequately well are therefore unsatisfactory and are either worthless or need to be punished to make them "shape up." Added to this is the significantly increased amount of care and special attention which they require. For the abusive caretaker, who is plagued with lifelong feelings of being unloved and ineffectual, this creates an unbearable situation, and maltreatment is more likely to occur. In our estimation, this is no different than other cases of abuse and neglect, except that there are more real reasons for considering the child to be unsatisfactory and, therefore, more stresses to the vulnerable parent, who in other less serious circumstances with a more rewarding baby might not be so abusive.

While it is perfectly true that some children are extremely difficult and, by their behavior, push their caretakers beyond their ability to cope, we deplore any tendency to accent the provocative behavior of the child at the expense of disregarding the parents' own deficiencies in caretaking abilities. It is quite similar to the frequently noted tendency of maltreating parents themselves to blame everything on the child. This is not a new phenomenon, as indicated by the following story which has been handed down from the fifth century B.C. in China (39).

> Tseng Tzu was one of the most famous disciples of Confucius. He was extremely dutiful toward his parents and became one of the 24 celebrated examples of filial piety. A story about him tells that once when he was hoeing melons for his father, he accidentally cut the root of one, and his father, becoming enraged, beat him so severely that he lost consciousness. Tseng Tzu submitted to this beating without complaint and, upon reviving, played his lute and sang as usual. It is said that when Confucius heard of this, he told his disciples that it would have been filial for Tseng Tzu to have submitted to a light thrashing, but he should have avoided such a severe beating because, by not doing so, he was involving his father in an unrighteous act which does not become a filial son.

Attachment

The infants and children described above are not at risk simply because of immaturity, physical defects, or emotional aberrancy. There is also a marked diminution or complete lack of parental attachment to such infants. These difficulties in attachment are most likely to occur with parents who have had difficult childhoods themselves and are hence already deficient in empathy. Such predispositions for poor attachment are markedly increased, especially in mothers, by troubles during pregnancy, complicated deliveries, prematurity, cesarean sections, or illness of the infant or mother that necessitates the separation of the mother and child for a significant time in the postnatal period. It can be extremely difficult for even the best-prepared parents to attach to a child if, in the postnatal period, they cannot, because of medical conditions, pick up, hold, feed, or otherwise care for the new baby. In this latter case, however, it is possible for such parents to develop fully normal attachments when the medical crisis is over and they assume the normal tasks of parenting.

Attachment behavior is also profoundly influenced by the kind of fantasies parents have during the pregnancy. This is to some extent true of fathers but is especially true of mothers, because the fetus is inside her and part of her, as well as a separate entity. Normally, such fantasies are of having a fine baby, possibly with some preference for sex, which will be a pleasurable addition to the family. Such essentially pleasant fantasies are not counteracted by the common anxieties concerning whether or not the baby will be normal and everything else all right. Parents at high risk for poor attachment and caretaking difficulties are, because of their own past lives, likely to have much more distressing fantasies during the prenatal period. One young mother described this clearly when she said early in pregnancy, "If it's a girl, it will be a mess. She will hate me as I hated my mother, and I will hate her like mother hated me." Another young mother, who could not be relieved of her anxiety that her baby might be born without arms or legs or might have defects in his back or head, delivered a normal baby, but she had seriously injured it several times before it was a year old. Often fantasies are of the baby *in utero* developing into the same kind of child which the mother was. And this, of course, is a bad omen if the mother remembers herself as an extremely difficult, bad child, who often had to be punished. More seriously psychologically disturbed mothers may have fantasies of the fetus being some kind of parasitic invader who is destructively eating her up from the inside. If carried to term, such a baby, even though apparently normal, is likely to be maltreated and thought of as some kind of "monster." It must be remembered not only that various organic difficulties during pregnancy can give rise to negative fantasies on the part of the mother, but also that negative daydreams, fantasies, and night dreams can be evidence of psychological states, which can, in turn, have profoundly disturbing effects on the pregnancy itself. Unrealistic expectations of the baby can be expressed in prenatal fantasy also. One young mother expressed the conviction that she would have a beautiful little girl who would help her overcome her emotional difficulties in life, and she looked forward with happy anticipation to birth. She delivered a boy, to whom she did not attach, as it was the wrong sex, and she could not mother him well. Other parents, including fathers, may have fantasies of the child growing up to be a disruptive influence in the family, making trouble between the parents, and causing serious conflicts with siblings. Such prenatal fantasies bear a very direct relationship to the parent's own childhood and certainly do not bode well either for full attachment or subsequent attitudes toward the infant by the caretaker.

The attachment of parents or other caretakers to their new infants is thus seen not as a simple, automatic process, but as one that is highly influenced for better or worse by many other factors, particularly those which have their roots in the parents' own earliest childhood experiences and how well they were lovingly, sensitively cared for with adequate empathy. Probably nearly all parents have, to some degree, the expectation that having a child will somehow be a rewarding, fulfilling experience which will make their lives happier and more complete. This is true for the majority of parents, and the rewards of parenthood outweigh the trials and tribulations. But it is likely that if caretakers have problems and discontents of any significant degree, having a child will not solve such problems but probably will make them worse. We believe this is one factor

which leads to the somewhat higher instance of maltreatment of adopted children. The adoptive procedure itself, in almost all instances, is undertaken to solve a parental problem, particularly the deficit of infertility and the inability to have natural children. Fortunately, most adoptive parents have inner strength and past experience and empathy enough to manage their caretaking skills quite well. A number of them, however, seem to have problems in low self-esteem, incompetence, and a sense of being defective that are too deep to be solved by the adoption of a child. Hence, the adopted child is unconsciously seen as failing to solve the parental problem, is therefore an unsatisfactory child, and is at high risk for maltreatment. The fact that so many adoptive mothers attach so effectively to their infants and become perfectly adequate mothers indicates attachment is not a purely biological phenomenon, which has to be accomplished in a critical period during the first few hours postpartum, although that period when the infant is in a quiet-alert state and the mother awake is possibly the most ideal time for attachment (40).

This discussion of attachment has primarily been concerned with the presence or absence of attachment, but there has also been the implication that, in some instances, there is not only a lack of positive attachment but what might be called antagonism or antipathy toward the infant, which is quite the opposite of positive attachment. Such negative attachments are often related to misperceptions of the child associated with fantasies of abnormality occurring during the prenatal period, or with excessive identifications of the child with the parent's own, bad, childhood self. They may also be related to the baby being unwanted, because it is a product of rape, incest, or, more commonly, the child of a now-discarded lover or a deserting, divorced spouse. The baby may also be unwanted because of being unplanned or coming at a time of extreme inconvenience to the family because of financial problems, geographic moves, or family tragedies. If attention is not paid to such replacement of attachment by negative attitudes, serious difficulties in the caretaker-infant relationship resulting in maltreatment may well occur. We have often seen children seriously injured, neglected, even killed by parents who loathed their child, who wanted to get rid of the child and give him or her up for adoption, but who were cajoled or shamed into keeping the child by relatives or health professionals. Negative attachments need special care. While it is sometimes true, in cases where mothers and fathers are unhappy about a child, that they will "learn to love it in time," such loving is far from automatic, and the negative feelings warrant serious attention if tragedy is to be avoided.

ATYPICAL ABUSE AND INFANTICIDE

There are some abusers, nearly all of them men in our experience, who repeatedly and cruelly injure the children with whom they are involved. They maltreat their charges much like other abusers but do not confine themselves to the usual patterns of attacking a child because of some specific error or unacceptable behavior. They also indiscriminately attack for no more apparent reason than that the child is there as a handy person upon whom to release aggression. They may pinch, slap, or punch a baby each time they see it or go by its crib, extinguish cigarettes by stubbing them out on a child's foot or arm, or routinely kick a child playing on the floor. They have been described as "torturing" their offspring. Often, they also abuse their wives or mistresses, get into fights, pass bad checks, and have frequent brushes with the law because of numerous traffic offenses and minor crimes. They may also be clever liars and manipulative "con men." Abuse of alcohol and drugs is common. Their personal relationships are shallow and exploitative. Such persons, who constitute possibly some 5% to 10% of the abusive population, can best be described as sociopaths. They are characterized by their free, unconflicted discharge of aggression, their self-centered, narcissistic demands, and especially by their extreme lack of empathic caring for other human beings and disregard of others' welfare. In childhood, they had very little love, warmth, or consistency from their caretakers and were exposed to excessive and frequent violence in their homes. They are quite similar in these respects to men who murder without apparent motive, as described by Satten et al. (41).

Not rarely, a child will die as a result of such persistent maltreatment by its sociopathic caretaker. Typically, the abuser shows little or no guilt or remorse, denies any possibility that his own actions might have contributed to the death, blames the death on his wife or other people, even including emergency room personnel, or assumes that the child had some previously unrecognized illness or defect. We consider it important to recognize such individuals as early as possible, since we have found it extremely difficult, if not impossible, to rehabilitate them to the point of being safe caretakers. Their abuse is repetitive and is easily transferred to other children in the family.

Mental illness may significantly interfere with parental abilities, either through disregard of the child or misperceptions of him. Severe depressive or schizophrenic psychosis may seriously compromise a caretaker's ability to perceive a child's needs and respond appropriately to them. Preoccupation with obsessive thoughts, delusions, and hallucinations or withdrawal into hopeless immobility results in profound neglect of the child, leading to delayed development, starvation, illness, and sometimes death. In other instances, the child is woven into the caretaker's delusional system and becomes a target of paranoid attacks. This is not unrelated to the severe beatings, sometimes fatal, administered by fanatic religious groups in order to "drive the devil out" of infants perceived as "evil." Toxic psychoses and delirious states induced by various hallucinogenic drugs such as LSD or by alcohol may also lead to se-

infants; in such cases, there is usually a history of significant preexisting emotional disturbance or mental illness.

The direct murder of children is predominantly the act of a psychotic or seriously mentally disturbed member of the family or a stranger (42). But infanticide, in general, which has existed throughout history and is still present all over the world, has much in common with the other forms of maltreatment (43, 44). It is essentially a human behavior which disregards the life and welfare of an infant and satisfies the needs and purposes of adults. The child is sacrificed for religious, military, or political purposes or for population control because of superstitions, parental convenience, or avoidance of shame and ostracism. Although legally considered as infanticide, there is a somewhat different kind of infant death which is the result of maltreatment (45) and death from prolonged failure to thrive. In the latter, there is less an open, direct wish or attempt to kill the child than a pervasive indifference and disregard for the child and subsequent failure to provide life maintenance. In the more frequent cases of death resulting from repeated physical abuse, parents, as a rule, do not intend to kill the child but, on the contrary, have an investment in a living child who must be punished to become more obedient and satisfying. Death is an unexpected, undesired, incidental result of the abuse. The abuser may be quite frightened by what has happened, may or may not seek immediate help, and may not understand that he has done something which would kill the child. He subsequently tends to feel guilt and great remorse, being quite opposite in this respect from the sociopath described above. There are also deaths which occur to children who are only occasionally mildly abused which are, in a sense, "quite accidental." For example, a small child may be forcefully hit on the back, causing him to stumble against a sharp corner of a coffee table, resulting in abdominal injury with ruptured liver and later death. The parent in such a case is likely to feel extremely guilty and be overwhelmed with grief, finding it quite

difficult to understand why he is put in jail and treated like a common murderer.

SEXUAL ABUSE

Although sexual abuse of children has been recognized for as long as any other form of maltreatment, it has been more concealed, less reported, and has attracted relatively little concern. Most attention has been directed toward statutory rape and toward the less serious problems of exhibitionism and pedophilia. A taboo of dealing with the common phenomenon of incest seems to have been as strong or stronger than the taboo of incest itself. However, with increasing public awareness and concern over the enormous number of cases of physical abuse and neglect, and the courage given by the women's rights movement, sexual abuse has also become a matter of public concern. Cases, especially of incest of all varieties, are now increasingly reported in numbers approaching those of other kinds of abuse (46-51).

In view of the great variety of forms of sexual abuse—heterosexual, homosexual, children of all ages, sexual acts of all kinds—it is impossible to give a simple description which covers all cases. There are significant, different, psychodynamic factors in, for instance, those men who abuse only very young girls, those men who confine their acts to early adolescent boys, and women who selectively seduce either sons or daughters. Such specific preferential sexual behaviors can be best understood in terms of the distortions of psychosexual development commonly seen in cases of perversion and neurosis and are well described in the psychiatric literature. But the basic abusive pattern is not dissimilar from that seen in other kinds of maltreatment, physical abuse, neglect and failure to thrive, and emotional abuse. Physical and sexual abuse often coexist; a caretaker may sometimes physically abuse and at other times sexually abuse the same child. Or the sexual abuse itself may be accompanied by physical violence and trauma. In very young children, especially, sexual abuse is often belatedly discovered only during investigation or treatment of the more obvious physical abuse which has been reported and which called attention to the case. Older children, from latency to adolescence, are more likely to be sexually abused by their caretakers without accompanying physical abuse, although there may have been physical abuse in earlier years.

Sexual abuse of children of all ages is not an isolated phenomenon occurring in an otherwise healthy life situation. It is the obvious, overt, symptomatic expression of seriously disturbed family relationships and has always been preceded by more or less emotional neglect or mistreatment. Parents or other caretakers involved in sexual abuse are, in most ways, quite similar to those who are only physically abusive and neglectful and, as noted above, may at different times express any of these destructive behaviors. They suffer from the same severe lack of self-esteem, have a poorly integrated sense of identity, tend to be somewhat socially isolated, and have a history of emotional deprivation, physical abuse, and often very chaotic family lives in their early years. As in physical abuse, there is often a history of generational repetition of sexual abuse, especially incest in various forms. Langsley, Schwartz, and Fairbairn (52) report a case of father-son incest in which the father was repeating his seduction by adult males experienced in his own childhood. Raybin (53) reported homosexual incest involving three generations, and Raphling, Carpenter, and Davis (54) described multiple incestuous relationships existing in a family for over three generations. Gebhard et al. (55) noted that men imprisoned for sexually molesting children had often been the subjects of sexual molestation themselves as children. Lukianowicz (47) and Yorokoglu and Kemph (56) also report sexual mistreatment of children by persons who had been sexually abused themselves. In addition to the obvious learning from role modeling which must occur in such family settings, there is also a deeper and compelling identification with the sexually abusive adults known in early childhood. This often gives incest a sort of moral approval in the subculture of some families and is clearly evident when we see some fathers say with some degree of righteous indignation, "My father had sex with all my sisters, so why should I not sleep with my daughters?" Mothers also, in identification with their own mothers, seem unable to protect daughters from sexual abuse and, in many instances, condone or actually promote the incestuous relationship between husband and daughter. Both fathers and mothers may righteously justify their incestuous activities by the rationalization that it is better for the child to learn about sex from a loving family member than from "no-good" peers.

The family backgrounds of those caretakers involved in sexual abuse of children are similar, in many respects, to the backgrounds of parents and others who have been involved in physical maltreatment and neglect. Several authors have accented the role of poverty (55, 57-59). There are also descriptions of the absence of reliable parental figures in early life, particularly fathers, and often the child was moved from one foster placement to another, either in or out of the family. The caretakers of early life are also described as punitive or uncaring (58, 60-63). Some sexual abusers describe extremely chaotic living conditions during their earliest years, with multiple changes of caretaking figures and exposure to extremely atypical, flamboyant sexual activities. For instance, one man said, "My father was a drunk and my mother was a whore. There were always other men and women coming into the house, and very free sexual activity of all kinds, both heterosexual and homosexual." We have, on the other hand, known sexual abusers who were brought up in extremely rigid, highly religious, but emotionally cold families, in which sex was a forbidden subject, even for education, and the children would become involved in aberrant sexual activity through seeking knowledge elsewhere. The common denominator in all these situations seems to be the absence of warm, loving, sexual relationships as a model for the child to emulate; lack of appropriate sexual education; and, most important for all, lack of empathic, sensitive care during the early impressionable, developmental years. Although we have no firm data, it is our impression that the more chaotic the sexual abuser's life has been in early childhood, the more likely he is to be sexually abusive to younger children, to be more aggressive in his abuse, and to show more perverse behavior and much less consideration for the victim. The more nearly the early life experience approached "normal," the more likely the abuser is to become involved with much older children and to do so only under periods of unusual stress or when drunk. Substance abuse, including alcohol, is certainly a fairly common precipitating factor to acts of sexual abuse of children. There seems to be a difference, however, between the chronic alcoholic who has been a frequent sexual abuser and the person who has indulged in sexual acts with children, either within or outside the family, only on very rare occasions when drinking as part of his futile attempts to solve the anxiety and loneliness resulting from marital conflict or the stress of other problems.

As in other forms of abuse, in sexual abuse, the child victim is often considered to be the one at fault or at least guilty of "contributory negligence," particularly if she gives any evidence of having had any pleasure in the activity. In cases of incest, the daughter is often said to have been quite seductive and not only willing to participate but ready to instigate the incestuous behavior with her father. Such concepts are given further support by the observations of girls as young as 3 and 4 who have been placed in foster care because of sexual abuse in their homes but who continue to approach all males very seductively and attempt to play with their genitals. There is no question about the accuracy of such observations. The question is how to interpret them.

We believe, with very rare exceptions, that it is impossible for a young child to have such strong sexual drives and such seductive abilities that he or she can overcome a healthy adult's concepts of what is appropriate interaction between a caretaker and a child. It must also be kept in mind that little girls are often encouraged to be cute and seductive and are admired for it. For a "normal," healthy adult to be unable to resist erotic advances of a child is patently ridiculous. The essential ingredient for sexually abusive behavior is the lack of empathic consideration by the adult for the child's stage of development and abilities, plus the adult's placing the satisfaction of his own needs above those of the child. In this, we see the essence of sexual abuse of children, the exploitation of the child for the purpose of satisfying the adult. It is the recognition of having been exploited and uncared for as an individual human being that leads to the long-lasting residual damages of sexual abuse in development, rather than the actual physical sexual act itself. As in physical abuse, it is not the bodily damage or hurt itself that is most traumatic, but the fact that one was uncared for and misused by the ones to whom one must look for comfort, care, and protection. The resulting ambivalence, lack of trust, and difficulty in human relationships are inevitable and severe.

Although relationships between fathers and daughters and stepfathers and stepdaughters are by far the most commonly reported forms of incest, it is quite likely that sexual activities between brothers and sisters are even more common, ranging from simple visual inspection of each other to intercourse. It would seem useful to describe two different patterns of brother-sister interactions. The first is the fairly common effort of children to find out something about themselves and their functions by comparing themselves with the opposite sex and understanding the differences. This can happen either within the family with siblings or with other children and may progress to various attempts to explore and to imitate the sexual behavior of adults, about which they have either heard or seen examples. Such exploratory "educational" activities between brothers and sisters are usually engaged in by mutual consent and are mutually rewarding, and, even though they may, in some instances, progress to actual intercourse in older children, they are of short duration and provide channels for expanding relationships into other heterosexual contacts with peers and are not ordinarily productive of long-lasting, psychosexual difficulties. Although children involved in such activities may have some awareness that they are being "naughty," they do not develop a serious sense of guilt or disturbance of their sexual relationships unless the disapproval and punishment by authorities who discover the activity is unusually severe. There is another group of brother-sister relationships which, although superficially like the preceding, are not only motivated by normal sexual curiosity and search for identity but, in addition, a search for love, care, and acceptance from somebody. This seems to occur most frequently with siblings who, for one reason or another, feel emotionally deprived, neglected, or misunderstood by both parents and who do not feel free in any way to discuss their problems of any kind, including sexual, with the caretaking figures. Such relationships between brother and sister, expressed in the sexual sphere, become endowed with very intense needs for love and affection and are then extremely vulnerable to betrayal and exploitation, as well as abandonment. In such instances, the incestuous behavior can become traumatic and a source of much difficulty later.

Homosexual incest, like father-daughter incest, is often related to the emotional, sexual, or geographical absence or the death of the mother. The father (or stepfather), preferring out of his own insecurity to keep his sexual activity within the family, turns to the son to satisfy his sexual urges; the son submits to the sexual advances hoping to find some of the love and acceptance he has not received from the mother, along with the satisfaction of some sexual needs. We believe the boy's gender identity has usually been at least partially compromised before the homosexual seduction occurs because of long-lasting disturbances in family relationships. Certainly, the father's homosexual tendencies existed in either open or covert form for many years.

The rarest type of incest is between mother and son; it seems to arouse more horror in people and has been the object of the most stringent taboo. In some ways, it is similar to other forms of incest occurring in families with preexisting problems of many kinds, including disturbed sexual relations of the parents. The father may be emotionally or physically absent, and the mother turns to the son for love and attention, while the father is indifferent or turns to a daughter. After a father's death, a teenage son may be told he is "now the man of the house and must take his father's place," and the advice is followed literally by both mother and son. Yet, it seems doubtful if such social pseudoapproval would be followed if there were not preexisting excessively intimate interactions between them. In a half-dozen mother-son incest cases with which we have been involved (one of which proceeded to full intercourse), and in most of the few cases reported in the literature, there is evidence of significant neurosis, intermittent psychosis, or a severe borderline state in the mother (47, 54, 64). She has had previous difficulty in allowing separation and individuation to occur and has in other ways exploited the mother-son relationship.

We have been accenting the role of object relationships in the genesis of sexual abuse of children, and we believe this is the most important element in such behavior. It is also useful to consider the psychodynamic consequences of the Oedipus complex experienced by the victims of abuse. In the first place, it seems unlikely, in view of the great extent of pregenital difficulty, that there was ever the development of the fully, erotically tinged, oedipal complex as it is classically understood. At the oedipal period, these boys and girls were still too involved with the yearning for basic, empathic love, care, and consideration and in the struggle to develop individual identity to be able to look to the parent of the opposite sex with strong, erotic yearning and a sense of concern over the reaction of the parent of the same sex. Most of them were still looking for basic care and protection in a nutritive framework. Both boys and girls turned to fathers or male figures for basic love and empathy, which they had not received in adequate quantities from their mothers. Boys thus tended to have homosexual tendencies, and girls turned toward their fathers, yearning for love and prematurely placing it in a heterosexual erotic context. The turning of girls to their fathers was not complicated by fears of loss of mother's love because mother's love had not been there to lose. Boys could not turn to their mothers with strong erotic feelings because they were still looking for the basic love and acceptance which was not there. Instead, they were afraid of their mother; she was felt to be an engulfing, castrating figure, and we believe this accounts in some degree for the relative rarity of mother-son incest compared to the great frequency of father-daughter incest.

In some families, the oedipal configuration may have definite bearing on the later pattern of abuse, although it would not be a complete determinant of it. For instance, a young man who sexually and physically abused his 2-year-old stepdaughter had grown up in a family in which he was severely physically abused by his father and mildly so by his mother. The father favored an older sister, for whom he bought more clothes than he did for the mother and with whom he had an incestuous relationship. He also beat up this girl when, as an unmarried teenager, she became pregnant. The son repressed his anger at his mother for not protecting and caring enough for him and became much closer to her, with her encouragement. He also competed with his father by buying nightgowns and robes for his mother and trying in other ways to please and gain her favor. Later, he became involved with women who were critical of his inability to satisfy their needs, materially or sexually, and once severely abused his wife, who indicated she might be pregnant by another man. The abuse of the stepdaughter occurred under the influence of alcohol, when the mother complained about the ineffectiveness of his efforts to care for her. It seemed to be a revengeful discharge of anger at females who would not be satisfied or let him love them—mother, wife, and baby. It was also a discharge of aggression in identification with the father who was incestuous and aggressive toward females and with whom he was competitive in his distorted oedipal struggles.

In most cases of sexual abuse of children, the problem is an extremely complex one, and no simple etiology will explain any one case. There is nearly always a clear history of deficient "mothering" or other neglect in early years, plus the added factors of distorted sexual behavior in the family, leading to the inability to be empathic with children and to the sexual exploitation of them.

▌ THE CLINICAL PICTURE ▌

The following condensed case history pictures with unusual clarity many of the commonly seen elements of physical and sexual abuse.

Laura G. was an attractive young woman, age 26, poised, friendly, and verbal. She was the wife of a noncommissioned career officer in the armed forces. Her reasons for coming to us were anxiety over marital problems, depression, and worry over abuse of her elder son.

Laura was the elder of two children of parents living in very marginal economic circumstances on the outskirts of a small, rural town. Her father was mildly alcoholic; her mother more severely so. Her parents frequently argued and occasionally fought rather violently. Laura had never felt her mother was interested in her, and the mother had seemed far away and inattentive when Laura tried to talk to her. She recalled that even as a little child, she worked very hard to do things to please her mother but never seemed able to do so and was often the subject of much criticism. She felt deprived, rejected, and hopeless. The younger brother, Joe, was her mother's favorite, the one to whom she gave all her love. Laura's relationship to Joe was always ambivalent—some love and companionship mixed with envy and hatred.

Laura was deeply attached to her father from her earliest years. She felt very close to him and believed he returned her warmth, cared for her, and listened to her. Father, however, was not always kind. He often beat her with his hands or a belt until she was black and blue, and his favorite saying was, "I'll knock you through the wall." Sometimes, he made her hold two bare electric wires in her hands while he turned on a current to give her a shock (he was an electrician by trade). He explained to her that he gave her these shocks to remind her that he was the boss and she must obey him. Despite such abuse, she felt close to him and liked to be around him and do things which pleased him. He would often praise her and give her credit for things she did well when she tried to help him. She spent much more time with him than she did with her mother, and by the time she was 4, father had begun to extend his affectionate cuddling into some degree of genital fondling. She remembers him asking, "You want me to make it feel good down there?" and her answering, "Yes." By the time Laura was 7, the father was having regular sex play with her, and this soon progressed to intercourse, which continued for several years. Laura enjoyed the closeness and pleasure of the sexual activity but also felt it was somehow wrong because her father admonished her not to tell other people. She was puzzled about just what was "wrong," as father seemed to gain pleasure from the activity and had asked her to do it, and she had always been taught to obey him. In addition, her mother did not seem to disapprove, even though she was aware of what was happening between Laura and her husband.

The mother and father were rarely affectionate with each other and were often in open conflict. The mother rejected the father sexually and repeatedly told him to leave her alone. They usually slept in different rooms. There was no doubt that mother was aware of the incest because sometimes after an argument with the father, she would encourage Laura to go and sleep with him. Sometimes, she had asked Laura to get money from the father after she slept with him and bring it back to her so that she could buy a bottle of liquor.

When Laura was 13, her father became depressed, as far as she knew, because of his endless difficulties in trying to make a living. He committed suicide in the bedroom of their home, using a shotgun to blow off part of his face and the top of his head, while Laura was helping her mother cook dinner. She was utterly devastated as well as shocked. Three days later, after the funeral, on a cold, gray, rainy day, Laura and her mother came back home and went into the bedroom. It smelled badly, and she opened the shutters and the windows to let in light and air, and she recalls, "I looked around the room, and there I saw bits of flesh and hair on the wall and the ceiling, all that was left of my father. He was the only one I ever loved, and the only person who ever loved me."

The next year, when she was 14, Laura acquired a steady boyfriend. He was friendly and affectionate to her and spoke in a way when they were alone that made her feel very beautiful and fine. She began having intercourse with him frequently and enjoyed it. In public, however, he fought with her and treated her as "something to wipe his feet on." She could not stand the mistreatment and broke up with him. Years later, she still dreamed about him and fantasized about him, even though she realized life with him would not have been good.

At 15, she began dating cadets at an air force base. She loved being treated "like a lady" by these somewhat older young men. Frequently, the relationships became sexual affairs, but they did not seem meaningful to her and did not last very long. She became more promiscuous, and between ages 18 and 21, she describes having affairs with 32 different men and had, at times, "carried on" with as many as three men in one day. At 22, she met and married a man who was very kind, patient, and considerate of her. He listened to her, tried to do things to please her and to make her happy. In spite of what seemed to her an ideal marriage, she continued periodically to have affairs and, at times, found her husband physically repulsive. By the time we knew her, she felt, by her behavior, that she had "ruined" him and changed him from a kindly person to an angry, punitive one. She avoided sex with him and was often very critical of him, despite all his efforts. Although it was not really necessary, Laura often worked part-time in order to "get money to help the family finances," thus reducing the financial burden on her husband, and also to get away from the house. At these jobs, she often met the men with whom she would become involved.

Toward Jimmy, the older of her two sons, Laura had been extremely ambivalent. At times, she had felt love for him and, in general, had taken good physical care of him. Yet, she was more likely to be filled with feelings of disgust and hatred and had often wished that she could get rid of him or that he would die. She expected him to be quite capable and obedient, and for various misbehaviors, she would beat him with her fists or whip him with a belt or board. She seemed to be aware that fundamentally, Jimmy was a rather normal little boy, but she said, "He has all my faults, and I have tried to beat all his phobias and other problems out of him. I know it's not sensible, but I can't control myself. I think he must be me, and I'm a combination of my mother and my father. My mother would never pay any attention to me, and my father would beat me. I say to Jimmy, 'I'll knock you through the wall,' just like daddy used to say to me." Laura had a curious mixture of feeling guilty over her mistreatment of the boy and yet, at the same time, feeling justifiably angry at him because of his deficits and failure. She also considered that she had brainwashed her husband into following her pattern of screaming and yelling at this boy, to whom he had previously been very good. Laura felt she had ruined both her husband and her son, but her guilty responsibility could not eliminate her anger. She would say, "I want to get rid of them both. I want them both to die. But I've thought of suicide

myself because I've been ruining them." Although Laura did not drink regularly or excessively, after a social evening with a few drinks, she was more likely to get into quarrels with her husband and have more trouble with Jimmy, with the likelihood of abuse.

With her younger son, Benny, Laura had a completely different relationship. She loved him dearly and had for him a warmth and affection she had not previously known she was capable of feeling. She surmised that he was like her younger brother, Joe, to whom her mother had given all her love and affection, and she was imitating her own mother in this. Laura was bewildered by these very intense and yet discrepant feelings. She was quite puzzled about her own identity, which she expressed at various times in such thoughts as, "I think Jimmy must be me, and I'm a combination of my mother and father. When I would talk to my mother, she would be far away and not answer. I do the same thing with Jimmy. It was father who used to beat me; now it seems Jimmy is me, and I'm beating him the way father beat me. Little Benny is my brother, Joe. Mother gave all her love and protection to Joe, and I am very kind and loving to him." Another time, she said, "I don't know yet who I really am. I am beginning to think I am somebody and I know a little bit about who I am, but I'm having trouble becoming it and being something. I don't know whether I am my mother or my father or my brother, Joe, or a combination of all of them or whether I am my children."

After her marriage, Laura periodically made an attempt to establish some sort of friendly relationship with her mother, and there were occasional visits. But they never did reach any true emotional rapport, nor could they discuss the events of Laura's earlier life. With her brother, Joe, she had a distant, hostile relationship. While there was no evidence of overt incestuous activity between Joe and his mother, she seemed to have exploitatively tried to keep him close to her and had hampered his separation and individuation. He eventually became seriously disturbed, and once, when he threatened to kill their mother, Laura offered her sanctuary and protection. At that time, there was some feeling of closeness, which was soon ruptured by her mother's inconsiderate disregard of her daughter's feelings and criticisms of her behavior.

Superficially, Laura appeared to be a popular, attractive, young married woman with two children, similar to many other young women who lived with their armed service-career husbands around a military base. Yet, she was seriously troubled, behaviorally and psychologically, both in her marriage and in her child-caring functions. In this tragic history are the themes of economic difficulty, alcoholism, social isolation, parental conflict, maternal deprivation, sibling rivalry, physical abuse, incest, and father-loss by suicide. As an adult, she shows many of the characteristics commonly met with in parents who maltreat children. She has a mild, chronic depression, very low self-esteem, inability to have pleasure or find satisfaction for her long-lasting emptiness and need for love and attention, lack of a coherent consistent sense of identity, and misperceptions of her children. The striking split between good and bad objects, uncoordinated ego functions, and unintegrated components of identity are similar to those described as characteristic of "borderline states." These psychological difficulties seem to be clearly related to the experiences she had with the caretakers of her early life and the necessity for her to adapt somehow to them. She has identified with the several parts of the inconsistent caretaking behaviors of both mother and father and also maintains a self-concept closely related to herself as a child. She transfers and attributes to adults in her present environment and to her own children the attitudes and feelings she had toward the important figures of her early life. Her sexual behavior seems to be a frantic, desperate, compulsive search for a man to love and be loved by and is at least partly due to unresolved grief over the death of her father by suicide. She overidealized her father, clinging especially to the loving side of her ambiva-

lence toward him, has never fully relinquished her attachment to him, and has been unable to find an adequate replacement for the warm closeness she had with him, including the incest. Her promiscuity is undoubtedly related to the sexualization of this early love relationship with the father. Yet, the desperateness of her search also suggests it has deep roots in an effort to find a substitute for the lack of basic, empathic love from her mother in her early life. Her inability to gain full satisfaction or pleasure from sexual activity stems partly from the fact that, in itself, sexual activity cannot replace this deep, early sense of being empathetically loved and cared for. It is also partly due to residual guilt in relationship to her father, which is not so much a feeling of having done something wrong sexually with him, but rather that she had not been able, even in her most warm and loving sexual surrender to him, to make him happy enough to prevent the suicide. Laura was aware that her sexual behavior was not really acceptable in society. Yet, this was not totally a feeling of guilt over sexuality but more a sense that she was ineffectual and never good enough for other people. It was not a strong, inner sense of having done something wrong for which she deserved punishment, nor did she give evidence of guilt over sexual behavior in relation to having displaced her mother in her father's affections. In fact, her earliest, powerful, superego identifications are with the mother who encouraged the sexual relationship with the father and with a father who instigated and appreciated the sexual relationship. Because she is still unconsciously fixated to the loving, sexual father of her childhood, who was also abusive, she has had the recurrent tendency to attach herself to men who not only love her but are also cruel to her, fight with her, or attack her physically. By criticizing and frustrating her husband, who was originally quite affectionate and considerate to her, she managed to change him into a person who is mean to her and maltreats their child, thus re-creating the father of her childhood.

Laura relives another part of the childhood drama in her ambivalent behavior toward her older son, Jimmy, whom she misperceives as almost a reincarnation of her own childhood self. In identification with her father, she loves Jimmy at times, but she also abuses him, hitting him, using a belt on him, and repeating to him the same words her father used, "I'll knock you through the wall." At other times, she repeats the behavior of her mother toward herself and is unresponsive, inattentive, and unempathic toward Jimmy. With her younger son, Benny, she repeats the kind, preferential care which her mother gave to her younger brother, Joe, and she also lavishes on Benny the love which she wishes she had had as a little girl, gaining some vicarious pleasure from this. In view of Laura's disturbing experiences in early life and the multiple, inconsistent identifications with her parents, it is not surprising that she is significantly hampered in her child-caring activities and has become what we call an abusive parent. Her tendency to repeat the past and get herself involved in unhappy experiences is an example of moral masochism in the sense described by Berliner as "self-defeating or destructive behavior" due to attachment to a sadistic love object. Difficulties in having pleasure or enjoying life generally, as well as constantly recurring patterns of getting into difficulty, are characteristic of most of the maltreating caretakers we have known. This masochistic tendency makes such persons increasingly vulnerable and unable to cope with the troublesome crises and difficulties that inevitably occur in all people's lives, especially in the care of children.

The process of responding to the parents of earliest years, the identification with them, and the persistence of these identifications into adult life is not in any way abnormal. It is a normal part of the psychic development of all children. As noted before, the problem lies in the kind of parent available for the identification process. Laura identified with both the punitive and loving aspects of her father and with the aloof, rejecting, uncaring aspects of her mother, as well as with her mother's loving care of a boy. In her social interactions, Laura maintained superficially close, sexualized relationships with men and more distant, often antagonistic, relations with women. In therapy, she established positive relationships with three successive male therapists whom she felt "understood" her but remained suspicious and cool toward female clinic personnel.

SUMMARY

Parents and others who maltreat the infants and children under their care are not haphazardly discharging destructive impulses in the form of abuse and neglect. They are following understandable and predictable patterns of parent-child interactions which have been basically determined by the way they themselves were cared for in infancy. Beginning with poor attachment in the perinatal period, followed in ensuing months and years by unempathic care, unrealistic demands, and excessive criticism, and punishment for failure, they developed poor self-esteem, poor basic trust, and fragmented identities. Deeply embedded identifications with their parents and their behaviors, which will surface most strongly in times of stress, lead to repetitions of the patterns in their own child-care behaviors. During the earliest, most impressionable period of life, while a child is under the exclusive care of its own family before contact is made with the wider culture, the patterns are transmitted from caretaker to child, and the potentials for physical abuse, neglect, and sexual exploitation are re-created for yet another generation.

REFERENCES

1. Kempe, C. H.; Silverman, F. N.; Steele, B. F.; Droegemueller, W.; and Silver, H. K. 1962. The Battered-Child Syndrome. *JAMA* 181: 17-24.

2. Steele, B., and Pollock, C. 1968. A Psychiatric Study of Parents Who Abuse Infants and Small Children. In *The Battered Child.* R. Helfer and C. H. Kempe. Chicago: University of Chicago Press.

3. Steele, B. F. 1970. Parental Abuse of Infants and Small Children. In *Parenthood: Its Psychology and Psychopathology,* ed. E. J. Anthony and T. Benedek. Boston: Little, Brown & Co.

4. Straus, M. A. 1979. Family Patterns and Child Abuse in a Nationally Representative American Sample. *Child Abuse and Neglect: International J.* 3: 213-25.

5. Curtis, G. 1963. Violence Breeds Violence—Perhaps? *Am. J. Psychiatry* 120: 386-87.

6. Fontana, V., and Besharov, D. 1977. *The Maltreated Child.* Springfield, IL: Charles C. Thomas.

7. Oliver, J. E., and Taylor, Audrey. 1971. Five Generations of Ill-treated Children in One Family Pedigree. *British J. Psychiatry* 119-552.

8. Silver, L. B.; Dublin, C. C.; and Lourie, R. S. 1969. Does Violence Breed Violence? Contributions from a Study of the Child Abuse Syndrome. *Am. J. Psychiatry* 126: 404-7.

9. Spinetta, J. J., and Rigler, D. 1972. The Child-Abusing Parent: A Psychological Review. *Psychology Bull.* 77: 296-304.

10. Morris, M. G., and Gould, R. W. 1963. Role Reversal: A Concept in Dealing with the Neglected/Battered Child Syndrome. In *The Neglected-Battered Child Syndrome.* New York: Child Welfare League of America.

11. Gray, J. D.; Cutler, C. A.; Dean, J. G.; and Kempe, C. H. 1977. Prediction and Prevention of Child Abuse and Neglect. *Child Abuse and Neglect: International J.* 1: 45-58.

12. Ainsworth, M. 1973. Development of Infant-Mother Attachment. In *Child Development and Social Policy. Review of Child Development Research,* ed. B. Caldwell and H. N. Ricciuti, vol. 3. Chicago: University of Chicago Press.

13. Bowlby, J. 1969. *Attachment.* New York: Basic Books.

14. Brazelton, T. B.; Kozlowski, B.; and Main, M. 1974. The Origins of Reciprocity: The Early Mother-Infant Interaction. In *The Effect of the Infant on Its Caregiver,* ed. M. Lewis and L. Rosenblum. New York: Wiley.

15. Kennell, J. H., et al. 1972. Maternal Behavior One Year after Early and Extended Post-Partum Contact. *Developmental Medicine and Child Neurology* 16: 172-79.

16. Klaus, M., and Kennell, J. 1976. *Maternal-Infant Bonding.* St. Louis: C. V. Mosby.

17. Lynch, M., and Roberts, J. 1977. Predicting Child Abuse: Signs of Bonding Failure in the Maternity Hospital. *British Med. J.* 1: 624-26.

18. Ounsted, C.; Oppenheimer, R.; and Lindsay, J. 1974. Aspects of Bonding Failure: The Psychopathology and Psychotherapeutic Treatment of Families of Battered Children. *Developmental Medicine and Child Neurology* 16: 447-52.

19. Melnick, B., and Hurley, J. R. 1969. Distinctive Personality Attributes of Child Abusing Mothers. *J. Consulting and Clinical Psychology* 33: 746-49.

20. Benedek, T. 1959. Parenthood as a Developmental Phase: A Contribution to the Libido Theory. *J. Am. Psychoanalytic Assn.* 7: 389-417.

21. Olden, C. 1953. On Adult Empathy with Children. *Psychoanalytic Study of the Child* 8: 111-26.

22. Olden, C. 1958. Notes on the Development of Empathy. *Psychoanalytic Study of the Child* 13: 505-18.

23. Josselyn, I. 1956. Cultural Forces, Motherliness and Fatherliness. *Am. J. Orthopsychiatry* 26: 264-71.

24. Bullard, D.; Glaser, H.; Heagarty, M.; and Pivchik, E. 1967. Failure to Thrive in the Neglected Child. *Am. J. Orthopsychiatry* 37: 680-90.

25. Spitz, R. 1945. Hospitalism. *Psychoanalytic Study of the Child* 1: 53-74.

26. Spitz, R. 1946. Hospitalism: A Follow-up Report. *Psychoanalytic Study of the Child* 2: 113-17.

27. Provence, S., and Lipton, R. 1962. *Infants in Institutions.* New York: International Universities Press.

28. Koel, B. S. 1969. Failure to Thrive and Fatal Injury as a Continuum. *Am. J. Diseases of Children* 118: 565-67.

29. Barbero, G.; Morris, M.; and Reford, M. 1963. Malidentification of Mother-Baby-Father Relationships Expressed in Infant Failure to Thrive. *Child Welfare* 42: 13.

30. Barbero, G., and Shaheen, E. 1967. Environmental Failure to Thrive. *J. Pediatrics* 71: 639.

31. Elmer, E. 1960. Failure to Thrive: Role of the Mother. *Pediatrics* 25: 717.

32. Fischoff, J.; Whitten, C.; and Pettit, M. 1971. A Psychiatric Study of Mothers of Infants with Growth Failure, Secondary to Maternal Deprivation. *J. Pediatrics* 79: 209-15.

33. Leonard, M. F.; Rhymes, J. P.; and Solnit, A. J. 1966. Failure to Thrive in Infants. *Am. J. Diseases of Children* 111: 600-612.

34. Glaser, D., and Bentovim, A. 1979. Abuse and Risk to Handicapped and Chronically III Children. *Child Abuse and Neglect: International J.* 3: 565-75.

35. deLissovoy, Vladimer. 1979. Toward the Definition of "Abuse Provoking Child." *Child Abuse and Neglect: International J.* 3: 341-50.

36. Friedrich, W. N., and Boriskin, J. A. 1976. The Role of the Child in Abuse: A Review of the Literature. *Am. J. Orthopsychiatry* 46: 580-90.

37. Johnson, B., and Morse, H. A. 1968. Injured Children and Their Parents. *Children* 15: 147-52.

38. Milowe, J. D., and Lourie, R. S. 1964. The Child's Role in the Battered Child Syndrome. *J. Pediatrics* 65: 1079-81.

39. Creel, H. G., ed. 1948. *Literary Chinese by the Inductive Method.* Chicago: University of Chicago Press.

40. deChateau, P., and Wiberg, B. 1977. Long-term Effect on Mother-Infant Behavior of Extra Contact dur-

ing the First Hour Post-partum. *Acta Pediatrica Scandinavica* 66: 137-51.

41. Satten, J.; Menninger, K.; Rosen, I.; and Mayman, M. 1960. Murder without Apparent Motive: A Study in Personality Disorganization. *Am. J. Psychiatry* 117: 48-53.

42. Adelson, L. 1961. Slaughter of the Innocents. *New England J. Med.* 264: 1345-49.

43. Piers, M. W. 1978. *Infanticide: Past and Present.* New York: Norton.

44. Resnick, P. J. 1969. Child Murder by Parents: A Psychiatric Review of Filicide. *Am. J. Psychiatry* 126: 325-34.

45. Steele, B. 1978. Psychology of Infanticide Resulting from Maltreatment. In *Infanticide and the Value of Life,* ed. M. Kohl. Buffalo: Prometheus Books.

46. Greenberg, N. H. 1979. The Epidemiology of Childhood Sexual Abuse. *Pediatrics Annals* 8: 289-99.

47. Lukianowicz, N. 1972. Incest. *British J. Psychiatry* 120: 301-13.

48. Meiselman, Karin C. 1978. *Incest: A Psychological Study of Causes and Effects with Treatment Recommendations.* San Francisco: Jossey-Bass.

49. Nakashima, I., and Zakus, G. 1977. Incest: Review and Clinical Experience. *Pediatrics* 60: 696-700.

50. Summit, R., and Kryso, J. 1978. Sexual Abuse of Children: A Clinical Spectrum. *Am. J. Orthopsychiatry* 48: 237-51.

51. Westermeyer, J. 1978. Incest in Psychiatric Practice: A Description of Patients and Incestuous Relationships. *J. Clinical Psychiatry* 39: 643-48.

52. Langsley, D. G.; Schwartz, M. N.; and Fairbairn, R. H. 1968. Father-Son Incest. *Comprehensive Psychiatry* 9: 218-26.

53. Raybin, J. B. 1969. Homosexual Incest. *J. Nervous and Mental Disorders* 148: 105-10.

54. Raphling, D. L.; Carpenter, B. L.; and Davis, A. 1967. Incest: A Genealogical Study. *Archives of General Psychiatry* 16: 505-11.

55. Gebhard, P. H., et al. 1965. *Sex Offenders: An Analysis of Types.* New York: Harper and Row.

56. Yorokoglu, A., and Kemph, J. P. 1966. Children Not Severely Damaged by Incest with Parent. *J. Am. Acad. Child Psychiatry* 51: 111-24.

57. Kaufman, I.; Peck, A. L.; and Tagiuri, C. K. 1954. Family Constellation and Overt Incestuous Relations between Father and Daughter. *Am. J. Orthopsychiatry* 24: 266-77.

58. Reimer, S. 1940. A Research Note on Incest. *Am. J. Sociology* 45: 566-75.

59. Weiss, J., et al. 1955. A Study of Girl Sex Victims. *Psychiatric Q.* 29: 1-27.

60. Hartogs, R. 1951-52. Discipline in the Early Life of Sex-Delinquents and Sex-Criminals. *The Nervous Child* 9: 167-73.

61. Lustig, N., et al. 1966. Incest: A Family Group Survival Pattern. *Archives of General Psychiatry* 14: 31-40.

62. Weiner, I. B. 1962. Father-Daughter Incest: A Clinical Report. *Psychiatric Q.* 36: 607-32.

63. Weiner, I. B. 1964. On Incest: A Survey. *Excerpt. Criminology* 4: 137-55.

64. Wahl, C. W. 1960. The Psychodynamics of Consummated Maternal Incest. *Archives of General Psychiatry* 3: 188-93.

Is Treatment Too Late?

What Ten Years of Evaluative Research Tells Us

ANNE HARRIS COHN
DEBORAH DARO *1987*

"Is Treatment Too Late? What Ten Years of Evaluative Research Tells Us" presented to the field, for the first time in the literature, a summary of what was known about the effectiveness of different treatment approaches for parents who had abused and neglected their children and for the children themselves. In this paper, Cohn and Daro describe the findings from four separate multi-year evaluation studies that included 89 different demonstration or pilot treatment programs and data on 3,253 families experiencing difficulties with abuse and neglect. Collectively the studies suggest directions for relatively more successful treatment approaches.

The importance of this paper can be seen from a number of perspectives. First, it elevates the value of applied research by presenting findings from research that sought to answer questions of direct applicability to front-line workers as well as policy makers and program designers.

Second, it presents findings from studies funded by the U.S. government through contracts to consulting firms—studies that would not ordinarily have ended up in the referenced literature, even though they were the only ones being conducted at the time.

Third, it synthesizes the findings of all such studies that had been done to date (e.g., 1987)—a task not typically undertaken. Historically, such studies remained, despite their similarities in purpose and design, as discrete undertakings; today, finding syntheses of previous work is relatively common in the referenced literature.

Fourth, it was the first paper in the literature to look at the value of studying subpopulations and not assuming that all families or all perpetrators are alike. Indeed, this paper makes clear that diverse interventions are needed and that effective treatment is that which is tailored to the needs of individual families.

And finally, the paper analyzed the implications of the studies' findings for subsequent policy as well as research. It is notable that a major conclusion is that treatment for parents who have already maltreated their children is relatively ineffective (e.g., has very low rates of success) and thus, a focus on earlier intervention and prevention is called for. By giving prevention advocates empirical evidence for the value of preventive approaches, it became a catalyst for more work in the prevention arena.

While the methodologies used in these early, large-scale evaluations were, relative to today's efforts, rudimentary—for example, none employed a randomized trial—they do represent the earliest efforts to make sense of the effectiveness of different interventions for different types of abuse and different types of families. By summarizing their collective findings in one location, the paper prompted both more and better subsequent research on this topic. And, in large measure, the key findings they present—notably that intensive lay counseling and various group services have the greatest chances of success—are not materially different from those appearing in the literature today.

K. O.

As early as 1961, Dr. Brandt Steele and his colleagues noted that the abuse of children "is not confined to people with a psychopathic personality or borderline socioeconomic status. It also occurs among people with good education and stable financial and social background." And, they suggested that a professional's duty and responsibility to the child "requires a full evaluation of the problem and a guarantee that the expected repetition of trauma will not be permitted to occur" [1]. Therein began an ever-growing battle to identify families from across all population groups in the United States who may be experiencing difficulties with abuse, to use investigative and diagnostic skills to determine if and why the maltreatment occurred, and to offer treatment services so the abuse would not recur.

In those early times, before reports of serious child abuse topped 1 million nationwide and before treatment workers carried caseloads of 50 to 60, with little or no supportive services to offer their clients, there appeared to be reason for optimism. Initially, treatment efforts looked promising with abuse families.

In discussing activities at what has come to be known as the C. Henry Kempe National Center for the Prevention and Treatment of Child Abuse and Neglect, Dr. Steele reported,

For the great majority of patients treatment was successful, highly so in some, moderately so in others. Criteria of success were multiple. Of primary importance was a change in the style of parent-child interaction to a degree which eliminated the danger of physical harm to the child and lessened the chance of serious emotional damage. . . . Of this treated group well over three-fourths showed significant improvement. [2:138, 145]

Even for those not experiencing positive outcomes, Dr. Steele offered some thoughts on why it might appear that clients were regressing, as treatment comes to a close and some clues on what to do about it:

Termination of treatment can arouse once more the feelings of being deserted and rejected, and not rarely these will be a mild transient recurrence of tendencies to demand too much and be too aggressive toward the infant. In response, "we let patients know we would be glad to hear from them again, after therapy had been tapered off and technically terminated." [2:141]

If only greater care had been taken to heed Dr. Steele's thoughtful remarks and to look upon treatment, not as a time-limited interaction between provider and client but as a

Originally published in *Child Abuse and Neglect,* 1987, Vol. 11, pp. 433-441. Reprinted by permission of Elsevier Science.

long-standing relationship, perhaps the development and testing of treatment approaches since 1981 would have proved more successful. The expanding scope of maltreatment and the diversity of behaviors and service needs among high-risk or abusive populations have tested the limits of interventions once thought to be productive. This paper takes a look at large-scale formal attempts undertaken in the last decade to improve our knowledge about effective treatment.

BACKGROUND

In the early 1970s, prior to the passage of the federal Child Abuse and Neglect Treatment Act, there was limited empirical research or program evaluations on how best to treat families experiencing child abuse. Ethnographic research, such as that of Dr. Steele [2], and clinical studies with small, nonrepresentative samples, undefined outcome variables, and a very narrow range of intervention strategies were all that was available. During the past 10 years, in large part because of the establishment of the federal child abuse program, a number of evaluative and longitudinal studies have been conducted on approaches to treatment, creating a rich base of empirical data. One particularly large effort has been the multiple site program evaluations funded by the federal government since 1974, which included four major studies:

- Study 1: Berkeley Planning Associates' evaluation of the 11 joint OCD/SRS demonstration programs in child abuse and neglect conducted between 1974 and 1977 with a client impact sample of over 1,600 families;
- Study 2: Abt Associates' evaluation of 20 demonstration and innovative treatment projects funded by the National Center on Child Abuse and Neglect (NCCAN) between 1977 and 1981 with a client impact sample of 488 families;
- Study 3: E. H. White's evaluation of 29 service improvement grants funded by

NCCAN between 1978 and 1981 with a client impact of 165 families; and

- Study 4: Berkeley Planning Associates' evaluation of 19 clinical demonstration projects funded by NCCAN between 1978 and 1982 with a client impact of 1,000 families.

Collectively, these four studies represent over a $4 million federal investment in child abuse and neglect program research over a 10-year period. A total of 89 different demonstration treatment programs, on which the government spent approximately $40 million, were studied; data on 3,253 families experiencing difficulties with abuse and neglect were gathered. Detailed findings and descriptions of the evaluations can be obtained from the U.S. National Child Abuse and Neglect Clearinghouse and the National Technical Information Service [3-6]. While each of these studies explored some unique questions about the child maltreatment spectrum [7], each addressed common questions regarding the relative efficacy of different treatment strategies.

METHODOLOGY

A variety of methodological techniques was utilized by the four evaluations, although sufficient similarity existed to allow for comparison of findings. Qualitative or descriptive approaches, such as case studies and in-depth interviews, were used both to explain the organizational and service structures of the individual demonstration projects [8, 9] and to highlight the key clinical issues raised in addressing the needs of multiproblem families and individuals [10]. These descriptive data provided a picture of what the projects did and how they did it. Quantitative approaches, primarily focusing on impact and outcome data, were used as well. These data were used to assess the most effective organizational and staffing patterns in working with maltreating families [11], to determine the relative costs of providing various services to maltreating families [12, 13], to determine the critical elements of a well-functioning community systems' response to maltreatment [14, 15], and to assess the attributes of quality case management [16, 17]. Specific studies also identified the key issues in addressing child neglect [18] and in providing therapeutic interventions to young children [19, 20].

Three of the evaluations employed multivariate statistical techniques to identify the specific service and client characteristics which accounted for positive client outcomes [21-23]. The dependent variables used in the evaluations included clinician judgments regarding continued abuse or neglect during treatment, future likelihood for maltreatment following termination, progress in overall functioning, and progress in resolving a number of specific behavioral or psychosocial problems exhibited at intake. Utilizing data collection instruments developed by the evaluators, individual project staff provided detailed assessment of their clients at both intake and termination. Each of the evaluations used a multiple comparison group design in which the performance of clients receiving one set of services was compared to the performance of clients receiving a different service package. Multiple regression was utilized in the analyses, with covariates entered to control for differences in client characteristics and in the types and severity of maltreatment [24].

The variety of interventions provided families with similar presenting problems and the utilization of a common data collection system and uniform outcome measures created a natural experiment for assessing the relative merits of different treatment strategies. While true causal relationships between services and outcomes are best determined through experimental research designs with random assignment to treatment and control groups, the multiple comparison group design offers a pragmatic alternative to the ethical and logistical problems inherent in experimental research. The breadth of interventions represented by the federal demonstration programs provided a program and client pool sufficiently diverse to effectively and appropriately use this research design to inform practice and policy development.

An additional methodological constraint is that the measures were limited to clinical judgment rather than direct behavior measures. The study design limited the researchers' ability to gather data directly from clients, and thus the reliance on professional observations was necessary.

Nature of the Study Population

The clients served by these 89 federally funded demonstration projects represented a broad spectrum of families. Wide variation in the types of maltreatment, household income, household composition, race, and presenting problems were noted in all four evaluation efforts. As summarized in Table 22.1, the four client impact samples represented a wide range of maltreatment [25]. The most notable differences among the four studies were the variations in the number of high-risk families included in each sample and in the recorded incidence of sexual abuse. While approximately one quarter of the clients included in Studies 2 and 3 were identified as high risk, this classification applied to only 5% of the Study 4 sample. Of the substantiated cases served by the projects, the percentage of families who had previously been reported for child maltreatment was 29% in the Study 1 sample and over 40% in Studies 2 and 4 samples. Variations in the percentage of sexual abuse cases were partially reflected in the selection criteria NCCAN employed in establishing each demonstration effort [26].

Despite this diversity in family characteristics and type of maltreatment, the major presenting problems identified in these families are remarkably similar across the four studies

TABLE 22.1 Type of Maltreatment

	Study 1 (1977)	Study 2 (1981)	Study 3 (1981)	Study 4 (1982)
High risk	28%	25%	42%	5%
Emotional maltreatment	14%			23%
Physical neglect	20%	26%	32%	27%
Physical abuse	31%	28%	21%	17%
Sexual maltreatment	4%	5%		28%
Emotional or sexual maltreatment			7%	
Neglect & physical abuse	3%	13%		
Sexual maltreatment, neglect and/or physical abuse		2%		
	(n = 1,686)	(n = 488)	(n = 164)	(n = 895)

and mirror the array of difficulties frequently cited in the literature for this population. As summarized in Table 22.2, contextual problems (such as financial difficulties or unemployment) and interpersonal problems (such as marital conflict, social isolation, substance abuse, and spouse abuse) were identified by sizable percentages of clients in each study population. As might be expected, since Studies 3 and 4 included more severe cases, the frequency of all of these problems was also greater. For example, financial difficulties were noted for 46% of the client population in Study 1 and over 80% in the client population in Study 4. Similarly, employment problems were identified in 18% and 36% of the respective clients samples.

STUDY FINDINGS

Study findings from three areas suggest the following: (1) the relative effectiveness of different services with abusers and neglecters, (2) the success rates in treatment for abusers and neglecters, and (3) the effectiveness of services for the abused and neglected children.

Service Effectiveness for Adults

While Study 2 found no notable correlation between a given set of services and positive client outcomes, both Studies 1 and 4 identified specific services as enhancing client outcomes. Study 1 concluded that, relative to any other discrete services or combination of ser-

TABLE 22.2 Major Presenting Problems of Maltreating Families

	Study 1 (1977)	Study 2 (1981)	Study 3 (1981)	Study 4 (1982)
Financial difficulties	46%	44%	62%	80%
Employment problems	18%	30%	n.a.	36%
Marital conflict	40%	36%	40%	74%
Social isolation	29%	23%	n.a.	67%
Substance abuse	19%	24%	25%	54%
Spouse abuse	11%	13%	n.a.	42%
	(n = 1,686)	(n = 488)	(n = 164)	(n = 903)

vices, the receipt of lay services—lay counseling and Parents Anonymous—as part of a treatment package resulted in more positive treatment outcomes. The study also noted that group services, such as group therapy and parent education classes, as supplemental services also produced significant effects, particularly for the physical abuser. Although Study 1 cautioned that the lay services provided by the projects participating in that study required intensive on-the-job training and ongoing professional back-up and supervision for the lay therapist, the study clearly indicated that expansion beyond a strictly therapeutic or counseling service model was both beneficial to the client as well as cost-effective for the project [27, 28].

Similar findings were noted in Study 4. Again, the provision of group counseling and educational and skill development classes showed a significant relationship to a client's achievement of both overall progress and the elimination of a propensity toward future maltreatment. After considering the possible impacts of initial severity and client characteristics on outcomes, adults who received group counseling were 27% less likely than those who did not receive this particular service to demonstrate a continued propensity for future maltreatment. Similarly, those clients who received educational or skill development classes, such as household management, health care, and vocational skills development, were 16% less likely than the clients who did not receive this service to demonstrate a continued propensity for future maltreatment. Clients receiving group counseling and educational or skill development classes were also significantly more likely than clients not receiving these services to demonstrate overall progress during treatment [29-32]. Similar findings regarding the efficacy of group therapy and parenting education classes have also been noted in other program evaluations.

Studies 1 and 4 both noted that clients engaged in treatment for less than 6 months were

less likely to make overall progress in treatment or to demonstrate a reduced propensity toward future maltreatment. In addition, Study 4 found that clients remaining in treatment over 18 months also performed less well on these indicators, suggesting that an optimal treatment period may be between 7 and 18 months. The Study 4 findings corroborates Study 2 findings.

On balance, the findings summarized above suggest that successful intervention with maltreating families requires a comprehensive package of services which address both the interpersonal and concrete needs of all family members. Strategies which continue to rely solely upon costly professional therapy, without augmenting their service strategies with group counseling efforts and other supportive or remedial services to children and families, will offer less opportunity for maximizing client gains. Also, projects should be aware of the diminishing rate of return on services over time and invest the most intensive resources during the initial months of treatment, as close to the point of initial referral as possible, in order to successfully engage the family and begin altering behavior.

Success Rates in Treatment for Adults

In three of the studies, client outcome was measured. Overall, the data suggest that federally funded demonstration projects have had their problems in achieving client success, both in terms of initially stopping the abuse and in reducing the likelihood for further maltreatment. As summarized in Table 22.2, continued abuse while in treatment occurred in 30% to 47% of the cases evaluated. While the definition of this outcome measure varied among the three samples (e.g., Study 2 noted only cases involving severe neglect or physical abuse during treatment while Study 2 recorded all instances of maltreatment occurring while the family received services), the collective impression of these findings suggests that, in the short run, existing treatment efforts have not been very successful in protecting children from further harm.

On the other hand, repeated maltreatment while receiving services is not, in and of itself, a sufficient predictor of eventual progress in treatment or long-standing propensity for future maltreatment. All three studies reported a relatively weak correlation between abusive behavior during treatment and other client outcome measures, such as propensity for future maltreatment and overall progress in resolving a range of personal and family functioning problems. In every respect, the projects most successful in immediately eliminating abusive behavior were projects which generally separated the child from the abusive parent, either by placing the child in temporary foster care or requiring the maltreating parent to move out of the home [33].

Reduced propensity toward future maltreatment was also measured. In Study 1, 42% of the clients demonstrated a reduced propensity for future maltreatment, compared to 80% of the clients included in Study 2. While these clients were found less likely to maltreat their children in the future than they had been prior to services, the likelihood for future maltreatment continued to exist among many of the clients. Study 4 identified 46% of the clients served as being unlikely to maltreat their children in the future.

Study 4 also noted a dramatic difference in the performance of clients involved in different types of maltreatment on this indicator. For example, 70% of the clients served by the sexual abuse treatment projects were viewed as being unlikely to further maltreat their children, but only 40% of the adults served by the child neglect projects were viewed in this manner. This suggests that greater gains have been made in achieving success with incestuous families than have been made in the more intractable area of child neglect [34-36]. Similar findings

have been noted by others evaluating sexual abuse interventions.

Measures of improved adult client functioning in behavior and attitudes associated with abuse were also used in three of the evaluation efforts. As summarized in Table 22.3, the projects in Study 4 fared better than the other demonstration efforts in resolving the key functioning problems of their adult clients. While roughly two thirds of the adults served by the 11 joint OCD/SRS demonstration projects (Study 1) experienced improvement in only one third or less of their functioning problems, 51% of the clients served by the most recent NCCAN-funded demonstration effort (Study 4) realized improvement on at least half of their problems, with 30% of these clients realizing gains on all of their presenting problems. Similarly, while Study 2 noted that 34% of its client sample achieved overall progress during treatment, over 60% of the adults included in Study 4 were identified at termination as having made progress.

The latest child abuse and neglect demonstration projects made more progress in reducing the propensity for future maltreatment and in improving client functioning than those funded a decade ago. The caseloads of these projects have included percentages of families experiencing severe maltreatment and multiple problems [37]. Expansions in the service package and the better targeting of services to specific child maltreatment subpopulations are among the factors which have most likely contributed to these successes [38].

Service Effectiveness for Children

In the earliest rounds of demonstration projects (Studies 1 and 2), very few children received direct services, making the assessment of the impacts of such efforts on remediating the physical and emotional effects of maltreatment difficult. For example, only 70 children

TABLE 22.3 Success Rates

Outcome Measure	Study 1	Study 2	Study 4
Reincidence	30% of all cases severe reincidence	44% reincidence for all cases	47% reincidence for all cases
Future likelihood to maltreat	42% reduced propensity	80% reduced propensity	46% unlikely to abuse in future
Improvement on functional problems adult clients exhibited at intake:			
Percentage showing any progress during treatment		33%	60%
Percentage of problems showing improvement:			
33%–0%	62%		
34%–66%	18%		
67%–00%	21%		
Less than 50%			49%
50%–74%			14%
75%–99%			7%
100%			30%

received direct services during the first federal demonstration effort (Study 1). Of the 70 children who did receive some form of therapy, over 50% demonstrated improvements in those developmental, emotional, or socialization areas noted to be serious problems at the time treatment began. In contrast to the relatively few number of children provided direct services by these early demonstration efforts, over 1,600 children and adolescents served by the demonstration projects assessed in Study 4 were provided a wide variety of direct services including individual therapy, group counseling, therapeutic day care, speech and physical therapy, and medical care. Over 70% of the young children and adolescents in Study 4 demonstrated gains across all functional areas during treatment.

IMPLICATIONS

The collective results of the federally funded research and demonstration efforts certainly provide useful and positive program guidelines. In addition to descriptive data, which provide greater clarity on how to differentiate among families experiencing various types of maltreatment when providing treatment and a better understanding of how to provide expanded intervention models which include direct services to both adults and children, the studies document

- approaches to improved client outcomes, especially in the areas of individual and family functioning with increasingly more severe forms of maltreatment; and
- methods for success in eliminating initial reabuse and future propensity among families involved in sexual abuse.

The studies also provide some cause for concern: Treatment efforts in general are not very successful. Child abuse and neglect continue despite early, thoughtful, and often costly intervention. Treatment programs have been relatively ineffective in initially halting abusive and neglectful behavior or in reducing the future likelihood of maltreatment in the most severe cases of physical abuse, chronic neglect, and emotional maltreatment.

One third or more of the parents served by these intensive demonstration efforts maltreated their children while in treatment, and over one half of the families served continued to be judged by staff as likely to mistreat their children following termination. Whether one views this level of success as notable or disappointing is largely a function of personal perspective and professional choice.

Assessing the overall success rate one can hope to achieve in working with abusive and neglectful families, Kempe and Kempe in their earlier work estimated that, regardless of the interventions used, 20% of the parents will be treatment failures, such that the child will not be returned home; 40% of the parents will grow and develop and eventually permanently change their parenting behaviors; and 40% of the parents will no longer physically abuse or neglect their children but will continue to be emotional maltreators [39]. More recent research experiences are less positive. While the combination of therapeutic and supportive services, such as group and family therapy, educational and skill development classes, in-home lay therapist, and self-help groups, have enhanced overall performance with families agreeable to intervention, a sizable core of parents now appear to remain unchanged, and their children remain at risk. In addition to suggesting clear treatment paths, therefore, the collective findings of these national program evaluations identify clear limitations on strategies which serve families only after abusive and neglectful patterns have surfaced.

If research findings are to be of any use in setting policies, the results of a decade of evaluative research on treatment programs suggest that putting all resources into intervention after the fact does not make sense. Perhaps intervention much earlier with families would produce better results. Dr. Brandt Steele said it best:

> We want to prevent not only the immediate, painful misery of children who are subjected to maltreatment, but also to prevent those lifelong disastrous consequences that are more and more difficult to treat as the person grows older. To work toward the prevention of all these unhappy lasting effects of maltreatment is one of the most valuable things we can do to benefit our fellow human beings [40].

NOTES AND REFERENCES

1. KEMPE, C. H., SILVERMAN, F. N. and STEELE, B. F., DROEGEMUELLER, W. and SILVER, H, K,. The battered child syndrome. *Journal of the American Medical Association* 181: 17-24 (1962).

2. STEELE, B. F. and POLLOCK, C. B. A psychiatric study of parents who abuse infants and small children. *The Battered Child,* R. E. HELFER and C. H. KEMPE (Eds.). University of Chicago Press, Chicago (1968).

3. BERKELEY PLANNING ASSOCIATES. *Evaluation of the Joint OCD/SRS Demonstration Projects in Child Abuse and Neglect* (Vols. 1-12). National Center for Health Services Research, Office of Assistant Secretary for Health, DHEW, under Contracts HRA 106-74-120 and HRA 230-76-076, Washington DC (1977).

4. ABT ASSOCIATES. *Impact Evaluation of Twenty Demonstration and Innovative Child Abuse and Neglect Treatment Projects* (Vols. 1-2). National Center for Child Abuse and Neglect, Office of Human Development Services, DHHS under Contract 105-77-1047. Washington DC. (1981).

5. WHITE, E. H. *Evaluation of Service Improvements Grants: Analysis of Client Case Reports.* National Center for Child Abuse and Neglect, Office of Human Development Services, DHHS, under Contract HEW 105-78-1107, Washington DC (1981).

6. BERKELLEY PLANNING ASSOCIATES. *Evaluation of the Clinical Demonstrations of the Treatment of Child Abuse and Neglect* (Vols. 1-9). National Center for Child Abuse and Neglect, Office of Human Development Services. DHHS, under Contract HEW 105-78-1108, Washington DC (1983).

7. Over the time period spanned by the four evaluations, fewer of the demonstration projects were housed in public protective service agencies; the client population became more dominated by substantiated rather than "high risk" families: the number and range of services provided by the projects to the children and adolescents in these maltreating families increased; and projects targeted their services to a more limited range of maltreatment behavior.

8. BERKELEY PLANNING ASSOCIATES. *Historical Case Studies: Eleven Child Abuse and Neglect*

Projects, (Vol. 12). Berkeley Planning Associates, Berkeley, CA (1974-1977).

9. BERKELEY PLANNING ASSOCIATES. *Historical Case Studies.* (Vol. 9). Berkeley Planning Associates, Berkeley, CA (1983).

10. BERKELEY PLANNING ASSOCIATES. *A Qualitative Study of Most Successful and Least Successful Cases,* (Vol. 3). Berkeley Planning Associates, Berkeley, CA (1983).

11. BERKELEY PLANNING ASSOCIATES. *Project Management and Worker Burnout* (Vol. 9). Berkeley Planning Associates, Berkeley, CA (1977).

12. BERKELEY PLANNING ASSOCIATES. *Cost Report* (Vol. 7). Berkeley Planning Associates, Berkeley, CA (1977).

13. BERKELEY PLANNING ASSOCIATES. *Resource Allocation Study* (Vol 7). Berkeley Planning Associates, Berkeley, CA (1983).

14. BERKELEY PLANNING ASSOCIATES. *Community Systems Impact* (Vol. 5). Berkeley Planning Associates, Berkeley, CA (1977).

15. BERKELEY PLANNING ASSOCIATES. *Guide for Planning and Implementing Child Abuse and Neglect Programs* (Vol. 10). Berkeley Planning Associates, Berkeley, CA (1977).

16. BERKELEY PLANNING ASSOCIATES. *Quality of the Case Management Process* (Vol. 6). Berkeley Planning Associates, Berkeley, CA (1977).

17. COHN, A. and DEGRAAF, B. Assessing case management in the field of child abuse. *Journal of Social Service Research* 5: 29-43 (1982).

18. BERKELEY PLANNING ASSOCIATES. *Child Neglect* (Vol. 4). Berkeley Planning Associates, Berkeley, CA (1983).

19. BERKELEY PLANNING ASSOCIATES. *Child Impact* (Vol. 11). Berkeley Planning Associates, Berkeley, CA (1977).

20. BERKELEY PLANNING ASSOCIATES. *Therapeutic Child Care: Approaches to Remediating the Effects of Child Abuse and Neglect* (Vol. 5). Berkeley Planning Associates, Berkeley, CA (1983).

21. BERKELEY PLANNING ASSOCIATES. *Methodology for Evaluating Child Abuse and Neglect Service Program* (Vol. 8). Berkeley Planning Associates, Berkeley, CA (1977).

22. ABT ASSOCIATES. *Detailed Account of Study Findings, Methods and Conclusion* (Vol. 2). Abt Associates, National Center for Child Abuse and Neglect. Office of Human Development Services, Washington DC (1981).

23. BERKELEY PLANNING ASSOCIATES. *Final Analysis Plan and Methodology for the Exploration of Client Characteristics, Services and Outcome* (Vol. 8). Berkeley Planning Associates, Berkeley, CA (1981).

24. This analytic method controls for all variation in the dependent variables explained by nonservice-related factors before considering the impact of the intervention. This method, while representing a very conservative approach to identifying significant service impacts, is one of the few analytic methods which can be used to determine service impact in the absence of a formal control or comparison group. To compensate for the lack of a true experimental research design, the method assumes services were randomly assigned to clients (i.e., no consistent relationship existed between client characteristics and the provision of services). Client characteristics and other nonservice variables are entered into the model first under this method as a means of controlling for their specific contribution to differential outcomes. Service impact is then determined to be the additional variance in the dependent variable of interest explained by the introduction of specific service variables.

25. Reviewing the demographic descriptions of these families, one would be hard-pressed to isolate patterns of maltreatment to a single socioeconomic class. For example, over 15% of the families in Study 1 had household incomes in excess of $12,000 while over 22% of the families in Study 4 had incomes in excess of $15,000. In addition, income was found in Study 4 to be highly correlated with the family's primary type of maltreatment.

26. Each project funded under this effort targeted services to one of five subpopulations including sexual abuse, adolescent maltreatment, substance abuse, remedial services for children, and child neglect.

27. BERKELEY PLANNING ASSOCIATES. *Adult Client Impact Reports* (Vol. 3). Berkeley Planning Associates, Berkeley. CA (1977).

28. COHN, A. Effective treatment of child abuse and neglect. *Social Work* 24: 513-519 (1979).

29. BERKELEY PLANNING ASSOCIATES. *The Exploration of Client Characteristics, Services and Outcomes: Final Report and Summary of Findings* (Vol 2). Berkeley Planning Associates, Berkeley, CA (1983).

30. BEAN, S. L. A multiservice approach to the prevention of child abuse. *Child Welfare* 50: 277-282 (1971).

31. MCNEIL, J. S. and McBRIDE, M. L. Group therapy with abusive parents. *Social Casework* 60: 36-42 (1979).

32. MOORE, J. B. Project Thrive: A supportive treatment approach to parents of children with nonorganic failure to thrive. *Child Welfare* 61: 389-398 (1982).

33. For treatment projects committed to working with the entire family, and in maintaining the family unit throughout the treatment process, this intervention strategy is less viable. Breaking the cycle of maltreatment is a difficult treatment issue that involves not only breaking the abusive or neglectful patterns but also cultivating different, more appropriate patterns of interaction and discipline. Prior to the completion of this process, families will likely fall back into those patterns that are familiar and comfortable. As each of these evaluations has

pointed out, reincidence in this context is not solely an outcome indicator but rather a continuum along which a family's progress may be monitored.

34. ANDERSON, L. M. and SHAFER, G. The character-disorder family: A community treatment model for family sexual abuse. *American Journal of Orthopsychiatry 49*: 436-445 [1979].

35. GIARRETTO, H. The treatment of father-daughter incest: A psychosocial approach. *Children Today 5*: 34-35 (1976).

36. GIARRETTO, H. Humanistic treatment of father-daughter incest. *Journal of Humanistic Psychology 18*: 59-76 (1978).

37. The increased percentage of severe maltreatment cases being served by the demonstration projects has both positive and negative aspects. To see that solid success can be achieved with multiproblem families is certainly encouraging. On the other hand, the focus on the more severe cases places child abuse and neglect treatment projects in the difficult position of working with families which have fewer and fewer material and personal resources.

38. Hypotheses regarding subpopulations of maltreatment were supported by all four evaluations. Each identified significant differences in demographic characteristics, presenting problems, and service needs among families and perpetrators involved in different types of maltreatment. Segmenting the population for service purposes along this dimension, however, is problematic. The continued funding of projects to serve only one segment of the maltreatment population may be difficult to justify in light of rising fiscal constraints and service demands. For years, one of the keys to a successful community response to child maltreatment has been establishing a coordination system which includes all professional and voluntary agencies concerned with child health and well-being.

39. KEMPE, R. S. and KEMPE, C. H. *Child Abuse.* Harvard University Press, Cambridge, MA (1978).

40. STEELE, B. F. Notes on the lasting effects of early child abuse. *Child Abuse & Neglect 10*: 283-291 (1986).

23

The Litany of the Smoldering Neglect of Children

RAY E. HELFER   *1987*

"The Litany of the Smoldering Neglect of Children," one of Ray Helfer's many seminal articles, offers an important and clear discussion of the form of maltreatment most neglected by policy makers, clinicians, and researchers alike—that of chronic or smoldering neglect. In his paper, Helfer discusses the incidence and manifestations of that lower grade form of neglect—harder to recognize and define—which occurs day in and day out and appears almost intractable.

While outlining the need to assess the whole family in responding to this form of maltreatment and to offer a wide variety of support services over a very long period of time, Helfer establishes the very real challenges of working with these families. The challenges he cited in 1987 are every bit as relevant today—notably finding funding to offer long-term services and funding for a person who can coordinate those services—expenses that cannot be covered by traditional fee for services systems. As Helfer points out, because these families require such a major investment—one that he argues is well worthwhile—an even better

approach would be to focus on prevention or early intervention. Few scholars had previously articulated the value of a preventive approach in dealing with chronic neglect, as Helfer does in this paper.

Stuart Hart reflects on the unique contributions of this paper. It makes a strong case for the development of minimal care standards for child rearing—a need still quite relevant today. It provides a good organizing structure for the causes or characteristics of parents who neglect, which still has strong heuristic value today. And it sets challenges for family evaluation and care, noting that society and the helping professions need to invest much greater resources in dealing with neglect. This also remains true today. Helfer recommends the kind of in-depth family assessments, intervention alternatives, and coordination of case management that we have yet to achieve. And in many ways, this paper is even more important today, as public policy tends to push us away rather than toward these recommendations.

Stephen Ludwig remarks that Helfer's ability to make a complex problem simple and his infectious optimism, hallmarks of all his work, are most evident in this paper. This work is vintage Helfer and is still as informative and instructive today as it was when it was published.

Besides its educational value, this piece also argues cogently and convincingly for a far more preventive approach to working with high-risk families, such as those smoldering in neglectful behavior. This is Helfer the visionary helping professionals put the value of different facets of their work into perspective. And, in fact, Helfer refers the reader of *The Battered Child,* in which this paper appears as a chapter, to other chapters in the book that deal with prevention and early intervention, citing how very important these are to reducing the incidence and effects of chronic neglect.

A. C. D. and K. O.

In this discussion of the neglect of children, special emphasis will be given to family interaction and long-term follow-up. There will be a few comments about some of the political issues relating to child neglect, since decisions have been made recently (1985-1986) to cut even further the funding for Medicaid, nutrition programs, and other supports for poor children in the United States. Primary emphasis will be given to how the medical care system responds over a long period of time to these neglected children and their families. Additional emphasis will be given to the personal issues that face all physicians, particularly those in family practice or pediatrics, who interact with the parents of neglected children. This chapter, however, is directed to all professionals involved with these difficult situations, including physicians for adults, social workers, psychologists, psychiatrists, public health nurses, and others. The goal is to put into perspective the process and results of the long-term neglect of children and how professionals can and should respond.

INCIDENCE

The true incidence of child neglect is unknown, since no consensus on the definition exists. The point at which a child slips from satisfactory care to neglected care is hard to define. Of course, there is little difficulty recognizing or defining severe child neglect; harder to define is low-grade, smoldering neglect, month after month, before one's very eyes in a neglected environment. Is neglect defined as something present or absent in the child, or something present or absent in the parent, or both? What *is* known about the incidence of child neglect is that approximately 65% of those children who are reported to social agencies throughout the United States each year as a result of child abuse reporting laws are categorized as neglected. This amounts to approximately 650,000 cases per year. While these reporting laws provide a definition of neglect, in reality, neglect is what the school teacher, physician, social worker, judge, psychologist, or police officer "says it is" at the time of the report. Whether or not a protective services worker or a judge agrees with the professional making the report depends on a variety of issues, including the worker's experience, caseload, ability to document the findings, comparison group, background, and training. However, one should not get hung up on the definition of child neglect but rather get on with helping these children, who are being cared for in a manner far below our society's accepted standards.

CLASSIFICATION

When child neglect is listed along with physical abuse, sexual exploitation, verbal abuse, and spouse abuse under the classification of family interaction, this moves the problem into proper perspective. When a comprehensive evaluation of a family is undertaken, emphasis must be given to the separate categories of how parents themselves manifest the problem of neglect—what parents do or do not do, what happens or does not happen to the children—and how these children manifest the problem to various professionals.

MANIFESTATIONS OF NEGLECTING PARENTS

Neglecting parents manifest themselves to those who deliver health care and other professional services in a variety of ways which are not mutually exclusive. These include (1) overt retardation, (2) psychiatric illness, (3) physical illness, (4) ecological problems, (5) development problems, (6) substance abuse, and (7) fanatical beliefs of one type or another. Harder to classify are those parents whose difficulties include several of these problem areas to a mild degree, which collectively create serious interactional problems, especially when their subculture is tolerant of inadequate child care standards.

Those who are overtly retarded may not remember to feed their babies, recall how much or when a child was fed, understand how to handle money, or know how to read or write. Some do not have the intellectual capacity to deal with the day-to-day demands of parenting. Parents who are clearly retarded are relatively easy to identify, especially if they have recently been discharged from a state institution as a result of a societal decision to encourage retarded adults to live in our communities, often within a communal setting. While this plan is commendable, our society has not considered what to do with the children that occur as a result of these communal relationships. Resolving one social problem has created another. Not uncommonly, a woman who lives in a communal setting and has a baby must leave and be on her own. These retarded parents and their babies have to fend for themselves. Few communities have considered the consequences of this outcome.

Other parents who often neglect their children are those with serious psychiatric illnesses. Adults who are psychotic or sociopathic commonly fail to interact appropriately with their children, placing these children at very high risk.

Many parents of neglected children are physically ill. They may have a variety of health-related problems, varying from gynecological issues and nutritional deficiencies to hypertension and obesity. Our medical care system has been most unresponsive to their needs. Finding physicians to care for the physical problems, many of which are chronic in nature, of neglecting parents in our current fee-for-service system is most difficult. Serious medical illnesses are so common among neglecting parents that any family care program must respond to these health care needs if comprehensive services are to be offered.

Neglecting parents often live in environments that are truly unfit, with insufficient food, shelter, heat, lights, and transportation to meet the basic needs of their families. Such devastated ecological environments may be such that no outcome for the child is possible other than neglect. These environments may occur through no fault of the parents, but rather as a result of social and political priorities.

Parents who neglect their children sometimes have development problems as a result of being neglected themselves when they were children. Their childhood environments and experiences have given them no model for positive child care. To them, negative, neglectful child rearing is normal; they raise their children the way they were raised.

Substance abuse by parents may present serious problems in caring for and interacting with their children. While alcohol abuse is most common, other forms of drug abuse are also prevalent among neglecting parents. Being under the influence of drugs is not the sole reason for child neglect problems; rather, the lifestyle that surrounds substance abuse and the constant drain on very severely limited financial resources to support a drug habit take their toll on child care.

Finally, some parents who neglect their children are true fanatics—religious, nutritional, or cultural. Such fanaticism may interfere with the rearing of their children. Some parents believe they should never give their children animal protein; others have bizarre religious beliefs about child discipline and training; others withhold medical care from their children and may even teach them that health care professionals are "instruments of the devil." These belief systems may result in long-term neglect of certain basic nutritional, medical, and educational needs of the children.

In spite of these separate but interrelated problems, neglecting parents often very sincerely want to do well by their children. Many parents who are retarded, psychiatrically ill, physically ill, ecologically deprived, or from neglectful families themselves are highly motivated to be better parents. This may become a most difficult personal problem confronting those who care for these children for any length of time. (This is discussed in more detail in the section on "personal issues" below.)

MANIFESTATIONS OF NEGLECTED CHILDREN

Neglected children most commonly exhibit delayed development and growth in addition to varying degrees of malnutrition. Neglected children have frequent illnesses, both major and minor, in any of many physical systems, from the ears, throat, lungs, chest, and gastrointestinal tract to neurological dysfunctions.

They have chronic, smoldering illnesses, many of which are not life-threatening or blatantly serious. If one reviews the medical records of neglected children, which list each incident, multiple visits with similar or related problems are common. As every visit or failure to show up for an appointment is tallied, as the children's heights and weights are graphed and tabulated, the litany of neglect sounds loud and clear.

Young infants who are neglected present the classic form of "failure to thrive," that is, failure over time to grow according to accepted standards for height, weight, and development.

The manner in which older neglected children are recognized depends upon the professional's perception of these children. From a teacher's point of view, they may be children with learning disorders and with latchkeys around their necks. From a physician's point of view, they may be children suffering malnutrition, physical illness, or behavioral problems.

FAMILY ASSESSMENT

Every component of a neglectful family's interaction must be fully assessed. When the family medical history is comprehensively evaluated, many family members may be found to have some type of ongoing medical problem. This is often one of the most difficult problems confronting those in the health care system who care for neglected children. All members of the household need to be assessed to understand how health problems affect this group of individuals. Assistance from a family practitioner or internist is essential, though difficult to achieve.

The children's heights, weights, and head circumferences are measured and plotted on a regular basis. Height/weight ratios are most useful. Persistent pursuit is the rule of the day when these families "don't show." Various agencies can be used to arrange transportation for families to their appointments for medical evaluation and follow-up.

Periodic photographs and videotapes are useful to record components of the family's interactional system, physical findings, and developmental capabilities. Surprisingly, parents rarely express concerns or refuse when asked permission to take photographs and videotapes. They should have the opportunity to see them from time to time.

Numerous laboratory studies are rarely necessary in most neglected children. What is required is a comprehensive, periodic medical history and physical examination, using only those diagnostic laboratory tests necessary to follow up on clues that are obtained in this process. Little is gained by shooting in the dark to find that rare disease. For example, one does not have to order multiple chemistries, chest X-ray, intravenous pyelogram, blood urea nitrogen, and creatinine tests on a neglected child who is 8 years old and still wetting the bed, assuming that a thorough history, physical, urinalysis, and culture failed to produce any additional leads. Very often, these children are overmedicated and overstudied, while their basic problem of neglect is overlooked.

Concurrently, a social worker needs to piece together the family's social history and their interactional system.

Children who are chronically neglected cannot be fully evaluated without an elaborate survey of the home in which they are being reared. Often, this can be the function of a well-trained public health nurse who plays an integral part in the evaluation and follow-up of these families. The presence of heat, food, lights, excessive animals, sufficient beds, and reasonably stimulating environment to meet the needs of children must be assessed. Emphasis is given to those environmental circumstances that lead to accidents, poisonings, and other catastrophes.

A logical long-term treatment plan is impossible unless the mental and psychological states of the parents and the children are understood. Because of the high incidence among neglecting families of mental retardation and psychiatric illness, a complete psychological evaluation administered by a trained child psychologist or psychiatrist is needed.

Once neglect has been recognized in a child, the law clearly mandates the intervention of a protective services unit. This is easiest to achieve by telling the parents that the magnitude of their problem is beyond the capabilities of any one person. The parent should be told up front that a call to the community social worker (i.e., protective services worker) and the public health nurse is necessary. While the law does not necessitate the involvement of a public health nurse, the care of these families does. If this is done with openness and sincerity, parents rarely object. A neglect report asks professionals for their assistance. The sooner this is done, the more help they can provide.

As the family's story unfolds during the comprehensive assessment, the nature and degree of the chronicity of the problem becomes clear. If the children are school age, one cannot complete the assessment or develop a long-term plan without involving the school system and reviewing the child's educational progress. Parents usually cooperate and give permission for the school's involvement. In fact, they are often flattered by the interest shown to them and their child when the physician, clinic nurse, or social worker asks permission to visit the school and talk with the child's teacher.

Once the evaluation of *all* systems has been completed, all those involved—the public health nurse, protective services worker, school nurse, psychologist, and physician—must sit down from time to time to talk. There is no way to assess the severity and chronicity of the problem without everybody meeting in the same room at the same time. Parents are informed of the meeting and who will be in attendance, and they are asked whom they would like to give them a summary of the meeting. There should be no secrets about these meetings or their outcomes. Parents must be dealt with fairly and frequently, given as many choices as possible during this assessment and follow-up period. They will choose the person with whom they are most comfortable to give them the information that emerges from these meetings. Without such periodic meetings, the follow-up and care for children who are suffering from smoldering, chronic neglect month after month, year after year, will not be adequate. This multidisciplinary team model also works well for other chronic conditions, such as children with severe rehabilitation problems, cleft palate, learning disorders, and the like. Those agencies that hesitate to share their information in these group meetings can be involved by asking the parents to sign a release for the sharing of information among professionals on the case. Again, rarely do the parents object, if approached fairly and openly.

FISCAL ASPECTS

One of the greatest obstacles confronting physicians, psychologists, and other professionals is that there is no way to make a living caring for these chronically neglected children and their families. The fee-for-service system collapses when professionals who depend on this system for payment try to deliver services to these children. Even pre-payment plans (e.g., HMOs and others) find it most difficult to afford the number of visits and the amount of work and evaluation required. There is no resolution to this problem unless community and social service systems are geared to offer the comprehensive services that are necessary, using multidisciplinary teams. If a community or state is able and willing to supplement the salaries of the professionals needed to provide the services of a public health nurse, physician, social worker, psychologist, and protective services worker, then the comprehensive assessment and long-term follow-up that is absolutely necessary for these families will occur. Without such a community commitment, these families will not receive the care they require.

This is not dissimilar to the collapse of the fee-for-service system for the treatment of most chronic diseases that affect children. Only through supplemental service funds is one able to make a living seeing children with problems that fall in this category. Even the Crippled Children's Service in most states is not structured to provide funds for the extensive type of evaluation and follow-up required by neglecting families (except in Florida). Physicians caring for neglected children should not be viewed any differently than those caring for children with chronic renal disease or chronic pulmonary disease. Pediatric cardiologists and gastroenterologists used to receive supplemental funds, but now they are able to make their own living because the high technology of sonography and fiber optics permits a payment system for such achievements. If a "neglectoscope" were available, a flexible tube with a light on the end to move through the family system to observe and record the interactional breakdown, maybe then, the health insurance systems would pay for this service. Since a "neglectoscope" does not and cannot exist, all the interdisciplinary teams must be funded externally. The cost is minimal compared to the expense of doing nothing and can be justified easily by the improved productivity of these children and the decreased cost of their education.

DETERMINING OUTCOME

The determination of the type of intervention required and the likely outcome for any given family whose children are being neglected requires the utilization of all the data gathered in the comprehensive assessment described above. Without each component, incorrect decisions and plans are common.

For example, a host of community services may be made available to a given family in an effort to reverse the neglect of their children, only to find much too late that the parents are masking significant retardation, illiteracy, or severe psychiatric illness. True psychotics, certain fanatics, sociopaths, multiple personalities, and addicts have major problems rearing children. Their treatment requires more time than the children can afford. On the other hand, poverty and health problems per se may improve greatly with support and medical care, resulting in a much more positive outcome.

The bottom line: The appropriate type of intervention and the likely outcome cannot be determined without an in-depth family assessment.

INTERVENTION

The amount of intervention necessary to help these children and their families is enormous. Some of the players on this intervention team are described above, since they are also involved in the family assessment. On the other hand, they are not sufficient. Some of the other disciplines and training that are necessary to work with these families are as follows:

1. A statewide home extension service (formerly called the cooperative or agricultural extension service). These individuals, often available through a state university, are trained to help families who find it difficult to understand how and what to feed their children or how to make plans for day-to-day living. They may actually take the mother to a store and help her through each step of providing food for her children—shopping, preparing, and serving the food.

2. Community infant development programs, often run by mental health services. These infant development specialists work with parents of limited capacity, giving high priority to mother/father/infant interactional methods to improve the mental health of the parents as well as the overall health and development of the infants.

3. Mental health services and other psychiatric services from private agencies and community agencies. These services vary from direct one-to-one counseling to small support groups.

4. Public health nurses. Ongoing home visits are necessary to assess the physical health of the children and the environment in which they are living, and to give the parents the assistance necessary to find their way into the health care system and the community.

5. The school system can provide very valuable services to children of all ages. Recently enacted public laws mandate schools to develop an extensive evaluation service for children who are likely to require ongoing support when they are in school. Without question, children who are neglected are a major financial burden for school systems because they usually have significant learning disorders and require excessive time and effort on the part of school personnel. Early involvement is to both the school's and the family's benefit.

6. Home visitors or parent aides. These lay volunteers come from various agencies to assist mothers and fathers in the development of day-to-day living skills.

7. A medical care system in which a physician will see the children and adults consistently on an ongoing basis. Careful records must be kept. Twenty four-hour services are necessary.

8. Financial planners from departments of social services.

9. Vocational rehabilitation services can assist some of the parents in getting retrained, relocated, and employed.

10. Protective services provide a valuable service during family assessment. Unfortunately, most protective service units are not able to stay involved over a long period of time, so their role is often intermittent and sporadic. Since neglecting families often generate multiple reports to protective services, may *different* protective service workers may be involved with the same family over a period of years. This method of delivery of service is outmoded and cannot be condoned. Ongoing, long-term service by a given pro-

tective service worker with a family can be invaluable.

None of the above services is feasible unless there is someone who is the overall coordinator of services. This position is probably the single most flagrant omission in most communities. It is the hardest to sell, the hardest to fund, and often the hardest to staff. One person who calls the shots and is seen positively by the various team members and the families is critical. This individual often works for the child protection team or the multidisciplinary team within the community. This is not a role for the physician, public health nurse, psychologist, or protective services worker, but it should be seen as a separate, critically important function which must be funded independently. Those who think about the importance of this individual will immediately see that the weakest link in any long-term care of neglecting families is the unavailability of such a coordinator. Considering all the manifestations of neglecting parents, there is little wonder why such a person is so necessary to coordinate all their activities. One cannot expect the retarded, psychiatrically ill, physically ill, or poor parents to coordinate their own multidisciplinary service system. The questions of how this individual is paid and for whom he or she works have never been adequately resolved. Clearly, this role cannot continue to be ignored. Equally clearly, the public sector thus far has not been willing to provide support for these individuals.

▌ PERSONAL ISSUES ▌

When a physician, psychologist, social worker, or nurse becomes involved with a family who is caught up in the litany of smoldering neglect, the personal conflicts that arise must not be underestimated. These families, without doubt, are the most difficult cases for any professional. Trying to decide who you are, what your role is, and whether you are the advocate for the child, for the parents, or for the whole family is most difficult.

One way of handling this difficult ambivalence is to get mad at the parents and stay mad at them throughout the follow-up period; this usually results in frequent missed appointments and excessive resistance to any interventions. Another way is to establish a close rapport with the parents; this ultimately leads to empathy, frustration, and anger. The anger mounts when the parents do not follow up, give medications, or come in 2 or 3 weeks late for medical problems. The anger mounts when the community services are insufficient or are withdrawn. One becomes upset and annoyed with the parents, many of whom are truly trying but clearly do not have the capabilities to change. If while developing a close relationship with the parents, one ignores the children's lack of progress and other obvious components of neglect, this leads to a variety of external pressures from school teachers, public health nurses, and others who are saying, "Why don't you do something? You're the doctor." One's objectivity may diminish as the closeness to these families increases. Seeing them frequently is very helpful, but some of the smoldering, slowly developing problems may become less obvious.

Directing one's attention solely to the children and dealing with their problems, ignoring the parents, leads to a rapid breakdown in the rapport and increases the problems of neglect.

The personal anguish that results, the sleepless nights of trying to determine the proper approach, is inevitable. Some families are followed from the birth of their children. Over a 2- to 3-year period, one may get used to the problem, "accepting the way in which the kids are handled." When a new public health nurse or an extension worker arrives in the home, they may be aghast at what they find and wonder why in the world the problem has been allowed to go on for so long.

Some neglecting families barely reach acceptable standards of care, even with the help of extensive intervention. All may hit the fan, as it did in the early 1980s, when our federal policies result in cutbacks of significant family services. Marginal families who were just meeting acceptable standards began to collapse. Extension workers were pulled out, protective service workers' caseloads were increased, public health nurses could no longer make twice-weekly visits, and school systems were losing professionals. As children's nutritional status declined, their growth became less and less acceptable.

The personal problems grow as the inevitable becomes clear. When children who are being neglected do not appear for several weeks or months at a time because of the lack of transportation and other social services available to them, and when they eventually arrive at the clinic underweight, with hollow sunken eyes, the dismay grows. At this point, one is not certain at whom the anger should be directed—At the nebulous "system"? At the retarded or psychiatrically and physically ill parents? At one's self?—but one certainly is angry. After becoming close to such a family during many years of follow-up, the next step then becomes extremely painful.

SEPARATION OF PARENTS AND CHILDREN

As all the interactions with a family are summarized by a review of the records and the litany of the failures of these parents is documented, the gnawing feeling that the children should be taken out of the home and placed into a foster home develops. The ensuing pain that results leads one to wonder how he or she ever got into this situation in the first place. The results of saying to a family, "You just can't hack it any more. I am going to court to testify about what lousy parents you have been all these years," can only be felt and not described. Of course, these are not the words actually used, but as the story unfolds, the truth of that crude message is heard over and over again. Is the professional an advocate for the children, the parents, or the family? As objectivity is questioned by one's

peers, nurses, the public health system, protective service workers, and oneself, the outcome is clear. Often, what is right is to say, "These children deserve a better environment." Without exception, the most difficult aspect of working with these families is when the physician and other professionals find themselves in court being asked to testify about a family they have known well for several years and recommending the ultimate, a "parentectomy," the separation of children from their parents.

This should not imply, or even hint, that most or even a small segment of children who are neglected over a long-term basis are removed from their homes. The court system often does not permit this to occur; the legal rules of evidence are often contrary to the best interests of these children. If separation does occur, and the children are still young and have the good fortune of being placed in a superb, warm, stimulating, "cuddly" foster home, the outcome can be truly amazing. A developmental unfolding occurs before one's eyes, as if by magic.

A brief vignette may help place these various issues into proper perspective. A family of three children with a retarded mother and father was followed for approximately 2 years. The ages of the children were 6 years, 3 years, and 18 months. During this period, they had visited the pediatric clinic and were seen by the same pediatrician or one of the residents on 52 occasions. The father consumed a good deal of alcohol but worked on a regular basis at a local bowling alley. The mother was retarded, functioning at a level of about 70 IQ. The father's IQ was not much greater. While the children did not have any serious physical problems, they did have recurrent, low-grade staphylococcal infections of the skin. The baby had stool retention, beginning at the age of 3 months. Growth and development were slow in all of the children, each falling below the third percentile for height and weight and well below the acceptable standards in their development.

Finally, over a period of time and after great pressures from the public health nurse, extension workers, schools, and others who were working with the family, a court hearing was sought. The petition was accepted, and a request by the parents' lawyer to have a jury trial was permitted.

The long-standing, close relationship between the health care providers and the parents broke apart as a result of the testimony in court. As the presentation of the litany of neglect that was documented in the children's record unfolded, one could legitimately criticize the providers of care, particularly the physician, for waiting so long to seek court involvement. The precipitating event was a staphylococcal infection in the mother which resulted in her hospitalization. A single episode of physical abuse (the first) to one of the children by the father followed. While this was relatively minor, it created great stress for the father and for those who were following the family.

At the meeting with the parents, when the physician told them of the upcoming court hearing, crying and wailing ensued as the 18-month-old child sat in the corner, rocking and playing with his fist. He had no language to speak, could not yet walk at that time, and still suffered from severe, ongoing stool impaction.

The jury trial resulted in the placement of the three children in two foster homes. The two youngest went to a superb home of an elderly "grandmother-type" woman who cared for them with great diligence. The children were seen in follow-up by the same physician. They began to make marked improvement, both physically and developmentally. The younger child blossomed in his development. At 22 months, while being measured, he insisted on standing up against the wall rather than lying on the table. When the triangle was placed on his head to check his height, he looked at it, and the first words the physician heard from this child after 55 outpatient visits were, "That's a triangle!" His stool impaction cleared within 6 weeks, his walking progressed so that within 3 months, he was running, and he was becoming very verbal in his interactions with others. One can compare this experience only to time-lapse photography as these children developmentally unfolded before everyone's eyes.

As the emotions and guilt that mounted during the court hearing and later during the breakup of the marriage after the children were removed are compared to the elation and satisfaction of seeing each of these children improve dramatically developmentally, socially, physically, each seems to counteract the other. As hard as it is to admit, this family structure was expendable. The children ultimately were permanently adopted. They improved dramatically. The parents' relationship collapsed, and now, they are trying to find their own way in our social system that provides minimal support for retarded adults.

EPILOGUE

There is no good ending to the story of the smoldering neglect of at least 650,000 children each year in our country. Cutbacks in the social service system by federal, state, and local agencies, the decrease in federal funding for nutritional programs, food stamps, Women, Infants, and Children, and the Medicaid system are all exacerbating the problem.

Without an intensive, multidisciplinary community assessment, follow-up, and treatment program, children who are neglected over long periods of time will continue to smolder and create an inordinate burden upon our societal structure, especially our school systems. The amount of time and money that it takes to educate these children is enormous. While separation from their parents is painful, it occasionally is the only resolution. Our courts and social systems must cooperate in this endeavor if it is going to be successful. Extensive and multifaceted intervention programs can be most successful if they become ongoing, long-term commitments. Interventions cannot be short term. For those children who remain with their families, these services must continue until they are old enough to fend for themselves. While the cost of this type of intervention, including that which is necessary for the school system, is almost prohibitive, the cost of not caring for these families is enormous.

READINGS

Lolly, J. R. 1984. Three Views of Child Neglect: Expanding Visions of Preventive Intervention. *Child Abuse and Neglect: International J.* 8: 243-54.

Polansky, N. A.; Chalmers, M. A.; Buttenwieser, E.; and William, D. P. 1981. *Damaged Parents.* Chicago: University of Chicago Press.

Polansky, N. A.; Guadin, J. M., Jr.; Ammons, P. W.; and Davis, K. B. 1985. The Psychological Ecology of the Neglectful Mother. *Child Abuse and Neglect: International J.* 9: 265-75.

Wolock, I., and Horowitz, B. 1979. Child Maltreatment and Maternal Deprivation among AFDC-Recipient Families. *Social Services Review* 53: 175-94.

24

Reliable and Fictitious Accounts of Sexual Abuse to Children

DAVID P. H. JONES
J. MELBOURNE McGRAW   1987

"Reliable and Fictitious Accounts of Sexual Abuse to Children" was published in 1987 on the heels of several years of extensive media attention in the United States to the issue of childhood sexual abuse in general, resulting in skyrocketing reports of suspected sexual abuse and growing concern about the possibility of children creating fictitious accounts of such abuse. This paper is seen as a landmark largely because it is the first to address the growing concerns through a differentiated examination of sexual abuse reports.

As explained by Kathleen Faller, in their analysis of data from the Denver County Children's Protective Services agency and the Kempe National Center, Drs. Jones and McGraw break down the widely used designation of "founded" and "unfounded" cases into reliable accounts, recantations of reliable accounts, insufficient information, unsubstantiated suspicions, fictitious reports by adults, and fictitious reports by children. In addressing two widely held concerns, the findings showed that the number of fictitious reports was a small proportion of all reports and that adults were more likely than children to offer such fictitious reports. Faller also notes that the study offers, for the first time, a list of factors generated by a group of experts (rather than a single individual) which could be used to differentiate false reports from true ones.

As Theresa Reid points out, the learning from this piece of work have as much value today as when it was published. For example, in discussing the implications of the findings, the authors points out that those making fictitious allegations are not just acting on whim or malice but are likely quite disturbed and thus as much in need of services as those making reliable reports.

The study's findings, as pointed out by the authors themselves, are not definitive. They are preliminary and as such should form the basis for further study—which they have done. Furthermore, the authors note that because there is no absolute test of truthfulness, the clinical findings, such as those offered in this study, must be viewed with caution. Concerns about the study's shortcomings rest with others in addition to the authors. Gary Melton notes, for example, that the study lacks measures of interrater reliability, resulting in conclusions based to a large extent on a particular clinician's opinions about the validity of allegations.

Melton also reflects on what a shame it is that among the "highly influential papers" of the past several decades is one that focuses on "whodunit" rather than on "what we can do." In response, this paper is very much a reflection of the times in which the research was done and the results were published. And, still today, even as questions of what to do about it abound with greater frequency, the public and the field still are very much caught up in whodunit.

A. C. D. and K. O.

Reporting suspected sexual abuse is mandated by law in most of the United States. Local social service departments break down these reports into two broad categories and label them "founded" or "unfounded," or substantiated/unsubstantiated, valid/invalid. Unfounded reports usually make up approximately half of any area's reports (National Committee for Prevention of Child Abuse, 1986). The implication has been made that such unfounded cases may represent false allegations of abuse (Renshaw, 1985) but, as yet, there is a lack of adequate data on which to base this assertion. On the other hand, from a clinical perspective, false reports of sexual abuse to children are generally considered to be an unusual occurrence (Goodwin, Sahd, & Rada, 1982; Horowitz, Salt, Gomes-Schwartz, & Sauzier, 1985; Peters, 1976).

The purpose of the present study was to discover what varieties of situations were included in the broad categories of founded and unfounded, to find out how often child sexual abuse reports were false, to describe the features of false cases, and to derive clinical and research implications from the study of these cases.

The study consisted of two phases. The first was a pilot investigation of the types of reports of suspected sexual abuse made to a city's social service department during 1 year. The second was a clinical study of allegations considered to be false after evaluation at a child abuse study center. The overall aim was to use clinical experience to review large numbers of reports as well as to evaluate cases in depth in order to see if common themes were evident in such cases.

PHASE 1

Sample

The Phase 1 sample consisted of all reports of suspected sexual abuse made to Denver Department of Social Services (DSS) during 1983 ($N = 576$). The reports were received from neighbors, relatives, day care providers, and professionals. Each report was investigated by the Sexual Abuse Team of Denver DSS before being designated founded or unfounded.

Method

We approached a local DSS and were granted permission to study all child sex abuse case records (provided the use of identifying information was avoided in our report). Preliminary discussions with the DSS Sexual Abuse Team caseworkers established that there were different categories of reports that were made to them. The caseworkers then classified all

---

Originally published in *Journal of Interpersonal Violence*, 1987, 2, 27-45. Reprinted by permission of *Journal of Interpersonal Violence*.

TABLE 24.1 Sexual Abuse Reports in Denver, 1983

Type of Report	N	Percentage	Denver Department of Social Services Category
Reliable	284	49	Founded
Recantation	25	4	(N = 309; 53%)
Insufficient information	137	24	Unfounded
Unsubstantiated suspicion	96	17	(N = 267; 47%)
Fictitious from adult	26	5	
Fictitious from child	8	1	
Total	576	100	

reports made during 1983 using the definitions set out below. When the caseworker was unsure, the record was reviewed by the researchers and placed into the appropriate category. The following categories were used:

- *Reliable accounts* were reports considered by the caseworkers to be convincing accounts of child sexual abuse. They included those cases that were corroborated in the legal sense.
- *Recantations* were reliable accounts that were subsequently retracted by the child. The retraction was considered to be falsely made under duress (Summit, 1983).
- *Unsubstantiated suspicions* were reported by an adult about a child. The adult reported his or her suspicion of child sexual abuse without malice. The reporter accepted the conclusion of DSS that sex abuse had not occurred. Abuse was not alleged, nor was an adult accused, merely suspicion reported.[1]
- *Insufficient information* reports were those for which DSS did not have enough data to conclude whether or not child sexual abuse had occurred.
- *Fictitious*[2] *reports by adults* were made about children, yet considered by DSS to have not occurred. Deliberate falsifications, misperceptions, and confused interpretations of nonsexual events were all potentially included in this category.
- *Fictitious reports by children* were those in which the child provided an account of sexual abuse that was considered falsely made. As in the previous category, falsifications

and misperceptions were included, as well as situations where the child had been coached by an adult to make a false account.

The caseworkers' classifications were reviewed by the research team for agreement. There was agreement between caseworkers and the research team on all cases categorized as recantations. Chosen at random were 10 cases from each of the categories insufficient information, unsubstantiated suspicion, and reliable accounts, and there was full agreement. The category fictitious account by an adult contained 11 cases out of 36 (31%) where the researchers considered there was insufficient evidence to allow a diagnosis to be made. These 11 were recategorized by the researchers as insufficient evidence. (One fictitious account by child case was in fact made by the child's parent on behalf of the child; this case was reviewed with the caseworker and categorized as fictitious account by adult.)

RESULTS

Table 24.1 shows the types of reports of suspected sexual abuse made to DSS during 1983. DSS considered that reliable reports and recantations constituted their overall category founded (N = 309; 53%). The remainder were considered unfounded reports (N = 267; 47%). Recantations (N = 25) made up

TABLE 24.2 Types of Sex Abuse
Allegation, Denver, 1983

Type of Allegation	N	Percentage
Reliable and recantations	309	70
Unsubstantiated suspicion	96	22
Fictitious by adult	26	6 ⎤ 8
Fictitious by child	8	2 ⎦
Total	439	100

9% of the total number of founded cases of sexual abuse (N = 309).

The proportion of fictitious allegations can be considered by subtracting reports where there was insufficient evidence and regarding the remainder as suspicions or allegations of possible sexual abuse (N = 439).

As can be seen in Table 24.2, 8 allegations were fictitiously made by children and 26 by adults on behalf of their children. There were 96 cases of unsubstantiated suspicion. Regarded in this way, 70% of the suspicions of sexual abuse turned out to be reliable cases. The fictitious cases are now looked at further.

There were eight fictitious allegations made by five individual children. One child made three separate allegations and another child made two. Four of these five were disturbed female teenagers who had been sexually victimized by an adult in the past but had made this current allegation fictitiously. The circumstances of the allegation, alleged event, and circumstances were incompatible with the allegation made. The youngsters had symptoms suggestive of posttraumatic stress disorder (PTSD) with sleep disturbance, recollection symptoms, and a disturbance of affect. The fifth child was 4 years old and produced an account with his mother that appeared fictitious by the criteria described below.

The case records of the fictitious cases made by an adult were inadequate, precluding a detailed review. However, two adults were parents with major psychiatric disturbance who appeared to have made an improbable allegation based upon their delusions. In other cases, allegations of sexual abuse had arisen in the context of a custody or visitation dispute.

PHASE 2

The Kempe Center is an institute of the University of Colorado Department of Pediatrics. It is involved in training and research and has a small clinical program to which cases are referred by local DSS and other professionals.

Before describing Phase 2 of the study in detail, we will describe the process of validation used at the Kempe Center.

The Process of Validation

All cases were carefully weighed, and a clinical decision made as to the validity of the allegation. We do not have an absolutely reliable test of the occurrence of child sexual abuse. As clinicians, we are usually faced with a child's statement that abuse has occurred, and an opposing adult statement that it has not. Thus, the clinical decision consisted of the gathering of relevant data, followed by deciding what degree of confidence could be applied to the conclusion as to whether sexual abuse had occurred or whether the allegation seemed fictitious. Hence, we avoided a simple true-or-false dichotomy and chose instead to consider allegations along a spectrum extending from reliable accounts on the one hand to fictitious allegations on the other.

The factors that were taken into account when making the clinical judgment about the veracity of suspicion of sexual abuse are outlined below. An assessment was also made as to whether the alleged events could possibly have taken place within the time frame and in the place described in the allegation. This involves liaison with police officers in order to assess such issues. If a child alleged vaginal penetration or the presence of other individuals during the abuse, corroboration was sought. In such situations, an absence of corroboration contributed to a decision that the report was fictitious. Some children said their account was false and gave a good reason (unlike the recantations of reliable accounts, in which statements sounded pressured and contrived). In the fictitious cases, we were able to reconstruct a dynamic sequence through which the fictitious allegation had probably arisen. Like Benedek and Schetky (1985), we considered the diagnosis, fictitious allegation, incomplete without such a formulation. Finally, we stress that one dubious factor alone did not lead to a diagnosis of fictitious; rather, the coexistence of several such factors was necessary.

Factors in Validation

The factors presented here are based upon clinical experience and review of those authors who have described their experience with this process of validation (Faller, 1984; Goodwin et al., 1982; Sgroi, Porter, & Blick, 1982; Trankell, 1972; Undeutsch, 1982).

The Child's Statement

The statement was examined for explicit detail of the alleged sexual abuse. Younger children, particularly under the age of 5, were not able to relate as much detail as older children (Goodman & Helgeson, 1985). Detailed description of sexual acts was considered unlikely without personal experience.

Unique or distinguishing detail was looked for in the description of the sexual encounter and/or in surrounding circumstances. Such detail included unpredicted, unique, or unusual aspects of the account, for example, descriptions of unusual smells and tastes associated with rectal, vaginal, or oral sex. Such detail was also found in the description of the room, surrounding circumstances, or the clothing people wore.

The child's *words and sentence formation* should have been congruent with the age and developmental status of the child. Children did not usually use adult or sophisticated words to describe body parts or sexual functions such as ejaculation. (However, as time passed, some children adopted their therapists' words.) Sentence construction should have been in keeping with age and developmental status. In this regard, early statements of the child were often more helpful than later ones. The sentence construction and words used by the child when describing sexual abuse were compared with those used by the child when describing less emotionally charged events.

A *child's perspective* was looked for in the statement. This revealed a perspective of the abuse that could have originated only from the child him- or herself, because of either a child's visual perspective or how a child organizes events.

The *emotion expressed* by the child during the interview was usually congruent with the events being described. However, two caveats were made. First, a child may have experienced one element of the abuse as more offensive than another, and this difference could have been different from the adult evaluator's notion as to what might have been the worst part of the abuse. Second, seriously traumatized children may have had a blunted emotional response. The way in which the account was given to the evaluator was examined. Accounts that were delivered in response to the slightest of prompts from the interviewer, or related in a rehearsed, packaged manner with an absence of appropriate emotion were considered with suspicion, as were those that lacked the usual difficulty, reserve, or hesitancy. We assessed whether the emotion expressed was apparently genuinely experienced or hollow in its character.

Quite apart from emotion expressed during the interview, the child's *psychological response* to the abusive incident was sought. We looked for typical emotional responses such as fear, anger, depression, guilt, dissociation, and feelings of low self-worth.

The *pattern of the abuse* was examined. Often, intercourse was not involved, and the abuse consisted of genital fondling or oral sex. When the abuse was committed by a person known to the child, it was common for there to be multiple incidents over time and a progression in the severity of the sexual contact over the time period involved. In many cases, the child was required to perform some sexual act upon the abuser.

An element of *secrecy* was usual, whereby the child was made to feel that the sexual activity had to be kept hidden either from specific individuals or from the outside world. The child may have been coerced into sexual activity and/or instructed not to tell about it afterward. Sometimes, children were told that they would be physically harmed or removed from people whom they loved, or that some dreadful fate would befall one of their relatives or friends. Such *coercion and threats* were covert or overt.

Other features were less common, but, if present, lent credence to the account. These included pornographic involvement, sadism, and ritualism. Pornographic involvement sometimes consisted of involvement in a sex ring. On occasion, it was produced for consumption within the family or by a group of families who shared sexual interests in their children.

Supporting Features

The features considered below either lent weight to or detracted from the child's statement itself.

The *history of the family* provided supportive information. The biography of individual family members, as well as the nature of family interaction, was helpful. The accused's track record of violence, spouse abuse, alcohol and substance abuse, or criminal involvement was sought. Similarly, the nonabusive parent's attitude and response to the allegation of sexual abuse was scrutinized to see if it was in keeping with the responses seen in other corroborated cases. The family may have had a prior history of neglecting or abusing children. Frequently, there was intergenerational abuse and neglect. The parent's attachment to the child provided

further data, as did family interaction and functioning. The parents often had a history of sexual abuse as children, such a history being more common among incestuous parents.

The *behavior of the child* during the period when abuse was occurring, or the phase directly afterward, often showed typical features. These included anxiety features, sexually inappropriate behaviors and knowledge, depression, sleep and appetite disturbances, and symptoms of a PTSD. Older children displayed more acting-out behavior, running away, lying, stealing, conduct disturbance, drug and alcohol abuse, and suicide or self-harming behaviors.

The child's *disclosure* of abuse was examined to see if it was similar to other confirmed and corroborated cases. We looked to see if the account unfolded in the familiar way, whereby the child gradually overcame his or her internal reluctance, reserve, and fear (Summit, 1983). The timing of the disclosure was examined to see if it was understandable in terms of the pressures to remain silent. We noted whom the child told and why.

The child's *statement to the other people* was examined. A child usually told one of his or her friends initially, or a neighbor, baby-sitter, trusted adult, teacher, or professional person. The content of this statement was then compared with other statements made by the child.

Consistency between different statements made by a single child was regarded as more complicated than it first appeared. We noted that there was usually, in truthful accounts, consistency with respect to the core elements of abuse, but there was often variation in the more peripheral aspects (Goodman & Helgeson, 1985). Thus, the question of consistency was not an either/or situation. It varied with the degree of personal poignancy of the particular experience and its meaning for that child. Similarly, violent elements such as coercion or threat may have been so terrifying for the child that disclosure would be delayed (Lister, 1982). Thus, inconsistencies such as these in a child's account over time could be more indicative of a reliable account than a false statement made with monotonous consistency and no variation over time.

The way in which a child used *toys, play things, and drawing materials* was often revealing. Drawings sometimes contained highly sexual themes. More commonly, play showed evidence of the emotional unavailability of parent figures, neglect and abuse that acted as a substrate to sexual abuse within the family. In cases of abuse by strangers, sexualized themes occurred commonly.

The child's *knowledge of sexual anatomy and function* was often asynchronous with those of similar age and social background. We took into account the subcultural setting in which the child lived, as there is much variation between families as to the degree of personal nudity and knowledge of sexual activity permitted.

Other children who were involved or in the same household may have had a viewpoint concerning the sexual abuse of the index child. Such children may have seen the abuse occurring, had knowledge of it, or have been additional victims, and so their statements were sought.

Physical and Physiological Evidence

Gross physical evidence of sexual abuse occurs in approximately 15% of cases (Kerns, 1981). Paul (1977) has provided a detailed description of the possible physical abnormalities in the sexually abused child. Evidence of ejaculation was sought in vaginal, rectal, and oral orifices, as well as evidence of tissue damage or abnormal stretching created by attempted or actual penetration (Krugman & Jones, 1986). Cantwell (1983) has pointed to more subtle findings in sexually abused girls that may give an indication of possible abuse. Physiological correlates of truthfulness, such as the polygraph examination, have not been subjected to sufficiently rigorous studies so as to provide a reliable measure of truthfulness.

Cases exist with clear evidence in which the abuser passes a polygraph with ease.

The approach presented above involved assessing as many of the above features as possible and the relative weight of the individual elements in any single case. At the time of writing, the major emphasis is on the child's statement itself.

Sample

Phase 2 consisted of the 21 false (fictitious) cases of child sexual abuse that were seen at the Kempe National Center between 1983 and 1985. During this period, 696 reliable cases were also seen. These latter cases provided a pool of clinical experience against which to make observations about the fictitious ones.

Method

All cases of child sexual abuse evaluated between 1983 and 1985 were subjected to the process of validation described above. The 21 cases described consist of all the cases considered to be fictitious seen during the years 1983-1985. The fictitious cases were classified into three groups: those made by the child, those made primarily by an adult, and those mixed cases in which both adult and child alleged that the child was a victim of sexual abuse, and it was unclear who first generated the allegation.

One of us (David Jones) categorized the quality of the investigative interview (DSS or police) that had preceded referral to the Kempe Center. The interview was regarded as *adequate* or *inadequate,* depending upon if it was too brief or developmentally inappropriate (e.g., interviewer used double negatives), if it contained excessive leading questions, if anatomically correct dolls were used in a leading manner, or if it simply was *not done* (i.e., no interview with the child).

Results

The Kempe Center sample of 21 fictitious cases consisted of 17 girls and 4 boys ages 1 to 10 years. Of the 21 cases, 5 were made by the child, 9 by an adult, and 7 were mixed.

The five *fictitious accounts from children* were made by girls between 3 and 9 years of age. Four children were documented to have been sexually abused before the current allegations and were suffering from untreated PTSD when the current allegation arose. One child's parents were involved in a custody dispute. All five children made their allegations with little or no accompanying emotion when they described the abuse. Similarly, descriptions of threats were absent from their accounts. In four cases, there were no distinguishing or unusual features described, and the expected child's perspective on the abuse was absent. However, the accounts contained considerable detail, even though adjudged fictitious. For example:

> Two children were in foster care because they had been physically and sexually abused by their stepfather. While in placement, they made a fresh allegation following a supervised visit that the stepfather had reabused them. The new allegations were detailed, yet were made with little accompanying emotion, no coercive or threatening elements, and simply could not have occurred during the time frame or setting of the supervised visit. Furthermore, each child described the original family home when asked to describe the place where reabuse had occurred. This was at variance with their allegation that they had been sexually abused at the DSS office. It later transpired that they had made this fictitious allegation in order to avoid being returned home from foster care.

Nine *fictitious accounts were made by adults.* The adults were all female, with seven being children's mothers and two being professionals. The children who were alleged to have been abused were between 1 and 6 years old—seven girls and two boys. In six of the

nine cases, there was no account provided by the child despite careful and repeated interviewing, and the other three provided minimal information at interview. In seven of the cases, there was a custody/visitation dispute between the mother and her ex-husband. Six of the adults had personal histories of abuse, deprivation, and/or neglect. Five of these showed significant emotional disturbance currently, including the two professionals. The diagnoses were hysterical or paranoid personality disorder and/or symptoms suggestive of PTSD.

There were seven *mixed* cases. In these, it was not clear who had first originated the allegation of sexual abuse. Of the children involved, two were male and five female. Ages ranged from 3 to 10 years. In all cases, there was a bitter custody or visitation dispute in process between the mother and her ex-husband. The allegation concerned the ex-husband in all these cases. All seven mothers were psychiatrically disturbed, with paranoid or hysterical personality disorders. Three of them had evidence of an unresolved PTSD based upon their own childhood experiences of being sexually abused. In these three cases, the mother's abuse had occurred at around the same age as the child who was currently alleged to have been abused. In all seven cases, the mother-child relationship was unusually intense and enmeshed. The child provided emotional support and care for the mother and could be noted frequently checking his or her mother's response and status whenever subjects suspected of upsetting the mother were discussed. In those children who did describe abuse, there was no accompanying emotion or description of coercion/threats in their allegations.

The *quality of the initial investigative interview* was judged. In 8 of the adult fictitious cases, no one had interviewed the child, and it seemed highly probable that the omission had contributed to the confusion about diagnosis. In 10 other cases out of the 21, the interview was judged inadequate, and in only 2 out of 21 was an adequate interview performed.

DISCUSSION

The two phases of this study suggest that fictitious allegations are unusual and that the majority of the suspicions of sexual abuse brought to professional attention prove to be reliable cases. We suggest caution with the interpretation and use of these results, as the DSS survey was a pilot, and the clinical survey was uncontrolled. The definition of *fictitious* used in this study was that professionals did not consider that abuse had occurred. This is subject to error, although in both phases of our study, the conclusion of fictitious always followed a consensus of professional opinion. We therefore suggest that the results be used as a base for further study and not as a definitive basis for proving that a case is or is not "true." (We are aware that our study has already been misused in court for this latter purpose.)

Types of Reports Made

In the first phase, 8% of the allegations were deemed fictitious (after these cases with insufficient information were removed). This figure compares with 7% fictitious allegations found by Goodwin et al. (1982), 6% by Peters (1976), and 5% by Horowitz et al. (1985). Katz and Mazur (1979) found a rate of 2% in their series of adult rape victims, compared with the 2% of fictitious child reports in this study. In Phases 1 and 2, children of all ages made fictitious allegations. The youngest to generate fictitious reports on their own initiative without prior coaching by an adult were a 12-year-old girl in Phase 1 and two 5-year-old girls in Phase 2.

In 24% of all the reports made to DSS, there was insufficient information for any further decision to be made as to their validity. Since 1983, we have heard anecdotally that several of these have surfaced as confirmed cases of sexual abuse in 1984 or 1985. Of the reliably made allegations, 9% were recanted by the children shortly after disclosure. Goodwin et al. (1982)

report a figure closer to 30% for this phenomenon, and we have searched for an explanation of this. Our figure may represent an underestimate because our classifications were made around the time of the initial investigation, whereas the process of recantation reflects the child's gradual capitulation to internal and external pressures (Summit, 1983). Additionally, the child victims in this study received counseling and group therapy through the DSS program, and the lower recantation rate in this study may be a positive reflection of such services. Of the reports, 17% turned out to be unsubstantiated suspicions, reflecting that the law requires individuals to report their suspicions of child sex abuse in Colorado. The other factor that may have generated this high number of unsubstantiated suspicions was the high level of public awareness with local media coverage that had occurred in recent years in Denver.

Features of Fictitious Allegations

There was no formally assigned comparison group for the 21 Kempe Center cases. However, 696 cases were seen during the same period, allowing us to draw preliminary conclusions about the features of fictitious reports that appear to distinguish them from reliable ones. Again, we stress that no one factor alone simply discriminated allegations into reliable and fictitious ones. A lack of accompanying emotion as the abuse was being described was frequently found in the fictitious reports. Other authors have also pointed out this feature (Benedek & Schetky, 1985; Brandt & Sink, 1984; Goodwin et al., 1982; Green, 1986; Undeutsch, 1982). However, blandly delivered accounts of sex abuse do occur in certain circumstances in reliable cases. For example, when children have been subjected to multiple interviews, they may begin to recount their experience with muted emotions over successive interviews. Similarly, children who have been severely traumatized and suffer from PTSD may show an attenuated emotional responsiveness in all areas of life. However, an evaluative interview, which includes a period of free play, appears to allow evidence of conflict and significant emotion to be elicited, even in situations such as those described above.

In children who had been sexually abused in the past, but later made an erroneous allegation that they had been reabused, there was an interesting difference in their emotional expression when describing earlier abuse compared with that when describing the most recent, fictitious incident. When describing the first incident, their attendant emotion was pained, fearful, and sometimes angry, while the current description was delivered blandly, with little expressed concern. This difference was observed in spite of the fact that the current allegation appeared to have arisen in the context of a flashback or recollection experience. The absence of threats or coercive elements in the fictitious allegations was again of interest because in these children's original, corroborated abusive incidents, there was significant violence described. However, in the current, fictitious allegation, the sexual elements were described in full but without a description of accompanying violence. We feel that care must be taken with this finding, because the violence involved in any sexually abusive act may not emerge at the time the child discloses that he or she has been sexually abused (Lister, 1982).

Fictitious reports frequently lacked detail, whereas the reliable ones contained an appropriate amount of detail for the age of the child. However, the maxim that if a child uses explicit detail, then the account must be a true one cannot be relied upon solely, because in this study, those children who were prior victims and suffering from PTSD often provided considerable detail of the current alleged incident. Presumably, this was because they indeed had a clear memory of a prior experience and attached this vivid memory to a new person in their life. As noted above, when children did this, the account lost its affective component and often the element of violence or threat. Hence, detail

alone may have to be treated with care as a discriminating factor. On the other hand, children who were coached, or those who were interviewed inappropriately, were not able to provide explicit details of their experiences. An interesting exception to this was a 3-year-old girl who was coached to make a false allegation, but she had the added factor of having been a prior victim of sexual abuse and thus had vivid personal memories to draw from.

The presence of unique or distinguishing features within the detail of the abuse was useful. Reliable accounts contained this element; however, those children who were suffering from an unresolved PTSD did sometimes include such distinguishing elements, especially concerning their surroundings, but rarely connected to the abuse itself. The language that the child used was often of help. Reliable children used personal pronouns and age-appropriate words and sentence formation when describing abuse. They used personal pronouns such as *I, we,* or *me* when describing their experience, whereas some children making fictitious statements used pronouns such as *they* throughout the interview. (In other cases, where sexual abuse was later corroborated, some children used the pronoun *they* when describing a portion of the abusive experience that was not experienced by them as hurtful, only to change dramatically to the use of the pronoun *I* or *me* when describing events that had a personal poignancy.) Yet again, cases of PTSD raised some problems because the account seemed very real at first. However, if the previous sexually abusive event occurred some years before, when the child was immature, then a careful review of the language used in the current allegation was revealing. For example, one child, age 5, who made a fictitious allegation, used words and sentence structure in keeping with her development when age 3. It turned out that she had been sexually abused when age 3 but by a different person, and this review of language used in the current allegation was one of the factors in determining that the current allegation was fictitious.

In addition to the report and statement of the child or adult, useful information was derived from an examination of the adult or parent-child interaction. In this study, acrimonious custody or visitation disputes were often connected with fictitious allegations. However, in a separate study of child sexual abuse allegations in the context of a custody dispute, there were more occasions when there were *both* a custody dispute and a reliable sex abuse account than cases of false allegation (Jones & Seig, n.d.). In the present study, the mother-child relationships were enmeshed and mutually overly dependent in custody cases, suggesting a possible mechanism for the origin of the report in the child's need to provide emotional nurturance for his or her parent.

The observation that adults who made fictitious reports and who became enmeshed with their children often had personality problems or symptoms of PTSD should be approached with caution, because many nonabusive parents in incest families are childhood incest victims, and the presence of such features per se does not discriminate reliable from fictitious. The presence of residual psychological symptoms related to this experience may be helpful, particularly if the adult gives a history of frequent flashback or recollection experiences. In such situations, the adult lives with a constantly elevated fear, sometimes constituting conviction that he or she is about to be sexually abused again, or that a person for whom he or she cares will meet the same fate.

IMPLICATIONS

Clinical Practice

First, this study suggests there is a need for professionals with specialist training in the areas of child development and the dynamics of child sex abuse to be involved in the initial investigative process. Such a response could be experimentally set up for investigation of cases involving young children or custody disputes and its effectiveness assessed.

Second, there are implications for the type of clinical evaluation required. In selected cases, there is a need for interviews with the child alone and with his or her parent and an assessment of the quality of interaction between child and each parent. Such an evaluation can reveal possible mechanisms and dynamics with which to understand a reliable or fictitious account, particularly in custody or visitation disputes.

Third, the investigation itself should include a clinical process of validation in all cases, so that professionals always keep an open mind and maintain what Goodwin et al. (1982) have termed a "don't yet know" stance while data are being gathered. All too frequently, we saw cases where it appeared that the professional mind had been made up well before sufficient information had been obtained. Fictitious cases can be diagnosed only if the evaluator entertains the possibility that such a situation is feasible.

Fourth, adults and children should be screened for the presence of prior victimization and PTSD. Such a past history should not be taken as a sign of falsehood; rather, it should raise caution in the evaluator's mind. In adults who have been sexually abused, symptoms of anxiety or panic episodes, combined with a fear of recurrence, sleep disturbances, and flashbacks, are seen (Horowitz, Wilner, Kaltreider, & Alvarez, 1980). In children, the symptoms are less well defined and include a similar recurrence conviction that may be expressed in play, anxieties about past and possible future abuse, and specific symptoms such as sleep disturbance and panic episodes (Goodwin, 1985). In addition, both adults and children may show an attenuated or muted emotional responsiveness to events that would create more emotion in other individuals.

Fifth, those involved in fictitious allegations, as well as the falsely accused, needed as much help as the reliable cases. The children may continue to believe that they have been sexually abused, especially when involved in overly close and enmeshed relationships with their mothers, as in the fused cases in this series.

Last, the absence of an absolute test of truthfulness implies that clinical conclusions should be offered with caution and due regard as to the degree of certainty that can be applied. In our present state of knowledge, in uncorroborated cases, it would be improper to offer conclusions without reference to what degree of doubt exists.

Research and Future Studies

These findings are presented as preliminary, yet provide a basis for future study. Further work on the cases reported to DSS could be done by researchers blind to the caseworkers' outcome categories in order to test the validity of these operationally defined categories. The impact of having specialist interviewers on specific cases could be explored on a comparative basis to see if diagnostic accuracy can be improved and, if so, which cases will benefit from such an approach. Further research into the physical sequelae of sexual abuse is needed, together with studies of polygraph examinations of accused adults in relation to case outcome. Research approaches could also include the rating of videotaped interviews of sexually abused children by clinicians who are blind to the eventual case outcome in order to test the reliability and validity of the factors used in validation of an allegation.

NOTES

1. For example, a divorced mother of a 5-year-old girl reported her suspicion of child sexual abuse on the recommendation of her pediatrician because of the girl's vaginal redness and irritation after weekend visits with her father. The investigation did not reveal evidence of sexual abuse from the child's account, from further medical assessment, or from the quality of interaction between child and each parent. The mother accepted the department's conclusion, and at no point was a false allegation of sexual abuse made, but a suspicion was appropriately reported and investigated.

2. The term *fictitious* is used instead of *false* to avoid a pejorative connotation and to include misperceptions and the like.

REFERENCES

Benedek, E. P., & Schetky, D. H. (1985). Allegations of sexual abuse in child custody and visitation disputes. In D. H. Schetky & E. B. Benedek (Eds.), *Emerging issues in child psychiatry and the law.* New York: Brunner/Mazel.

Brandt, R.S.T., & Sink, F. (1984, October). *Dilemmas in court ordered evaluation of sexual abuse charges during custody and visitation proceedings.* Paper presented at 31st Annual Meeting of American Academy of Child Psychiatry, Toronto.

Cantwell, H. (1983). Vaginal inspection as it relates to young girls. *Child Abuse and Neglect, 7,* 171-176.

Faller, K. C. (1984). Is the child victim of sexual abuse telling the truth? *Child Abuse and Neglect, 8,* 473-481.

Goodman, G. S., & Helgeson, V. S. (1985) Child sexual assault: Children's memory and the law. *University of Miami Law Review, 40,* 181-208.

Goodwin, J. (1985) Post-traumatic symptoms in incest victims. In S. Eth & R. S. Pynoos (Eds.), *Post traumatic stress disorder in children* (pp. 155-168). Washington, DC: American Psychiatric Press.

Goodwin, J., Sahd, D., & Rada, R. T. (1982). False accusations and false denials of incest: Clinical myths and clinical realities. In J. Goodwin (Ed.), *Sexual abuse: Incest victims and their families* (pp. 17-26). Boston: John Wright.

Green, A. H. (1986). True and false allegations of sexual abuse in child custody disputes. *Journal of the American Academy of Child Psychiatry, 25,* 449-456.

Horowitz, J. M., Salt, P., Gomes-Schwartz, B., & Sauzier, M. (1985). *False accusations of child sexual abuse.* Unpublished manuscript.

Horowitz, M. J., Wilner, N., Kaltreider, N., & Alvarez, W. (1980). Signs and symptoms of post traumatic stress disorder. *Archives of General Psychiatry, 37,* 85-92.

Jones, D. P. H., & Seig, A. (n.d.). *Fictitious accounts of sexual abuse in child custody and visitation disputes.* Unpublished manuscript.

Katz, S., & Mazur, M. A. (1979). The false rape report. In S. Katz & M. A. Mazur, *Understanding the rape victim* (pp. 205-214). New York: John Wiley.

Kerns, D. L. (1981). Medical assessment in child sexual abuse. In P. B. Mrazek & C. H. Kempe (Eds.), *Sexually abused children and their families* (pp. 126-141). Oxford: Pergamon.

Krugman, R., & Jones, D. P. H. (1986). Incest and other forms of sexual abuse. In R. Helfer & R. S. Kempe

(Eds.), *The battered child* (4th ed.). Chicago: University of Chicago Press.

Lister, E. D. (1982). Forced silence: A neglected dimension of trauma. *American Journal of Psychiatry, 139,* 867-872.

National Committee for Prevention of Child Abuse. (1986). *What do we know about unsubstantiated child abuse reports.* Chicago: Author.

Newsweek. (1985, February). *The youngest witness: Is there a witch hunt mentality in sex abuse cases?*

Paul, D. M. (1977). The medical examination in sexual offenses against children. *Medicine Science and the Law, 17,* 251-258.

Peters, J. J. (1976). Children who are victims of sexual assault and the psychology of offenders. *American Journal of Psychotherapy, 30,* 598-642.

Renshaw, D. C. (1985). When sex abuse is falsely charged. *Medical Aspects of Human Sexuality, 19,* 44-52.

Sgroi, S. M., Porter, F. S., & Blick, L. C. (1982). Validation of child sexual abuse. In S. M. Sgroi (Ed.), *Handbook of clinical intervention in child sexual abuse* (pp. 39-79). Lexington, MA: D. C. Heath.

Summit, R. (1983). The child sexual abuse accommodation syndrome. *Child Abuse and Neglect, 7,* 177-193.

Trankell, A. (1972). *The reliability of evidence.* Stockholm: Rotobeckmans.

Undeutsch, V. (1982). Statement reality analysis. In A. Trankell (Ed.), *Reconstructing the past: The role of psychologists in criminal trials* (pp. 27-56). Stockholm: P. A. Norsted & Sons.

25

Does Violence Beget Violence?
A Critical Examination
of the Literature

CATHY SPATZ WIDOM   1989

W hat makes parents abuse their children? It is human nature to want to seek simple answers to complex problems, but complex problems such as child abuse have no simple answers. In this paper, Widom challenged the widely held view that abuse in one generation causes abuse to reappear in the next. She achieved this by a comprehensive, critical review of the literature including an analysis of the methodology used in many studies that claimed to support the intergenerational transmission hypothesis.

Widom pointed out that the evidence that abuse breeds abuse is problematic and limited by overdependence on self-reports, retrospective data, and infrequent use of control groups.

One of the most widely cited observations to support the intergenerational hypothesis is Steele and Pollock's (1968) "A Psychiatric Study of Parents Who Abuse Infants and Small Children." However, Widom points out that although this paper is often cited by those who support the

intergenerational transmission view, Steele and Pollock were careful to acknowledge the limitations of their observations, as they were based on a series of clinical investigations.

Charles Wilson points out that besides challenging the prevailing dogma about the intergenerational transmission of abuse, this paper brings together and reviews three decades of research on this topic. He says that, in addition, Widom gives the reader a review of research design, pointing out the methodological limitations of the often-cited studies that have been used to support the intergenerational hypothesis.

It is not that Widom denies that there is intergenerational transmission of abuse, but rather that she points out that it is an oversimplification and that it applies only to a minority of cases. This leads to the notion that although parents who were physically abused in their childhood are at greater risk of becoming abusive parents, the majority do not. Widom's review shows that most adults who abuse their children were not abused in their own childhoods.

Widom also called for studies that distinguish neglected from abused children rather than studies that include abused and neglected children as a single group, a problem that still occurs today.

Finally, Widom demonstrated that abuse can have results other than aggressive behavior, such as withdrawal and self-destructive behavior, and she then calls for more studies directed at finding why some children from violent, abusive families appear to be invulnerable to these effects. What is it that protects them?

Charles Wilson points out that Widom showed that abuse experiences are but one part of a complex model that includes other life experiences and that places some families at risk for abusive behavior. This paper encouraged others to explore these complex relationships.

A. C. D. and K. O.

Violence increasingly affects all of us. According to a recent report by Langan and Innes (1985), 3% of Americans each year are victims of violent crime, the equivalent of approximately 6 million people. During 1984, a violent crime—murder, rape, robbery, or an aggravated assault—occurred every 25 seconds.

Of the total instances of violent crime, domestic violence is considered to be the most common. Severe violence may be a chronic feature of almost 13% of all marriages in the United States (Straus, 1977). A U.S. Department of Justice (1980) survey estimated that there were 1.2 million occurrences of violence among relatives, and another more recent survey estimates that at least 1,200 children died in 1986 as a result of abuse and neglect. According to Straus, Gelles, and Steinmetz (1980), between 1.4 million and 2.3 million children have been beaten up by a parent at some time during their childhood.[1]

Considerable uncertainty and debate remain about the extent of family violence, yet, even less is known about its effects. For children who have been abused or neglected, the immediate consequences may involve physical injuries or psychological trauma. The emotional and developmental scars that these children and those who witness severe family violence receive may persist.

One of the most pervasive claims that appears in the scholarly and popular literature refers to the cycle of violence: Abused children become abusers, and victims of violence become violent victimizers. Over 25 years ago, in a brief clinical note entitled "Violence Breeds Violence—Perhaps?", Curtis (1963) expressed the concern that abused and neglected children would "become tomorrow's murderers and perpetrators of other crimes of violence, if they survive" (p. 386).

The idea that violence begets violence is firmly established in the minds of professionals and the general public alike. In the words of Garbarino and Gilliam (1980),

> The premier developmental hypothesis in the field of abuse and neglect is, of course, the notion of intergenerational transmission, the idea that abusing parents were themselves abused as children and that neglect breeds neglect. (p. 111)

The idea is appealing; it makes intuitive sense. To paraphrase Garbarino and Gilliam (1980), however, the alleged relationship has not really "passed scientific muster" (p. 111). Because many other events in the child's life (such as natural abilities, physiological predispositions, social supports, and so on) may mediate the effects of child abuse and/or ne-

Originally published in *Psychological Bulletin*, 1989, *106*, 3-28. Used by permission.

glect, the long-term consequences of such childhood victimization are difficult to determine and remain unclear.

Much has been written about the context of violence in our culture (McCall & Shields, 1986) and the importance of force and violence in our society. A number of writers have argued that societal approval of such behaviors legitimates and reinforces the use of violence (Gil, 1973; Huggins & Straus, 1980; Steinmetz, 1977) and that the norms prohibiting violent behavior represent "legal" rules adopted by certain subcultures, rather than the informal codes of conduct practiced by others (Wolfgang & Ferracuti, 1967). There also is evidence of a high degree of acceptance of interpersonal violence in our society (R. A. Stark & McEvoy, 1970). Thus, given this cultural context of violence, learning to become violent through "normal" child-rearing experiences might not be too difficult or unusual (Goldstein, 1986).

From a social learning perspective, physical aggression between family members provides a likely model for the learning of aggressive behavior as well as for the appropriateness of such behavior within the family (Bandura, 1973; Feshbach, 1980). Children learn behavior, at least in part, by imitating someone else's behavior. Thus, children learn to be aggressive through observing aggression in their families and the surrounding society (Feshbach, 1980). According to this view, "each generation learns to be violent by being a participant in a violent family" (Straus et al., 1980, p. 121).

Over the last 10 years, the scholarly literature on family violence has grown enormously. A number of reviews have appeared that focus on child abuse (Belsky, 1980; Parke & Collmer, 1975; Vasta, 1982), the abused child (Friedrich & Einbender, 1983), child-abusive parents (Friedrich & Boriskin, 1976; Friedrich & Wheeler, 1982; Wolfe, 1985), and family violence (Lystad, 1975; Straus et al., 1980). Few, however, address the "violence breeds violence" hypothesis. Those that do are often unpublished conference papers (Potts, Herz-

berger, & Holland, 1979), not readily available (C. P. Smith, Berkman, & Fraser, 1980), or out of print (Hunner & Walker, 1981). Two recent exceptions are a review by Kaufman and Zigler (1987), which focuses on the intergenerational transmission of violence from abused child to abusive parent, and one by Garbarino and Plantz (1986), which examines the link between child abuse and juvenile delinquency.

The purpose of this article is to assess the "violence breeds violence" hypothesis by drawing on empirical evidence from a number of different disciplines—psychology, sociology, criminology, psychiatry, social work, and nursing. Researchers and professionals have used the phrases *cycle of violence* and *intergenerational transmission of violence* rather loosely to refer to assumptions or hypotheses about the consequences of abuse and neglect in relation to a number of different dependent variables. Some writers refer exclusively to the idea that abused children become abusive parents (Kaufman & Zigler, 1987). Others focus on the relationships between child abuse and neglect and later delinquent, adult criminal, or violent behaviors. At present, there is a need for a comprehensive and critical assessment of the existing empirical literature on the "violence begets violence" hypothesis broadly defined.

To facilitate this review, I have organized the literature into sections that represent hypotheses implicitly subsumed within the broader "cycle of violence" hypothesis. The first section summarizes writings that address the "abuse breeds abuse" question directly, and the second describes reports of abuse in the backgrounds of small numbers of violent or homicidal offenders. The next sections review studies relating abuse and neglect to delinquency and those linking abuse and neglect to violent behavior. Studies from the developmental psychology literature that examine the relationship between abuse, neglect, and aggressive behavior in infants and young children are reviewed next. A short section follows that reviews research on abuse, withdrawal, and self-destructive behavior, and the last section broadens the examination to include studies of the impact of witnessing or observing violent behavior, drawing upon surveys and studies of children of battered women, and of the impact of television violence on aggressive behavior. After briefly summarizing the findings, I draw conclusions about the strength of the cycle of violence.

The literature on child abuse and neglect encompasses a number of distinct phenomena: physical abuse, sexual abuse, neglect, severe physical punishment, and psychological maltreatment. This review focuses on the first four. Despite occasional references to the destructive impact of psychological abuse, the focus here is primarily on physical abuse and severe neglect. Psychological maltreatment is beyond the scope of this article and merits its own extensive coverage (Brassard, Germain, & Hart, 1987; Garbarino, Guttman, & Seeley, 1986).

Also excluded are medical reports that primarily describe proximate or distal physical sequelae of early childhood trauma (cf. Martin, Beezley, Conway, & Kempe, 1974). I conducted computerized searches of psychological and educational abstracts, as well as of the national database on child abuse and neglect through 1985; however, although this review is intended to be representative and comprehensive, it does not purport to be exhaustive.

Finally, because many of the studies included suffer from serious methodological shortcomings, a general discussion of these concerns is necessary to provide a context for the evaluation. Thus, prior to the literature review, I examine methodological considerations.

METHODOLOGICAL CONSIDERATIONS

Over the last several years, scholarly reviews of the child abuse literature have criticized existing research as methodologically flawed and limited in its generalizability, scientific validity, and, ultimately, its policy rel-evance (e.g., Berger, 1980; Newberger, Newberger, & Hampton, 1983). Many of the same limitations characterize studies relevant to the postulated cycle of violence. A number of problems are discussed here that characterize the cycle of violence literature, and they are summarized in the Appendix.

The first problem concerns the lack of specificity in defining predictor and/or outcome variables. Because "child abuse is a community-defined phenomenon which must be viewed in the context of community norms and standards governing the appropriate conduct of adults in their interactions with their own and others' children" (Parke & Collmer, 1975, p. 513), one well-recognized problem in the literature is that of defining the phenomenon. Criteria for child abuse and/or neglect are often questionable, vary widely, and include unsubstantiated cases. Basic differences in the definitions or criteria for abuse or neglect affect not only estimates of its frequency but also the replicability of assessment and research.[2]

In some cases, child abuse is limited to a clinical condition (broken bones or severe physical trauma). For example, a common definition of child abuse is "non-accidental physical injury (or injuries) that are result of acts (or omissions) on the part of the parents or guardians that violate the community standards concerning the treatment of children(170) (Parke & Collmer, 1975). In other cases, criteria might refer to a wider range of activities, milder forms of physical punishment, or even *neglect* (the failure to provide adequate food or clothing or proper care for the child). Most studies restrict their subjects to the victims of excessive physical force by parents, usually in the home environment. Abuse outside the home is rarely addressed, and sexual abuse is typically treated as a separate topic. In some research, sexual abuse cases are included, whereas in others, they are excluded.

Much of the research in this area is based on designs weakened by questionable accuracy of information owing to the retrospective nature of the data or to reliance on second-hand information (e.g., parental reports) rather than on directly observed or validated behaviors. Often, there is no medical or direct evidence of the severity, frequency, or chronicity of abuse.

Although the term *retrospective* usually refers to the time at which data were collected or analyzed, I use the term *retrospective recall bias* to emphasize the risk of distortion and loss of information that result from recalling events from a prior time period. Retrospective data are notoriously unreliable (Yarrow, Campbell, & Burton, 1970). Descriptions of the incidence of certain phenomena differ depending on whether self-reports are made in the context of retrospective or prospective studies (Koeske, 1981; Sommer, 1978).

Studies based on retrospective accounts of abuse or neglect are open to a number of potential biases. If asked to recall events after a period of years, people perceive and describe these events in the context of later circumstances and their present situations, from which they derive much of the events' meaning and significance. Despite people's best intentions, there is a considerable degree of slippage in accuracy in retrospective reporting.

Social desirability factors may also influence people to report behaviors in more favorable terms. Given society's disapproval of various forms of family violence, adults being asked to provide retrospective accounts of earlier experiences might reconstruct their own childhood histories to be consistent with or to explain their present behavior. In designs dependent on retrospective recall for information, then, respondents might "forget" or redefine their behaviors in accord with their current situations. This is of particular concern here because much of the child abuse research tends to be based on self-reports by parents (often mothers) who are typically participants, either voluntarily or involuntarily, in groups for abusing parents. Similarly, defendants charged with serious crimes might believe they would benefit from special leniency or increased empathy from others by claiming early child abuse or severe childhood neglect. In recent

work, the role of social desirability has been recognized and productively incorporated into research designs (Herrenkohl, Herrenkohl, & Toedter, 1983).

Another problem is the use of weak sampling techniques involving opportunity or convenience samples, data gathered from cases that medical or psychiatric practitioners have at hand, or anecdotal clinical accounts or small-scale case studies. A related concern is the ex post facto nature of many of the studies, which offer little predictive power. This is particularly problematic if the design involves a reverse records check—that is, starts with groups that have previously been labeled delinquent. In some cases, this can produce a conservative bias in studies dependent on archival records. The low incidence of abuse recorded before it was mandatory to keep such records probably underestimates rather than overestimates the actual occurrence of abuse (Widom, 1988).

There is an almost universal reliance on correlational studies in the child abuse literature. Although a reasonable place to begin inquiries into new areas of investigation, research based on nonexperimental and correlational studies rarely addresses etiology or causality.

Most studies fail to distinguish between abused and neglected children, treating them as one group. Although there is often overlap in reality, with some children experiencing both abuse and neglect, the practice of routinely treating them as indistinguishable may obscure important behavioral or psychological distinctions.

Research on this topic is also characterized by a widespread lack of appropriate comparison or control groups and a failure to consider statistical base rates. Several researchers have argued that official reports of child abuse overrepresent low-income families (e.g., Newberger, Reed, Daniel, Hyde, & Kotelchuck, 1977). This represents a serious concern because it is clear that abuse and neglect occur in all social classes. However, national surveys of family violence have found that those with the lowest incomes are more likely to abuse their children (Straus et al., 1980). Phrased somewhat differently, low socioeconomic status (SES) characterizes the largest portion of abusive families (Gil, 1973; Pelton, 1978).

Low-income families may have many problems, child abuse being only one of them. Because other factors—poverty, unemployment, parental alcoholism, drug problems, or otherwise inadequate social and family functioning—are often present in such multiproblem homes, control groups matched on SES and other relevant variables become vital components of this research. Being reported for child abuse may be a function of also being poor or unemployed. Such confounding of correlated characteristics needs to be avoided.

Appropriate control groups are also important for another reason. Because many of these same family and demographic characteristics relate to delinquency and later criminality (Friedrich & Einbender, 1983; Loeber & Dishion, 1983; Loeber & Stouthamer-Loeber, 1986), control groups are necessary to assess the independent effects of abuse and neglect. Without control groups to provide a rough estimate of such base rates, it is difficult to assess the magnitude of relationships.

Furthermore, as Monahan (1981) so convincingly argued, the most important single piece of information we can have in the prediction of violence is the base rate for violent behavior in the population with which we are dealing. Particularly in the area of abuse and neglect, there is a tendency to overemphasize individual case information at the expense of base rates. Webster (1978) published base rates of arrests for violent crime for the U.S. population, illustrating that different subgroups have different base rates. Men were arrested for violent crimes nine times more frequently than women, blacks more often than whites, and people in urban areas more often than those in the suburbs. In determining whether particular early childhood experiences lead to later violent behavior, base rates—from the same population of people at the same time period—must be taken into account.

In terms of outcome variables, most studies relate child abuse and neglect to generalized delinquent behavior, depending almost exclusively on juvenile court records. Blind assessments of outcomes are made only rarely. When violent behaviors are examined, criteria range from evidence of assaultive and aggressive behaviors to convictions for violent offenses. For example, Steinmetz (1986) defined violence as "an act carried out with the intention of, or perceived as having the intention of, physically hurting another person" (p. 52). In actuality, this definition includes actions ranging from a slap (slight pain) to murder. On the other hand, Strasburg (1978) defined violent behavior as "illegal use or threat of force against a person" (p. 6). Included here are assault, aggressive assault, robbery, aggressive robbery, gross sexual impositions, rape, arson, threatening behavior, menacing, kidnaping, injury to the person, aggressive burglary, burglary and entering an inhabited building, and murder.

Finally, of the studies that focus on violent behavior, most do not address the long-term consequences of early abuse and neglect. Few have traced the effects of abuse or neglect through adulthood (or adult court records).

ABUSE BREEDS ABUSE

One of the most commonly held beliefs in both the scholarly and popular literature is that adults who were abused as children are more likely to abuse their own children. Early writers called attention to what they perceived to be the cycle of violence within the family, and a number of reports were published suggesting that abused children grow up to be abusing parents (Spinetta & Rigler, 1972). A typical example is that found in a review of research on family violence in which Gelles (1980) noted,

One of the consistent conclusions of domestic violence research is that individuals who have experienced violent and abusive childhoods are more likely to grow up and become child and spouse abusers than individuals who have experienced little or no violence in their childhood. (p. 878)

On the other hand, a number of researchers have questioned the validity of the hypothesis (Cichetti & Aber, 1980; Herzberger, 1983; E. Stark, 1985). After reviewing the literature, both Kadushin (1974) and Jayaratne (1977) concluded that little convincing evidence supported the theory that abusive parents were themselves abused as children. Most recently, Kaufman and Zigler (1987) concluded that the unqualified acceptance of the intergenerational transmission of violence hypothesis is unfounded.

What is the evidence that abuse leads to abuse or that abuse is transmitted across generations? Support for the hypothesis is based on four types of evidence: case histories, agency records, clinical interviews, and self-report studies.

One of the earliest observations of the intergenerational transmission of abuse was made by Steele and Pollock (1968):

> Without exception in our study group of abusing parents, there is a history of having been raised in the same style which they have recreated in the pattern of rearing their own children. Several had experienced severe abuse in the form of physical beating from either mother or father; a few reported "never having had a hand laid on them." All had experienced, however, a sense of intense, pervasive, continuous demand from their parents. (p. 111)

It is interesting that although Steele and Pollock (1968) were careful to acknowledge the limitations of their observations (based on clinical interview materials) and that they were "not to be thought of as useful for statistical proof" (p. 104), their study is probably the one most widely cited in support of the intergenerational transmission hypothesis.

One case history, offered as evidence for the intergenerational transmission hypothesis, described a study of five generations of ill-treated children in one family pedigree (Oliver & Taylor, 1971). Of a total of 49 individuals considered, 6 died before the age of 2 years, 3 were battered, 10 were subjected to physical cruelty or starved, 10 were abandoned, and 11 were unsupervised. Only 7 children were "obviously not ill used," and an additional 6 were cases in which the information was unclear.

Another often cited study by Silver, Dublin, and Lourie (1969) describes the follow-up of 34 emergency-room cases of suspected or proven child abuse. In this agency record study, data for 6 months in 1963 from the social services department of a Washington, D.C., hospital were reviewed retrospectively in 1967 to study the families as well as community agency practices. In more than half of the cases, abuse on the part of one or both parents toward each other or siblings was found. Of the 19 cases in which siblings were abused, 15 were in families where the child under study had a history of abuse prior to the 1963 episode. More than one episode of abusive behavior toward the child had occurred in 20 of the 34 cases, and even after the child's referral to community services, abuse or neglect continued or recurred in 12 cases during the 4-year period. The critical finding, however, which is often neglected, is that "in four of the cases there was sufficient evidence to show that the abuser had been abused as a child" (Silver et al., 1969, p. 405).

Most of the studies relevant to the "abuse breeds abuse" hypothesis are based on self-reports of a history of abuse. For example, in a nationwide survey of almost 10,000 reports of child abuse, Gil (1973) found that for the 1967 sample cohort of 1,380 families, at least 14% of mothers and 7% of fathers had been victims of abuse in their own childhoods. In an analysis of the child-rearing practices of 214 parents of battered babies, S. M. Smith and Hanson

(1975) found a higher incidence of self-reported rejecting and harsh upbringing in index mothers and fathers (27% and 32%, respectively) than in control parents (0% and 8%, respectively).

Straus et al. (1980) interviewed a nationally representative sample of 1,146 American couples who had children between the ages of 3 and 17 living at home. One child in each family was randomly selected as the "referent" child. The rate of abusive violence by fathers who grew up in the most violent homes (16%) was about double the rate for those who grew up in nonviolent homes; for mothers, the rate of abusive violence was 30%. For a number of reasons, however, these estimates are ambiguous with respect to the intergenerational transmission of abuse. First, the definition of "violent home" (a proxy for a history of abuse) is based on a question assessing how often the respondents' parents hit them as teenagers. There are no data on whether their parents hit them prior to their teens, as would be the case in child abuse. Second, these findings are based on interviews with adults who were married or cohabiting with a member of the opposite sex. Single parents and parents of children under age 3 were omitted from the survey. Because these two groups are at higher risk for child abuse, this exclusion is especially problematic. A third concern relates to the survey's reliance on retrospective accounts of prior and current family violence. Depending on their current family situation, adults may reconstruct their recollections of their families of origin. Despite these shortcomings, these findings provide a benchmark for the magnitude of the hypothesized relationship.

Adopting a very different approach involving a prospective design, Hunter and Kilstrom (1979) studied mothers of 282 premature or ill newborns who were admitted to a regional newborn intensive care unit. The "abuse breeds abuse" hypothesis was tested by an examination of the relationship between the independent variable (self-reported parental history of abuse or neglect) and the dependent variable (abuse or neglect reports filed and subsequently substantiated within the child's first year of life). At the admission interview, 49 of these families reported a history of abuse or neglect for one or both parents. During the child's first year of life, of the 255 mothers (whose infants had been discharged home from the hospital), 10 had abuse or neglect reports filed against them that were subsequently substantiated. Nine of the 10 mothers revealed a "family history of abuse or neglect" in the initial interview, whereas only 17% ($n = 42$) of the comparison mothers gave such a history. A number of other differences existed between reported and nonreported mothers. Nonreported mothers had a "fuller" social network and a higher frequency of adequate child care arrangements. Reported mothers, on the other hand, were more likely to have contemplated abortion (less adaptation to the pregnancy) and were less likely to have obtained minimal prenatal care. Infants born to the reported versus nonreported families also differed in gestational age, birth weight, congenital defects, and period of time in the hospital, indicating that infants born to nonreported families were healthier in a number of ways.

The findings from this study appear to demonstrate powerful intergenerational transmission effects; however, it is important to examine the findings carefully. Nine of the 49 families reporting a history of abuse or neglect were identified as abusers. This means that the rate of intergenerational transmission was 18% and that the remainder of the families (40 out of the original 49, or 80%) were not reported for abuse during this time period. If only abusing parents had been included in the sample, the estimate of the rate of transmission would have been much higher (90%) and deceptive. By using a prospective design, with families chosen prior to the abuse or neglect, Hunter and Kilstrom increased the validity of their estimates of the strength of the association.

Despite the strength of this prospective design, these findings are limited because of the reliance on mothers' or fathers' reports of a "history of abuse or neglect" without substantiation or validation. In addition, because of its fairly short follow-up time, this study may underestimate the actual amount of abuse across generations. Hunter and Kilstrom's (1979) 18% transmission rate may be low because the families were only followed for 1 year. Had the sample been followed for more than 1 year, it is likely that more cases of abuse would have been reported. Furthermore, the criterion for current abuse status was a confirmed report of abuse registered in the state welfare agency. This contrasts with the parents' history of abuse, which was based on self-reports in the context of interviews. Thus, the criteria for a history of abuse in the parents were much less stringent than those used to determine current abuse status. Had the criteria been the same for each generation, the rate of transmission might have been higher.

Generalizing from these findings is also problematic because of the unique nature of the sample (families of premature or ill newborns). Because of the importance of the questions addressed and the strength of the prospective design, further follow-up studies over a longer time period should be done, as well as other studies to assess whether the results from these premature or ill newborns are generalizable to other families with infants. The differences between reported and nonreported mothers and their infants suggest other important avenues of inquiry to pursue.

Using a different design involving a sample of 529 heads of households (composed of 251 from families characterized by abuse, 89 by neglect, and the remainder from families with preschool children served by various community programs), Herrenkohl et al. (1983) compared parent's experiences of being disciplined as a child with the type and severity of their disciplinary practices with their own children. An important design feature of this research was the inclusion of three control variables (social desirability, number of children, and income level of parents) that are of frequent concern to researchers in the field.

In simple bivariate analyses, 56% of those who abused their own children reported having one or more abusive caretakers as a child, in contrast to 38% of those parents who denied abusing their children. On the other hand, 53% (124) of those who reported experiencing abuse did not abuse their children. Because the control variables were all significantly related to the dependent variable (parent's discipline of own children), they were entered into the regression equation before each of the independent variables. Reported abuse by the respondent's mother alone and mother and father together and the number of caretaking situations in which the respondent had lived and been subjected to physical abuse were significantly related to the respondent's disciplining of his or her own child. These findings support the hypothesis that "exposure to abusive discipline as a child increases the risk for reliance on severe discipline techniques as a parent" (Herrenkohl et al., 1983, p. 315). However, the authors emphasized that other past and current life stresses or supports seem to be important in affecting parental behavior positively or negatively.

Despite the limitations imposed by this study's dependence on retrospective self-reports, the inclusion of the three control variables is notable because it provides an empirical estimate of the importance of social desirability, number of children, and income level. The significance of the three control variables in these analyses demonstrates clearly the need to include (or at a minimum, to consider) these variables in future research.

Egeland and Sroufe and colleagues (Egeland & Brunquell, 1979) designed a prospective longitudinal study to assess the consequences of child maltreatment. The original sample consisted of 267 mothers enrolled in the study during their last trimester of pregnancy. The families were selected not because maltreatment had occurred, but because they (and presumably their children) were at high risk for developmental problems because of poverty, limited parental knowledge about child care, lack of education, or the mother's young age (40% were teenagers). In approximately 200 cases from the total at-risk sample on whom data were available for the first 2 years, Egeland and Sroufe (1981b) identified, on the basis of several sources of information, four groups of maltreated children whose abuse included physical abuse, hostile/verbal abuse, psychological unavailability, and neglect. (Thirty-one mothers were identified as seriously neglecting or abusing their infants [Egeland & Sroufe, 1981a]). In a later report, Egeland and Jacobvitz (1984) described findings from 160 of the mothers (high-risk, low-income, predominantly single-parent), using data from semistructured interviews designed to obtain information about their childhood histories and current disciplinary practices. A history of abuse in the parents was defined by incidents of severe physical punishment such as being thrown against the wall, being hit repeatedly with an object, or being intentionally burned. According to the authors, 70% of the mothers with a history of severe physical abuse engaged in current abuse. However, in addition to mothers who used severe punishment ("physical abuse"), this 70% figure also included mothers in the "borderline" (30%, regular spanking that did not cause bruises) and "other" (6%, mothers whose children were being cared for outside the home) categories.

Although this study is limited by an overreliance on self-reports for a history of abuse among the mothers, overly broad definitional criteria for current abuse, and relatively small sample sizes for abuse and neglect, it has a number of methodological strengths. Because the families in this study—including those who were not abusive and who had not maltreated their children—were all high risk and presumably suffered from multiple problems (see "Methodological Considerations"), the results are not confounded with the effects of poverty, stress, and so forth. This study also has the advantage that the nonmaltreated children from the sample serve as a strong control

group, allowing the authors to distinguish the consequences of maltreatment from those of poverty and other high-risk characteristics.

Overall, the empirical evidence for the notion that abuse breeds abuse is methodologically problematic and limited by an overdependence on self-report and retrospective data and infrequent use of control groups. However, existing studies suggest that there is a higher likelihood of abuse by parents if they themselves were abused as children. Among abusing parents, estimates range from a low of 7% (mothers in Gil's, 1973, sample) to a high of 70% (Egeland & Jacobvitz, 1984). In most studies included here, the majority of abusive parents were not abused in their own childhoods.

A similar conclusion was reached by Kaufman and Zigler (1987). On the basis of their literature review, Kaufman and Zigler estimated the rate of intergenerational transmission of abuse to be 30% plu 5%. This means that about one third of the individuals who are abused or neglected will abuse their own children and that two thirds will not. "Being maltreated as a child puts one at risk for becoming abusive but the path between these two points is far from direct or inevitable" (Kaufman & Zigler, 1987, p. 190).

REPORTS OF SMALL NUMBERS OF VIOLENT OR HOMICIDAL OFFENDERS IN CLINICAL SETTINGS

The second type of evidence offered to substantiate the "violence breeds violence" hypothesis is based on case histories of small numbers of violent or homicidal offenders in clinical settings. These seven reports describe prior abuse in the family backgrounds of adolescents who attempted or succeeded in killing their parents or in the backgrounds of convicted murderers or those charged with murder. For example, Easson and Steinhilber (1961) provided clinical accounts of eight boys who had committed murderous assaults. All were from socially normal families, yet two of the eight had a clear history of habitual brutal beating by their parents, and the histories of three others led the authors to "wonder if brutality to the child was being concealed." Duncan and Duncan (1971) reported a preliminary study of six adult male prisoners convicted of first-degree murder. All were from middle-class families of good standing. In four of the six, there was "continuous, remorseless brutality during childhood" at the hands of one of the parents. The remaining two prisoners were overtly psychotic, and no childhood histories were obtained. In a study of nine adolescent boys who had committed homicide as teenagers, King (1975) found that as children, they were subjected to more beatings than their siblings. Sendi and Blomgren (1975) compared case histories and current behavior of three groups of adolescents: 10 who had committed homicide, 10 who had threatened or attempted homicide, and a control group of 10 hospitalized adolescents. Both homicide groups were more likely than the hospitalized control adolescents to come from "unfavorable home environments" (defined as "one in which a considerable amount of stress was present, including parental neglect, abuse, or absence" [Sendi & Blomgren, 1975, p. 425]).

On the other hand, in a study of 10 mothers who murdered their children (Tuteu & Glotzer, 1966), there was no suggestion of abuse in the mothers' backgrounds. Rather, according to the authors, these women grew up in emotionally cold and often directly rejecting family environments.

More recently, Ressler and Burgess (1985) described the extent of early abuse in a sample of sexual murderers who were part of the Federal Bureau of Investigation's study of sexual homicide and crime scene patterns. Thirteen of these 31 murderers reported physical abuse in their childhood histories; 23 of the 31 reported psychological abuse; and 12 reported sexual abuse in childhood.

Finally, M. Rosenbaum and Bennett (1986) reported on six homicidal depressed patients and compared them with nonhomicidal depressed control subjects, drawn from a caseload of 120 patients treated over the course of 5 years. Preliminary findings were that the homicidal depressed patients were more likely than the nonhomicidal depressed patients to have been physically abused as a child, to have personality disorders, to abuse alcohol and drugs, and to be suicidal.

These reports provide informative, provocative, and often detailed clinical accounts by astute observers. Yet, they suffer many of the shortcomings of uncontrolled case studies, including the general lack of appropriate control groups, confounding factors, small numbers, and dependence on retrospective self-reports of prior abuse. Two of these studies have control groups (M. Rosenbaum & Bennett, 1986; Sendi & Blomgren, 1975). However, the definition of the independent variable in the first study—"unfavorable home environment"— incorporates a number of confounds because it includes "stress and parental absence" in addition to parental neglect or abuse. In the second study (M. Rosenbaum & Bennett), the small number of homicidal subjects ($n = 6$) and the uniqueness of both samples (depressed patients) limit the generalizability of the findings.

Although these small-scale clinical reports have been especially helpful in stimulating further research and generating hypotheses, their own statistical usefulness is limited. Recognizing the limitations of these clinical accounts, researchers have examined the consequences of abuse and neglect in the context of larger and more controlled investigations.

CHILD ABUSE, NEGLECT, AND DELINQUENCY

The third set of nine studies addresses the relationship between child abuse, neglect, and delinquency, but not necessarily violent behavior. Table 25.1 presents basic information about these studies—subjects, criteria for abuse and/or neglect, and findings. Of the nine studies included in Table 25.1, three are prospective and six are retrospective.

Prospective Studies

Each of the three prospective studies (Alfaro, 1981; Bolton, Reich, & Gutierres, 1977; McCord, 1983) has design problems that seriously limit the validity of the findings. It is important to note that two of the three studies had no control group (Alfaro, 1981; Bolton et al., 1977).

In a report of the New York State Select Committee on Child Abuse, Alfaro (1981) described a study of 4,465 children who had been referred to protection agencies for suspected abuse or neglect in eight counties in New York State during 1952-1953. Traced through 1967, 17.2% of these youths had had at least one subsequent contact with the juvenile court for juvenile delinquency or ungovernability. As many as 50% of the families reported for child abuse or neglect had at least one child who was later taken to court as a delinquent or ungovernable.

The strength of Alfaro's study lies in its prospective design. That is, the time order of the two factors—abuse and delinquency—is clear. Unfortunately, this strength is offset by the lack of a control group. Alfaro (1981) was not unaware of this problem (pp. 177-178).

Using a similar design, Bolton et al. (1977) studied a sample of 5,392 children who had been referred to the Arizona State Department of Economic Security for child abuse. Of this group, 873 (16.2%) were subsequently identified in juvenile court records, but 99 of these were eliminated because they were dependency cases rather than cases of juvenile crime or status offenses. Thus, 774 (or 14.3%) of the original group were involved with the juvenile court. The time period over which this study

was conducted is not known, and once again, there is no control group.

Control groups are critical because it is otherwise impossible to determine what percentage of youths not referred for child abuse subsequently became delinquent or were referred to the juvenile court. As Newberger et al. (1983) pointed out in regard to Alfaro's (1981) research, but which is equally true of the Bolton et al. (1977) work,

> Left open in the discussion, and unfortunately not susceptible to definitive analysis in this sample, is the extent to which the preferential selection of poor children both for reporting for maltreatment and for delinquency may have affected the perceived association and the extent to which poverty per se may have determined both problems. (p. 263)

The third prospective study, by McCord (1983), is based on 232 males first studied in the years 1939 through 1945 (in a project designed to prevent delinquency) and then followed up between 1975 and 1979, providing a 40-year perspective. In the original study, social workers visited the boys' homes two times per month for 5 years. The counselor's description of how the boy and his parent interacted provided the basis for coding the attitude of each parent toward his or her child. The subjects were then divided into four groups (loved, abused, neglected, and rejected) on the basis of these case reports originally written by social workers between 1939 and 1945.

Criteria for assigning the boys to groups were as follows: *loving*—if the parent seemed genuinely concerned for the child's welfare and if criticism was absent from most of the parent-child interactions; *rejecting*—if the parent demonstrated repeated displeasure with the child; *neglecting*—if there tended to be little emotional commitment to the child; *punitive*—if corporal punishments formed the reg-

TABLE 25.1 Child Abuse, Neglect, and Delinquency

Study	Subjects	Criterion for Abuse/Neglect	Findings
		Prospective	
Bolton, Reich, & Gutierres (1977)	5,392 children referred to AZ State Dept. Economic Security, Child Protective Services	Referral for sexual, physical, or emotional abuse	14.3% (774) had been referred to juvenile court
Alfaro (1981)	Cases referred to public and private child protective agencies in 1952-53 (n = 4,465)	Referral to child protection agencies for possible abuse/neglect	17% had had at least one subsequent contact with juvenile court for juvenile delinquency or ungovernability
McCord (1983)	201 males originally studied thru 1945; retraced in 1975 and 1979: 48 neglected, 49 abused, 34 rejected, and 101 loved	Abuse, neglect, or rejection in social workers' case reports	Juvenile delinquency: rejected children, 29%; neglected, 15%; abused, 10%; loved, 7%
		Retrospective	
Glueck & Glueck (1950)	500 delinquents in juvenile institution; 500 nondelinquents (matched for age, race, IQ, and neighborhood)	Families needed help from service agencies for abuse/neglect of children	85% delinquent families needed help, in contrast to 44% of nondelinquent families
Lewis & Shanok (1977)	109 delinquents referred from juvenile court; 109 nondelinquents (matched on age, sex, race, and socioeconomic status	Hospital use because of abuse	9% delinquents used hospital services versus 1% controls
Alfaro (1981)	1,960 cases referred as delinquents or ungovernable to probation intake departments and family courts in New York state in 1971-72	Prior contact with child protective agencies for abuse/neglect	21% of boys and 29% of girls had been reported, when younger, for abuse or neglect as a child
Wick (1981)	50 records of cases referred to Central Texas Youth Services Bureau	Author's analysis of youth's case files	29% judged to have early abuse or neglect as source of their problem
Mouzakitis (1981)	60 female adjudicated delinquents or status offenders in Arkansas Girls Training School (1977)	Self-reported childhood discipline by physical means	86% reported discipline by physical means: 13% hands, 23% hands/belts, 50% objects and hands
Kratcoski (1982)	863 case files of delinquent youth incarcerated in four Ohio institutions for serious male offenders	Physical abuse or neglect in case files	26% had experienced some form of physical abuse or neglect

ular basis for the parent's attempt to control the boy. (Interrater reliability was 76% for the fathers and 80% for the mothers for the coding of the first three parental attitudes toward the boy; the corresponding figures for the latter coding were 88% and 100%.)

This resulted in 49 men classified as abused, 48 as neglected, 34 as rejected, and 101 as loved. McCord (1983) described the groups as follows:

> Men who had been subjected to consistently punitive, physical punishments were classified as *abused*. Those whose parents interacted with them infrequently, showing neither affection nor rejection, were classified as *neglected*. Among those not abused, the ones who had at least one parent who seemed concerned for the child's welfare and generally pleased with his behavior were classified as *loved*. And the remaining group, those neither abused nor neglected but also not loved, were classified as *rejected*. (p. 267)

McCord found that serious crimes (i.e., theft, auto theft, breaking and entering, burglary, or assault) were committed in childhood by 50% of the rejected children, about 20% of the abused and neglected children, and 11% of the loved children. More important, she called attention to the fact that many of the males appeared to be relatively invulnerable to the adverse effects of parental abuse and neglect. "Among the 97 neglected or abused children, 44 had become criminal, alcoholic, mentally ill, or had died before reaching age 35, and 53 showed none of these signs of having been damaged" (McCord, 1983, p. 269).

Although this study in general has many design strengths, it has one major limitation as an assessment of the consequences of abuse and neglect. The problem concerns McCord's)1983) definition of and criteria for abuse, neglect, and rejection. The ratings are prospective and based on observed behavior in the homes of the boys, and these represent design

strengths. However, considering the operational definitions for group assignment (detailed above), the severity of the abusive or neglectful behaviors is questionable, as is the extent to which these boys were appropriately labeled *rejected*. For example, neglect here refers to little interaction, affection, and emotional commitment by parents. Although certainly reflecting a form of psychological neglect, this description differs markedly from the studies of neglected children whose lives are characterized by extreme neglect due to lack of adequate food, clothing, shelter, or medical attention. In addition, the meaning of the label *rejected*—defined as neither abused nor neglected nor loved—is highly ambiguous and would be difficult to replicate with another sample. Thus, although McCord's work offers a number of provocative findings and is the only study to extend into adulthood, concerns about the severity of the abuse limit the generalizability of the findings.

Retrospective Studies

In contrast to the three prospective studies, the other six studies in Table 25.1 are retrospective (Alfaro, 1981; Glueck & Glueck, 1950; Kratcoski, 1982; Lewis & Shanok, 1977; Mouzakitis, 1981; Wick, 1981). These six identify samples of delinquent youths and use reverse records checks to determine the incidence of abuse or neglect in the delinquents' backgrounds.

In terms of the methodological problems listed in the Appendix, all six are retrospective; all fail to distinguish between abused and neglected children; all focus on generalized delinquent behavior (although more specific analyses are provided subsequently for two of the samples: Alfaro, 1981; Kratcoski, 1982; and all fail to address the long-term consequences of abuse and neglect into adulthood. Only two of these studies used control groups (Glueck & Glueck, 1950; Lewis & Shanok, 1977). Two depend on weak sampling techniques (Mouzakitis, 1981; Wick, 1981), and four represent ex post facto analyses (Kratcoski, 1982; Lewis & Shanok, 1977; Mouzakitis, 1981; Wick, 1981). Only one (Alfaro, 1981) is clearly not correlational.

Retrospective studies face particular threats to validity in terms of inaccuracies in recording and other biases. On the other hand, there may be a bias toward minimization. For example, Alfaro (1981) identified 1,963 children reported to Family Court or Probation Intake Services across eight counties in New York state as delinquent or ungovernable in 1971 or 1972, and then he examined earlier records for a history of abuse. Thus, histories of delinquent or ungovernable youths were traced backward for prior involvement in abuse or neglect case records, which would have been recorded in the 1950s and 1960s. At that time, most communities did not have child protection services, and because there were no mandatory child abuse reporting laws as we currently have, many cases of abuse may have gone unreported. Considering the time from which the abuse data were obtained, it is noteworthy that about one fifth (21%) of the boys and almost one third of the girls (29%) who had been reported as delinquent or ungovernable in the early 1970s were found to have been reported, when younger, as abused or neglected children. In some counties, the figures were much higher: 41% of the boys and 36% of the girls in Erie County, 36% of the boys and 53% of the girls in Monroe County, and 31% of the boys and 45% of the girls in New York County.

Two studies frequently cited as supporting the relationship between child abuse and delinquency warrant further description beyond that in Table 25.1. Wick (1981) examined 50 randomly selected case files from a total of 3,027 cases of "troubled youth," ages 5 to 18. Files with complete information were then analyzed to determine the source and severity of the youths' problems and were then coded by the author into eight categories of potential causes. On the basis of this process, Wick determined

29% of the cases (13) to be primarily due to abuse or neglect. Although this figure of 29% is in line with those of other studies, a number of major limitations detract from the validity of this study: retrospective analysis of case files, inability to generalize from 50 randomly selected cases to over 3,000 troubled youth of widely divergent ages, and the lack of reliability information on the coding of case files.

In the study by Mouzakitis (1981), graduate students administered questionnaires to a group of 60 female adjudicated delinquents in the Arkansas Girls Training School. The mean age of the girls was 14.8 years (range = 12 to 17 years). Two thirds of the girls were white; one third were black. Eighty-six percent (51) reported that they had received physical punishment by the use of hands, objects, or belts. As a result of this punishment, 51% of the girls recalled bruises, 25% recalled scars, and 38% recalled bleedings. A fifth of the girls recalled no apparent physical effects. Of the girls receiving physical punishment, the majority (37 of the 51) described receiving this punishment when they were younger than 10. Thirteen reported that they had been physically punished since infancy, and only 3 since age 14. Given that these girls were punished so early (before age 10), it does not seem likely that punishment occurred as a response to the incorrigibility, running away, or delinquency of the girls. However, because there is no comparison group with which to compare these percentages and because these data are based on self-reports (there is no substantiated evidence for the physical abuse), these findings remain provocative but inconclusive.

Another study based on an analysis of existing case files avoids the pitfalls of a number of the other studies but suffers from the lack of an appropriate control group and from dependence on retrospective information. Kratcoski (1982) surveyed case files of delinquent male adolescents incarcerated in four institutions for serious offenders in Ohio. Here, abuse was carefully defined as "any nonaccidental physical injury inflicted on a child by a parent or other caretaker deliberately or in anger" (Justice & Justice, 1976, p. 18). According to Kratcoski, only clear-cut instances of physical maltreatment were considered. Most of the physical abuse took the form of severe beatings with objects, such as belts, whips, paddles, or fists. In a few cases, sexual abuse occurred, and there were cases of other forms of severe abuse such as stabbing, burning, and so on. Of the 863 cases in the population, 26% (or 223) had experienced physical abuse in some form.

This work by Kratcoski, as well as a number of the other studies, represents after-the-fact analyses of preexisting records or depends on the retrospective recall of the subjects for information. For example, Kratcoski (1982) abstracted information about abuse experiences by reading case summaries written by psychologists or social workers. These findings may be distorted and reflect a conservative bias because, in many cases, the psychologists or social workers who interviewed the youths never brought up issues about parent relationships, thus missing the chance to uncover possible abuse. Furthermore, the parents had rarely been officially charged with child abuse. In some instances, determinations about whether abuse had occurred were made by the researchers. Thus, we are left with questions regarding the substantiation or validation of the abuse experiences.

In sum, the nine studies summarized in Table 25.1 address the relationship between abuse, neglect, and delinquent behavior. Only three are prospective; only three have control groups. All have design problems. In studies using a prospective design, among those who had been abused or neglected as children, delinquency occurred in fewer than 20% of the cases. In the McCord (1983) study, rejected children had the highest rates of recorded juvenile delinquency. In studies using a retrospective design, rates of abuse in the backgrounds of delinquents ranged from 8% to 26%, with two exceptions (Glueck & Glueck, 1950; Mouzakitis, 1981).

ABUSE, NEGLECT, AND VIOLENT BEHAVIOR

Twelve studies, summarized in Table 25.2, specifically address the relationship between abuse, neglect, and violent behavior. For the sake of clarity, these studies are further subdivided into those that involve delinquents and those that use patient groups in their investigations.

With three exceptions (Alfaro, 1981; Gutierres & Reich, 1981; Lewis et al., 1985), the studies in this group suffer from questionable criteria for abuse or neglect, including nonsubstantiated cases; are weakened by retrospective designs or reliance on second-hand information; and rely on ex post facto and correlational designs. In addition, two depend on weak sampling techniques (Blount & Chandler, 1979; Jenkins, 1968). Most refer to physical abuse only (three exceptions are Gutierres & Reich, 1981; Hartstone & Hansen, 1984; Jenkins, 1968). Three studies incorporated control groups (Climent & Ervin, 1972; Gutierres & Reich, 1981; Lewis et al., 1985). Only one (Climent & Ervin, 1972) examined the long-term consequences of abuse and neglect into adulthood.

Delinquents

The most common design used delinquents, who were then divided into more specialized groups: abused and nonabused (Alfaro, 1981; Gutierres & Reich, 1981; Kratcoski, 1982), socialized and unsocialized aggressives (Jenkins, 1968), and violent and nonviolent (Lewis, Shanok, Pincus, & Glaser, 1979; Hartstone & Hansen, 1984). In each of these studies, the author(s) examined differences between delinquent subgroups in the extent to which they engaged in violent behavior or in the extent to which they experienced or witnessed child abuse.

A number of these studies provide support for a relationship between abuse and later violent behavior. For example, in the study by Lewis et al. (1979), 97 boys who were incarcerated at a correctional school in Connecticut during the time of the project were evaluated by a clinical team. Each child was rated on a scale of violence from 1 *(least violent)* to 4 *(most violent)* using data only from behavior and offenses, not from psychiatric or neurological assessments. Children were rated 1 if there was no evidence of having committed any offense against a person or having committed arson ($n = 8$); 2 if there was some indication of a potential for violence ($n = 11$); 3 if they had committed a serious offense against a person such as murder, rape, multiple episodes of arson, armed robbery, or assault ($n = 55$); or 4 if they had demonstrated extreme brutality toward others ($n = 23$). All ratings were subjective, and, according to the authors, there was agreement among raters in almost all cases.

These boys were also evaluated by a child psychiatrist and neurologist, who attempted to obtain as detailed a medical history as possible and, in particular, to determine whether the child had been the victim of abuse or had witnessed extreme violence. As can be seen in Table 25.2, the more violent boys were more likely to have experienced abuse or witnessed extreme physical abuse than the nonviolent boys. The correlation between the degree of child violence and "ever having been abused" was .37 ($P < .001$)

A small-scale prospective study by Lewis et al. (1985) indicates a strong relationship between early abuse and later murder by documenting the childhood and family characteristics of nine males who were clinically evaluated as adolescents (when they were between the ages of 12 and 18 years) and then later when they were arrested for murder (at ages 15 through 26). The majority (78%) of the nine young murderers had experienced severe abuse by one or both parents, compared to about 60% of the nonviolent youths. Nevertheless, given the very small number of subjects, there is a need for caution in interpreting these findings and a strong need for replication with larger samples.

Adopting a very different approach, Hartstone and Hansen (1984) studied 114 violent juvenile male offenders from four cities who had been found legally guilty of an excessively violent offense against a person and had a prior adjudication for a felonious crime against a person or property (i.e., repeat offenders). The mean age of the offenders was 16.3 years (range = 14 to 18). Seventy-three percent were black, 18% were white, and 10% were Hispanic or Chicano. Information was gathered from three sources: official records in the subject's case file and structured interviews with the youth and the youth's mother or mother figure.

Overall, 30% of the study youths had witnessed or experienced at least one form of family violence; 15% had suffered from prior child abuse, and 2% were sexually abused in the home. Hartstone and Hansen (1984) cautioned that these figures may be conservative, given the common underreporting of family violence in both client and case folders. However, because many of the incidents were based on retrospective self-reports by the offenders, whether these percentages represent under- or overestimates of the extent of abusive histories remains an empirical question.

Geller and Ford-Somma's (1984) work represents one of the most detailed and statistically sophisticated analyses of the relationship between specific forms of violent behavior and a history of abuse. In their study, 226 incarcerated juvenile offenders (182 boys, 42 girls) in training schools in New Jersey completed self-report questionnaires. Interviews were also conducted with a subsample of 22. In simple descriptive frequencies, the extent of family violence was high. Two thirds of the offenders reported being beaten with a belt or an extension cord, and 32% reported being beaten at least five times. One fifth were threatened with a knife or a gun, and 12% were assaulted with a knife or a gun. Thirty-three percent were

TABLE 25.2 Child Abuse, Neglect, and Violent Behavior

Study	Subjects	Criterion for Abuse/Neglect	Outcome Measure	Findings
	Delinquents			
Jenkins (1968)	445 unsocialized, aggressive, assaultive delinquents; 231 socialized delinquents	Psychiatric judgments of parents	Child guidance clinic record	Unsocialized aggressives: Punitive and rejecting families, who used extreme forms of physical punishment; Socialized: Families were poorer, larger, and neglectful
Lewis, Shanok, Pincus, & Glaser (1979)	97 incarcerated boys: extremely and less violent groups	Medical history from psychiatric and neurological examination	Violent behavior scale rating (1-4)	More violent Less violent Abuse by mother 44% (21) 14% (2) Abuse by father 55% (29) 29% (5) Abuse by others 45% (23) 14% (2) Ever abused 75% (52) 33% (6) Witnessed violence 79% (44) 20% (3)
Guitierres & Reich (1981)	Of original group referred, 471 abused and siblings and 900 juvenile offenders and siblings	Physical, emotional, sexual, or abuse/neglect	Type of crime: escape and aggressive	Escape Aggressive Abused 40% 3% Siblings 29% 6% Offenders 18% 5% Siblings 12% 5%
Alfaro (1981)	Delinquents from 1970s sample divided into two groups: abused/neglected and nonabused/neglected	Prior contact with child protective agencies for abuse/neglect	Referral to juvenile court for violent act	Of abused/neglected, 26% referred for violence; of nonabused/neglected, 21% referred for violent acts
Kratcoski (1982)	863 incarcerated delinquent youths divided into abused and nonabused groups	Analysis of case files for clear-cut indication of physical maltreatment	Violent acts: illegal use or threat of force against persons	Abused delinquents were not more violent than nonabused delinquents
Geller & Ford-Somma (1984)	224 juvenile offenders in New Jersey training schools; 182 boys, 43 girls	Responses to self-report questionnaire	Violent delinquency (arrests and self-report)	The more offenders were abused, the more violent crimes they committed and the more they engaged in expressive violence (based on multiple regression analyses)

Study	Sample	Method	Definition of violence	Findings
Hartstone & Hansen (1984)	114 violent males in 4 states, ages 14 to 18	Case files and structured interview of youth and mother	Legal definition as violent offender	15% of study youths had suffered from prior child abuse; 2% had been sexually abused in the home
Lewis et al. (1985)	9 young murderers, ages 15-26, evaluated prior to murder; 24 males with no record of violent crime 6 years after evaluation	Medical and family history from psychiatric and neurological examination	Police arrest records	At least 7 (about 78%) of murderers had been severely abused by one or both parents, compared to about 60% of nonviolent youths
Patients				
Climent & Ervin (1972)	40 emergency-room patients (mean age = 32) presenting complaints of violence; 40 relatives of other patients matched on sex, race, religion, and marital status (age = 28)	Patient self-report during emergency room interview	Self-reported present or past history of repeated violent behavior	Violent subjects were more likely to have been beaten as children by fathers (40%) and mothers (23%) than were control group subjects (15% and 3%).
Blount & Chandler (1979)	30 randomly selected adolescent state hospital patients ages 13-18; 15 admitted for assault; 15 no evidence of assaultive behavior	Hospital medical records, including reports of previous placements, agencies, treatments	Assaultive behavior outside and within state hospital	Assaultive patients: 8 of 15, prior abuse; nonassaultive patients: 3 of 15, prior abuse.
Tarter, Hegedus, Winstein, & Alterman (1984)	101 delinquent adolescents referred consecutively to psychiatric institute and clinic: 276 abused, 74 nonabused	Information from past records and probation officer reports, psychiatric interview	Commission of assaultive crime	Abused delinquents were more likely to commit crimes of assaultive nature than nonabused (44% versus 16%)
Monane, Leichter, & Lewis (1984)	Unselected sample of 166 children and adolescents admitted to psychiatric services of large city hospital in 1 year, divided into abused and nonabused groups (ages 3-17)	Physical abuse coded from hospital records	Violent behavior rating scale (Lewis et al., 1979)	Most significant factor distinguishing groups was violent behavior, 72% of abused had been extremely violent, as compared with 42% of nonabused group

NOTE: The majority of the studies refer to physical abuse only. Exceptions are Jenkins (1968), Gutierres and Reich (1981), Alfaro (1981), and Hartstone and Hansen (1984).

beaten so severely they were bruised, 29% so severely they bled, and 8% so severely that they received hospital care.

These juvenile offenders had not only experienced violence as victims but had also perpetrated violence. Although 22% punched their fathers, 5% attacked their fathers with a knife or gun, and almost 12% reported hitting siblings with a stick or other hard object or had beaten siblings so severely they bled (9%), very few of the offenders reported violence directed at their mothers (only 5%).

Given the predominance of violent offenders in this study (only 21% of this group had never been arrested for a violent offense, and nearly 20% had been arrested for violent offenses at least five times), the authors chose not to divide their sample into groups but rather to conduct regression analyses to determine the relationship between experiencing and committing violence. The dependent variable was violent delinquency, measured by the number of times an offender was arrested for murder and reported having robbed someone with a weapon, robbed someone without a weapon, raped someone, attacked someone with a weapon, and beat someone for no reason. Three different forms of family violence represented the independent variables. Routine family violence was measured by the number of times an offender was hit with a belt or stick or some other hard object, life-threatening violence by the number of times an offender was threatened or assaulted with a knife or gun, and injurious violence by the number of times offenders were beaten so badly they were bruised or bled (Geller & Ford-Somma, 1984, pp. 54-55).

These three independent variables in the regression equation explained 10% of the variance in violent delinquency. The more the offenders were victimized by routine violence, the more violent crimes they committed. (Life-threatening and injurious family violence had no significant effects on violent delinquency.) Thus, the most common form of family violence—routine family violence—led to violent acts outside the home.

In another regression analysis using expressive violent crimes (murder, rape, attacking someone with a weapon, and beating someone for no reason) as the dependent variable, 14% of the variance was explained, with both routine and life-threatening family violence contributing significantly. In contrast, none of the independent variables was significant in a regression on instrumental violence (robbery and armed robbery). On the basis of these findings, Geller and Ford-Somma (1984) suggested that family violence affects violent delinquency but is useful primarily in explaining expressive violence.

The Geller and Ford-Somma (1984) study is important because of its statistically sophisticated analysis using a number of clearly defined independent variables to predict violent behavior. However, like many of the other studies reviewed here, because of its dependence on retrospective information and on self-reports of abuse and neglect from incarcerated delinquents, as well as its lack of control-group data, these findings must remain tentative.

Patients

In the smaller subset of studies in Table 25.2, groups of patients were compared. In one of the only studies in this group with a nonpatient or nondelinquent control group, Climent and Ervin (1972) studied 40 violent patients who were brought or came to the Boston City Hospital Emergency Room with the chief complaint of violent behavior and with a reported present or past history of repetitive, severe, violent acts against persons. Thoughts, verbalizations, or fantasies alone would disqualify a patient for inclusion in the study. However, no confirmation of violent behavior by a witness was required. Patients were interviewed in the emergency room by a research assistant, as were a matched control group of relatives of other emergency room patients (n = 40). (Patients were somewhat older than controls [mean age of 32 versus 28 years]; the majority of both groups were male [approximately 75%]; and the racial composition was equivalent, approximately two thirds white and one third black.) Violent patients were more likely to report having been beaten as children: Physical assaults by fathers were more likely in violent patients (16/40) than nonviolent subjects (6/40), as were physical assaults by mothers (9/40 versus 1/40). Despite the strengths of this study, its exclusive reliance on retrospective self-reports for a prior history of abuse and the unique nature of the violent sample necessitate caution in assessing the validity and generalizability of these findings.

Monane, Leichter, and Lewis (1984) divided an unselected sample of children and adolescents receiving psychiatric services at a large city hospital in 1 year in the late 1970s into abused and nonabused groups and compared their violent behavior. Monane et al. (1984) defined abuse as "deliberate aggressive acts by family members or others outside the home that caused or could have been expected to cause serious injury (e.g., hit with a wooden board, thrown down a flight of stairs)" (p. 654). Ordinary spankings or beatings on the buttocks with a strap or switch were not considered abuse. Overall, there was a high incidence of physical abuse (42%) in the medical histories of these patients, with similar percentages of abuse for boys (42%) and girls (41%). However, the most significant factor distinguishing the abused from nonabused psychiatrically hospitalized children and adolescents was the violence. Among the abused patients in the sample, 72% had been extremely violent (rated 3 or 4 on the Lewis et al., 1979, scale), compared with only 46% of the nonabused patients. Homicidal behavior was slightly more common in the abused than in the nonabused groups (33% vs. 24%).

So far, these studies with delinquents and patients provide tentative support for the cycle of violence. Other studies do not support the cycle of violence hypothesis and offer contradictory evidence. For example, Gutierres and

Reich (1981) found that children who were physically abused were less likely to engage in later aggressive crimes (assault, assault with a deadly weapon, fighting, armed robbery, and so on) than their siblings and nonabused controls (nonabused juvenile offenders and their siblings). Abused children were more likely to be arrested for escape acts (truancy, missing juvenile, and runaway).[3] In the 1970s sample of abused and nonabused delinquents studied by Alfaro (1981), only slightly more of the abused delinquents (25.8%) than the nonabused delinquents (21.3%) committed crimes involving violence. In Kratcoski's (1982) study, abused delinquents were not more violent than nonabused delinquents. More than three quarters of the youths in both groups (abused and nonabused delinquents) had committed at least one act that would be considered violent, but the two groups did not differ significantly.

In sum, 12 studies address the relationship between abuse and violent behavior. Although some provide support for the relationship, others offer contradictory evidence. Eight studies involved delinquents; four used a variety of patient groups. Young murderers had more abuse in their backgrounds, the more violent delinquents reported more abuse in their backgrounds, and violent and assaultive patients reported higher incidences of having been beaten in their childhoods. Certain forms of family violence predicted violent delinquency and were particularly useful in explaining expressive violence. In contrast, other studies found no differences between abused and nonabused delinquents in the extent of violent crime, and at least one study found abused delinquents were less likely to engage in aggressive crimes.

Most of the studies in this group (Table 25.2) suffer from methodological limitations. Some used small samples (Blount & Chandler, 1979; Lewis et al., 1985). Most important, all but one (Climent & Ervin, 1972) lack a normal (that is, nondelinquent or nonpsychiatric patient) control group. For this reason, it is difficult to assess whether the percentages reported are meaningful and beyond base rates typically associated with youths of similar demographic characteristics. Finally, because these are studies of youths and adolescents, the findings do not address the long-term consequences of abuse and neglect into adulthood.

ABUSE, NEGLECT, AND AGGRESSIVE BEHAVIOR IN YOUNG CHILDREN

Eighteen experimental and laboratory studies addressing the relationship between abuse, neglect, and aggressive behavior in young children are summarized in Table 25.3. Because children's behavior is the focus of this examination, studies of adult behavior or of interactions of adults and children that did not report separate findings for the children were omitted.

By and large, these studies indicate with some consistency that abused children manifest more aggressive and problematic behavior, even at early ages. Abused infants ignored or refused maternal distractions (Wasserman, Green, & Allen, 1983); abused toddlers physically assaulted peers and harassed caregivers (George & Main, 1979); abused children (ages 6-7) were more aggressive in fantasy and free play and in school settings (Reidy, 1977); and abused 5- to 12-year-olds were deficient in emotional development, particularly self-concept and aggressiveness (Kinard, 1980).

There were also contradictory findings. In one study (Friedrich, Einbender, & Luecke, 1983), although abused preschoolers differed cognitively, they did not differ in terms of behavior. In another (Rohrbeck & Twentyman, 1986), abused children (ages 4-5) did not differ from control children in measures of impulsivity. In some studies, although abused and neglected children behaved differently from controls, they were similar to one another; in others, neglected children were different from abused children in prosocial and aggressive behaviors (Bousha & Twentyman, 1984; Herrenkohl, Herrenkohl, Toedter, &

Yanushefski, 1984; Hoffman-Plotkin & Twentyman, 1984; Reidy, 1977; Rohrbeck & Twentyman, 1986).

Generally, these studies do not suffer from the same methodological problems as the studies included in Tables 25.1 and 25.2. With two exceptions, studies in Table 25.3 have control groups. Control children are generally well matched with abused children for age, sex, racial composition, socioeconomic status, and other relevant parental background characteristics (cf. Friedrich & Wheeler, 1982).

Most of the studies of older children and delinquents (reviewed in earlier sections of this article) did not separate abused and neglected children. However, the results of this set of studies (Table 25.3) suggest the importance of distinguishing between the early experiences of abuse and neglect when examining later outcomes. For example, neglected children displayed a depressed rate of positive social behavior, less verbal and nonverbal interaction, and fewer social initiations than other children (Bousha & Twentyman, 1984). Neglected children also demonstrated high rates of physical aggression. "These data imply that abuse and neglect represent fundamentally different forms of child maltreatment and that combining maltreating groups, as has frequently been done, may actually obscure the important differences" (Bousha & Twentyman, 1984, p. 113).

For studies in Table 25.3, age groups vary, as do definitions of abuse and neglect. However, definitions of abuse and neglect are more careful, cases of abuse and neglect are substantiated and validated, and there is less dependence on retrospective data. Several outcome measures are used: videotapes and direct observations of social interaction in the home and in day care settings; levels of aggression as reflected in projective tests, in free-play environments, or on a variety of psychological, behavioral, or intelligence tests; or ratings by observers, teachers, and mothers or from caseworker reports. Assessment strategies range from those that depend exclusively on mother's reports of the child's behavior (Aragona & Eyberg, 1981; Perry, Doran, & Wells, 1983; Wolfe & Mosk, 1983) to those that involve multimodal assessment of behavior, based on teacher and parent ratings and direct observations or assessment of the child's behavior (Rohrbeck & Twentyman, 1986).

There are, however, two methodological limitations that are relatively unique to this group of studies. First, a number were conducted while the child's parent was in treatment (Perry et al., 1983; Wolfe & Mosk, 1983) or in training programs specifically related to the abuse or neglect incident (Aragona & Eyberg, 1981; Wasserman et al., 1983). Given the earlier discussion and the empirically demonstrated role played by social desirability (Herrenkohl et al., 1983), it is possible that abusive parents may redefine their behaviors or their description of their child's behavior in line with their current situations. This is particularly problematic when mothers' reports are the only source of information about the child. Second, with two exceptions (Morse, Sahler, & Friedman, 1970; Martin & Beezley, 1977), these studies are cross-sectional, and the time between the abuse or neglect incident and the laboratory testing or assessment was rather short.

The Minnesota Mother-Child Project, a prospective study of a sample of poor mothers and their infants (see earlier description of study), overcomes this last methodological problem (Egeland & Sroufe, 1981b). The original sample consisted of 267 mothers enrolled in the study during their last trimester of pregnancy, that is, before any maltreatment had occurred. Egeland and Sroufe (1981b) identified three forms of maltreatment in addition to physical abuse in approximately 35 children. On the 2-year problem-solving situation, the physical abuse group had significantly higher scores on the frequency of observed aggressive behaviors, frustration, and noncompliance and lower scores on positive affect. Although the children with different forms of maltreatment had evidence of negative consequences at 2

years, for most of the outcome variables, the outcomes were related to the particular patterns of maltreatment. Furthermore, the results of Egeland and Sroufe indicated a noticeable decline in functioning over the first 2 years for the maltreated children, who were not distinguished from control infants in the early assessments.

With a few exceptions (e.g., Egeland & Sroufe, 1981b), most of the developmental psychology studies are primarily correlational and cannot address issues of causality. However, there is other evidence which suggests that aggressiveness is a fairly stable personality trait. For example, a 3-year follow-up of sixth-grade boys showed that there was a high degree of stability in aggressive behavior over time (Olweus, 1977). After reviewing 16 longitudinal studies of aggression (excluding those based on self-report), Olweus (1979) concluded that stability of aggressive reaction patterns over time was not much lower than that typically found in studies of the stability of intelligence. Commenting on this pattern, Olweus (1980) wrote, "A preadolescent or adolescent boy characterized by an aggressive reaction pattern is not very likely to outgrow his mode of reaction, and his behavior may fairly easily develop into more directly antisocial forms of behavior" (p. 645).

A number of other authors also found that early aggressiveness, often manifesting as early as 8 to 12 years, was predictive of later antisocial behavior (Farrington, 1978; Robins, 1978). Physical and verbal aggression of the type measured by peer nominations has been found to predict adult physical aggression, criminal behavior, and serious crimes (Farrington, 1979; Huesmann, Eron, Lefkowitz, & Walder, 1984; Parke & Slaby, 1983).

Abuse, Withdrawal, and Self-Destructive Behavior

Given our strong belief that violence breeds violence, it is not surprising that most of the

(text continues on page 336)

TABLE 25.3 Abuse, Neglect, and Aggressive Behavior in Children

Study	Subjects	Age, Sex, Race	Design Comments	Outcome Measures	Findings
Morse, Sahler, & Friedman (1970)	25 children treated for suspected child abuse or gross neglect at Strong Memorial Hospital during 1963-1966	Median age at follow-up = 5 years	Follow-up approximately 3 years after hospitalization for injury or illness	Comprehensive record check—hospital, social service agencies, criminal courts	Six judged to be emotionally disturbed (frightened, withdrawn, temper tantrums, aggressive, disciplinary problems, hyperactive); nine judged to be mentally retarded
Martin & Beezley (1977)	50 abused children	Mean age = 6 years	Assessed 4 years after physical abuse first identified	Observations of nine characteristics during physical and neurological examinations, intelligence testing, and interviews	Characteristic Frequency Impaired ability for enjoyment 33 Behavioral symptoms 31 Low self-esteem 26 Withdrawal 12 Opposition 12 Hypervigilance 11 Compulsivity 11 Precocious behavior 10 School learning problems 9
Reidy (1977)	20 abused (A), 16 neglected (N), 22 control (C)	Age: 6-7 years Sex: F, M Race: B, W	Cross-sectional design	Aggressive fantasies, observer and teacher ratings during free play (Behavior Problem Checklist)	Thematic Apperception Test: A > N and C Free play: A > and C Teacher rating: A and N > C
Burgess & Conger (1978)	17 abusive (A) families, 17 neglectful (N) families, 19 control (C) families	Age: 6.5 years	Matched for age, income, number of children, education; authenticated abuse/neglect	Observations collected in home over four visits	A interacted less verbally and physically with mother than C; no differences in responsiveness to fathers. N spoke less often, interacted less positively, and initiated fewer physical contacts with fathers than C; with mothers no differences in responsiveness in N and C

Study	Subjects	Subject characteristics	Source/Matching	Measures	Results
George & Main (1979)	10 abused toddlers, 10 matched controls from families experiencing stress	Age: 1-3 years; Sex: 6 females, 4 males	Matched age, race, mother and father education and occupation, marital status, living situation	Observations of social interactions by trained observers in day care center	Abused more likely to physically assault peers, harass caregivers verbally, assault or threaten to assault caregivers, and avoid other children, and less likely to approach caregivers in response to friendly gestures
Kinard (1980)	30 physically abused, 30 nonabused	Age: 5-12 years; Sex: 8 female, 22 male; Race: 90% white, 10% black	Matched for age, sex, race, welfare status, birth order, parent structure and residence	Piers Harris Children's Self-Concept Scale; Rosenzweig Picture Frustration Study; Tasks of Emotional Development (TED)	Significant differences between A and C on Rosenzweig extrapunitive and impunitive child-child items and on TED self-concept, socialization, and separation from mother task
Aragona & Eyberg (1981)	27 mother-child dyads: 9 neglect (N; 6 female, 3 male), 9 behavior problem (BP; 3 female, 6 male, 9 nonproblem (C; 4 female, 5 male)	Age: 5-6 years; Race: Caucasian	Dyads selected from clinical and research files (1976-78); income < $10,000	Eyberg Child Behavior Inventory (mother's description of child's behavior problems)	Child behavior problems: BP > N > C
Barahal, Waterman, & Martin (1981)	17 abused (5 females, 12 males), 16 controls (4 females, 12 males)	Age: 6-8 years; Race: Caucasian (1 nonwhite each group)	Referrals from Department of Social Services, controls from local summer day camp run by same agency	Locus of control; social sensitivity; cognitive perspective taking (Flavell); understanding social roles; moral judgment	Abused more likely to attribute external control, less social sensitivity; controls better at understanding complex roles and at decentering; no differences in moral judgment
Straker & Jacobson (1981)	19 abused (A), 19 nonabused (C)	Age: 5-10 years; Sex: 8 females, 30 males; Race: Caucasian	Physical abuse (verified by MD or parent's admission)	Rosenzweig Picture Frustration Test, Children's Apperception Test, Affective Situations Test	Aggression: No differences; Emotional maladjustment: A > C; Empathy: C > A
Baird (1982)	63 physically abused (A), 96 neglected (N), 34 noninvolved siblings		Child Protective Services, caseworkers completed checklist	Aggressiveness, antisocial behavior, cognitive deficits, psychopathology	A higher on dependent variables (psychopathology) than N or noninvolved siblings. However, differences were due to age, sex, and family problems, not to abuse per se

TABLE 25.3 Continued

Study	Subjects	Age, Sex, Race	Design Comments	Outcome Measures	Findings
Wasserman, Green, & Allen (1983)	12 physically abused, 12 control infant-mother pairs	Age: 14 months (Matched for age, sex, race, socioeconomic status	Videotaping of mother-infant pairs during free play situation	Measures of cognitive and social competence	Abused infants more likely to ignore or refuse maternal distractions, but not less likely to comply to orders by mother, than controls
Friedrich, Einbender, & Luecke (1983)	11 physically abused, 10 nonabused	Age: preschool Sex: male Race: Caucasian	Matched for age, family income, mother's education and age	McCarthy Scales of Children's Abilities, Wide Range Achievement Test, Performance on persistence task	Differences on verbal, memory, and general cognitive index; no behavioral differences
Perry, Doran, & Wells (1983)	21 physically abused	Age: 4.6 years Sex: 9 females, 12 males	Mother's report about child	Child's Adjustment: Washington Symptom Checklist	Abused children reported by their mothers to have more nonnormal behaviors or poorer self- and school adjustment than controls
	21 nonabused	Age 5.5 years Sex: 10 females, 11 males			
Wolfe & Mosk (1983)	35 physically abused (A)	Age: 10 years Sex: 17 females, 18 males	Documented and recorded physical abuse	Child Behavior Profile: Social Competence & Behavior Problem sacles competed by parent or parent surrogate	Social competence: Activities—no difference; Social: C > A and NA. School: C > A and NA. Total: C > A and NA. Behavior problem variables: A and NA > C except on somatic complaints. No difference by length of agency involvement
	36 nonabused (NA), agency	Age: 11.6 years Sex: 18 females, 18 males			
	35 controls (C), nonabused	Age: 11.1 years Sex: 19 females, 16 males			

Study	Sample	Age/Race	Method	Measures	Results
Bousha & Twentyman (1984)	12 abused (A) child-mother pairs 12 neglected (N) child-mother pairs 12 control (C) child-mother pairs	Age: 4.7 years Race: 10 white, 2 black Age: 4.3 years Race: 9 white, 3 black Age: 4.2 years Race: 10 white, 2 black	Naturalistic observation in home for 3 consecutive days @ 90 min/day	Raters' coding of interactions of mother and child	A and N children showed fewer positive behaviors such as verbal and nonverbal affection and play behavior; A and N showed more aggressive behaviors, such as physical, verbal, and vocal aggression; N differed from A and C, showed less verbal and nonverbal instruction as well as fewer social interactions
Herrenkohl, Herrenkohl, Toedgter, Yanushefski (1984)	Interactions of 182 maltreated children: 58 harsh discipline (A), 78 neglect (N), 50 both (B), 58 control (C)	Age: 50 months; controls from child welfare agencies, day care programs, Head Start	Observation of parent-child interactions in home in play sessions	Ratings of verbal and nonverbal behavior on six child factors: task involvement, negative and visual behavior, talking to observer, positive affect, child helps other	N showed more talking to observers but did not differ on other ratings. A talked more to observers and had more negative global ratings of interactions. N and A did less speaking than C, showed less task involvement, had more negative global ratings of interactions and less warmth as rated.
Hoffman-Plotkin & Twentyman (1984) Race: 5 blacks, 9 whites	14 abused (A) 14 neglected (N) 14 controls	Age: 49 months Age: 51 months Sex: 4 females, 10 males Race: 6 blacks, 8 whites Age: 51 months Sex: 5 females, 9 males Race: 4 blacks, 10 whites	Behavioral observation (30 minutes) in classroom; Child Behavior Form	Behavioral ratings, parent and teacher ratings	Interactions: N < C; prosocial behavior: A and N < C; social maturity: A and N < C; readiness to learn: A and N < C; aggressiveness: A > N or C; discipline received: A > N or C; no differences on measures of social interaction with teacher, noncompliance, disruptive behavior, or affection to others
Rohrbeck & Twentyman	12 abused (A; 5 females, 7 males), 12 neglected (N; 5 females, 7 males), 12 controls (C; 7 females, 5 males)	Age: 58 months	Multimodal assessment, impulsivity	Child Impulsiveness Measures: walk slowly and draw a line slowly; Kansas Reflective Impulse Scale for preschoolers; Conners Teachers Rating Scales	Teachers' ratings: N more dysfunctional on 11 of 12 scales; mothers' ratings: N more conduct problems than C (A and N not different); child measures of impulsivity: no differences noted by day-care teachers or mothers on Revised Conners Parent Rating Scale.

work in this area examines attitudinal and behavioral outcomes related to violence. Indeed, most of the research on the consequences of various forms of family violence focuses on aggression, delinquency, and violent behavior. However, a number of writers have suggested that severe abuse or neglect in childhood leads not only to aggression directed outwardly but to aggression directed inwardly (Gutierres & Reich, 1981). Often overlooked evidence suggests that abuse may lead to withdrawal or to severe self-destructive behavior and suicide attempts. Thus, not only might abused children be destructive and abusive toward others, but they might also be damaging to themselves.

Evidence comes from a number of diverse sources. Sears (1961) described accident proneness, suicidal tendencies, and excessive concern with self-punishment in 12-year-old boys who had been punitively handled during toilet training. The frequent occurrence of physical abuse during childhood was noted in case histories of suicidal black adults (Hendin, 1969). Martin and Beezley (1977) found that a number of the abused children they studied became withdrawn. Kagan (1977) reported that repeated abuse, as opposed to one or two isolated incidents, resulted in docile, withdrawn children. George and Main (1979) found that physically abused children in a day care setting were quite similar to anxious/avoidant children, showing similar patterns of approach/avoidance conflicts with peers and with adults.

In their study of violent emergency room patients, Climent and Ervin (1972) found that violent subjects had thought about suicide (73%) and had attempted suicide (25%) more often than had controls (20% and 0%, respectively). Similarly, Bach-y-Rita and Veno (1974) reported a high incidence of self-destructive behaviors and self-mutilation in a group of 62 habitually violent patients/inmates from a California prison population. Over half of the inmates/patients admitted to having seriously attempted to hurt themselves; 42% had

mutilated their bodies in such a way as to leave scars.

In a direct examination of this relationship, Green (1978) found that a group of 59 physically abused children, ages 5 to 12, had a higher incidence (41%) of self-destructive behavior (including suicide attempts as well as self-mutilation) than a group of neglected but nonabused children (17%) and a group of normal controls (7%). According to Green (1978), in the majority of the cases, "self-destructive behavior was precipitated by parental beatings, or occurred in response to actual or threatened separation from key parental figures" (p. 580). Although this body of work is not extensive, these diverse findings suggest that in some individuals, abuse may lead to self-abuse and self-destructive behavior.

IMPACT OF OBSERVING OR WITNESSING VIOLENCE

Up to this point, I have focused primarily on the direct effects of abuse or neglect on later behavior. For some time, it has been recognized that witnessing violence—children witnessing their parents engage in physical or severe mental fights or children viewing extreme television violence—may have serious consequences for children.

Although early laboratory studies demonstrated that children and young adults imitated the behavior of aggressive models in experimental situations (Bandura, 1973; Bandura, Ross, & Ross, 1963), these studies did not address the long-term consequences of such modeling. Similarly, questions remained about the generalizability of aggressive play in the laboratory to assaultive behavior in the street, or from primarily middle-class nursery school children to abused children of different backgrounds.

Bach-y-Rita and Veno (1974) reported that 53% of their 62 cases of habitually violent offenders had observed their parents engaged in physical combat. Sorrells (1977) noted that the families of 31 youths charged with homicide or attempted homicide in California were "violent and chaotic." Lewis et al. (1979) noted that 79% of the violent children they studied reported witnessing extreme violence between their parents, whereas only 20% among the nonviolent offenders witnessed such violence. Hartstone and Hansen (1984) found that 23% of the fathers of violent youths had engaged in wife battering.

Studies that address the impact of witnessing violence on children's later behavior fall into three basic types: (a) large-scale surveys that correlate self-reports of exposure to violence with adult approval of violence or marital violence, (b) studies of the children of battered women, and (c) studies of television violence and aggressive behavior.

Survey Findings

Owens and Straus (1975) analyzed data from a national sample survey (representing 1,176 interviews conducted in 1968 of persons 18 years of age and older) to examine the relationship between three aspects of early exposure to violence (observing violence, being a victim of violence, and committing violence) in relation to approval of violence as an adult. Correlations among the three ranged from .52 to .59. Exposure to violence was also related to approval of interpersonal violence as an adult, although at a much lower level (correlations were .31 for commission of violence, .21 for being a victim, and .29 for observing violence). On the basis of these findings, Owens and Straus (1975) concluded that the "amount of violence experienced in childhood by members of a society is one of the factors contributing to the development and maintenance of cultural norms supporting the use of violence in face-to-face situations" (p. 193).

Kalmuss (1984) used data from another nationally representative sample of adults to explore the relationship between two types of family aggression (parent to teen and parent to parent) and severe marital aggression in the next generation (measured by items involving severe physical aggression carrying a high risk of serious injury: being kicked, bit, hit, beat up, and so on). These data are based on interviews conducted in 1976 with 2,143 adults who were married or cohabiting with a member of the opposite sex (Straus et al., 1980). The measure of parent-child hitting is based on a question assessing how often respondents' parents hit them as teenagers.[4]

Observing hitting between one's parents was more strongly related to involvement in severe marital aggression than was being hit as teenagers. However, the probability of marital aggression increased dramatically when respondents had experienced both types of family aggression. Kalmuss found that when neither form of exposure to teenage aggression occurred, the probability of husband-wife aggression was 1%. With only parent-teen hitting, the probability increased to 3%. With only parental hitting, it increased to 6%, and with both types, the probability increased to 12%. (A similar pattern was found for wife-husband aggression: 2%, 4%, 8%, and 17%, respectively.)

Unfortunately, a serious limitation of this otherwise elegant analysis is its reliance on retrospective accounts of family and marital aggression.

Given social disapproval of marital aggression, adults involved in such behavior may reconstruct their childhood families as aggressive to be consistent with and explain their present behavior. Similarly, adults who do not engage in marital aggression may be ashamed of an aggressive family of origin and, thus, may reconstruct their family as nonviolent. Both these sources of measurement error would systematically inflate the intergenerational transmission effects. (Kalmuss, 1984, p. 18)

Despite this limitation, these results indicate that children model family behaviors that are not directed at them. "As with research on the intergenerational transmission of marital instability and of fertility behavior, the cross-generational patterns of marital aggression are consistent but weak" (Kalmuss, 1984, p. 18).

Kratcoski (1985) explored violent behavior among youth by administering questionnaires to students from four high school classes and to youths referred to a juvenile justice center for engaging in delinquent behaviors. The self-report questionnaire asked for demographic data and information on the youth's family functioning, parental aggressive behavior toward the youth, peer-group relations, violence committed while in a peer-group setting, and school functioning. In addition, students were asked to give the number, types, and frequencies of various acts.

Kratcoski found that youths who were violent toward their parents ($n = 62$) had experienced violence from their parents (78% vs. 30%), had expressed violence toward siblings (83% vs. 59%), and had observed their parents reacting in a violent way to each other (33% vs. 11%) to a much higher degree than those who were not violent toward their parents ($n = 232$).

Because these findings are based on retrospective recall data, they suffer the limitations associated with such designs. Recognizing this problem, however, Kratcoski (1985) commented that it was possible to corroborate the family violence the youths reported with evidence in the youths' case records for some of the cases:

> In some cases, the violent youth who struck a parent was acting in self-defense or was trying to protect a parent or a sibling who was being beaten by a spouse, boyfriend, or other person in the household. In many cases, the violence of the youth toward a parent resulted from a parent trying to assert authority over the youth and the youth re-

jecting the attempt and reacting with physical violence. (p. 155)

Studies of the Children of Battered Women

Taking a different approach to assessing the effects of observing violence on children, A. Rosenbaum and O'Leary (1981) compared three groups of mothers who were asked to complete the Peterson-Quay Behavior Problem Checklist (BPC) to indicate the presence of behavioral and emotional problems in their male children. Fifty-two women—self-referred victims of physical marital violence in treatment—made up the battered-women group. Twenty satisfactorily married women were selected at random from the county telephone directory to compose one comparison group, and a second comparison group was made up of 20 women who were not battered but who were in discordant marriages and involved in marital therapy. The three groups were reasonably well matched for age, number of years married, number of children, and average family income. In this study, A. Rosenbaum and O'Leary failed to find significant differences between the three groups on the BPC. These results were similar to those of Hughes and Barad (1983), who reported that children of abused wives living at a shelter scored within normative ranges on several measures of child functioning.

A second investigation, by Hershorn and Rosenbaum (1985), used a similar design to study the impact of marital violence on male children with information provided by three groups of mothers: maritally abused (15); nonviolent, maritally discordant (12); and satisfactorily married (18). Current behavioral problems were again assessed by maternal report on the BPC, although mothers were also asked to complete a self-report questionnaire on marital adjustment, overt marital hostility, and child-rearing style. Here, the abused and nonviolent groups differed significantly from the satisfactorily married group but did not differ from each other, suggesting that the detrimental effects of parental marital violence may be attributable to the marital discord inherent in such relationships, not to the marital violence per se.

Using the Achenbach Child Behavior Checklist, which provides ratings of a child's social competence (e.g., activities, social participation, school performance) and behavior problems (e.g., hyperactivity, aggression, withdrawal), Wolfe, Jaffe, Wilson, and Zak (1985) studied a sample of 198 children (ages 4-16 years) from violent and nonviolent families. Mothers rated their child's or their children's behavior and also completed measures of family violence and maternal stress. Children of battered women (in transition houses or shelters for abused women) were rated as significantly higher on behavior problems and lower in social competence than children in the comparison group. Among the sample of 102 children from violent families, 34% of the boys and 20% of the girls fell within the clinical range of behavior problems. On the basis of the findings that maternal stress and family violence variables accounted for 19% of the variance in child behavior problems and for 16% in social competence (using multiple regression analyses). Wolfe and his colleagues suggested that the impact on the child of witnessing family violence may be partially mediated by factors associated with maternal stress. This explanation is not inconsistent with the Hershorn and Rosenbaum (1985) findings described earlier.

Going a step further, Jaffe, Wolfe, Wilson, and Zak (1986) compared the impact of direct and indirect exposure to family violence on school-aged boys. Boys who had witnessed violence between their parents (32 boys obtained from shelters for battered women) were compared with a sample of 18 male children from a provincial child welfare agency who had been physically abused by their parents. A third group of 15 children—a community comparison—was obtained through a newspaper advertisement asking women and children to par-

ticipate in a study on family relations. Mothers rated their child's or children's behavior on the Achenbach Child Behavior Checklist. Significant differences were found between the groups on measures of internalizing and externalizing problems, but not on social competence. Both the abused and the exposed-to-violence groups differed from the control group on internal and external scores. Abused boys also showed more externalizing symptoms than the exposed-to-violence children. Thus, boys who were exposed to family violence had behavior problems similar to those shown by abused children but different from those shown by children from nonviolent families. Cautious about the implications of these findings, Jaffe et al. (1986) pointed out,

> Although the results of this study suggest that exposure to family violence may be as harmful to the child as physical abuse, one cannot rule out the existence of common factors that may account for this finding. For example, the problems exhibited by the boys from violent families may be related to variables such as family stress, disadvantage, abrupt school and home changes, disrupted social supports, inadequate child management, and parental separations that are indirectly linked to family violence. (p. 145)

The relatively few studies that have assessed the effects of witnessing or observing family violence have yielded fairly consistent but modest findings. Among those witnessing severe family aggression, about 16% to 17% reported marital aggression. Observing hitting between one's parents was more highly related to marital aggression than was being hit as a teenager, although experiencing both types of violence yielded the highest risk of marital violence in the next generation. Studies of the children of battered women suggest that observing marital violence or extreme marital discord may be as harmful to the child as physical abuse. These studies are, however, limited because of an almost exclusive reliance on self-reports (in surveys) and mothers' reports of children's behavior (in studies of children of battered women). This dependence on self-reported, retrospective data and indirect measures of child problem behaviors detracts importantly from the validity of these findings.

Studies of Television Violence and Aggressive Behavior

The final consideration in assessing the empirical evidence for the cycle of violence hypothesis concerns the potential effects of viewing television violence on the attitudes and aggressive behavior of young children. This extensive literature, replete with ongoing and vigorous debates, will not be reviewed here (e.g., Freedman, 1984; Friedrich-Cofer & Huston, 1986). However, because viewing violence and later violent behavior are part of the cycle of violence hypothesis, a few brief comments are worth noting.

A number of writers have questioned whether the aggression or aggressive behavior measured in the television violence studies[5] can be generalized beyond the laboratory to real-life behaviors of delinquency or criminality (Cook, Kendziersky, & Thomas, 1983; Freedman, 1984). In their recent review of television violence and aggression, Friedrich-Cofer and Huston (1986) concluded that forms of aggression measured in studies of television violence are clearly relevant to serious behavioral aggression. As an example, they cited Belson's (1978) study in which the category most clearly related to television violence was "serious acts of aggression," which included firing a revolver at someone, attacks with a knife, setting fire to a building, hitting someone in the face with a broken bottle, and knocking someone off a bike (p. 369). In a 10-year follow-up of over 200 children (Lefkowitz, Eron, Walder, & Huesmann, 1972), the amount of violent

television watched at age 9 was the best single predictor of juvenile delinquency offenses related to aggression at age 19.

Exposure to television violence has been found to increase levels of aggression in the viewer, to have long-term effects as well as effects immediately after exposure, and to lead to emotional desensitization, making the viewer less likely to respond both physiologically and behaviorally to aggression in others (Slaby & Quarfoth, 1980). For example, children with a history of high levels of exposure to television have been found to show lower levels of emotional arousal (as measured by skin conductance and blood volume pulse amplitude) in response to a moderately violent television program than children with a history of low levels of television exposure (Cline, Croft, & Courier, 1973). There is some evidence to suggest that this emotional indifference toward violence may also appear as behavioral indifference in young children (Thomas, Horton, Lippincott, & Drabman, 1977). And a growing body of evidence suggests that heavy television viewing may lead to distorted perceptions about real-life violence in both adults and children (Slaby & Quarfoth, 1980). These findings—increased levels of aggression after viewing television violence, emotional insensitivity, and a distorted perception of reality—bear marked resemblance to findings from research on delinquent and violent offenders (Wilson & Herrnstein, 1985).

Recent work on television and violent criminal behavior by Heath, Kruttschnitt, and Ward (1986) returns us directly to the cycle of violence. This study was designed to examine the relationship between self-reported television viewing at ages 8, 10, and 12 years and the subsequent commission of violent criminal acts. The authors interviewed 48 male inmates incarcerated for violent crimes and 45 nonincarcerated, nonviolent males matched on age, race, and neighborhood of residence during adolescence. These authors found that the extent of a respondent's reported television viewing was not, in and of itself, predictive of violent criminal acts. Rather, it was the interaction of large amounts of television viewing and exposure to either maternal or paternal abuse that related to violent crime.

SUMMARY AND CONCLUSION

Despite tougher child abuse laws, increased public awareness, and an increase in social service agencies to deal with the problem, more than 25 years after Curtis (1963) called attention to the intergenerational transmission of violence, our knowledge of the long-term consequences of abusive home environments remains limited. Methodological problems play a major role in handicapping our efforts toward further understanding. In many instances, the reported relationships of violence across generations may represent underestimates of the actual relationship.

Empirical evidence demonstrating that abuse leads to abuse is fairly sparse. That which exists is methodologically problematic and limited because of an overdependence on self-report and retrospective data, inadequate documentation of childhood abuse or neglect, and the infrequent use of control groups. Existing studies suggest that there is a higher likelihood of abuse by parents if the parents themselves were abused as children. However, among adults who abused their children, the majority were not abused in their own childhood.

The second type of evidence offered in support of the "violence breeds violence" hypothesis is based on case histories of small numbers of violent or homicidal offenders in clinical settings. Although these have contributed to stimulating further research, their own statistical usefulness in elucidating the relationship between abuse and later behavior is obviously limited.

Nine studies addressed the relationship between abuse, neglect, and delinquency. The majority were retrospective; of the three prospective studies, two had no control groups. In prospective studies with children who were abused or neglected, the incidence of later delinquency was about 20%. In studies using a retrospective design—where delinquents were asked about their early backgrounds—estimates of abuse ranged from 8% to 26% (with two exceptions). Thus, among those abused, the majority did not become delinquent; among delinquents, the majority in most studies were not abused as children. In at least one study, rejected children had the highest rates of delinquency. Without appropriate control groups and improved methodology, however, conclusions remain tenuous.

With regard to the relationship between child abuse, neglect, and violent criminal behavior, 12 studies are relevant. Eight of these involved delinquents, and four involved varied groups of patients. All have some methodological problems, not the least of which is the universal lack of normal control groups. Findings are contradictory: Some provide strong support for the cycle of violence; in others, abused and nonabused delinquents did not differ; and in at least one study, abused delinquents were less likely to engage in later aggressive crimes. In most of the studies reviewed, the majority of abused children became neither delinquent nor violent offenders. Because most of the work reviewed here examines violence among delinquents or adolescents, there is little evidence that these childhood experiences have lasting consequences for the commission of violent crimes into adulthood.

Recent work in developmental psychology indicates that abuse and neglect are related to aggressive behavior in children as young as infants and toddlers. Although relatively short-term, these developmental studies provide serious ground for concern, given the literature which suggests that aggressiveness is a fairly stable personality trait and that early aggressiveness (as early as 8 to 12 years old) is predictive of later antisocial behavior.

The developmental studies also reinforce the need to consider the experience of neglect as distinct from abuse. Neglected children may not be the same—conceptually or empirically—as abused children. Neglected children may actually show higher levels of subsequent violent behavior than abused children. The larger scale studies examining the relationship between abuse and neglect and delinquency or violent behavior have typically aggregated abused and neglected children or have restricted their samples to those who were physically abused. With one exception (McCord, 1983), only the developmental studies in Table 3 have systematically examined and reported differences between separate samples of abused and neglected children. Combining the abused and neglected groups or studying only physically abused children may obscure important differences in consequences. On the other hand, accomplishing this purity of design and analysis is difficult given the reality of considerable overlap in the experiencing of abuse and neglect by children.

In addition to examining the direct effects of abuse and/or neglect on later behavior, I briefly reviewed three additional types of studies assessing the consequences of observing or witnessing violence. In large-scale national surveys, a weak but rather consistent association was found between observing violence and later marital aggression. That is, among those witnessing severe family aggression, about 16% to 17% reported marital aggression. From studies of the children of battered women, it was learned that observing marital violence or extreme marital discord may be as harmful to the child as physical abuse. These two types of studies, however, are limited because of an almost exclusive reliance on self- reports (in surveys) and mothers' reports of children's behavior (in studies of children of battered women). The A. Rosenbaum and O'Leary (1981) study

is an example of the possible underestimation of the extent of intergenerational transmission of violence. They found no relationship; however, their criterion for aggression in children was the mother's ratings of the child on a parent rating scale. How good are these mothers at judging the behavior of their children? There is some evidence to suggest that parents, particularly in multiproblem families, are poor judges of their children's behavior. I mentioned the literature on television violence and aggressive behavior briefly in an attempt to call attention to the diverse research methods used and to suggest similarities between its substantive findings and those of the delinquency and criminality literatures.

Most of the research on the consequences of family violence focuses on subsequent abusive behavior and aggression. Evidence that is often overlooked suggests that abuse or neglect in early childhood leads not only to further aggressive behavior but also to depression, withdrawal, and self-punishing behavior. Although this body of work is not at all extensive, this diverse set of findings suggests that in some individuals, abuse may lead to self-abuse and seriously self-destructive behavior, in contrast to outward manifestations of aggression.

Although we are beginning to have some perspective on the cycle of violence, the magnitude of the relationship remains difficult to interpret because of pervasive methodological problems, not the least of which is the general lack of control groups or base rate information with which to compare these figures. With the exception of the developmental studies (and these are somewhat limited because of their small sample sizes), less than a third of the other studies reviewed here have control groups, and many of the control groups are problematic.

How do we interpret existing research findings? Being abused as a child may increase one's risk for becoming an abusive parent, a delinquent, or an adult violent criminal. However, on the basis of the findings from the existing literature, it cannot be said that the pathway is straight or certain. It is likely that our conceptualization of the relationship between child abuse and violence has been overly simplistic. Indeed, Curtis (1963) long ago recognized the unlikely possibility that there would be a simple causal relationship between early child abuse and later crimes of violence.

Abusive parenting, delinquency, or criminality may be direct by-products of these early experiences. These outcomes may also reflect the interaction of a number of other causal factors, child abuse or neglect among them. In addition to the importance of a childhood history of abusive discipline, Herrenkohl et al. (1983) emphasized that other past and current life stresses were also important in determining the positive or negative direction of parenting behavior. Similarly, Heath et al. (1986) found that the interaction of large amounts of television viewing and exposure to parental abuse related to violent criminal behavior.

There are further clues within the literature that the path from early abusive or neglectful experiences may not lead simply or directly to violence and that the effects of these early experiences may be manifested in different ways. Evidence often forgotten suggests that abuse may also lead to withdrawal or self-destructive behavior. Thus, one explanation for the lack of a more substantial relationship between childhood abuse and later abuse, delinquency, or violent behavior may lie in more subtle manifestations of emotional damage such as severe anxiety, depression, withdrawal, or—in the extreme—suicide. Indeed, given the attrition that typically occurs in longitudinal studies, examination of cases lost due to early death, hospitalizations, and so forth would be revealing. In some ways, our almost exclusive focus on violence may have been shortsighted, precluding examination of more subtle forms of damage.

Now is the time to undertake a more discriminating analysis of the different effects likely to result from early experiences with abuse and neglect. Although clear cases of the cycle of violence are often foremost in our minds, the ultimate outcome may depend on a variety of factors, including the characteristics of the abuse or neglect incident (nature and severity of the abuse), the age of the child when the abuse occurred (Rutter, 1983), the characteristics of the perpetrator (Adams-Tucker, 1982), and characteristics of the child, such as IQ (Frodi & Smetana, 1984) or the child's perception of the event (Herzberger, Potts, & Dillon, 1981).

Not all children who grow up in violent homes become violent adults. In McCord's (1983) study, a number of the men appeared to be relatively invulnerable to the adverse effects of parental abuse and neglect. Certainly, a wide variety of environmental stresses, potential triggering mechanisms, and many other factors are involved in the learning process. Nevertheless, because many children appear not to succumb to the adverse effects of abuse or neglect, it is important to determine why this is so and what it is that protects them from these negative consequences. Studies are needed that examine the role of what have been called *protective factors* (Garmezy, 1981)—those dispositional attributes, environmental conditions, biological predispositions, and positive events that can act to mitigate against early negative experiences. Why some children succumb and others do not remains an open question. In the meantime, we need further research that builds on our current knowledge and increasing methodological awareness and sophistication.

Finally, it is important to draw attention to the persistent transmission of confident conclusions in this literature with little regard to data or lack thereof. Unqualified repetitions of the "cycle of violence" theme persist, despite the recognition of serious shortcomings in these studies. In support of the cycle of violence hypothesis, citations are often made of reports that present no data at all. My foremost suggestion for further research is to avoid the errors identified in this review, and I have described study methods and findings in detail in hopes of averting the intergenerational transmission of misinformation.

APPENDIX

Summary of Methodological Problems Characteristic of Cycle of Violence Literature

1. Questionable criteria for abuse and neglect, including nonsustantiated cases.
2. Designs weakened by questionable accuracy of information due to retrospective nature of data or reliance on second-hand information.
3. Weak sampling techniques, involving convenience or opportunity samples.
4. Ex post facto nature of studies, offering little predictive power.
5. Reliance on correlational studies.
6. Failure to distinguish between abused and neglected children, treating them as one group.
7. Lack of appropriate comparison or control groups and failure to consider statistical base rates.
8. Tendency to examine generalized delinquent behavior, with less focusing on violent criminal behavior.
9. Lack of knowledge of long-term consequences of abuse and neglect into adulthood.

NOTES

1. Estimates of the number of child abuse and neglect cases in the United States range from approximately 500,000 per year (Burgdorf, 1980; Gil, 1973; Light, 1974; Zalba, 1971) to as high as 2.3 million (Straus et al., 1980). In terms of incidence rates, it has been estimated that 10.5 of 1,000 children under age 18 in the United States are abused and/or neglected annually.

2. For a more complete discussion of the extent to which sampling decisions influence outcomes in child abuse research, see Widom (1988).

3. An unpublished follow-up to the Gutierres and Reich (1981) study indicated that the difference reported disappeared after 3 years.

4. This variable is limited to the respondents' teenage experiences with parent-child hitting because there are no data on whether their parents hit them prior to their teens.

5. In contrast to the cycle of violence research, the television and aggression literature is full of a variety of designs, viewing stimuli, circumstances (cartoons, actual TV broadcasts, live models, naturalistic viewing, and single-exposure situations), and measures of aggression (punching Bobo dolls, interpersonal aggression in play groups or classrooms, analog measures, and measures of naturally occurring aggression).

REFERENCES

Adams-Tucker, C. (1982). Proximate effects of sexual abuse in childhood: A report on 28 children. *American Journal of Psychiatry, 139,* 1252-1256.

Alfaro, J. (1981). Report on the relationship between child abuse and neglect and later socially deviant behavior. In R. J. Hunner & Y. E. Walker (Eds.), *Exploring the relationship between child abuse and delinquency* (pp. 175-219). Montclair, NJ: Allanheld, Osmun.

Aragona, J. A., & Eyberg, S. M. (1981). Neglected children: Mothers' report of child behavior problems and observed verbal behavior. *Child Development, 52,* 596-602.

Bach-y-Rita, G., & Veno, A. (1974). Habitual violence: A profile of 62 men. *American Journal of Psychiatry, 131,* 1015-1017.

Baird, D. A. (1982). A comparative study of abused and neglected children and their siblings. *Dissertation Abstracts International, 43,* 1276-B. (University Microfilms No. 82-18998)

Bandura, A. (1973). *Aggression: A social learning analysis.* Englewood Cliffs, NJ: Prentice Hall.

Bandura, A., Ross, D., & Ross, S. A. (1963). Imitation of film-mediated aggressive models. *Journal of Abnormal and Social Psychology, 66,* 3-11.

Barahal, R. M., Waterman, J., & Martin, H. P. (1981). The social cognitive development of abused children. *Journal of Consulting and Clinical Psychology, 49,* 508-516.

Belsky, J. (1980). Child maltreatment: An ecological integration. *American Psychologist, 35,* 320-335.

Belson, W. (1978). *Television violence and the adolescent boy.* Hampshire, England: Saxon House.

Berger, A. M. (1980). The child abusing family: I. Methodological issues and parent-related characteristics of abusing families. *American Journal of Family Therapy, 8,* 53-66.

Blount, H. R., & Chandler, T. A. (1979). Relationship between childhood abuse and assaultive behavior in adolescent male psychiatric patients. *Psychological Reports, 44,* 1126.

Bolton, F. G., Reich, J., & Gutierres, S. E. (1977). Delinquency patterns in maltreated children and siblings. *Victimology, 2,* 349-359.

Bousha, D. M., & Twentyman, C. T. (1984). Mother-child interactional style in abuse, neglect, and control groups: Naturalistic observations in the home. *Journal of Abnormal Psychology, 93,* 106-114.

Brassard, M., Germain, R., & Hart, S. (1987). *Psychological maltreatment of children and youth.* New York: Pergamon Press.

Burgdorf, K. (1980). *Recognition and reporting of child maltreatment.* Rockville, MD: Westat.

Burgess, R. L., & Conger, R. D. (1978). Family interaction in abusive, neglectful, and normal families. *Child Development, 49,* 1163-1173.

Cichetti, D., & Aber, L. A. (1980). Abused children-abusive parents: An overstated case? *Harvard Educational Review, 50,* 244-255.

Climent, C. E., & Ervin, F. R. (1972). Historical data in the evaluation of violent subjects: A hypothesis generating study. *American Journal of Psychiatry, 27,* 621-624.

Cline, V. B., Croft, R. G., & Courier, S. (1973). Desensitization of children to television violence. *Journal of Personality and Social Psychology, 27,* 360-365.

Cook, T. D., Kendziersky, D. A., & Thomas, S. V. (1983). The implicit assumptions of television: An analysis of the 1982 NIMH Report on Television and Behavior. *Public Opinion Quarterly, 47,* 161-201.

Curtis, G. C. (1963). Violence breeds violence-perhaps? *American Journal of Psychiatry, 120,* 386-387.

Duncan, J. W., & Duncan, G. M. (1971). Murder in the family: A study of some homicidal adolescents. *American Journal of Psychiatry, 127,* 74-79.

Easson, W. M., & Steinhilber, R. M. (1961). Murderous aggression by children and adolescents. *Archives of General Psychiatry, 4,* 27-35.

Egeland, B., & Brunquell, D. (1979). An at-risk approach to the study of child abuse: Some preliminary findings. *Journal of the American Academy of Child Psychiatry, 18,* 219-235.

Egeland, B., & Jacobvitz, D. (1984). *Intergenerational continuity of parental abuse: Causes and consequences.* Paper presented at the Conference on Biosocial Perspectives in Abuse and Neglect, York, Maine.

Egeland, B., & Sroufe, A. (1981a). Attachment and early maltreatment. *Child Development, 52,* 44-52.

Egeland, B., & Sroufe, A. (1981b). Developmental sequelae of maltreatment in infancy. In R. Rizley & D. Cicchetti (Eds.), *Developmental perspectives on child maltreatment, new directions for child development* (pp. 77-92). San Francisco: Jossey-Bass.

Elmer, E. (1967). *Children in jeopardy: A study of abused minors and their families.* Pittsburgh, PA: University of Pittsburgh Press.

Farrington, D. P. (1978). The family backgrounds of aggressive youths. In L. A. Hersov, M. Berger, & D. Shaffer (Eds.), *Aggression and antisocial behavior in childhood and adolescence* (pp. 73-93). Oxford, England: Pergamon Press.

Farrington, D. P. (1979). Longitudinal research on crime and delinquency. In N. Morris & M. Tonry (Eds.), *Crime and justice: An annual review of research, Volume I* (pp. 289-348). Chicago: University of Chicago Press.

Feshbach, S. (1980). Child abuse and the dynamics of human aggression and violence. In J. Gerbner, C. J. Ross, & E. Zigler (Eds.), *Child abuse: An agenda for action.* New York: Oxford University Press.

Freedman, J. L. (1984). Effects of television on aggressiveness. *Psychological Bulletin, 96,* 227-246.

Friedrich, W. H., & Boriskin, J. A. (1976). The role of the child in abuse. A review of the literature. *American Journal of Orthopsychiatry, 46,* 580-590.

Friedrich, W. H., & Einbender, A. J. (1983). The abused child: A psychological review. *Journal of Clinical Child Psychology, 12,* 244-256.

Friedrich, W. H., Einbender, A. J., & Luecke, W. J. (1983). Cognitive and behavioral characteristics of physically abused children. *Journal of Consulting and Clinical Psychology, 51,* 313-314.

Friedrich, W. H., & Wheeler, K. K. (1982). The abusing parent revisited: A decade of psychological research. *Journal of Nervous and Mental Disease, 170,* 577-588.

Friedrich-Cofer, L., & Huston, A. C. (1986). Television violence and aggression: The debate continues. *Psychological Bulletin, 100,* 364-371.

Frodi, A., & Smetana, J. (1984). Abused, neglected, and nonmaltreated preschoolers' ability to discriminate emotions in others: The effects of IQ. *Child Abuse and Neglect, 8,* 459-465.

Garbarino, J., & Gilliam, G. (1980). *Understanding abusive families.* Lexington, MA: Lexington Books.

Garbarino, J., Guttman, E., & Seeley, J. (1986). *The psychologically battered child: Strategies for identification, assessment, and intervention.* San Francisco: Jossey-Bass.

Garbarino, J., & Plantz, M. C. (1986). Child abuse and juvenile delinquency: What are the links? In J. Garbarino, C. Schellenbach, & J. Sebes (Eds.), *Troubled youth, troubled families* (pp. 27-39). New York: Aldine de Gruyter.

Garmezy, N. (1981). Children under stress: Perspectives on antecedents and correlates of vulnerability and resistance to psychopathology. In A. I. Rabin, J. Aronoff, A. M. Barclay, & R. A. Zucker (Eds.), *Further explorations in personality* (pp. 196-269). New York: Wiley.

Geller, M., & Ford-Somma, L. (1984). *Violent homes, violent children. A study of violence in the families of juvenile offenders* (New Jersey State Department of Corrections, Trenton. Division of Juvenile Services). Report prepared for the National Center on Child Abuse and Neglect, Department of Health and Human Services, Washington, DC.

Gelles, R. J. (1980, November). Violence in the family: A review of research in the seventies. *Journal of Marriage and the Family, 42*, 873-885.

George, C., & Main, M. (1979). Social interactions of young abused children: Approach, avoidance, and aggression. *Child Development, 50*, 306-318.

Gil, D. (1973). *Violence against children: Physical child abuse in the United States.* Cambridge, MA: Harvard University Press.

Glueck, S., & Glueck, E. (1950). *Unraveling juvenile delinquency.* Cambridge, England: Cambridge University Press.

Goldstein, J. (1986). *Aggression and crimes of violence.* New York: Oxford University Press.

Green, A. H. (1978). Self-destructive behavior in battered children. *American Journal of Psychiatry, 135*, 579-582.

Gutierres, S., & Reich, J. A. (1981). A developmental perspective on runaway behavior: Its relationship to child abuse. *Child Welfare, 60*, 89-94.

Hartstone, E., & Hansen, K. V. (1984). The violent juvenile offender: An empirical portrait. In R. A. Mathias (Ed.), *Violent juvenile offenders: An anthology* (pp. 83-112). San Francisco, CA: National Council on Crime and Delinquency.

Heath, L., Kruttschnitt, C., & Ward, D. (1986). Television and violent criminal behavior: Beyond the Bobo doll. *Violence and Victims, 1*, 177-190.

Hendin, H. (1969). Black suicide. *Archives of General Psychiatry, 21*, 407-422.

Herrenkohl, E. C., Herrenkohl, R. C., & Toedter, L. J. (1983). Perspectives on the intergenerational transmission of abuse. In D. Finkelhor, R. J. Gelles, G. T. Hotaling, & M. A. Straus (Eds.), *The dark side of families* (pp. 305-316). Beverly Hills, CA: Sage.

Herrenkohl, E. C., Herrenkohl, R. C., Toedter, L., & Yanushefski, A. M. (1984). Parent-child interactions in abusive and nonabusive families. *Journal of the American Academy of Child Psychiatry, 23*, 641-648.

Hershorn, M., & Rosenbaum, A. (1985). Children of marital violence: A closer look at the unintended victims. *American Journal of Orthopsychiatry, 55*, 260-266.

Herzberger, S. D. (1983). Social cognition and the transmission of abuse. In D. Finkelhor, R. J. Gelles, G. T. Hotaling, & M. A. Straus (Eds.), *The dark side of families* (pp. 317-329). Beverly Hills, CA: Sage.

Herzberger, S. D., Potts, D. A., & Dillon, M. (1981). Perceptions of abused and nonabused children toward their parents. *Journal of Consulting and Clinical Psychology, 49*, 81-90.

Hoffman-Plotkin, D., & Twentyman, C. (1984). A multimodel assessment of behavioral and cognitive deficits in abused and neglected preschoolers. *Child Development, 55*, 794-802.

Huesmann, L. R., Eron, L. D., Lefkowitz, M. M., & Walder, L. O. (1984). Stability of aggression over time and generations. *Journal of Abnormal Psychology, 20*, 1120-1134.

Huggins, M. D., & Straus, M. A. (1980). Violence and the social structure as reflected in children's books from 1850 to 1970. In M. A. Straus & G. T. Hotaling (Eds.), *The social causes of husband-wife violence.* Minneapolis: University of Minnesota Press.

Hughes, H., & Barad, S. (1983). Psychological functioning of children in a battered women's shelter: A preliminary investigation. *American Journal of Orthopsychiatry, 53*, 525-531.

Hunner, R. J., & Walker, Y. E. (1981). *Exploring the relationship between child abuse and delinquency.* Montclair, NJ: Allanheld, Osmun.

Hunter, R. S., & Kilstrom, N. (1979). Breaking the cycle in abusive families. *American Journal of Orthopsychiatry, 136*, 1320-1322.

Jaffe, P., Wolfe, D. A., Wilson, S., & Zak, L. (1986). Similarities in behavioral and social maladjustment among child victims and witnesses to family violence. *American Journal of Orthopsychiatry, 56*, 142-146.

Jayaratne, S. (1977, January). Child abusers as parents and children: A review. *Social Work, 22*, 5-9.

Jenkins, R. L. (1968). The varieties of children's behavioral problems and family dynamics. *American Journal of Psychiatry, 124*, 1440-1445.

Justice, B., & Justice, R. (1976). *The abusing family.* New York: Human Sciences Press.

Kadushin, A. (1974). *Child welfare services.* New York: Macmillan.

Kagan, J. (1977). The child in the family. *Daedalus: Journal of the American Academy of Arts and Sciences, 106*, 33-56.

Kalmuss, D. (1984, February). The intergenerational transmission of marital aggression. *Journal of Marriage and the Family, 46*, 11-19.

Kaufman, J., & Zigler, E. (1987). Do abused children become abusive parents? *American Journal of Orthopsychiatry, 57*, 186-192.

Kinard, E. M. (1980). Emotional development in physically abused children. *American Journal of Orthopsychiatry, 50*, 686-696.

King, C. H. (1975). The ego and the integration of violence in homicidal youth. *American Journal of Orthopsychiatry, 45*, 134-145.

Koeske, R. D. (1981). Theoretical and conceptual complexities in the design and analysis of menstrual cycle research. In J. A. Noack & S. N. Elder (Eds.), *The menstrual cycle: Volume 2. Research and implications for women's health.* New York: Springer-Verlag.

Kratcoski, P. C. (1982). Child abuse and violence against the family. *Child Welfare, 61*, 435-444.

Kratcoski, P. C. (1985). Youth violence directed toward significant others. *Journal of Adolescence, 8*, 145-157.

Langan, P. A., & Innes, C. A. (1985). *The risk of violent crime* (Bureau of Justice Statistics Special Report,

NCJ-97119). Washington, DC: U.S. Government Printing Office.

Lefkowitz, M. M., Eron, L. D., Walder, L. O., & Huesmann, L. R. (1972). Television violence and child aggression: A follow-up study. In G. A. Comstock & E. A. Rubinstein (Eds.), *Television and social behavior* (Vol. 3, pp. 35-135). Washington, DC: U.S. Government Printing Office.

Lewis, D. O., Moy, E., Jackson, L. D., Aaronson, R., Restifo, N., Serra, S., & Simos, A. (1985). Biopsychological characteristics of children who later murder: A prospective study. *American Journal of Psychiatry, 142,* 1161-1167.

Lewis, D. O., & Shanok, S. S. (1977). Medical histories of delinquent and nondelinquent children. *American Journal of Psychiatry, 134,* 1020-1025.

Lewis, D. O., Shanok, S. S., Pincus, J. H., & Glaser, G. H. (1979). Violent juvenile delinquents: Psychiatric, neurological, psychological and abuse factors. *Journal of the American Academy of Child Psychiatry, 18,* 307-319.

Light, R. J. (1974). Abused and neglected children in America: A study of alternative policies. *Harvard Educational Review, 43,* 556-598.

Loeber, R., & Dishion, T. (1983). Early predictors of male delinquency: A review. *Psychological Bulletin, 94,* 68-99.

Loeber, R., & Stouthamer-Loeber, M. (1986). Family factors as correlates and predictors of juvenile conduct problems and delinquency. In M. Tonry & N. Morris (Eds.), *Crime and justice* (Vol. 7, pp. 219-339). Chicago: University of Chicago Press.

Lystad, M. H. (1975). Violence at home: A review of the literature. *American Journal of Orthopsychiatry, 45,* 328-345.

Martin, H. P., & Beezley, P. (1977). Behavioral observations of abused children. *Developmental Medicine and Child Neurology, 19,* 373-387.

Martin, H. P., Beezley, P., Conway, E. F., & Kempe, C. H. (1974). The development of abused children. *Advances in Pediatrics, 21,* 25-73.

McCall, G. J., & Shields, N. (1986). Social and structural factors in family violence. In M. Lystad (Ed.), *Violence in the home: Interdisciplinary perspectives* (pp. 98-123). New York: Brunner/Mazel.

McCord, J. (1983). A forty-year perspective on effects of child abuse and neglect. *Child Abuse and Neglect, 7,* 265-270.

Monahan, J. (1981). *Predicting violent behavior: An assessment of clinical techniques.* Beverly Hills, CA: Sage.

Monane, M., Leichter, D., & Lewis, D. O. (1984). Physical abuse in psychiatrically hospitalized children and adolescents. *Journal of the American Academy of Child Psychiatry, 23,* 653-658.

Morse, C. W., Sahler, O. J., & Friedman, S. B. (1970). A 3-year follow-up study of abused and neglected children. *American Journal of Diseases of Children, 120,* 439-446.

Mouzakitis, C. M. (1981). An inquiry into the problem of child abuse and juvenile delinquency. In R. J. Hunner & Y. E. Walker (Eds.), *Exploring the relationship between child abuse and delinquency* (pp. 220-232). Montclair, NJ: Allanheld, Osmun.

Newberger, E. H., Newberger, C. M., & Hampton, R. L. (1983). Child abuse: The current theory base and future research needs. *Journal of the American Academy of Child Psychiatry, 22,* 262-268.

Newberger, E. H., Reed, R. B., Daniel, J. H., Hyde, J. N., & Kotelchuck, M. (1977). Pediatric social illness: Toward an etiological classification. *Pediatrics, 50,* 178-185.

Oliver, J. E., & Taylor, A. (1971). Five generations of ill-treated children in one family pedigree. *British Journal of Psychiatry, 119,* 473-480.

Olweus, D. (1977). Aggression and peer acceptance in adolescent boys: Two short-term longitudinal studies of ratings. *Child Development, 48,* 1301-1313.

Olweus, D. (1979). Stability of aggressive reaction patterns in males: A review. *Psychological Bulletin, 86,* 852-875.

Olweus, D. (1980). Familial and temperamental determinants of agressive behavior in adolescent boys: A causal analysis. *Developmental Psychology, 16,* 644-660.

Owens, D. J. & Straus, M. A. (1975). The social structure of violence in childhood and approval of violence as an adult. *Aggressive Behavior, 1,* 193-211.

Parke, R. D., & Collmer, C. W. (1975). Child abuse: An interdisciplinary analysis. In M. E. Hetherington (Ed.), *Review of child development research* (Vol. 5, pp. 509-590). Chicago: University of Chicago Press.

Parke, R. D., & Slaby, R. G. (1983). The development of aggression. In P. H. Mussen & M. E. Hetherington (Eds.), *Handbook of child psychology: Vol. 4. Socialization, personality, and social development* (pp. 547-641). New York: Wiley.

Pelton, L. H. (1978). Child abuse and neglect: The myth of classlessness. *American Journal of Orthopsychiatry, 48,* 608-617.

Perry, M. A., Doran, L. D., & Wells, E. A. (1983). Developmental and behavioral characteristics of the physically abused child. *Journal of Clinical Child Psychology, 12,* 320-324.

Potts, D. A., Herzberger, S. D., & Holland, A. E. (1979, May). *Child abuse: A cross-generational pattern of child rearing?* Paper presented at the annual meetings of the Midwestern Psychological Association. Chicago.

Reidy, T. J. (1977). The aggressive characteristics of abused and neglected children. *Journal of Clinical Psychology, 33,* 1140-1145.

Ressler, R. K., & Burgess, A. W. (1985). The men who murdered. *FBI Law Enforcement Bulletin, 54,* 2-6.

Robins, L. N. (1978). Sturdy childhood predictors of adult antisocial behavior: Replications from longitudinal studies. *Psychological Medicine, 8,* 611-622.

Rohrbeck, C. A., & Twentyman, C. T. (1986). Multimodal assessment of impulsiveness in abusing, neglecting, and nonmaltreating mothers and their preschool children. *Journal of Consulting and Clinical Psychology, 54,* 231-236.

Rosenbaum, A., & O'Leary, K. D. (1981). Children: The unintended victims of marital violence. *American Journal of Orthopsychiatry, 51,* 692-699.

Rosenbaum, M., & Bennett, B. (1986). Homicide and depression. *American Journal of Psychiatry, 143,* 367-370.

Rutter, M. (1983). Stress, coping, and development: Some issues and some questions. In N. Garmezy & M. Rutter (Eds.), *Stress, coping, and development in young children* (pp. 1-41). New York: McGraw-Hill.

Sears, R. R. (1961). Relation of early socialization experience to aggression. *Journal of Abnormal and Social Psychology, 63,* 466-492.

Sendi, I. B., & Blomgren, P. G. (1975). A comparative study of predictive criteria in the predisposition of homicidal adolescents. *American Journal of Psychiatry, 132,* 423-427.

Silver, L. R., Dublin, C. C., & Lourie, R. S. (1969). Does violence breed violence? Contributions from a study of the child abuse syndrome. *American Journal of Psychiatry, 126,* 152-155.

Slaby, R. G., & Quarfoth, G. R. (1980). Effects of television of the developing child. In B. W. Camp (Ed.), *Advances in behavioral pediatrics* (Vol. 1, pp. 225-266). Greenwich, CT: JAI Press.

Smith, C. P., Berkman, D. J., & Fraser, W. M. (1980). *A preliminary national assessment of child abuse and neglect and the juvenile justice system: The shadows of distress* (Reports of the National Juvenile Justice Assessment Centers). Washington, DC: U.S. Department of Justice, Office of Juvenile Justice and Delinquency Prevention.

Smith, S. M., & Hanson, R. (1975). Interpersonal relationship and childrearing practices in 214 parents of battered children. *British Journal of Psychiatry, 127,* 513-525.

Sommer, B. (1978). Stress and menstrual distress. *Journal of Human Stress, 4,* 5-47.

Sorrells, J. M. (1977). Kids who kill. *Crime and Delinquency, 23,* 312-320.

Spinetta, J. J., & Rigler, D. (1972). The child-abusing parent: A psychological review. *Psychological Bulletin, 77,* 296-304.

Stark, E. (1985). Women battering, child abuse, and social hereditary: What is the relationship? *Marital Violence: Sociological Review Monographs, 31,* 147-171.

Stark, R. A., & McEvoy, J. (1970, November). Middle class violence. *Psychology Today,* pp. 52-54, 110-112.

Steele, B. J., & Pollock, C. B. (1968). A psychiatric study of parents who abuse infants and small children. In R. E. Helfer & C. H. Kempe (Eds.), *The battered child* (pp. 103-147). Chicago: University of Chicago Press.

Steinmetz, S. K. (1977). *The cycle of violence: Assertive, aggressive, and abusive family interaction.* New York: Praeger.

Steinmetz, S. K. (1986). The violent family. In M. Lystad (Ed.), *Violence in the home: Interdisciplinary perspectives* (pp. 51-70). New York: Brunner/Mazel.

Straker, G., & Jacobson, R. S. (1981). Aggression, emotional maladjustment, and empathy in the abused child. *Developmental Psychology, 17,* 762-765.

Strasburg, P. (1978). *Violent delinquents.* New York: Monarch.

Straus, M. (1977, March 12). *Normative and behavioral aspects of violence between spouses: Preliminary data on a nationally representative USA sample.* Paper presented to Symposium on Violence in Canadian Society, Simon Fraser University, Burnaby, British Columbia, Canada.

Straus, M., Gelles, R., & Steinmetz, S.K. (1980). *Behind closed doors: Violence in the American family.* Garden City, NY: Anchor Press.

Tarter, R. E., Hegedus, A. M., Winsten, N. E., & Alterman, A. I. (1984). Neuropsychological, personality, and familial characteristics of physically abused delinquents. *Journal of the American Academy of Child Psychiatry, 23,* 668-674.

Thomas, M. H., Horton, R. W., Lippincott, E. C., & Drabman, R. S. (1977). Desensitization to portrayal of real-life aggression as a function of exposure to television violence. *Journal of Personality and Social Psychology, 35,* 450-458.

Tuteur, W., & Glotzer, J. (1966). Further observations on murdering mothers. *Journal of Forensic Sciences, 11,* 373-383.

U.S. Department of Justice. (1980). *Intimate victims: A study of violence among friends and relatives.* Washington, DC: U.S. Government Printing Office.

Vasta, R. (1982). Physical child abuse: A dual-component analysis. *Developmental Review, 2,* 125-149.

Wasserman, G. A., Green, A., & Allen, R. (1983). Going beyond abuse: Maladaptive patterns of interaction in abusing mother-infant pairs. *Journal of the American Academy of Child Psychiatry, 22,* 245-252.

Webster, W. (1978). *Crime in the United States-1977* (Federal Bureau of Investigation). Washington, DC: U.S. Government Printing Office.

Wick, S. C. (1981). Child abuse as causation of juvenile delinquency in central Texas. In R. J. Hunner & Y. E. Walker (Eds.), *Exploring the relationship between child abuse and delinquency* (pp. 233-239). Montclair, NJ: Allanheld, Osmun.

Widom, C. S. (1988). Sampling biases and implications for child abuse research. *American Journal of Orthopsychiatry, 58,* 260-270.

Wilson, J. Q., & Herrnstein, R. J. (1985). *Crime and human nature* New York: Simon & Schuster.

Wolfe, D. A. (1985). Child-abusive parents: An empirical review and analysis. *Psychological Bulletin, 97,* 462-482.

Wolfe, D. A., Jaffe, P., Wilson, S. K., & Zak, L. (1985). Children of battered women: The relation of child behavior to family violence and maternal stress. *Journal of Consulting and Clinical Psychology 53,* 657-665.

Wolfe, D. A., & Mosk, M. D. (1983). Behavioral comparisons of children from abusive and distressed families. *Journal of Consulting and Clinical Psychology, 51,* 702-708.

Wolfgang, M. E., & Ferracuti, F. (1967). *The subculture of violence.* London: Tavistock.

Yarrow, M. R., Campbell, J. D., & Burton, R. V. (1970). Recollections of childhood: A study of the retrospective method. *Monographs of the Society for Research in Child Development. 35* (5, Serial No. 138).

Zalba, S. (1971). Battered children. *Transaction, 8,* 58-61.

List of Commentators

The following individuals, all widely respected clinicians, researchers, and academicians working in the child abuse field, assisted in reviewing the papers in this volume, offering their views about why these papers have come to be regarded as classics, and commenting on their relevance in today's world. Their thoughts were woven into the editors' commentaries before each of the papers in this volume.

Helen Agathonos, Ph.D., Greece

Randall Alexander, M.D., Ph.D. United States

Donald Bross, J.D., United States

Kevin Browne, Ph.D., England

David Chadwick, M.D., United States

Diane Depanfilis, PhD, M.S.W., United States

Jaap E. Doek, J.D., The Netherlands

Howard Dubowitz, M.D., M.S., United States

Martha F. Erickson, Ph.D., United States

Kathleen Coulborn Faller, Ph.D., United States

Martin Finkel, D.O., United States

Stuart Hart, Ph.D., United States

Susan Hiatt, Ph.D., United States

Susan Kelley, Ph.D., R.N., United States

Kari Killen, Ph.D., Norway

Jill Korbin, Ph.D., United States

Richard Krugman, M.D., United States

John Leventhal, M.D., United States

Stephen Ludwig, M.D., United States

Gary Melton, Ph.D., United States

Theresa Reid, M.A., United States

Jacquie Roberts, M.A., M.Sc., Scotland

Donna Rosenberg, M.D., United States

Patricia Schene, Ph.D., United States

Charles Wilson, M.S.W., United States

List of Classic Papers

Browne, A., & Finkelhor, D. (1986). Impact of child sexual abuse: A review of the research. *Psychological Bulletin, 99,* 66-76.

Caffey, J. (1946). Multiple fractures in the long bones of infants suffering from chronic subdural hematoma. *American Journal of Roentgenology, 56,* 163-173.

Caffey, J. (1972). On the theory and practice of shaking infants: Its potential residual effects of permanent brain damage and mental retardation. *American Journal of Diseases of Children, 124,* 161-169.

Cohn, A. H. & Daro, D. (1987). Is treatment too late: What ten years of evaluative research tells us. In *Child abuse and neglect* (Vol. 11, pp. 433-441). Oxford, UK: Elsevier Science.

Egeland, B., & Vaughan, B. (1981). Failure of "bond formation" as a cause of abuse, neglect, and maltreatment. *American Journal of Orthopsychiatry, 51,* 78-84.

Finkelhor, D. (1984). Four preconditions: A model. In *Child sexual abuse: New theory and research* (pp. 53-68). New York: Free Press.

Garbarino, J. (1978). The elusive "crime" of emotional abuse. In *Child abuse and neglect* (Vol. 2, pp. 89-99). Oxford, UK: Elsevier Science.

Gelles, R. J., & Edfeldt, A. W. (1986). Violence toward children in the United States and Sweden. In *Child abuse and neglect* (Vol. 10, pp. 501-510). Oxford, UK: Elsevier Science.

Gil, D. G. (1975). Unraveling child abuse. *American Journal of Orthopsychiatry, 45,* 346-356.

Goldstein, J., Freud, A., & Solnit, A. J. (1973). On continuity, a child's sense of time, and the limits of both law and prediction. In Goldstein et al., *Beyond the best interests of the child* (pp. 31-52). New York: Free Press.

Gray, J. D., Cutler, C. A., Dean, J. G., & Kempe, C. H. (1979). Prediction and prevention of child abuse and neglect. In *Child abuse and neglect* (Vol. 1, pp. 45-58). Oxford, UK: Elsevier Science.

Helfer, R. E. (1987). The litany of the smoldering neglect of children. In R. E. Helfer & C. H. Kempe (Eds.), *The battered child* (4th ed., pp. 301-311). Chicago: University of Chicago Press.

Hufton, I. W., & Oates, R. K. (1977). Nonorganic failure to thrive: A long-term follow-up. *Pediatrics, 57,* 73-77.

Jones, D. P. H., & McGraw, J. M. (1987). Reliable and fictitious accounts of sexual abuse to children. *Journal of Interpersonal Violence, 2,* 27-45.

Kempe, C. H. (1978). Sexual abuse: Another hidden pediatric problem. *Pediatrics, 62,* 383-389.

Kempe, C. H., Silverman, F. N., Steele, B. F., Droegemueller, W., & Silver, H. K. (1962). The battered-child syndrome. *Journal of the American Medical Association, 181,* 17-24.

Klaus, M. H., Jerauld, G., Kreger, N. C., McAlpine, W., Steffa, M., & Kennell, J. H. (1972). Maternal attachment: Importance of the first post-partum days. *New England Journal of Medicine, 286,* 460-463.

Meadow, R. (1977). Munchausen syndrome by proxy: The hinterland of child abuse. *Lancet, 2,* 343-345.

Olds, D. L., Henderson, C. R., Jr., Chamberlin, R., & Tatelbaum, R. (1986). Preventing child abuse and neglect: A randomized trial of nurse home visitation. *Pediatrics, 78,* 65-78.

Pelton, L. H. (1978). Child abuse and neglect: The myth of classlessness. *American Journal of Orthopsychiatry, 48,* 608-617.

Polansky, N., Chalmers, N., Buttenwieser, E., & Williams, D. P. (1979). Isolation of the neglectful family. *American Journal of Orthopsychiatry, 49,* 146-152.

Russell, D. E. H. (1983). The incidence and prevalence of intrafamilial and extrafamilial sexual abuse of female children. In *Child abuse and neglect* (Vol. 7, pp. 133-146). Oxford, UK: Elsevier Science.

Steele, B. F. (1987). Psychodynamic factors in child abuse. In R. E. Helfer & C. H. Kempe (Eds.), *The battered child* (4th ed., pp. 81-114). Chicago: University of Chicago Press.

Summit, R. C. (1983). The child sexual abuse accommodation syndrome. In *Child abuse and neglect* (Vol. 7, pp. 177-193). Oxford, UK: Elsevier Science.

Widom, C. S. (1989). Does violence beget violence? A critical examination of the literature. *Psychological Bulletin, 106,* 3-28.

Index

About the Editors

Anne Cohn Donnelly, who holds a doctorate in public health from the University of California (Berkeley) School of Public Health, is an adjunct professor at the Kellogg Graduate School of Management, Northwestern University, Evanston, Illinois. Prior to this position, and for 17 years, she served as executive director of the National Committee to Prevent Child Abuse. She directed the first national evaluation study of child abuse and neglect treatment programs and has published widely on this and related topics. She served for 8 years as the secretary of the International Society for the Prevention of Child Abuse and Neglect (ISPCAN).

Kim Oates is a pediatrician with his medical degree from the University of Sydney. Currently the chief executive of The New Children's Hospital in New South Wales, he has had a long-standing interest in child abuse as a clinician and researcher. He has published widely in this area, particularly about longer-term studies of abused and neglected children. He has served as acting director of the Kempe Center in Denver, he is past president of ISPCAN, and he currently chairs the Australian Government's National Council for the Prevention of Child Abuse.

Please remember that this is a library book,
and that it belongs only temporarily to each
person who uses it. Be considerate. Do
not write in this, or any, library book.

DATE DUE

OC 26 '06			